PENGUIN CLASSICS

THE JEWISH WAR

ADVISORY EDITOR: BETTY RADICE

JOSEPHUS was born in about 37 A.D. He was one of the Jewish leaders at the time of the revolt of the Jews in the reign of Nero. He commanded in Galilee and was captured by the Romans, but his life was spared. Spending the rest of his life in Rome, he was given Roman citizenship and became a friend of Titus and Vespasian. His two most important works are *The Jewish War* and *The Jewish Antiquities*

.

G. A. WILLIAMSON was born in 1895 and was a Classical Exhibitioner at Worcester College, Oxford, graduating with a First Class Honours degree. He was Senior Classics Master at Norwich School from 1922 to 1960. He also translated *Eusebius: The History of the Church* (1965) and *Procopius: The Secret History* (1966) for the Penguin Classics. He died in 1982.

.

E. MARY SMALLWOOD was born in 1919 and was a Classical Scholar at Girton College, Cambridge, graduating with a First Class Honours degree in 1942. She was later a Research Fellow at Girton College, where she obtained her Ph.D in 1951. Since then she was on the staff of the Queen's University of Belfast, where she held a Personal Chair as Professor of Romano-Jewish history from 1978 until her retirement in 1983. Two of her other books are listed in the bibliography.

JOSEPHUS

The Jewish War

TRANSLATED BY

G. A. WILLIAMSON

REVISED

WITH A NEW INTRODUCTION,

NOTES AND APPENDIXES,

BY E. MARY SMALLWOOD

PENGUIN BOOKS

PENGUIN BOOKS

Published by the Penguin Group
Penguin Books Ltd, 80 Strand, London WC2R 0RL, England
Penguin Putnam Inc., 375 Hudson Street, New York, New York 10014, USA
Penguin Books Australia Ltd, 250 Camberwell Road, Camberwell, Victoria 3124, Australia
Penguin Books Canada Ltd, 10 Alcorn Avenue, Toronto, Ontario, Canada M4V 3B2
Penguin Books India (P) Ltd, 11 Community Centre, Panchsheel Park, New Delhi – 110 017, India
Penguin Books (NZ) Ltd, Cnr Rosedale and Airborne Roads, Albany, Auckland, New Zealand
Penguin Books (South Africa) (Pty) Ltd, 24 Sturdee Avenue, Rosebank 2196, South Africa

Penguin Books Ltd, Registered Offices: 80 Strand, London WC2R 0RL, England

www.penguin.com

This translation first published 1959
Revised edition 1970
Revised edition, with new Introduction, notes and appendixes
by E. Mary Smallwood, 1981
29

Copyright © G. A. Williamson, 1959, 1970
Introduction and editorial matter copyright © E. Mary Smallwood, 1981
All rights reserved

Printed in England by Clays Ltd, St Ives plc
Set in Monotype Bembo

ISBN-13: 978–0–140–44420–9

www.greenpenguin.co.uk

Contents

Foreword to this Edition

THE translation here given is that of the first edition, Mr Williamson's eminently lucid and readable rendering, unaltered except for minor amendments, mostly merely editorial. His division of the work into twenty-three chapters, unrelated to the seven books of the original, presents it in much more easily digestible chunks than Josephus does.

The familiar Hebrew forms of Old Testament names such as Elijah are substituted for Josephus' Grecized forms, and the name Jesus, common in his period, is given its Hebrew form Jeshua. The historian, however, is referred to by the Greek/Latin form of his name, Josephus, to distinguish him from other men with the same name, who appear as Joseph. I have taken the liberty of correcting Josephus' mis-spelling of Sosius and Cerealis throughout.

In the notes (pp. 409–60) I have attempted to explain historical and other allusions which are likely to puzzle the non-specialist and make it difficult for him to follow the story. In the interests of brevity I have frequently made categorical statements unsubstantiated by evidence; full argument or documentation seems inappropriate here. It would have been easy – and tempting – to produce copious notes to pp. 27–149, where the *Antiquitates Judaicae* (*AJ*) overlaps the *Bellum Judaicum* (*BJ*), giving the parallel references in the *AJ* and the differences between the two accounts. But I have tried to resist that temptation, and to confine such references to essential or highly significant additions or variations in the *AJ*. The Loeb edition of *AJ* xii–xx, has full and valuable notes. My notes also include many cross-references within the *BJ*, especially in cases where the appropriate passage cannot readily be found through the index, in the hope of saving time and reducing the frustration of search for the reader.

To avoid repeated explanations or back-references to earlier notes, a few frequently used technical terms are explained in a glossary. Questions which would have produced cumbersome notes, points which are interdependent, explanations of recurrent details, and some peripheral matters are relegated to appendixes.

As regards the introduction, the student seeking enlightenment on the finer points or deeper questions of Josephan scholarship will look in vain for it there. The introduction is designed, like the notes and other aids, for the general reader to whom Josephus is as yet a closed book and the ancient world as a whole is largely unfamiliar territory. It is no more than an attempt to set the writer and his works in their context, to explain some facets of ancient historiography which the newcomer may find strange, and to guide the reader towards some assessment of Josephus as a historian. After that the reader is left to encounter the *BJ* for himself and to form his own judgement on it.

Belfast   E. MARY SMALLWOOD
September, 1979

Introduction

THE *Bellum Judaicum*, 'The Jewish War', was the first written of the four works of Josephus which have come down to us. In the course of it he describes, at disproportionate length, his own by no means wholly creditable exploits as commander in Galilee in A.D. 66–7. In that account he says not a word about his personal enemy, Justus, son of Pistus, from Tiberias, and their differing attitudes and policies. But some twenty years after the publication of the *BJ* Justus also produced a history of the war (not extant) which contained what Josephus regarded as such a distorted picture of his command that he felt impelled to produce the short work misleadingly called the *Vita*, his life, to clear his name. This composition is no full and balanced autobiography but is little more than a detailed account of his command, written with the avowedly apologetic purpose of defending himself against what he saw as slanders by Justus, very much longer even than the account in the *BJ* (though the siege of Jotapata, which provides one of the most extensive purple passages in the earlier work, gets only a few passing references). It is prefaced by a brief survey of his earlier life (five pages out of a total of eighty in the Loeb edition) and rounded off with an even shorter sketch of his fortunes after 67. But thanks to the first and last few pages of this distinctly unsatisfactory work, we have more detailed, and (presumably) reliable, information about the personal life of this historian than we have about many other ancient writers.

Josephus, son of Matthias, was born in A.D. 37 to a priestly family which proudly traced its pedigree back to the early Hasmonaeans. The year was ill-omened for both Romans and Jews in seeing the accession of the emperor Gaius (as a toddler nicknamed Caligula, 'little boot', when he was brought up in a camp on the Rhine, where his father was commander, and dressed in a miniature soldier's uniform). He was already mentally unbalanced when he came to the throne, and he was probably, in our terminology, 'certifiable' by the time he was assassinated, less than four years later, for behaviour intolerable to the Romans. One of the outrageous actions of the last year of his life was an attempt to desecrate the Jewish Temple (pp. 139–41), which, if carried through, would undoubtedly have precipitated a full-scale revolt a generation earlier than the one of which Josephus writes.

Destined by his birth for the priesthood, Josephus was educated in a rabbinic school in Jerusalem, where, he tells us, by the age of about fourteen he had become such an authority on the intricacies of the Jewish Law that even senior priests and laymen prominent in the administration of the city came to him for the elucidation of knotty points. At about sixteen he spent some months studying successively with the Pharisees, the Sadducees and the Essenes (the monastic sect described on pp. 133–7) in the hope of deciding which sect to join. But he was unable to make up his mind, and so went to live with an ascetic hermit in the desert for three years' meditation. He returned to Jerusalem at nineteen, a Pharisee.

Of the next seven years, presumably spent uneventfully on priestly duties, Josephus says nothing, but at the age of twenty-six he began to see the world: he took upon himself (apparently; he does not say that he was chosen by higher authorities) the minor but delicate diplomatic mission of sailing to Rome in the hope of securing the release of some fellow priests who had been sent to Nero to answer a charge which Josephus does not specify but describes as 'trivial'. After a shipwreck en route which nearly deprived us of the *BJ*, he succeeded in getting his friends acquitted through the good offices of Nero's wife Poppaea, to whom he was introduced by a Jewish actor he had met on landing in Italy. (One would like to know more about Jews in the theatrical profession. This one surely was an apostate, and the fact that Nero and Poppaea were among his 'fans' is not evidence, as has been argued, that Poppaea had an interest in Judaism.)

Josephus must have stayed in Rome for a couple of years or done an unrecorded 'grand tour' on the way home, for he did not return until 66, when the war clouds had already gathered and were about to break. He did his best to prevent the revolt, of which he was to be the historian, at the eleventh hour by arguing with the nationalist leaders and trying to make them see that the outcome of war with Rome would inevitably be disaster; but to no avail. On the contrary, he made himself so unpopular that he had to take refuge in the inner court of the Temple to avoid being arrested and executed on suspicion of collusion with the Romans, and only dared to re-emerge after the murder of one of the prominent extremists, Menahem (pp. 166–7), in September brought Jerusalem back under the control of the moderate party, to which he belonged.

But by this time the die was cast; the extreme nationalists had carried the day, the Jews were in revolt against what they, with some justification, regarded as Roman oppression, and the Roman military forces had been driven out of Jerusalem. In November a legion which came from Syria to attempt to re-establish control was heavily defeated, and this irrevocably committed the Jews to war. The moderates, the peace party, now had no choice but to accept as inevitable the conflict which they had failed to prevent; but they tried to keep the direction of it out of the hands of the extremists and in their own hands, in the vain hope that, by ostensibly supporting them in preparing for full-scale warfare, they might win their confidence and then be able to persuade them to abandon a struggle foredoomed to failure. An ex-high priest (not the sort of man whom one would regard as an obvious military leader) assumed supreme control of operations in Jerusalem, and the rest of the country was divided into six regional commands. Josephus, a priest and a scholar, was appointed commander of the most northerly of the regions, Galilee.

Despite his unpromising background, Josephus turned out to be a man of considerable natural military ability, but he was in the uncomfortable position of being commissioned to prepare for a war of which he did not approve. For some time his policy was to carry out his mandate by fortifying a large number of towns and training an army but neither to give nor to respond to any provocation to conflict. This of course did not please the extremist leaders in the area, Justus of Tiberias among them, who were thirsting for action, and their attempts first to murder him and then to get the Jerusalem authorities to deprive him of his command, albeit unsuccessful, made life very difficult for him. By the spring of 67, however, he could sit on the fence no longer: when a large Roman force invaded Galilee and his army ran away, he threw in his lot with the rebels and retreated into the town of Jotapata. The siege of that strongly fortified and fanatically defended fortress lasted for nearly two months and ended with the capture of Josephus by the Romans in circumstances which redounded little to his credit (p. 220).

As a valuable prisoner Josephus was to have been sent to Nero, but he hastily turned the situation to his own advantage by prophesying to Vespasian, the Roman commander, that he would soon become emperor. Information that other predictions by Josephus had come true impressed Vespasian sufficiently for him to keep the encouraging prophet in honourable custody at his headquarters for the next two years, until in July 69 (by which time Nero had been dethroned and his two short-lived successors had met equally inglorious ends) his troops took a hand in the current game of emperor-making and proclaimed their popular and able commander emperor as a more worthy candidate for the throne than the effete glutton then occupying it. Josephus' foresight was thus vindicated – and promptly rewarded with freedom. He was to spend the rest of the war with the Roman forces, the only safe place for a man treated with such favour by the enemy that he was inevitably an object of the gravest suspicion to his own people.

In the autumn of 69 Josephus accompanied Vespasian as far as Alexandria on the first stage of his journey to Rome to claim the throne, returning from there with Vespasian's son Titus, now commander-in-chief, for the campaign which was to culminate in the siege and sack of Jerusalem the following summer, and incidentally with a new wife (the wife whom Vespasian had been kind enough to provide for him during his two years as a prisoner, a captive Jewish girl from Caesarea, having abandoned him when he set out for Alexandria). During the siege he was used on several occasions as an intermediary to appeal to the Jews, by oratory addressed to the defenders on the walls, to give up their futile resistance and save their city by surrender. His words, far from having the desired effect, served only to infuriate the Jews, who regarded him, with good reason, as a traitor and answered him with missiles, one of which found its target, though not fatally.

After the fall of the city Titus offered to reward Josephus for his services by inviting him to help himself to anything he liked from the wreckage. The scholar in him accepted some copies of the Scriptures from Titus' own hand, but – to his credit – he took no loot, asking as his reward merely the release of his brother, fifty friends, and a number of women and children of his acquaintance whom he found among the many lined up in the Temple court for deportation and enslavement. Later he used his influence to get three friends whom he saw being crucified reprieved and taken down. But such minor services as these could not wipe out his years on the Roman side, and although Titus, who had promised that after the war he would restore the land of all Jews who had not joined the revolt, gave Josephus an estate outside Jerusalem in lieu of his former property in the city, which lay in the area now earmarked for the camp of the new legionary garrison (p. 374), Josephus thought it prudent to decamp for good to Rome. And it turned out to be also highly advantageous personally; for when he reached Rome with Titus (and with his wife, who unlike her predecessor did not refuse to accompany him away from home), he was given the house in which Vespasian had lived as a private citizen, a pension for life, and Roman citizenship. Following the normal practice of enfranchised provincials, he took the family name of the emperor to whom he owed the grant of citizenship, Flavius Vespasianus, and Joseph, son of Matthias, became Flavius Josephus.

The rest of Josephus' life is largely the story of his literary works, to which we must soon turn. He gives us only one domestic detail: in 73 or 74 he divorced his wife soon after the birth of their third and only surviving child because 'he was displeased with the way she behaved' (a phrase on which he lets our imaginations loose) and married a Jewess from Crete, who quickly presented him with two more sons. He apparently never revisited his native land, though Vespasian later gave him a second estate in Judaea, a large one, and Domitian (emperor from 81 to 96) exempted his property from the land-tax payable by all provincials, a highly coveted honour. Besides suffering the mendacious attack made on him *c.* 72 by one of the Jewish extremists who had escaped to Cyrenaica to stir up trouble there (p. 408), he was subject up to the 80s to accusations from Jews jealous, he says, of his good fortune. No doubt they in their devastated country were jealous. But the conduct which had resulted in that good fortune will surely have rankled still more deeply, and it was not safe to set foot again among people who could not let bygones be bygones.

The date of Josephus' death is not known. He finished the *AJ* towards the end of 93 and wrote both the *Vita* (*V*) and the *In Apionem* (*Ap.*) after that. It is clear from the way in which he speaks of king Agrippa II in *V* 359–60 that he outlived him; but that is of little help, since the date of Agrippa's death is uncertain.*

JOSEPHUS' WORKS

Provided with a comfortable house and freed by his pension from financial worries and the need to earn a living, Josephus settled down in Rome to write a full account of the war of 66–70 in which the Jews had attempted, and failed miserably, to shake off the Roman yoke under which they had spent the previous sixty years, and to recover their political independence. His title in full, 'The History of the Jewish War against the Romans', views it from the Roman angle as a war fought against the Jews. From the Jewish angle it would have been 'The History of the Roman War against the Jews'; indeed in Jewish tradition it appears as 'the war of Vespasian'. But Josephus does not throw his readers in at the deep end with the 'immediate cause' of the war, the trivial incident at Caesarea in the spring of 66 that triggered off the revolt which soon became a full-scale war, or even start with its 'fundamental cause', tracing the ever-increasing friction that had developed between the Jews and their Roman masters since part of the country had been annexed as a province in A.D. 6. He devotes nearly the first third of his work to a survey of the period of well over two hundred years during which the Jews came under Syrian domination, freed themselves from it and achieved political independence, enjoyed that

* A medieval bibliographer who had access to a general history starting with Moses by Justus of Tiberias says categorically that that work ended with Agrippa's death in 100; but the cumulative evidence of other, and on the whole more reliable, scraps of information points to 92/3 for his death.

independence for some eighty years, constantly enlarging their territory, fell under Roman domination as a client kingdom on the fringe of the expanding Roman empire, and finally were brought right into that empire as a province governed by Roman officials, with whom relations steadily deteriorated until they exploded into war.

The *BJ* is divided into seven books (p. 31), though it is not certain that the sevenfold division in our MSS. is Josephus' division. In an ancient work a 'book' sometimes corresponded roughly to a chapter in a modern one, dealing with a unit of subject-matter. But in a long continuous work such as a history it tended to be rather the amount of material that could conveniently be contained in one ancient 'book', a papyrus roll. The twenty-three chapters under which the present translation is presented, and their headings, owe nothing to Josephus.

In his preface to the *BJ* Josephus explains that he wrote it first in Aramaic for circulation among the Jews of the eastern Diaspora – those living beyond the Euphrates, under Parthian rule – and later translated it into Greek in order to make it accessible to the peoples of the Roman empire. Greek had by then been the *lingua franca* of Asia Minor, Syria and the eastern part of north Africa for over three centuries, and the educated Latin-speaking Italian, if not bilingual, was at least competent in Greek. (The titles of Josephus' works were, of course, all Greek; but we still follow the renaissance convention of translating the titles of Greek works into Latin for purposes of reference.) Josephus talks about the composition of the *BJ* also in *V* 361–7 and in *Ap*. i. 49–56, and with the information there supplementing what is said in the preface we get a fairly clear picture of how and when the work was written and translated.

The translation was completed in or after 75, the year of the dedication of the Temple of Peace mentioned on p. 386 – a reference almost certainly not in the original but inserted into the translation. Although there can be no proof, it seems inherently likely that while making the translation Josephus used the opportunity to revise the whole work, perhaps extensively. As Josephus, though no doubt fluent in Greek, was not completely bilingual (he admits in *AJ* xx. 263 that his pronunciation was imperfect), he got the assistance of a number of native Greek speakers to ensure that the translation was idiomatic.

Josephus' purpose in making his translation was to correct the distorted picture of the war given in inaccurate accounts which had been published by writers without first-hand knowledge of it. Josephus professes accuracy. And he certainly should have achieved it. Not only was he a participant in the early stages of the war and a spectator of its final stages at close quarters, but he tells us that he 'kept a careful record of what went on before his eyes in the Roman camp', and that while there he 'was in a unique position to understand the information brought by deserters' (of whom there were a great many). This second point explains how he was able to give detailed and graphic accounts of events and conditions in Jerusalem both before and during the siege, although he had left the city in the winter of 66–7, never to return till after it had fallen. He also had access in Rome to Vespasian's and Titus' *Commentaries*, their factual records of military operations written while on campaign and, though not published, as Julius Caesar's famous commentaries on his Gallic war had been, preserved in the archives, where, apparently, any serious student was at liberty to peruse them. At two points in his *Vita* (342, 358) Josephus appeals explicitly to the *Commentaries* as confirmation of his veracity.

When the translation was complete, Josephus presented copies to Vespasian and Titus, who pronounced them to be an accurate and reliable record, Titus going so far as to sign the copies and give them his explicit *imprimatur*. Josephus then sent a copy of part of the work to king Agrippa II, a descendant of Herod the Great who was ruling non-Jewish territory north of Palestine and who, after failing to dissuade the Jews from rebelling, had contributed troops to the Roman force and had been present in Titus' camp at the siege of Jerusalem. He wrote congratulating Josephus on his care and accuracy and asking for the remaining volumes, and then penned no fewer than sixty letters (we are not told to whom) recommending the work and vouching for its truthfulness. Copies were later given to a number of Romans who had taken part in the war, and others were sold to prominent Jews in Palestine, all of whom joined in the chorus of praise. But few authors escape without any bad reviews, and Josephus was not among the lucky ones. The *BJ* was attacked by what he describes as 'certain despicable persons' on the grounds of inaccuracy, to which his answer was that even if, as they declared, they had read the imperial *Commentaries*, they had not been eyewitnesses as he had.

Josephus' next work was his biggest, *Antiquitates Judaicae*, 'The Jewish Archaeology' in Greek, which we should be more inclined to entitle 'The History of the Jews'; for such it is, going all the way from Adam to the eve of the revolt in A.D. 66 in twenty books. The first half is a summary of Biblical history down to the Exile in 587 B.C. The next book and a half cover the return from exile in 538 and the period down to the early second century B.C. Then from the middle of book twelve to the end, the *AJ* runs parallel to the first book and a half of the *BJ* (pp. 33–149), covering the same ground but obviously in much more detail. For example, when dealing with Judaea as a Roman province in the *AJ*, Josephus gives more episodes illustrating the increasing tension between the Jews and the Roman authorities and the growing disorder, eventually amounting to anarchy, of the country in the years leading up to the revolt than he does in the *BJ*, and when he relates an episode in both works, the *AJ* account is usually rather fuller.

Josephus wrote the *AJ*, he tells us in the preface, at the instigation of a certain Epaphroditus, who evidently became his patron after the deaths of Vespasian in 79 and Titus in 81. Epaphroditus is most credibly identified with a scholar of that name from Alexandria, who settled in Rome under the Flavians, where he amassed a vast library and enjoyed a high reputation. If this is correct, Josephus may well have learnt from him much of what he knows of Greek literature and mythology (see, for example, his references to Greek legends in *BJ*, pp. 108, 137, 223). But the idea of such a work as the *AJ* was already in Josephus' mind, for when composing the *BJ* he had contemplated writing a complete history of the Jews to precede the story of the war, though he had abandoned the idea on the grounds that it would have produced too cumbersome a work. Now, however, it was to be an independent work, on a much larger scale than would have been practicable before, written with the aim of making the whole of Jewish history accessible to the Greek-speaking world.

On reaching the end of book twenty and the completion of 60,000 lines (rather shorter than those of the Loeb text; counting was necessary because the scribes who copied manuscripts for publication were paid so much a hundred lines), Josephus remarks with a superb lack of modesty: 'And now, having finished what I set out to do, I can say with confidence that no one else, Jew or gentile, would have been capable, even if he had been willing, to carry out this task so accurately for the benefit of the Greek world; for my fellow Jews agree that I far excel them in both Jewish and gentile learning'. In the final two sentences of the *AJ* Josephus outlines his future plans – a continuation, in effect, of the *AJ*, carrying the history of the Jews on from 66, through the war (presumably with a summary of the long *BJ* account) to the present day (it was now late in 93, and Domitian's reign was, fortunately, nearing its end), and then a work in four books on Jewish theology and law. There is no evidence to suggest that either of these projects was ever carried out; for at this point, as has been explained above, Josephus' attention was diverted to the writing of the *Vita*.

The general character and purpose of the *Vita* have already been mentioned. It certainly is not the proposed continuation of the *AJ*, dealing as it does with only a few months of the war and that from a wholly personal point of view; and yet Josephus evidently regarded it as a kind of appendix to that work, for at the end of the *AJ* as we have it, immediately before the statement about Josephus' plans for future major works, stands a sentence which looks like an alternative conclusion inserted, without the removal of the original conclusion, when it became necessary to produce the *Vita*: Josephus says that it would be a good idea to give a brief account of his own life while there are still people alive to refute or corroborate his statements. The *Vita* then opens with a conjunction, perhaps most naturally translated 'Now my family is ...', implying that this sentence is not the start of an independent work; and it closes with the words 'Having given you a complete account of our archaeology' (the Greek title of the *AJ*), 'my good Epaphroditus, I end my narrative here for the time being.'

Justus of Tiberias had apparently represented Josephus as the instigator and organizer of the revolt in Galilee, or at least of the revolt of Tiberias. This was worse than embarrassing for a pensioner of the imperial family: it could have been positively dangerous. His patrons Vespasian and Titus were dead; Domitian was becoming more and more of a tyrant as his reign proceeded, hostile to converts to Judaism for their refusal to participate in the worship which he as a living emperor demanded; and there was a risk of his hostility extending to the Jews, despite their official exemption from participation in the imperial cult. Josephus needed to defend himself. But he could hardly deny the well-known fact of his military command in Galilee. According to the *BJ*, written before there was need for self-justification, Galilee was already in revolt when Josephus was sent there, and his mission was to prepare for the inevitable Roman reprisals. But in the *Vita*, where Josephus wants to play down his anti-Roman stance, he opens the account of his command with the statement, irreconcilable with the *BJ*, that 'the whole of Galilee had not yet risen in revolt' and his mission was 'to try to persuade the bad men to lay down their arms' (*V* 28–9). This surely is self-justification by falsification. Other discrepancies follow, great and small (the latter perhaps venial and due to no more than lapse of memory or carelessness). Given the circumstances of the composition of the *Vita*, it seems on the whole safer to accept the *BJ* when the two accounts conflict.

Josephus' last work was one in two books entitled 'Concerning the Antiquity of the Jews' but always known now by the title which it has held since the time of St Jerome, *Contra* or *In Apionem*, 'Against Apion'. The title is explained on the first page, where Josephus expresses surprise that even after the publication of the *AJ*, which shows Jewish history stretching back over a period of 5,000 years, some people still insist on regarding the Jews as a very young race. But as the work progresses, it becomes far more than an argument for the antiquity of the Jewish people. It develops into an impassioned but well-written and well-argued comprehensive *apologia* for the Jews and Judaism, a defence of his people, their religion, their law and their customs against the malicious and often ill-informed attacks made on them by anti-Semitic writers of the previous three centuries. One of the most vicious of these was Apion, an Alexandrian scholar and rhetorician a generation or more older than Josephus, whose calumnies are torn to pieces in the first half of book two, and whose name has been adopted in the title to denote the 'type' of the anti-Semite. The work is very valuable not only for what Josephus tells us in it about Judaism but also for his verbatim quotation of numerous excerpts from writers whose works are no longer extant. The work is dedicated to Epaphroditus as 'a devoted lover of the truth' and to anyone who, like him, 'wishes to know the facts about our race'.

JOSEPHUS AS A HISTORIAN

It is indeed to Josephus that we turn for many 'facts about the Jewish race'. In the Victorian household a copy of William Whiston's translation of the whole of Josephus' works, first published in 1737 and reprinted many times, and to us virtually unreadable in its prolixity and pomposity (not to mention its inaccuracy), stood beside the family Bible. And while Josephus' standing is not so high nowadays as that collocation implied, he is still invaluable. Thanks to Josephus, supplemented by the New Testament and Philo,* we know more about

* Philo was a Greek-speaking Alexandrian Jew, a member of a very wealthy family prominent in the Jewish community there. His brother is mentioned on p. 303; and that brother's son disgraced the family by giving up Judaism and as an apostate entering the Roman government service to act as procurator of Judaea in the 40s, prefect of Egypt in the 60s, where he had to deal with an anti-Semitic riot, and Titus' chief of staff at the siege of Jerusalem (pp. 143, 152, 172, 290). Philo was a religious thinker and philosopher, and most of his copious works are attempts to make Jewish thought, law and theology accessible and at the same time intelligible to gentiles by interpreting them in terms of Greek philosophy. His last two works, written shortly before his death in the 40s A.D., are quite different. *In Flaccum*, 'Against Flaccus', is largely a detailed account of anti-Semitic riots in Alexandria in 38, and takes its title from the name of the prefect under whom they happened and who, in Philo's view, helped to cause them and did little to stop them. *Legatio ad Gaium*, 'The Embassy to Gaius', takes its name from the central episode in what is really an attack on the emperor Gaius for the atrocities of his reign, the fortunes of an embassy sent to Rome by the Alexandrian Jews in the hope of getting redress for their sufferings in 38. Woven into that episode is the full story of Gaius' attack on the Temple in the form of a report to the embassy by messengers from Palestine, and other odd pieces of information about the provinces are included incidentally.

Palestine in the first century A.D. than we do about any other part of the Roman Empire at that period – or indeed at many others. Through Josephus the Jews are unique among Rome's subjects at that time in being articulate to us. But of course, despite Josephus' defection to Rome, it is largely from the Jewish point of view that events are presented to us. On the Roman side there is almost complete silence. One longs in vain for Pontius Pilate's version of the clashes with his subjects which Josephus records, and indeed for his angle on the Crucifixion of Christ. Roman historians were in general more interested in what went on in Rome and Italy than in the material and cultural development of the provinces or the attitude of the provincials towards their mistress, and they recorded only major events outside Italy, such as foreign wars and serious revolts. Judaea was small, distant, and most of the time uninteresting and unimportant, becoming 'news' only in 66. The sole event of the years 6–66 in Palestine which finds a place in the (admittedly incomplete) *Annals* of Tacitus, the greatest historian of the first century A.D., is the clash between the Galilaeans and the Samaritans under Cumanus (pp. 144–6); and Tacitus' version differs from that of Josephus at so many points that it raises a host of problems. The outbreak of the war in 66 can hardly have been omitted from the latter part of Tacitus' *Annals*, which went up to the end of 68; but the end of that work is lost. In his *Histories*, which dealt with the period from 69 to (probably) 96, Tacitus gave an account of Titus' siege of Jerusalem, preceding it with a thumbnail sketch of Jewish history, customs and religion – an extraordinary amalgam of fact, nonsense, and anti-Semitic slander – a description of the defences of Jerusalem, and a brief survey of the Jewish factions; but while that preamble survives as the opening chapters of book five, the text then breaks off and the siege is lost with the whole of the rest of the work. Suetonius, surprisingly, has little to say about the Jewish war in his biography of Vespasian and less in his biography of Titus. Much of the long history written by Dio Cassius early in the third century survives only in excerpts and epitomes, and the only passage of any length on the Jews, three pages on the siege of Jerusalem, does not provide a check on Josephus. Thus not only for the war of 66–70 but also for the history of the province of Judaea, and for the story of the reigns of Herod the Great, his sons and his grandson, Josephus stands virtually alone, and must be judged on his own merits.

Serious discrepancies occur, as has already been said, between the *Vita* and the *BJ*. Less serious ones occur between accounts of the same episodes in the *BJ* and the *AJ* – possibly implicit corrections in the later work of errors in the earlier. There are even internal discrepancies within individual works. All this is enough to raise the suspicion that we are not on wholly firm ground even where there are accounts which agree or single accounts; but in the absence of external controls we must perforce accept Josephus' word, however uneasily.

Factual accuracy, however, is not the sole criterion by which the quality of a historian is judged. The accuracy of Livy and even of Tacitus can at times be impugned, yet few would deny them the accolade of greatness. A totally accurate factual record may be useful but it is likely to be utterly dull and lifeless, a mere chronicle, not a literary work. An essential feature of a history is literary artistry, and presentation in its many aspects is as vital an ingredient in determining a historian's standing as is his choice of material, the accuracy of his facts, and his critical judgement.

One feature of Josephus' writing which may be disconcerting to the modern reader and appear inartistic is the way in which at times the narrative is proceeding at a spanking pace when it is unceremoniously cut short by a paragraph or a longer passage of material unrelated or only marginally related to the subject in hand, and then resumed equally abruptly. Basically these interruptions are of two types, with different reasons behind them, and it may therefore be helpful if a word is said here about the conventions of ancient historiography, which differed considerably from ours.

One type of interruption, such as a sudden move to another theatre of war, occurs because ancient historians usually wrote annalistically – literally, by years. This convention was established in the late fifth century B.C. by the first scientific historian, Thucydides, who wrote his account of the war between Athens and Sparta 'by summers and winters'. It is a conveniently tidy method by which the reader knows exactly where he is chronologically throughout, and it is reasonably satisfactory in Thucydides' own work, since many of the episodes in the war he is narrating were short and began and ended within one summer or winter. But it is less satisfactory for a historian relating, for example, both events at home and a foreign war lasting for several years (as Tacitus does on occasion); if he follows the annalistic principle strictly, he inevitably has to chop the war, and also domestic events of any length, up into a number of sections, and the narrative loses continuity.

In relating the war of 66–70 Josephus writes annalistically, though events come so thick and fast that his unit is not formally a year. He turns aside from his main narrative whenever he feels it necessary, inserting an episode from elsewhere which happened to be contemporaneous, with or without the definite chronological link 'at this time'. To pick out just a few examples: on p. 179 the massacre of the Jews in Damascus is inserted into the story of the reaction in Jerusalem to the defeat of Cestius; on pp. 190–91 the Jewish attack on Ascalon comes in the middle of Vespasian's preparations for his first campaign; and on pp. 212-14 the revolt of Japha and an incipient rising in Samaritis cut into the siege of Jotapata. In these cases the intrusive episodes are, it is true, germane to the main theme. But this is not always so. On pp. 171-3 we turn from the early stages of the revolt to a riot in Alexandria which, even if contemporary, had no apparent connection with events in Palestine. Going even further away from the main topic, on p. 277 we have a paragraph on the civil war in Italy without any indication of the impact it was soon to have on Palestine by removing Vespasian from the scene of action; and then on pp. 280-86 there is an unnecessarily long account of the proclamation of Vespasian as emperor and the events which established him on the throne. In the case of these and other similar passages on Roman history one is in the border-land between annalistic insertions and outright digressions, which will be discussed shortly.

Josephus does not, however, follow the annalistic method through-out the *BJ*. His account of the reign of Herod the Great is constructed more nearly as it would be by a modern historian, by topics – first external events and accessions of territory, then Herod's building programme in his own country and his benefactions, and finally the quarrels and executions within his family, with earlier episodes of domestic history woven in where necessary as explanations. And towards the end of the work attacks on the Jews in Antioch in 67 and 70-71 are brought together (pp. 377-83, though the account of the later incident suffers an unfortunate and irrelevant interruption).

A quite different explanation lies behind other interruptions to the flow of the narrative. The ancient world never invented those useful lay-bys in which the modern author can park essential but intractable material and thus avoid breaking the main thread of his argument, the footnote and the appendix. Indeed, given the format of the ancient book – a papyrus roll usually some eight to ten inches wide and any-thing up to thirty feet long (or even longer, occasionally), held hori-zontally with the text in columns down its width, and gradually wound off the right-hand roller on to the left by the reader or writer – reference forward or back was very inconvenient. Appendixes at the end of a roll would have been more trouble than they were worth (though footnotes would have been practicable, if anyone had thought of them). All material therefore had to be incorporated in the text, and what we relegate to notes and appendixes appeared as digressions. Herodotus, the 'father of history' in the mid fifth century B.C., was also the father of the digression and a past master at its use. By means of digressions ranging from a few lines to many pages he managed to include all the wide assortment of miscellaneous knowledge that he had accumulated in what was ostensibly the history of a single war.

Josephus does not rival Herodotus in the number or prolixity of his digressions but they are still a noticeable feature of the *BJ*. Leaving aside awkward insertions like the reference to Vespasian's and Titus' movements on p. 243, we have very obvious 'footnotes' in the description on p. 140 of Ptolemais and its crystalline sand, too short to be called an appendix, and in the much briefer explanations of minor points such as those on pp. 45, 59 and 99, which are bracketed in this translation. Three long geographical passages – the survey of the districts of Palestine (pp. 192–3), and the descriptions of the Sea of Galilee and the source of the Jordan (pp. 230–31) and of Jericho and the Dead Sea (pp. 271–3) – can clearly be classified as appendixes, as can the story of Onias (pp. 406–7) and the long accounts of the Jewish sects (pp. 133–8) and of the organization, training, equipment and marching order of the Roman army (pp. 194–7). The description of the fortifications of Jerusalem (pp. 298 ff.) is obviously essential to an understanding of the siege, as is the description of the defences of Masada (pp. 395–6); but from the walls of Jerusalem Josephus is diverted into a detailed description of the Temple and the high priests' vestments which in the context is a digression, though it could have formed an integral part of the narrative under Herod's building programme. It is hard to know whether to classify as long footnote or short appendix the passage on the rue plant at Machaerus with its supernatural powers (p. 388), which appears to serve no purpose but to reveal Josephus' apparently remarkable credulity.

But what of the passages on Roman history mentioned above? Though inserted into the chronological scheme annalistically, they are in character digressions, and two later passages, the first on the German revolt and the Sarmatian raid of 70 (pp. 381–2) and the second on the campaign which led to the annexation of Commagene in 72–3 and an unrelated episode on the eastern fringe of the empire (pp. 391–3), which have no bearing whatever on Jewish history, can only be condemned as unnecessary and irrelevant digressions. And this brings us to the question of Josephus' historical judgement.

How able is Josephus to evaluate critically the evidence before him, to weigh the relative importance of one fact against another, and to see events in true historical perspective? It is not only in his mistaken inclusion of a few irrelevant episodes that he betrays a lack of historical balance. It is shown also in the relative weight which he gives to various topics. The quarrels in Herod's family were of course important in leading ultimately to his final choice of heirs and the division of his kingdom; and they reveal to us his increasingly twisted and suspicious nature. But do they merit three times as much space as is devoted to all the other events of his reign? The saga of the quarrels is vivid, dramatic

and horrifying, and a history devoid of vividness and drama would be
dull indeed. But it appears that once Josephus gets hold of a good story
he cannot summarize but must retail it in full, at the price of giving it
disproportionate prominence. Trivial but colourful incidents of far
less historical significance than Herod's family history receive similarly
full treatment – the circumstances of Aristobulus' death (p. 39), for
instance, and the fate of Simon the Jew at Scythopolis (p. 170), as well
as very many episodes of the war, where at times Josephus passes into
the sensational and the melodramatic. (Are we seriously expected on
p. 209 to believe that a Roman cannon-ball knocked a man's head off
and flung it six hundred yards?) It is perhaps forgivable that Josephus'
personal direction of the siege of Jotapata led him to recount it at extreme length, but we would willingly trade in some of the more
disgusting details of the depths of degradation to which both sides
descended during the siege of Jerusalem (e.g. pp. 334–5) for fuller
information than the eight lines on p. 391 afford us on the reorganiza-
tion of the province of Judaea after the war.

In a number of long episodes, for instance the quarrels in Herod's
family, a good deal of space is given to speeches, in the direct and not
the reported form; and even lengthier speeches punctuate the narrative
of the war. The thoughtful reader may be puzzled by this apparent
verbatim reporting from an age not blessed with shorthand typists
and tape-recorders, and perhaps especially puzzled by Josephus'
acquaintance with such things as a private conversation between Herod
and Octavian (pp. 79–80) and a remark made to Herod by his wife
in their bedroom (p. 87). Of the war speeches, some Josephus cannot
possibly have heard, and even those which he probably did hear,
like Agrippa II's appeal to the citizens of Jerusalem (pp. 156–62), or
made himself, it would have been out of the question for him to remember word for word. But Josephus is merely following the practice
introduced into historiography by Thucydides, who says of the speeches
in his history that, since verbatim reporting was impossible, he has
put into each speaker's mouth what he 'thought was required by the
occasion, keeping as near as possible to the general drift of what was
actually said'. Such speeches add life and variety to the factual narrative, and points can be made more forcibly in this dramatic form than
in impersonal argument. Some later historians were less scrupulous
than Thucydides and did not confine themselves to producing their
own versions of speeches of which records or memories survived.
Tacitus, for instance, invents pre-battle pep-talks for Boudicca and the
Scottish tribal chieftain Calgacus, who harangued their warriors, if at
all, in a language wholly incomprehensible to any Roman within ear-
shot.

As regards the speeches in the *BJ*, those attributed to Herod need not be rejected as pure Josephan fantasy. In writing of his reign Josephus depended very heavily on the work of Nicolas of Damascus, the king's close friend and court chronicler, who is likely to have had fairly reliable records of the speeches made on various occasions (though no doubt Josephus made his own contributions to the rhetoric); he also had access to Herod's *Memoirs* (mentioned in *A J* xv. 174), which could have provided even more intimate details than an account of his interview with Octavian. Josephus' own hand is obvious throughout the war speeches; in most cases it is hard to see how any written record could have survived, and memories would quickly have got blurred. Many are of an unconvincing length and polish, and two in particular, Agrippa II's appeal in 66 and the first of Josephus' own two speeches to the defenders of Jerusalem (pp. 318–22), with their extended arguments from history and contemporary politics, read more like literary set-pieces than actual speeches; for, however valid their logic, one can hardly imagine the audience on either occasion having the patience to listen to them.

It is hard to like Josephus as a person. He was conceited, not only about his own learning but also about the opinions held of him as commander both by the Galilaeans and by the Romans; he was guilty of shocking duplicity at Jotapata, saving himself by the sacrifice of his companions; he was too naive to see how he stood condemned out of his own mouth for his conduct, and yet no words were too harsh when he was blackening his opponents; and after landing, however involuntarily, in the Roman camp, he turned his captivity to his own advantage, and benefited for the rest of his days from his change of side. An unpleasant personality is, of course, not incompatible with high qualities as a historian, but in that role Josephus has been shown to have deficiencies. Yet, when all is said, Josephus has left us in the *BJ* – to borrow, with him (*Ap.* i. 53), Thucydides' assessment of his own work – 'not a mere ephemeral prize essay but an everlasting possession'. Whether it deserves to be called 'great' is at least partly a matter of opinion, but even its severest critics cannot deny that it gives us an outstandingly vivid picture of the death-throes of a proud but unhappy city, of the fanaticism of the rival factions and the tensions between them, of the miseries of the ordinary people caught up willy-nilly in events which they could not control, and of the horrors of siege, sack, fire and pillage. In setting out to make the tragedy of his people known to the gentile world Josephus succeeded beyond his wildest dreams. His story has lived down the centuries as a treasured legacy from antiquity and now reaches those to whom his own tongue is inaccesible in translations made into languages unborn in his day.

THE JEWISH WAR

Preface

THE war of the Jews against the Romans was the greatest of our time; greater too, perhaps, than any recorded struggle whether between cities or nations. Yet persons with no first-hand knowledge, accepting baseless and inconsistent stories on hearsay, have written garbled accounts of it, while those of eyewitnesses have been falsified either to flatter the Romans or to vilify the Jews, eulogy or abuse being substituted for factual record. So for the benefit of the Emperor's subjects I have decided to translate into Greek the books which I wrote some time ago in my native language[1] for circulation among non-Greek speakers inland. I myself, Josephus, son of Matthias, am a Hebrew by race, and a priest from Jerusalem[2]; in the early stages I fought against the Romans, and of the later events I was an unwilling witness.

This upheaval, as I said, was the greatest of all time; and when it occurred Rome herself was in a most unsettled state. Jewish revolutionaries took advantage of the general disturbance; they had vast resources of men and money; and so widespread was the ferment that some were filled with hope of gain, others with fear of loss, by the state of affairs in the East; for the Jews expected all their Mesopotamian brethren to join their insurrection.[3] From another side Roman supremacy was being challenged by the Gauls on their borders, and the Celts were restive – in fact after Nero's death disorder reigned everywhere. Presented with this opportunity many aspired to the imperial throne, while the soldiery were eager for a transference of power as a means of enriching themselves.[4]

I therefore thought it inexcusable, when such issues were involved, to see the truth misrepresented and to take no notice. Parthians, Babylonians, Southern Arabians, Mesopotamian Jews, and Adiabenians,[5] thanks to my labours, were accurately informed of the causes of the war, the sufferings it involved, and its disastrous ending. Were the Greeks and those Romans who took no part in it to remain ignorant of the facts, deluded with flattery or fiction? Yet the writers I have in mind claim to be writing history, though besides getting all their facts wrong they seem to me to miss their target altogether. For they wish to establish the greatness of the Romans while all the time disparaging and deriding the actions of the Jews. But I do not see how men can prove themselves great by overcoming feeble opponents! Again, they are not impressed by the length of the war, the vastness of the Roman forces which endured such hardships, and the genius of their commanders, whose strenuous endeavours before Jerusalem will bring them little glory if the difficulties they overcame are belittled.

However, it is not my intention to counter the champions of the Romans by exaggerating the heroism of my own countrymen: I shall state the facts accurately and impartially.. At the same time the language in which I record the events will reflect my own feelings and emotions; for I must permit myself to bewail my country's tragedy. She was destroyed by internal dissensions, and the Romans who so unwillingly set fire to the Temple were brought in by the Jews' self-appointed rulers,[6] as Titus Caesar,[7] the Temple's destroyer, has testified. For throughout the war he pitied the common people, who were helpless against the partisans[8]; and over and over again he delayed the capture of the city and prolonged the siege in the hope that the ringleaders would submit. If anyone criticizes me for the accusations I bring against the party chiefs and their gangs of bandits,[9] or for my laments over the misfortunes of my country, he must pardon my weakness, regardless of the rules of historical writing. For it so happened that of all the cities under Roman rule our own reached the highest summit of prosperity, and in turn fell into the lowest depths of misery; the misfortunes of all other races since the beginning of history, compared with those of the Jews, seem small; and for our misfortunes we have only ourselves to blame. How then could I master my feelings? If anyone is disposed to pass harsh judgement on my emotion, he must remember that the facts belong to the story and that only the grief is the writer's.

On the other hand criticism may fairly be levelled at those Greek scholars who, knowing that the wars of the past fade into insignificance beside the astonishing events of their own times, sit in judgement upon the latter and severely censure those who make an effort to record them. For though their own flow of words is greater, their historical sense is inferior. They write histories themselves about the Assyrians and Medes, implying that the earlier writers did not do the work properly. Yet they are no more a match for them as writers than as thinkers. For the old historians were all eager to set down the events of their own lifetimes, and their participation in these events gave vitality to their accounts, while it was impossible to depart from the truth without being detected. Surely to leave a permanent record of events not previously recorded for the benefit of posterity is worthy of the highest praise; and the real worker is not the man who merely changes the order and arrangement of another man's work, but the one who has something new to say and constructs a historical edifice of his own. I myself have gone to great trouble and expense, though an alien, so that I may offer to the Greeks and Romans a permanent record of their triumphs: native writers, on the other hand, though the chance of profit from litigation finds them possessed of ready tongue and an unlimited flow of words, when they turn to history (which requires them to speak the truth after laboriously collecting the facts) appear to be gagged, and pass over to inferior writers unaware of the facts the task of recording the achievements of the great. I am determined therefore to respect the truth of history, though it has been neglected by the Greeks.

An account of the early history of the Jews, their origin, their exodus from Egypt, the extent of their wanderings and subsequent conquests, and their removal from their country, would, I think, be out of place here, and in any case unnecessary[10]; for many Jews before me have accurately recorded the doings of our ancestors, and their accounts have been translated into Greek with very few mistakes.[11] But where the Greek historians and our own prophets left off I shall begin my story; and I shall relate the events of the war which I witnessed in great detail and with all the completeness of which I am capable, whereas events before my time will be run over in brief outline.

Starting with Antiochus Epiphanes, who stormed Jerusalem and after holding it for three and a half years was driven out of the country by the Hasmonaeans, I shall explain how their descendants by their struggles for the throne forced Pompey and the Romans to intervene; how Antipater's son Herod brought in Sosius[12] and put an end to the Hasmonaean dynasty; how the people revolted after Herod's death, when Augustus was Roman Emperor and Quintilius Varus the local governor; and how in the twelfth year of Nero's reign the war broke out, with disastrous results to Cestius and remarkable successes for Jewish arms in the early encounters.

The fortification of the neighbouring towns will occupy us next; and the decision of Nero, in whom Cestius' defeats had aroused fears for the whole Empire, to give Vespasian supreme command; the invasion of Jewish territory by Vespasian assisted by his elder son; the size of the Roman army and allied contingents with which he overran Galilee; and the capture of the Galilaean towns, some by all-out assault, some by negotiation. At this point I must explain the Roman system of military discipline and legionary training, and describe the dimensions and features of the two Galilees[13] and the limits of Judaea, with the peculiarities of the country, especially the lakes and springs. Of the fate of each of the captured towns I shall give an exact account based on my own observations and the part I played. It would be pointless to draw a veil over my own misfortunes, with which my readers are familiar.[14]

Next will come the death of Nero at the moment when Jewish hopes were waning; the interruption of Vespasian's advance on Jerusalem by his summons to the throne; the encouragement he received from portents, and the upheavals in Rome; the insistence of his soldiers on making him emperor despite his protests; the outbreak of party strife among the Jews following his departure for Egypt to settle the affairs of the Empire; and the tyranny and dissensions of the party chiefs.

An account must next be given of the second invasion, mounted in Egypt by Titus; the method, place, and size of his troop concentrations; the state of the party-riven City when he arrived; the series of assaults and the erection of the platforms; the siting and measurements of the three protecting walls[15]; the defences of the City and the plan of the Temple and Sanctuary[16]; all the exact measurements of these and of the altar; certain customs of the feasts, the seven grades of purity, the priestly ministrations, the priestly and high-priestly vestments; and a description of the Holy of Holies. I shall conceal nothing, and add nothing to the published facts.

Then I shall contrast the brutality of the party chiefs towards their countrymen with the clemency of the Romans towards aliens, and the persistence with which Titus showed his anxiety to save the City and the Sanctuary[17] by inviting the insurgents to come to terms. In discussing the sufferings of the people and the calamities that led to their final defeat, I shall consider how far they were due to enemy action, how far to party strife, and how far to starvation. My account will include the misfortunes of the deserters and the punishments inflicted on the prisoners; the burning of the Sanctuary despite Caesar's disapproval and the number of sacred treasures snatched from the flames; the capture of the entire City and the signs and wonders that preceded it; the arrest of the party chiefs, the number of people enslaved and the fates that befell them; the way in which the Romans disposed of the last remnants of the war, demolishing the ramparts of every fort; the progress of Titus through the whole country to establish order, and his return to Italy and triumphal celebrations.

All this I have embraced in seven books. To those who took part in the war or have ascertained the facts I have left no ground for complaint or criticism; it is for those who love the truth, not those who seek entertainment, that I have written. I will now begin my story where I began my summary.

CHAPTER I

Herod's Predecessors

AT the time when Antiochus Epiphanes[1] was disputing the control of Palestine[2] with Ptolemy VI, dissension broke out among the leading Jews, who competed for supremacy because no prominent person could bear to be subject to his equals. Onias, one of the chief priests, forced his way to the top and expelled the sons of Tobias from the City. They fled to Antiochus and implored him to use them as guides and invade Judaea.[3] This was just what the king wanted; so setting out in person with a very large force he stormed the City, killed a large number of Ptolemy's adherents, gave his men permission to loot as they liked, took the lead in plundering the Sanctuary, and stopped the continuous succession of daily sacrifices for three and a half years.[4] The high priest Onias fled to Ptolemy, from whom he obtained a site in the district of Heliopolis. There he built a little town on the lines of Jerusalem and a Sanctuary like the one he had left. All this will be referred to again in due course.[5]

Antiochus was far from satisfied with his unexpected capture of the City, the loot, and the long death-roll. Unable to control his passions and remembering what the siege had cost him, he tried to force the Jews to break their ancient Law by leaving their babies uncircumcised and sacrificing swine on the altar. Meeting with a blank refusal he executed the leading recusants; and Bacchides, who was sent by him to command the garrison,[6] finding in these monstrous instructions scope for his savage instincts, plunged recklessly into every form of iniquity, torturing the most worthy citizens one by one, and publicly displaying day after day the appearance of a captured city, till by the enormity of his crimes he drove his victims to attempt reprisals.

Matthias, son of Asamonaeus,[7] a priest from the village of Modein, raised a tiny force consisting of his five sons and himself, and killed Bacchides with cleavers. Fearing the strength of the garrison he fled to the hills for the time being, but when many of the common people joined him he regained confidence, came down again, gave battle, defeated Antiochus' generals and chased them out of Judaea. By that success he achieved supremacy, and in gratitude for his expulsion of the foreigners his countrymen gladly accepted his rule, which on his decease he left to Judas,[8] the eldest of his sons.

As Judas did not expect Antiochus to take this lying down, he not only marshalled the available Jewish forces but took the bold step of allying himself with Rome.[9] When Epiphanes again invaded the country he counter-attacked vigorously and drove him back; then striking while the iron was hot, he hurled himself against the garrison of the City, which had not yet been dislodged, threw the troops out of the Upper City, and shut them into the Lower – the part of the town called the Citadel. Then taking possession of the Temple he cleansed the whole area and walled it round, ordered a new set of ceremonial vessels to be fashioned and brought into the Sanctuary as the old ones were defiled, built another altar, and resumed the sacrifices. No sooner was Jerusalem once more the Holy City than Antiochus died, leaving as heir – both to his throne and to his hatred of the Jews – his son Antiochus.

The new king got together 50,000 foot, about 500 horse, and 80 elephants, and marched through Judaea into the hill country. Bethsaron, a small town, fell into his hands, but at a place called Bethzachariah,[10] where the road narrows, he was met by Judas and his army. Before the main bodies engaged, Eleazar, Judas' brother, noticed the tallest of the elephants fitted with a large howdah and gilded battlements, and assuming that Antiochus was on its back, ran out a long way ahead of his own lines, and hacking a way through the enemy's close array got near to the elephant. To reach the supposed king was impossible because of his height from the ground, so he struck the beast's under-belly, bringing it down on himself so that he was crushed to death. He had done no more than make a heroic attempt, putting glory before life itself. The rider of the elephant was in fact a commoner; even if he had happened to be Antiochus, Eleazar would have achieved nothing by his daring but the reputation of having gone to certain death in the mere hope of a brilliant success. To his brother the tragedy was a presage of the final issue. Determined and prolonged as was the Jews' resistance, superior numbers and fortune's favour gave the king's soldiers the victory; with most of his own men dead, Judas fled with the remnant to the toparchy of Gophna. Antiochus went on to Jerusalem, where he remained only a few days, till lack of supplies compelled him to withdraw, leaving a garrison that he thought adequate, and taking the rest of his forces to winter quarters in Syria.

After the king's retreat Judas did not let the grass grow under his feet. Large numbers of Jews flocked to his standard, and he had already rallied the survivors of the battle; so near the village of Acedasa he challenged Antiochus' generals. In the battle that followed he fought magnificently and inflicted heavy casualties on the enemy, but lost his own life.[11] Only a few days later his brother John fell victim to a plot of the pro-Syrian party.

Judas was succeeded by another brother, Jonathan, who did everything possible to strengthen his authority in his own country, securing his position by his friendship with Rome[12] and by making a truce with Antiochus' son.[13] Unfortunately none of these precautions could guarantee him security. Trypho, guardian of the young Antiochus and virtually regent, had long been plotting against the boy and endeavouring to eliminate his friends; and when Jonathan came with a very small escort to Ptolemais to see Antiochus, he treacherously seized and imprisoned him, and launched a campaign against the Jews. Then repulsed by Simon, Jonathan's brother, he avenged his defeat by murdering Jonathan.

Simon's conduct of affairs was most efficient. He reduced Gazara, Joppa, and Jamnia in the neighbourhood of Jerusalem, and demolished the Citadel after overwhelming the garrison.[14] Later he allied himself with Antiochus[15] against Trypho, whom Antiochus was besieging in Dora before marching against the Parthians. But he did not cause the king to modify his ambitions by helping him to destroy Trypho: it was not long before Antiochus sent an army under his general Cendebaeus to ravage Judaea and reduce Simon to subjection. Simon in spite of his years showed a young man's vigour in his conduct of the campaign; he sent his sons ahead with his stoutest men, while he himself at the head of a section of his army took the offensive in another direction. He also placed large numbers of men in ambush all over the hill country and was successful in every onset; so brilliant was his victory that he was appointed high priest,[16] and after 170 years of Macedonian control[17] gave the Jews their freedom.

He too was the victim of a plot: he was assassinated at a banquet by Ptolemy, his son-in-law, who after locking up Simon's wife and two of his sons sent a party to murder the third son, John Hyrcanus.

Warned of their approach the youngster made a dash for the City, having great confidence in the people, who remembered what his father had achieved and were disgusted with Ptolemy's iniquitous conduct. Ptolemy hurled himself against another gate but was thrown back by the citizens, who had already welcomed Hyrcanus with open arms. Ptolemy at once retired to one of the forts above Jericho, called Dagon; Hyrcanus, invested with the high priesthood[18] like his father before him, offered sacrifice to God and then hurried after Ptolemy to rescue his mother and brothers.

His attack on the fort started promisingly enough, but was held up by his natural feelings. Every time Ptolemy was in a difficulty, he brought out John's mother and brothers on to the ramparts where they could be seen by all, and began to torture them, threatening to throw them headlong unless John broke off the siege forthwith. This atrocity filled Hyrcanus with anger, and still more with pity and fear; but neither torture nor the threat of death could make his mother flinch – she stretched out her arms and implored her son on no account to let her cruel sufferings induce him to spare the vile creature; better death at Ptolemy's hands than life without end, so long as he paid for his wrongs to their house. Whenever John, thrilled by his mother's fortitude, listened to her entreaties, he launched a fresh attack; but when he saw her flesh torn with the lash, his resolution weakened and his feelings overcame him. This dragged out the siege till the Year of Rest came round, for like the seventh day, the seventh year is observed by the Jews as a time of rest. This freed Ptolemy from the siege, and after putting John's mother and brothers to death he fled to Zeno Cotulas, the autocrat of Philadelphia.

Antiochus, eager to avenge his defeat at Simon's hands, marched into Judaea and pitching his camp before Jerusalem besieged Hyrcanus. Hyrcanus opened the tomb of David, the wealthiest of kings, and removed more than 3,000 talents. With a tenth of this sum he bribed Antiochus to raise the siege.[19] With the balance he did what no Jew had ever done before; he maintained a body of mercenaries.

When later Antiochus marched against the Parthians,[20] giving him a chance to retaliate, Hyrcanus at once launched a campaign against the towns of Northern Palestine, correctly assuming that he would find no first-class troops in them. Medabe and Gamaea with the towns nearby submitted, as did Shechem and Gerizim. He was successful also against the Cuthaeans, the people living round the copy of the Temple

at Jerusalem.[21] In Idumaea a number of towns submitted, including
Adora and Marisa.[22]

Advancing to Samaria, where now stands Sebaste, the city built by
King Herod,[23] he constructed a wall right round and entrusted the
siege to his sons Aristobulus and Antigonus. They pressed it relentlessly, bringing the inhabitants so near to starvation that they resorted
to the most unwonted food. They appealed for aid to Antiochus the
Aspendian.[24] He readily agreed, but was defeated by Aristobulus and
his men. Chased by the brothers all the way to Scythopolis he
managed to escape; they, returning to Samaria, again shut the people
inside the walls, then took the city, demolished it, and enslaved the
inhabitants. As success followed success they lost none of their ardour,
but marching their forces as far as Scythopolis overran that region
and ravaged all the country inland from Mount Carmel.

Jealousy of the continued success of John and his sons aroused the
bitter hostility of their fellow countrymen, who gathered in large
numbers and engaged in active opposition, which at last flared up in
open war and ended in defeat. For the rest of his natural life John
enjoyed prosperity, and after no less than thirty-one[25] years of admirable administration he died leaving five sons, blessed if ever a man
was and with no cause to blame fortune as far as he was concerned. He
alone enjoyed the three greatest privileges at once – political power,
the high priesthood, and the prophetic gift. So constant was his
divine inspiration that no future event was hidden from him; for
instance, he foresaw and foretold that his two eldest sons would not
retain control of the state. Their overthrow is a story worth telling, so
far did they fall below their predecessor's prosperity.

When their father died,[26] the eldest of them, Aristobulus, turned
the constitution into a monarchy, and was the first to wear a crown,
471 years and three months after the return of the nation to their own
land, set free from slavery in Babylon.[27] To the next brother, Antigonus, of whom he seemed very fond, he assigned equal honours; the
rest he imprisoned in fetters. In fetters too he placed his mother, who
contested his claim to supremacy, as John had left her in supreme
charge, going so far in brutality as to let her die of starvation in the
dungeon.

Vengeance overtook him in the loss of his brother Antigonus, of
whom he was so fond that he had made him sharer of his royal authority. He killed even him as the result of slanders invented by

unscrupulous courtiers. At first their tales were disbelieved by Aristobulus, who, as we have said, was very fond of his brother and put down most of their lies to jealousy. But when Antigonus returned with full ceremony from a campaign to attend the feast at which it is an old custom to put up tabernacles to God,[28] it happened that Aristobulus was ill at the time. At the end of the feast Antigonus went up to the Temple with his bodyguard and in full regalia to offer prayers, mainly for his brother's recovery. Meanwhile the unscrupulous courtiers went to the king and told him all about the escort of soldiers and the proud bearing of Antigonus, improper in a subject; he was coming, they said, with a huge force to murder him, unable to rest content with the shadow of royalty when he could grasp the substance.

These tales by degrees overcame the reluctance of Aristobulus, who took care to hide his suspicions but at the same time to guard against any unseen danger. While he himself was confined to bed in the fort at first called Baris and later Antonia,[29] he stationed his bodyguard in one of the underground passages, with orders to leave Antigonus alone if unarmed, but to kill him if he came in arms; then he sent men to warn his brother to come unarmed. To counter this the queen contrived a very cunning plot with the conspirators. They bribed the messengers to suppress the king's warning and tell Antigonus that his brother had heard he had secured some wonderful armour and military equipment in Galilee.[30] Owing to his unfortunate illness he could not come and see them himself; 'However,' he went on, 'now that you are just leaving, I should very much like to see you in your outfit.' Hearing this, and aware of nothing in his brother's disposition to make him suspect any harm, Antigonus set off in his armour to have it inspected. When he came to the dark passage called Strato's Tower, the bodyguard killed him – convincing evidence that no natural affection is proof against slander, and that none of our better feelings are strong enough to hold out against envy indefinitely.

The incident had another surprising feature. Judas was an Essene[31] born and bred, who had never been wrong or mistaken in any of his predictions. On this occasion, when he saw Antigonus passing through the Temple, he called out to his acquaintances – a number of his pupils were sitting there with him – 'O God! the best thing now is that I should die, since truth is dead already, and one of my predictions has proved false. There, alive, is Antigonus, who was to have been killed today. The place where he was fated to die was Strato's Tower, and that is seventy miles away; and it is already ten o'clock! The time has made nonsense of my prophecy.' Having said this the old man remained lost in gloomy thoughts – and a few minutes later came the news that Antigonus had been murdered in the underground strong-point, which was actually called Strato's Tower, like the coastal town of Caesarea.[32] So the prophet's mistake was natural.

Aristobulus, bitterly regretting this foul crime, at once fell into a swift decline; at the thought of the murder his mind became un-hinged and he wasted away, until his entrails were ruptured by his uncontrollable grief and he brought up quantities of blood. While carrying this away one of the servants waiting on him, impelled by divine providence, slipped at the very spot where Antigonus had been struck down, and on the blood-stains – still visible – of the murdered man he spilt the blood of the killer. At once a shriek went up from the spectators, as if the servant had poured the blood there on purpose. Hearing the cry the king asked the reason, and when no one dared tell him he insisted on being informed. At last by threats he compelled them to tell him the truth. His eyes filled with tears, and groaning with the little strength that was left he murmured: 'So it is. I could not hide my unlawful deeds from God's all-seeing eye. Swift retribution pursues me for the blood of my kinsman. How long, most shameless body, will you contain the soul that has been adjudged my mother's and my brother's? How long shall I pour out my blood to them, drop by drop? Let them take it all at once: let heaven mock them no more with these libations from my entrails.' The next moment he was dead,[33] having reigned no more than a year.

His widow released his brothers and enthroned Alexander, the eldest,[34] and seemingly the most balanced character. But on ascending the throne he executed one brother as a rival claimant: the survivor, who preferred to keep out of the public eye, he held in honour. He also came into conflict with Ptolemy Lathyrus, who had seized the town of Asochis; he inflicted many casualties but Ptolemy had the advantage. But when Ptolemy was chased away by his mother Cleopatra and withdrew to Egypt, Alexander besieged and took Gadara and Amathus,[35] the biggest stronghold east of the Jordan, where were stored the most valuable possessions of Zeno's son Theodorus. But by a sudden counter-attack Theodorus not only recovered his property but captured the king's baggage-train, killing some 10,000 Jews. However, the blow was not fatal, and Alexander turning towards the coast captured Gaza, Raphia, and Anthedon,[36] which King Herod later renamed Agrippias.

After his enslavement of these towns there was a Jewish rising at one of the feasts – the usual occasion for sedition to flare up. It looked as if he would be unable to crush this conspiracy, but his foreign troops came to the rescue. These were Pisidians and Cilicians: Syrians[37] he did not recruit as mercenaries because of their innate detestation of all Jews. After putting to the sword over 6,000 of the insurgents he attacked Arabia, overruning Gilead and Moab and imposing tribute on the inhabitants. Then returning to Amathus he found that Theodorus had taken fright at his victories and abandoned the fortress; so he demolished it. He next took the field against Obodas of Arabia. But the king had laid an ambush near Gaulane and Alexander fell into the trap, losing his entire army, which was crowded together at the bottom of a ravine and crushed by a mass of camels. He made good his own escape to Jerusalem, but the completeness of the disaster fanned the smouldering fires of hatred and the nation rose in revolt – only to be worsted again in a succession of battles which lasted six years and cost the lives of as many as 50,000 Jews. He had little cause to rejoice over these victories, so ruinous to his kingdom; so suspending warlike operations he attempted to reach an understanding with his subjects by persuasion. But they were still more embittered by his change of front and unstable behaviour; and when he asked in what way he could satisfy them, they replied: 'By dying; even a dead man would be hard to forgive for such monstrous crimes.' Without more ado they called on Demetrius the Unready[38] for help. He at once agreed – in the hope of enlarging his kingdom – and arrived with an army, joining his Jewish allies near Shechem.

The combined army was opposed by Alexander with 1,000 cavalry and an infantry force of 8,000 mercenaries, reinforced by loyal Jews to the number of 10,000. The other side consisted of 3,000 cavalry and 14,000 infantry.[39] Before battle was joined the two kings issued proclamations intended to detach supporters from the other side, Demetrius hoping to win over Alexander's mercenaries, Alexander Demetrius' Jewish contingent. As the Jews would not abandon their bitterness nor the Greeks their loyalty, there was nothing for it but an appeal to force. The victor in the battle was Demetrius, in spite of a magnificent display of determination and prowess by Alexander's mercenaries. The outcome of the engagement, however, was not at all what either side had expected. Demetrius, the victor, was deserted by those who had called him in, whereas through sympathy for the man who was down Alexander, after fleeing to the hills, was joined by 6,000 Jews! This swing of the pendulum was too much for Demetrius: convinced that Alexander was now fit to take the field again and that the whole nation was flocking to his standard, he withdrew. The departure of their allies did not cause the rest of the people to lay aside their quarrel: they waged war unremittingly with Alexander till after very heavy losses the remnant were driven into Bemeselis; when this town fell, the survivors were taken as prisoners to Jerusalem. So unbridled was Alexander's rage that from brutality he proceeded to impiety. Eight hundred of the prisoners he crucified[40] in the middle of the City, then butchered their wives and children before their eyes; meanwhile cup in hand as he reclined amidst his concubines he enjoyed the spectacle. Such terror gripped the people that the next night 8,000 of the king's opponents fled right out of Judaea, and remained in exile till his death. By such deeds he at last gave his kingdom an uneasy peace, and hung up his weapons.

But fresh troubles were in store for him – the work of Antiochus Dionysius, brother of Demetrius and last heir of Seleucus.[41] This man launched a campaign against the Arabs, alarming Alexander, who dug a deep trench stretching from the hillside above Antipatris to the beach at Joppa, raising a high wall in front of the trench with wooden towers built into it to ward off attacks at the weak points. But Antiochus was not to be stopped: he burnt the towers, filled in the trench, and marched his army across. Deciding to deal later with the man who had tried to stop him, he went straight on to attack the Arabs. Their king retired to better defensive positions, then suddenly faced about with his cavalry force of 10,000 men and fell upon the army of Antiochus while it was in disarray. A bitter struggle followed. While Antiochus survived his men fought on, though they suffered appallingly at Arab hands; when at last he fell as a result of risking his life all the time in the forefront to help his struggling soldiers, the entire line broke. Most of his army was destroyed in the engagement or in the subsequent flight; the survivors took refuge in the village of Cana, where lack of food killed off all but a handful.

At this point the people of Damascus, through hatred of Ptolemy, son of Mennaeus,[42] brought in Aretas[43] and made him king of

Coele Syria.[44] He promptly marched into Judaea, defeated Alexander in battle, agreed on terms, and withdrew. Alexander took Pella and advanced against Gerasa, once more coveting Theodorus' possessions.[45] After shutting up the garrison within a triple wall he occupied the place without a battle. He went on to overwhelm Gaulane and Seleucia and the 'Valley of Antiochus', and captured the strong fortress of Gamala,[46] dismissing its commander Demetrius who was accused of many crimes. Then he returned to Judaea, after three whole years in the field, and was warmly welcomed by the nation in view of his successes. But the end of the war proved to be the beginning of physical decay. Afflicted with a quartan ague he thought he could get rid of his sickness by resuming a strenuous life. He threw himself into ill-judged campaigns, and by making impossible demands on his bodily strength wore himself out completely. He died in the midst of storm and stress, after reigning for twenty-seven years.[47]

He had left his throne to his wife Alexandra, confident that the Jews would most readily submit to her, since by her freedom from any trace of his brutality and her constant opposition to his excesses she had gained the good-will of the people. And he was right in his expectations; woman though she was, she established her authority by her reputation for piety. She was most particular in her observance of the national customs, and offenders against the Holy Law she turned out of office. Of the two sons she had borne Alexander she appointed the elder, Hyrcanus, high priest,[48] in view of his age and his natural disinclination to interfere with state affairs; the younger, Aristobulus, who was an impulsive character, she kept out of the public eye.

Alongside her was the growing power of the Pharisees, a Jewish sect that appeared more pious than the rest and stricter in the interpretation of the Law.[49] Alexandra, being devoted to religion, paid too great heed to them and they, availing themselves more and more of the simplicity of the woman, ended by becoming the effective rulers of the state, free to banish or recall, to release or imprison, at will. In short, the privileges of royal authority were theirs, the expenses and vexations Alexandra's. She was very shrewd, however, in making major decisions, and by regular recruiting doubled the size of her army, collecting also a large mercenary force, so that beside making her own country strong she inspired a healthy respect in foreign potentates. But while she ruled others, the Pharisees ruled her. Thus

Diogenes, an eminent man who had been a friend of Alexander, was put to death by them on the charge of having abetted the king in his crucifixion of eight hundred citizens. Then they pressed Alexandra to execute the rest of those who had incited Alexander against them: her superstitious nature made her give way, and they killed whom they would. The most prominent of the threatened citizens sought the aid of Aristobulus, and he persuaded his mother to spare them in view of their station, expelling them from the City if not sure of their innocence. Thus granted impunity, they scattered over the country.

Alexandra dispatched an army to Damascus on the ground that Ptolemy was regularly meddling there; but the army returned with no particular success to its credit. However, while Tigranes the Armenian king was encamped before Ptolemais besieging Cleopatra, she won him over by bargaining and bribery. But he had to withdraw in hot haste to deal with troubles at home, Lucullus having invaded Armenia.[50] Meanwhile Alexandra sickened; the younger son Aristobulus seized his chance, and with his numerous servants – all devoted to him because of his impulsive character – got all the strongholds[51] into his power, and with the money found there raised a force of mercenaries and proclaimed himself king. This so upset Hyrcanus that his mother felt very sorry for him, and locked up the wife and children of Aristobulus in Antonia. This was a fortress adjoining the Temple on the north side; as stated already, it was first called Baris and later renamed when Antony was supreme, just as the cities of Sebaste and Agrippias were named after Sebastos (Augustus) and Agrippa.[52] But before Alexandra could proceed against Aristobulus for the unseating of his brother, she died, after ruling the country for nine years.[53]

The heir to the throne was Hyrcanus. While still alive Alexandra had put the kingdom in his hands, but in ability and enterprise he was no match for Aristobulus. Near Jericho the two met in battle for the crown, but the bulk of Hyrcanus' army deserted him and went over to Aristobulus. Hyrcanus with those who stuck to him immediately sought shelter in Antonia, and seized as hostages for his security the wife and children of Aristobulus. However, final disaster was averted by a compromise: Aristobulus was to be king[54] and Hyrcanus, having abdicated, was to retain his other dignities as the king's brother. On these terms they were reconciled in the Temple, and surrounded by the people they warmly embraced each other and exchanged residences, Aristobulus taking over the Palace, Hyrcanus Aristobulus' house.

Fear seized the enemies of Aristobulus when he so unexpectedly triumphed, most of all Antipater, whom he had long detested. He was by race an Idumaean, and ancestry, wealth, and other sources of strength made him the natural leader of his nation.[55] He advised Hyrcanus to seek the protection of Aretas, king of Arabia, and so win back his kingdom, at the same time urging Aretas to receive Hyrcanus and restore him to his throne. He heaped abuse on the character of Aristobulus and lavished praise on Hyrcanus, and argued that it was the right thing for the ruler of so splendid a kingdom to extend his aid to the wronged; wronged indeed was Hyrcanus, deprived as he was of the crown that was his by right of birth. Having prevailed on both men, he slipped out of the City in the dark with Hyrcanus, and making all speed arrived safely at Petra, the capital of Arabia. There he handed over Hyrcanus to Aretas, whom by dint of much persuasion and carefully chosen presents he induced to provide an army to restore the exile – 50,000 horse and foot. For such a force Aristobulus was no match; worsted in the first clash he was chased into Jerusalem, where he would quickly have been captured after a successful assault had not Scaurus the Roman commander intervened in the nick of time and ended the siege.

Scaurus had been sent into Syria from Armenia by Pompey the Great, who was at war with Tigranes. Arriving at Damascus immediately after its capture by Metellus and Lollius, he packed off these officers, and learning how things were in Judaea lost no time in seizing this heaven-sent opportunity.[56] As soon as he set foot on Jewish soil delegates arrived from both brothers to request his aid. The rights of the case were outweighed by Aristobulus' gift of three hundred talents. Accepting this sum Scaurus sent a herald to Hyrcanus and the Arabs, threatening them with Pompey and the Romans unless they raised the siege. Back from Judaea to Philadelphia fled Aretas in a panic, and back to Damascus went Scaurus. Aristobulus was not satisfied with his escape, but collected his entire army and pursued the enemy; near Papyron he engaged them and killed over 6,000, among whom was Antipater's brother Phallion.

Hyrcanus and Antipater, deprived of Arab help, transferred their hopes to the other side, and when Pompey entered Syria and arrived at Damascus[57] they sought his protection. They brought no presents but relied on the same arguments as they had used with Aretas, begging him to repudiate the violent methods of Aristobulus and to restore to his throne the man to whom, as the elder and better of the two, it belonged. Nor was Aristobulus behindhand, knowing that Scaurus could be bribed. He too presented himself, decked out in all his royal splendour. But he became sick of servility and could not bear to abase himself in order to secure his ends at the cost of his dignity; so at the city of Dium he turned back.

This conduct stung Pompey, who yielding to the importunity of Hyrcanus and his friends set off in pursuit of Aristobulus at the head of the Roman army and numerous auxiliaries from Syria. By-passing Pella and Scythopolis he came to Coreae, where travellers from the interior cross into Judaea. Informed that Aristobulus had sought safety in Alexandreum, a most elaborately equipped fortress perched on a lofty eminence, he sent orders to him to come down. Summoned thus peremptorily the king was more inclined to try a fall than to submit, but he saw that the people were frightened to death, and his friends begged him to realize that Roman power was irresistible. Taking their advice he came down to Pompey, attempted at great length to justify his claim to the throne, and went back to his stronghold. At his brother's invitation he came down again, argued the rights and wrongs of the case, and went away without hindrance from Pompey. Hovering between hope and fear, he came down repeatedly in the expectation of talking Pompey into putting everything into his hands, and as often returned to his citadel to avoid the appearance of yielding too soon. Finally however Pompey insisted on his evacuating the forts, and as the commanders had instructions to take no notice of any order not written by Aristobulus himself, he forced him to send each one of them a written order to march out. Aristobulus complied, but withdrew to Jerusalem in a rage and prepared for war with Pompey.

Pompey allowed him no time for these preparations but followed at once, stimulated by news of Mithridates' death, received when he was near Jericho. (This is the most fertile spot in Judaea, rich in palms and in balsam: the stems of the balsam trees are slashed with sharp stones and the resin collected where it is exuded from the cuts.) After spending one night in camp there, at dawn he set off rapidly for Jerusalem. Panicking at his approach Aristobulus met him as a suppliant, and by promising money and putting the City and himself in his hands appeased his anger. But no part of this agreement was carried out: the officer sent to receive the money, Gabinius, was prevented by Aristobulus' partisans from even entering the City.

Stung once more by this treatment, Pompey kept Aristobulus in custody, and advancing to the City reconnoitred the possible lines of attack, observing the almost impregnable strength of the walls, the formidable ravine in front of them, and within the ravine the Temple, with its fortifications so strong that if the town was captured it would provide a further refuge for the enemy. While Pompey took time to make up his mind, party strife broke out in the City, the supporters of Aristobulus calling for war and the rescue of the king, those of Hyrcanus urging the opening of the gates to Pompey. The numbers of the latter were swelled by fear, when they saw the perfect discipline of the Romans. Worsted in the struggle, the opposite faction retired into the Temple, destroyed the bridge linking Temple and City,[58] and prepared to fight to the death. The others invited the Romans into the City and surrendered the Palace, to which Pompey sent Piso, one of his senior officers, and a large body of men. Piso posted sentry-groups about the City, and as none of the men sheltering in the Temple could be persuaded to come to terms, he removed all obstacles in the vicinity in readiness for an assault, finding the supporters of Hyrcanus most free with advice and assistance.

Pompey himself on the north side was busy filling in the trench[59] and the entire ravine[60] with material collected by the troops. This was a formidable task, as the depth was immense and the Jews interfered from above in every possible way. The Romans would never have reached the end of their labours if Pompey had not availed himself of the Seventh Day, on which for religious reasons the Jews will not set their hands to any work, raising the level of his platform[61] while keeping his men out of all armed clashes; for only in self-defence will Jews fight on the Sabbath. When at last the ravine was filled in, he erected high towers on the platform, brought up the engines he had fetched from Tyre, and began to batter the walls while the stone-throwers prevented any interference from above. But for a long time little impression was made on the towers, which in this sector were massive and splendid to a degree.

While the Romans were suffering severely Pompey was amazed at the unshakable endurance of the Jews, especially their maintenance of all the religious ceremonies in the midst of a storm of missiles. Just as if deep peace enfolded the City the daily sacrifices, offerings for the dead, and every other act of worship were meticulously carried out to the glory of God. Not even when the Temple was being captured and they were being butchered round the altar did they abandon the ceremonies ordained for the day. In the third month of the siege[62] the Romans at last overthrew one of the towers and swarmed into the Temple. The first who ventured to surmount the wall was Sulla's son, Cornelius Faustus. Next came two centurions, Furius and Fabius, followed by their respective units, which completely surrounded the Temple court and killed some as they fled to the Sanctuary, others as they put up a short-lived resistance. Many of the priests, though they saw the enemy approaching sword in hand, quietly went on with the sacred rites and were cut down as they poured libations and offered incense, putting the service of God before their own preservation. Most who fell were killed by their own countrymen of the rival faction; others beyond number threw themselves over the precipices; some, maddened by their hopeless position, fired the buildings round the wall and perished in the flames. The Jews lost 12,000 dead; of the Romans very few were killed, though a good many were wounded.

Among the disasters of that time nothing sent such a shudder through the nation as the exposure by aliens of the Holy Place, hitherto screened from all eyes. Pompey and his staff went into the Sanctuary, which no one was permitted to enter but the high priest, and saw what it contained – the lampstand and the lamps, the table, the libation cups and censers, all of solid gold, and a great heap of spices and sacred money totalling 2,000 talents.[63] Neither on this nor on any other of the sacred treasures did he lay a finger, and only one day after the capture he instructed the custodians to purify the Temple and perform the normal sacrifices. He appointed Hyrcanus high priest[64] again, because he had shown himself most helpful during the siege, especially by holding off the crowds of countryfolk anxious to fight for Aristobulus. In such ways he proved his worth as a general, and by relying on considerateness rather than severity won the goodwill of the citizens. The prisoners included Aristobulus' father-in-law, who was also his uncle. The chief authors of the war were beheaded. Faustus and the men who had given him such splendid support received magnificent rewards. The country and its capital were laid under tribute.[65]

Pompey next deprived the Jews of the towns they had occupied in Coele Syria, putting them under a Roman governor specially appointed; this meant that the nation was confined within its own boundaries. He rebuilt Gadara, which the Jews had razed to the ground, as a favour to a Gadarene among his own freedmen. He also freed from their rule all such inland towns as they had not already destroyed – Hippus, Scythopolis, Pella, Samaria, Jamnia, Marisa, Azotus, and Arethusa; likewise the coastal towns, Gaza, Joppa, Dora, and the city which at first was called Strato's Tower[66] and later was rebuilt by King Herod on the most magnificent scale and renamed Caesarea. All these towns he gave back to their legitimate citizens and added to the province of Syria,[67] which with Judaea and the whole area as far as Egypt and the Euphrates he entrusted to Scaurus, with two of his legions. He himself marched rapidly through Cilicia on his way to Rome, taking with him Aristobulus and his family as prisoners. Of the two sons and two daughters, one son, Alexander, escaped en route; the younger, Antigonus, and his sisters were conveyed to Rome.

Meanwhile Scaurus invaded Arabia, but was held up at Pella by the difficult terrain, and though he ravaged the country around he suffered severely in doing so as he ran out of food completely. From this plight he was saved by Hyrcanus, who sent supplies by Antipater. He as an old friend of Aretas was dispatched by Scaurus to persuade him to buy peace. The Arab agreed to pay three hundred talents, and on those terms Scaurus removed his army from Arabia.

The son of Aristobulus who had slipped out of Pompey's hands, Alexander, in time collected a large force which undermined Hyrcanus' position by overrunning Judaea, and it looked as if he would quickly dethrone him; for he advanced to Jerusalem and brazenly began rebuilding the section of the wall thrown down by Pompey.[68] But Gabinius had been sent to Syria as successor to Scaurus,[69] and after showing his worth on many other occasions he marched against Alexander. In alarm at his approach, Alexander recruited vigorously till he had 10,000 heavy infantry and 1,500 cavalry, and fortified carefully chosen positions, Alexandreum, Hyrcania, and Machaerus near the Arabian hills. Gabinius sent Mark Antony ahead with a detachment of his army, and followed in person with the main body. Antipater and his picked men, with the other Jewish forces under Malichus and Peitholaus, put themselves under the command of Mark

Antony's officers and made contact with Alexander. Soon afterwards the heavy infantry arrived with Gabinius at their head. The united forces of his enemies were too much for Alexander, who retreated until near Jerusalem he was forced to give battle, losing in the engagement 6,000 men, half of them killed, half of them prisoners. With the survivors he fled to Alexandreum, where Gabinius on his arrival found many of them encamped. Before using force he tried to win them over by promising to pardon their past offences; but when they refused any compromise, he killed a large number and shut the rest into the stronghold. In this battle Mark Antony displayed superlative courage; on every field he had invariably proved his worth, but never so convincingly as now.

Gabinius left enough men to reduce the fort and went off himself to settle the towns that had not been sacked and to rebuild those that had been destroyed. On his instructions Scythopolis, Samaria, Anthedon, Apollonia, Jamnia, Raphia, Marisa, Dora, Gaza, Azotus, and many other towns were re-established, each of them attracting an influx of eager colonists.[70] These arrangements complete, he returned to Alexandreum and intensified the siege till Alexander, abandoning hope entirely, sent a herald to implore pardon for his offences and to surrender his remaining fortresses of Hyrcania and Machaerus. Finally he handed over Alexandreum as well. All these Gabinius demolished at the instigation of Alexander's mother, that they might never be used as bases for a second war. The lady had come to ingratiate herself with him in her anxiety for the prisoners at Rome, her husband and remaining children. Gabinius next reinstated Hyrcanus in Jerusalem, entrusting him with the custody of the Temple, and set up a political system based on aristocracy. He divided the whole nation into five unions, one centred on Jerusalem, one on Gazara,[71] one under the protection of Amathus, the fourth assigned to Jericho, and the fifth based on Sepphoris, a town in Galilee. Only too pleased to be freed from the domination of one man, the Jews were thenceforth ruled by an aristocracy.[72]

It was not long before trouble broke out for them. Aristobulus escaped from Rome, and again rallied a number of Jews, some eager for political change, others long devoted to him. His first act was to seize Alexandreum and to attempt its refortification; but when he learnt that Gabinius had sent an army under Sisenna, Antony, and Servilius to attack him, he retired towards Machaerus. Shaking off a mass of useless followers he kept only those properly equipped, about 8,000. Among these was Peitholaus, chief of staff in Jerusalem, who had deserted to him with 1,000 men. The Romans followed close behind, and battle was joined. For a long time Aristobulus and his men offered a fierce and successful resistance, but in the end they were overwhelmed by the Romans and lost 5,000 killed. Some 2,000 escaped on to a hill and the remaining thousand led by Aristobulus hacked their way through the Roman ranks and drove on to Mach- aerus. There, as he bivouacked the first night among the ruins, the king dreamt of raising another army, if only he was granted a breath- ing-space, and he began to fortify the position after a fashion; but the Romans soon attacked, and after holding out for two days beyond his strength he was captured, and with Antigonus, the son who had escaped with him from Rome, he was brought in fetters to Gabinius and by Gabinius sent back to Rome. He himself was imprisoned by the Senate, but his children were allowed to return to Judaea, as Gabinius sent a written statement that he had promised this to Aristobulus' wife in return for the surrender of the strongholds.

Gabinius had already sent off an expedition against the Parthians when he was stopped by Ptolemy.[73] He turned back from the Euphrates and restored that monarch to the Egyptian throne, sup- ported throughout the campaign by all the resources of Hyrcanus and Antipater. Money, weapons, corn, and auxiliaries were furnished by Antipater, who also persuaded the Jewish frontier guards at the Pelusian Approaches[74] to let Gabinius pass. In the absence of Gabinius there were risings all over Syria, and the Jews were again stirred to revolt by Alexander, Aristobulus' son, who collected a huge army and started a massacre of all the Romans in the country. This alarmed Gabinius, who had already hurried back from Egypt on hearing of the upheaval in Palestine. He had sent Antipater ahead to win over the rebels, and met with some success; but 30,000 remained loyal to Alexander, and he was determined to fight. So when Gabinius took the field, the Jews met him, and in a battle near Mount Tabor lost 10,000 killed, the rest fleeing in all directions. Gabinius visited Jeru- salem, where he reconstituted the government according to Anti- pater's wishes[75]; setting out from there he defeated the Nabataeans in battle. Mithridates and Orsanes, refugees from Parthia, got away with his connivance, 'giving him the slip', as he informed the soldiers.

At this point Crassus arrived to take over the governorship of

Syria. For the campaign against the Parthians he removed all the gold from the Sanctuary in Jerusalem, including the 2,000 talents Pompey had not touched.[76] He crossed the Euphrates and perished with his army, but that is irrelevant to our story. After their victory the Parthians swept forward to cross the river into Syria, but were driven back by Cassius,[77] who had escaped to the Roman province. Having secured the province he hurried towards Judaea, capturing Tarichaeae, where he enslaved some 30,000 Jews and at Antipater's suggestion executed Peitholaus, who was trying to rally Aristobulus' partisans. Antipater had married a distinguished lady from Arabia called Cypros, who bore him four sons, Phasael, the future King Herod, Joseph, and Pheroras, and a daughter Salome. He had won influential support on every side by kindness and hospitality; above all he had by his marriage made the Arab king his friend, and when he undertook the war against Aristobulus it was to him that he sent his children for safe keeping. Cassius, after forcing Alexander to give a written undertaking to keep the peace, went back to the Euphrates to prevent a Parthian crossing. A fuller account will be given in a later work.[78]

When Pompey and the Senate fled across the Adriatic, Caesar became master of Rome and the Empire.[79] He at once released Aristobulus from prison, put two legions at his disposal, and sent him post-haste to Syria, in the hope that he would easily bring over that province and the whole Judaean area to his side. But malice frustrated both Aristobulus' enthusiasm and Caesar's hopes: Aristobulus was poisoned by Pompey's adherents, and for a long time was even denied burial in his native land, his body lying preserved in honey till Antony delivered it to the Jews to be buried in the royal sepulchres. Death came also to his son Alexander by the axe of Scipio in Antioch, by order of Pompey, after he had been tried for the damage he had done the Romans. His brother and sisters were taken under the wing of Ptolemy, son of Mennaeus and ruler of Chalcis under Lebanon, who sent his son Philippion to fetch them from Ascalon. Philippion tore Antigonus and his sisters away from Aristobulus' widow, and after taking them to his father fell in love with the younger and married her – only to be killed on her account by his father, who after murdering his son married Alexandra himself! This marriage made him take still greater care of her brother and sister.

On Pompey's death Antipater changed sides[80] and courted Caesar, and when Mithridates of Pergamum while leading an army to Egypt was warned off the Pelusian Approaches and held up at Ascalon, as a friend of the Arabs he persuaded them to assist, and arrived himself with 3,000 Jewish infantry. He further won the support of two influential Syrians, the Ptolemy resident in Lebanon, and Jamblichus,[81] who easily induced the towns in their neighbourhood to join the war. All doubt dispelled by the additional strength which Antipater had provided, Mithridates pushed on to Pelusium, and finding the way barred laid siege to the town. In the assault too chief honours went to Antipater; he broached the wall in front of him and was the first to dash into the town followed by his men. Pelusium fell; but as Mithridates advanced he was again held up by the Egyptian Jews who occupied the district called after Onias.[82] But Antipater induced them not only not to oppose the army but even to furnish supplies; consequently at Memphis too the people refrained from opposition and volunteered to serve under Mithridates. He now rounded the Delta and met the rest of the Egyptians in battle at a place called 'Jews' Camp'. As the fight raged he with the entire right wing was in grave danger, when he was rescued by Antipater who, after routing his opponents on the left where he was in command, made his way round by the river bank. He fell on Mithridates' pursuers, killed a great many and pursued the survivors so far that he even took their camp. He lost only eighty of his own men, whereas Mithridates in the rout had lost about eight hundred. Saved thus from imminent destruction, he bore whole-hearted testimony before Caesar to Antipater's achievements.

Thereupon Caesar by praise and promise incited the veteran to face further hazards on his behalf. In all these he proved himself the most intrepid of fighters, and wounded again and again he bore on almost every part of his body the marks of his valour. Later, when order had been restored in Egypt and Caesar returned to Syria,[83] he bestowed Roman citizenship on him[84] and exempted him from taxation, and by other honours and marks of friendship made him an object-lesson to all. For his sake also Caesar confirmed the high priesthood of Hyrcanus.[85]

CHAPTER 2

Herod's Rise to Power

SOON after this Antigonus, son of Aristobulus, had an interview with
Caesar which had the unexpected result of winning Antipater further
advancement. His wisest course would have been to express grief for
his father, who was thought to have been poisoned because of his
differences with Pompey, and indignation at Scipio's brutal treatment
of his brother, and not to mix his appeals for sympathy with an outburst of bitterness. But he went on to accuse Hyrcanus and Antipater,
openly alleging that in a most iniquitous fashion they had driven him
and his sisters right out of their native land; that in their insolence
they had treated the whole nation outrageously; that they had sent
assistance to Caesar in Egypt, not out of loyalty to him, but through
fear springing from old differences and in the hope that their friendship with Pompey would be forgotten. Antipater retorted by throwing off his garments and exposing his countless scars. Of his loyalty to
Caesar, he said, he need say nothing; his body shouted it aloud without his saying a word. The impudence of Antigonus passed belief;
the son of an enemy of Rome – and a fugitive from Rome – inheriting
from his father a craving for revolution and sedition, he had the sauce
to accuse other people before the Roman commander, and to try and
feather his own nest when he was lucky to be alive! His present lust
for power did not arise from his being in want; his ambition was to
stir up sedition among the Jews and so to bite the hand that fed him.
Having listened to both, Caesar declared Hyrcanus the better candidate for the high priesthood, and allowed Antipater to choose his own
office. Antipater left it to the bestower of the honour to decide its
magnitude, and was appointed commissioner[1] for all Judaea, with
authority to rebuild the demolished walls of the mother-city. These
honours Caesar ordered to be engraved in the Capitol, to commemor-
ate his own justice and Antipater's splendid services.

As soon as Antipater had escorted Caesar out of Palestine he returned
to Judaea. There he began by re-erecting the wall of the capital which
Pompey had demolished, and proceeded to suppress disturbances in
various parts of the country, using in every case both threats and

advice – if they supported Hyrcanus they would live in prosperity and quiet, enjoying their own property and general peace; but if they were deluded by the frigid hopes of those who for private profit were eager for revolution, they would find him not a protector but a master, Hyrcanus not a king[2] but an autocrat, and Caesar and the Romans not leaders and friends but enemies; they would never stand by while the Jews turned out of office the man they had appointed. While he talked in this way he was organizing the country along his own lines, knowing that Hyrcanus was too lethargic and spineless to be a real king. Phasael, his eldest son, he appointed governor of Jerusalem and district; the next one, Herod, he sent with equal authority into Galilee, though he was quite young.[3]   *Antipater*

Herod, overflowing with energy, soon found scope for his active spirit. Finding that Hezekiah, a bandit chief, was overrunning the district adjoining Syria with a very large gang, he caught and executed him along with many of his bandits.[4] This stroke won Herod the gratitude of the Syrians; in all the villages and in the towns his praises were sung – had he not won back for them their peace and property? A further result was that he became known to Sextus Caesar, a kinsman of the great Caesar and governor of Syria. His reputation also served to arouse a spirit of friendly rivalry in his brother Phasael, who became steadily more popular in Jerusalem and by force of personality kept the City quiet without any blundering misuse of his powers. Consequently Antipater was revered by the nation as if he were king, and honoured by all as undisputed head of the state; yet his own loyalty and faithfulness to Hyrcanus remained unchanged.

But in prosperity there is no way of avoiding jealousy. Hyrcanus, though he did not show it, was cut to the heart by the fame of the young men; he was grieved most of all by Herod's achievements, and by the stream of messengers announcing one success after another. His bitterness was aggravated by the malignity of numerous courtiers, offended by the moderation either of the sons or of Antipater; to the three of them had gone by default the management of affairs, while Hyrcanus sat helpless, retaining only the name of king without the authority. How long would he be so foolish as to rear kings to his own hurt? They no longer pretended to be viceroys but were the un-questioned heads of the state, while he had ceased to count; for with-out his giving any order, verbal or written, Herod had put all these people to death in defiance of the Jewish Law. If he was not king but a private citizen still, he ought to be put in the dock and in the king's presence justify his breach of the ancestral laws which forbade execution without trial.[5] By these suggestions Hyrcanus was gradually inflamed, and at last in an outburst of fury he sent for Herod to stand his trial. Advised by his father and emboldened by the success of his own policy, Herod posted garrisons about Galilee and presented himself in Jerusalem, accompanied by a strong escort – not so swollen a force as to suggest the intention of dethroning Hyrcanus, nor small enough to leave him helpless in face of jealousy. But Sextus Caesar, fearing that the young man would run into a hornets' nest, sent Hyrcanus a categorical order to acquit Herod of the charge of homicide.[6] The king, who as an admirer of Herod was in any case anxious to do this, found him not guilty.

Herod, believing that the king was mortified by his escape, withdrew to Sextus' headquarters in Damascus, with the intention of disobeying if summoned again. The malignant courtiers renewed their incitement of Hyrcanus, alleging that Herod had gone away in a rage and was ready to attack him. Swallowing the bait the king was at a loss what to do, as he saw the superiority of his opponent. But when Sextus Caesar actually appointed Herod commander-in-chief of Coele Syria and Samaria[7] and not only the loyalty of the people but the forces at his disposal made him formidable, Hyrcanus was paralysed with fear, every minute expecting Herod to march against him with an army at his back. And he guessed right. Herod, furious at the threat implied in his trial, collected an army and set out for Jerusalem to dethrone Hyrcanus. And he would soon have done it, if his father and brother had not hurried out and calmed him down, urging him to confine his revenge to threats and ferocity and to spare the king under whom he had grown so powerful. If he felt sore at being put in the dock, he ought at the same time to be grateful for his acquittal, and not, when the sword had been hanging over his head, to be ungrateful for his escape. And if it was true that in war God held the balance, Herod's military strength would be outweighed by the wrong he was doing. So he had better not be too certain of victory when he was going to join battle with his king and comrade, often his benefactor, who had never been harsh, except when he had been driven by malignant advisers to try to scare him with a shadow of injustice. Thus advised Herod gave way, satisfied that he had made his future secure by giving the people a demonstration of his power.

Meanwhile near Apamea peace was shattered for the Romans and civil war broke out. Caecilius Bassus in loyalty to Pompey treacherously killed Sextus Caesar and took over his army. Caesar's other generals in revenge for the murder assailed Bassus with all their forces. Antipater, for the sake of the dead Caesar and the living, both friends of his, sent them assistance by his sons.[8] While the war dragged on, Murcus arrived from Italy as successor to Sextus. It was at this time that Rome's great war broke out through the action of Cassius and Brutus, who treacherously murdered Caesar when he had held supreme power for only three years and seven months.[9] A tremendous upheaval resulted from the murder and the most powerful citizens were divided into two camps, every man joining the party that promised him most. Cassius in particular went to Syria to take over the forces near Apamea. He patched up the quarrel between Bassus and Murcus and between the opposing legions, and brought the siege of Apamea to an end. Then taking command of the troops himself, he went from town to town levying tribute and demanding more money than they were in a position to pay. When the Jews were ordered to contribute 700 talents, Antipater, frightened by Cassius' threats, divided the responsibility for its speedy collection among his sons and some of his acquaintances, including Malichus, one of his enemies, in view of the pressing necessity. The first to satisfy Cassius was Herod, who brought his quota of one hundred talents from Galilee and earned Cassius' hearty approval. The others Cassius abused for their slowness, and then poured forth his fury on the unfortunate towns. Gophna, Emmaus,[10] and two less important places he enslaved, and he was on the point of executing Malichus for his failure to levy the tribute at once, when his death and the destruction of the other towns were prevented by Antipater's prompt appeasement of Cassius with a present of one hundred talents.[11]

When, however, Cassius was out of the way, Malichus, so far from showing gratitude to Antipater, devised a plot against the man who had so often saved him, anxious as he was to remove this obstacle to his career of crime. Antipater, alarmed at the strength and cunning of the man, crossed the Jordan with the intention of raising a force to crush the plot. Caught in the act, Malichus by sheer impudence got the better of Antipater's sons: Phasael, warden of Jerusalem, and

Herod, responsible for arms and equipment, were deceived by a stream of excuses and oaths into undertaking to intercede on his behalf with their father. Thus Malichus was saved a second time by Antipater, who persuaded Murcus, then governor of Syria, to abandon his intention of executing him as a revolutionary.

When war was declared on Cassius and Brutus by young Caesar [12] and Antony, Cassius and Murcus raised an army in Syria, and as they hoped for valuable assistance from Herod they put him for the time being in charge of Coele Syria [13] with a body of horse and foot under his command, Cassius promising that when the war was won he would make him king of Judaea. [14] Antipater's destruction was the direct outcome of the actual and prospective dominance of his son. Fearing Herod's rise, Malichus bribed one of the royal cup-bearers to give Antipater poison. It was a triumph for the scheming Malichus; for after the banquet Antipater died. He had at all times shown energy and initiative in the management of affairs, above all in putting Hyrcanus back on his throne and keeping him there. Malichus, suspected of the poisoning, quieted the angry citizens by denying it and made himself more secure by raising a body of infantry; he did not suppose that Herod would take it lying down, and indeed Herod arrived almost instantaneously with an army to avenge his father. But as his brother Phasael advised him not to settle accounts with the man openly, for fear of provoking a riot, he accepted Malichus' explanation for the time being and agreed that no suspicion attached to him. Then he performed the funeral rites for his father with magnificent ceremonial.

He next turned his attention to Samaria which was torn by party strife, and after putting matters there to rights turned back to Jerusalem to attend the feast, accompanied by his armed forces. Hyrcanus, at the instance of Malichus who had panicked at Herod's approach, sent orders that he was not to bring foreigners among the nationals when they were purified. Herod showed his contempt for the pretext and for the man who issued the order by entering during the night. Malichus again approached him and bewailed Antipater. Herod met cunning with cunning, though he could hardly contain his anger; but he sent letters deploring his father's murder to Cassius, who hated Malichus already. Cassius wrote back that he should settle accounts with his father's killer, and gave secret instructions to his tribunes to help Herod 'pay a debt of honour'.

After Cassius' capture of Laodicea[15] the leading men of every district gathered at his headquarters, bringing him crowns and other gifts. This was the moment chosen by Herod for his revenge. Malichus was suspicious, and when he was in Tyre, where his son was held as a hostage, he determined to get him out by stealth, and made arrangements for his own escape to Judaea. His slender chances of survival acted as a spur; his ambitions soared, and he saw himself leading his nation in revolt against the Romans while Cassius had his hands full with the war against Antony, and setting the crown on his own brow after quickly disposing of Hyrcanus.

But fate had the last laugh. Herod, perceiving his game, invited him and Hyrcanus to dinner, and then calling one of his attendant slaves sent him home as if to prepare the meal, but really to warn the tribunes to come out and put the ambush into effect. They had not forgotten Cassius' instructions and came out to the sea-shore in front of the city sword in hand, and there surrounded Malichus and hacked him to death. Hyrcanus promptly fainted from shock and collapsed; when at last he recovered consciousness and asked Herod who had killed Malichus, one of the tribunes answered 'Cassius' orders'. 'Then Cassius,' replied Hyrcanus, 'has saved me and my country too, by destroying the mortal enemy of both.' Whether he really thought this or was too frightened to dispute an accomplished fact, will never be known. Anyway, Herod's account with Malichus was now settled.

When Cassius withdrew from Syria[16] strife again broke out in Jerusalem. Helix, backed by a body of soldiers, rose against Phasael with the intention of avenging Malichus by punishing Herod through his brother. As it happened, Herod was with Fabius the Roman general at Damascus, and though anxious to help he was immobilized by sickness. Meanwhile Phasael overpowered Helix without assistance, and denounced the ingratitude of Hyrcanus in collaborating with Helix and permitting Malichus' brother to seize the forts. He had indeed seized many of these, among them the strongest of all, Masada. But he was helpless against the might of Herod, who as soon as he was well again recaptured all the forts and kicked him out of Masada grovelling. Next he expelled from Galilee Marion the autocrat of Tyre, who had already possessed himself of three of the strongholds, sparing every Tyrian he captured and even sending some away laden with gifts, so ensuring that the citizens were devoted to him and bitterly hostile to their own ruler. Marion had received his authority from Cassius, who had appointed an autocratic ruler of every district; through hatred of Herod he had brought back from exile Aristobulus' son Antigonus – in any case he could not resist Fabius, who had been bribed by Antigonus to work for his recall. All expenses were met by Ptolemy, the brother-in-law of Antigonus.[17] These confederates Herod met and defeated at the approaches to Judaea; then banishing Antigonus again he went back to Jerusalem to receive universal congratulations on his success. Even those who had hitherto regarded him coldly now warmed towards him in view of his marriage into the family of Hyrcanus. He had previously married a Jewess of good birth named Doris, who had borne him a son, Antipater; now he wedded Mariamme, daughter of Alexander the son of Aristobulus, and grand-daughter of Hyrcanus, so becoming a connection of the king.[18]

When at Philippi Cassius had met his end, Caesar went back to Italy and Antony to Asia. Numerous cities sent deputations to Antony in Bithynia, and with them came influential Jews to accuse Phasael and Herod of obtaining control of affairs by force and leaving Hyrcanus a mere figurehead. To counter this propaganda Herod appeared on the scene, and by coaxing Antony with huge bribes so worked upon him that he would not let Herod's enemies say a word. Thus for the time being they were silenced. But later on a hundred Jewish officials arrived at Daphne near Antioch to appeal to Antony, now a slave to his passion for Cleopatra. They put forward the most highly esteemed and eloquent men among them to accuse the two brothers. Messala replied for the defence, backed by Hyrcanus because of the marriage-connection. Antony listened to both sides, and then asked Hyrcanus which party was the more fit to govern. When Hyrcanus recommended Herod and his associates, Antony was delighted. (Years before he had been the guest of Herod's father, who had given him a right royal welcome when Gabinius and he were invading Judaea.[19]) So he appointed the two brothers tetrarchs, with the task of administering all Judaea.

The delegates exploded with fury, and Antony arrested fifteen and locked them up, with the fixed intention of putting them to death; the rest he sent packing with a flea in their ear. The result was greater turmoil in Jerusalem. A second delegation – a thousand strong – was sent to Tyre, where Antony was resting on his way to Jerusalem. His reply to their clamour was to send out the governor of Tyre with instructions to execute all he could catch and to back up the authority of the men he had appointed tetrarchs. This procedure was forestalled by Herod, who went on to the beach with Hyrcanus and strongly advised them not to bring about their own destruction and land their country in war by senseless strife. This made them more furious still, so Antony dispatched a body of infantry, who killed or wounded many of them: Hyrcanus saw to it that the dead were buried and the wounded cared for. Even so the survivors would not keep quiet, but created such disorder in the City that Antony was actually goaded into executing the prisoners.

Two years later Barzapharnes, the Parthian satrap, serving under Pacorus the king's son, seized Syria.[20] Lysanias, who had succeeded his late father, Ptolemy son of Mennaeus, by promising 1,000 talents and five hundred women, persuaded the satrap to bring back Antigonus and make him king, dethroning Hyrcanus.[21] Pacorus accepted the bribe, and choosing the coastal route for himself, instructed Barzapharnes to drive through the interior. Of the seaside towns Tyre would not admit Pacorus, though Ptolemais and Sidon did so. Then to one of the royal cup-bearers who had the same name as himself he entrusted a detachment of cavalry, ordering him to gallop on into Judaea, to reconnoitre the enemy position and give all necessary aid to Antigonus.

While the troopers plundered Carmel, Jews flocked to Antigonus' standard, eager to take part in the invasion. He sent them ahead to seize a position called The Oaks. Here they clashed with the enemy, drove them back and chased them helter-skelter to Jerusalem, and having attracted strong support advanced to the Palace. Hyrcanus and Phasael met them with a powerful force and battle raged in the market-place. Routing the enemy, Herod's forces herded them into the Temple, and to keep watch on them posted sixty men in the houses nearby. These guards the party opposed to the brothers assailed and burnt to death; Herod, furious at their destruction, attacked and killed many of the citizens; and day after day they sallied out against each other in small groups and bloodshed continued without pause.

Now came the Feast of Pentecost, and all the vicinity of the Temple – in fact the whole City – was filled with people from the countryside, most of them armed. Phasael was guarding the wall, Herod, with a handful of men, the Palace. The latter sallied out against the disordered enemy in the northern suburb, inflicted very heavy casualties, routed them all, and herded some into the City, some into the Temple, and others into the entrenched camp outside. At this stage Antigonus requested the admission of Pacorus[22] as mediator, and Phasael agreed to open the gates to the Parthian with an escort of five hundred horse, and made him welcome. Pacorus had come avowedly to end the strife, but in reality to assist Antigonus; he cunningly persuaded Phasael to go and discuss with Barzapharnes ways of re-establishing peace, though Herod did his best to dissuade him and urged him to kill the schemer, not walk into his trap: one should never trust a foreigner's word. Phasael went, taking Hyrcanus with him. Pacorus, to silence suspicion, left with Herod some of the so-called Yeomen Cavalry, and with the rest escorted Phasael.

On reaching Galilee they found the inhabitants in a state of armed revolt. They had an interview with the satrap, a very subtle rogue who wrapped up his scheming in friendly protestations. He bestowed gifts on them, and then as they departed set a trap for them. The nature of the plot dawned on them when they arrived at one of the seaside towns, called Ecdippon. There they heard of the promised 1,000 talents, and learnt that most of the five hundred women dedicated by Antigonus to Parthian use were of their own race, and that they themselves were spied on by the foreign troops every night, and would have been kidnapped long ago if the plotters had not been waiting to seize Herod in Jerusalem first, before news of what had happened to them put him on the look-out. This was no longer just a rumour: they could now see sentries not far away. But though Ophellius, who had learnt every detail of the plot from Saramalla, the richest Syrian of his generation, did his best to persuade Phasael to make his escape, nothing could induce him to desert Hyrcanus. He went straight to the satrap and told him plainly what he thought of the plot, and especially of his sinking so low for the sake of money; moreover, he himself was prepared to pay more for his life than Antigonus for his crown. The Parthian made a cunning and plausibly reply, denying the suspicion on oath, and then went to Pacorus. In accordance with his orders some of the Parthians left behind at once kidnapped Phasael and Hyrcanus, who cursed them bitterly for their perjury and broken faith.

Meanwhile the cup-bearer who had been sent to kidnap Herod was trying to carry out the plot by enticing him outside the walls, as instructed. He, however, had from the beginning suspected the invaders, and, learning now that a letter notifying him of the plot had fallen into enemy hands, he refused to go outside, though Pacorus argued most convincingly that he ought to meet the bearers of the dispatch, which had not come into the enemy's possession and made no reference to a plot, but merely recorded Phasael's doings. But as it happened, Herod had previously learnt from another informant that his brother had been kidnapped; and he was visited by Hyrcanus' daughter Mariamme,[23] the shrewdest of women, who implored him not to go outside or trust himself to the foreigners, now openly trying to bring him down. Pacorus and his staff were still seeking some crooked means of carrying out their scheme, as it was impossible to get the better of so alert a man openly, when Herod forestalled them by setting out at night with those to whom he was most attached, in the hope of reaching Idumaea[24] undetected. The Parthians, learning what had happened, went in pursuit. Herod made his mother and sisters,[25] the girl he had promised to marry, with her mother, and the youngest of his brothers, go straight on, while he and his servants protected them by vigorous rearguard actions. Every time he attacked the enemy he inflicted heavy casualties, finally making a dash for Masada.

In his flight he had less trouble with the Parthians than with the Jews, who harried him all the way, and seven miles from the City began a pitched battle, which lasted quite a long time and ended in their utter defeat. Here later on Herod commemorated his victory by building a city graced with a palace on which no expense was spared, and defended by a citadel of enormous strength. This city he called Herodium[26] after himself. For the rest of his flight he was daily joined by large numbers, and at Thresa in Idumaea his brother Joseph met him and advised him to disburden himself of most of his followers, as Masada could never hold so large a number – over 9,000. Herod agreed, and sent those who were of no use to him to various parts of Idumaea, providing them with food for their journey; then keeping the toughest fighters as well as his family and close friends, he arrived safely at the fortress. Leaving eight hundred men there to protect the women, with provisions sufficient for a siege, he hurried on to Petra in Arabia.

The Parthians in Jerusalem turned to looting, breaking into the houses of those who had fled and into the Palace, and sparing only Hyrcanus' money, which did not exceed three hundred talents. The total sum found fell short of their expectations; for Herod, long suspicious of Parthian trustworthiness, had already transferred the most valuable of his treasures to Idumaea, an example followed by all his friends. The looting finished, the Parthian conduct became so outrageous that they filled the whole country with war to the death, blotted out the city of Marisa, and after making Antigonus king, actually handed Phasael and Hyrcanus over to him in fetters to be tortured. When Hyrcanus fell down at his feet, Antigonus with his own teeth mutilated his ears, in order that he might never again resume the high priesthood in any circumstances; for a high priest must be physically perfect.

Phasael, however, was too quick for him; he bravely dashed his head against a rock, as he was not free to use sword or hand. Thus he showed himself a true brother of Herod and Hyrcanus a cowardly poltroon; he died like a hero, crowning his life's work with a fitting end. A rival version of the incident states that he revived after the first shock, but that a doctor sent by Antigonus 'to look after him' filled the wound with noxious drugs and finished him off. Whichever version is correct, all honour to him for his attempt. It is said that before he breathed his last he was told by some woman that Herod had escaped. 'Now,' he whispered, 'I shall die happy, as I'm leaving behind me a living man to avenge me.' So he died. The Parthians had missed their main target – the women – but put Antigonus at the head of affairs in Jerusalem and carried off Hyrcanus in fetters to Parthia.

Herod was driving on farther towards Arabia, thinking his brother was still alive and anxious to get money from the king, as without it he could not hope to save Phasael by appealing to Parthian cupidity. He reckoned that if the Arab was too forgetful of his friendship with Herod's father and too close-fisted to make him a gift, he could borrow the ransom from him by leaving in pledge the son of the man to be ransomed. (He had his nephew with him, a boy of seven.) He was further prepared to give him 300 talents, putting forward Tyrian intermediaries. But fate had forestalled his earnest efforts; Phasael was dead, and Herod's brotherly affection was of no avail. Nor did he find any friendship now among the Arabs. Their king Malchus[27] sent him orders to leave the country forthwith, on the pretext that the Parthians had formally demanded the expulsion of Herod from Arabia; in actual fact he had made up his mind to keep what he owed Antipater, and not to be shamed into repaying Antipater's generosity

by any kindness to his children in their distress. He was abetted in his
shameless behaviour by men equally anxious to embezzle the money
which Antipater had deposited with them – the most powerful of his
courtiers.

Meeting with the hostility of the Arabs for the very reason that had
led him to expect their warmest friendship, Herod gave the messengers the answer suggested by his disappointment and turned back towards Egypt.[28] The first night he bivouacked at one of the country's
temples, after picking up the men he had left behind. The next day he
went on to Rhinocorura, where the story of his brother's death
reached him. With anxiety for what might happen now displaced by
grief for what had happened already, he marched straight on. Be-
latedly regretting his behaviour, the Arab king hastily sent messengers
to recall the man he had wronged. But Herod had already reached
Pelusium, where he was refused a passage by the sailors in the harbour,
and so appealed to their superiors; they, impressed by his rank and
reputation, conducted him to Alexandria. When he entered the city
he received a splendid welcome from Cleopatra, who hoped to
employ him as commander in a projected campaign[29]; but he evaded
the queen's pressing request, and fearing neither a voyage in mid-
winter[30] nor the turmoil in Italy sailed for Rome.[31]

In serious danger off Pamphylia he jettisoned the bulk of the cargo
and with difficulty made Rhodes, which had suffered grievously in
the war against Cassius. There he was received by his friends Ptolemy
and Sapphinius. Shortage of money did not prevent his having a very
large trireme built; in this he sailed with his friends to Brundisium.
From there he hurried on to Rome, where he first applied to Antony
as the friend of his father, telling him of his own and his family's misfortunes, and how he had had to leave his nearest and dearest besieged
in a fortress while he endured a winter crossing to appeal for his
assistance.

Antony was very grieved at the change in his fortunes: recalling
Antipater's hospitality and filled with admiration for the heroic
character before him, he decided on the spot that the man he had once
made tetrarch should now be king of the Jews.[32] If regard for Herod
moved him, dislike of Antigonus moved him just as much; he considered him an agitator and an enemy of Rome. Caesar Herod found
even more ready to help than Antony: the Egyptian campaigns which
Antipater had shared with his father[33] were fresh in his mind, as were

his hospitality and unshakable loyalty; and he could see Herod's appetite for action. He convened the Senate, to which Messala, supported by Atratinus, introduced Herod, and gave a full account of his father's services and his own loyalty to Rome, at the same time making it clear that Antigonus was their enemy, not only because he had quarrelled with them before, but because he had now accepted the crown from the Parthians in defiance of the Romans. These revelations angered the Senate, and when Antony rose to suggest that the Parthian war was an added reason for making Herod king, they all voted in favour. The House adjourned, and Antony and Caesar went out with Herod between them, the consuls and other magistrates leading the way in order to offer sacrifice[34] and to deposit the decree[35] in the Capitol. This first day of Herod's reign Antony celebrated with a banquet.

CHAPTER 3

·Herod Master of Palestine

ALL this time Antigonus was besieging Masada, whose defenders had plenty of supplies of every other kind but were short of water. In view of this, Joseph, Herod's brother,[1] with two hundred of his men planned to make a dash for Arabia, being informed of Malchus' desire to make amends to Herod. He would actually have left the fortress had it not happened that on the night of his departure rain fell in torrents; the reservoirs were filled to the brim, and he had no further wish to escape. They began to make sorties against Antigonus' forces, and now engaging them in the open, now luring them into ambushes, destroyed large numbers. Of course they did not succeed every time; sometimes they were worsted and had to retreat.

Meanwhile Ventidius, the Roman commander sent from Syria to check the Parthians,[2] after dealing with them had crossed into Judaea, professedly to assist Joseph, but really to get money out of Antigonus. He encamped very close to Jerusalem, and after lining his pockets to his satisfaction withdrew with most of his troops; but he left Silo in command of a detachment, for fear that the removal of the whole army might make it only too evident what he had been after. Antigonus meanwhile, in the hope of further help from the Parthians, courted Silo to avoid any interference with the fulfilment of this hope.

But by this time Herod had sailed from Italy to Ptolemais, and having raised a substantial force of Jews and foreigners was marching through Galilee against Antigonus, with the cooperation of Ventidius and Silo, whom Dellius on Antony's behalf had induced to assist Herod's return. But Ventidius was busy settling sporadic disturbances resulting from the Parthian occupation, and Silo remained in Judaea, bribed with Antigonus' money. Not that Herod lacked support: as he moved on his strength steadily grew, and apart from a few localities all Galilee took up his cause. The most urgent task facing him was Masada; he must first of all rescue his family and friends from the siege. Joppa[3] stood in the way; it was in enemy hands and must be reduced first; otherwise while he went on to Jerusalem his opponents would remain in possession of a stronghold behind his back. He was joined by Silo, who was only too pleased to have found a pretext for leaving Jerusalem. The Jews followed in pursuit but Herod swooped on them with a handful of men, routing them easily and rescuing Silo, whose efforts at defence were feeble. He then took Joppa and hurried on to Masada to rescue his friends. Some of the country-folk were drawn to him by their friendship with his father, some by his own fame, some by the desire to repay the kindnesses of both, but the largest number by the prospect of a stable monarchy; consequently he had now got together an almost invincible army. Antigonus tried to check his progress by laying ambushes at suitable points on his route, very ineffectively, as it turned out. Herod had no difficulty in freeing his friends in Masada and recovering the fortress of Thresa. He then set out for Jerusalem, and was joined by Silo's men and many Jews from the City, alarmed at his strength.

Having pitched their camp west of the town, Herod's men became the target for the arrows and javelins of the guards on that side, while others made organized sorties to test the strength of his outposts. Herod at once had a proclamation made all round the walls that he came for the good of the people and the preservation of the City, and that he would take no action even against his undisguised enemies but would grant even his bitterest foes an amnesty. Antigonus' staff countered this appeal by forbidding anyone to listen to the proclamations or to cross over; so Herod gave his men leave from then on to return the shots from the battlements, and they hurled their missiles to such effect that the towers were quickly cleared of defenders.

At this point Silo's venality became evident. He put up a number of his men to raise a clamour about short rations and demand money for food, and to insist on being marched to winter quarters[4] in a suitable locality; there was nothing to be had anywhere near the City, as Antigonus' men had taken the lot! Silo thereupon began to strike camp in an attempt to withdraw. But Herod approached the Roman officers, and then appealed to the rank and file not to leave him in the lurch when he had come with the authority of Caesar, Antony, and the Senate. That very day he would supply their wants. He had no sooner ended this appeal than he set out in person for the country-side, returning with supplies in such abundance as gave the lie to all Silo's pretexts; and to guard against any possible shortage in the coming days he requested the people living round Samaria – that city having espoused his cause[5] – to bring corn, wine, oil, and cattle to Jericho.

Hearing of this, Antigonus sent orders round the country to block or ambush the food-convoys. The people obeyed, and a large number of armed men gathered above Jericho, and stationed themselves on the hills to watch for the supply column. However Herod was not idle; he set off with ten cohorts, five Roman, five Jewish, with a sprinkling of mercenaries and a few of the cavalry, and arrived at Jericho, which he found deserted; but the high ground had been occupied by five hundred men with their wives and families. These he captured but set free, while the Romans poured into the rest of the town and looted it, as they found the houses full of luxuries of every kind. Leaving a garrison in Jericho the king returned, and sent away the Roman contingent to winter in places that had come over to him – Idumaea, Galilee, and Samaria. Antigonus for his part by taking advantage of Silo's venality persuaded him to billet a portion of his army in Lydda – a sop to Antony.

While the Romans enjoyed every comfort and a complete rest from fighting, Herod was not idle. He occupied Idumaea with 400 horse and 2,000 foot led by his brother Joseph, to forestall any movement in support of Antigonus. His own task was to transfer his mother, and all the kinsmen and friends he had brought out of Masada, to Samaria; when he had settled them safely there, he marched on to secure the remainder of Galilee and expel Antigonus' garrisons. Forcing his way through a blizzard to Sepphoris he occupied the city without opposition, the defenders fleeing at his approach. There he refreshed his followers, battered by the storm, with the plentiful supplies available, setting out next against the bandits who lived in caves[6] and overran a great part of the country, causing the inhabitants as much misery as a war could have done. Sending on three infantry brigades and one troop of cavalry to the village of Arbela, he joined them six weeks later with the rest of his army. His coming failed to frighten the enemy, who went out armed to meet him with all the skill of warriors as well as the fearlessness of bandits, and joining battle routed Herod's left wing with their right. Promptly swinging round his own right wing, Herod came to the rescue, made his fleeing troops face about, and falling on the pursuers brought their advance to a halt, finally breaking their resistance by frontal attacks and putting them to flight. He pursued them to the Jordan, attacking all the way and destroying a large proportion of them, the survivors scattering beyond the river. Galilee could now breathe again; the only bandits left were lurking in caves, and it would take time to deal with them. So Herod's next act was to bestow on his soldiers the fruits of their toil, awarding each man 150 silver drachmas and sending much larger sums to the officers in the various camps in which they were wintering. Pheroras, his youngest brother, he appointed to lay in stores of provisions for them and to fortify Alexandreum. Both tasks Pheroras faithfully performed.

At this period Antony was living near Athens, and Ventidius sent for Silo and Herod to take part in the Parthian war, instructing them first to settle the problem of Judaea. Herod was delighted to second Silo to Ventidius, while he himself took the field against the bandits in the caves. These caves opened on to almost vertical slopes and could not be reached from any direction except by winding, steep, and very narrow paths; the cliff in front stretched right down into ravines of immense depth dropping straight into the torrent-bed. So for a long time the king was defeated by the appalling difficulty of the ground, finally resorting to a plan fraught with the utmost danger. He lowered the toughest of his soldiers in cradles till they reached the mouths of the caves; they then slaughtered the bandits with their families and threw firebrands at those who proved awkward. Wishing to save some of them, Herod invited them to come up to him. Not a man voluntarily surrendered, and of those who were brought out forcibly many preferred death to captivity. One old man, father of seven children, was begged by the children and their mother to let them come out as their lives were guaranteed. His response was terrible. One by one he ordered them to come out, while he stood at the cave-mouth and killed each son as he emerged. Herod, in a good position to watch, was cut to the heart, and stretched out his hand to the old man, begging him to spare his children; but he, treating the suggestion with contempt, went so far as to sneer at Herod for his lack of guts, and after disposing of the last of his sons and killing his wife too, flung their bodies down the precipice and finally leapt over the edge himself.

Master now of the caves and the cave-dwellers, Herod left what he deemed a sufficient force to deal with any rising, with Ptolemy in command, and turned back towards Samaria with 600 cavalry and 3,000 heavy infantry to settle accounts with Antigonus. His departure removed all restraint from the habitual trouble-makers in Galilee; they killed his general Ptolemy in a surprise attack and systematically ravaged the country, establishing their lairs in the marshes and other inaccessible places. Informed of the rising Herod speedily came to the rescue, destroyed a large number of the insurgents, reduced all their fortresses by siege, and as a penalty for their fickleness made the towns pay a fine of 100 talents.

By now the Parthians had been driven out and Pacorus killed[7]: so Ventidius was able at Antony's suggestion to send support to Herod in his struggle with Antigonus – two legions and 1,000 horse. Their commander Machaeras received a letter from Antigonus begging him to come to his aid instead, complaining bitterly of Herod's unscrupulous use of force against his kingdom, and promising to make it worth his while. Machaeras however was not prepared to disobey higher authority – especially as Herod was offering more; so he refused to turn traitor, and simulating friendship went to spy out Antigonus' position, disregarding Herod's warnings. Antigonus was not deceived, but shut the City gates in his face and shot at him from the ramparts as an enemy, till the crestfallen general returned to Herod at Emmaus, so furious at his failure that he killed every Jew he met on the way, not sparing even Herod's men but treating everyone as a supporter of Antigonus. This made Herod so angry that he was on the point of attacking Machaeras as an enemy, but mastering his rage he set out for Antony's headquarters to expose the outrageous conduct of his subordinate. Machaeras, realizing his mistake, followed on the king's heels and by eating humble pie mollified him. But Herod continued his journey all the same; and when he heard that Antony was conducting a large-scale attack on Samosata,[8] a well-fortified city near the Euphrates, he increased his speed, seeing an excellent chance of showing his mettle and placing Antony under an obligation. And so it proved. As soon as he arrived he finished the siege for them, killing masses of the enemy and capturing quantities of booty, so that Antony's old admiration for his prowess was greatly strengthened, and he heaped new honours upon him, confirming his hopes of mounting the throne, while King Antiochus was forced to surrender Samosata.

Meanwhile a heavy blow befell Herod's fortunes in Judaea. He had left his brother Joseph in complete charge, instructing him to make no move against Antigonus till his return, since the unreliability of Machaeras as an ally was evident from what he had done. But as soon as Joseph heard that his brother was a long way off, he disregarded his

instructions and marched towards Jericho with five cohorts contributed by Machaeras; he went with the intention of seizing the corn-
crop at the height of summer. In hilly and difficult country he was set
upon by his adversaries; he himself was killed after playing a hero's
part in the battle, and the Romans perished to a man. The cohorts
were new levies from Syria, with no stiffening of veterans to
strengthen the morale of raw recruits. Not satisfied with his victory,
Antigonus went to such an extreme of fury that he even mutilated
Joseph's corpse. Having got possession of the bodies of the dead he cut
off his head, although his brother Pheroras offered to redeem it for
fifty talents. Antigonus' victory was followed by such an upheaval in
Galilee that his partisans dragged the more important of Herod's
adherents to the lake and drowned them. Many parts of Idumaea too
changed sides, though Machaeras was there, rebuilding a stronghold
called Gittha.

Not a word of all this had yet come to Herod's ears. After the fall of
Samosata Antony had made Sosius governor of Syria, instructing him
to assist Herod against Antigonus, while he himself returned to
Egypt.[9] Sosius accordingly sent two legions ahead to reinforce Herod
in Syria, following on his heels with the rest of his army. But while
Herod was at Daphne near Antioch, vivid dreams informed him of his
brother's death, and as he sprang in alarm from his bed messengers
came in with news of the disaster. For a brief while he gave vent to his
distress, then postponing further mourning hurried off at a killing
pace in the direction of his enemies. Arriving at Lebanon he was
reinforced by eight hundred of the hillmen and joined by one Roman
legion. Without waiting for daylight he led this mixed force into
Galilee, where he was met by the enemy but drove them back to their
base and began a continuous assault on its fortifications. Before he
could take it a phenomenal storm compelled him to seek shelter in the
village nearby. When a few days later the second legion sent by
Antony joined forces with him, his increased strength alarmed the
enemy, and in the night they abandoned the stronghold. Herod next
passed through Jericho, determined to take the speediest vengeance on
his brother's killers. There thanks to providence he had an astonishing
and miraculous escape, which gained him the reputation of being the
darling of heaven. Many of the local magistrates had dined with him
that evening, and when the banquet was over and everyone had left,
the building immediately caved in. Deeming this a joint portent of

dangers and deliverance in the coming campaign, at dawn he moved forward with his army. About 6,000 of the enemy charged down from the hills and engaged his advance guard: they did not feel inclined to meet the Romans hand to hand, but pelted them at long range with stones and javelins, wounding a large number, including Herod himself, who as he rode along was struck by a javelin in the side.

It was the wish of Antigonus to give the impression that his men were superior not only in daring but also in numbers; so he sent Pappus, one of his associates, with an army to Samaria. Their task was to oppose Machaeras. Herod for his part overran the enemy country, reduced five little towns, destroyed 2,000 of the inhabitants, fired the houses, and returned co his camp near the village of Isana.[10] He was joined by a steady stream of Jews from Jericho and other places, some through hatred of Antigonus, others impressed by Herod's successes, but most in the grip of an unaccountable longing for change. Herod was impatient for a fight, and Pappus, completely confident in the face of superior numbers and Herod's extraordinary energy, advanced against him eager for the fray. When the clash came, most of the enemy line stood firm for a time; but Herod, remembering his murdered brother and risking everything to get his revenge on the murderers, quickly mastered the troops facing him and then attacked in turn all the groups that still held out, till in the end the whole army was in flight. The carnage was frightful, with the enemy driven back into the village from which they had set out and Herod mercilessly assailing their rear and killing more than could be counted. Along with the enemy he rushed into the village, where every house was packed with armed men and the roofs crowded with defenders who threw missiles down at him. First defeating those outside, he tore the houses to pieces and dragged out those within. On a great many he pulled down the roofs, destroying them en masse; those who crawled out of the ruins were met by the soldiers sword in hand: so vast were the piles of corpses that the streets were blocked to the victors. Such a blow the enemy could not survive; those who reassembled after the battle, seeing the destruction in the village, fled in all directions. Emboldened by his victory, Herod would at once have driven on to Jerusalem, if he had not been held up by a most violent storm. This circumstance robbed him of his crowning success and final defeat of Antigonus, who was already planning to abandon the City.

In the evening Herod dismissed his weary comrades to refresh themselves while he himself, still hot from the fight, went to take a bath like any other soldier, attended by a single slave. He was on the point of entering the bath-house when one of the enemy dashed out in front of him sword in hand, then a second and a third, with others in their train. These men had fled from the battlefield into the bath-house fully armed. There they had cowered unnoticed for a time, but when they saw the king, they lost their nerve entirely and ran past him, unarmed as he was, shaking with fear, and dashed for the exits. As it happened, no one else was there to seize the men and Herod was content to have come to no harm, so they all got away. Next day he cut off the head of Pappus, Antigonus' general, who had perished in the fighting, and sent it to his brother Pheroras as reparation for their murdered brother; for it was Pappus who had killed Joseph.

When the storm died down [11] Herod drove on towards Jerusalem and brought his army up to the walls. It was now the third year since he had been proclaimed king in Rome. He pitched his camp opposite the Temple, as from that direction an attack could be launched, and it was from there that Pompey had captured the City. Dividing the task among the troops, he stripped the suburbs of trees and ordered three artificial platforms to be raised and towers erected on them. Then, leaving his most competent subordinates to supervise the work, he went off to Samaria to fetch Alexander's daughter, whom he had promised to marry, as mentioned before. [12] He made his wedding incidental to the siege – he no longer took the enemy seriously. The wedding over, back he went to Jerusalem with still stronger forces. Sosius too joined him at the head of a very large army of horse and foot which he had sent on by the inland route while he himself marched through Phoenicia. The combined forces totalled eleven infantry brigades and 6,000 cavalry, not counting the Syrian auxiliaries, who added considerably to the strength. They encamped together near the north wall, Herod relying on the senatorial decrees appointing him king, Sosius on Antony's decision to send the army under his command to support Herod.

The Jewish masses throughout the City showed their agitation in various ways. Crowding round the Sanctuary the feebler creatures behaved as if possessed, and feigning inspiration poured out a mass of 'prophecies' to fit the situation; the bolder spirits went out in gangs to carry out raids of every kind, and especially to seize all supplies within reach of the City, leaving no food for man or beast. Of the fighting-men the more disciplined were organized to resist the besiegers; from the ramparts they hindered the raising of the platforms and countered the engines with a succession of new devices: in nothing did they score so much over the enemy as in their mining operations. The king parried the raids by devising ambushes which put a stop to their excursions; he overcame the food shortage by fetching supplies from a distance; and he got the better of the fighting-men by using Roman tactical skill, though they showed amazing audacity. In broad daylight they would hurl themselves against the Roman lines to certain death, and through their mine-shafts they would suddenly appear in the middle of Herod's men; and before any section of the wall was battered down they would build another in its stead – in short, with neither hand nor brain did they show the slightest weariness, determined as they were to hold out to the last. Indeed, despite the overwhelming strength of the besieging army, they maintained their resistance for more than four months.[13]

Finally some of Herod's storm-troopers ventured to scale the wall and leap into the City, followed by Sosius' centurions. First to be captured was the area round the Temple; then the army poured in and there was frightful carnage everywhere, as the Romans were furious at the length of the siege, and Herod's Jewish soldiers determined that not one opponent should survive.[14] They were massacred by the thousand, crowded together in streets and houses or fleeing to the Sanctuary. No mercy was shown to infants or the aged, or to defenceless women. Although the king sent round imploring them to discriminate, no one stayed his hand, but as if raging mad they vented their fury on every age alike. At this point Antigonus, paying no regard to his past or to his present position, came down from his Palace and fell at Sosius' feet. The Roman, not in the least moved by his changed situation, laughed uproariously and called him Antigone.[15] But he did not treat him like a woman and let him go free: he put him in fetters and kept him in custody.

Herod's first problem after mastering his enemies was to master also his foreign allies; for the alien masses were determined to see the Temple and the sacred things inside the Sanctuary. The king appealed to some, threatened others, and drove yet others back by force of arms, thinking victory more terrible than defeat if such people got a glimpse within the Veil. At the same time he stopped all looting in the City, telling Sosius with the utmost emphasis that if the Romans stripped the City of money and men, they would leave him king of a desert, and that for the slaughter of so many citizens he would regard a worldwide empire as inadequate compensation. When Sosius insisted that after the strain of the siege it was only right to let the men pillage, Herod undertook to distribute rewards to the whole army out of his own pocket. Ransoming thus what was left of his mother-city, he kept his promises; he rewarded every soldier handsomely, and the officers in proportion, Sosius himself right royally, so that no one went short of money. Sosius dedicated a golden crown to God[16] and then bade farewell to Jerusalem, taking Antigonus in fetters to Antony. The fallen ruler, clinging to life to the very end though hope was dead, died as such a coward deserved – by the axe.

King Herod[17] did not make the mistake of treating all the citizens alike: by bestowing honours on those who had taken his side he increased their devotion; the supporters of Antigonus he liquidated. As money was now tight, he turned all his personal treasures into cash and sent it to Antony and his staff. Even so he could not buy freedom from all trouble: Antony, ruined by his passion for Cleopatra, had become the complete slave of his desire, while Cleopatra had gone right through her own family till not a single relation was left alive, and thirsting now for the blood of strangers, was slandering the authorities in Syria and urging Antony to have them executed, thinking that in this way she would easily become mistress of all their possessions. She even extended her acquisitiveness to Jews and Arabs and worked in secret to get their kings, Herod and Malchus, put to death.

Antony was sober enough to realize that one part of her demands – the killing of honest men and famous kings – was utterly immoral; but he cut them to the heart by withdrawing his friendship. He sliced off large parts of their territory, including the palm-grove at Jericho in which the balsam is produced, and gave them to Cleopatra along with all the cities except Tyre and Sidon south of the river Eleutherus.[18] Mistress now of this domain she escorted Antony as far as the Euphrates on his way to fight the Parthians,[19] and then came via Apamea and Damascus into Judaea. Herod placated her hostility with costly gifts, and leased back from her the lands broken off from his kingdom, at two hundred talents a year! Finally he escorted her all the way to Pelusium, showing her every attention. It was not long before

Antony reappeared from Parthia, bringing a prisoner – Artabazes the son of Tigranes – as a present for Cleopatra, to whom, along with the money and all the booty, the unfortunate Parthian was immediately handed over.

When the war that ended at Actium broke out,[20] Herod prepared to take the field with Antony, having settled all disturbances in Judaea and captured Hyrcania, a fortress till then in the hands of Antigonus' sister. But he was prevented by Cleopatra's cunning from sharing Antony's dangers; as mentioned already, she was scheming against the kings, and now she persuaded Antony to entrust Herod with the war against the Arabs – if he won she would become mistress of Arabia, if he lost, of Judaea, and she would be using one ruler to get rid of the other.[21]

It was Herod, however, who benefited by her scheme. He began by plundering enemy country, then he got together a large force of cavalry and sent them into battle near the city of Dium,[22] emerging victorious despite determined resistance. This defeat led to feverish activity among the Arabs, who gathered at Canatha in Coele Syria in enormous strength and awaited the Jews. There Herod arrived with his army, and endeavouring to conduct his campaign with great circumspection ordered a camp to be fortified. His soldiers, however, disregarded his commands, and elated by their earlier success attacked the Arabs, routed them at the first charge and followed in pursuit. But in the pursuit Herod was the victim of treachery, the inhabitants of Canatha being sent against him by Athenio, one of Cleopatra's generals who was permanently hostile. Their onslaught restored the morale of the Arabs, who turned about, and joining forces on rocky, difficult ground routed Herod's men, slaughtering them wholesale. Those who escaped from the battle sought shelter in Ormiza, but their camp was surrounded and captured with all its defenders by the Arabs.

Soon after this disaster Herod brought up reinforcements, but he was too late. Responsibility for the tragedy rested with his undisciplined subordinates; if battle had not been joined prematurely, Athenio would have found no opportunity for treachery. Still, Herod got even with the Arabs later by repeatedly overrunning their country, so that they often had reason to remember ruefully their one victory. But while he was settling accounts with his enemies another disaster befell him, an act of God occurring in the seventh year of his reign[23] at the height of the Actian War. At the beginning of spring

there was an earthquake which destroyed 30,000 people and innumerable cattle. The army escaped unhurt, as it was camping in the
open. At once Arab confidence was stimulated by rumour, which
always makes disasters seem worse than they are. Convinced that
Judaea was one vast ruin, the land deserted and at their mercy, they
descended on it, first offering as sacrificial victims the envoys who had
just arrived from Judaea. This invasion completely demoralized the
people – their spirit was broken by the succession of overwhelming
disasters; so Herod brought them together and tried by the following
appeal to awaken the spirit of resistance.[24]

'It is surely quite unnecessary to take fright like this. To be upset by
an act of God was natural enough; to be equally upset when men
attack you shows a very poor spirit. I for one am so far from being
alarmed because the enemy have come after the earthquake that I
believe God sent it to trap the Arabs, and make them pay us the
penalty for what they have done. It was not so much their own
strength and skill as our accidental misfortunes that gave them
confidence to come here – and it is a poor hope that depends not on
one's own ability but on other people's troubles! No one can count on
either bad luck or good going on for ever – everybody knows how
fickle fortune is. You can see an example of that very near home. You
won the first battle, they won the second; now they expect to win
and are pretty certain to lose. Cocksure people are caught napping,
while those who scent danger keep their eyes open; so your nervous-
ness makes me feel all the safer. When you were overbold and went
for the enemy against my wishes, Athenio seized his chance to catch
us out; now that you hang back and seem down in the mouth, I am
dead certain we shall win. That is how you *should* feel while waiting
for something to happen: when it does happen, you must see red,
and show these dirty louts that nothing God or man can do to us will
ever damp the fighting spirit of Jews as long as they have breath in
their bodies, and that no Jew will stand by while his property goes to
an Arab who time and time again has only just missed becoming his
prisoner.

'Again, you needn't turn a hair at the upheavals of the physical
world, or imagine that the earthquake is a warning of another disaster
to come. These elemental disturbances are quite natural and do us no
harm beyond the immediate damage. Plague, famine, and earth
tremors may perhaps be foreshadowed by some slighter indication,

but the actual calamities are too big to go beyond their own limits. Do you think we could suffer more than we did in the earthquake, even if we lost the war? No; it is our enemies that have received the clearest warning of the coming crash, not from some natural occurrence or the action of someone else, but from their own guilty consciences. In defiance of international law they have brutally murdered our envoys[25]; such are the victims they have sacrificed to get God on their side! But they will not escape His all-seeing eye and invisible right arm; they will soon pay us the penalty, if we show something of the spirit of our fathers and rouse ourselves to give these treaty-breakers what they deserve. Let every man take up arms to champion, not his wife, his children, or his threatened country, but our murdered envoys; they will be more inspiring leaders in the war than we who are alive can ever be. For my part, if you will obey my orders, I will be in the forefront of the battle; you know well enough that unless by some rash act you injure your own cause, your gallantry is irresistible.'

By this speech Herod put new spirit into his soldiers, and satisfied with their enthusiasm he sacrificed to God, immediately afterwards crossing the Jordan with his army. Pitching his camp near Philadelphia quite close to the enemy, he began skirmishing with them for the possession of a fort in No Man's Land, being anxious for an early trial of strength. It happened that the enemy had sent a party forward to seize this strongpoint; the king's men quickly drove them back and occupied the hill. Herod himself daily led out his forces, deployed them for battle, and challenged the Arabs. Not a man came forward to oppose him – they were in a state of utter panic, and even more than the rank and file their general Elthemus was incapacitated by terror – so Herod advanced to their palisade and began to tear it down. At that they had to do something, and they came out to battle in disorder, infantry mixed with cavalry. In numbers they had the advantage of the Jews, but in enthusiasm they could not be compared, though desperation made even them show reckless courage. So as long as they stood their ground their losses were few, but when they turned tail many were killed by the Jews and many trampled to death by their friends. 5,000 fell in the rout; the remainder lost no time in crowding within their palisade. Surrounded and besieged by Herod, they would have fallen to an assault if the failure of their water-supply had not forced them to send envoys at once. These the king treated with contempt, and the offer of five hundred talents only made him intensify his attacks. Parched with thirst, the defenders came out en masse and voluntarily gave themselves up, so that in five days 4,000 were taken prisoner. Next day in desperation the remainder came out to give battle. Herod engaged them and killed about 7,000 more. By this overwhelming blow he settled his account with Arabia and humbled the pride of her people so triumphantly that the nation chose him as their Protector.[26]

No sooner was that difficulty overcome than Herod's whole future was in the melting-pot because of his friendship with Antony, whom Caesar had defeated at Actium. Actually he occasioned more alarm than he felt; for Caesar was not sure that Antony was finished while his ally Herod remained.[27] But the king determined to come to grips with his danger, and sailing to Rhodes where Caesar was at the time, sought an audience without his crown, in the dress and with the appearance of a commoner, but with the haughtiness of a king. He kept back nothing and spoke as man to man.[28]

'It was Antony, Caesar, who set me on the throne, and I freely admit that to Antony I have rendered every possible service. Nor do I hesitate to say that you would certainly have found me fighting loyally by his side if the Arabs had not prevented it. As it was I sent him all the reinforcements I could and many thousand sacks of corn; and not even after his defeat at Actium did I desert my benefactor – I gave him the best possible advice, as it was no use sending any more soldiers; I told him there was only one way of retrieving his disasters – Cleopatra's death.[29] If he would kill her I promised money, protecting walls, an army, and my active participation in the war against you. But there it is! His ears were stopped by his insane passion for Cleopatra – and by God who has given the victory to you. I am defeated with Antony and with his fall I lay aside my crown. I have come to you placing my hope of safety in my unblemished character, and believing that you will wish to know not whose friend, but what sort of friend, I have been.'[30]

Caesar replied: 'You are perfectly safe, and your throne is now more securely yours. You deserve to rule over many subjects after showing such loyalty to your friend. Try to be as faithful to those who enjoy better success; for my part, I see a dazzling prospect for such a bold spirit as yourself. It is a very good thing that Antony listened to Cleopatra and not to you: we have gained you through his folly. It seems I am already in your debt, as Quintus Didius writes to tell me you have sent a contingent to help him deal with the gladiators.[31] I now therefore issue a decree that the throne is securely yours. Before long I shall endeavour to show you some further favour, so that you may not miss Antony.'

After addressing these gracious words to the king and setting the crown on his head, he published a decree announcing the award and expressing with the utmost generosity his high opinion of the beneficiary. After placating him with presents Herod interceded on behalf of Alexas, a friend of Antony, who had asked for mercy. But Caesar's anger brooked no opposition; he vigorously and bitterly condemned the petitioner, firmly rejecting Herod's appeal. Later, when Caesar travelled to Egypt via Syria, Herod welcomed him for the first time with all his kingly wealth, rode by his side when he inspected his army near Ptolemais, and gave a banquet for him and all his friends, finally providing a feast of good things for the rest of the army.[32] As the troops were to march through the desert to Pelusium and back, he took care to supply water in abundance, and the army lacked nothing in the way of supplies. The thought naturally occurred to Caesar and his men that in view of his generosity Herod's kingdom was far too small. So when Caesar arrived in Egypt, and Cleopatra and Antony were now dead, he showered honours upon him, restored to his kingdom the area sliced off by Cleopatra, and added Gadara, Hippus, and Samaria, with the coastal towns Gaza, Anthedon, Joppa, and Strato's Tower.[33] He further made him a present of four hundred Gauls, to be his bodyguard as they had formerly been Cleopatra's.[34] Of all his liberality there was no more potent cause than the openhandedness of the recipient.

After the first Actiad[35] Caesar added to Herod's kingdom Trachonitis, Batanaea that adjoined it, and Auranitis. This is how it came about. Zenodorus had leased the estate of Lysanias,[36] and he never stopped sending bandits from Trachonitis to waylay the Damascenes. These sought the protection of Varro, governor of Syria, and begged him to bring their plight to the notice of Caesar; Caesar's response was to authorize the destruction of the nest of bandits. Varro therefore mobilized his forces, cleared the district of these rogues, and dispossessed Zenodorus; to prevent it from again becoming a base for raids on Damascus, Caesar later transferred it to Herod. When after an interval of ten years he paid a second visit to the province, he made him procurator of all Syria,[37] with power to veto any decision of the other procurators; and when Zenodorus died he assigned to him also the whole area between Trachonitis and Galilee.[38] What counted still more with Herod was that in Caesar's affections he was second only to Agrippa, in Agrippa's second only to Caesar.[39] From then on he climbed to the very heights of prosperity, while his moral stature increased and his superb generosity was largely devoted to works of piety.

In the fifteenth year of his reign[40] he restored the existing Sanctuary and round it enclosed an area double the former size, keeping no account of the cost and achieving a magnificence beyond compare. This could be seen particularly in the great colonnades that ran round the entire Temple and the fortress that towered over it to the north. The former were completely new structures, the latter an extremely costly reconstruction, as luxurious as a palace, and named Antonia in honour of Antony. His own Palace, built in the Upper City, consisted of two very large and very lovely buildings which made even the Sanctuary seem insignificant: these he named after his friends, one Caesareum, one Agrippeum.[41]

But it was not in buildings only that he enshrined their memory and names; through his lavish generosity whole cities came into being. In the district of Samaritis he built a city with magnificent walls over two miles long, settled in it 6,000 colonists, allotted to them some land of excellent quality, and in the centre of the new town erected a vast shrine with precincts three hundred yards in length dedicated to Caesar.[42] The town he called Sebaste,[43] and to the citizens he granted a very special charter. At a later date, when Caesar had enriched him by the addition of further lands, there also he erected a shrine of white marble dedicated to his patron, near the sources of the Jordan at a place called Paneum.[44] There is a mountain here whose top is lost in the clouds; in the lower slopes is a cavern with its mouth concealed by vegetation, inside which a sheer precipice descends, nobody knows how far, to a cavity filled with still water: no plummet has ever reached the bottom, however long the cord. From the roots of the cavern outside well up the springs which some consider to be the head-waters of Jordan. A true account will be given later.[45] At Jericho, between the fortress of Cypros[46] and the old palace, he built other new buildings, better and more comfortable for visitors, named after the same friends. In fact I cannot think of any suitable spot in his kingdom that he left without some tribute of esteem for Caesar. When he had filled his own country with temples[47] these tributes overflowed into the province,[48] and in city after city he erected a Caesareum.[49]

He noticed on the coast a town called Strato's Tower, in a state of decay, but thanks to its admirable situation capable of benefiting by his generosity. He rebuilt it entirely with limestone and adorned it with a most splendid palace. Nowhere did he show more clearly the liveliness of his imagination. The city lies midway between Dora and Joppa, and hitherto the whole of that shore had been harbourless, so that anyone sailing along the Phoenician coast towards Egypt had to ride the open sea when threatened by the south-west wind; even when this is far from strong, such huge waves are dashed against the rocks that the back-wash makes the sea boil up a long way out. But the king by lavish expenditure and unshakable determination won the battle against nature and constructed a harbour bigger than the Piraeus, with further deep roadsteads in its recesses. The site was as awkward as could be, but he wrestled with the difficulties so triumphantly that on his solid fabric the sea could make no impression, while its beauty gave no hint of the obstacles encountered. He first marked out the area for a harbour of the size mentioned, and then lowered into 20 fathoms of water blocks of stone mostly 50 feet long, 9 deep and 10 broad, but sometimes even bigger. When the foundations had risen to water-level he built above the surface a mole 200 feet wide; half this width was built out to break the force of the waves and so was called the Breakwater; the rest supported the encircling stone wall. Along this were spaced massive towers, of which the most conspicuous and most beautiful was called Drusium after Caesar's step-son.[50]

There was a row of arched recesses where newly-arrived crews could land, and in front of these was a circular terrace forming a broad walk for those disembarking. The harbour-mouth faced north, as in that locality the north wind is the gentlest, and on either side rose three colossal statues standing on pillars; those on the left of ships entering were supported by a solid tower, those on the right by two upright stones clamped together, even higher than the tower on the other side. Adjoining the harbour were houses, also of limestone, and to the harbour led the streets of the town, laid out the same distance apart. On rising ground opposite the harbour-mouth stood Caesar's temple, of exceptional size and beauty; in it was a colossal statue of Caesar, no whit inferior to the Olympian Zeus[51] which it was intended to resemble, and one of Rome[52] comparable with the Hera of Argos. Herod dedicated the city to the province, the harbour to those who sailed these seas, and the honour of his new creation to Caesar: Caesarea was the name he gave it. The rest of the buildings – theatre, amphitheatre, and market-place – were on a scale worthy of that name. The king also instituted four-yearly games and called them too after Caesar, gracing the first contest – held in the 192nd Olympiad – with the personal gift of very valuable prizes, the royal bounty extending not only to the winners but to those who came second and third.[53]

Herod also rebuilt Anthedon, a coastal town destroyed in war, and renamed it Agrippeum. So devoted was he to his friend Agrippa that he even engraved his name over the gate which he had erected in the Temple.[54]

If ever a man was full of family affection, that man was Herod. In memory of his father he founded a city, choosing a site in the loveliest plain in his kingdom with an abundance of rivers and trees, and naming it Antipatris; and the fortress overlooking Jericho he re-fortified, making it outstandingly strong and beautiful, and dedicated it to his mother under the name Cypros. To his brother Phasael he erected the tower in Jerusalem that took his name; its design and tremendous size we shall describe later.[55] He also founded another city in the valley running north from Jericho and called it Phasaelis.

Having immortalized his family and friends he did not neglect to make his own memory secure. He built a fortress in the hills facing Arabia and called it Herodium after himself, and seven miles from Jerusalem he gave the same name to an artificial hill, the shape of a woman's breast, adorning it more elaborately than the other. He encircled the top with round towers, filling the enclosed space with a palace so magnificent that in addition to the splendid appearance of the interior of the apartments the outer walls, copings, and roofs had wealth lavished on them without stint. At very heavy cost he brought in an unlimited supply of water from a distance, and furnished the ascent with 200 steps of the whitest marble; the mound was of considerable height, though entirely artificial. Round the base he built other royal apartments to accommodate his furniture and his friends, so that in its completeness the stronghold was a town, in its compactness a palace.[56]

After this spate of building he extended his generosity to a great many cities outside his boundaries. For Tripolis, Damascus, and Ptolemais he provided gymnasia, for Byblus a wall, for Berytus and Tyre halls, colonnades, temples, and market-places, for Sidon and Damascus theatres, for the coastal Laodicea an aqueduct, and for Ascalon baths, magnificent fountains, and cloistered quadrangles remarkable for both scale and craftsmanship; in other places he dedicated woods and parks. Many towns, as if they belonged to his kingdom, received gifts of land; others he endowed with revenues to finance for all time the annual appointment of a gymnasiarch[57] – Cos, for instance – that the office might never lapse. Corn he bestowed on all who needed it. To Rhodes he over and over again gave money for naval construction, and when the temple of Apollo was burnt down he rebuilt it with new splendour out of his own purse. What need be said of his gifts to Lycia or Samos, or of his liberality to the whole of Ionia, sufficient for the needs of every locality? Even Athens and Sparta, Nicopolis and Mysian Pergamum are full of Herod's offerings, are they not? And the wide street in Syrian Antioch, once avoided because of the mud, did he not pave – two and a quarter miles of it – with polished marble, and to keep the rain off furnish it with a colonnade from end to end?[58]

It may be suggested that all these benefits were enjoyed only by the particular community favoured; but his endowment of Elis was a gift not only to Greece in general but to every corner of the civilized world reached by the fame of the Olympic Games. Seeing that the games were declining for lack of funds and that the sole relic of ancient Greece was slipping away, he not only acted as president of the four-yearly meeting held when he happened to be on his way to Rome, but endowed them for all time with an income big enough to ensure that his presidency should never be forgotten.[59] We should go on for ever if we tried to list the debts and dues he paid for others, as when he relieved Phaselis, Balanea, and the smaller Cilician towns of part of the burden of their annual taxation. However, his superb generosity was severely limited by the fear of arousing jealousy, or of being suspected of an ulterior motive for doing more for the cities than did their own masters.

Herod's bodily strength was as great as his power of mind. He had always excelled in hunting, owing his success mainly to his horsemanship. On a single day he once brought down forty beasts: the country breeds boars, and stags and wild asses are still commoner. He was also an incomparable fighter; on the training-ground many were amazed to see his accuracy in throwing the javelin, and the regularity with which his arrows found the target. Beside his bodily and mental advantages he enjoyed the best of luck; he met with very few military defeats, and for these he was not to blame – they were due either to his soldiers' rashness or to someone's treachery.

CHAPTER 4

Herod's Murder of Mariamme and her Children

FOR his public successes fortune made Herod pay a terrible price in his own house.[1] His woes began with a woman whom he loved passionately. At the start of his reign he had divorced the wife he had married when a commoner, a native of Jerusalem called Doris, and wedded Mariamme, the daughter of Aristobulus' son Alexander.[2] She was the cause of the divisions in his house, which began early and grew worse after his return from Rome.[3] First of all he banished from the City his son by Doris, Antipater, for the sake of his children by Mariamme, permitting him to return for the festivals alone. Next he executed his wife's grandfather Hyrcanus on his return from Parthia, accusing him of conspiracy. Hyrcanus had been taken prisoner by Barzapharnes when he overran Palestine, but freed at the request of his sympathetic countrymen beyond the Euphrates. If only he had taken their advice not to go across the river to Herod, he would not have perished when innocent; but he was lured to his death by his grand-daughter's marriage, relying on that and unable to resist the pull of his homeland. He provoked Herod not by claiming the throne, but because the throne was really his.[4]

Of Herod's five children by Mariamme two were girls and three boys. The youngest of the boys died while at school in Rome; the two eldest he brought up in royal style on account of their mother's noble birth and because he was king when they were born.[5] A more compelling reason was his passionate love of Mariamme, which every day consumed him more fiercely, blinding him to the calamities that his beloved was bringing upon him; for Mariamme hated him as passionately as he loved her. She had good reason to be revolted by his actions and could speak freely because of her hold upon him, so she openly took him to task for what he had done to her grandfather Hyrcanus and her brother Jonathan. For he had not spared even him, child as he was; he had given him the high priesthood in his seventeenth year and after bestowing the honour had immediately executed him, because when he put on the sacred vestments and approached the altar during a feast, the whole crowd had burst into tears. The boy was therefore sent at night to Jericho and there, by Herod's command, the Gauls took him to a swimming-pool and drowned him.[6]

These were the things for which Mariamme took Herod to task; she then turned her attention to his mother and sister and heaped abuse upon them. Herod was muzzled by his infatuation, but the women were furious, and knowing that it was the most likely way of rousing Herod brought against her the baseless charge of adultery. Among much false evidence concocted to convince him, they accused her of having sent a portrait of herself to Antony in Egypt, and in her over-mastering licentiousness exposed herself, in spite of the distance, to a man who was woman-mad and able to get his way by force. Herod was thunderstruck; in his passionate love he was tormented by jealousy; and he thought of the terrible skill with which Cleopatra had disposed of King Lysanias[7] and the Arab Malchus – he knew he was in danger of losing not only his queen but his own life. So, as he was bound for foreign parts, he put Mariamme in the care of Joseph, husband of his sister Salome, a trustworthy man, loyal because of their kinship, giving him secret instructions to kill her if Antony killed Herod himself. Joseph, with no evil intention but simply to prove to her how passionately the king loved her, as he could not bear that even death should part them, disclosed the secret. On his return Herod, during intercourse, protested with many oaths his devotion to her, the only woman he had ever loved. 'And a nice way,' she exclaimed, 'to show your love for me – giving Joseph instructions to kill me!' When he learnt that the secret was out, Herod was frantic, and declared that Joseph would never have revealed his instructions unless he had seduced her. Blind with rage he leapt from the bed and rushed wildly about the palace. This opportunity for slander his sister Salome seized with both hands, assuring him that his suspicion of Joseph was true. Driven mad by uncontrollable jealousy he ordered the instant execution of them both.[8] But rage quickly gave way to remorse, and as anger died down love was rekindled. So hot was the flame of his desire that he could not believe her dead, but in his sickness of mind talked to her as if still alive, until time revealed to him the terrible truth, and filled his heart with grief as passionate as his love had been while she lived.[9]

The mother bequeathed her bitterness to her sons, who, aware of the blood on their father's hands, viewed him as an enemy, first at the time of their schooling in Rome, and still more when they returned to Judaea.[10] As they approached manhood this feeling grew steadily stronger; and when they reached an age to marry and one (Aristobulus) wedded the daughter of his aunt Salome, the accuser of their mother, and the other (Alexander) the daughter of King Archelaus of Cappadocia (Glaphyra), they made no further attempt to conceal their hatred. This boldness gave slanderers their chance, and more open suggestions were made to the king that both sons were plotting against him, and that the son-in-law of Archelaus, relying on his father-in-law, was getting ready to flee in order to accuse his father before Caesar. Stuffed with these slanders Herod, as a bulwark against his other sons, recalled his son by Doris, Antipater, and began in every way to show him preference.[11]

This new attitude was more than the two sons could stomach: when they saw the commoner's son promoted, pride in their own birth made their anger uncontrollable, and every new annoyance called forth an outburst of wrath; as a result they provoked increasing hostility, while Antipater was now winning favour by his own efforts. He was very clever at flattering his father, and concocted a variety of slanders against his brothers, putting some of them into circulation himself and getting his close friends to broadcast others, till he destroyed any chance of his brothers' coming to the throne. Both in his will and by his public actions Herod declared him to be the heir[12]: he was sent in royal state to Caesar, with the robes and all the other trappings except the crown.[13] In time he was in a position to bring back his mother to Mariamme's bed; and by employing two weapons against his brothers, flattery and slander, he cleverly coaxed Herod into contemplating the execution of his sons.

Alexander was dragged by his father to Rome to be charged before Caesar with an attempt to poison him.[14] Having at last a chance to bring his grievances into the open before a judge more experienced than Antipater and better balanced than Herod, the accused kept a respectful silence about his father's faults, but vigorously combated the imputations against himself. Having next made it clear that his brother and companion in danger was as innocent as he was, he went on to denounce the villainy of Antipater and the wrong done to his brother and himself.[15] He was aided not only by a clear conscience but by the vigour of his oratory – he was a very effective speaker. Declaring as his peroration that his father was free to put them both to death if he was satisfied that the accusation was true, he reduced the whole court to tears, and so moved Caesar that he dismissed the charges and effected an immediate reconciliation, on the understanding that the sons should obey their father in everything and that he should be free to choose his successor.[16] The king then took his leave of Rome, to all appearance abandoning the charges against his sons, but still retaining his suspicions; for he was accompanied by Antipater, who had inspired his hate, but dared not openly reveal his enmity through respect for the reconciler. As he skirted Cilicia Herod landed at Eleusa and was hospitably entertained by Archelaus, who expressed delight at his son-in-law's acquittal and the greatest satisfaction at the reconciliation: he had previously written to his friends in Rome to stand by Alexander at his trial. He escorted Herod to Zephyrium and gave him presents to the value of thirty talents.

Back in Jerusalem Herod assembled the citizens, presented his three sons, explained his absence, and expressed his deep gratitude to God and to Caesar for setting his troubled household to rights and bestowing on his sons something more precious than the throne – concord. 'That concord,' he went on, 'I shall myself knit together. Caesar made me lord of the realm and judge of the succession, and I while acting in my own interest will requite his kindness. I proclaim these three sons of mine kings, and call first on God, then on you, to confirm my decision. The succession belongs to one by priority of birth, to the others by their noble parentage: my kingdom is big enough for more than three.[17] Those whom Caesar has joined together and whom their father nominates you must defend, honouring them justly and equally, but each according to his birthright: to pay one more respect than his age entitles him to would give less pleasure to him than annoyance to the one neglected. The Counsellors and Gentlemen of the Household[18] who are to attend each king I shall myself choose, appointing them securities for the preservation of concord, since I am well aware that divisions and rivalries are engendered by the malignity of the companions of princes, but if companions are good men they encourage feelings of affection.

'I must insist, however, that not only these officials but also the officers in my army place their hopes for the present in me alone: it is not kingship, but the honour due to kingship that I am bestowing on my sons. The sweets of power they will enjoy, but the burden of responsibility is mine, however unwelcome. Let each of you consider my age, my way of life and my piety. I am not so old that an early end is in sight, or given up to self-indulgence, which cuts men off even in their prime, and I have served the Almighty with such devotion that I may hope for a very long life.[19] So any man who puts himself at the service of my sons in order to bring me down I shall punish for their sakes too: it is not meanness towards my own children that makes me limit the reverence to be paid them; it is the knowledge that to the young, adulation is a temptation to presumption. If everyone who comes into contact with these young men reflects that if he upholds what is right, I shall reward him, but that if he promotes division, not even the man he is serving will give him any recompense for his malice, then everyone, I think, will be loyal to me – and that means to my sons; for it is in their interest that I should be on the throne, and in mine that their concord should be unbroken.

'You, my good sons, turn your thoughts first to the sacred laws of nature, which keep even beasts in the bonds of affection; then to Caesar, who brought about our reconciliation; and lastly to me, who entreat when I might command – and continue as brothers. I give you henceforth the robes and attendants of kings; and I pray that God will maintain my settlement, if your concord remains.'

So saying he gave each of his sons an affectionate embrace and dismissed the people, some of whom said Amen to his prayer, and others, who wanted a change, pretended they had not even heard it!

However, the brothers did not leave their divisions behind but parted still more suspicious of each other, Alexander and Aristobulus resenting the confirmation of Antipater's rights as the eldest, Antipater grudging even second place to his brothers. Antipater however was extremely shrewd and kept his mouth shut, concealing with the utmost cunning his detestation of the other two; whereas they, proud of their birth, made no secret of their feelings, goaded all the time by their 'friends', many of whom nosed their way in to spy on them. Every word uttered in Alexander's circle was immediately repeated in Antipater's, and passed on, with additions, by Antipater to Herod. The young man could not make the most innocent remark without getting into trouble; everything he said was given an incriminating twist, and if he spoke unguardedly, mountains were manufactured out of molehills. Antipater employed a succession of agents to draw him on, so that his own lies should have some foundation of truth, and if any one of the statements attributed to Alexander was proved authentic, the rest were taken for granted. All his own friends were either naturally secretive or induced by gifts to divulge absolutely nothing: Antipater's life might fairly be described as a mystery of wickedness. Alexander's companions, on the contrary, had succumbed to bribery or subtle flattery, Antipater's invariable weapon, and become informers who betrayed all his actions and words. By the most adroit stage-management Antipater showed himself a pastmaster in the art of making slander sink into Herod's ears, himself acting the part of an affectionate brother and leaving the tale-bearing to others. Whenever a story was told to the discredit of Alexander, he would make his entrance and act his part, first tearing the story to pieces, then subtly confirming it and stirring the king to anger. Everything was turned into proof of conspiracy, and nothing did so much to win acceptance for the slanders as Antipater's appeals on his brother's behalf.

Thus deceived Herod grew savage, and every day cared less for the youths and proportionately more for Antipater. The courtiers followed his example, some willingly, some under compulsion, for instance Ptolemy his most valued friend, the king's brothers,[20] and all his family. Antipater was everything and – the bitterest pill for Alexander to swallow – so was Antipater's mother, his fellow-conspirator and the cruellest of stepmothers, who hated her stepsons the more because their mother had been a princess. It followed that everyone fawned on Antipater now in the hope of advantage, and was encouraged to turn against Alexander and his brother by a command of the king forbidding his most distinguished subjects to go near them or have anything to do with them. His word was law not only in his own kingdom but among his friends abroad: to no other king had Caesar given the right to demand the extradition from another sovereign state of a fugitive national.

Blissfully ignorant of these slanders the youths exposed themselves to them all the more, as their father never openly took them to task; but gradually the truth dawned on them, as they perceived his coldness and growing exasperation over petty annoyances. Antipater also poisoned against them the mind of their uncle Pheroras and aunt Salome, whom he coaxed and prodded as if she had been his wife! Her enmity was further stimulated by Alexander's wife Glaphyra, who vaunted her noble lineage and claimed precedence over all the ladies at court, as the descendant of Temenus[21] through her father and of Darius son of Hytaspes through her mother, while she was never tired of sneering at the low birth of Herod's sister and wives, all of them chosen for their looks, not their parentage. He had many wives, as Jewish custom had always allowed polygamy,[22] and the king was strongly in favour! Every one of these, provoked by Glaphyra's contemptuous boasting, detested Alexander.

Salome, enraged already by Glaphyra's abuse, was alienated by her own son-in-law Aristobulus, who was constantly sneering at his wife for her humble origin, and lamenting that he had married a commoner and his brother Alexander a princess. Between her sobs she repeated this to her mother Salome, adding that Alexander and Aristobulus were threatening, when they succeeded to the throne, to force the mothers of the other brothers to work at the loom with the slaves, and to make the brothers village clerks – a mocking allusion to their careful schooling. Unable to contain herself Salome repeated the whole story to Herod: she was naturally believed as it was her son-in-law she was accusing. A further slander was brought at the same time to the king's ears, adding fuel to the flames. He was informed that the two brothers were constantly invoking their mother, bewailing her loss while they called down curses on him, and that often, when he distributed some of Mariamme's garments among his newer wives, they would threaten that instead of royal robes they would soon be wearing haircloth.

These tales made Herod fear the temper of the young men, but he still had hopes of correcting their faults; and on the eve of a voyage to Rome[23] he summoned them before him, and after briefly threatening them as their king, admonished them at great length as their father, urging them to love their brothers, and overlooking their offences in the past on condition that they behaved better in the future. They replied with a complete denial of the charges, declaring them to be baseless, and assuring him that they would prove their statements true by their actions; at the same time it was his duty to put a stop to tittle-tattle by being less ready to swallow it; there would never be an end to the lies told about them, as long as there was someone to believe them.

As he was their father, they soon convinced him by these declarations and rid themselves of their immediate fears; but their anxiety for the future was increased now that they knew of the hostility of Salome and their uncle Pheroras. These two were dangerous enemies, especially Pheroras, who shared all the appurtenances of royalty except the crown. He had a private income of a hundred talents, and enjoyed the revenue of all trans-Jordan, a gift from his brother, who beside obtaining Caesar's permission to appoint him tetrarch, honoured him with a royal marriage by giving him the hand of his own wife's sister.[24] On her death he promised him his eldest daughter with a dowry of three hundred talents; but Pheroras ran away from the royal marriage for love of a slave-girl. This enraged Herod, who married his daughter to his nephew, later killed by the Parthians.[25] But before long he got over his annoyance with Pheroras and pardoned his love-sickness.

Pheroras had at an earlier date, when the queen[26] was still alive, been falsely accused of conspiring to poison Herod; and now great numbers of informers came forward, so that Herod, though a most devoted brother, began to believe their stories and to take fright. After torturing many suspected persons he came finally to Pheroras' friends. None of these made a direct admission that there was a conspiracy, but they said that Pheroras was preparing to snatch up his loved one and make a dash for Parthia, partnered in his projected flight by Costobar, Salome's husband, to whom the king had given her hand after the execution of her former husband for adultery.[27] Salome herself did not escape slander: her brother Pheroras accused her of pledging herself to marry Syllaeus, regent for Obodas, king of Arabia and a bitter enemy of Herod.[28] Found guilty of this and every other offence with which Pheroras charged her, she was nevertheless pardoned. Pheroras himself was acquitted by the king on all counts.

The storm that threatened Herod's house then struck Alexander, bursting about his head with all its violence. There were three eunuchs whom the king valued most highly, as is plain from the offices entrusted to them. One was detailed to pour out his wine and one to serve his dinner, while the third put him to bed and slept in his room. These Alexander had induced by large presents to minister to his unnatural lust. When this came to the king's ears he put them to the torture, and they at once confessed their criminal association, disclosing also the promises which had tempted them to it; they had been deceived by Alexander, who told them not to rest their hopes on Herod, a shameless old man who dyed his hair (unless that made them really think he was young), but to turn to Alexander, who would succeed to the throne whether Herod liked it or not, and at no distant date would settle accounts with his enemies and bring prosperity and happiness to his friends, above all to themselves. They added that

leading citizens had secretly offered their services to Alexander, and
that the generals and other officers of the army were conferring with
him behind closed doors.

These revelations so alarmed Herod that he dared not immediately
publish them, but sent out secret spies, night and day, to investigate
all that was done or said; all suspects were at once executed. Complete
anarchy reigned in the Palace; to suit his personal animosity or hatred
everyone invented slanders, and many availed themselves of the royal
lust for blood to get rid of their rivals. Any lie found immediate
acceptance, and the punishment came more swiftly than the slander.
The man who had just accused another was himself accused; and he
and his victim were led off to execution together; for the king's
enquiries were cut short by the danger to his life. He became so embittered that he never smiled even at those not accused and was ready
to bite the heads off his friends; many of these he debarred from the
court, and those who were safe from his hand felt the lash of his
tongue. On top of Alexander's misfortunes came Antipater, who with
the collaboration of his Counsellors slandered him in every imaginable way. To such a pitch of terror was the king reduced by his
ingenious lies and fabrications that he was convinced that Alexander
stood over him sword in hand.[29] So he suddenly arrested and imprisoned him and proceeded to put his Gentlemen to the torture.
Many died without a word, or after saying only what they knew to
be true; others were driven by their agonies to tell lies, and said that
Alexander and his brother Aristobulus were plotting against him and
awaiting a chance to kill him while out hunting and make a dash
for Rome. This improbable story, extemporized under pressure, the
king was glad to accept, feeling more comfortable about the imprisonment of his son now that it seemed justified.

When Alexander saw there was no way of shaking his father's
belief, he determined to come to grips with his perils, and composed
a four-volume indictment of his enemies, admitting the plot but
naming most of them as accomplices, of whom the chief were
Pheroras and Salome; the latter, he alleged, had one night actually
forced her way into his room and had intercourse with him against
his will. These volumes, full of clamorous and dreadful allegations
against the highest in the land, came into Herod's hands, and Archelaus then made a hurried journey to Judaea, in alarm for his daughter
and son-in-law. In assisting them he showed remarkable tact, and by

using guile he brought the king's threats to nothing. The moment he met Herod he let fly. 'Where is that perishing son-in-law of mine? Where shall I find that damned parricide? I will flay him alive with my own hands; and I will do the same to my daughter along with her charming husband! Even if she had no finger in the pie, she is his wife, and tarred with the same brush. I can't understand how you, the intended victim, can take it so calmly – if it is true that Alexander is still alive! *I* came full speed from Cappadocia expecting to find that he had paid the penalty long ago, and to ask your advice about my daughter, whom I gave away to that scoundrel because of your great name; but now we must put our heads together about the pair of them, and if you are too much of a father or haven't the nerve to give your son what he deserves, we had better change places and carry out each other's sentences.'

Herod was taken in by this tirade of Archelaus, although against his better judgement. At any rate, he gave him the documents compiled by Alexander to read and went through them with him, dwelling on each section. Archelaus then seized the chance of furthering his own scheme and gradually shifted the blame on to the people mentioned in them, especially Pheroras. When he saw that the king believed him, he said: 'We must be sure that the young man really is plotting against you and is not the victim of a plot by these villains. For there is no obvious reason why he should have plunged into such a foul crime, when he was already enjoying a royal position and expecting to succeed you, unless there were people working on him and taking advantage of the instability of youth. People like that can impose on the elderly as well as on the young and overthrow illustrious families and whole kingdoms.'

Seeing the force of this argument Herod for a time transferred his anger from Alexander to Pheroras, the chief villain of the four volumes. Pheroras, observing this sudden change in the king's attitude and his complete acceptance of the suggestions of his friend Archelaus, saw no hope of saving himself by honest means, so decided to do it by sheer impudence. He dropped Alexander and applied to Archelaus. That monarch answered that he did not see how he could plead for a man mixed up in such a shady business – which made it as plain as could be that he had plotted against the king and brought all the lad's present troubles on him – unless he was prepared to abandon his tricks and denials and plead guilty to the crimes he was charged with, and then ask pardon of his brother, who was still fond of him: if Pheroras would do that, he would help him in every possible way.

Pheroras took his advice, and after making careful preparations to look as woebegone as possible, clothed in black and with streaming eyes, grovelled at Herod's feet and begged for mercy – as he had done successfully on several previous occasions! He admitted he was a dirty scoundrel, guilty on every count, but blamed his unbalanced and frenzied state of mind, brought on, he said, by his passionate love for his wife. Having thus brought Pheroras to accuse and give evidence against himself, Archelaus now began to plead for him, and to mitigate Herod's anger by quoting parallels in his own house: why, he himself had suffered much worse treatment at his brother's hands, but had never let revenge weaken the ties of blood; kingdoms were like fat men – one member or another was always getting inflamed because of the weight it carried; but this called, not for the surgeon's knife, but for a dose of medicine.

These arguments and others to the same effect softened Herod's anger with Pheroras, but Archelaus continued to fume against Alexander, insisting that he would get his daughter divorced and take her home, until he brought Herod round to the point of pleading with him on the lad's behalf, and once more requesting the hand of his daughter for his son. With a most convincing appearance of sincerity Archelaus gave him leave to marry her to anyone he pleased – except Alexander; he was most anxious to preserve the marriage links between himself and Herod. The king replied that he would be receiving back his son as a gift from him if he refrained from breaking the marriage; they already had children and the lad was most devoted to his wife; if she stayed with him she would help him to be ashamed of his misdeeds, but if she was torn from him his despair would be complete: a reckless spirit was tamed when diverted by domestic affection. After long hesitation Archelaus gave in, was reconciled to the young man, and reconciled his father to him. However, he said that it was necessary to send him to Rome for an audience with Caesar,[30] to whom he had himself dispatched a detailed report.

Thus the stratagem by which Archelaus rescued his son-in-law was a complete success. After the reconciliation they spent their time in feasting and mutual entertainment. When he said goodbye Herod made him a present of seventy talents, a golden throne set with precious stones, eunuchs, and a concubine called Pannychis, and rewarded all his Gentlemen according to their rank. By the king's command all his Counsellors similarly gave Archelaus magnificent gifts. Finally he was escorted by Herod and the nobility all the way to Antioch.

Alas! it was not long before Judaea was visited by a man who could do far more than the stratagems of Archelaus, and who not only brought to an end the reconciliation which Archelaus had contrived for Alexander but actually compassed that young man's destruction. He was a Spartan by birth named Eurycles, whose intrusion into the kingdom was due to his passion for money: Greece no longer satisfied his extravagance. He brought splendid gifts for Herod as a bait to secure his ends, instantly receiving much bigger ones in return; but he had no use for a straightforward gift unless he could make a profit out of the kingdom by bloodshed. So he got round the king by compliments, subtle suggestion, and hollow flattery. He quickly summed up Herod's character, and playing up to him in all he said and did he soon became one of his closest friends: the king and all his court were only too glad to show special regard for this Spartan for his country's sake.

He soon became thoroughly acquainted with the rotten state of the royal house, the brothers' quarrels and their father's attitude to each, and though Antipater in view of his hospitality had the first claim on his gratitude, he professed friendship for Alexander, falsely claiming that he had long been an intimate friend of Archelaus. This won him instant acceptance as a proved ally, and an early introduction to Alexander's brother Aristobulus. Playing first one part and then another, in various ways he won the confidence of everybody; but his favourite rôles were those of hireling to Antipater and traitor to Alexander. He cried shame on Antipater if he, the eldest son, stood by while other people were after his expectations; and on Alexander if he, whose mother and wife were kings' daughters, allowed the crown to pass to a commoner's son, and that when he had the influential backing of Archelaus! The lad trusted him as a counsellor since he claimed the friendship of Archelaus; so, keeping nothing back, he told him of all the wrongs Antipater had done him, and of the likelihood that after killing their mother Herod would deprive him and his brother of her kingdom. With these grievances the tender-hearted Eurycles pretended to sympathize. Then he tricked Aristobulus into saying the same things, and having involved both in criticism of their father he went off to repeat their private conversation to Antipater, adding the lie that his brothers were after his blood and on the point of swooping on him sword in hand. These efforts having earned him a handsome dividend, he sang the praise of Antipater to his father. Finally terms were agreed for him to compass the death of Aristobulus and Alexander, and he undertook to accuse them before their father.

Presenting himself before Herod he declared that he was offering him life in return for his kindness, the light of day to repay his hospitality; a sword had long since been sharpened against him and Alexander had braced his arm – he himself had delayed the blow by feigned collaboration. He had heard Alexander say that Herod was not content to sit on a throne belonging to others, and after murdering their mother to squander her empire, but was actually dragging in a bastard as his successor and offering the kingdom of their grandfather[31] to that worm Antipater. But he would take the law into his own hands and avenge the spirits of Hyrcanus and Mariamme: he would never stoop to succeed such a father on the throne without bloodshed. Day after day he was subjected to constant annoyance, so that he could not make the most casual remark without its being turned against him. If other people's ancestry was mentioned, his father went out of his way to make insulting remarks such as 'Only Alexander has any ancestors: he thinks his father came out of the gutter!' At the hunt his very silence gave offence; if he paid a compliment he was accused of sarcasm. Everywhere he found his father impossible to please, and with no feeling for anyone but Antipater; so he would gladly die if he failed in his attempt. If he succeeded, his safety was guaranteed, first by Archelaus his father-in-law, to whom he could easily escape, then by Caesar, who was not yet aware of Herod's true character; he would not, as on a former occasion,[32] stand before him intimidated by his father's presence, or confine himself to the discussion of his personal grievances; he would first of all openly proclaim the miseries of his people, bled white by taxation, and then reveal the luxuries and excesses on which all this blood-money was spent, the character of the men enriched at the expense of himself and his brother, and the means by which certain towns had won privileges. And while he was there he would demand an enquiry into the fate of his grandfather[33] and his mother, and mercilessly expose the filth and corruption pervading the whole kingdom. There would be no question then of his being adjudged a parricide!

When he had concluded this scandalous diatribe against Alexander, Eurycles delivered a lengthy eulogy of Antipater as the only son with any affection for his father, and for that reason an obstacle to the plot hitherto. The king, who had not yet completely got over the earlier shocks, boiled over with uncontrollable anger. Antipater again seized his chance, and sent a fresh set of hush-hush informers to accuse his brothers of having held secret conferences with Jucundus and Tyrannus, once officers of the king's cavalry, but now because of some offences deprived of their commissions. At this Herod lost his temper completely and at once had the two men tortured. They admitted none of the charges; but a letter was produced from Alexander to the commandant at Alexandreum, requesting him to admit Aristobulus and himself to the fortress when he had killed their father, and to let them use the weapons and other resources of the place. Alexander protested that this letter had been forged by Diophantus the king's secretary, a man without scruples and very clever at imitating any hand. (After a lifetime of forgery he was ultimately executed for that very offence.) Herod put the commandant to the torture, but failed to extract any information from him about the allegations. He found the evidence unconvincing, but nevertheless kept his sons under surveillance though still at liberty. The curse of his house and stage-manager of the whole filthy business, Eurycles, he called 'saviour' and 'benefactor' and rewarded with fifty talents. Thus enriched Eurycles did not wait for the truth to come out, but hurried off to Cappadocia, where he got money out of Archelaus too by brazenly asserting that he had reconciled Herod to Alexander. Then crossing to Greece he employed his ill-gotten gains in promoting further mischief. Twice accused before Caesar of fostering sedition all over Greece and fleecing the townships, he was deported. So he paid the penalty for what he had done to Alexander and Aristobulus.

How different from the Spartan was Evarestus of Cos! One of Alexander's closest friends, he was in the country at the same time as Eurycles, and when the king put to him the allegations made by the latter he declared on oath that he had not heard the youngsters say any such thing. But he could do nothing to help the unfortunate pair: Herod was only too eager to listen to evil tongues and no others, and welcomed only men as gullible and irascible as himself.

His savage treatment of his children received a further impetus from Salome, the aunt and mother-in-law of Aristobulus. Aristobulus wanted to involve her in his own dangers and so sent her a hint to look after herself; the king, he said, was ready to kill her on the charge previously brought against her – that in her determination to wed the Arab Syllaeus she had treacherously disclosed to him the secrets of the king his enemy. This proved to be the final gust that sent the storm-tossed youths to the bottom. Salome ran to the king and reported the hint she had received. Herod, finally giving way, put both his sons in fetters and in solitary confinement; then losing no time he sent Volumnius the military tribune[34] and one of his Gentlemen, Olympus, to Caesar with Salome's report in writing. They sailed for Rome and delivered the king's dispatches. Caesar was very grieved for the youths, but did not think that he ought to undermine the father's authority over his sons; so he wrote back leaving the matter to Herod's discretion, but recommending him to convene a joint committee of his own Counsellors and the provincial governors to enquire into the alleged conspiracy: if the charges were proved, he should put his sons to death; if they had merely intended to abscond, a lesser penalty would suffice.

Accepting this suggestion Herod went to Berytus, the place indicated by Caesar, and convened the court. In obedience to the Emperor's written instructions the bench was occupied by Roman officers, Saturninus and his legates (Pedanius and others), together with Volumnius the procurator.[35] Also present were the king's Counsellors and Gentlemen, Salome, and Pheroras, and finally the nobility of all Syria, with the sole exception of King Archelaus, who as Alexander's father-in-law was distrusted by Herod. The sons were not brought into court – Herod was too shrewd for that, knowing they had only to be seen to melt all hearts, and if in addition they were allowed to speak Alexander would easily refute the charges. So they were kept in custody at Platana, a village near Sidon.

The king rose and, as if they were present, launched out into a bitter attack. His attempts to prove the charge of conspiracy were weak, owing to the lack of evidence; but he emphasized the insults, mocking speeches, outrages, and offences without number directed against him, harder to bear than death itself, as he told the court. Then he invited his silent audience to pity him, in that he himself was the sufferer even if he did win a bitter victory over his sons. Finally he asked them for their several opinions. First to reply was Saturninus, who was for condemning the youths, but not to death: it would not be right for a man with three children in court to vote for the execution of another man's children. His two legates voted the same way, and several others followed their lead. Volumnius was the first to advocate the death sentence, and all who spoke after him were for condemning the lads to death, some from flattery and some from hatred of Herod, but no one from conviction that the accused were guilty. And now all Syria and Judaea were in suspense, waiting for the last scene of the drama; but no one guessed that Herod would be so barbarous as to murder his children. He however dragged his sons to Tyre, and after sailing from there to Caesarea weighed the possible methods of putting the lads to death.

There was an old soldier of the king called Tiro, whose son was a bosom friend of Alexander, and who was very fond of both lads himself. He was so overcome with indignation that his reason gave way and he went round shouting that justice had been trampled underfoot, truth was no more, nature in confusion, life in a state of anarchy – and anything else that occurred to a man deeply moved and without a thought for his own life. At length he went boldly to the king: 'You miserable wretch!' he thundered, 'that is what I think of you! To turn against your own flesh and blood at the bidding of utter scoundrels! Over and over again you have condemned Pheroras and Salome to death – and now you take their word against your children! Don't you see that they are cutting off your legitimate heirs and leaving you with only Antipater, choosing a king they can twist round their little finger? Take care, take care the army doesn't one day hate him as it hates you, because of his brothers' death: there is not one private who doesn't pity the lads, and many of the officers are cursing you openly.' He proceeded to give their names; and the king at once arrested them, along with Tiro and his son.

Directly after this one of the court barbers, called Trypho, sprang forward in the grip of some frenzy and informed against himself. 'I am in it too,' he shouted, 'Tiro here told me to cut your throat with my razor when I was shaving you, and promised that Alexander would pay me well.' Hearing this Herod examined Tiro, with his son and the barber, under torture, and when the first two denied everything and the other had nothing to add, ordered Tiro to be racked still more severely. At last the son, greatly distressed, promised to tell the king everything if he would spare his father, and when

Herod agreed he stated that his father had been persuaded by Alexander to plan his death. Some people thought that he had made this up in order to end his father's agony, others that it was true.

Herod called a mass meeting, at which he accused the officers and Tiro and enlisted the help of the people to dispose of them; along with the barber they were killed then and there with clubs and stones. Then he sent his sons to Sebaste, which was not far from Caesarea, giving orders that they should be strangled. The order being instantly carried out, he gave instructions for the bodies to be brought to the fortress of Alexandreum, to be buried by the side of Alexander,[36] their mother's father. So ends the story of Alexander and Aristobulus.[37]

CHAPTER 5

Herod's Murder of his Heir, and Death

ANTIPATER, now undisputed heir, had called down on his own head the utter loathing of the nation; for everyone knew that all the slanders directed against his brothers had originated with him. And he was filled with secret but terrible fear when he saw the dead men's children growing up. Glaphyra had borne Alexander two sons, Tigranes and Alexander; Berenice, Salome's daughter, had borne Aristobulus three sons, Herod,[1] Agrippa,[2] and Aristobulus, and two daughters, Herodias[3] and Mariamme. Glaphyra Herod sent back to Cappadocia with her dowry after the execution of Alexander; Aristobulus' widow Berenice he married to the brother of Antipater's mother: it was to placate the hostility of Salome that Antipater arranged this marriage. He tried also to get round Pheroras with gifts and other attentions, and round Caesar's friends by sending large moneys to Rome. Saturninus and his staff in Syria all received more than enough of his presents. But his gifts made him the more hated, as it was obvious they were not spontaneous expressions of generosity but insurances against foreseen dangers. The result was that while the recipients liked him no better than before, those to whom he gave nothing became more bitter enemies. Yet he made his largesse daily more lavish, as he saw the king negativing his efforts by taking care of the orphans and showing his remorse for the murder of his sons by his tenderness towards their offspring.

One day Herod assembled his Counsellors and the Gentlemen of his Household, set the children before them, and with brimming eyes began: 'The fathers of these children were snatched from me by some malignant spirit: they themselves are commended to my care both by natural ties and by pity for their orphanhood. I will try, though I have been most unfortunate as a father, at any rate to show myself a more devoted grandfather, and when I die to leave in charge of them those most dear to me. I betroth your daughter, Pheroras, to the elder of Alexander's two boys, and so make you automatically his guardian; and to your son, Antipater, I give Aristobulus' daughter (Mariamme), so that you will become father to the orphan girl. Her

sister (Herodias) my own Herod shall have, since on his mother's side
he had a high priest for grandfather.[4] Let my wishes be carried out
in this way, and let no one who cares for me go against them. I pray
God to seal these unions to the good of my kingdom and of my
descendants, and to look with gentler eyes on these little children here
than He ever looked on their fathers.' And now the tears flowed
faster and he joined the children's hands; then after warmly embracing
each in turn he dismissed the gathering.

His decision struck a sudden chill into Antipater, who made no
attempt to hide his mortification. He felt that the honour shown by his
father to the orphans meant the end of his hopes, and that his prospects of succession would again be in danger if not only Archelaus
but Pheroras, a tetrarch,[5] supported Alexander's heirs. He thought of
the nation's hatred for himself and compassion for the orphans, of the
devotion the Jews had felt for his brothers while they lived, and their
tender memories of them now that, thanks to him, they were dead.
So he made up his mind by fair means or foul to break these be-
trothals. He was afraid to try any tricks on a father so difficult and so
prone to suspicion, so he took the bull by the horns and asked him
directly not to rob him of the honour already conferred, or to give
the name of king to him and the power to others; he would never
be in control if, with Archelaus as his grandfather, Alexander's son
should also have Pheroras as his father-in-law; as the royal family
was so large, would he please reconsider the proposed marriages?

The king, indeed, had nine wives[6] and children by seven of them.
Antipater himself was the son of Doris, Herod of Mariamme, the
high priest's daughter, Antipas and Archelaus of Malthace the
Samaritan, their sister Olympias being married to Herod's nephew
Joseph. By Cleopatra, a girl from Jerusalem, he had Herod and Philip,
and by Pallas Phasael. He had other daughters also, Roxane and Salome, the first by Phaedra, the second by Elpis. Two wives were
childless, a cousin and a niece. Apart from these there were the two
sisters of Alexander and Aristobulus, children of Mariamme.[7] The
family being of such exceptional size, Antipater asked for the marriage
arrangements to be reconsidered.

On realizing how Antipater regarded the orphans the king was
extremely angry, and it flashed across his mind that the murdered men
might also be victims of Antipater's slanders. So for the moment he
made a long and bitter reply and sent the fellow packing. Later how-

ever he succumbed to his flatteries and altered the arrangements, marrying Aristobulus' daughter (Mariamme) to Antipater himself and Pheroras' daughter to his son. How effective was his flattery in this instance can be seen from Salome's failure in a like case. She was Herod's sister, and was backed by Caesar's wife Livia[8] in her repeated requests to marry the Arab Syllaeus; but Herod swore he would count her his worst enemy if she did not abandon this ambition, and ended by marrying her against her will to Alexas, one of his Gentlemen, and one of her daughters to Alexas' son, the other to Antipater's mother's brother. Of his own daughters by Mariamme,[9] one wedded his sister's son Antipater, one his brother's son Phasael.

Having cut off the orphans' hopes and arranged the marriages for his personal benefit, Antipater felt that his own hopes were safely in port, and, as confident now as he was wicked, became insufferable. To overcome the detestation in which he was universally held was beyond him, so he relied on terror to maintain his security. He was aided by Pheroras, who had no doubt now that he would be king. There was also a group of women who stirred up fresh troubles at court. Pheroras' wife, with the cooperation of her mother and sister and of Antipater's mother, began to throw her weight about in the palace, even daring to affront two of the king's daughters – which made him thoroughly disgusted, though his aversion did not prevent their tyrannizing over the rest. The only person to stand up to this conspiracy was Salome, who denounced the gang to the king as a danger to himself. Informed of this denunciation and of Herod's displeasure, they left off meeting openly and exchanging friendly greetings, and instead pretended to quarrel with each other in the king's hearing: Antipater joined in the pretence by publicly disagreeing with Pheroras. But they held secret meetings and caroused in the night, the watch kept over them only serving to strengthen the conspiracy. But every detail of their doings was known to Salome and duly passed on to Herod.

The king blazed with anger, especially against Pheroras' wife, whom Salome accused most vehemently. He convened a committee of his Counsellors and Gentlemen and laid a great many things to the woman's charge, especially the affront to his daughters, accusing her also of paying money to the Pharisees[10] to spite him, and turning his brothers against him by the use of powerful drugs. Finally he turned to Pheroras and told him he must choose one or the other, his brother or his wife. When Pheroras replied that he would die rather than give up his wife, Herod, at a loss, went off to Antipater and forbade him to hold any converse with Pheroras, his wife, or anyone connected with her. Antipater conformed with this command in public, but in secret he spent the night with them. Afraid however of Salome's watchful eye, he arranged through friends in Italy to visit Rome. They wrote that Antipater ought in the near future to be sent to Caesar, and without hesitation Herod sent him off with a splendid retinue, a vast sum of money, and his will, which named Antipater as the next king, and as Antipater's successor Herod, son of Mariamme the high priest's daughter.

Syllaeus the Arab also sailed to Rome, in disregard of Caesar's commands and with the intention of arguing against Antipater the case about which he had previously been arraigned by Nicolas.[11] There was also a serious dispute between him and Aretas,[12] his own king, as he had executed a number of his friends, among them Soaemus, the most powerful man in Petra. By a heavy bribe he won over Fabatus, Caesar's treasurer, using his help against Herod too. But Herod by a still heavier bribe detached him from Syllaeus and attempted with his aid to extract from that rogue the money Caesar had ordered him to pay. Syllaeus would not pay a penny, and even accused Fabatus to Caesar, saying his treasurer treasured not his interests but Herod's! Furious at this, and still high in Herod's favour, Fabatus betrayed Syllaeus' secrets, telling the king that Syllaeus had bought the services of his bodyguard Corinthus, on whom he must keep an eye. As Corinthus, though brought up in his kingdom, was by birth an Arab, the king took the hint and immediately arrested both him and two other Arabs found with him, one a friend of Syllaeus and the other a tribal chief. Under torture they admitted that Corinthus had given them heavy bribes to murder Herod. After further examination by Saturninus, governor of Syria, they were sent under escort to Rome.

Herod maintained his relentless pressure on Pheroras to divorce his wife, but could find no means of punishing the woman, many as were his motives for hating her, till he lost his temper and banished her, along with her brother. Pheroras swallowed the insult and went off to his tetrarchy swearing that the only end to his exile would be the death of Herod – never while he lived would he go back to him! He did not return even when his brother was sick, despite the most pressing invitation; for Herod wanted to leave him certain instructions, believing himself on the point of death. But he unexpectedly recovered, and soon afterwards Pheroras fell sick. Herod showed himself less adamant; he went to him and looked after him sympathetically. But he could not master the sickness and after a few days Pheroras died. Herod had loved him till his dying day, but for all that it was rumoured that he had poisoned him. However, he conveyed the body to Jerusalem, ordered prolonged mourning by the whole nation, and honoured him with the most magnificent funeral. Such was the end that came to one of the murderers of Alexander and Aristobulus!

But arising out of Pheroras' death retribution was at last finding the true author of that crime. Some of the dead man's freedmen came in a dejected state to the king and declared that his brother had been deliberately poisoned; his wife had brought him a most unusual dish, and as soon as he had eaten it he had been taken ill. Two days earlier her mother and sister had called in an Arab woman with a knowledge of drugs to prepare a love-potion for Pheroras; instead she had given him deadly poison at the instance of Syllaeus, to whom she was known.

Plagued with suspicions of every kind, the king put the maid-servants and several free women to the torture. One of them in her agony cried out: 'May God, the ruler of heaven and earth, visit our sufferings on their author, Antipater's mother!' Seizing on this hint the king went still further in his search for the truth. The woman disclosed the friendship of Antipater's mother with Pheroras and his womenfolk, and their surreptitious meetings. She told how Pheroras and Antipater, after returning from the king, drank with them all night, rigidly excluding every servant whether man or woman. It was one of the free women who gave this information.

The slave-girls Herod tortured one at a time. Their evidence in every case tallied with that already given, with the addition that it was by agreement that Antipater had gone off to Rome and Pheroras to Peraea; for they had said again and again that, having disposed of Alexander and Aristobulus, Herod would be after them and their wives. After killing Mariamme and her sons he would spare no one, so it was better to put as many miles as possible between them and the beast. Again, Antipater had often grumbled to his mother that he was grey-haired already while his father got daily younger; as likely as not he would die without ever actually being king. When his father died – if he ever did – his enjoyment of the succession would be terribly short. And those hydra-heads[13] were shooting up, the sons of Aristo-bulus and Alexander. He had been robbed by his father of his hopes for his children, as the person nominated to succeed him when he died was not to be one of his own sons but Mariamme's Herod. In that respect anyway the king must be a complete dotard, if he imagined that in this matter his will would be carried out; he himself would see that none of the family survived. Hating his children more than any father had ever done, Herod hated his brother far more. Only a day or two ago he had given him, Antipater, a hundred talents to hold no converse with Pheroras. When Pheroras asked: 'What harm were we doing him?' Antipater had replied: 'I only wish he would strip us of everything, and leave us to live naked. But there is no way to escape such a murderous beast, who will not even let us show affection openly. Now we meet in secret: we shall be able to meet openly if ever we have the arms and spirits of men.'

To these disclosures, wrung from them by torture, they added that Pheroras had planned to fly with them to Petra. Herod believed every word because of the hundred talents, which he had mentioned to nobody but Antipater. His anger descended first on Doris, Antipater's mother; he stripped her of all the adornments he had lavished on her at fantastic expense and sent her packing a second time. Pheroras' women-folk he made as comfortable as he could after their ordeal, having no further quarrel with them. But he was in constant terror and blazed up on the tiniest suspicion, dragging many guiltless persons off to torture for fear of missing any of the guilty.

He now turned to the Samaritan Antipater, Antipater's chief agent. By torturing him he found out that Antipater had sent one of his companions to Egypt for a noxious drug meant for him; Antiphilus had handed it to Theudion, Antipater's uncle, who had passed it on to Pheroras, Pheroras being required by Antipater to assassinate Herod while he himself was at Rome out of reach of suspicion; and Pheroras had put the drug in his wife's hands. The king sent for her and com-manded her to fetch that very moment what she had received. She went out as if to fetch it, but threw herself from the roof, to forestall inquisition by the king's torturer. However, by the providence of God who, it would seem, was resolved to punish Antipater, she did not fall on her head but on other parts of her body, and survived. She was taken to the king, who had her revived, as she was unconscious after her fall, and pressed her for the explanation, swearing that if she told the truth she would be immune from any punishment, but if she held anything back he would tear her to pieces by torture and leave nothing for burial.

After a brief hesitation the woman answered: 'Well, why should I go on keeping these secrets, now Pheroras is dead? To save Antipater, who has ruined us all? Listen, Your Majesty, and may God listen too and witness the truth of my words, for there is no deceiving him! When Pheroras was dying and you sat beside him in tears, he called me to him and whispered: "I have been badly mistaken, my dear, about my brother's attitude to me. He loves me like this and yet I hated him, and planned to kill a man who is so terribly distressed about me even before my death. I am only receiving what I deserve for my disloyalty; you go and fetch the drug you are keeping to poison him with, that Antipater left with us, and destroy it at once before my eyes, for fear I go to Hades with a devil on my back." Thus bidden, I fetched it and emptied most of it into the fire before his eyes, but kept a little for myself in case of emergency and because I was afraid of you.'

So saying she produced the box, containing very little indeed of the poison. The king then turned his tortures against Antiphilus' mother and brother, who both admitted that he had fetched the box from Egypt, and stated that he had obtained the drug from a brother who practised medicine in Alexandria. The ghosts of Alexander and Aristobulus were prowling around the whole Palace, ferreting out hidden things and bringing them to light, and dragging those most remote from suspicion before the inquisitor. Even the high priest's daughter Mariamme was found to be privy to the conspiracy; torture extracted this information from her brothers. The king punished the mother's criminal intention through her son: the name of her Herod, who was to succeed Antipater, was blotted out of his father's will.[14]

On top of this Bathyllus came under inquisition and clinched the evidence of Antipater's conspiracy. He was a freedman of Antipater and he came with another concoction, a noxious compound of the poison of asps and the secretions of other reptiles, so that if the first drug proved ineffectual, Pheroras and his wife should be armed with this weapon against the king. As a sideline to the intended attack on the father he brought letters forged by Antipater to incriminate his brothers Archelaus and Philip, sons of the king at school in Rome, now adolescent and proud-spirited.[15] Determined to nip in the bud this growing danger to his hopes, Antipater forged incriminating letters in the names of their friends in Rome, and bribed others to write that they regularly criticized their father, openly denouncing the fate of Alexander and Aristobulus and protesting against their own recall; for their father had already sent for them, and this was the chief cause of Antipater's alarm.

Even before his absence from the country, while still in Judaea, he had paid for similar incriminating letters to be written in Rome, and to avoid suspicion had gone to his father on purpose to excuse his brothers' conduct, maintaining that some of the things were untrue, and others merely boyish indiscretions. Having disbursed vast sums to the writers of these incriminating letters, his task now was to cover up his tracks; so he bought up costly wardrobes, elaborate tapestries, cups of silver and gold and many other valuables, in order that his huge expenditure under these heads might conceal the more dubious items. His accounts showed outgoings totalling two hundred talents, attributed mostly to his legal battle with Syllaeus. But all his rascalities, however small, had come to light with the major crime, now that all the tortures cried aloud 'Parricide!' and the letters 'Fratricide a second time!' – yet no one arriving in Rome told him what had happened in Judaea, though between the discovery of his guilt and his homecoming seven months went by; so great was the detestation with which all regarded him. Perhaps, too, the mouths of those prepared to tell him were stopped by the ghosts of his murdered brothers. Anyway he wrote from Rome announcing the good news of his imminent arrival, and of the honour paid him by Caesar at his final interview.

Itching to lay hands on this murderous scoundrel and afraid of his being forewarned and on the look-out, the king replied in a letter which suppressed his real feelings, and with much show of affection urged him to hurry home; if he came quickly, Herod would say no more about his mother's misdoings. For Antipater was now aware of her banishment from the court. He had earlier received at Tarentum a letter describing Pheroras' death and had made a great show of grief, which much impressed those who thought it was for his uncle. It is more likely that he was upset by the failure of the conspiracy and was weeping not for Pheroras but for his tool; and he was already assailed by terror at what he had done: perhaps the poison had been discovered! Now when he received in Cilicia[16] the letter from his father mentioned above, he pushed on without delay; but as he sailed into Celenderis he was overcome by the thought of his mother's fate, his unaided soul giving him a premonition of disaster. The more far-seeing of the Gentlemen of his Household advised him not to put himself in his father's power till he knew for certain the grounds of his mother's banishment: they were afraid there might be something attached to the charges against her. The less prudent, more anxious to see their own country again than interested in Antipater's welfare, urged him to push on and not by lingering to give his father an excuse for base suspicion and his enemies a handle for slander. Even if there had been a movement against him, it was due to his absence: no one would have dared if he had been there. It was ridiculous to let doubtful suspicions deprive him of unmistakable benefits, and not to put himself as soon as possible in his father's hands to take over the kingdom which depended on him alone. It was to these advisers that Antipater, guided by his evil genius, listened: he made the crossing and landed at the Augustan Harbour of Caesarea.[17]

He was amazed to find himself utterly alone: everyone avoided him and no one ventured near him; for while he had been hated just as much in the past, now at last this hatred was not afraid to show itself. Many too were kept away by fear of the king, since every city was now full of rumours about Antipater, and the only person unaware of his situation was Antipater himself. No one ever had a more wonderful send-off than he when he sailed for Rome, or a more miserable welcome back. He now began to suspect the disasters at home, but he was cunning enough to hide it, and by a tremendous effort maintained a haughty demeanour though inwardly dead with fear. There was no possibility now of running away or of getting his head above water; but he had no definite news of events at home because of the king's threats, and a glimmer of hope was left – perhaps nothing had been discovered; perhaps, even if it had, he might put things right by brazenness and trickery, by which alone he could survive.

Armed with these vain hopes he came into the palace without his Gentlemen, who had been rudely turned back at the outer gate. It happened that inside was Varus, governor of Syria.[18] Antipater went in to his father and in an attempt to brazen it out went up to him as if to embrace him. Herod put his hands in front of him and turned away his head, crying: 'How like a parricide, to want to put his arms round me with so much on his conscience! To hell with you, disgusting wretch! Don't touch me till you have disproved the accusations! You shall have a fair trial, and Varus has come at the right time to be your judge. Go and think out your defence for tomorrow; I will give you a chance to prepare some of your little tricks.' Too taken aback to answer a word Antipater turned and went, and his wife[19] and mother came to him with full details of the charges. Then having recovered his composure he got to work on his defence.

Next day the king summoned a court consisting of his Counsellors and Gentlemen, inviting Antipater's Gentlemen to come too. Presiding jointly with Varus, he had all the witnesses brought in. These included some servants of the accused's mother who shortly before had been caught carrying a note from her to her son as follows: 'Your father has found out everything, so don't go near him unless you can count on help from Caesar.' When these had been brought in with the rest, Antipater entered and fell on his face at his father's feet. 'I beg you, father,' he began, 'not to condemn me in advance but to lend an unbiased ear to my defence: I shall prove my innocence, if you will let me.'

Interrupting him with a peremptory call for silence, Herod turned to Varus. 'That you, Varus, and every upright judge will condemn Antipater as a hopeless scoundrel I am quite certain. But I am afraid my own wretchedness will disgust you, and you will judge me worthy of every calamity for having fathered such sons. Yet for that very reason you ought to feel the more sorry for me, because I have been the most affectionate of parents to such foul wretches. My other sons I named kings when they were quite young, and in addition to having them educated in Rome I made them Caesar's friends, the envy of other kings – and I found them plotting against me! They are dead, chiefly for Antipater's sake; for he was young and he was the heir, so that his safety was my principal concern. And this filthy beast, gorged with my indulgence, has poured out his swollen insolence on me! He thought I lived too long; he was bored with my old age; he could not bear to become king except by parricide! It serves me right for bringing him back to the City after throwing him out, and thrusting aside the sons of a princess to make *him* heir to my throne! I freely admit, Varus, that I have been an utter fool: I provoked those other sons against me, robbing them of their just expectations for Antipater's sake. When did I ever show them the kindness I showed him? I very nearly abdicated in his favour; I openly named him in my will as heir to my throne with a yearly allowance of fifty talents; I showered gifts upon him from my privy purse; when he recently sailed for Rome I gave him three hundred talents, and commended him, alone of all my family, to Caesar, as his father's preserver! What crime did the others commit to compare with Antipater's? What evidence was brought against them as strong as that which reveals this fellow's conspiracy?

'And now this parricide has dared to speak, and hopes to cover up the truth again with his tricks! Varus, be on the look-out! I know the little beast; and I can guess what specious pleas and crocodile tears he will produce! This is the man who in the days when Alexander was alive warned me to beware of him and not to trust my person to all and sundry; this is the man who escorted me to my bed and searched the room for any lurking assassin; this was the guardian of my sleep, my protector from anxiety, my comforter when I grieved for my dead sons, my surety for the loyalty of his surviving brothers, my shield, my bodyguard! When I remember, Varus, his cunning hypocrisy on every occasion, I can hardly believe I am alive and wonder how I escaped so deep a conspirator. But since some evil genius desolates my house and makes my dearest ones rise against me one by one, I shall indeed lament my cruel fate and inwardly grieve for my loneliness, but I will let no one escape who thirsts for my blood, not even if judgement finds every one of my children guilty!'

Overcome by emotion he could say no more, so he beckoned to Nicolas,[20] one of his Gentlemen, to repeat the depositions. But at this point Antipater, who had remained prone at his father's feet, raised his head and cried: 'You, father, have made my defence for me. How can I be a parricide if, as you agree, I have been your protector through thick and thin? You call my devotion to my father a hypocritical defence: how could I, so cunning in other ways, have been such a fool as not to realize that it was hard enough to hide from human eyes the preparation of so hideous a crime, and quite impossible to hide it from the Judge above, who sees everything and is everywhere present? Was I unaware of my brothers' end, and the terrible punishment they received from God for their evil designs against you? and what provoked me to injure you? the hope of being king? but I *was* a king! suspicion of your hate? but wasn't I most tenderly loved? fear of you

on some other ground? but my care of you made others fear me!
~~shortage of money? but who had more to spend than I? Suppose I~~
had been the most degraded of men with the soul of a savage beast,
father, should I not have been tamed by your kindness when you
brought me back from exile, as you yourself said, preferred me to
your many sons, proclaimed me king in your own lifetime, and by
showering on me honours of all kinds made everyone envy me?

'Oh, what a pity I went abroad, opening the doors wide to envy
and playing into the hands of intriguers! Yet it was for your sake,
father, I went abroad; I went to fight your battles, so that Syllaeus
should not treat your old age as a joke.[21] Rome can bear witness to
my love of my father; and so can the ruler of the whole world,
Caesar, who often called me "Philopator".[22] Here is the letter he has
sent you. This is more trustworthy than local slander; this is my sole
defence; this I put forward as testimony to my warm affection for
you. Remember that I undertook the voyage against my will, knowing only too well the enmity against me lurking in this kingdom. It
was you, father, who unintentionally ruined me by forcing me to
give envy an opportunity for slander. However, here I am to face
the charges; I have travelled over land and sea, nowhere coming to
grief as a parricide should! But do not take me back into favour now
because of *that* evidence; for I am convicted in God's eyes and in
yours, father. But convicted as I am, I beg you not to base your beliefs
on what others have admitted under torture. Let the fire be used
against me; let the instruments of torture pass right through my entrails; do not spare this foul body! If I am a parricide, I ought not to
die without being tortured!'

At these cries, laments, and tears Varus and all the rest were overcome with emotion. Herod alone was too angry to weep – he knew
that the charges were true.

Then Nicolas rose, and on the king's instructions began with a
thoroughgoing exposure of Antipater's duplicity, scattering all
sympathy for him to the winds. Next he poured out a torrent of bitter
accusations, holding him responsible for all the crime in the kingdom,
and especially the murder of his brothers, proving that their deaths
were due to his slanders. He further charged him with conspiring
against the survivors in the line of succession. Was it likely that one
who had prepared poison for his father would spare his brothers?
Dealing next with the poisoning charge he gave an orderly exposition

of the sworn statements; on the subject of Pheroras he could hardly contain himself – to think that Antipater should have turned him of all people into a fratricide, and by bribing the king's nearest and dearest filled the whole palace with corruption! After putting forward many other arguments and demonstrating their truth, Nicolas resumed his seat.

Varus now called on Antipater to make his defence; but he only said 'God is witness of my complete innocence', and remained prone and silent. So Varus sent for the poison, gave it to a prisoner sentenced to death, and made him drink it. Death was instantaneous. He then conferred with Herod in private, wrote a report of the proceedings for Caesar, and left Jerusalem next day. The king threw Antipater into prison and dispatched messengers to Caesar to inform him of these calamitous events.[23]

Shortly afterwards it was discovered that Antipater had plotted against Salome too. One of Antiphilus' manservants arrived from Rome with letters from a maidservant of Livia, Acme by name. From her the king learnt that she had found among Livia's papers letters from Salome and was sending them to him as she wished to help him. These letters, containing the most bitter abuse of the king and the most vehement accusations, had been forged by Antipater, who had bribed Acme to send them to Herod. His guilt was proved by her letter to him; for the woman had written to him too. 'In accordance with your wishes I have sent those letters to your father with a covering note; I am certain he will not spare his sister when he reads them. When it is all over, kindly remember your promise.'

When this letter was discovered along with those forged to ruin Salome, it occurred to the king that perhaps the documents inculpating Alexander[24] had not been genuine either, and his emotions were painful indeed when he thought how near he had been to executing his sister too through Antipater's machinations. So he decided to lose no time in punishing him for all his crimes. But as he was taking action against Antipater he was crippled by a severe illness[25]; however, he sent word to Caesar about Acme and the crooked attempt to involve Salome. He also sent for his will and altered it; as his successor he nominated Antipas, cutting out the two eldest, Archelaus and Philip, both of whom had been slandered by Antipater. To Caesar, in addition to gifts other than money, he bequeathed 1,000 talents; to the emperor's wife, children, friends,[26] and freedmen about 500 talents; to the rest of his own children generous legacies in land and money. He set aside most splendid gifts as a special honour to his sister Salome. These were the amendments he made to his will. His illness was getting steadily worse, the disease having attacked him when old and despondent. He was now nearly seventy, and his spirit had been broken by the dreadful troubles with his children, so that even in health the good things of life meant nothing to him. His sickness was intensified by bitterness that Antipater was still alive: he was determined that the execution should be no hole and corner affair, and so must wait for his own recovery.

In the midst of his troubles there occurred a popular rising. There were two rabbis[27] in the City with a great reputation as exponents of national tradition, and for that reason held in the highest esteem by the whole nation – Judas, son of Sepphoraeus, and Matthias, son of Margalus. Many young students came to them for instruction in the laws; in fact they daily attracted a host of men in their prime. When they learnt that the king was succumbing to his sickness of body and mind, they dropped a hint to their acquaintances that here was a wonderful chance to strike a blow for God and to pull down the works erected contrary to the laws of their fathers. Although it was unlawful to have in the Sanctuary images or portrait-busts or the likeness of any living thing, the king had put up over the Great Gate a golden eagle.[28] This the rabbis now urged them to cut down, saying that even if danger was involved, it was a glorious thing to die for the laws of their fathers: for those who came to such an end there was a sure hope of immortality and the eternal enjoyment of blessings, whereas the poor-spirited, knowing nothing of the rabbinical wisdom, through ignorance clung to life and chose death by disease rather than death in a righteous cause.

While they were preaching thus, it was rumoured that the king was actually dying, so that the young men undertook the task with more confidence. At mid-day, when masses of people were walking about the Temple courts, they lowered themselves by stout ropes from the roof and began to cut down the golden eagle with axes. The news quickly reached the king's officer, who hurried to the spot with a large force, seized about forty young men and took them before the king. He began by asking them whether they had dared to cut down the golden eagle. They said they had. Who told them to do it? The law of their fathers. What made them so cheerful when they were about to be executed? The knowledge that they would enjoy greater blessings after their death. At this the king exploded with rage, and forgetting his sickness went out to address a public meeting. He attacked the men at great length as temple-robbers, who pleading the Law as an excuse had some ulterior purpose, and demanded their punishment for sacrilege. The people, fearing punitive measures on a wide front, begged him to punish first those who had suggested the attempt, then those who had been caught in the act, and to take no action against the rest. The king reluctantly agreed: those who had lowered themselves from the roof together with the rabbis he burnt alive[29]; the rest of the men seized he handed over to his attendants for execution.

From then on the sickness spread through his entire body, accompanied by a variety of painful symptoms. He had a slight fever, an unbearable itching all over his body, constant pains in the lower bowel, swellings on the feet as in dropsy, inflammation of the abdomen, and mortification of the genitals, producing worms, as well as difficulty in breathing, especially when lying down, and spasms in all his limbs.[30] The diviners said that his many diseases were a punishment for what he had done to the rabbis. But though he was wrestling with so many disorders he hung on to life, hoped for recovery, and planned his own treatment. He crossed the Jordan and tried the hot baths at Callirrhoe, which empty their water into the Dead Sea,[31] water sweet enough to drink. The doctors there decided to warm his whole body with hot oil by lowering him into a full bath; but he fainted and turned up his eyes as if dead. The loud cries of his attendants brought him back to consciousness, but having no further hope of recovery he ordered the distribution of fifty drachmas a head to the soldiers and large gratuities to the officers and to the Gentlemen of his Household.

By the time he arrived at Jericho on the return journey he was melancholy-mad, and in a virtual challenge to death itself he proceeded to devise a monstrous outrage. He brought together the most eminent men of every village in the whole of Judaea and had them locked up in the hippodrome.[32] Then he sent for his sister Salome and her husband Alexas and said: 'I know the Jews will greet my death with wild rejoicings; but I can be mourned on other people's account and make sure of a magnificent funeral if you will do as I tell you. These men under guard – as soon as I die, kill them all – let loose the soldiers amongst them; then all Judaea and every family will weep for me – they can't help it.'³³

While he was giving these instructions a dispatch arrived from his ambassadors at Rome to notify him that at Caesar's command Acme had been executed and Antipater condemned to death; it went on to say that if his father preferred merely to banish him, Caesar had no objection. For a while Herod felt rather more cheerful, but later he was so tormented by lack of food and a racking cough that his sufferings mastered him and he made an effort to anticipate his appointed end. He took an apple and asked for a knife, it being his habit to cut up apples when he ate them; then looking round to make sure there was no one to stop him he raised his hand to stab himself. But his cousin Achiab dashed up and stopped him by grasping his wrist. At once loud cries went up in the palace as if the king had gone. Antipater soon heard the cheering news, and in his delight offered his jailers a handsome bribe to loose him and let him go. But the prison governor not only put a stop to this but ran and told the king of his attempt. Herod uttered a shout louder than seemed possible in so sick a man, and at once sent his bodyguard to put Antipater to death. After ordering his body to be interred at Hyrcania he again modified his will, naming as heir Archelaus, his eldest son, and as tetrarch Archelaus' brother Antipas.³⁴ He survived his son's execution by only five days.³⁵ Reckoning from the date when he put Antigonus to death and became master of the state, his reign had lasted thirty-three years; reckoning from his proclamation by the Romans as king, thirty-six.³⁶ In most respects he enjoyed good fortune if ever a man did: he came to the throne though he was a commoner, occupied it a very long time, and left it to his own children; but in his family life he was the most unfortunate of men.

Before the military knew that Herod was dead, Salome went out with her husband and freed the prisoners whom the king had ordered to be murdered. She told them the king had changed his mind and was permitting them all to go home again. When they were safely out of the way, she informed the soldiers of the true situation and summoned them to a joint meeting with the civilian population in the amphitheatre at Jericho. Here Ptolemy came forward, displaying the signet-ring entrusted to him by the king, to whom he paid the warmest tribute, followed by words of advice to the civilians present. Next he read aloud the letter Herod had left for the troops, in which he made a lengthy appeal for loyalty to his successor. After the letter he opened and read the final will, in which Philip was named as heir to Trachonitis and the neighbouring districts, Antipas as tetrarch,[37] as explained above, and Archelaus as king. Archelaus was to take Herod's ring to Caesar, with the state documents under seal, as Caesar was in sole charge of all his dispositions and executor of his will. All other provisions of the earlier will remained valid.

Vociferous congratulations were at once heaped upon Archelaus, and the soldiers came forward in companies with the civilians, pledged their loyalty, and joined in prayers for the blessing of God. Then they turned to the task of the king's burial. Everything possible was done by Archelaus to add to the magnificence: he brought out all the royal ornaments to be carried in procession in honour of the dead monarch. There was a solid gold bier, adorned with precious stones and draped with the richest purple. On it lay the body wrapped in crimson, with a diadem resting on the head and above that a golden crown, and the sceptre by the right hand. The bier was escorted by Herod's sons and the whole body of his kinsmen, followed by his Spearmen, the Thracian Company, and his Germans and Gauls,[38] all in full battle order. The rest of the army led the way, fully armed and in perfect order, headed by their commanders and all the officers, and followed by five hundred of the house slaves and freedmen carrying spices. The body was borne twenty-four miles to Herodium, where by the late king's command it was buried.[39] So ends the story of Herod.

CHAPTER 6

The Rise and Fall of Archelaus

ARCHELAUS was involved in fresh disturbances by the necessity of visiting Rome. He had spent a week mourning his father, and had provided the funeral feast for the populace on the most lavish scale – a custom which is the ruin of many Jews: they are obliged to feed the populace to escape the charge of impiety. Now he changed into white garments and proceeded to the Temple, where the people received him with varied acclamations. In reply he waved to the crowd from a golden throne on a raised platform, and thanked them heartily for the great pains they had taken with his father's funeral, and the respect they had already shown to himself as if he were already established as king. However, for the present he was not going to assume the royal power or even the title until his succession was confirmed by Caesar, who by the terms of Herod's will was in supreme control. At Jericho also, when the army had tried to set the crown on his head, he had refused it; however, for their enthusiastic loyalty he would render full payment to soldiers and people alike, as soon as the supreme authorities had established him as king; he would endeavour in every way to show himself kinder to them than his father had been.

This promise delighted the crowd, who at once tested his sincerity by making large demands. Some clamoured for a lightening of direct taxation, some for the abolition of purchase-tax,[1] others for the release of prisoners. He promptly said Yes to every demand in his anxiety to appease the mob. Then he offered sacrifices and sat down to a banquet with the Gentlemen of his Household. But in the afternoon a number of men with revolutionary ideas collected, and began lamentations of their own when the public mourning for the late king was over, bewailing those who had been executed by Herod for cutting down the golden eagle from the gate of the Sanctuary. These were not secret lamentations but piercing wails, weeping in chorus, and beating of breasts, that resounded throughout the whole City, as they were for men who, they said, had died for the laws of their country and for the Sanctuary. To avenge them they clamoured for the punishment of Herod's placemen, and above all the removal of the man whom he had appointed high priest; for it was their duty to choose a man of greater piety and with cleaner hands.[2]

This infuriated Archelaus, but he held his hand in view of his anxiety to begin his journey, fearing that if he aroused the hostility of the populace the consequent disturbance might delay his departure. He therefore tried to quieten the rebels by persuasion rather than by force, and privately sent his commander-in-chief to ask them to desist. The officer came to them in the Temple, but before he could utter a word the rioters stoned him and drove him away, doing the same to many others whom Archelaus sent after him to secure quiet. To every appeal they made a furious response, and it was evident that if they received general support there would be no holding them. To make things worse the Feast of Unleavened Bread was approaching – known to the Jews as the Passover, and celebrated with sacrifices on a vast scale – and there was a huge influx from the country for the festival. Meanwhile those who were bewailing the dead rabbis massed in the Temple and so provided fuel for sedition. This frightened Archelaus, who, to prevent the disease infecting the whole population, sent a tribune with his cohort[3] to restrain by force the leaders of the sedition. Their approach infuriated the huge mob, who pelted the cohort with stones and killed most of the men, wounding the tribune, who barely escaped with his life. Then as if nothing strange had occurred, they turned to sacrifice. Archelaus realized that the crowd could no longer be restrained without bloodshed; so he sent his whole army against them, the infantry in a body through the City, the cavalry through the fields.[4] As all the men were sacrificing the soldiers suddenly swooped on them, killing about 3,000, and scattered the remainder among the neighbouring hills. Archelaus' heralds then followed, ordering everyone to go home; and home they all went, abandoning the Feast.

Archelaus with his mother and three of his Gentlemen – Poplas, Ptolemy, and Nicolas – went down to the sea, leaving Philip as governor of the Palace and custodian of his property. He was accompanied by Salome and her children and by the late king's nephews and sons-in-law, who professed the intention of supporting his claim to the throne, but whose real purpose was to denounce him for his lawless actions in the Temple.

At Caesarea they were met by Sabinus the procurator of Syria,[5] who was on his way to Judaea to take charge of Herod's estate but was prevented from going further by the arrival of Varus, whom Ptolemy on Archelaus' behalf had begged to come. So for the time being Sabinus, in deference to Varus' wishes, neither hastened to the citadels nor locked Archelaus out of his father's treasuries, but promised to postpone any action until Caesar had reached a decision, and remained at Caesarea. But as soon as restraint was removed by the return of Varus to Antioch and the departure of Archelaus for Rome, he promptly set out for Jerusalem, where he took possession of the Palace, and sending for the garrison commanders and comptrollers tried to sort out the property accounts and to take possession of the citadels. However, the officers were loyal to Archelaus' instructions and continued to guard everything in the name of Caesar rather than of Archelaus.

Meanwhile Antipas also was strenuously laying claim to the kingdom, insisting that Herod's earlier will, not the later one, was valid, and that this named him king.[6] He had a promise of support from Salome and many of the relatives who were sailing with Archelaus. He tried also to win over his mother and Nicolas' brother Ptolemy, who seemed a weighty supporter in view of the trust Herod had reposed in him; for he had been the most honoured of Herod's Gentlemen. But he placed most confidence in the extraordinary skill of Irenaeus the orator; he therefore disregarded those who advised him to give way to Archelaus as the elder brother, named in the later will. In Rome all the relatives, who detested Archelaus, transferred their allegiance to Antipas. Their first preference was for autonomy under the protection of a Roman official[7]; failing that they were prepared to accept Antipas as king.

In these endeavours they were aided by Sabinus, who sent letters denouncing Archelaus to Caesar and lavishing praise on Antipas. Salome and her friends collected all the charges and put the file in Caesar's hands. Then Archelaus in his turn sent Ptolemy with a written summary of his own claims, his father's ring, and the official records. Caesar, having considered in private the rival dossiers, the size of the kingdom, the value of the revenue, and also the number of Herod's children, read the dispatches from Varus and Sabinus about the matter. Then he summoned a council of Roman officials,[8] giving a seat on it for the first time to Gaius – son of Agrippa and his own daughter Julia, and adopted by him – and invited the disputants to put their case.

Salome's son Antipater at once rose. The cleverest speaker among Archelaus' opponents, he pointed out that, though professedly Archelaus was only laying claim to the throne, actually he had been reigning for a long time, so that it was mockery now to seek an audience of Caesar, whose decision on the succession he had anticipated. As soon as Herod was dead he had secretly bribed certain persons to crown him; he had sat in state on the throne and given audience as a king; he had altered the organization of the army and granted promotions. Furthermore he had conceded to the people everything for which they had petitioned him as king, and had released men whom his father had imprisoned for shocking crimes. And now he had come to ask his master for the shadow of that kingship of which he had himself snatched the substance, allowing Caesar control not of realities but of names. Antipater also alleged that his mourning for his father was a sham – that in the daytime he assumed an expression of grief and at night indulged in drunken orgies, which had aroused indignation and caused popular unrest. The speaker directed the whole force of his argument to the number of persons killed around the Sanctuary, who had come to the Feast only to be brutally murdered alongside their own sacrifices – such a huge pile of corpses in the Temple courts as one would scarcely have expected to see if a foreign invader had descended upon them without warning. Recognizing this vein of cruelty in his son, Herod had never given him the least hope of succeeding to the throne till his mind became more decayed than his body, and he was incapable of logical thought and did not realize what sort of man he was making his heir by his new will, though he had no fault to find with the heir named in the earlier one, written when his health was good and his mind quite unimpaired. If however anyone was inclined to attach more weight to the decision made when his health was failing, the answer was that Archelaus had proved himself unfit to rule by his illegalities; what would he be like after receiving authority from Caesar, when he had put so many to death before receiving it?

After continuing in this vein at considerable length and bringing forward most of the relatives to witness the truth of each accusation, Antipater sat down. Then Nicolas rose to defend Archelaus and argued that the slaughter in the Temple was unavoidable, for those killed had been enemies not only of the crown but of Caesar who was now awarding it.[9] The other measures with which he was charged had been taken on the advice of the accusers themselves! As for the later will, he claimed that it was proved valid primarily by the fact that in it Caesar was appointed executor; a man sensible enough to put the management of his affairs into the hands of the supreme ruler was not likely to choose the wrong man for his heir, and one who knew the authority that made the appointment was likely to show good sense in choosing the person to be appointed.

When Nicolas too had had his say, Archelaus came forward and fell down at Caesar's knees without saying a word. The emperor raised him up in the most gracious manner and declared that he deserved to succeed his father, but made no definite announcement. After dismissing those who had formed his council that day, he thought over in private what he had been told, considering whether to appoint one of those named in the wills to succeed Herod, or to divide the power among the whole family; for it seemed necessary to provide support for the mass of interested persons.

Before Caesar could reach a decision, Archelaus' mother Malthace died of an illness, and letters arrived from Varus in Syria about the revolt in Judaea. He had seen this coming, and so when Archelaus had sailed, he had gone to Jerusalem to restrain the prime movers, as it was obvious that the populace would not remain quiet. Then, leaving in the City one of the three legions he had brought from Syria, he returned to Antioch. However, as soon as he had gone, Sabinus arrived and promptly gave the people an excuse for sedition. He tried to compel the garrison to hand over the forts and made a ruthless search for the king's money, employing not only the soldiers left by Varus but a gang of his own slaves, arming them all and using them as instruments of his avarice. On the eve of Pentecost – a Jewish feast which takes place seven weeks after the Passover: 'Pentecost' means 'fiftieth day' – the people assembled, not to conduct the usual rites but to vent their wrath. An enormous crowd gathered from Galilee and Idumaea, from Jericho and Peraea east of Jordan; but they could not equal in number and enthusiasm the swarm of natives from Judaea itself. The whole mass split up into three divisions which established themselves in separate camps, one to the north of the Temple, one to the south by the hippodrome,[10] and the third near the Palace to the west. Thus they surrounded the Romans and began to blockade them.

Their numbers and determination alarmed Sabinus, who sent a

stream of messengers to Varus to request immediate assistance: if it was delayed the legion would be cut to pieces. He himself went up to the highest tower of the fortress, the one called Phasael after Herod's brother who had died at the hands of the Parthians. From there he signalled to the legionaries to attack the enemy, for he was too panic-stricken even to go down to his own men. Doing as they were told, the soldiers dashed into the Temple and engaged in a fierce combat with the Jews, in which, as long as no one shot at them from above, their experience of war gave them the advantage. But when many of the Jews climbed on to the top of the colonnades and threw their missiles on to their heads, casualties were heavy, and it was difficult either to reply to this attack from above or to resist those who fought them hand to hand.

Hard pressed from both directions the soldiers set fire to the colonnades, works remarkable for both size and magnificence. The men on top were suddenly hemmed in by the flames: many of them were burnt to death; many others jumped down among the enemy and were destroyed by them; some turned about and flung themselves from the wall; a few, seeing no way of escape, fell on their own swords and cheated the flames; a number who crept down from the walls and rushed in among the Romans were easily overpowered in their confused state. As the survivors fled in terror the soldiers swooped on the unguarded treasury of God and carried off about four hundred talents; what they did not steal Sabinus collected.

The effect on the Jews of this loss of life and property was to bring together a far bigger and better equipped force to oppose the Romans. They surrounded the Palace and threatened to destroy all its occupants unless they withdrew forthwith, but promised safe conduct to Sabinus if he was prepared to take his legion away. They were reinforced by the bulk of the royal troops, who deserted to them. But the most warlike section, 3,000 men from Sebaste with their officers, Rufus and Gratus, attached themselves to the Romans.[11] Gratus commanded the royal infantry, Rufus the cavalry; each of them, even without the men under him, was brave and intelligent enough to turn the scales in war. The Jews conducted a vigorous siege, assaulting the walls of the fortress and at the same time vociferously urging Sabinus and his soldiers to withdraw, and not to hinder the Jews, now that at long last they were recovering their traditional independence. Sabinus would have been only too glad to withdraw quietly, but he distrusted their promises and suspected that their soft words were a bait to catch him. As he was also expecting Varus' reinforcements, he continued to hold out.

Meanwhile in the country districts also there were widespread disturbances and many seized the opportunity to claim the throne. In Idumaea 2,000 of Herod's veterans reassembled with their arms and proceeded to fight the royal troops. They were opposed by Achiab, a cousin of the late king; he sheltered behind the strongest fortifications and would not risk a battle in the open. At Sepphoris in Galilee Judas, son of Hezekiah – a bandit chief who once overran the country and was suppressed by King Herod[12] – collected a considerable force, broke into the royal armoury, equipped his followers, and attacked the other seekers after power. In Peraea Simon, one of the royal slaves, considered that his good looks and great stature entitled him to set a crown on his own head. Then he went round with a band of robbers and burnt down the palace at Jericho and many magnificent country residences, securing easy plunder for himself out of the flames. He would indeed have reduced every notable building to ashes had not Gratus, commander of the royal infantry, taken the archers from Trachonitis and the best of the troops from Sebaste and gone to meet the adventurer. The Peraeans suffered heavy losses in the battle: Simon himself fled up a ravine but was cut off by Gratus, and as he fled a blow from the side broke his neck. The palace at Betharamatha near the Jordan was burnt down by another gang from Peraea.

A third claimant to the throne was a shepherd called Athrongaeus, whose hopes were based on his physical strength and contempt of death, and on the support of four brothers like himself. Each of these he put in charge of an armed band, employing them as generals and satraps on his raids, and reserving to himself as king the settlement of major problems. He set a crown on his own head, but continued for a considerable time to raid the country with his brothers. Their principal purpose was to kill Romans and the royal troops; but not even a Jew could escape if he fell into their hands with anything valuable on him. Once they ventured to surround an entire century of Romans near Emmaus, when they were conveying food and munitions to their legion. Hurling their spears they killed the centurion Arius and forty of his best men; the rest were in danger of meeting the same fate until the arrival of Gratus with the troops from Sebaste enabled them to escape. Such was the treatment that they meted out to natives and foreigners alike throughout the war; but after a while three of them were defeated, the eldest by Archelaus, the next two in an encounter with Gratus and Ptolemy; the fourth submitted to Archelaus on terms. It was of course later that their career came thus to an end: at the time we are describing they were harassing all Judaea with their brigandage.

When Varus received the dispatches of Sabinus and the officers, he was naturally afraid for the whole legion and hurried to the rescue. He picked up the other two legions and the four troops of horse attached to them and marched to Ptolemais, giving instructions that the auxiliaries provided by kings and local potentates should meet him there. In addition he collected 1,500 heavy infantry as he passed through the city of Berytus. At Ptolemais he was joined by a great number of allies. Prominent among these was Aretas the Arab, who because he had hated Herod brought a considerable force of infantry and cavalry. Varus at once dispatched a portion of his army to the part of Galilee near Ptolemais, under the command of his friend Gaius. Gaius routed those who blocked his way, captured the city of Sepphoris and burnt it, enslaving the inhabitants. With the rest of his forces Varus himself marched into Samaria,[13] but kept his hands off the city[14] as he learnt that, when the whole country was in a ferment, there had been complete quiet there. He encamped near a village called Arus, which belonged to Ptolemy and for that reason was plundered by the Arabs, who were angry with Herod and his friends too. From there he went on to Sappho, another fortified village, which they plundered in the same way, seizing all the revenues they found there. Fire and bloodshed were on every side, and nothing could check the depredations of the Arabs. Emmaus too, abandoned by its inhabitants, was destroyed by fire at the command of Varus to avenge Arius and those who had perished with him.

Then Varus marched on to Jerusalem, where at the first sight of him and his forces the Jewish armies melted away, the fugitives disappearing into the countryside. The citizens however welcomed him and disclaimed all responsibility for the revolt, declaring that they had not lifted a finger but had been forced by the occurrence of the Feast to receive the swarm of visitors, so that far from joining in the attack they had, like the Romans, been besieged. Before this he had been met by Joseph, the cousin of Archelaus, by Rufus and Gratus at the head of the men from Sebaste as well as the royal army, and by the

members of the Roman legion with the normal arms and equipment –
for Sabinus, not daring to come into Varus' sight, had already left the
City for the sea. Varus sent portions of his army about the countryside
in pursuit of those responsible for the upheaval, and great numbers
were brought in: those who seemed to have taken a less active part
he kept in custody, while the ringleaders were crucified – about two
thousand.

Information reached him that in Idumaea there still remained a
concentration of 10,000 men, heavily armed. But he found that the
Arabs were not behaving as allies but campaigning in accordance with
their own ideas, and ravaging the countryside contrary to his wishes
through their hatred of Herod. So he sent them away, and with his
own legions hurried to meet the rebels. But, before a blow was
struck, they took the advice of Achiab and gave themselves up. Varus
acquitted the rank and file of any responsibility, but sent the leaders to
Caesar to be examined. Caesar pardoned most of them, but some of
the king's relatives – a few of the prisoners being connected with
Herod by birth – he sentenced to death for having fought against a
king of their own blood. Varus, having thus settled matters in Jerusalem, left as garrison the same legion as before and returned to
Antioch.[15]

At Rome Archelaus was involved in a new dispute with some Jews
who before the revolt had been permitted by Varus to come as
ambassadors and plead for racial autonomy.[16] These numbered fifty
and were backed by more than 8,000 of the Jews in Rome.[17] Caesar
summoned a council of Roman officials and his own friends[18] in the
temple of Apollo which he himself had built on the Palatine and
decorated regardless of expense. The Jewish mob stood with the
ambassadors facing Archelaus and his friends: his relatives' friends
stood apart from both; for hatred and envy made them unwilling to
be associated with Archelaus, while they did not wish Caesar to see
them with his accusers. They had also the support of Philip the brother
of Archelaus, who had been sent by the kindness of Varus for two purposes – he was to co-operate with Archelaus, and if Caesar divided
Herod's estate among all his descendants, he was to secure a share of it.

When the accusers were called upon they first went through
Herod's crimes, declaring that it was not to a king that they had submitted but to the most savage tyrant that had ever lived. Vast numbers
had been executed by him, and the survivors had suffered so horribly

that they envied the dead. He had tortured not only individual subjects but whole cities; for he had pillaged his own to adorn those of other races, and had shed Jewish blood to gratify foreigners. Depriving them of their old prosperity and their ancestral laws he had reduced his people to poverty and utter lawlessness.[19] In fact the Jews had endured more calamities at Herod's hands in a few years than their ancestors had endured in all the time since they left Babylon in the reign of Xerxes[20] and returned home. But they had become so subservient and inured to misery that they had submitted without a struggle to the continuance of their appalling slavery under Herod's successor. Archelaus, the son of that cruel tyrant, they readily acclaimed as king on the death of his father: they joined with him in mourning Herod's death and in praying for the success of his own reign. But, as though anxious to prove himself the true son of his father, he had inaugurated his reign by putting 3,000 citizens to death, offering to God that number of sacrifices for his enthronement, and filling the Temple with that number of dead bodies during a Feast! Those who had survived such a succession of calamities had naturally already reflected on their sufferings and wished like soldiers to receive their blows in front; they begged the Romans to pity the remnant of the Jews, and not to throw what was left of them to the savage beasts who would tear them to pieces, but to unite their country with Syria and administer it through their own officials.[21] This would show that men now falsely accused of sedition and aggression knew how to submit to reasonable authority.

With this request the Jews brought their accusation to an end. Nicolas then rose and refuted the charges brought against the kings, accusing the populace of anarchic tendencies and habitual disloyalty to their kings. Lastly he abused those of Archelaus' relatives who had gone over to the accusers.

After hearing both sides Caesar adjourned the meeting; but a few days later he gave half the kingdom to Archelaus, with the title of ethnarch and the promise that he should be king if he showed that he deserved it: the other half he divided into two tetrarchies which he bestowed on two other sons of Herod, one on Philip, the other on Antipas who was disputing the kingship with Archelaus. Under Antipas were placed Peraea and Galilee with a revenue of two hundred talents, while Batanaea, Trachonitis, Auranitis, and some parts of Zenodorus' domain round Paneas, with a revenue of a hundred talents, were put under Philip.[22] Archelaus' ethnarchy comprised Idumaea, all Judaea, and Samaritis, which was excused a quarter of its taxes as a reward for not joining in the revolt. The cities placed under his rule were Strato's Tower, Sebaste, Joppa,[23] and Jerusalem: the Greek cities of Gaza, Gadara, and Hippus were detached from the kingdom and added to Syria. The revenue from the territory assigned to Archelaus amounted to four hundred talents. Salome, in addition to what the king had left her in his will, was appointed mistress of Jamnia, Azotus, and Phasaelis, and as a gift from Caesar she received the palace at Ascalon.[24] From all these she collected a revenue of sixty talents; but her domain came under the general control of Archelaus. Each of Herod's other descendants received what had been left to him in the will. On the two unmarried daughters Caesar bestowed in addition 500,000 silver drachmas, and arranged that they should marry the sons of Pheroras. After dividing up Herod's estate he also shared out among them all the legacy bequeathed to him by Herod – the sum of 1,000 talents – after picking out a few treasures of no intrinsic value in memory of the departed.

At this period a young man, Jewish by birth but brought up at Sidon by a Roman freedman, took advantage of his physical resemblance to pass himself off as Alexander, the son whom Herod had executed, and thinking himself safe from detection came to Rome. Assisting him was a fellow-countryman who knew all that went on in royal circles, and who instructed him to say that the men detailed to execute him and Aristobulus had been moved by pity to smuggle them away, leaving instead bodies resembling theirs. With this pretence he deceived the Jews in Crete, who provided him with the means to travel in luxury to Melos. There by his amazing plausibility he collected a much greater sum, and induced his backers to sail with him to Rome. Landing at Dicaearchia[25] he obtained very large contributions from the Jews there, and was escorted on his way like a king by his 'father's' friends. So convincing was the physical likeness that men who had seen Alexander and remembered him well swore it was he. The whole Jewish community in Rome poured out to see him, and an enormous crowd gathered in the narrow streets through which he was carried; for so completely had the Melians lost their wits that they carried him in a litter and furnished him with royal splendour at their own expense.

Caesar, acquainted with Alexander's features since he was accused

by Herod before him, realized even before seeing the man that it was
a case of impersonation; but on the chance that there was something
behind these sanguine hopes he sent one Celadus, who remembered
Alexander well, with orders to bring the young man to him. As soon
as Celadus set eyes on him he observed the differences in his face, and
noticing that his whole body was tougher and more like a slave's he
saw through the whole plot, and was most indignant at the impudence of the fellow's story; for when asked about Aristobulus he
insisted that he too was alive, but had been left in Cyprus on purpose
for fear of treachery: they were safer apart. Celadus took him aside
and said: 'Caesar will spare your life in return for the name of the
man who persuaded you to tell such monstrous lies.' The youth
replied that he would give him the required information and accompanied him into Caesar's presence, where he pointed to the Jew who
had made use of his likeness to Alexander for profit: he himself had
received more gifts in every city than Alexander received in his whole
lifetime. Caesar was highly amused, and in view of his splendid
physique sent the pseudo-Alexander to join his galley-slaves, but
ordered the man who led him astray to be put to death. The Melians
were sufficiently punished for their folly by the loss of their money![26]

Once established as ethnarch Archelaus was unable to forget old
quarrels but treated not only Jews but even Samaritans so brutally that
both peoples sent embassies to accuse him before Caesar, with the
result that in the ninth[27] year of his rule he was banished to Vienne in
Gaul, and his property transferred to Caesar's treasury. Before he was
summoned by Caesar, so we are told, he dreamt that he saw nine large,
full ears of corn devoured by oxen. He sent for the seers and some of
the Chaldaeans and asked what they thought this foretold. Various
interpretations were given, Simon, one of the Essenes,[28] suggesting
that the ears denoted years and the oxen a political upheaval, because
by ploughing they turned the soil over. Archelaus would rule one year
for every ear, and would pass through various political upheavals
before he died. Five days after hearing this the dreamer was called to
his trial.

I think I might also mention the dream of his wife Glaphyra,
daughter of Archelaus, king of Cappadocia. She had first married
Alexander, the brother of Archelaus about whom I have been writing,
and son of King Herod, who put him to death as already explained.
When he died she married Juba, king of Libya, and when he too died,

she returned home and lived as a widow in her father's house until the ethnarch Archelaus saw her, and fell so deeply in love with her that he instantly divorced his wife Mariamme[29] and married her. Shortly after her arrival in Judaea she dreamt that Alexander stood over her and said: 'Your Libyan marriage was quite enough; but you were not satisfied with it; you came back again to my home after choosing a third husband and, you impudent woman, my own brother at that! I shall not overlook the insult; I will fetch you back to me whether you like it or not.' She related this dream, and in less than two days she was dead.[30]

CHAPTER 7

Judaea under Roman Rule

THE territory of Archelaus was brought under direct Roman rule, and a man of equestrian rank at Rome, Coponius, was sent as procurator[1] with authority from Caesar to inflict the death penalty.[2] In his time a Galilaean named Judas tried to stir the natives to revolt, saying that they would be cowards if they submitted to paying taxes to the Romans, and after serving God alone accepted human masters. This man was a rabbi with a sect of his own, and was quite unlike the others.[3]

Among the Jews there are three schools of thought, whose adherents are called Pharisees, Sadducees, and Essenes respectively. The Essenes profess a severer discipline: they are Jews by birth and are peculiarly attached to each other. They eschew pleasure-seeking as a vice and regard temperance and mastery of the passions as virtue. Scorning wedlock, they select other men's children while still pliable and teachable, and fashion them after their own pattern – not that they wish to do away with marriage as a means of continuing the race, but they are afraid of the promiscuity of women and convinced that none of the sex remains faithful to one man. Contemptuous of wealth, they are communists to perfection, and none of them will be found to be better off than the rest: their rule is that novices admitted to the sect must surrender their property to the order, so that among them all neither humiliating poverty nor excessive wealth is ever seen, but each man's possessions go into the pool and as with brothers their entire property belongs to them all. Oil they regard as polluting, and if a man is unintentionally smeared with it he scrubs himself clean; for they think it desirable to keep the skin dry and always to wear white. Men to supervise the community's affairs are elected by show of hands, chosen for their tasks by universal suffrage.

They possess no one city but everywhere have large colonies.[4] When adherents arrive from elsewhere, all local resources are put at their disposal as if they were their own, and men they have never seen before entertain them like old friends. And so when they travel they carry no baggage at all, but only weapons to keep off bandits. In every town one of the order is appointed specially to look after strangers and issue clothing and provisions. In dress and personal appearance they are like children in the care of a stern tutor. Neither garments nor shoes are changed till they are dropping to pieces or worn out with age. Among themselves nothing is bought or sold: everyone gives what he has to anybody in need and receives from him in return something he himself can use; and even without giving anything in return they are free to share the possessions of anyone they choose.

They show devotion to the Deity in a way all their own. Before the sun rises they do not utter a word on secular affairs, but offer to Him some traditional prayers as if beseeching Him to appear.[5] After this their supervisors send every man to the craft he understands best, and they work assiduously till an hour before noon, when they again meet in one place and donning linen loincloths wash all over with cold water. After this purification they assemble in a building of their own which no one outside their community is allowed to enter; they then go into the refectory in a state of ritual cleanliness as if it was a holy temple and sit down in silence. Then the baker gives them their loaves in turn, and the cook sets before each man one plateful of one kind of food. The priest says grace before meat: to taste the food before this prayer is forbidden. After breakfast he offers a second prayer; for at beginning and end they give thanks to God as the Giver of life. Then removing their garments as sacred they go back to their work till evening. Returning once more they take supper in the same way, seating their guests beside them if any have arrived. Neither shouting nor disorder ever desecrates the house: in conversation each gives way to his neighbour in turn. To people outside the silence within seems like some dread mystery; it is the natural result of their unfailing sobriety and the restriction of their food and drink to a simple sufficiency.

In general they take no action without orders from the supervisors, but two things are left entirely to them – personal aid, and charity; they may of their own accord help any deserving person in need or supply the penniless with food. But gifts to their own kinsfolk require official sanction. Showing indignation only when justified, they keep their tempers under control; they champion good faith and serve the cause of peace. Every word they speak is more binding than an oath; swearing they reject as something worse than perjury, for they say a man is already condemned if he cannot be believed without God being named. They are wonderfully devoted to the work of ancient writers, choosing mostly books that can help soul and body; from them in their anxiety to cure disease they learn all about medicinal roots and the properties of stones.[6]

Persons desirous of joining the sect are not immediately admitted. For a whole year a candidate is excluded but is required to observe the same rule of life as the members, receiving from them a hatchet,[7] the loin-cloth mentioned above, and white garments. When he has given proof of his temperance during this period, he is associated more closely with the rule and permitted to share the purer waters of sanctification, though not yet admitted to the communal life. He has demonstrated his strength of purpose, but for two more years his character is tested, and if he is then seen to be worthy, he is accepted into the society. But before touching the communal food he must swear terrible oaths, first that he will revere the Godhead, and secondly that he will deal justly with men, will injure no one either of his own accord or at another's bidding, will always hate the wicked and co-operate with the good, and will keep faith at all times and with all men – especially with rulers, since all power is conferred by God. If he himself receives power, he will never abuse his authority and never by dress or additional ornament outshine those under him; he will always love truth and seek to convict liars, will keep his hands from stealing and his soul innocent of unholy gain, and will never hide anything from members of the sect or reveal any of their secrets to others, even if brought by violence to the point of death. He further swears to impart their teaching to no man otherwise than as he himself received it, to take no part in armed robbery, and to preserve the books of the sect and in the same way the names of the angels. Such are the oaths by which they make sure of their converts.

Men convicted of major offences are expelled from the order, and the outcast often comes to a most miserable end; for bound as he is by oaths and customs, he cannot share the diet of non-members, so is forced to eat grass till his starved body wastes away and he dies. Charity compels them to take many offenders back when at their last gasp, since they feel that men tortured to the point of death have paid a sufficient penalty for their offences. In trying cases they are most careful and quite impartial, and the verdict is given by a jury of not less than a hundred: when they reach a decision there is no appeal.

What they reverence most after God is the Lawgiver,[8] and blasphemy against him is a capital offence. Obedience to older men and to the majority is a matter of principle: if ten sit down together one will not speak against the wish of the nine.

They are careful not to spit into the middle of other people or to the right, and they abstain from seventh-day work more rigidly than any other Jews; for not only do they prepare their meals the previous day so as to avoid lighting a fire on the Sabbath, but they do not venture to remove any utensil or to go and ease themselves. On other days they dig a hole a foot deep with their trenching-tool (for such is the hatchet they give to the novices) and draping their cloak round them so as not to affront the rays of the god, they squat over it; then they put the excavated soil back in the hole. On these occasions they choose the more secluded spots; and though emptying the bowels is quite natural, they are taught to wash after it, as if it defiled them.

They are divided into four grades, according to the stage they have reached in their preparation[9]; and so far are the juniors inferior to the seniors that if they touch them the persons touched must wash as though contaminated by an alien. They are long-lived, most of them passing the century, owing to the simplicity of their daily life, I suppose, and the regular routine. They despise danger and conquer pain by sheer will-power: death, if it comes with honour, they value more than life without end. Their spirit was tested to the utmost by the war with the Romans, who racked and twisted, burnt and broke them, subjecting them to every torture yet invented in order to make them blaspheme the Lawgiver or eat some forbidden food, but could not make them do either, or ever once fawn on their tormentors or shed a tear. Smiling in their agony and gently mocking those who tortured them, they resigned their souls in the joyous certainty that they would receive them back.[10]

It is indeed their unshakable conviction that bodies are corruptible and the material composing them impermanent, whereas souls remain immortal for ever. Coming forth from the most rarefied ether they are trapped in the prison-house of the body as if drawn down by one of nature's spells; but once freed from the bonds of the flesh, as if released after years of slavery, they rejoice and soar aloft. Teaching the same doctrine as the sons of Greece, they declare that for the good souls there waits a home beyond the ocean, a place troubled by neither rain nor snow nor heat, but refreshed by the zephyr that blows ever gentle from the ocean. Bad souls they consign to a darksome, stormy abyss, full of punishments that know no end. I think the Greeks had the same notion when they assigned to their brave men, whom they call heroes or demigods, the Islands of the Blest,[11] and to the souls of the wicked the place of the impious in Hades, where according to their stories certain people undergo punishment – Sisyphus and Tantalus, Ixion and Tityus,[12] and the like. They tell these tales firstly because they believe souls to be immortal, and secondly in the hope of encouraging virtue and discouraging vice, since the good become better in their lifetime through the hope of a reward after death, and the propensities of the bad are restrained by the fear that, even if they are not caught in this life, after their dissolution they will undergo eternal punishment. This then is the religious teaching of the Essenes about the soul, providing an inescapable inducement to those who have once tasted their wisdom.

Some of them claim to foretell the future, after a lifelong study of sacred literature, purifications of different kinds, and the aphorisms of prophets; rarely if ever do their predictions prove wrong.

There is a second order of Essenes, which agrees with the other in its way of life, customs, and rules, and differs only in its views on marriage. They think that the biggest thing in life – the continuance of the race – is forfeited by men who do not marry, and further, if everyone followed their example mankind would rapidly disappear. However, they put their brides on probation for three years, and do not marry them till the regularity of their periods proves them capable of child-bearing.[13] When conception has taken place intercourse ceases – proof that the object of the marriage was not pleasure but the begetting of children. When women bathe they wear a dress just as the men wear a loincloth. Such are the customs of the order.

Of the two schools named first, the Pharisees are held to be the most authoritative exponents of the Law and count as the leading sect.[14] They ascribe everything to Fate or to God: the decision whether or not to do right rests mainly with men, but in every action Fate takes some part. Every soul is imperishable, but only the souls of good men pass into other bodies,[15] the souls of bad men being subjected to eternal punishment. The Sadducees,[16] the second order, deny Fate altogether and hold that God is incapable of either committing sin or seeing it; they say that men are free to choose between good and evil, and each individual must decide which he will follow. The permanence of the soul, punishments in Hades, and rewards they deny utterly. Again, Pharisees are friendly to one another and seek to promote concord with the general public, but Sadducees, even towards each other, show a more disagreeable spirit, and in their relations with men like themselves they are as harsh as they might be to foreigners.

This is all I wish to say about the Jewish schools of thought.

When the ethnarchy of Archelaus came under Roman rule his brothers, Philip and Herod Antipas, continued to rule their respective tetrarchies. When Salome died, she left to Julia, Augustus' consort, her toparchy, with Jamnia and the palm-groves at Phasaelis.[17] Later, when on the death of Augustus, who had been in supreme control for fifty-seven years, six months and two days,[18] the empire passed to Tiberius, the son of Julia, Antipas and Philip remained in their tetrarchies. Philip founded the city of Caesarea near the sources of the Jordan in Paneas and Julias in Lower Gaulanitis; Antipas founded Tiberias in Galilee and a city called after Julia in Peraea.[19]

As procurator of Judaea Tiberius sent Pilate,[20] who during the night, secretly and under cover, conveyed to Jerusalem the images of Caesar known as standards. When day dawned this caused great excitement among the Jews; for those who were near were amazed at the sight, which meant that their laws had been trampled on – they do not permit any graven image to be set up in the City – and the angry City mob was joined by a huge influx of people from the country. They rushed off to Pilate in Caesarea, and begged him to remove the standards from Jerusalem and to respect their ancient customs.[21] When Pilate refused, they fell prone all round his house and remained motionless for five days and nights.

The next day Pilate took his seat on the tribunal in the great stadium and summoned the mob on the pretext that he was ready to give them an answer. Instead he gave a pre-arranged signal to the soldiers to surround the Jews in full armour, and the troops formed a ring three deep. The Jews were dumbfounded at the unexpected sight, but Pilate, declaring that he would cut them to pieces unless they accepted the images of Caesar, nodded to the soldiers to bare their swords. At this the Jews as though by agreement fell to the ground in a body and bent their necks, shouting that they were ready to be killed rather than transgress the Law. Amazed at the intensity of their religious fervour, Pilate ordered the standards to be removed from Jerusalem forthwith.[22]

After this he stirred up further trouble by expending the sacred treasure known as Corban[23] on an aqueduct fifty miles long.[24] This roused the populace to fury, and when Pilate visited Jerusalem they surrounded the tribunal and shouted him down. But he had foreseen this disturbance, and had made the soldiers mix with the mob, wearing civilian clothing over their armour, and with orders not to draw their swords but to use clubs on the obstreperous. He now gave the signal from the tribunal and the Jews were cudgelled, so that many died from the blows, and many were trampled to death by their friends as they fled.[25] The fate of those who perished horrified the crowd into silence.

At about this time Agrippa, son of that Aristobulus who had been put to death by his father Herod, sought an audience of Tiberius in order to accuse Herod the Tetrarch.[26] When the accusation was not accepted, he remained in Rome and made approaches to many eminent men, and particularly to Germanicus' son Gaius, as yet a private citizen. One day he invited him to dinner and, after entertaining him lavishly, finished by stretching out his hands and openly praying that Tiberius might die soon, so that he could see Gaius lord of the world.[27] One of his domestics passed this on to Tiberius, who was enraged and had Agrippa locked up, keeping him in rigorous confinement for six months until his own death.[28] He had reigned twenty-two years, six months and three days.

On being proclaimed Caesar, Gaius released Agrippa and set him over the tetrarchy of Philip, recently deceased,[29] as king. Agrippa's acquisition of this title awoke jealous ambitions in Herod the Tetrarch. Herod's hopes of a crown were inspired chiefly by his wife Herodias, who kept nagging him for his inertia and declared that only his unwillingness to make the journey to Caesar prevented his acquiring a better title. Having promoted Agrippa from private citizen to king, the emperor would surely not hesitate to promote Herod from tetrarch. Yielding to this pressure Herod came to Gaius, who punished his ambition by banishing him to Spain. For he had been followed by Agrippa, who brought accusations against him[30] and was rewarded by Gaius with the addition of Herod's tetrarchy. Herod, whose wife shared his exile in Spain, died there.

Gaius Caesar's accession to power so completely turned his head that he wished to be thought of and addressed as a god, stripped his country of its noblest men, and proceeded to lay sacrilegious hands on

Judaea.[31] He ordered Petronius[32] to march with an army to Jerusalem and erect his statues in the Temple: if the Jews refused them, he was to execute the objectors and enslave all the rest of the population. But God evidently took note of these instructions. Petronius, with three legions and a large body of Syrian allies, began a swift march from Antioch to Judaea. Some of the Jews disbelieved the rumours of war; others who did believe were at a loss how to defend themselves. But soon a shudder ran through them all; for the army was already at Ptolemais. (This is a seaside town of Galilee,[33] built on the edge of the Great Plain and shut in by mountains. To the east, seven miles away, is the Galilaean range; to the south is Carmel, fifteen miles distant; to the north is the highest range, called 'The Ladder of Tyre' by the natives: the distance in this case is twelve miles. About a quarter of a mile from the town flows the Beleus, a very tiny stream on whose banks is the Tomb of Memnon. Near this is an area fifty yards wide which is of great interest; it is a round hollow which yields crystalline sand. A large number of ships put in and clear this out; but the place fills up again thanks to the winds, which as if on purpose blow into it common sand from outside. This is at once converted by the mine into crystal. Still more wonderful, I think, is the fact that crystal which overflows from the basin reverts to ordinary sand. A most unusual spot.)

The Jews with their wives and children massed on the plain near the city, and appealed to Petronius first for their ancestral laws and then for themselves. He yielded to the demands of such a formidable crowd, and left the army and the statues in Ptolemais. Then he advanced into Galilee, and summoning the populace with all the notables to Tiberias[34] he enlarged on the power of Rome and the threats of Caesar. He demonstrated too the unreasonableness of their demands; for when all the subject races had set up the images of Caesar in their cities among the other gods, for Jews alone to object was tantamount to rebellion and deliberate disloyalty. When they pleaded their Law and ancestral customs and explained that it was not permissible for a graven image of God, much less of a man, to be placed in the Temple or even in some ordinary place in their country, Petronius retorted: 'Quite so; but I too am bound to keep the law of my sovereign lord: If I break it and spare you, I shall perish as I deserve. It will be the Emperor himself who will make war on you, not I. I am subject to authority just as you are.' In reply the crowd roared that they were ready to suffer anything for their Law. When he had secured silence Petronius asked: 'Will you then go to war with Caesar?' The Jews replied that for Caesar and the people of Rome they sacrificed twice a day.[35] But if he wished to set up the images in their midst, he must first sacrifice the whole Jewish race: they were ready to offer themselves as victims with their wives and children. This reply filled Petronius with wonder and pity for the unparalleled religious fervour of these brave men and the courage that made them so ready to die. So for the time being they were dismissed with nothing settled.

During the next few days he got the leading men together privately and assembled the people publicly, and tried first persuasion and then advice. But for the most part he relied on threats, emphasizing the strength of the Romans, the fury of Gaius, and the necessity imposed on himself. Nothing that he could think of had any effect, and he saw that the land was in danger of remaining unsown; for it was at seed-time[36] that the crowds had wasted seven weeks in idleness. So at last he got them together and said: 'It is better for me to take the risk. With God's help I shall convince Caesar and we can all breathe again: if he is exasperated, I will gladly give my life to save so many.' Then he dismissed the throng, who offered many prayers on his behalf, withdrew the army from Ptolemais, and returned to Antioch. From there he at once sent a dispatch to Caesar, informing him of his invasion of Judaea and the appeals of the nation, and adding that unless he wished to destroy both the men and the land they tilled, he must let them keep their law and withdraw his instructions. To this dispatch Gaius replied in no gentle terms, threatening Petronius with death for his slowness in carrying out his orders. But as it happened the messengers who carried this reply were held up for three months by storms at sea, while others who brought news of Gaius' death had a good voyage, so that Petronius received intimation of this event four weeks earlier than the denunciation of himself.[37]

When after a reign of three years and eight months Gaius was treacherously murdered, the armies in Rome forced the empire on Claudius.[38] The Senate however, on the motion of the consuls Sextus Saturninus and Pomponius Secundus, ordered the three remaining cohorts to protect the City and assembled in the Capitol, where in view of the savagery of Gaius they voted to take military action against Claudius. They resolved to restore the aristocracy that had ruled the country in the past,[39] or else to choose by vote a man worthy to be emperor.

As it happened that Agrippa was then on a visit to Rome,[40] the Senate sent and invited him to discuss the situation with them, and at the same time Claudius summoned him to his camp to assist him as occasion arose.[41] Realizing that he was virtually Caesar already, Agrippa went to Claudius, who dispatched him as ambassador to the Senate to explain his intentions. In the first place his hand had been forced by the soldiers, but he felt that to disregard their enthusiasm would be unfair, and to disregard his own future most unsafe; for the fact that he had been summoned to the imperial throne placed him in great danger. He added that he would carry on the government like a good popular leader, not like a dictator; for he was satisfied with the honour of the imperial title, and on every matter at issue he would follow the wishes of the people. Indeed, if he had not been a moderate man by inclination, he would have had a sufficient inducement to self-restraint in Gaius' death.

This message was delivered by Agrippa. The Senate answered that they relied on the army and on wise counsels and would not voluntarily submit to slavery. When Claudius heard this answer, he sent Agrippa back to inform them that he would never consent to betray those who had given him unanimous support, and must therefore fight, though most unwillingly, against those who should have been his best friends. However, they must choose a battlefield outside the City; for it would be sacrilege if by their folly they polluted their ancestral shrines with the blood of their countrymen. This message Agrippa conveyed to the Senate.

Meanwhile one of the soldiers with the Senate drew his sword and cried: 'Look here, you fellows; why should we think of killing our friends and attacking men just like ourselves who happen to be with Claudius? We have an emperor with nothing against him, and the closest ties with those we are proposing to march against.' With these words he strode through the middle of the Senate with his entire unit behind him. Left in the lurch the patricians[42] immediately panicked; and as they could find no means of escape they went the way of the soldiers and hurried off to join Claudius. But before the walls they were met by the naked swords of those who had been quicker than they to back the winning side; and the men who led the way might have been in danger before Claudius was aware of the soldiers' violent intentions, had not Agrippa run to him and shown him how dangerous the situation was, pointing out that, unless he restrained the violence of his men, who were furious with the patricians, he would lose the very people who could make his reign glorious, and find himself ruler of a desert.[43]

When Claudius heard this, he put a stop to the violent behaviour of the soldiery and received the Senate into the camp, making them welcome and then immediately going out with them to present to God thankofferings for his accession. On Agrippa he at once bestowed the entire kingdom of his forbears, adding the outer districts given by Augustus to Herod, Trachonitis, and Auranitis,[44] and also another kingdom called that of Lysanias. The people he informed of this bestowal by an edict; the magistrates he ordered to engrave the award on bronze tablets to be set up in the Capitol. He then bestowed on Agrippa's brother Herod – who was also his son-in-law, having married Berenice – the kingdom of Chalcis.

From such wide dominions wealth poured into Agrippa's treasury, which he very quickly emptied; for he began to surround Jerusalem with fortifications so huge that had they been finished they would have made it futile for the Romans to attempt a siege.[45] But before the wall reached its full height he died in Caesarea, after three years as king following three as tetrarch.[46] He left three daughters born to him by Cypros, Berenice, Mariamme, and Drusilla, and one son by the same wife, Agrippa. As Agrippa was quite a child Claudius brought the kingdom under direct rule again,[47] dispatching as procurator Cuspius Fadus, followed by Tiberius Alexander.[48] These two left native customs severely alone and kept the nation at peace. After this Herod King of Chalcis died leaving two sons, children of his niece Berenice, Berenicianus and Hyrcanus, and one son, the child of his former wife Mariamme, Aristobulus. A third brother, Aristobulus, a private citizen, also died, leaving a daughter Jotape. The three brothers, as I said before, were sons of Aristobulus and grandsons of Herod; Aristobulus and Alexander were born to Herod by Mariamme and put to death by their father. Alexander's descendants established a dynasty in Greater Armenia.[49]

After the death of Herod, King of Chalcis, Claudius gave the throne to his nephew Agrippa, son of the first Agrippa.[50] In the other districts, which were under direct rule, the procurator Alexander was succeeded by Cumanus, whose governorship[51] was marked by disturbances and further disaster to the Jews. The people had assembled in Jerusalem for the Feast of Unleavened Bread, and the Roman cohort stood on guard over the Temple colonnade, armed men always being on duty at the feasts to forestall any rioting by the vast crowds. One of the soldiers pulled up his garment and bent over indecently, turning his backside towards the Jews and making a noise as indecent as his attitude. This infuriated the whole crowd, who noisily appealed to Cumanus to punish the soldier, while the less restrained of the young men and the naturally tumultuous section of the people rushed into battle, and snatching up stones hurled them at the soldiers. Cumanus, fearing that the whole population would rush at him, sent for more heavy infantry. When these poured into the colonnades the Jews were seized with uncontrollable panic, turned tail and fled from the Temple into the City. So violently did the dense mass struggle to escape that they trod on each other, and more than 30,000 were crushed to death.[52] Thus the Feast ended in distress to the whole nation and bereavement to every household.

This disaster was followed by a further disturbance, the work of bandits. On the Beth-horon highroad bandits[53] swooped down on one of the emperor's slaves, a certain Stephen, and robbed him of the baggage that he was carrying. Cumanus sent out men with orders to bring the inhabitants of the neighbouring villages in chains to his headquarters, blaming them for their failure to pursue and capture the bandits. In one village a soldier found a copy of the sacred Law, tore it in two and threw it on to the fire. The Jews, as if their whole country was in flames, assembled in frantic haste, religious fervour drawing them together irresistibly, and on a single summons ran in their thousands from all directions to Caesarea, where they besought Cumanus not to let the man who had thus insulted God and their Law go unpunished. Cumanus, seeing that the mob could only be appeased by a conciliatory answer, agreed that the soldier should be produced, and ordered him to be led between the lines of his accusers to execution. Then the Jews went home.

Next came a clash between Galilaeans and Samaritans. In the village of Gema, situated in the great plain of Samaritis, a Galilaean was murdered when numbers of Jews were going up to the Feast. This brought swarms of Galilaeans to the spot to attack the Samaritans; but their leading men came to Cumanus and begged him to cross into Galilee before the situation got beyond control and punish those responsible for the crime: in no other way could the mass of men be dispersed and war avoided. Cumanus, however, made their petitions take second place to matters then in hand, and promised the petitioners nothing.[54]

When news of the murder reached Jerusalem the crowds were infuriated, and abandoning the Feast they instantly set out for Samaria without generals, paying no heed to the appeals of their magistrates. The bandit and revolutionary element among them was led by one Eleazar, son of Dinaeus, and Alexander. These men swooped on their neighbours in the toparchy of Acrabata and slaughtered them, sparing neither infants nor the aged, and setting fire to the villages.

Cumanus, taking from Caesarea one troop of horse, called the Augustans,[55] went to the rescue of those who were being plundered, and rounded up many of Eleazar's followers, killing still more. As for the rest of the crowd that had set out to fight the Samaritans, the Jerusalem magistrates, rushing out clad in sackcloth and with ashes poured on their heads, besought them to return and not to provoke the Romans to attack Jerusalem by reprisals on the Samaritans: they must spare their country and their Sanctuary, and their own wives and children, who were all in danger of being destroyed for the sake of avenging one Galilaean. These appeals induced the Jews to disperse; but many turned to banditry as there was no one to stop them, and all over the country plundering went on and the bolder spirits rose in revolt. On the Samaritan side the leading men went to Ummidius Quadratus, governor of Syria,[56] at Tyre, and demanded the punishment of those who had ravaged their land. On the other hand prominent Jews, among them the high priest Jonathan, son of Ananus,[57] presented themselves and declared that it was the Samaritans who had begun the disturbance by the murder, but that blame for what had followed lay at Cumanus' door, since he had refused to take action against the actual killers.

Quadratus for the time being put off both delegations with the promise that when he visited the area he would enquire into all the circumstances. But he went to Caesarea, and finding there those whom Cumanus had taken alive he crucified them all. From there he went on to Lydda, where he heard the Samaritan version again; then he sent for eighteen Jews who were reported to have taken part in the fighting and cut off their heads. Besides two other men in important positions, the high priests Jonathan and Ananias,[58] with the latter's son Ananus[59] and several other leading Jews, were sent to Caesar, as were the most eminent of the Samaritans. He further instructed Cumanus, with Celer the military tribune,[60] to sail for Rome and report to Claudius what had occurred. After making these arrangements he went from Lydda to Jerusalem, and finding that the people were celebrating the Feast of Unleavened Bread[61] in an orderly manner, he returned to Antioch.

At Rome Caesar heard what Cumanus and the Samaritans had to say. Agrippa was there too, enthusiastically supporting the Jews while Cumanus too had many powerful advocates. Claudius found the Samaritans guilty and ordered their three most powerful men to be executed; Cumanus he banished, and Celer he sent in chains to Jerusalem with orders that he should be handed over to the Jews for torture, dragged round the City and finally beheaded.

After this he sent Felix, the brother of Pallas,[62] as procurator of Judaea, Samaria, Galilee, and Peraea. From Chalcis he transferred Agrippa to a larger kingdom, giving him Philip's old province of Trachonitis, Batanaea and Gaulanitis, together with the kingdom of Lysanias and the old tetrarchy of Varus.[63] He himself, having ruled the Empire for thirteen years, eight months and twenty days, died, leaving his throne to Nero. His wife Agrippina had tricked him into adopting Nero as his heir,[64] though he had a son of his own, Britannicus, by Messalina his former wife, and a daughter, Octavia, whom he had married to Nero. He also had a daughter, Antonia, by Paetina.

Through excess of prosperity and wealth Nero lost his balance and abused his good fortune outrageously. He put to death in succession his brother,[65] wife, and mother, turning his savage attention next to his most eminent subjects. The final degree of his madness landed him on the stage of a theatre. But so many writers have recorded these things[66] that I will pass over them and turn to what happened to the Jews in his time.

Lesser Armenia Nero gave to Herod's[67] son Aristobulus, with the title of king, while to Agrippa's kingdom he added four cities with their toparchies, Abila and Julias in Peraea, Tarichaeae and Tiberias in Galilee. Over the rest of Judaea he appointed Felix procurator.[68] Felix captured the bandit chief Eleazar, who had been plundering the country for twenty years, with many of his men, and sent them as prisoners to Rome; the bandits whom he crucified, and the local inhabitants in league with them whom he caught and punished, were too many to count. When the countryside had been cleared of them, another type of bandit sprang up in Jerusalem, known as 'Sicarii'.[69] These men committed numerous murders in broad daylight and in the middle of the City. Their favourite trick was to mingle with festival crowds, concealing under their garments small daggers with which they stabbed their opponents. When their victims fell, the assassins melted into the indignant crowd, and through their plausibility entirely defied detection. The first to have his throat cut by them was Jonathan the high priest,[70] and after him many were murdered every day. More terrible than the crimes themselves was the fear they aroused, every man hourly expecting death, as in war. They watched at a distance for their enemies, and not even when their friends came near did they trust them; yet in spite of their suspicions and precautions they were done to death; such was the suddenness of the conspirators' attack and their skill in avoiding detection.

In addition to these there was formed another group of scoundrels, in act less criminal but in intention more evil, who did as much damage as the murderers to the well-being of the City. Cheats and deceivers claiming inspiration, they schemed to bring about revolutionary changes by inducing the mob to act as if possessed, and by leading them out into the desert on the pretence that there God would show them signs of approaching freedom.[71] Thereupon Felix, regarding this as the first stage of revolt, sent cavalry and heavy infantry who cut the mob to pieces.

A greater blow than this was inflicted on the Jews by the Egyptian false prophet. Arriving in the country this man, a fraud who posed as a seer, collected about 30,000 dupes, led them round from the desert to the Mount of Olives, and from there was ready to force an entry into Jerusalem, overwhelm the Roman garrison, and seize supreme power with his fellow-raiders as bodyguard. But Felix anticipated his attempt by meeting him with the Roman heavy infantry,[72] the whole population rallying to the defence, so that when the clash occurred, the Egyptian fled with a handful of men and most of his followers were killed or captured; the rest of the mob scattered and stole away to their respective homes.[73]

When this fever too had died down, another festering sore appeared in the body politic. The religious frauds and bandit chiefs joined forces and drove numbers to revolt, inciting them to strike a blow for freedom and threatening with death those who submitted to Roman rule; men who willingly chose slavery would be forcibly freed. Then splitting up into groups they ranged over the countryside, plundering the houses of the well-to-do, killing the occupants, and setting fire to the villages, till their raging madness penetrated every corner of Judaea. Day by day the fighting blazed more fiercely.

Another disturbance broke out round Caesarea, the Jewish settlers coming to blows with the Syrian inhabitants. The Jews claimed the city as their own on the ground that it had been built by a Jew, King Herod. The Syrians agreed that the founder was a Jew, but declared that the city belonged to the Greeks; Herod would not have set up statues and temples in it if he had meant it for the Jews.[74] These were the arguments put forward by the two sides, and the dispute led to blows, the bolder spirits on both sides daily rushing forth to battle; for the elder Jews were unable to restrain their own partisans, and the Greeks could not bear to be worsted by Jews. The Jews had the advantage in material resources and bodily prowess: the Greeks enjoyed the help of the soldiers; for the greater part of the Roman force there had been raised in Syria, and they were ready to help their own flesh and blood.[75] The city magistrates, anxious to quell the disturbance, constantly arrested the more pugnacious and punished them with whipping and imprisonment. However, the pains of those arrested failed to check or frighten the remainder, who plunged still more furiously into the rioting. One day the Jews were victorious, and Felix came into the market-place and ordered them with threats to retire. When they refused, he sent his soldiers against them and killed a large number, whose property was promptly plundered. As the rioting, however, continued, he picked out the leading men of both communities and sent them as ambassadors to Nero, to argue the merits of the case.

CHAPTER 8
War Clouds

THE next procurator, Festus,[1] tackled the chief curse of the country; he killed a considerable number of the bandits and captured many more. Albinus, who followed him,[2] acted very differently, being guilty of every possible misdemeanour. Not content with official actions that meant widespread robbery and looting of private property, or with taxes that crippled the whole nation, he allowed those imprisoned for banditry by local courts or his own predecessors to be bought out by their relatives, and only the man who failed to pay was left in jail to serve his sentence. Now too the revolutionary party in Jerusalem cast off all restraint, and its leaders bribed Albinus to shut his eyes to their subversive activities, whilst any of the common people who did not care for peace and quiet joined forces with the procurator's associates. Every scoundrel, surrounded by his own gang, stood out from his followers like a bandit chief or dictator and used his henchmen to rob respectable citizens. The result was that the victims kept their wrongs to themselves while those still immune, through fear of the same fate, flattered[3] those they should have battered.[3] In short, free speech was completely suppressed and tyranny reigned everywhere; from then on the seeds of the coming destruction were being sown in the City.

Such a man was Albinus,[4] but his successor Gessius Florus made him appear an angel by comparison. Albinus for the most part did his mischief with secrecy and dissimulation; Gessius boasted of the wrongs he did to the nation and, as if sent as public executioner to punish condemned criminals, indulged in every kind of robbery and violence.[5] When pitiable things happened, he showed himself the most heartless of men; when disgraceful things, the most disgusting. No one ever had less use for truth or thought out more subtle methods of crime. Making a profit out of individuals he considered poor sport: he stripped whole cities, ruined complete communities, and virtually announced to the entire country that everyone might be a bandit if he chose, so long as he himself received a rake-off. The result

of his avarice was that every district was denuded, and many people
left their old homes and fled to foreign provinces.

As long as Cestius Gallus was in Syria administering his province,[6]
no one dared even to approach him with complaints against Florus;
but when he appeared in Jerusalem on the eve of the Passover, the
people crowded round – at least 3,000,000 of them[7] – imploring him
to pity the nation in its distress and shouting against Florus, the ruin
of their country. Florus, who was present and stood at Cestius' side,
laughed at their protests. Cestius, however, quieted the excited crowd
by assuring them that he would guarantee more reasonable conduct
on Florus' part in the future. Then he returned to Antioch. But
Florus accompanied him as far as Caesarea, disguising the intention
he had already formed of making war on the nation, his only hope of
diverting attention from his own crimes; for if peace lasted, he
foresaw that he would have the Jews accusing him to Caesar, but if
he contrived to make them revolt, the greater outrage would forestall
any enquiry into lesser ones. So to ensure a nation-wide revolt he
daily added to the general distress.

Meanwhile the Greeks of Caesarea secured from Nero control of
the city and returned with the decision in writing. War broke out in
the twelfth year of Nero's reign and the seventeenth of Agrippa's, in
the month of Artemisios.[8] In comparison with the fearful disasters to
which it led its pretext was insignificant. The Jews in Caesarea had
a synagogue alongside a piece of ground belonging to a Greek
citizen. This they had repeatedly tried to acquire, offering many times
the real value. Scorning their requests, the Greek further insulted them
by beginning to build a factory right up to the dividing line, leaving
them a narrow and utterly inadequate passage. The immediate result
was that the more hot-headed of the young men jumped in and
interfered with the builders. When this display of force was suppressed by Florus, the leading Jews, among them John the tax-
collector, having no other way out, gave Florus a bribe of eight silver
talents to put a stop to the work. As nothing mattered to him but
money, he promised full co-operation; but as soon as the money was
his, he left Caesarea for Sebaste, allowing party strife to take its
course as if he had sold the Jews permission to fight it out!

The next day was a Sabbath, and when the Jews gathered in the
synagogue a Caesarean partisan had placed a chamber-pot upside
down at the entrance and was sacrificing birds on it.[9] This infuriated

the Jews, who felt that their Law had been violated and the site desecrated. The steadier, gentler people advised an appeal to the authorities; the quarrelsome element and youthful hotheads burned for a fight. The Caesarean partisans stood waiting for them, for they had sent the men to sacrifice by prearrangement, and the clash soon came. Jucundus, the cavalry officer detailed to prevent it, stepped forward, picked up the pot, and attempted to end the strife. But he was no match for the violence of the Caesareans, so the Jews seized the rolls of the Law and retired to Narbata, a Jewish area seven miles from Caesarea. John and twelve other influential citizens followed Florus to Sebaste, where they complained bitterly of what had happened and implored him to help, tactfully reminding him of the eight talents. He actually arrested these men and put them in prison, on the ground that they had removed the rolls of the Law from Caesarea.[10]

This new outrage caused anger in Jerusalem, but passions were still kept under control. Florus, however, as if he had contracted to fan the war into flame, sent to the Temple treasury and removed seventeen talents on the pretext that Caesar required it. Uproar followed at once and the people rushed in a body into the Temple, where with piercing yells they called on the name of Caesar, imploring him to free them from Florus' misrule. Some of the rioters shouted the most scandalous abuse at the latter, and going round with a basket begged coppers for the poor starveling! This did not cure his avarice but increased his determination to get rich quickly. So instead of going to Caesarea to extinguish the conflagration that was breaking out there and to remove the causes of the trouble – as he had been paid to do – he dashed off to Jerusalem with an army of horse and foot, in order that he might get what he wanted with the help of Roman arms,[11] and by intimidation skin the City. The people, anxious to make him ashamed of his attempt, met the soldiers with friendly greetings and prepared to receive Florus submissively. He, however, sent ahead fifty horsemen commanded by Capito, and ordered them to retire and not to mock with new-found cordiality the man they had abused so scandalously. If they were fearless and outspoken, they ought to make fun of him to his face, and show by force of arms as well as words that they loved liberty. This took the crowd aback, and when Capito's troops charged into their midst, they scattered before they could salute Florus or convince the soldiers of their readiness to obey. Returning to their homes they passed the night in fear and dejection.

Florus slept in the Palace, and the next day had a dais erected outside and took his seat. The chief priests,[12] political leaders, and eminent citizens lined up before this tribunal. Florus ordered them to give up the men who had abused him, declaring that they themselves would feel the weight of his hand if the culprits were not forthcoming. The Jewish leaders insisted that the people were peacefully disposed and apologized for the offending remarks; in such a mass of people there were bound to be some impudent juveniles, and it was impossible to identify the miscreants when everyone was conscience-stricken and afraid to confess his guilt. If Florus cared anything about the peaceful state of the nation and wished to save the City for the Romans, it would be better for the sake of the many innocent to pardon the few guilty than because of a few scamps to wreck the lives of so many loyal subjects.

This plea made Florus still more furious, and he shouted to the soldiers to sack the area known as the Upper Market-place[13] and kill all they met. Their acquisitiveness thus stimulated by their general's encouragement, they not only sacked the area to which they had been sent but burst into all the houses and murdered the occupants. There followed a flight through the narrow streets, the slaughter of those who were caught, and rapine in all its horror. Many peaceful citizens were seized and taken before Florus, who had them scourged and then crucified. The total number that perished that day, including women and children – for not even infants were spared – came to about 3,600. The disaster was made the more crushing by the unheard-of character of the Roman brutality. No one had ever before dared to do what Florus did then – to scourge men of equestrian rank before the judgement-seat and nail them to the cross, men who were indeed Jews, but all the same enjoyed Roman status.[14]

At this time it happened that King Agrippa had travelled to Alexandria to congratulate Alexander, who had been entrusted with Egypt by Nero and sent there as governor.[15] However, his sister Berenice was in Jerusalem, and seeing the criminal conduct of the soldiers she was cut to the heart, and repeatedly sent her cavalry commanders and bodyguards to Florus to beg him to stop the slaughter. He, caring nothing for the number of the victims or the high rank of the petitioner, but only for the profit which he made out of the loot, was deaf to her appeals; and the mad fury of the soldiers did not even spare the queen – not only did they torture their prisoners to death before her eyes; they would actually have killed her if she had not escaped in time into the royal palace[16] and spent the night there with her guards, in fear that the soldiers would attack. She was staying in Jerusalem to perform a vow to God; it is usual for those who are sick or in distress to vow that for thirty days before they intend to sacrifice they will abstain from wine and shave their heads.[17] These vows Berenice was then performing, and she stood barefoot before the judgement-seat appealing to Florus, but no respect was paid to her and she went in danger of her life.

These events occurred on the 16th of Artemisios. The next day the crowd in great distress swarmed into the Upper Market-place, shrieking and lamenting for the dead and still more vociferously calling down curses on Florus. This alarmed the influential citizens and chief priests, who rent their clothes and, falling down before one man after another, begged them to desist and not, after all they had suffered, to provoke Florus to commit some irreparable outrage. The crowd at once complied out of respect for the petitioners and in the hope that Florus would commit no more crimes against them.

The extinction of the disturbance annoyed the procurator, who in order to rekindle the flames summoned the chief priests and prominent citizens, and said that the only way of proving that the people would not revolt again was to go out and meet the troops approaching from Caesarea – two cohorts were on the way. While the people were still being collected, he sent orders to the centurions of the cohorts to instruct their men not to return the Jews' salutes, and if they uttered a word against him to use their weapons. The chief priests assembled great numbers in the Temple and urged them to meet the Romans and to avert irreparable disaster by welcoming the cohorts. This appeal failed to influence the insurgent element, and the thought of the fallen swung the majority to the side of the bolder spirits.

Thereupon every priest and every minister of God brought out the sacred vessels and put on the robes they always wore when officiating, the harpers and singers appeared with their instruments, and they all fell down and implored the people to preserve their sacred ornaments and not provoke the Romans to plunder the treasures of God. The chief priests themselves could be seen heaping dust on their heads, their clothes rent and their breasts bared. They appealed by name to each of the prominent citizens and collectively to the crowd not by some trifling offence to betray their country to men who were anxious to sack it. What advantage would it be to the soldiers to be saluted by the Jews? What compensation for past wrongs not to go out now? If they gave them the usual welcome, Florus would be deprived of all pretext for war, and they themselves would enjoy their country and immunity from further wrong. Again, to give way to a handful of insurgents, when with their overwhelming numbers they could compel even them to behave sensibly, would be feeble in the extreme.

With these arguments they quietened the crowd while the insurgents yielded, some to threats, others to authority. Then leading the way they went quietly and in good order to meet the column, and when the soldiers came near saluted them; but when they met with no response, the Jews began to vilify Florus. This was the agreed signal to attack them. In a flash the soldiers had surrounded and begun to club them; when they fled, the cavalry pursued them and trampled them down. Many fell under the blows of the Romans, more were crushed by their friends. Round the gates there was frightful congestion; as everyone raced to get in first the flight was slowed down for them all, and those who stumbled met a horrible end; suffocated and crushed to pulp beneath countless feet, they were unrecognizable when their kinsfolk came to bury them. The soldiers poured in with the fugitives, raining blows on any they caught, and drove the crowd through Bezetha, in an effort to force their way through and seize the Temple and Antonia. For the same purpose Florus led his own men out of the Palace and endeavoured to reach the fortress. But the attempt failed; for the people swung round to face him and blocked his advance, then lined up on the roofs and pelted the Romans. Suffering severely from the falling missiles and too weak to hack a way through the crowds that blocked the narrow streets, they retreated to their camp near the Palace.[18]

The insurgents, afraid that Florus would come on again and seize the Temple by way of Antonia, climbed up at once and cut a gap in the colonnades that linked Antonia with the Temple. This cooled the avarice of Florus; for it was the treasures of God he was after, and for this reason he was anxious to get into Antonia, so that when the colonnades were broken down he was diverted from his attempt. He sent for the chief priests and the Sanhedrin, and told them that he was going to quit the City but would leave them as big a garrison as they wanted. In reply they solemnly promised to maintain order and prevent any rising, if he left them one cohort, but not the one that had been engaged,[19] as the people hated it because of what it had done to them. So he changed the cohort as requested, and with the rest of his forces went back to Caesarea.

As a further inducement to hostilities he sent Cestius a false report of a Jewish revolt, alleging that they had started the recent fighting and charging them with violence of which they had in reality been the victims. The Jerusalem magistrates did not take this lying down; they and Berenice too wrote to Cestius about the crimes which Florus had committed against the City. Cestius read the communications from both parties and consulted his staff. They advised him to go at once to Jerusalem at the head of an army, and either punish the revolt, if real, or strengthen the allegiance of the Jews, if they were indeed loyal; but he thought it better to send one of his colleagues first to examine the position and to bring a reliable report of the state of Jewish feeling. So he sent the tribune Neapolitanus, who at Jamnia met King Agrippa on his way home from Alexandria, and told him who had sent him and why.

There too the Jews' chief priests, with the leading citizens and the Sanhedrin, arrived to welcome the king. After paying homage they began to bewail their own calamities and to describe the savagery of Florus. This shocked Agrippa, but he discreetly turned his indignation on the Jews, whom he inwardly pitied, wishing to humble their pride and, by refusing to see that they had suffered any wrong, to damp their ardour for revenge. They, being men of position and property-owners with a personal interest in peace, realized that the king's rebuke was kindly meant. But the people came seven miles out of Jerusalem to welcome Agrippa and Neapolitanus, with the widows of the slain running in front and wailing, and the people replying to their groans with lamentations. They implored Agrippa to help them, and dinned into the ears of Neapolitanus all that Florus had done to them. When they entered the City the Jews pointed to the desolate Market-place and sacked houses. Then with Agrippa's help they persuaded Neapolitanus to walk round the City as far as Siloam with one attendant, and see for himself that the Jews were submissive to all other Romans and only bitter against Florus because of his appalling savagery. Going through the City Neapolitanus found proof enough of their docility; so he went up into the Temple. There he assembled the people, praised them highly for their loyalty to Rome, and urged them strongly to keep the peace. Then he made obeisance to the Sanctuary of God from the outer court[20] and returned to Cestius.

The Jewish crowd now turned to the king and the chief priests, begging them to send envoys to Nero to denounce Florus, and by protesting against his wholesale massacres to end suspicions of a Jewish revolt. For they would be thought to have started hostilities if they were not quick to point out the real aggressor. It was evident that they would not take it quietly if anyone tried to block the embassy. Agrippa realized that to choose men to accuse Florus would be to ask for trouble, but that to stand by till Jewish fury flared up into actual hostilities was dangerous even for himself. So he summoned the crowd into the Gymnasium[21] and placed his sister Berenice conspicuously on the roof of the Hasmonaean Palace. This was above the Gymnasium on the other side of the Upper City; the Gymnasium was linked with the Temple by a bridge. Then he began[22]:

'If I had found you all eager for war with the Romans, whereas in fact the most honest and sincere section of the people are bent on keeping the peace, I should not have come forward to address you or ventured to give advice, for it is a waste of breath to say anything in favour of a wise course when the audience is unanimously in favour of a foolish one. But some of you are young men with no experience of the horrors of war, others are too sanguine about the prospects of independence, and others are led on by selfish ambition and the profit to be made out of weaker men if the explosion occurs. So in the hope that these men may learn sense and change their ways, and that the folly of a few may not be visited on good citizens, I felt obliged to call you all together and tell you what I think is best. Please do not interrupt me if you disapprove of what I say; for those who have absolutely made up their mind to revolt will be free to feel the same after hearing my views, but my words will be lost even on those who want to listen unless everyone keeps quiet.

'Now I am aware that many rant against the insolence of the procurators and rhapsodize about the wonders of liberty; but before I go into the question of who you are and whom you are planning to fight, I must first sort out your jumble of pretexts. If you are trying to avenge your wrongs, why do you prate about liberty? If on the other hand slavery seems unbearable, it is a waste of time to blame your rulers; if they were the mildest of men, it would still be disgraceful to be slaves.

'Consider these pretexts one at a time, and see how feeble are your grounds for war. First, the charges against the procurators. You should flatter, not provoke, the authorities; when for trifling errors you pile on reproaches, it is yourselves you hurt by your denunciation of the offenders; instead of injuring you secretly and shamefacedly they plunder you openly. Nothing damps an aggressor like patient submission, and the meekness of the persecuted puts the persecutor to shame. I grant that the ministers of Rome are unbearably harsh; does it follow that all the Romans are persecuting you, including Caesar? Yet it is on them that you are going to make war! It is not by their wish that an unscrupulous governor comes from Rome, and western eyes cannot see the goings-on in the east; it is not easy in Rome even to get up-to-date news of what happens here.[23] It would be absurd because of the trifling misdemeanours of one man to go to war with a whole nation, and such a nation – a nation that does not even know what it is all about! Our grievances can be quickly put right; the same procurator will not be here for ever, and his successors are almost sure to be more reasonable.[24] But once set on foot, war cannot easily be either broken off or fought to a conclusion without disaster.

'As for your new passion for liberty, it comes too late; you ought to have made a supreme effort to retain it long ago. For the experience of slavery is a painful one, and to escape it altogether any effort is justified; but the man who has once submitted and then revolts is a refractory slave, not a lover of liberty. Thus the time when we ought to have done everything possible to keep the Romans out was when the country was invaded by Pompey. But our ancestors and their kings, with material, physical, and mental resources far superior to yours, faced a mere fraction of the Roman army and put up no resistance; will you, who have learnt submission from your fathers and are so ill provided compared with those who first submitted, stand up to the whole Roman Empire?

'Think of the Athenians. To preserve the liberty of Greece they once consigned their city to the flames. When proud Xerxes sailed across land and marched across water and counting the seas no barrier led an army too big for Europe to hold, they chased him away in a single ship like a runaway slave.[25] Near little Salamis they broke the might of Asia – and today they are slaves of Rome, and the city that once lorded it over Greece takes her orders from Italy! Think of the Spartans; after Thermopylae and Plataea, after Agesilaus who swept across Asia,[26] they are happy under the same masters. Think of the Macedonians. They still dream of Philip and see visions of the goddess[27] who with Alexander sowed for them the seeds of world-empire; yet they endure this complete transformation and loyally serve the new recipients of Fortune's favours. Other nations by the thousand, bursting with greater determination to assert their liberty, no longer resist. Will you alone refuse to serve the masters of the whole world?

'Where are the men, where are the weapons you count on? Where is the fleet that is to sweep the Roman seas? Where are the funds to pay for your expeditions? Do you think you are going to war with Egyptians and Arabs? Look at the far-flung empire of Rome and contrast your own impotence. Why, our forces have been worsted even by our neighbours again and again, while their arms have triumphed over the whole world! And even the world is not big enough to satisfy them; the Euphrates is not far enough to the east, or the Danube to the north, or Libya and the desert beyond to the south, or Cadiz to the west; but beyond the Ocean they have sought a new world, carrying their arms as far as Britain, that land of mystery. Why not face facts? Are you richer than the Gauls, stronger than the Germans, cleverer than the Greeks, more numerous than all the nations of the world? What gives you confidence to defy the power of Rome?

'It is terrible to be enslaved, it will be said. How much worse for Greeks, who surpass every nation under the sun in nobility and fill such a wide domain, and yet bow before the *fasces*[28] of a Roman governor, as do the Macedonians, who have a better right than you to demand their liberty! And what of the five hundred cities of Asia?[29] Do they not without a garrison bow before one governor and the consular *fasces*? Need I mention the Heniochi, the Colchians, and the Tauric race, the peoples near the Bosporus, the Black Sea, and the Sea of Azov?[30] At one time they recognized not even a native ruler, and now they submit to 3,000 legionaries, while forty warships keep the peace on the sea where before none but pirates sailed. How justly Bithynia, Cappadocia, Pamphylia, Lycia, and

Cilicia[31] might demand liberty! Yet without armed pressure they pay their dues.

'Then there are the Thracians, spread over a country five days' march in width and seven in length, more rugged and much more defensible than yours, a country whose icy blasts are enough to halt an invader. Yet 2,000 Roman guards suffice to maintain order.[32] Their neighbours the Illyrians, whose land extends from Dalmatia to the Danube frontier, need only two legions to keep them quiet; in fact Illyrians unite with Romans to halt Dacian raids.[33] The Dalmatians again, who have so often tried to shake off the yoke and have always been driven by defeat to rally their forces and revolt again, now live peaceably under one Roman legion!

'But if any people might reasonably be tempted to rebel by its peculiar advantages, that people is the Gauls, provided as they are with such marvellous natural defences, on the east the Alps, on the north the Rhine, on the south the Pyrenees, and on the west the Ocean. Yet in spite of these immense obstacles, in spite of their huge total of three hundred and five tribes, in spite of the prosperity that wells up from their soil and enables them to flood the whole world with their goods, they submit to being the milch cow of Rome and receiving from her hands what they themselves have produced! And this they tolerate, not from effeminacy or racial inferiority – they fought for eighty years[34] to save their liberty – but because they are overawed by the might of Rome and still more by her destiny, which wins her more victories than do her arms. So Gaul is kept in order by 1,200 soldiers – hardly more men than she has cities!

'Then Spain – in the fight for independence the gold from her soil could not save her, nor could the vast stretch of land and sea that separates her from Rome, nor the tribes of Lusitania and Cantabria with their passion for fighting, nor the neighbouring Ocean that terrifies even the natives with its tides. Crossing the cloud-capped Pyrenees and advancing their arms beyond the Pillars of Hercules,[35] the Romans enslaved Spain too. Yet to guard this remote and almost invincible nation requires but one legion!

'Which of you has not heard of the Germans, with their inexhaustible manpower? You have, I am sure, seen their magnificent physique on many occasions, for on every side Roman masters have German slaves; yet this people occupies an immense area, their physique is surpassed by their pride, from the bottom of their hearts they despise death, and when enraged they are more dangerous than the fiercest of wild beasts. Yet the Rhine is the limit of their aggression and the Romans with eight legions have tamed them, enslaving the prisoners and driving the entire nation to seek refuge in flight.

'Consider the defences of the Britons, you who feel so sure of the defences of Jerusalem. They are surrounded by the Ocean and inhabit an island as big as the land which we inhabit; yet the Romans crossed the sea and enslaved them, and four legions keep that huge island quiet. But why should I say more about that, when even the Parthians, the most warlike race of all, rulers of so many nations and protected by such vast forces, send hostages to Rome, and on Italian soil may be seen, humbly submitting for the sake of peace, the aristocrats of the east.[36]

'Almost every nation under the sun bows down before the might of Rome; and will you alone go to war, not even considering the fate of the Carthaginians, who boasted of great Hannibal and their glorious Phoenician ancestors, but fell beneath Scipio's hand? The Cyrenians (Spartans by descent), the Marmaridae (a race that extends to the waterless desert), Syrtes, whose very mention terrifies, Nasamonians, Moors, Numidians with their vast numbers[37] – none of them could resist Roman skill at arms. This third of the whole world, whose nations could hardly be counted, bounded by the Atlantic and the Pillars of Hercules, and supporting the millions of Ethiopia as far as the Indian Ocean, is subdued in its entirety; and apart from the regular crops which for eight months of the year feed the whole population of Rome, these peoples pay tribute of every kind, and for the needs of the Empire willingly submit to taxation; and unlike you they take no offence when given orders, though only a single legion is quartered in their midst.

'But why should we go so far for evidence of the Roman power when we can find it in Egypt, our nearest neighbour? She stretches as far as Ethiopia and Arabia Felix; she is the port for India; she has a population of seven and a half million (excluding the citizens of Alexandria), as is shown by the poll-tax returns. But she does not repudiate the rule of Rome – yet what a stimulus to revolt she has in Alexandria with its size, its population and its wealth! a city three and a half miles long and over a mile wide, which pays Rome every month more tribute than you pay in a year, and apart from money sends her corn for four months, and which is protected on every side by track-less deserts or harbourless seas or rivers or marshes. Yet none of these things proved equal to the fortune of Rome, and two legions stationed in the city curb the remotest parts of Egypt and the nobility of Mace-don as well.[38]

'Whom, I ask you, will you find in the uninhabited wilds to be your allies in this war? for in the inhabited world all are Romans – unless you extend your hopes beyond the Euphrates and imagine that your kinsmen from Adiabene will come to your aid![39] But they will not without good reason get involved in a full-scale war, and if they should decide on anything so foolish, the Parthian king would put a stop to it; for he is anxious to preserve his armistice with the Romans, and will consider it a breach of the truce if any of his tributaries takes the field against them.[40]

'So there is no refuge left except to make God your ally. But He too is ranged on the Roman side, for without His help so vast an empire could never have been built up. Think too how difficult it would be, even if you were fighting feeble opponents, to preserve the purity of your religion, and how you will be forced to transgress the very laws which furnish your chief hope of making God your ally, and so will alienate Him. If you observe the custom of the Sabbath with its complete cessation of activity, you will promptly be crushed, as were your ancestors by Pompey, who was most active in pressing the siege on the days when the besieged were passive.[41] But if in the war you transgress your ancestral Law I don't see what you have left to fight for, since your one desire is that none of your ancestral customs should be broken. How will you be able to call the Deity to your aid, if you deliberately deny Him the service that is due?

'Everyone who engages in war relies on either divine or human help; but when, as is probable, both are denied, the aggressor is bringing certain destruction on himself. What prevents you from killing your wives and children with your own hands and from consigning your ancestral home, the most beautiful in the world, to the flames? By such madness you would at least avoid the shame of defeat! It is wise, my friends, it is wise, while the vessel is still in harbour, to foresee the approaching storm, and not to sail out into the middle of the hurricane to sure destruction. For those on whom disaster falls out of the blue are at least entitled to pity, but a man who plunges into destruction with his eyes open earns only contempt.

'Possibly some of you suppose that you are making war in accordance with agreed rules, and that when the Romans have won they will be kind to you, and will not think of making you an example to other nations by burning down your Holy City and destroying your entire race. I tell you, not even if you survive will you find a place of refuge, since every people recognizes the lordship of Rome or fears that it will have to do so. Again, the danger threatens not only ourselves here but also those who live in other cities; for there is not a region in the world without its Jewish colony.[42] All these, if you go to war, will be massacred by your opponents, and through the folly of a few men every city will run with Jewish blood.[43] There would be an excuse for such a massacre; but if it did not take place, think how wicked it would be to take up arms against such kindly people! Pity your wives and children, or at least pity your mother city and its sacred precincts. Spare the Temple and preserve for your use the Sanctuary with its sacred treasures. For the Romans will no longer keep their hands off when they have captured these, since for sparing them hitherto they have received no thanks at all. I call to witness all you hold sacred, the holy angels of God, and the Fatherland we all share, that I have not kept back anything that is for your safety; if you make a right decision, you will share with me the blessings of peace, but if you are carried away by your passions, you will go without me to your doom.'

At the end of his speech he burst into tears as did his sister, and with his tears considerably damped the ardour of his hearers. But they shouted that it was not Rome they were fighting, it was Florus – the man who had done them such wrong. To this King Agrippa replied: 'But you have acted as if you were already at war with Rome; you have paid no tribute to Caesar[44] and you have cut down the colonnades leading to Antonia. You can refute the charges of insurrection by joining up the colonnades again and paying the tax; for, you know, Florus doesn't own the fortress, and Florus will not receive your money.'

Accepting this advice, the people with the king and Berenice went up into the Temple and began to rebuild the colonnades, while the magistrates and councillors went to the various villages and collected the tribute, quickly getting together the forty talents due. In this way Agrippa delayed for the moment the threatened war; but when he tried further to persuade the mob to obey Florus until Caesar sent a successor to replace him, they were furious and abused the king and announced his banishment from the City. Some of the insurgents even dared to throw stones at him. The king saw that the passions of the revolutionaries could no longer be controlled, and wounded by the insults he had received, he sent their magistrates and influential citizens to Florus at Caesarea, in order that he might choose some of them to collect the tribute from the countryside. Then he retired to his own kingdom.

CHAPTER 9
The Outbreak of War

MEANWHILE some of those most anxious for war made a united attack on a fort called Masada, captured it by stealth, and exterminated the Roman garrison, putting one of their own in its place.[1] At the same time in the Temple courts Eleazar, son of Ananias the high priest and a very confident young man, who was Temple Captain,[2] persuaded the ministers of the Temple to accept no gift or offering from a foreigner. This it was that made war with Rome inevitable; for they abolished the sacrifices offered for Rome and Caesar himself,[3] and in spite of the earnest appeals of the chief priests and prominent citizens not to cancel the customary offerings for the government they would not give in. Their numbers made them supremely confident, backed as they were by the toughest of the revolutionaries, but chiefly they pinned their faith on Eleazar, the Temple Captain.

The prospect of irreparable disaster brought together the leading citizens, the chief priests, and the most prominent Pharisees to discuss the crisis. They decided to try an appeal to the insurgents and summoned a public meeting in front of the Bronze Gate,[4] the eastern entrance to the inner courts of the Temple. They began by vehemently denouncing the folly of a revolt which would involve their country in total war, and went on to ridicule the pretext. Their ancestors had adorned the Sanctuary at foreign expense for the most part, never refusing a gentile gift, and so far from debarring any man from sacrifice, a most irreligious thing to do, had set up votive offerings all round the Temple in conspicuous and prominent positions. And now these men were inviting the Romans to intervene and courting disaster at their hands by an alien innovation in their religion, and apart from the danger were condemning the City as irreligious, if among the Jews alone no foreigner might sacrifice or worship. If this law was brought in to debar a single individual, they would be indignant at such organized inhumanity, but they cared nothing when the Romans and even Caesar were shut out! But there was a danger that if they abolished the sacrifices offered for Rome, they might be forbidden to sacrifice even for themselves, and that the City would be shut out of the Empire – unless they quickly recovered their common sense, restored the sacrifices, and wiped out the insult before it was reported to those they had insulted.

While they pleaded thus they brought forward priests with expert knowledge of the traditions, who testified that all their ancestors had accepted offerings from aliens. But none of the revolutionaries would listen and not even the Temple ministers came forward – they were too busy making war inevitable. So seeing that the insurrection was now beyond their control and that the vengeance of Rome would fall upon them first, the most influential citizens determined to establish their own innocence and sent delegations to Florus and Agrippa, the former led by Simon, son of Ananias, the other distinguished by the inclusion of Saul, Antipas, and Costobar, kinsmen of the king. They begged both to come to the City with large forces and suppress the insurrection before it got beyond control. Florus was delighted with the news, and in his eagerness to start the conflagration gave no answer to the delegates. But Agrippa, equally concerned for the rebels and their opponents, anxious to preserve the Jews for the Romans, and the Temple and capital for the Jews, and aware that he himself stood to lose by the strife, sent to the help of the people 2,000 horsemen from Auranitis, Batanaea, and Trachonitis[5] under Darius the cavalry commander and Philip, son of Jacimus, the general.

Thus encouraged the leading citizens, the chief priests, and all the peace-loving section of the populace occupied the Upper City, the Lower City with the Temple being in the hands of the insurgents. There followed an all-day exchange of stones from hand and sling, a continuous stream of missiles from both quarters. Sometimes they even sallied forth in company strength and fought hand to hand, the insurgents showing the greater courage, the king's troops the greater skill. The latter fought chiefly to get possession of the Temple and to drive out those who were polluting the Sanctuary, Eleazar and the insurgents to hold what they had and to capture the Upper City in addition. The result was seven days of mutual slaughter, without either side being dislodged from its original position.

The next day was the Feast of Wood-carrying, on which the custom was that everyone should bring wood for the altar, so that there should never be a lack of fuel for the fire which is always kept alight. The Jews excluded their opponents from this ceremony; but when an unarmed crowd poured in and with them numbers of the

Sicarii – brigands who took their name from a dagger carried in their bosoms – they joined forces with these ruffians and pressed their attacks more confidently. The king's troops, inferior now in numbers as well as courage, were driven out of the Upper City. Their opponents rushed in and burnt down the house of Ananias the high priest and the palace[6] of Agrippa and Berenice; then they took their fire to the Record Office, eager to destroy the money-lenders' bonds and so make impossible the recovery of debts, in order to secure the support of an army of debtors and enable the poor to rise with impunity against the rich. The keepers of the records fled and the building was set on fire. When the nerve-centre of the City had gone up in flames, the insurgents went after their foes. Some of the leading citizens and chief priests plunged into the sewers and disappeared from view, others with the king's troops fled to the Upper[7] Palace and lost no time in bolting the doors. Among these were Ananias the high priest, his brother Hezekiah, and those who had gone as delegates to Agrippa. So for the moment, satisfied with their victory and with the destruction they had wrought, the enemy called off the pursuit.

The next day however, the 15th of Loös, they assaulted Antonia, and after a two-day siege captured and killed the garrison and set fire to the fortress. Then they went off to the Palace where the king's men had taken refuge, and breaking up into four bodies began to assail the walls. None of the defenders dared attempt a sortie in face of the swarm of attackers; but they lined the breastworks and towers and pelted all who approached, so that many of the bandits fell at the foot of the walls. Night and day the struggle continued without a break, the insurgents hoping to starve out the defenders, the defenders to wear down the besiegers.

Meanwhile one Menahem, son of Judas the Galilaean, the very clever rabbi who in the time of Quirinius had once reproached the Jews for submitting to the Romans after serving God alone,[8] took his friends with him and went off to Masada,[9] where he broke open King Herod's armoury and distributed weapons to his fellow-townsmen and other bandits. With these as bodyguard he returned like a king to Jerusalem, put himself at the head of the insurgents, and took charge of the siege. But they had no engines, and to undermine the wall under the enemy's eyes was impossible while they were pelted from above. So starting at a distance they dug a mine as far as one of the towers, transferred the weight of the tower to wooden props, set the props on fire and withdrew. When the supports were burnt through the tower suddenly collapsed, only to reveal another wall built further back; for the defenders had detected the stratagem in good time – possibly the tower had moved while it was being undermined – and had furnished themselves with a second barrier. This unexpected sight was a bitter blow to the assailants, who had felt sure that victory was theirs already. However, the defenders sent to Menahem and the leaders of the insurrection, requesting leave to come out under an armistice. This was granted only to the king's troops and Jewish nationals, who then came out. Left unsupported, the Romans lost heart; they could not force their way through such a host, and were ashamed to ask for terms – besides, they might not be kept, even if granted. So they evacuated their camp as indefensible and fled to the King's Towers, Hippicus, Phasael, and Mariamme.[10] Menahem and his men charged into the position thus deserted, caught and killed all who had not been quick enough to escape, looted the baggage, and fired the camp. This happened on the 6th of Gorpiaios.

On the next day the high priest Ananias was caught hiding near the Palace canal,[11] and murdered by the bandits along with his brother Hezekiah. Then the insurgents invested the towers and kept guard so that no soldier should escape. But Menahem, his head swelled by the overthrow of such strong positions and by the high priest's death, turned to savagery, and thinking he had no rival in the conduct of affairs became unbearably tyrannical. Eleazar and his men rose against him,[12] agreeing that it was absurd to revolt from Rome for love of liberty and then hand over that liberty to a Jewish executioner and submit to a master who, even if not violent, was certainly inferior to themselves. If they must put everything in one man's hands, anyone would be preferable to this fellow! So they formed their plans and attacked him in the Temple when he entered in pomp to worship, decked with kingly robes, and followed by a train of armed Zealots.[13] Eleazar and his men rushed at him while the rest of the people seized stones and began to pelt the rabbi, thinking that his overthrow would put a final end to the revolt. Menahem and his men held out for a while, but when they saw the whole populace rushing towards them they fled in all directions. Those who were caught were massacred, those who hid were ferreted out. A very few escaped by slipping away to Masada, among them Eleazar,

son of Jairus, who was related to Menahem[14] and later became autocrat of Masada. Menahem himself fled to Ophel and while hiding
ignominiously there was taken alive, dragged into the open, and put
to death by prolonged torture. A like fate befell his lieutenants,
including the chief instrument of his domination, Absalom.

The people, as I said, took part in this massacre, in the hope of
suppressing the insurrection altogether; the conspirators were in no
hurry to end hostilities – it was for the sake of a free hand in the
campaign that they had put Menahem to death. In fact the more the
people urged them to abandon the siege of the soldiers, the more
vigorously they pressed it, until unable to hold out any longer
Metilius, the Roman commander, sent officers to Eleazar to ask only
that their lives should be guaranteed, as they were ready to surrender
their arms and all their possessions. The Jews jumped at the proposal
and sent to them Gorion, son of Nicomedes, Ananias, son of Zadok,
and Judas, son of Jonathan to promise them safety on oath. On this
Metilius marched the soldiers down. As long as they were armed the
insurgents left them alone and gave no sign of treachery; but when
as agreed they laid down their shields and swords, and without a
suspicion in their minds were marching away, Eleazar and his men
rushed at them, surrounded them and cut them down, while they
neither resisted nor begged for mercy, but merely appealed loudly to
the agreement and the oaths. Thus they were all brutally murdered
except Metilius, who begged for mercy and by promising to turn
Jew and even be circumcised managed to save himself alone.[15] This
setback meant little to the Romans, whose immense numbers were
unaffected by so trifling a loss, but to the Jews it seemed the prelude
to their destruction. They saw no way to undo the provocation they
had given for war; and the City was stained by such guilt that they
must expect a visitation from heaven if not the vengeance of Rome.
So there was universal lamentation and the streets were full of long
faces, every decent citizen being terrified at the prospect of paying
for the misdeeds of the insurgents. For it so happened that the
massacre was carried out on the Sabbath, on which for religious
reasons not even right deeds may be done.

On the same day and at the same hour, as if divinely ordained, the
people of Caesarea had massacred the Jewish colony, in less than an
hour slaughtering more than 20,000 and emptying Caesarea of the
last Jew; for those who might have escaped were seized by Florus

and sent in chains to the dockyards. This blow made the whole nation wild with anger, and parties sacked the Syrian villages and the neighbouring cities, Philadelphia, Heshbon, Gerasa, Pella, and Scythopolis. Next they swooped on Gadara, Hippus, and Gaulanitis, destroying some places and firing others. Then on to Kedasa near Tyre, Ptolemais, Gaba, and Caesarea. There was no resistance to their onslaughts in either Sebaste or Ascalon, both of which they burnt to the ground, going on to demolish Anthedon and Gaza.[16] Round each of these cities a number of villages were looted, and the adult captives mercilessly slaughtered.

The Syrians on their side killed just as many Jews; they too slaughtered those they caught in the cities, not only through hatred as before, but now to avert their own peril. The whole of Syria was filled with hopeless confusion, and every city was divided into two camps, the survival of the one depending on the destruction of the other. The days were spent in bloodshed, the nights – still more terrible – in fear. For though they thought they were rid of the Jews, every community was suspicious of Jewish sympathizers,[17] and while they hesitated to exterminate on the spot the doubtful element in their midst, they feared these nondescripts as much as complete foreigners. To the slaughter of their opponents even those who had always been deemed the most harmless of men were tempted by avarice; for they plundered the property of their victims with impunity, and as if from a battlefield carried off the spoils of the slain to their own homes, special honour being paid to the man who grasped the most, as if he had overcome more powerful enemies. The cities could be seen full of unburied corpses, the dead bodies of the aged flung down alongside those of infants, women without a rag to conceal their nakedness, and the whole province full of indescribable horrors. Even worse than the atrocities continually committed were the threats of terrors to come.

So far the Jews had been attacking foreigners, but when they raided Scythopolis[18] they found the Jews there opposed to them; for they lined up with the Scythopolitans, and treating their own safety as of more importance than the ties of blood, they joined battle with their countrymen. But suspicion was aroused by this excess of zeal – the citizens feared that these men would attack the city in the night and bring a great disaster upon them, in order to compensate their fellow-Jews for their failure to support them. So they ordered them, if they wished to prove their loyalty and demonstrate their fidelity to their foreign neighbours, to go with their families into the Grove. The Jews carried out the order, suspecting nothing, and for two days the Scythopolitans made no move, thus deceiving them into thinking themselves safe; but on the third night they watched their opportunity when some were off their guard and others asleep, slaughtered them all – more than 13,000 of them – and looted the property of the whole colony.

An account must be given of the fate of Simon, son of a not undistinguished father, Saul. His bodily strength and personal courage were exceptional, but to the injury of his countrymen he abused both. He went out every day and killed many of the Jews attacking Scythopolis; often he routed their whole army and won the battle almost unaided. But he was overtaken by the punishment he had deserved by the slaughter of his own flesh and blood. When the men of Scythopolis surrounded the Grove and began to shoot down the men inside, he drew his sword but made no move towards the enemy as he saw their overwhelming numbers. Instead he exclaimed with great emotion: 'It serves me right for what I have done – I and the rest who have murdered so many of our own kith and kin to prove our loyalty to you Scythopolitans. Small wonder we have found foreigners treacherous when we have utterly betrayed our own nation; so let us die in disgrace by our own hands; we are not fit to die by those of the enemy. The same act can be the punishment my foul deeds deserve and the proof of my courage, so none of my foes shall boast of my death or gloat over my body.' So saying he glanced round with a look of mingled pity and rage at his own family – wife, children, and aged parents. Then first seizing his father by his grey hairs he ran him through with his sword; next he killed his unresisting mother, and finally his wife and children, each of them almost falling on the sword, so eager were they to forestall the enemy. Then Simon, having gone through all his family, stood over the bodies in view of everyone, and raising his right hand aloft for all to see plunged the whole length of the blade into his own throat. We may well feel pity for the young man in view of his prowess and courage; but his trust in foreigners made his tragic end inevitable.

The wholesale slaughter at Scythopolis caused all the other cities to take arms against their Jewish colonies. In Ascalon 2,500 were put to death, in Ptolemais 2,000, and many were thrown into prison. At

Tyre large numbers were killed and still more put under lock and key. At Hippus and Gadara the same thing happened, the bolder spirits being destroyed and the timid kept in custody, and so with the other cities of Syria, according to the hate or fear with which each regarded the Jewish race. Only in Antioch, Sidon, and Apamea were the settlers spared, there being no inclination to kill or imprison any of the Jews. Perhaps their vast populations made them indifferent to the possibility of a Jewish rising, but the chief reason as it seems to me was pity for men in whom they detected no sign of revolution. At Gerasa not only were those who remained left unmolested, but those who wished to leave were escorted to the frontiers.

Even in Agrippa's kingdom a plot was formed against the Jews. He himself had gone to see Cestius Gallus at Antioch, leaving in charge of affairs a friend of his called Noarus, a blood-relation of King Soaemus.[19] Seventy men then came from Batanaea, citizens outstanding in birth and ability, to ask for an army so that, if there should be any disturbance in their district, they would have adequate forces to suppress the rising. Noarus sent out by night some of the king's heavy infantry and massacred all seventy, committing this dastardly crime without reference to Agrippa, and through his un-limited avarice deliberately playing the traitor to his countrymen, with calamitous effect on the kingdom. He continued to outrage the nation cruelly till Agrippa heard of his conduct, and though unwilling to hurt Soaemus' feelings by putting him to death, deprived him of his regency.

The insurgents seized a fortress called Cypros overlooking Jericho, exterminating the garrison and razing the defences to the ground. At about the same date the mass of Jews at Machaerus urged the Roman garrison to leave the fortress and hand it over to them. The Romans, afraid that it would be taken away from them by force, agreed to withdraw under a truce, and accepting the guarantees provided handed over the fortress, which was promptly occupied and gar-risoned by its inhabitants.[20]

At Alexandria there had been constant strife between the natives and the Jewish colony ever since Alexander, finding the Jews very ready to help against the Egyptians, rewarded their active support with permission to reside in the city with the same rights as the Greeks.[21] They retained this privilege under his successors who in addition assigned them a quarter for their exclusive use,[22] so that they could preserve their own way of life uncorrupted by needless contact with other races, and allowed them to call themselves Macedonians.[23] When the Romans became masters of Egypt, neither the first Caesar[24] nor any of his successors allowed the privileges granted to the Jews from Alexander's time onwards to be diminished. But there were continual clashes between Jews and Greeks, and as the authorities punished many of both sides, the strife became ever more acute. At this time, when everywhere else confusion reigned, the fires were fanned into flame in Alexandria too. It happened that the citizens were holding a public meeting to consider a proposal to send an embassy to Nero, when there poured into the amphitheatre along with the Greeks a great stream of Jews. As soon as they caught sight of them their opponents yelled: 'Enemy spies!'[25] Then they sprang up and went for them tooth and nail. Most of the Jews fled and dispersed, but three of them were seized and hauled off to be burnt alive. The whole Jewish colony sprang to their defence; first they pelted the Greeks with stones; then they snatched up torches and rushed to the amphitheatre, threatening to burn to death every single person there. And they would actually have done it had their ardour not been checked by Tiberius Alexander, the governor of the city.[26] He employed no force in his first attempt to teach them sense, but unobtrusively sent respected figures among them to appeal to them to desist and not provoke the Roman army to attack them. But treating this appeal with contempt the insurgents heaped abuse on Tiberius.

Realizing that nothing less than a major calamity would halt the rebels, he then let loose among them the two Roman legions, and with them 2,000 soldiers who happened to have come from Libya, with fearful consequences for the Jews. He gave the men leave not merely to kill them but also to plunder their property and burn down their houses. The soldiers rushed into the area called Delta where the Jews were concentrated, and proceeded to carry out their orders, but not without bloodshed on their own side; for the Jews stood shoulder to shoulder with their most heavily armed men in front and held their ground magnificently, but when once the line gave they were destroyed wholesale. Death came upon them in every form; some were overtaken in the open, others driven into their houses, which the Romans first looted and then burnt down. They felt no pity for infants, no respect for the aged; old and young were slaughtered right and left, so that the whole district was deluged with blood and 50,000 corpses were heaped up[27]; even the remnant would not have survived had they not begged for mercy till Alexander, pitying them, ordered the Romans to retire. They with their habitual obedience broke off the massacre on the instant, but the populace of Alexandria through the bitterness of their hate were disinclined to obey and could hardly be dragged away from the bodies.

Such was the calamity that befell the colony at Alexandria. Cestius felt the necessity of action now that on every side the Jews were involved in war. He set out from Antioch at the head of the Twelfth Legion[28] at full strength, 2,000 picked men from each of the others, six infantry cohorts, and four troops of cavalry,[29] reinforced by contingents sent by the kings, Antiochus[30] furnishing 2,000 horse and 3,000 foot, all bowmen, Agrippa the same number of foot and nearly 2,000 horse, while Soaemus followed with 4,000 men, of whom a third were mounted and the majority bowmen. With this force Cestius advanced towards Ptolemais. Very large reinforcements were collected from the cities. Their skill was inferior to that of the soldiers, but their enthusiastic hatred of the Jews made up for their lack of training. Agrippa was there in person to guide and advise Cestius. At the head of a portion of his troops Cestius marched against a stronghold in Galilee called Zebulon, a frontier town between Jewish territory and Ptolemais. This he found deserted, as the population had fled to the mountains; but it was full of valuables of every kind, which he allowed the soldiers to loot. The town, as he realized, was very beautiful, the architecture being similar to that of Tyre, Sidon, and Berytus, but he set fire to it nevertheless. Then he overran the district, looted everything he came across, burnt down the surrounding villages, and returned to Ptolemais. But while the Syrians, especially the men from Berytus, were busy looting, the Jews plucked up courage on learning that Cestius had gone, and swooping without warning on the units he had left behind destroyed about 2,000 men.

Cestius left Ptolemais and marched to Caesarea, sending part of his army ahead to Joppa. If they could surprise the city, they were to garrison it; if their approach was observed, they were to wait for him to bring up the rest of the army. However, they divided into two parties, and advancing rapidly by sea and land attacked from both directions and easily captured the city: the inhabitants had no time to escape, much less to prepare for battle, so the Romans burst in and slaughtered them all with their families, and looted and burnt the city. The number killed was 8,400. In the same way Cestius sent a large force of cavalry into the toparchy of Narbata, near Caesarea; they ravaged the land and destroyed a great number of the inhabitants, looting their property and burning down their villages.

He dispatched Caesennius Gallus, commander of the Twelfth Legion, to Galilee, giving him such forces as he thought sufficient to deal with that part of the country. He had an enthusiastic reception in Sepphoris,[31] the strongest city in Galilee, and the good sense shown there caused the other towns to remain quiet. The insurgents and bandits all fled to the mountain in the very middle of Galilee situated opposite Sepphoris and known as Asamon. Against these Gallus led his troops. As long as the Galilaeans held a position of advantage they easily repulsed the advancing Romans, killing some two hundred of them; but when the Romans by a turning movement reached higher ground still, they were quickly worsted; men lightly armed could not withstand heavy infantry in a hand-to-hand struggle, nor could they escape the cavalry when routed, so that while a few took advantage of the difficult ground to elude capture, the killed numbered 2,000.

Gallus saw no further signs of revolt in Galilee, so he led his army back to Caesarea. Cestius then set out with his whole force and entered Antipatris. There he learnt that in a town called Aphek a large force of Jews had collected; so he sent on a detachment to attack it. But before a blow was struck the Jews scattered in panic, leaving their camp open to the attackers, who burnt it with the surrounding villages. From Antipatris Cestius went on to Lydda, which he found empty; the whole population had gone to Jerusalem to keep the Feast of Tabernacles. Fifty of those who did appear were killed and the town burnt down; then Cestius continued his advance, climbed up through Beth-horon and encamped in a place called Gibeon, six miles from Jerusalem.

The Jews, seeing that war was now approaching the Capital, abandoned the Feast and rushed to arms; and with complete confidence in their numbers but without any organization they leapt boisterously into the fray, utterly disregarding the seventh day's rest, although this was the Sabbath, which they usually observed most carefully.[32] But the passion that shook them out of their piety carried them to victory in the battle; they fell upon the Romans with such fury that they drove a wedge into their ranks and charged through the gap, inflicting heavy casualties. Had not the cavalry, with those infantry units that were not too hard pressed, made a detour and come to the aid of the broken line, the whole of Cestius' army would have been in peril. The Romans lost five hundred and fifteen killed – four hundred infantry and the rest cavalry; the Jews twenty-two, of whom the most splendidly courageous were two kinsmen of Monobazus the king of Adiabene,[33] Monobazus and Cenedaeus, closely followed by the Peraean Niger and Silas the Babylonian; the latter had deserted to the Jews from King Agrippa, in whose army he had served. Their frontal attack halted, the Jews turned back to the City; but as the Romans went up the slope to Beth-horon Simon, son of Gioras,[34] fell upon them from behind, severely mauled their rearguard, and carried off numbers of their baggage-animals, which he then drove into the City. Cestius remained immobile for three days; meanwhile the Jews seized the heights and kept watch on the approaches, making it clear that they would react promptly if the Romans began to march.

At this point Agrippa, seeing that not even a Roman army was safe when such a huge enemy force occupied the hills around, decided to try an appeal to the Jews – either he would persuade them all to cease hostilities or he would detach the peace party from their opponents. He therefore chose from his staff the two men best known to the Jews, Borcius and Phoebus, and sent them to promise that Cestius would grant them a treaty, and to guarantee that the Romans would overlook their offences if they threw away their arms and made their submission. But the insurgents, fearing that in the hope of indemnity the entire host would accept Agrippa's terms, violently assaulted his emissaries. Before he had uttered a word, Phoebus was murdered: Borcius was wounded but managed to escape. Those citizens who protested at this outrage were attacked with stones and clubs and chased into the City.

Cestius, seeing that their internal divisions invited attack, brought up his entire army, routed the Jews, and pursued them to Jerusalem. He pitched his camp on Mount Scopus,[35] three quarters of a mile from the City, but for three days he launched no attack, perhaps expecting that the occupants would move towards surrender. Meanwhile he sent out many of his soldiers to seize corn in the surrounding villages. On the fourth day, the 30th of Hyperberetaios, he formed up his army and marched into the City. The people were under the thumb of the insurgents, and the insurgents, demoralized by the discipline of the Romans, withdrew from the outskirts of the City and retreated into the Inner City and the Temple. Cestius on arrival set fire to Bezetha (also known as 'The New City') and the Timber Market, and then went on to the Upper City and encamped in front of the Palace.[36] If he had chosen at that very hour to force his way inside the walls, the City would have been his immediately and the war brought to an end. But his camp prefect Tyrannius Priscus and most of the cavalry officers had been bribed by Florus[37] to turn him from the attempt; thus it came about that the war lasted so long and the Jews were overwhelmed by irretrievable disasters.

At this juncture many of the prominent citizens, at the suggestion of Ananus, son of Jonathan,[38] sent invitations to Cestius, assuring him that they would open the gates to him. He however, filled with anger, contempt, and incredulity, played for time until the insurgents, finding themselves betrayed, threw Ananus and his associates down from the wall, pelted them with stones and drove them into their houses, then formed a long line and showered missiles from the towers on those who were trying to climb the wall. For five days the Romans kept up their attacks from all directions and made no progress; on the next day Cestius, at the head of a large force of picked men and all the archers, began to assault the Temple from the north. The Jews resisted from the roof of the colonnade, and repeatedly drove back those who approached the wall, but at length they were overwhelmed by the hail of missiles and withdrew. The front rank of the Romans then rested their shields against the wall, and on these the second row rested theirs and so on, till they formed a protective covering known to them as a 'tortoise'.[39] When the missiles fell on this they glanced off harmlessly, so that the soldiers received no hurt as they undermined the wall and prepared to set the Temple gate on fire. Utter panic seized the insurgents, and many now began to run from the City in the expectation that it would fall at any moment. This served to revive the people's hopes, and as the scoundrels retreated, better men went forward to open the gates and welcome Cestius as a benefactor. If only he had persevered with the siege a little longer he would have captured the City at once; but I think that because of those scoundrels God had already turned His back even on the Sanctuary, and would not permit that day to witness the end of the war.

At any rate Cestius, aware neither of the despair of the besieged nor of the feelings of the people, suddenly called off his men, abandoned hope though he had suffered no reverse, and flying in the face of all reason retired from the City. In view of this change of plan the bandits' hopes revived, and dashing out to attack his rearguard they destroyed numbers of cavalry and infantry. That night Cestius passed in his camp on Mount Scopus; the next day by retreating still further he invited fresh attacks, and the enemy pursuing relentlessly inflicted many casualties on his rearguard. They also pushed ahead on both sides of the road and hurled their spears at both flanks of the column. The rear files dared not turn and face those who were striking them down from behind, as they thought an enormous army was pursuing them; and those who were attacking them from the flanks they did not venture to drive back, as they themselves were heavily armed and afraid to open their ranks, while they saw that the Jews were lightly armed and adapted for sudden swoops. This meant that they suffered severely without doing any corresponding damage to the other side. Throughout the march the battering continued, and men who lost their places in the column were killed. At last when many were dead, among them Priscus the commander of the Sixth Legion,[40] Longinus the tribune, and a cavalry officer named Aemilius Jucundus, they managed to reach their old camp at Gibeon, after abandoning the bulk of their baggage. There Cestius remained two days at a loss what to do; on the third, seeing the numbers of the enemy greatly swelled and all the ground on every side swarming with Jews, he realized that he had lost by the delay and that if he remained any longer he would have more enemies still.

To speed his flight he ordered everything that slowed down the column to be reduced to a minimum. The mules and asses were slaughtered and even the wagon-horses, except those conveying missiles and artillery; these they determined to keep for their own use, especially as they feared the Jews would capture them and turn them against themselves. Then Cestius led his army on towards Beth-horon. In the wide spaces the Jews pressed them less vigorously, but when they were crowded together in the defiles of the descending road, one group got in front of them and barred their egress, others pushed the rearmost down into the ravine, and the main body lined the high ground overlooking the waist of the pass and showered missiles on the massed Romans. At this point the infantry were unable to defend themselves, and the danger to the cavalry was still greater; for the infantry could not keep their formation and march down the road while being pelted, and the steep slope made it impossible for mounted men to charge the enemy; on both sides there were cliffs and ravines into which they fell to destruction. No one could find a way to flee or a means to defend himself; in their helplessness they turned to lamentation and despairing groans. The Jews retorted with cheers and shouts of mingled joy and rage; and they would certainly have captured Cestius and his whole army had not darkness descended, enabling the Romans to take refuge in Beth-horon, while the Jews ringed them in and waited for them to come out.

Despairing now of openly continuing the march, Cestius decided on ignominious flight. He picked out some 400 of his most courageous soldiers and posted them on the roofs, instructing them to shout the watchwords of the camp sentries so that the Jews would believe the entire force to be still in position. He himself with the rest of his men advanced without a sound three and a half miles. At dawn the Jews observed that the Roman quarters were empty, and rushing at the 400 who had tricked them quickly disposed of them with javelins, then set off in pursuit of Cestius. He had gained a long lead in the night, and as soon as it was light put on such a turn of speed that the soldiers in utter panic dumped the battering-rams and spear-throwers[41] and most of the other engines. These the Jews promptly seized, later using them against their original owners.[42] They pursued the Romans all the way to Antipatris but failed to catch them; so turning back they carried off the machines and despoiled the dead, collected the booty that had been left behind, and with hymns of victory marched back to the Capital. Their own casualties were negligible, but the Romans and their allies had lost 5,300 infantrymen and 480 cavalrymen killed. This action was fought on the 8th of Dios in the twelfth[43] year of Nero's reign.

CHAPTER 10

Josephus Governor of Galilee

AFTER the disastrous defeat of Cestius many prominent Jews fled from the City like swimmers from a sinking ship. Costobar with his brother Saul and Philip, son of Jacimus, the commander of King Agrippa's army, slipped out of the City and went over to Cestius. But their companion in the siege of the Palace, Antipas, declined to flee and was put to death by the insurgents, as I shall describe later.[1] Cestius sent Saul and his friends at their own wish to Nero in Greece,[2] to acquaint him with their own plight and to lay the blame for the war on Florus; Nero's anger against Florus would, he hoped, lessen the danger to himself.

At this time the people of Damascus, learning of the destruction of the Roman force, were eager to exterminate the Jews in their midst. As they had had them cooped up in the gymnasium for a long time now, taking this precaution as a result of suspicion, the task appeared perfectly simple; but they were afraid of their own wives, who had almost all gone over to the Jewish religion, so that their chief anxiety was to keep them in the dark. Accordingly they fell upon the Jews, crowded together and unarmed, and though they numbered 10,500, they slaughtered them all in one hour without any trouble.

Those who had pursued Cestius returned to Jerusalem, where by force or persuasion they won over those who still favoured Rome, and at a mass meeting in the Temple appointed additional generals for the army. They chose Joseph, son of Gorion, and the high priest Ananus[3] to take full charge of all arrangements in the City, with special responsibility for increasing the height of the walls.[4] Eleazar, son of Simon,[5] had in his possession the Roman booty and the money captured from Cestius, together with vast public funds; but they did not put him in charge of affairs as they saw that he had dictatorial tendencies, and that his Zealots[6] were behaving like an armed body-guard. Gradually, however, the shortage of money and Eleazar's trickery induced the people to submit to him completely. For Idumaea they chose two other generals, Jeshua, son of Sapphas, one of the chief priests, and Eleazar, son of the high priest Neus; the then governor of Idumaea, Niger, a native of Peraea, east of Jordan, and therefore known as the Peraean, was instructed to accept orders from these two. The rest of the country was not neglected: Joseph, son of Simon, was sent to take command at Jericho, Manasseh in Peraea, and John the Essene[7] in the toparchy of Thamna, to which were attached Lydda, Joppa, and Emmaus. The districts of Gophna and Acrabata were put under the command of John, son of Ananias, while both parts of Galilee were assigned to Josephus, son of Matthias,[8] together with Gamala, the strongest city in that area.

Each of these generals carried out the task assigned to him with all the energy and ability he possessed. Josephus on arriving in Galilee gave first priority to securing the good-will of the inhabitants, knowing that this would serve him in very good stead even if some things went wrong. He saw that he would win the support of the leading men if he shared his authority with them, and of the people in general if he issued his instructions mainly through the channel of well-known residents. So he chose seventy elderly men, the most sensible he could find in the country, and put them in charge of the whole of Galilee, appointing also seven magistrates in every town to settle petty quarrels, on the understanding that major disputes and cases of homicide should be referred to himself and the seventy. When he had made these rules for settling the internal problems of the cities, he turned his attention to their safety from external foes. Realizing that the Romans would invade Galilee first, he fortified the most defensible positions, Jotapata, Bersabe and Selame, Caphareccho, Japha and Sigoph, Mount Tabor, Tarichaeae and Tiberias, next fortifying the caverns[9] near Lake Gennesaret in Lower Galilee, and in Upper Galilee the rock called Acchabaron, Seph, Jamnith, and Mero. In Gaulanitis he strengthened the defences of Seleucia, Sogane, and Gamala. Only in Sepphoris were the citizens invited to build a wall on their own responsibility: Josephus saw that they had ample means and that their enthusiasm for the war needed no stimulus. In the same way Gischala was fortified by John, son of Levi,[10] on his own responsibility at the request of Josephus. The building of all the other strongholds was personally supervised by Josephus, who directed the work and himself lent a hand. He also raised in Galilee a force of over 100,000 young men, equipping them all with old weapons that he had got together.

Josephus knew that the invincible might of Rome was chiefly due to unhesitating obedience and to practice in arms. He despaired of providing similar instruction, demanding as it did a long period of training; but he saw that the habit of obedience resulted from the number of their officers and he now reorganized his army on the Roman model,[11] appointing more junior commanders than before. He divided the soldiers into different classes, and put them under decurions and centurions, those being subordinate to tribunes, and the tribunes to commanders of larger units. He taught them how to pass on signals, how to sound the advance and the retreat, how to make flank attacks and encircling movements, and how a victorious unit could relieve one in difficulties and assist any who were hard pressed. He explained all that contributed to toughness of body or fortitude of spirit. Above all he trained them for war by stressing Roman discipline at every turn: they would be facing men who had conquered almost the entire world by physical prowess and unshakable determination. He would feel certain of their soldierly qualities even before they went into action, if they refrained from their besetting sins of theft, banditry, and looting, from defrauding their countrymen, and from regarding as personal gain the misfortunes of their closest friends. For if those who went to war had a clear conscience, victory was certain; but men whose private life was smirched had not only human enemies but God to contend with. To this effect he exhorted them continually. The army he had raised and trained for battle numbered 60,000 foot and 250 horse, together with the troops he trusted most, about 4,500 professional soldiers. He had also 600 picked men as a personal bodyguard. Maintenance for all except the professionals was easily obtained from the towns, as only half the conscripts from each town served with the colours, the rest staying behind to supply them with rations; thus one party was detailed for combatant duty, the other for fatigues, and those who provided the food were repaid by the combatants with security.

While Josephus was busy organizing the defence of Galilee, there appeared on the scene a plotter from Gischala, the son of Levi, John by name, the most unprincipled trickster that ever won ill fame by such vicious habits. He began as a poor man and for a long time his propensities were held in check by lack of means; but being a ready liar and clever at winning the trust of his victims, he made a virtue of deceit and practised it on his closest friends, and while parading his humanity was prepared to murder anybody for his money; there was

no limit to his ambitions, but his hopes were nourished by contemptible misdemeanours. He started as a solitary bandit but later found
associates for his ventures, a handful at first but more and more
numerous as he grew more successful. He was careful to accept no
one who would give in easily, and chose men for their physique,
sticking-power, and military experience, till he got together a gang
four hundred strong, consisting mainly of outlaws from Tyre and the
neighbouring villages. With their help he plundered all Galilee and
preyed upon the masses, distracted as they were by the imminence
of war.

He already pictured himself as general or something greater still,
and only shortage of money kept him down. When he saw that
Josephus was delighted with his energy, he first persuaded him to
entrust him with the rebuilding of the walls of his home-town,
thereby enriching himself at the expense of the well-to-do. Next he
contrived a remarkable piece of roguery. Pretending that he wished to
save all the Jews in Syria from using oil from non-Jewish sources,[12] he
obtained leave to deliver it to them at the frontier. Then he cornered
the available supplies, paying Tyrian currency worth four Attic
drachmas for four amphoras[13] and reselling at eight times that price.
As Galilee is renowned for its olives and the harvest had been exceptional, John, by exploiting his monopoly and supplying large
quantities wherever there was a shortage, amassed untold wealth,
which he promptly used to injure the man who had put this commerce
in his hands.[14] Supposing that if he brought Josephus down he would
himself become master of Galilee, he ordered the members of his
gang to put still more vigour into their raids; in the general turmoil
that would follow, if the governor went to the rescue, he could be
ambushed and finished off; if he failed to deal with the gang, he could
be slandered to the people of the country. Finally he had long been
spreading a rumour that Josephus was betraying the country to
the Romans, and devising many similar expedients to bring him
down.

At this time some young men from the village of Dabarittha,
members of the guard stationed in the Great Plain, waylaid Ptolemy,
chief minister of Agrippa and Berenice, and robbed him of all his
baggage, which included a large quantity of expensive clothing, a
number of silver goblets and six hundred gold coins. Unable to dispose of the loot secretly they brought it all to Josephus at Tarichaeae.[15]

He condemned their violence to the king's servants, and deposited the stolen goods with the chief citizen of Tarichaeae, Annaeus, intending to take the first opportunity of restoring them to their owners. This was a most dangerous thing to do; for the robbers were furious at receiving no share of the loot, and realizing that Josephus meant to present the king and queen with the fruits of their labours, they hurried off to the villages at night and everywhere denounced Josephus as a traitor. They further put the neighbouring cities in an uproar, so that when day broke 100,000 armed men gathered to attack him. The crowd packed the hippodrome at Tarichaeae and filled the air with yells of rage, some clamouring to stone the 'traitor', others to burn him alive. The fury of the mob was whipped up by John, backed by Jeshua, son of Sapphias, then governor of Tiberias.[16] The friends and bodyguard of Josephus, terrified by the huge crowd out for blood, fled with the exception of four men. He himself was asleep and did not wake till the house was on the point of being set on fire. The four who had remained urged him to fly, but, though he saw himself alone in the midst of a howling mob, he showed no trace of fear. He sprang forward, his clothes rent and his head sprinkled with ashes, his hands behind him and his sword dangling from his neck. Seeing this his friends, especially the Tarichaeans, were sorry for him, but the country-folk and those from the neighbourhood who resented his rule heaped abuse on him, insisting that he should instantly produce the public money and admit his compact to betray them. For they had gathered from his appearance that he would not deny any of the things they suspected, and that it was in order to obtain pardon that he had grovelled thus abjectly.

But the real purpose of this self-abasement was to prepare the way for a stratagem by which he would induce his enraged critics to quarrel among themselves. He promised to give a full explanation of the actions that had angered them, and when he was given leave to speak he began: 'I had no intention of either returning this money to Agrippa or of lining my own pockets. I trust I shall never treat your enemy as my friend or turn the country's loss to private gain. But I saw that your city of Tarichaeae stood more in need of defence than other cities and that it could not build walls for lack of funds; and fearing that in Tiberias and other places people had their eyes on these spoils, I intended to keep the money and say nothing till I had given you the protection of a wall. If you are not satisfied, I will produce what was brought to me and give it you to share out. But if I have acted in your interest, why punish your benefactor?'

On hearing this the Tarichaeans expressed their approval, but the people of Tiberias and elsewhere yelled abuse and threats. Then both parties let Josephus alone and turned to each other, while he, confident of his new supporters – nearly 40,000 Tarichaeans – proceeded to address the whole throng in bolder terms. He condemned their head-strong behaviour in no uncertain fashion, and then declared that with the money in hand he would fortify Tarichaeae and provide equal security for the other cities as well. There would be no lack of funds if only they made up their minds whom they were going to fight, instead of letting fly at the man who provided the means.

At this the bulk of the deluded crowd withdrew, though still very angry; but 2,000 men rushed at him, weapons in hand, and though he got back into the house in time, they besieged the doors and shouted threats. In this crisis Josephus resorted to a second trick. He went up on the roof, silenced them with a gesture and declared that he had no idea what they wanted, as he could not hear when they all shouted at once. But he would do whatever they demanded, if they would send in a delegation to talk things over with him quietly. On hearing this the leading men and the magistrates came in. Josephus then dragged them into the inmost recesses of the house, shut the outer door and flogged them all till he had torn their flesh to ribbons. Meanwhile the mob waited outside thinking the delegates were arguing their case at length. But Josephus suddenly flung open the doors and pushed the men out covered with blood, striking such terror into the threatening crowd that they threw down their weapons and fled.

This triumph made John more jealous still, and he framed a second plot against Josephus. Feigning sickness, he sent a letter begging his permission to seek a cure by taking the hot baths at Tiberias. Not yet suspecting a plot, Josephus wrote to his representatives in the city to accommodate John and provide everything necessary.[17] John made himself comfortable, and two days later got his scheme under way. Deceiving some and bribing others, he strove to induce the citizens to revolt from Josephus. When this came to the ears of Silas, whom Josephus had appointed guardian of the city, he reported the plot to his superior without a moment's delay. Josephus, on receiving this dispatch, set off on a swift night march which brought him at dawn to Tiberias, where he was met by the whole population except John.

John had little doubt that this visit was directed against him; nevertheless he sent one of his friends to make the excuse that he was unwell and confined to bed, and so could not pay his respects. But when Josephus had collected the citizens in the stadium and was trying to tell them about the report he had received, John quietly sent armed men with orders to assassinate him. These men drew their swords, but the people saw what was coming and gave a shout. Hearing the noise Josephus swung round, and seeing the bare steel within inches of his throat took a flying leap on to the beach – while addressing the people he had been standing on a mound nine feet high – and jumping into a boat moored near by with two members of his bodyguard made a dash for the middle of the lake.

His soldiers instantly seized their weapons and charged the conspirators. Then Josephus, fearing that if civil war broke out through the jealousy of a few the city would be ruined, sent a message to his men that they were only to see to their own safety, and neither kill anybody nor bring the guilty to trial. In obedience to this injunction the soldiers refrained from action; but when the people of the neighbourhood learnt of the plot and of the person responsible, they massed together to deal with John. He however slipped away in time and fled to Gischala, his home-town. From every city in Galilee the people streamed to the support of Josephus till the number swelled to thousands and thousands of armed men, who proclaimed that they had come to settle accounts with John, the enemy of the nation; they would burn him alive, and burn any city that received him. Josephus expressed his appreciation of their loyalty but restrained their fury, choosing to outwit his enemies rather than to kill them. He found out the names of those in every city who had revolted with John, their fellow-citizens being delighted to give the information, and made a public announcement that anyone who failed to sever his connection with John in the next five days would have his property seized and his house burnt together with his family. The immediate result was that 3,000 deserted John, came to Josephus and threw down their weapons at his feet, while with the rest, about 2,000 Syrian outlaws, John again took refuge in secret plots, abandoning open hostilities. He sent messengers to Jerusalem by stealth to allege that Josephus was growing too powerful, and to say that he might at any moment set himself up as dictator in the Capital itself, if his attempt was not forestalled.

The people were prepared for this story and took no notice; but

leading citizens, including some of the magistrates, were moved by
jealousy to send money secretly to John, so that he could raise a force
of mercenaries and make war on Josephus. They further issued a
decree on their own authority recalling him from his command; but
as they doubted its validity they dispatched 2,500 armed men with
four distinguished citizens, Joesdrus son of Nomicus, Ananias son of
Zadok, and Simon and Jude sons of Jonathan, all gifted speakers, in
order to deprive Josephus of popular support. If he came quietly, they
were to let him give an account of himself; if he insisted on remaining,
they must treat him as an enemy. Josephus had been warned by his
friends that an army was on the way, but the reason was not explained
as his enemies had taken their decision in secret. The result was that he
took no countermeasures, and four towns promptly went over to the
other side, Sepphoris, Gabara,[18] Gischala, and Tiberias. But he quickly
recovered these without the use of force,[19] and then by stratagems got
the four commanders into his hands and sent them back with the most
efficient of their soldiers to Jerusalem. They met with a most hostile
reception from the people, who would have killed them and those
who had sent them out, had they not immediately fled.

From that time on John was kept within the walls of Gischala by
fear of Josephus. A few days later Tiberias again revolted,[20] the
citizens having called in King Agrippa. Agrippa failed to arrive on the
date fixed, but a few Roman cavalry turned up unexpectedly that
very day and the gates were shut against Josephus. He was at Tarichaeae, where he was promptly informed of this revolt; but he had
sent out all his soldiers in search of food, and could neither take the
field alone against the rebels nor stay where he was, for fear that this
delay might enable the royal troops to slip into the city before him.
Furthermore he would be unable to make any move on the next day
owing to the Sabbath restrictions. However, he thought of a ruse to
circumvent the rebels. He ordered the gates of Tarichaeae to be shut,
to prevent any warning of his intentions from reaching those he was
planning to attack; then he collected all the boats there were on the
lake – two hundred and thirty, with not more than four sailors in
each – and made at full speed for Tiberias. He kept far enough from
the city to make clear vision impossible, ordering the vessels to ride
in deep water unmanned, while he himself with only seven armed[21]
guards went near enough to be seen. On sighting him from the walls
his opponents, who had not ceased to vilify him, were so amazed

that they assumed that all the craft were packed with armed men, flung down their weapons, and waving olive-branches begged him to spare the city.

Josephus gave vent to threats and reproaches. First, after taking up arms against Rome they were dissipating their strength beforehand in civil strife and so playing into their enemies' hands; secondly, they were striving to get rid of their one bulwark against destruction, and were not ashamed to close their city to the architect of its defences. Nevertheless he declared his willingness to receive a delegation that would offer an apology and co-operate in making the city secure. Ten citizens at once came down, the most important men in Tiberias. These he took on board one of the vessels and carried out to sea; fifty others, leading members of the city council, he ordered to come forward, on the ground that he wished to obtain a pledge from them. Then, by inventing one pretext after another, he called out group after group as if to arrange terms. As the boats were filled he ordered the masters to make with all speed for Tarichaeae and to clap the men into prison. In this way the whole council, 600 strong, and about 2,000 private citizens were arrested and conveyed in boats to Tarichaeae. The remainder shouted that the real author of the revolt was one Clitus, and urged Josephus to vent his wrath on him. Josephus was anxious to put no one to death; so he ordered Levi, one of his guards, to step ashore and cut off Clitus' hands. The soldier, taking fright, refused to go alone into the hostile crowd. At this Josephus boiled with rage and was on the point of jumping overboard to carry out the sentence himself when Clitus, watching from the beach, besought him to leave him one of his hands. Josephus agreed, on condition that he cut off the other himself, whereupon Clitus drew his sword with his right hand and cut off his left; so completely had Josephus terrified him. Thus with unmanned boats and seven guards the whole population was made prisoner and Tiberias brought back to its allegiance. But a few days later Josephus found that the city had revolted again in conjunction with Sepphoris, so he handed it over to the soldiers to pillage. However, he collected all the plunder and gave it back to the townspeople. He did the same at Sepphoris; for he subdued that town as well and decided to give the citizens a sharp lesson by pillaging it, and then by giving back their possessions to recover their good-will.

In Galilee all was now quiet, and abandoning internal dissension the people turned to preparations for war with Rome. In Jerusalem Ananus the high priest and all the leading men who did not favour Rome were repairing the walls and piling up munitions. All over the City they were forging missiles and suits of armour, most of the young men were receiving haphazard training, and there was tumult everywhere. Among the more stable, however, there was utter dejection; many saw only too well the approaching calamity and openly lamented. There were omens too, which to the peace-lovers portended disaster, but for which those who had lit the fires of war could easily invent a happy interpretation. In fact the whole condition of the City before the arrival of the Romans proclaimed the coming destruction. Ananus, indeed, nourished the hope that, if he gradually abandoned the preparations for war, he would incline the insurgents and the crazy men called 'Zealots' to take a wiser course; but he yielded to their violence, and his tragic end will be related below.[22]

Finally, in the toparchy of Acrabata Simon, son of Gioras, collected a large band of revolutionaries and gave himself up to pillage. He not only looted the houses of the rich, but he ill-used them personally; and it was evident from the start that his aim was despotism.[23] When a force was sent against him by Ananus and the magistrates, he fled with his followers to the bandits at Masada, and there till the death of Ananus and his other enemies he remained, joining in the pillage of Idumaea and forcing the authorities there, in view of the number murdered and the constant raids, to muster an army and garrison the villages. So much for events in Idumaea.[24]

CHAPTER 11

The Coming of Vespasian and Titus

WHEN Nero was informed of the reverses in Judaea he was naturally filled with consternation and alarm. This he was careful to conceal, treating the matter in public with anger and contempt: it was the commander's negligence, he said, not the enemy's prowess, that had caused the trouble. No doubt he felt that the majesty of empire obliged him to treat bad news with lordly disdain and to show himself superior to all eventualities. Nevertheless the turmoil of his spirit was betrayed by his furrowed brow. He was wondering to whom he could entrust the East in its disturbed state, with responsibility for punishing the Jewish upheaval and preventing the spread of the infection to the surrounding nations. He found no one but Vespasian equal to the task and capable of undertaking a war on such a tremendous scale. Vespasian had been a soldier all his life and was now a veteran [1]; years before he had pacified the West and crushed the rebellion against Rome which the Germans had provoked; by force of arms he had added Britain,[2] till then unknown, to the empire, so enabling Nero's father[3] Claudius, who had not lifted a finger himself, to celebrate a triumph.

Such a record was highly auspicious, and a man of Vespasian's age and experience could obviously be trusted. His sons moreover were hostages for his good faith, and being in the prime of life could provide the hands if their father provided the brains.[4] Perhaps also God was already planning the future of the world. For whatever reason, Nero sent this man to assume command of the armies in Syria, paying him in view of the urgent situation every smooth compliment that necessity can suggest. From Greece, where he was on Nero's staff, Vespasian dispatched his son Titus to Alexandria to fetch the Fifteenth Legion[5] from there; he himself crossed the Dardanelles and travelled overland to Syria. There he concentrated the Roman forces and large allied contingents provided by the neighbouring kings.

After the defeat of Cestius the Jews were so elated by their unexpected success that they were wild with excitement, and as if carried off their feet by this stroke of luck they determined to send their armies further afield. Without loss of time all their most warlike elements joined forces and marched to Ascalon. This is an old town sixty miles from Jerusalem, though the Jews hated it so bitterly that when they made it the object of their first attack it seemed much nearer than that! The expedition was led by three men of unequalled prowess and ability, Niger from Peraea, Silas the Babylonian, and John the Essene. Ascalon was strongly fortified, but the defenders were miserably few; it was garrisoned by a cohort of foot and one troop of horse, commanded by Antonius.[6]

The Jews in their fury marched at a most unusual pace, and as if their starting-point had been quite near they suddenly appeared before the city. Antonius however had been well aware of their approach: he led out his cavalry, and in utter disregard of the numbers and determination of the enemy stood up manfully to their first onslaught and beat off an attack on the wall. When raw levies were confronted by veteran troops, infantry by cavalry, undisciplined individuals by regulars who fought as one, men with nondescript weapons by fully armed legionaries, men guided by passion rather than reason by men who instantly responded to every signal, the issue could never be in doubt. When once the front ranks of the attackers were broken, they were routed by the cavalry and collided with units pushing forward from behind to assault the wall. Thus Jew fought Jew till the entire mass gave way before the cavalry charges, and scattered all over the plain. This was very large and ideal for cavalry tactics, a fact which weighted the scales in favour of the Romans and led to frightful carnage on the Jewish side; for the fugitives were headed off and turned back, and when they were herded together in their flight the horsemen charged right through and slaughtered them by the hundred. Whichever way they turned the Romans encircled them, group by group, and as they galloped round struck them down with javelins that could not miss.

In spite of their vast numbers, the Jews felt in their helpless state that they were terribly alone; the Romans were succeeding so wonderfully that, few as they were, they never doubted that they actually outnumbered the enemy. The Jews battled against their reverses, ashamed of their swift defeat and hoping for a change of fortune; the Romans relentlessly followed up their success. So the struggle continued till dusk, by which time 10,000 Jewish soldiers had fallen with two of their commanders, John and Silas. The survivors, wounded for the most part, with the one general left, Niger, fled to a little town in Idumaea called Chaallis. Roman casualties in this encounter amounted to a few men wounded.

So far from being broken-hearted by this fearful disaster, the Jews were stimulated by defeat to still greater determination, and disregarding the dead bodies at their feet they were lured by their earlier successes to a second disaster. Without even waiting for their wounds to heal they mustered all their forces and with greater fury than before, and much greater numbers, tore back to Ascalon. But together with their inexperience and other military deficiencies their old ill luck went with them. For Antonius laid ambushes in the passes, and taking no precautions they fell into these traps. Before they could take up battle stations they were encircled by the cavalry and again lost over 8,000. The survivors all fled, including Niger, who during the flight gave many proofs of his heroism. In the end the enemy pressure drove them into a strong fort in a village called Belzedek. Antonius and his men, to avoid wearing themselves out in an assault on this almost impregnable fort or else leaving the enemy's heroic commander alive, lit a fire at the foot of the wall, and the fort was soon ablaze. The Romans then withdrew, satisfied that Niger had perished with it, and blissfully unaware that he had leapt down from the fort and escaped into a cave in the very centre of the position. Three days later his friends were seeking his body in order to bury it and were lamenting aloud when they heard a muffled voice. Niger emerged, and joy undreamed-of filled every Jewish heart: had not the providence of God preserved him to lead them into battle again?[7]

At Antioch, the capital of Syria and by virtue of its size and prosperity undoubtedly the third city of the Roman Empire, Vespasian had found King Agrippa awaiting his arrival with the whole of his own army. He put himself at the head of all the available forces and advanced swiftly to Ptolemais.[8] There he was met by the inhabitants of Sepphoris, the only people in Galilee who desired peace. With their own safety and Roman supremacy in mind, they had already before Vespasian arrived given guarantees to Caesennius Gallus, received his assurances, and admitted a garrison.[9] Now they gave an enthusiastic reception to the supreme commander and pressed him to accept their help against their own countrymen. In response to their request he allotted them for the time being a defensive force of horse and foot, adequate in his opinion to defeat any incursions the Jews might choose to make; for he thought it would seriously endanger the campaign he was about to open if he lost Sepphoris, the biggest city in Galilee, ideally sited to be a bulwark against attack and to keep the whole area quiet.

There are two Galilees, known as Upper and Lower, shut in by Phoenicia and Syria. They are bounded on the west by Ptolemais with its border region and Carmel, a mountain that once belonged to Galilee but now belongs to Tyre; adjoining Carmel is Gaba, known as Cavalry Town because King Herod's cavalry settled there on their discharge.[10] The southern limit is formed by Samaritis and Scythopolis as far as the streams of Jordan, the eastern by the districts of Hippus, Gadara, and Gaulanitis, where Agrippa's kingdom begins. Beyond the northern frontier lie Tyre and the Tyrian lands. Lower Galilee stretches in length from Tiberias to Zebulon, the neighbour of Ptolemais on the coast, in breadth from the village of Xaloth in the Great Plain to Bersabe. Here begins Upper Galilee, which stretches in width as far as Baca, a village on the Tyrian frontier; in length it extends from Meroth to Thella, a village near Jordan.

Small as they are, and encircled by such powerful foreign neighbours, the two Galilees have invariably held out against enemy attack; for the Galilaeans are fighters from the cradle and at all times numerous, and never has cowardice afflicted the men or a declining population the country. The whole area is excellent for crops or cattle and rich in forests of every kind, so that by its adaptability it invites even those least inclined to work on the land. Consequently every inch has been cultivated by the inhabitants and not a corner goes to waste. It is thickly studded with towns, and thanks to the natural abundance the innumerable villages are so densely populated that the smallest has more than 15,000 inhabitants.[11]

In short, it may be true that Galilee is smaller in size than Peraea, but it takes the palm for productivity; for the whole country is cultivated, and fruitful from end to end, while Peraea though much greater in extent is mostly a stony desert, too wild to produce cultivated crops. Some parts however have workable soil that can bear crops of every kind, and in the plains grow trees of many species, those chiefly planted being the olive, vine, and palm. The country is watered by mountain torrents, and by perennial springs that suffice even in the dog-days[12] when the torrents dry up. In length it stretches from Machaerus to Pella, in breadth from Philadelphia to the Jordan.[13]

Pella, just mentioned, forms the northern boundary, Jordan the western; the southern limit is Moab, and on the east it shares a frontier with Arabia, Silbonitis, Philadelphia, and Gerasa.

Samaritis lies between Galilee and Judaea; beginning at a village in the Great Plain called Ginaea, it ends at the toparchy of Acrabata. In character it is exactly like Judaea: both are made up of hills and plains, with soil easily worked and amply repaying cultivation. They are well wooded and prolific in fruit, both wild and cultivated; for nowhere is the soil arid by nature and rain is generally ample. All their streams are remarkably sweet, and lush grass is so plentiful that the milk-yield of their cows is exceptionally heavy. The final proof of their outstanding productivity is the swarming population of both countries.

On their common frontier lies the village of Anuath Borceos, the limit of Judaea on the north. The southern region, to go to the other end, terminates at a village close to the Arabian frontier known as Jardan to the Jews of the locality. In breadth it stretches from the River Jordan to Joppa. Right in the middle lies the City of Jerusalem, so that some have quite appropriately called her the navel of the country. Judaea is not cut off from seaside delights, since it has a coastal strip that stretches all the way to Ptolemais.[14] It is divided into eleven districts, of which the royal City, Jerusalem, has the primacy, raised above the whole neighbourhood as the head above the body. The other districts or toparchies are less highly esteemed. Gophna ranks second, followed by Acrabata, Thamna, Lydda, Emmaus, Pella,[15] Idumaea, Engedi,[16] Herodium, and Jericho. We must include also Jamnia and Joppa, which control their neighbourhood, and finally the Gamala district, Batanaea and Trachonitis, though they are in Agrippa's dominions. These begin at Mount Lebanon and the sources of the Jordan, and in width stretch to Lake Tiberias, in length from a village called Arpha to Julias.[17] The population is a mixture of Jews and Syrians.

The foregoing must serve as the briefest possible description of Judaea and its neighbours.

The support that Vespasian sent to Sepphoris consisted of 1,000 horse and 6,000 foot, commanded by the tribune Placidus. After camping in the Great Plain the force divided, the foot moving into the city as a garrison and the horse remaining encamped outside. Both arms made a series of sorties, overrunning the whole district and doing great damage to Josephus and his men. If they remained inactive in their towns, the surrounding country was plundered; whenever they ventured to sally forth, they were driven back. Josephus actually assailed the city in the hope of capturing it, though before it seceded from the Galilaeans he had himself fortified it so strongly that even the Romans would have found it almost impregnable; and so the attempt failed, for he proved too weak to bring Sepphoris over to his side either by force or by persuasion. Moreover he provoked more vigorous attacks on his country; night and day in retaliation for his attempt the Romans ceaselessly ravaged the plains and plundered the villagers' belongings, killing everyone fit to bear arms and enslaving those who could not resist. From one end of Galilee to the other there was an orgy of fire and bloodshed; no horror, no calamity was spared; the only safety for the fugitive inhabitants was in the towns which Josephus had fortified.

Titus meanwhile had sailed from Greece to Alexandria in less time than is usual for a winter crossing. There he took over the force for which he had been sent, and marching at a great pace quickly reached Ptolemais. There he found his father, and to the two legions that accompanied him, the world-famous Fifth and Tenth, he united his own Fifteenth.[18] To these legions were attached eighteen cohorts; they were joined also by five cohorts and one troop of horse from Caesarea,[19] and five troops from Syria. Of the cohorts ten were 1,000 infantry strong, the other thirteen 600 infantry and 120 cavalry. A large allied contingent was also contributed by the kings, Antiochus, Agrippa, and Soaemus each providing 2,000 unmounted bowmen and 1,000 horse, while the Arab Malchus sent 1,000 horse as well as 5,000 foot, most of them bowmen. Thus the whole force, cavalry and infantry, including the men contributed by the kings, totalled 60,000,[20] apart from servants who followed in great numbers and who, in view of their sharing in the military training, ought not to be distinguished from the combatants – in peace they always took part in their masters' exercises, in war they shared their dangers, so that in skill and prowess none but their masters surpassed them.

The Romans showed remarkable foresight in making their domestic staff useful to them not only in the services of everyday life but also in war. Anyone who will take a look at the organization of their army in general will recognize that they hold their wide-flung empire as the prize of valour, not the gift of fortune. They do not wait for war to begin before handling their arms, nor do they sit idle in peacetime and take action only when the emergency comes – but as if born ready armed they never have a truce from training or wait for war to be declared. Their battle-drills are no different from the real thing; every man works as hard at his daily training as if he was on active service. That is why they stand up so easily to the strain of battle: no indiscipline dislodges them from their regular formation, no panic incapacitates them, no toil wears them out; so victory over men not so trained follows as a matter of course. It would not be far from the truth to call their drills bloodless battles, their battles bloody drills.

They never give the enemy a chance to catch them off their guard; for whenever they invade hostile territory they rigidly refuse battle till they have fortified their camp. This they do not construct haphazardly or unevenly, nor do they tackle the job with all their manpower or without organized squads; if the ground is uneven it is thoroughly levelled, then the site is marked out as a rectangle. To this end the army is followed by a large number of engineers with all the tools needed for building. The inside is divided up ready for the huts. From outside the perimeter looks like a wall and is equipped with towers evenly spaced. In the gaps between the towers they mount spear-throwers, catapults, stone-throwers, and every type of ordnance, all ready to be discharged. Four gates are constructed, one in each length of wall, practicable for the entry of baggage-animals and wide enough for armed sorties, if called for. The camp is divided up by streets accurately marked out; in the middle are erected the officers' huts, and in the middle of these the commander's headquarters, which resembles a shrine. It all seems like a mushroom town, with market-place, workmen's quarters, and orderly-rooms where junior and senior officers can settle disputes as they arise. The erection of the outer wall and the buildings inside is accomplished faster than thought, thanks to the number and skill of the workers. If necessary a ditch is dug all round, six feet deep and the same width.

The fortifications completed, the men go to their quarters unit by unit in a quiet and orderly manner. All other duties are carried out with attention to discipline and security, wood, food, and water as required being brought in by the units detailed. They do not have supper or breakfast just when they fancy at their individual discretion, but all together. Times for sleep, guard-duty, and reveille are announced by trumpet-calls, and nothing whatever is done without orders. At dawn the private soldiers report by units to their centurions, the centurions go to their tribunes to salute them, and the tribunes accompany all their superior officers to headquarters, where the commander-in-chief, in accordance with routine, gives them the password and other orders to communicate to their subordinates. They act in the same orderly way on the battlefield, changing direction promptly as required, and whether attacking or retreating move as one man.

When camp is to be struck, the trumpet sounds and every man springs to his duty. Following the signal huts are instantly dismantled and all preparations made for departure. The trumpet then sounds 'Stand by to march!' At once they load the mules and wagons with the baggage and take their places like runners lined up and hardly able to wait for the starter's signal. Then they fire the camp, which they can easily reconstruct if required, lest it might some day be useful to the enemy. For the third time the trumpets give the same signal for departure, to urge on those who for any reason have been loitering, so that not a man may be missing from his place. Then the announcer, standing on the right of the supreme commander, asks three times in their native language whether they are ready for war. They three times shout loudly and with enthusiasm 'Ready', hardly waiting for the question, and filled with a kind of martial fervour they raise their right arms as they shout. Then they step off, all marching silently and in good order, as on active service every man keeping his place in the column.

The infantry are armed with breastplate and helmet and carry a blade on each side; of these by far the longer is the one on the left,[21] the other being no more than nine inches long. The general's bodyguard of picked infantry carry lance and buckler, the other units javelin and long shield, together with saw and basket, axe and pick, as well as strap, reaphook, chain, and three days' rations, so that there is not much difference between a foot-soldier and a pack-mule! The cavalryman carries a long sword on his right hip and an enormous pike in his hand, a shield slanted across his horse's flank, and in a quiver slung alongside three or more darts, broad-pointed and as big as spears. Helmets and breast-plates of infantry pattern are worn by all arms. Equipment is exactly the same for the general's mounted bodyguard as for the other cavalry units. Lots are always drawn for the legion that is to head the column. So much for Roman routine on the march and in quarters, and for the variety of equipment.

In battle nothing is done without plan or on the spur of the moment; careful thought precedes action of any kind, and to the decisions reached all actions must conform. As a result they meet with very few setbacks, and if anything does go wrong, the setbacks are easily cancelled out. They regard successes due to luck as less desirable than a planned but unsuccessful stroke, because victories that come of themselves tempt men to leave things to chance, but forethought, in spite of occasional failures, is good practice in avoiding the same mistake. Good things that come of themselves bring no credit to the recipient, but unfortunate accidents that upset calculations have at least this comfort in them, that plans were properly laid.

Military exercises give the Roman soldiers not only tough bodies but determined spirits too. Training methods are partly based on fear; for military law demands the death penalty not only for leaving a post but even for trivial misdemeanours; and the generals inspire more fear than the law, since by rewarding good soldiers they avoid seeming harsh towards the men they punish. So complete is their submission to their superiors that in peace they are a credit to Rome and in the field the whole army is a single body; so knit together are their ranks, so flexible their manoeuvres, so ready their ears for orders, their eyes for signals, their hands for the tasks to be done. Thus it is that they are as quick to act as they are slow to give way, and never was there an engagement in which they were worsted by numbers, tactical skill, or unfavourable ground – or even by fortune, which is less within their grasp than is victory. When planning goes before action, and the plans are followed by so effective an army, who can wonder that in the east the Euphrates, in the west the ocean, in the south the richest plains of Africa, and in the north the Danube and the Rhine are the limits of the Empire? One might say with truth that the conquests are less remarkable than the conquerors.

The purpose of the foregoing account[22] has been less to eulogize the Romans than to console their defeated enemies and to deter any who may be thinking of revolt; and possibly those of an enquiring frame of mind who have not studied the matter may find it useful to get an insight into the Roman military set-up. This is all that I propose to say on the subject.

While Vespasian with his son Titus spent some time at Ptolemais organizing his forces, Placidus swept through Galilee destroying great numbers of men who fell into his hands, these being the feebler members of the Galilaean community and the faint-hearted. Then seeing that the warlike spirits regularly took shelter in the towns that Josephus had fortified, he set out to attack the strongest of them, Jotapata, in the expectation that it would easily fall to a surprise assault. This would establish his reputation with his superiors and greatly improve their chances in the coming campaign; for the other towns would take fright and surrender once the most powerful had gone. But his hopes were completely dashed. As he approached Jotapata the citizens saw him in good time and laid an ambush before the town. Then they pounced upon the unsuspecting Romans. With superior numbers, ready for battle and eager to ward off the danger that menaced their homes, their wives, and their children, they routed them at once. Many Romans were wounded but only seven killed, thanks to the orderliness of their retreat, the superficial nature of their wounds (their bodies being completely protected), and the fact that the Jews launched their missiles at long range and with their light armour dared not close with heavy infantry. Jewish casualties did not exceed three killed and a handful wounded. So Placidus decided that to attack the town was beyond his strength, and took to his heels.

Vespasian, eager to invade Galilee himself, set out from Ptolemais with his army arranged in the usual Roman marching order. The light-armed auxiliaries and bowmen formed the vanguard, with orders to repel sudden enemy rushes and reconnoitre woods suspected of concealing ambushes. Next came a body of heavy-armed Roman troops, mounted and unmounted. These were followed by ten men from every century carrying, besides their own kit, the instruments for marking out the camp-site. After them came roadmakers to straighten out bends in the highway, level rough surfaces, and cut down obstructive woods, so that the army would not be exhausted by laborious marching. In the rear of these the personal baggage of the commander and his senior officers was concentrated under the protection of a strong cavalry force, behind which rode Vespasian himself with the cream of his horse and foot and a body of spearmen. Next came the legionary cavalry; for each legion has its own troops of 120 horse. These were followed by the mules that carried the battering-rams and other artillery. After them came the generals, the prefects of the cohorts, and the tribunes, with a bodyguard of picked troops, and behind them the standards surrounding the eagle, which is at the head of every legion, as the king of birds and most fearless of all: this they regard as the symbol of empire and portent of victory, no matter who opposes them. The sacred emblems were followed by the trumpeters, and in their wake came the main body, shoulder to shoulder, six men abreast, accompanied as always by a centurion to maintain the formation. The servants of every legion marched in a body behind the infantry, looking after the soldiers' baggage carried by the mules and other beasts. In the rear of all the legions marched the bulk of the mercenaries,[23] followed by a protective rearguard of light and heavy infantry with a strong body of cavalry.

Marching in this way Vespasian arrived with his army at the frontiers of Galilee. There he pitched his camp, and restraining his soldiers' ardour for battle he made a show of force to inspire terror in the enemy and give them time for second thoughts in the hope that before battle was joined they would change their minds; at the same time he got ready to besiege their strongholds. The sight of the commander-in-chief did indeed lead to second thoughts in many, and to terror in them all. The troops of Josephus who were in camp not far from Sepphoris, seeing the war approaching and the Romans on the point of swooping upon them, did not wait for a battle but even before seeing their opponents fled in all directions. Left behind with a handful of men, Josephus saw that he had not got a force capable of stopping the enemy, that the morale of the Jews had collapsed, and that if they could get the Romans to trust them, the majority would be only too pleased to ask for terms. He already saw disaster looming ahead, but for the time being he decided to keep as far away as possible from danger, and with those who had stuck to him sought shelter in Tiberias.

Vespasian descended on Gabara, and finding it almost without defenders took it at the first assault. He marched into the town and put to the sword all except small children, the Romans showing mercy to neither young nor old through hatred of the nation and the memory of the way they had treated Cestius. He burnt down not only the town itself but all the hamlets and villages around. Some of these he found completely abandoned; from others he carried off all the occupants as slaves.

Josephus' hurried arrival produced panic in the city he had chosen as a refuge. The people of Tiberias concluded that if he had not completely written off the war, he would never have taken to flight. In this they were perfectly right about his opinion; for he saw the inevitable end awaiting the Jews, and knew that their one safety lay in a change of heart. He himself, he felt sure, would be pardoned if he went over to the Romans, but he would rather have died over and over again than betray his motherland and flout the trust reposed in him in order to make himself at home with those he had been sent to fight. So he determined to write a detailed appreciation of the situation for the Jerusalem authorities, without either exaggerating the strength of the enemy and so later finding himself abused as a coward, or minimizing it and thereby reviving their hopes just when they were having second thoughts. He suggested that if they were ready to sue for terms, they should write back at once; if they were determined to fight the Romans, they must send him adequate forces.²⁴ Having set down these proposals he dispatched the letter to Jerusalem by express messengers.

Vespasian was eager to destroy Jotapata; for he was informed that the biggest number of the enemy had taken refuge there, and that in addition it was a strong base for their activities. He therefore sent infantry and cavalry ahead to level the road, which was a stony mountain track, difficult for infantry and for cavalry quite impossible. They took only four days to complete their task, opening a broad highway for the army. On the fifth day – the 21st of Artemisios – Josephus left Tiberias and slipped into Jotapata just in time, awakening new courage in the sinking hearts of the Jews. Vespasian heard the good news of his arrival from a deserter, who urged him to attack the city with all speed, for when it submitted all Judaea would submit, provided Josephus fell into his hands.²⁵ Vespasian seized on this news as a most marvellous piece of luck. It must be by divine providence that the man who was considered the most able of his enemies had put his own head into the noose. Without losing a moment he sent 1,000 horsemen under Placidus and the decurion Aebutius, a man with a reputation for energy and ability, with orders to put a ring round the town and prevent the secret escape of Josephus. Next day the general himself followed with his entire force, and after marching till dusk arrived before Jotapata. He led the army to the north of the town and pitched his camp on rising ground three quarters of a mile from the walls, trying to make himself as conspicuous as possible in order to demoralize the enemy. The effect was immediate, and so overwhelmed the Jews that no one dared to go outside the walls. The Romans did not feel inclined to make their onslaught at once, after marching all day, but they put a double line of infantry round the town, stationing a third line outside them, formed from the cavalry, and so blocking all the enemy's means of egress. Thus robbed of all hope of escape, the Jews were stimulated to deeds of daring; for in war there is nothing like necessity to rouse the fighting spirit.

Next morning the assault began. At first the Jews stood their ground, remaining where they were encamped before the wall opposite the Romans.[26] So Vespasian brought up against them his bowmen and slingers and all who were equipped with long-range weapons, with instructions to keep up a barrage while he himself with the infantry pushed up the slope where the wall was easy to surmount. Then Josephus, seeing disaster threaten the city, made a vigorous sortie at the head of the whole Jewish garrison. Falling in a body on the Romans they drove them back from the wall, performing many remarkable deeds of prowess and daring. However, the enemy's losses were equalled by their own; the Jews were spurred on by the hopelessness of their situation, the Romans just as effectively by a sense of shame; one side was armed with experience as well as prowess, the other had no weapon but animal courage, no captain but blind fury. All day long they were locked in battle till night parted them. Roman casualties were very heavy, and included thirteen killed: on the Jewish side the dead numbered seventeen and the wounded six hundred.

On the next day the Romans attacked again, and the Jews, sallying out against them, met their advance with greatly increased determination, emboldened by their surprisingly effective resistance on the previous day. But they found the Romans too more aggressive than before; for shame put them into a blazing passion and they considered a failure to win quickly equivalent to a defeat. For five days the Roman attacks were incessant, and the sallies of the defenders and their fighting on the walls grew more and more determined; the Jews were not dismayed by the strength of the enemy, nor the Romans put off by the difficulty of capturing the town.

Jotapata is almost entirely perched on a precipice, cut off on three sides by ravines of such extraordinary depth that when people look down into them their sight cannot reach the bottom.[27] The only access is from the north, where the town is built up to the lowest slope of the mountain. This slope Josephus had included when he built the walls, so that the enemy could not occupy the ridge which commanded the town. A ring of heights screened this so effectively that until a man was actually inside, it could not be seen at all. Such were the bastions of Jotapata.[28]

Vespasian was not going to be defeated either by the natural strength of the place or by the daring resistance of the Jews; he determined to prosecute the siege more vigorously and called a meeting of senior officers to plan the assault. It was resolved to build a platform against the approachable section of the wall, so Vespasian sent out the whole army to collect material. The heights round the town were stripped of their trees, and along with the timber a mountain of stones was piled up. Then as a shelter from missiles descending from above a second party erected a line of hurdles supported by uprights and constructed the platform under their shelter, the bombardment from the walls causing few if any casualties. A third party tore up the hillocks near by and kept up a constant supply of earth to the builders. Thus with the men working in three groups nobody was idle. Meanwhile the Jews launched great rocks from the walls on to the enemy's screens, together with every kind of missile; even when they failed to reach their mark the noise was frightful and hindered the work.

Vespasian next set up his artillery in a ring – a hundred and sixty engines in all – and gave instructions to bombard the men on the wall. In a synchronized barrage the catapults shot lances into the air, and stones weighing nearly a hundredweight were discharged from stone-throwers, together with firebrands and a dense shower of arrows, driving the Jews not only from the wall but also from the area inside traversed by the missiles; for a host of Arab bowmen with all the javelin-men and slingers let fly at the same time as the artillery. The defenders, however, though unable to retaliate from the ramparts, were by no means idle. They made swift sallies in company strength guerrilla-fashion, tore away the screens that sheltered the working-party, and assailed them in their unprotected state; and whenever the Romans retired, they broke up the platform and set light to the uprights and hurdles. This continued till Vespasian realized that the lack of continuity in the earthworks was the cause of the trouble, since the gaps provided the Jews with an avenue of attack. He then linked the screens together and at the same time concentrated his forces, bringing to an end the Jewish penetrations.

As the platform was now rising and had almost reached the battlements, Josephus, thinking it disgraceful if he failed to invent some counter-device to save the town, collected stone-masons and instructed them to raise the wall higher. When they declared that it was impossible to build under such a hail of missiles, he devised protection for them as follows. He ordered the men to fix railings to the wall and over these to stretch raw oxhides, so that when the stones hurled by the engines fell on them, they would give without splitting; other types of missile would glance off them and firebrands would be quenched by their moisture. Thus protected the builders worked in safety day and night. They raised the wall to a height of thirty feet, built towers on it at short intervals, and completed it with a stout parapet. At this the Romans, who had fancied themselves already inside the town, were plunged into despondency; the resourcefulness of Josephus and the determination of the defenders amazed them. Vespasian was exasperated both by the cleverness of the stratagem and by the fearlessness of the townsmen, who, encouraged by the new fortifications, resumed their night sorties against the Romans and in the daytime engaged them at company strength. Every device of guerrilla war was brought into play, everything in their path was plundered, and the rest of the besiegers' works were set on fire. At length Vespasian recalled his troops from the battle and determined to blockade the town till starvation forced it to surrender; for the defenders would either be compelled by lack of provisions to beg for mercy, or if they held out to the bitter end, would die of starvation. He was confident that he would overwhelm them much more easily on the battlefield if he waited awhile and made a fresh onslaught when they were exhausted. He therefore ordered watch to be kept on the sally-ports.

Inside there was plenty of corn and all other necessities except salt, but the water-supply was inadequate as there was no spring within the walls and the townsfolk depended on rainwater – and little or no rain falls in the district during summer. As it was at that season that the siege took place, they were terribly despondent at the prospect of having nothing to drink, and fretting already as if the water-supply had failed completely. For Josephus, seeing that the town had all other necessities in abundance and that morale was high, and wishing to pin down the besiegers longer than they expected, had rationed his men's drink from the beginning. They, however, found this husbanding of resources harder to bear than actual shortage; unable to please themselves, they felt the craving the more acutely and began to flag as if they had already reached the last degree of thirst. Their condition could not be hidden from the Romans. From the rising ground they looked over the wall and saw the Jews collecting in one spot to receive their water-ration; so they made this spot the target for their spear-throwers, causing very heavy losses. Vespasian hoped that before long the tanks would be empty and the surrender of the town would inevitably follow. But Josephus, determined to shatter this hope, ordered numbers of men to soak their outer garments and hang them round the battlements, so that the whole wall suddenly ran with water. The result was despondency and consternation in the Roman ranks, when they saw such a quantity of water thrown away in jest by men who were thought to have nothing to drink. The commander-in-chief himself despaired of capturing the town through shortage and reverted to armed onslaught. Nothing could have pleased the Jews better; for they had long despaired of saving the town or themselves, and dreaded hunger and thirst far more than death in battle.

Josephus, however, devised a second stratagem to obtain more supplies that he needed. Down a gully leading to the western part of the valley, well-nigh impassable and consequently neglected by the Roman guards, he sent out messengers who delivered letters to Jews outside with whom he wished to make contact and brought back their answers, together with ample supplies of all the necessities that the town lacked. The messengers were instructed to crawl past the guard-posts as a rule, and to cover their backs with sheepskins so that if anyone did see them in the night they would be mistaken for dogs. But after a while the pickets detected the device and blocked the gully.

CHAPTER 12

Josephus the Prisoner of Vespasian

AT this point Josephus realized that the town could not hold out long
and that his own survival was doubtful if he stayed, so he discussed
with the leading citizens how they could escape. The people saw
what was afoot and poured round him, imploring him not to forget
that they depended on him alone. He was the one hope of survival
for the town if he stayed; if it fell, he would be their one comfort. It
would be unforgivable in him to run away from his enemies and
abandon his friends – to leap overboard when the ship on which he
had embarked in a calm was tossed by a storm. For he would sink
their town, as no one would venture to oppose the enemy any more,
once their only source of confidence was gone. Josephus concealed
his anxiety for his own safety and declared that it was for their sakes
he was arranging to leave. By staying in the town he could give them
little help if they survived; if they fell into enemy hands, he would
be but one more victim. On the other hand, by escaping from the
siege he could send them help from outside on the greatest scale; he
would at once assemble an army from the whole of Galilee, and by a
diversionary campaign draw off the Romans from their town. He
did not see how by staying with them he could be of any use to them
in present conditions. The most likely result would be to drive the
Romans to increase the vigour of the siege, as their chief desire was
to capture him. If on the other hand they learnt that he had fled, they
would greatly reduce the pressure on the town.

This appeal fell on deaf ears; it simply made the people more
determined to hold on to him. Children, old men, women with infants in their arms wept and fell down before him. They all grasped
him by the feet and held him fast, imploring him with sobs to remain
and share their lot – not through envy of his escape, I think, but in
the hope of their own; for they felt perfectly safe so long as he remained. Josephus realized that if he yielded, no further appeals would
be made, but that if he refused he would be watched. Furthermore his
determination to desert them was badly shaken by pity for their tears.
So he made up his mind to stay, and turning the general despair into a

weapon he exclaimed: 'Now is the time to begin the fight, when there is no hope of escape left. It is a glorious thing to win renown at the cost of one's life, and by some splendid deed to make oneself remembered by future generations.' Then he fell to work, and making a sortie with his toughest fighters he scattered the guards and dashed as far as the Roman camp, where he tore to pieces the skin tents which sheltered the troops on the platforms and set fire to their works. The next day and the day after that he repeated his exploit, and for many days and nights he fought on without rest.

Vespasian saw that the Romans were damaged by these sorties. They felt sore at being worsted by Jews, and when the Jews were worsted, pursuit was hampered by the weight of their armour. Again, the enemy after striking their blow always got back to the town before the Romans could retaliate. He therefore ordered the legionaries to avoid Jewish attacks and not become involved with men who wanted to die. Nothing was so productive of heroism as despair, but like a fire without fuel their enthusiasm would fizzle out when there was no new target for their attacks. And even Romans should avoid needless risks in winning their victories, since they were fighting not for survival but to enlarge their dominions. He made the Arab bowmen and the Syrian slingers and stone-throwers[1] bear the brunt of the Jewish onslaughts, and kept most of his artillery constantly in action. These did such damage that the enemy had to give way, but once inside the minimum range of the far-flung missiles they assailed the Romans furiously without a thought for life or limb, exhausted units being constantly replaced by fresh waves of attackers.

As time dragged on and the sorties continued, Vespasian felt it was he who was being besieged, and as the platforms were now getting near the walls he decided to bring up 'the ram'.[2] This is a huge baulk like the mast of a ship, fitted at the end with a great lump of iron in the shape of a ram's head, whence the name. It is supported at the middle, like the beam of a balance, by ropes passing over another baulk which rests on posts fixed on the ground on either side. The ram is drawn back by a great number of men, who then with a gigantic united heave swing it forward again so that it strikes the wall with the projecting iron. The first blows may be ineffective, but no wall is so thick that it can stand up to a prolonged battering. This was the method the Roman commander resolved to adopt in his anxiety to take the town by storm; for the blockade was sapping the vigour of his army and the Jews had the initiative. So in order to bring within range the Jews on the wall who were trying to stop them, the Romans pushed forward their catapults and other artillery and began to bombard them. The bowmen and slingers moved forward at the same time. As a result no one dared mount the rampart, and this enabled other troops to bring up the ram under the protection of overlapping hurdles covered with skins to safeguard both men and machine. The very first blow rocked the wall, and piercing shrieks were raised by those within, as if the town had been captured already.

Under the relentless battering of the same spot, Josephus saw that at any moment the wall would be laid flat, so he devised a scheme to counter for a time the force of the machine. Sacks were to be filled with chaff and lowered by ropes to the spot where they saw that the next blow was coming, so that the head would be deflected and the blows cushioned into ineffectiveness. This tactic held up the Romans completely, for to whatever spot they directed their engine, the defenders above put their sacks in the way and intercepted the strokes, so that the impact did no damage to the wall – till the Romans retaliated by attaching reaping-hooks to the ends of long poles and cutting down the sacks. The effectiveness of the battering-ram was thus restored, and the wall, so recently built, began to give way; so now Josephus and his helpers had recourse to fire. Setting light to all the dry wood they could lay their hands on, they rushed out in three columns and made a bonfire of the enemy's engines, hurdles, and platforms. The Romans made little effort to save them: they were paralysed by the Jews' astonishing courage and beaten by the flames in their race to the rescue. For the wood was dry, and mixed with bitumen, pitch, and even brimstone, so that the flames flew in every direction faster than thought, and what had cost the Romans many hours of toil was consumed in a single hour.

In this struggle one of the Jews distinguished himself in a way that calls for very special mention. His father's name was Samias, his own Eleazar, and his birthplace Saba in Galilee. This man raised a huge stone and flung it from the wall at the battering-ram with such tremendous force that he broke off its head. Then he leapt down and seizing the head under the noses of the enemy carried it back to the wall without turning a hair. A target now for all his foes and with no armour to protect his body from the rain of missiles, he was pierced by five shafts; but paying not the slightest regard to them he climbed the wall and stood there for all to admire his daring; then writhing with the pain of his wounds he fell to the ground with the head of the ram still in his grip. Most conspicuous for courage after him were two brothers, Neiras and Philip, from the village of Ruma, Galilaeans like Eleazar. They charged the ranks of the Tenth Legion, falling upon the Romans with such dash and fury that they broke through their lines and routed all who stood in their path.

Inspired by their example Josephus and the rest of the defenders again snatched up firebrands and set light to the engines, shelters, and constructions of the Fifth Legion and the routed Tenth. The other units were quick to cover their tackle and all their timber with earth. In the evening they again set up the ram and brought it against the place where the earlier battering had weakened the wall. At this juncture one of the defenders on the battlements hit Vespasian with an arrow in the sole of his foot. The wound was superficial, as the impact of the shaft was weakened by the long range, but the occurrence produced the utmost consternation in the Roman ranks; for the sight of the blood badly shook those nearest to Vespasian, and the news ran through the whole army, with the result that most of the men forgot the siege and in dismay and terror came running towards their commander. First to arrive was Titus, in fear for his father's life, so that the rank and file were agitated both by their regard for their leader and by the evident distress of his son. However it was quite easy for the father to put an end to his son's fears and the consternation of the army. Rising above his pain and showing himself instantly to all who were alarmed on his behalf, he stimulated them to yet more furious onslaughts; every man in his eagerness to avenge his commander was anxious to be in the forefront of danger, and shouting encouragement to each other they dashed towards the wall.

Josephus and his men, although falling in heaps under the barrage of spears and stones, clung stubbornly to the battlements and with fire, steel, and stones continued to pelt those who under cover of their hurdles were swinging the ram. But they accomplished little or nothing, and they themselves were continually falling, because the enemy could see them without being seen; for their own fires lit them up from every side, making them as conspicuous a target for the enemy as in daylight, and since the engines were too far off to be visible, it was difficult to avoid the missiles. The force of the spear-throwers and catapults was such that a single projectile ran through a row of men, and the momentum of the stones hurled by 'the engine'[3] carried away battlements and knocked off corners of towers. There is in fact no body of men so strong that it cannot be laid low to the last rank by the impact of these huge stones. The effectiveness of 'the engine' can be gathered from incidents of that night: one of the men standing near Josephus on the rampart got into the line of fire and had his head knocked off by a stone, his skull being flung like a pebble from a sling more than six hundred yards; and when a pregnant woman was struck in the belly on leaving her house at daybreak, the unborn child was carried away a hundred yards; so tremendous was the power of that stone-thrower. Even more terrifying than the actual engines and their missiles was the rushing sound and the final crash. There was a constant thudding of dead bodies as they were thrown one after another from the rampart. Within the town rose the terrible shrieks of the women, echoed from without by the groans of dying men. The whole strip of ground that encircled the battlefield ran with blood, and it was possible to climb up the heap of corpses on to the battlements. The din was made more terrifying by the echoes from the mountains around, and on that night nothing was wanting that could horrify ear or eye. Hundreds of those engaged in Jotapata's death-struggle fell like heroes; hundreds were wounded. Not till the time of the morning watch did the wall yield to the continual blows of the artillery; and then the Jews filled the breach with their bodies and their weapons to block the way before the Romans could rush the scaling-gangways into position.

At daybreak Vespasian assembled his army for the final assault, refreshed by a short rest after the toils of the night. As he wished to draw off the defenders from the breaches, he dismounted the pick of his horsemen and ranged them in three groups against the gaps in the wall, completely encased in armour and with long spears in rest, in order that as soon as the gangways were in position they might force the first entry. Behind them he ranged the flower of his infantry. (The rest of the cavalry he extended opposite the wall across the whole slope to intercept any man who might escape when the town was captured.) Still further back he stationed the bowmen in a curving line, ordering them to have their arrows ready to discharge; the slingers and artillerymen received similar instructions. Other men were to carry ladders and set them up against the undamaged portions of the wall, in the hope that some Jews in their efforts to hold them off would abandon the defence of the breaches, while the rest would be forced by the deluge of missiles to leave the way in unguarded.

Josephus, realizing what was afoot, stationed the older men and the battle-weary on the undamaged parts of the wall, where they were unlikely to suffer any hurt: where the wall had been broken through he posted the fittest of his men, each group headed by six officers, among whom he himself drew a place in order to be in the thick of the fight. He issued instructions that when the legions raised their battle-cry, the men were to stop their ears to avoid panic, and when the hail of arrows fell, they were to bend double under cover of their long shields and withdraw a little way, until the bowmen had emptied their quivers. But as the gangways fell into position they were to leap forward at once, hurling themselves at the enemy across his own apparatus. Every man must fight to the death, not for a birthplace that could still be saved, but for one that was already lost yet must be avenged. 'Picture to yourselves,' he concluded, 'old men butchered, women and children slaughtered by the foe at any moment now. These impending disasters arouse fury in your breasts. Seize that fury and hurl it against those who will cause the disasters.'

Such were the arrangements Josephus made for the two classes of defenders. But when the useless section of the community, the women and children, saw the triple line that encircled the town – none of the guards posted earlier had been moved into the battle – and saw too before the fallen ramparts the enemy, sword in hand, and the slope above them flashing with arms, and above them again the arrows of the Arab bowmen, they raised a last united shriek at their capture, as if ruin was no longer a threat but a present reality. Josephus, for fear that their lamentation might weaken the resolution of their menfolk, locked them in their homes, threatening them with punishment if they did not hold their tongues. Then he strode into the breach and took his stand where the lot had fallen to him. Of those who were bringing up the ladders elsewhere he took no notice, his thoughts intent on the coming rain of arrows.

At one and the same moment the trumpets of all the legions blared and a hair-raising battle-cry burst from ten thousand throats. This was the signal for a volley of arrows from every side that darkened the sky. Not forgetting Josephus' instructions the men under him stopped their ears against the shout and shielded their bodies from the volleys;

as the gangways were dropped into position, they charged over them
before the men who were dropping them could set foot on them.
Then pouncing upon the enemy as they struggled up, they gave a
magnificent display of prowess and fighting spirit, striving in the
midst of utter ruin to prove themselves the equals of those who with
so much less at stake showed such remarkable courage. No one broke
off his struggle with an opponent until one or the other was dead.
But while the Jews were being steadily worn out by the non-stop
battle and were unable to replace their front-line officers, on the
Roman side exhausted units were relieved by fresh troops, and as
soon as one group was forced back another came forward; they
cheered each other on, and standing shoulder to shoulder under cover
of their long shields they formed an unbreakable mass,[4] which with
the whole formation pushing as one man forced the Jews up the slope
and a minute later would have been on the wall.

The situation was critical, and Josephus taught by necessity – always
quick to improvise when despair applies the spur – ordered boiling
oil to be poured on the soldiers under the shields. As his men had it
ready, numbers of them from every side poured quantities of it on the
Romans, followed by the vessels still hissing from the flames.[5] Scalded
and burnt, the Romans broke up their formation and in agonizing
pain rolled down from the wall; for the oil instantly ran under their
armour and over their entire bodies from head to foot, consuming
their flesh as relentlessly as a fire, being by nature quick to grow hot
and slow to cool because of its fattiness. Imprisoned in their cuirasses
and helmets they could not escape from the scalding fluid. Leaping
into the air and contorted with pain they fell from the wooden
bridges one after another, while those who retired ran into their own
men as they pressed forward, making themselves an easy target for
the enemy shafts.

The Romans in their sorry plight displayed as much fortitude as
ever, the Jews as much resource. The Romans, though they saw the
pitiable sufferings of those who had been drenched with oil, continued
their relentless advance against those who had drenched them, everyone abusing the man in front for blocking his way. The Jews, however, employed a second ruse, to trip them up as they advanced: they
poured boiled fenugreek[6] on the boards of the gangways, so that the
enemy slithered and lost their footing. Whether retiring or advancing
nobody could stand upright; some fell on their backs while still on

the gangways and were trodden to death, many tumbled off on to the platform, where they were at the mercy of the Jews; for as the Romans could not stand, their opponents were no longer involved in hand-to-hand fighting and so could take careful aim. As they had been badly mauled in this assault, the commander towards evening called off his troops. Of the Romans many were dead and more were wounded; of the defenders of Jotapata only six had been killed, but over three hundred wounded were brought back from the battle. This fighting took place on the 20th of Daisios.

Vespasian tried to console his army for its misfortunes, but when he saw that the men were angry and needed not exhortation but work to do, he ordered them to raise the platforms higher and to erect three towers, each fifty feet high, encased in iron on all four sides, so that they would be too heavy to overturn and almost proof against fire. These he pushed forward on to the platforms, placing on top spearmen, bowmen, the light artillery, and also the most powerful of the slingers. These men, concealed by the height of the towers and the breastworks, proceeded to pelt the defenders exposed on the ramparts. The Jews found it almost impossible to dodge the missiles launched at their heads or to retaliate on their invisible assailants, and seeing that the tops of the towers were beyond the reach of weapons thrown by hand, while the iron that encased them was proof against fire, they abandoned the wall and sallied out to meet any attack that might be attempted. In this way Jotapata held out, though every day many lost their lives and the survivors could do no damage to the enemy in return, and could only block their advance at great risk.

While all this was happening, one of the towns in the neighbourhood, called Japha,[7] revolted in the excitement aroused by the astonishing way that Jotapata held out. Vespasian therefore dispatched Trajan,[8] commander of the Tenth Legion, at the head of 1,000 horse and 2,000 foot. Trajan saw that the town would be difficult to capture; for beside the natural strength of its position it was surrounded by two separate walls. But the inhabitants came out to meet him in their eagerness for battle, and when he saw them he attacked, quickly broke their resistance and drove them back. They took refuge inside the outer wall, but the Romans followed on their heels and burst in with them. When they made a new dash for the inner wall they were shut out of the town by their own friends, who feared the enemy would charge in with them. It was God without a doubt who made the

Romans a present of the unfortunate Galilaeans: it was God who at this moment allowed the population of the town to be shut out by the hands of their own kinsmen and handed over, every man of them, to their bloodthirsty foes for destruction. For hurling themselves in a body at the gates and frantically appealing to the keepers, they were butchered in the midst of their supplications. The outer wall was closed to them by the enemy, the inner by their friends. Crushed between the two ramparts so that they could not move, many were impaled on their comrades' swords, many on their own: immense numbers were slaughtered by the Romans, having no mind even to defend themselves; for as well as being terrified by the enemy they were heartbroken at being abandoned by their friends. They died cursing not the Romans but their own people, till in the end they were all destroyed, 12,000 of them.

Assuming that there were no fighting men left in the town, and taking it for granted that even if there were a few inside they would be too frightened to make any resistance, Trajan reserved the actual capture for the commander-in-chief, and dispatched messengers to Vespasian inviting him to send his son Titus to put the finishing touches to the victory. Vespasian, suspecting that the struggle was not yet over, sent his son with a force of 500 horse and 1,000 foot. Titus marched to the town with all speed, drew up his forces with Trajan posted on the left wing and himself in command on the right, and led them to the attack. The soldiers brought up ladders to the wall on every side, and for a short while the Galilaeans on the battlements tried to fight them off; but they soon abandoned their defences, and at once Titus' men sprang on to the battlements and a moment later were in possession of the town. Those inside the wall, however, rallied to oppose them and a furious struggle broke out. In the narrow streets the men of action fell upon the legionaries; and from the house-tops the women pelted them with anything they could lay their hands on. For six hours they kept up their resistance; but when the fighting men had been expended, the rest of the population were butchered in the open and in the houses, young and old together. For no male was left alive apart from infants in arms, who with the women were sold into slavery. Those who had been slaughtered, either in the town or in the preceding engagement, totalled 15,000, the slaves 2,130. This catastrophe befell the Galilaeans on the 25th of Daisios.

Even the Samaritans did not remain immune from disaster. They assembled on Mount Gerizim, which they regard as sacred, and though they made no move, there was a threat of war in this concentration of manpower and militant attitude.[9] Not even the calamities of their neighbours could teach them sense; in face of the Roman successes they took an illogical pride in their own weakness and were thrilled at the prospect of a head-on collision. Vespasian thought it wisest to forestall the rising and nip their attempt in the bud; for though every corner of Samaritis was garrisoned, the size and organization of the assembled host was alarming. So Cerealis,[10] commanding the Fifth Legion, was sent at the head of 600 horse and 3,000 foot. In this officer's opinion it was unsafe to ascend the mountain and join battle, as so many of the enemy occupied still higher ground; so encircling the whole base of the mountain with his troops he kept the enemy under observation all day long. It happened that just when the Samaritans were growing short of water they were burnt up by a terrible heatwave – it was summertime, and the mass of men were without essential supplies. As a result some of them died of thirst that very day, and many, feeling that such a death was worse than slavery, deserted to the Romans. From their condition Cerealis inferred that those who still held together were broken by their sufferings, and proceeded to climb the mountain and post his men in a ring round the enemy. Then as a first step he invited them to come to terms, urging them to save their lives and guaranteeing their safety if they threw down their arms. When his proposals were rejected he fell upon them and slew them all to the number of 11,600. It was on the 27th of Daisios that the Samaritans suffered this terrible calamity.

In Jotapata the defenders still held out, bearing up under their sufferings longer than seemed possible. But on the forty-seventh day[11] the Roman platforms overtopped the wall, and that very day a deserter informed Vespasian how few men were left in the city and how weak they were, and assured him that they were spent with total lack of sleep and constant fighting and could no longer withstand an assault, but would fall to a ruse if one was attempted. In the last hour of the night, when they counted on some respite from their sufferings and when exhausted men are most easily overcome by morning sleep, the sentries, he said, used to drop off; so that was the best time for an assault. Vespasian mistrusted the deserter, knowing how loyal the Jews were to each other and how contemptuous of punishment; for earlier on when a man from Jotapata had been captured he had borne up in the face of the most horrible tortures and even when the enemy used flames to extort information had refused to say a word about conditions in the town, finally going to death by crucifixion with a smile on his face. On the other hand the traitor's story was too convincing to be disbelieved, and thinking that possibly he was speaking the truth, and that even if he was laying a trap, the consequences to the Romans would not be serious, the general ordered him to be closely guarded but got his army ready for the capture of the town.

At the hour indicated they moved forward noiselessly to the wall. The first to climb up was Titus, accompanied by one of the tribunes, Domitius Sabinus, and followed by a handful of men from the Fifteenth Legion. Quickly disposing of the sentries they entered the town. In their rear Sextus Calvarius, a tribune, and Placidus introduced the units they commanded. Soon the citadel had been captured, the enemy were sweeping through the centre of the town, and it was broad daylight – and yet the vanquished defenders had no idea that the town had fallen! For most of them were helpless with fatigue and fast asleep; if anyone did rouse himself, he could not see for a dense mist which at the critical moment happened to envelop the town. At last, when the whole army had streamed in, they jumped up, only to discover that all was lost: they did not realize that the town had fallen till the massacre began.

The Romans, remembering what the siege had cost them, showed neither mercy nor pity for anyone. They drove the people down the slope from the citadel and slaughtered them. There even those still capable of resistance were deprived by the difficult ground of any chance to defend themselves. Jostling each other in the narrow streets and slipping down the steep face, they were swamped by the wave of destruction sweeping down from the citadel. Many even of Josephus' picked soldiers were driven to suicide; for when they saw that they could not kill a single Roman, they made sure that at least they should not die at Roman hands, and collecting at the far edge of the town they killed themselves.

Some of the sentries, realizing that the end had come, had got away in time. They went up into one of the northern towers and held out there for a time; but when they were hemmed in by a large enemy force they at last put up their hands and offered their throats to their opponents without flinching. The Romans might well have claimed that the final stage of the siege was a bloodless victory, if one man had not fallen at the time of the capture – the centurion Antonius, victim of a trick. One Jew who with a great many others had taken refuge in the caves begged Antonius to give him his hand as a pledge of protection and to help him climb out. The Roman incautiously gave him his hand, and with a swift upward thrust the man stabbed him in the groin and killed him instantly.

On that day the Romans killed all who were in the open; on the next few days they searched the hiding-places, falling on all whom they found in the sewers and caves, and destroying them regardless of their age, except women and babies. 1,200 prisoners were taken, while the dead, including those killed in the battles preceding the capture, were reckoned at 40,000. Vespasian ordered the city to be demolished and set fire to all the guardposts. Such was the end of Jotapata, captured on the 1st of Panemos in the thirteenth year of Nero's reign.

The Romans sought everywhere for Josephus both because their blood was up and because it was their commander's express wish, since the war would be virtually over once Josephus was in his hands.[12] So they searched carefully among the dead bodies and the men who had gone into hiding. But while the capture was taking place, Josephus, helped by some divine providence, had stolen away from the midst of the enemy and jumped into a deep pit communicating on one side with a wide cave which could not be seen from above. There he had found forty persons of importance concealed, and essential supplies that would last for many days. So in the daytime he lay hid as the enemy were everywhere, but at night he came out and looked for an escape route and scrutinized the sentry-posts; but as every avenue was blocked on his account and there was no possibility of escape, he went down into his cave again. So for two days he escaped detection, but on the third a woman of his party was captured and gave him away. Vespasian without a moment's hesitation sent two tribunes, Paulinus and Gallicanus, with orders to offer Josephus safe conduct and persuade him to come out.

When these arrived they gave him a warm invitation and guaranteed his safety, but without avail. The probable fate of one who had struck so many blows blinded him to the habitual gentleness of those who invited him, and made him highly suspicious; and he continued to fear that they were summoning him to punishment until Vespasian sent a third tribune, Nicanor, known to Josephus – in fact an old friend.[13] He came forward and enlarged on the habitual kindness of the Romans towards the vanquished. Josephus' prowess made him admired rather than hated by the generals, and the commander-in-chief was anxious to bring him out, not for punishment – he could inflict that even without Josephus coming forth – but because he preferred to save so excellent a man. He added that if Vespasian had been laying a trap he would not have sent a friend, hiding the foulest crime – perfidy – behind the fairest virtue – friendship; and if he himself had been required to deceive his friend, he would never have agreed to come.

While in spite of Nicanor's assurances Josephus still hesitated, the rank and file in their fury were eager to roast him out of the cave, but they were restrained by the tribune, who was determined to take him alive. As Nicanor urged his appeals and the threatening attitude of the enemy masses became evident to Josephus, the memory came to him of those dreams in the night by which God had forewarned him both of the calamities coming to the Jews and of the fortunes of the Roman emperors. Moreover in the matter of interpreting dreams he was capable of divining the meaning of equivocal utterances of the Deity: he was familiar with the prophecies of Holy Scripture, being a priest himself and the descendant of priests. At this very moment he was inspired to understand them, and seizing on the terrifying images of his recent dreams he sent up a secret prayer to God: 'Inasmuch as it pleaseth Thee to visit Thy wrath on the Jewish people whom Thou didst create, and all prosperity hath passed to the Romans, and because Thou didst choose my spirit to make known the things to come, I yield myself willingly to the Romans that I may live, but I solemnly declare that I go, not as a traitor, but as Thy servant.'

With these words he was on the point of giving in to Nicanor. But the Jews who had taken refuge along with him realized that he was accepting the invitation and crowded round him shouting: 'Well may a cry go up to heaven from the laws of our fathers, ordained by God Himself, who endowed our race with spirits that despise death! Are you so in love with life, Josephus, that you can bear to live as a slave? How quickly you have forgotten yourself! How many you have persuaded to lay down their lives for liberty! False, utterly false, was the reputation you won for courage and shrewdness, if you really

expect to be spared by those you have hit so hard, and if, even supposing their offer of pardon is genuine, you stoop to accept it! But if *you*
have been dazzled by Roman success, *we* must take care of our country's good name. We will lend you a sword and a hand to wield it.
If you die willingly, you will die as commander-in-chief of the Jews;
if unwillingly, as a traitor.' As they said this, they pointed their swords
at him and threatened to run him through if he gave in to the Romans.

Fearing the threatened assault and believing that it would be a
betrayal of the commands of God if he died before imparting his
message, Josephus in his critical situation began to philosophize. 'Why,
my friends,' he began, 'are we so anxious to commit suicide? Why
should we make those best of friends, body and soul, part company?
It is suggested that I have changed. Well, the Romans know all about
that. I am told it is a glorious thing to die in war. Quite so; but by the
laws of war – that is, by the hands of the victors. If I am shrinking
from the Roman swords, I fully deserve to die by my own hand; but
if they are disposed to spare an enemy, how much more justified
should we be in sparing ourselves? It would be absurd to do to ourselves what we are fighting to prevent their doing to us! You say it
is glorious to die for freedom; I say so too, but on the battlefield and
at the hands of those who are trying to take freedom from us. But
now they are not coming to do battle with us or to kill us. The man
who doesn't want to die when he ought is no more cowardly than
the man who does want to when he ought not. What fear keeps us
from going up to the Romans? Isn't it fear of death? Well, then, shall
we, because we fear possible death at the hands of our foes, inflict
certain death on ourselves? "No, it is fear of slavery," someone will
say. As if we were free men now! "It is a brave act to kill oneself,"
another will suggest. Not at all! It is a most craven act. *I* think a pilot
would be a most arrant coward, if through fear of bad weather he
did not wait for the storm to break but sank his ship on purpose.

'Again, suicide is contrary to the instincts shared by all living
things, and towards the God who made us it is sheer impiety. Of all
living things there is not one that dies on purpose or by its own act;
it is an irresistible natural law that all should wish to live. For that
reason if men openly attempt to rob us of life, we treat them as
enemies; if they lay a trap for us, we punish them. And do you suppose God isn't angry when a man treats His gift with contempt? It
is from Him we have received our being, and it is to Him we must

leave the right to take it away. The bodies of all men are mortal and have been fashioned out of perishable matter; the soul is immortal for ever, a fragment of God dwelling in our bodies.[14] If a man destroys something entrusted to him by another man or misuses it, he is judged a faithless rogue, is he not? then if a man throws away what God has entrusted to his personal keeping, does he think the One he has wronged is unaware? To punish runaway slaves is considered right, even if the masters they are leaving are rogues; if we ourselves run away from the best of masters, God, shan't we be judged impious? Don't you know that those who depart this life according to the law of nature, and repay the loan they received from God at such time as the Lender chooses to claim it back, win everlasting glory? that their homes and families are safe? and that their souls remain unspotted and obedient, having won the most holy place in heaven, from which when time's wheel has turned full circle they are again sent to dwell in unsullied bodies?[15] But if men go mad and lay hands on themselves, Hades[16] receives their souls into the shadows, and God their Father visits the sins of the fathers upon the children.[17] For that reason suicide is hateful in God's sight and the wisest of lawgivers has declared it a punishable offence. Those who destroy themselves must by our rules be exposed unburied till sundown,[18] though even our enemies are thought to be entitled to burial. In other lands it is laid down that the right hands of those who die thus should be cut off, since they have made war on themselves, on the ground that as the body has been divorced from the soul, so the hand must be divorced from the body.

'It is our duty then, comrades, to choose the honourable course and not to add to our human sufferings impiety towards our Creator. If we think it right to accept life when it is offered, let us accept it; for an offer of life brings no discredit if it comes from those whom we have convinced of our mettle by our tremendous resistance; if we choose to die, how better than at the hands of our conquerors? I shall not go over to the Roman side in order to be a traitor to myself; if I did, I should be much sillier than those who desert to the enemy; for to them desertion means life, to me it means death, my own death. However, I pray that the Romans may prove traitors: if after giving me their word they put me to death, I shall die happy, finding in the broken faith of such liars a consolation greater than victory itself.'

On these lines Josephus argued at great length in his desire to avert mass suicide. But desperation made his hearers deaf; they had long ago devoted themselves to death, and now they were furious with him. Running at him from all directions sword in hand, they reviled him for cowardice, everyone appearing to be about to strike him. But he called one by name, glared like a general at another, shook hands with a third, pleaded with a fourth till he was ashamed, and, distracted by conflicting emotions in his critical situation, he kept all their swords away from his throat, turning like an animal at bay to face each assailant in turn. Even when he was at his last gasp, they still respected their commander; their arms were enfeebled, their blades glanced off him, and many while thrusting at him with their swords spontaneously lowered their points.

In this predicament his resourcefulness did not fail him. Putting his trust in divine protection he staked his life on one last throw. 'You have chosen to die,' he exclaimed; 'well then, let's draw lots and kill each other in turn. Whoever draws the first lot shall be dispatched by number two, and so on down the whole line as luck decides. In this way no one will die by his own hand – it would be unfair when the rest were gone if one man changed his mind and saved his life.' The audience swallowed the bait, and getting his way Josephus drew lots with the rest. Without hesitation each man in turn offered his throat for the next man to cut, in the belief that a moment later his commander would die too. Life was sweet, but not so sweet as death if Josephus died with them! But Josephus – shall we put it down to divine providence or just to luck[19] – was left with one other man. He did not relish the thought either of being condemned by the lot or, if he was left till last, of staining his hand with the blood of a fellow Jew. So he used persuasion, they made a pact, and both remained alive.

Having thus come safely through two wars – one with the Romans and one with his own people – Josephus was brought by Nicanor before Vespasian. The Romans all rushed to see him, and as the noisy mob milled round their commander they raised conflicting cries, some exulting over the prisoner, some threatening him, some elbowing their way forward to get a nearer view. Those at the back clamoured for the execution of their enemy; those at the front remembered his exploits and were astounded at the change in his fortunes. As for the officers, the anger they had felt before was entirely forgotten now that they saw him. More than anyone else Titus was impressed by the courageous bearing of Josephus in his misfortunes and by pity for his youth.[20] When he remembered how he had fought in time past and saw him now a prisoner in enemy hands, he had occasion to reflect on the power of fortune, the sudden tilting of the scales in war, and the absence of any certainty in human affairs. So at this time he led very many Romans to feel for Josephus the pity he felt himself, and he was chiefly responsible for his father's decision to spare the prisoner's life. However, Vespasian gave instructions that he should be kept in the closest custody, as he intended to send him as soon as possible to Nero. Hearing this, Josephus asked to say a word to him in private. Vespasian ordered everyone except his son Titus and two friends to withdraw, and Josephus began thus:

'You suppose, sir, that in capturing me you have merely secured a prisoner, but I come as a messenger of the greatness that awaits you. Had I not been sent by God Himself, I knew the Jewish law and how a general ought to die. Are you sending me to Nero? How so? Will Nero and those who succeed him before your turn comes remain on the throne? You, Vespasian, are Caesar and Emperor, you and your son here. So load me with your heaviest chains and keep me for yourself; for you are master not only of me, Caesar, but of land and sea and all the human race; and I ask to be kept in closer confinement as my penalty, if I am taking the name of God in vain.'[21]

At the time Vespasian seemed unwilling to take these suggestions seriously, assuming that Josephus was lying to save his skin. But gradually he became convinced, for God was already awakening in him imperial ambitions and foreshowing the sceptre by other portents. Moreover he found that the prophecies of Josephus had proved correct on other occasions; for one of the friends present at the private interview expressed surprise that he had not warned the defenders of Jotapata that the town would fall or foreseen his own captivity – unless he was now talking nonsense to avert the anger he had brought on himself. But Josephus replied that he had predicted to the people of Jotapata that the town would fall after forty-seven days and that he himself would be taken alive by the Romans. Vespasian took the prisoners aside and questioned them about these claims; when he found that they were true, he began to take seriously the predictions about himself. So, although he kept Josephus locked up in prison, he presented him with clothing and other valuable gifts and treated him with kindness and consideration at all times, Titus showing the same eagerness to do him honour.

CHAPTER 13

Vespasian's Conquering Advance

ON the 4th of Panemos Vespasian marched his army to Ptolemais and thence to the coastal city of Caesarea, one of the largest in Judaea, with a predominantly Greek population. Army and generals alike were received with loud applause and in the friendliest spirit, partly through good will towards the Romans, but still more through hatred of the vanquished, hatred which caused a howling mob to clamour for Josephus to be executed. But this demand, proceeding as it did from mass ignorance, Vespasian dismissed with contemptuous silence. Two of the legions he settled for the winter at Caesarea, as he found the city convenient; the Fifteenth he sent to Scythopolis, to avoid burdening Caesarea with his whole army. That city too is as mild in winter as it is suffocatingly hot in summer, being situated on the plain and near the sea.[1]

Meanwhile those Jews who had been expelled from their towns in faction fights joined with those who had survived the recent defeats, forming a sizeable force, and proceeded to rebuild Joppa (recently devastated by Cestius[2]), to serve as their base. Then, as they were cut off from the land, which had been overrun by the enemy, they decided to turn to the sea. They built a large pirate fleet and began to raid the Syrian and Phoenician waters and the route to Egypt, making it impossible for anyone to sail those seas.[3] Vespasian, on hearing of this organization, sent horse and foot to Joppa. As the town was unguarded, this force entered it at night. The inhabitants were forewarned of the attack, but in their terror they abandoned all hope of keeping out the Romans, and fleeing to their ships spent the night out of range.

There is no natural harbour at Joppa, which ends in an uneven beach straight for most of its length but curving gently at both ends. These are formed by lofty cliffs and reefs running out into the sea, where the marks of Andromeda's chair are still shown as proofs of the antiquity of the legend.[4] Beating full on this shore and dashing the waves high against the opposing rocks, the north wind makes the anchorage more dangerous than a landless sea. Here the men from

Joppa were riding at anchor when just before daylight they were struck by a violent gale, known to sailors in those parts as 'the black northerly'. Some of the ships it dashed against the others then and there, others it drove on to the rocks. Many in the face of the oncoming surge forced their way into deeper waters, so great was the fear of this rocky shore and the enemy in possession of it; but even in the open sea the mountainous waves overwhelmed them. There was no way of escape, and no safety if they stayed: the power of the wind kept them from the sea, the power of the Romans from the land. There were agonizing shrieks as the vessels collided; when they broke up the noise was deafening. Of the men on board many were submerged by the waves and drowned, many lost their lives entangled in the wreckage, while some, thinking it less painful to die by the sword, cheated the sea by killing themselves. But most of them were cast up by the waves and dashed to pieces against the cliffs, so that a wide stretch of sea was stained with their blood and the beach was covered with corpses; for the Romans set upon those who were cast up on the shore and destroyed them. The number of bodies washed up was 4,200. The Romans captured the town without any fighting and demolished it.

Thus in a short period Joppa twice fell to the Romans. To prevent the pirates from again settling there Vespasian established a camp on the acropolis and left his cavalry in it along with a small infantry force. The latter were to stay where they were and guard the camp while the cavalry plundered the surrounding country and destroyed the villages and little towns in the neighbourhood of Joppa. These orders were duly executed: the countryside was overrun and devastated day after day till it was utterly desolate.

When Jerusalem received news of the catastrophe at Jotapata, at first very few believed it – the disaster was so overwhelming, and no eyewitness was available to confirm the report. No one had survived to relate what had happened, but a spontaneous rumour – for rumour delights in tragic news – announced the fall of the town. But by degrees the truth trickled through, and everyone knew that there was no longer room for doubt. Truth, however, was supplemented by invention; for instance, it was stated that among those killed when the town fell was Josephus himself. This report caused extreme distress in Jerusalem; whereas the lamentation for each of the dead was confined to his own household and kindred, the mourning for the commander was nationwide – some grieved for acquaintances, some for kinsmen, some for close friends, some for brothers, but the loss of Josephus distressed them all. For a whole month the wailing never stopped in the City, and a great many hired professional mourners to lead their lamentations. But before long the truth came to light, and what had really happened at Jotapata. When the people found out that the tragic fate of Josephus was an invention, and learnt that he was alive and with the Romans, and that he was receiving from the officers treatment no prisoner could expect, they were as furious with him living as they had been kind about him when believed dead. Some reviled him as a coward, some as a traitor; the City seethed with indignation and nothing was too bad to say about him. The people were maddened by the blows they had suffered and inflamed by their disasters. A setback, which among sensible people is an inducement to caution and to the avoidance of similar occurrences, for them was a spur to new calamities; and the end of one misery was invariably the beginning of another. So they were still more eager to get at the Romans in the hope that in damaging them they would requite Josephus. Such was the excitement that held Jerusalem in its grip.

Vespasian decided to acquaint himself with Agrippa's kingdom. He had been invited by the king himself, who was anxious to entertain the commander-in-chief and his army to the full extent of his privy purse, and at the same time to use them to settle the troubles within his borders. Starting therefore from Caesarea on the coast he marched to Caesarea Philippi. There he rested his troops for three weeks while he himself attended state banquets and offered sacrifices to God in gratitude for his successes. But when he was informed that Tiberias was in a rebellious state and Tarichaeae had revolted already[5] (the two cities formed part of Agrippa's dominions), resolved as he was to crush the Jews everywhere, he decided that this was the moment to march against the rebels, and to repay Agrippa's hospitality by subduing his cities for him. So he sent his son Titus to Caesarea to bring the forces still there to Scythopolis – the biggest city of the Decapolis,[6] not far from Tiberias – where he himself met him. Advancing at the head of three legions he encamped three and a half miles from Tiberias at a station well within view of the rebels, called Sennabris. Then he sent the decurion Valerianus with a troop of horse to make proposals of peace to the townsfolk and induce them to give pledges; for he had heard that the people were anxious for peace, but were being driven into war by a powerful faction.

Valerianus rode to Tiberias, and when he was near the wall dismounted and made his men do the same, that they might not be thought to have come to skirmish. But before any words were exchanged the leading rebels sallied out against him weapons in hand, led by one Jeshua, son of Sapphias,[7] the supreme head of the terrorist[8] gang. Valerianus thought it unsafe to join battle against the general's orders even if victory was certain, and very dangerous indeed for a handful of men caught off their guard to engage a large force which had the initiative. Besides, he was disconcerted by the unexpected daring of the Jews. So he fled on foot, and five others similarly abandoned their horses, which Jeshua and his men brought back to the city as delighted as if they had captured them in battle, not by surprise. This so alarmed the elder citizens and acknowledged leaders that they fled to the Roman camp, and calling the king to their aid threw themselves at Vespasian's feet, entreating him not to reject their appeal, or impute the madness of a few to the entire city, but to spare the citizens, who had been friendly to the Romans at all times, and punish only those responsible for the revolt, but for whom they themselves would have been only too glad to make their submission long ago. To these entreaties the general yielded, though the seizure of his horses made him angry with the whole city; for Agrippa's concern for his subjects was evident. As the delegates had made their submission in the name of all the citizens, Jeshua and his supporters decided that Tiberias was no longer a healthy place to stay in, and made a dash for Tarichaeae.

Next day Vespasian sent forward a body of horse under Trajan[9] as far as the ridge to find out whether the whole population was peacefully inclined. As soon as he felt sure that the citizens were unanimous in supporting their representatives, he marched his army to the city. The people opened their gates to him and met him with acclamations, calling him their saviour and benefactor. As the army was held up by the narrowness of the entrances, Vespasian ordered his men to break through the south wall, and thus made a wide passage for them. Plundering and violence, however, he ruled out in deference to the king, who induced him also to spare the walls by guaranteeing the future loyalty of the inhabitants. Thus after suffering grievously from its internal divisions the city received a new lease of life.

Then marching to a spot between Tiberias and Tarichaeae Vespasian pitched his camp, making it unusually strong, in case he was held up there by prolonged fighting; for an endless stream of insurgents was pouring into Tarichaeae, relying on the strength of the town and the protection of the lake known locally as Gennesaret. The town was situated, like Tiberias, at the foot of the mountains, and except where it was washed by the lake it had been fortified all round by Josephus – strongly, but not as strongly as Tiberias; for there the rampart had been built in the early stages of the revolt when he had unlimited money and power, but Tarichaeae had only enjoyed the remnants of his munificence.[10] The occupants had a large number of boats ready on the lake to evacuate them if defeated on land, and equipped for a sea fight if necessary. While the Romans were fortifying their camp, Jeshua and his supporters, fearless in the face of the numbers and perfect discipline of the enemy, made a sortie and at the first onset scattered the working-party and tore down a short length of the wall. But when they saw the legionaries forming up, they avoided all loss by a rapid withdrawal to their own lines. When the pursuing Romans forced them to take to their boats, they put out from shore but kept the Romans within bowshot, then dropped anchor with their vessels side by side like infantrymen standing shoulder to shoulder, and engaged in a sea fight with their enemy on land.

Meantime Vespasian, learning that the great bulk of them were formed up on the plain before the town, sent his son with six hundred picked cavalry. Titus, finding himself seriously outnumbered, sent a request to his father for reinforcements. In the meantime, seeing that while most of his men were eager to fight without waiting for help to arrive, some few could not hide their consternation at the Jews' advantage in numbers, he took his stand where all could hear him and began:

'Romans, I cannot begin better than by reminding you of the name you bear, that you may realize how different we are from the men we are going to fight. From our hands nothing in the wide world has hitherto escaped, though the Jews, we must admit, have not yet shown any sign of lying down under defeat. It would be a shocking thing if, when they stand unbowed in the midst of disaster, we should flag in the midst of success. The enthusiasm you outwardly display I am delighted to see, but I fear that the enemy's advantage in numbers may produce in a few of you a secret alarm. If so, they should again ponder the difference between their opponents and themselves, and the fact that the Jews, though extremely bold and contemptuous of death, have neither discipline nor experience of war, and are nothing but a rabble, not fit to be called an army. Of our own experience and discipline nothing need be said. But our object in being the one people to undergo military training in peacetime is that in war we may not have to compare our numbers with those of our opponents. What should we gain by being constantly on active service, if we needed equal numbers to oppose a mob of raw recruits?

'Remember again that you are fighting in full armour against men who have none, that you are horse and they are foot, that you have leaders and they are leaderless. These advantages make you in effect far more numerous than you are, while the enemy's disadvantages make their numbers count for very little. Wars are won, not by the size of an army however skilful, but by courage, however tiny the forces available. Small forces can be quickly deployed and can readily support each other, while swollen armies do themselves more damage than the enemy can do. The Jews are inspired by reckless audacity and desperation, emotions that invigorate while things go well but are extinguished by the smallest setback. We are inspired by disciplined courage and fortitude, which in prosperity reaches its greatest heights and in adversity endures to the end. And you will be fighting for a greater prize than the Jews; for though they face the dangers of war to defend the liberty of their country, what greater prize could you win than glory and the assurance that, after mastering the whole world, we do not acknowledge the Jews as rivals? Observe too that there is no fear of our suffering any irretrievable disaster. Ample reinforcements are at hand; but we can snatch the victory ourselves, and we must not wait for the men my father is sending to support us: if no one shares it, our triumph will be the greater.

'My own feeling is that at this moment my father is on trial, so am I, and so are you. Does he deserve his past triumphs? Do I deserve to be his son, and you to be my soldiers? With *him* victory is a habit; I could not bear to return to him if you abandoned me; would *you* not be ashamed if your commander led the way into danger and you

failed to follow? I *shall* lead the way, you may be sure, and shall be
the first to charge the enemy. So don't you fail me, or doubt for a
moment that with God at my side my efforts are bound to succeed.
I tell you plainly in advance that in fighting here outside the walls
we shall win a far-reaching triumph.'[11]

As Titus delivered this address a sudden wave of enthusiasm swept
the men off their feet; and when Trajan arrived before the battle
with 400 horse they were vexed that the victory would bring them
less credit through being shared. Vespasian also sent Antonius Silo
with 2,000 bowmen, who were to seize the hill opposite the town
and pin down the defenders on the wall. These orders were carried
out, and every attempt to bring help from within was frustrated.
Meanwhile Titus galloped to the front and charged the enemy; with
loud hurrahs the rest followed, extending their line across the plain
to the length of the enemy front, and so giving the impression of
much greater numbers than they possessed. The Jews, though taken
aback by their discipline and dash, for a time stood up to the onslaught; but pierced by lances and overborne by the momentum of
horses and men they were trampled underfoot, and death reigned
everywhere. The survivors scattered and fled to the town, every man
as fast as he could run. Titus, hard on their heels, cut down the
stragglers, drove through tight masses, rode past other groups and
charged them from the front, pulverized many by leaping among
them as they got in each other's way, headed them all off as they fled
towards the walls, and turned them back towards the plain until by
weight of numbers they forced their way through and sought safety
in the town.

Once within the walls they were again involved in party strife.
The residents clung to their possessions and their town, and had been
opposed to the war from the first; now after the defeat they were still
more opposed to it. But the newcomers, who were very numerous,
insisted all the more, both sides lost their tempers, and the shouting
and uproar made it evident that they would soon be at each other's
throats. Hearing the commotion Titus, who was not far from the
wall, exclaimed: 'Now is your chance, men; why hesitate, when the
Jews are ours for the asking? Seize your opportunity! Do you not
hear the row? The men who have slipped through our fingers are
fighting each other! The town is ours if we make haste; but we shall
have to work hard and fight hard too. Great prizes cannot be won

without taking risks. We must not wait for the enemy to make up their quarrel – necessity will reconcile them soon enough; and we must not wait for reinforcements either – we have beaten a whole army with a handful of men, and now we will capture the town by ourselves.'

With these words he leapt into the saddle and led the way to the lake. Riding through the water he entered the town at the head of his men. His audacity filled the defenders with terror, and not a man stayed to offer the least resistance. Abandoning their posts Jeshua and his supporters fled across country, while the rest rushed down to the lake where they ran into the enemy advancing to meet them. Some were killed as they got into their boats, others as they tried to swim to those who had put out before. In the town the streets ran with blood, the same fate befalling newcomers who had not escaped in time and now tried to resist and the residents who offered no resistance at all, refusing to fight in the hope of their submission being accepted and in the knowledge that they had opposed the war. At last Titus, having disposed of the culprits, took pity on the residents and put an end to the slaughter. Those who had taken refuge on the lake, when they saw that the town had fallen, put out as far from the enemy as they could.

Titus sent a dispatch-rider to give his father the good news of what had happened. Vespasian was naturally delighted at his son's prowess and at the resounding victory, thinking that a very important chapter of the war had been brought to a close. Going at once to the scene he ordered the town to be encircled by guards: if anyone slipped out he must be killed. The next day he went down to the lake and ordered rafts to be put together for the pursuit of the fugitives. These were soon ready, as there was abundance of wood and no lack of carpenters.

Lake Gennesaret takes its name from the region adjoining it. Though it measures sixteen miles by four and a half, its water is most delicious; for it is clearer than cloudy marsh water and quite pure, as on every side it ends in a sandy beach. When drawn it is pleasantly warm, more agreeable than river or spring water but always cooler than one would expect from a lake of that size. It becomes as cold as snow when it is exposed to the air, as is the regular local practice on summer nights. The species of fish that live in the lake differ in taste and appearance from those found elsewhere. Right through the middle flows the Jordan. The Jordan appears to rise at Paneum, but actually it flows out of sight underground from the pool called Phiale, 'the Bowl', to Paneum. Anyone going up into Trachonitis will find this pool fourteen miles from Caesarea Philippi,[12] not very far to the right of the road. It is very aptly called the Bowl because of its shape, which is a perfect circle. The water always remains level with its brim, neither sinking nor running over. For a long time it was not known that the Jordan rose there, but the truth was established by the tetrarch of Trachonitis, Philip, who threw chaff into the Bowl and found that it came to the surface at Paneum, which earlier generations had believed to be the source of the river. Paneum, naturally beautiful, has been further embellished by royal bounty, being adorned at Agrippa's expense. The visible course of the Jordan begins at this cavern, cuts through the still, marshy waters of Lake Semechonitis,[13] covers another fourteen miles, and after passing the city of Julias goes straight through the middle of Lake Gennesaret; then after a long journey through desert country it finishes up in the Dead Sea.

Alongside Lake Gennesaret is a stretch of country with the same name, wonderful in its characteristics and in its beauty. Thanks to the rich soil there is not a plant that does not flourish there, and the inhabitants grow everything: the air is so temperate that it suits the most diverse species. Walnuts, most winter-loving of trees, flourish in abundance, as do palms, which thrive on heat, side by side with figs and olives, for which a milder air is indicated. One might deem it nature's crowning achievement to force together into one spot natural enemies and to bring the seasons into healthy rivalry, each as it were laying claim to the region. For not only does it produce the most surprisingly diverse fruits but it maintains a continuous supply. Those royal fruits the grape and the fig it furnishes for ten months on end, the rest ripening on the trees all year round; for apart from the temperate atmosphere it is watered by a spring with great fertilizing power, known locally as Capernaum. Some have thought this an off-shoot of the Nile, as it breeds a fish very like the perch caught in the lake of Alexandria. The length of the region measured along the shore of the lake that bears the same name is three and a half miles, the width two and a half. Such is the character of the locality.

Preparations completed, Titus put on board as much of his force as he thought adequate to deal with their opponents in the boats, and the pursuit began. Thus encircled the Jews could neither escape to land, where the enemy were in full possession, nor fight it out on the water with any hope of success. Their boats were small and built for piracy, and were weak in comparison with the rafts, and the men on board each one were so few that they dared not come to grips with the Romans, who attacked them in mass formation. However, they circled round the rafts and sometimes even approached, pelting the Romans with stones at long range, then scraping past and attacking them at close quarters. In either case they got the worst of it: their shower of stones merely rattled on the Roman armour while they themselves were targets for Roman arrows; and when they ventured to approach, they had no time to do anything before disaster overtook them and they went down, boats and all. Some tried to break through, but the Romans were near enough to transfix many of them with their lances, killing others by leaping into the boats sword in hand. Some, as the rafts closed in, were caught in the middle and destroyed along with their craft. If any of those who had been plunged into the water came to the surface, they were dispatched with an arrow or caught by a raft. If in their extremity they attempted to climb on board, their heads or hands were severed by the Romans. Vast numbers of Jews perished in countless ways on every side, until the fleeing remnant were driven to the shore, their craft completely surrounded. As they poured out of them many were struck down while still in the water; many who had leapt clear were destroyed by the Romans on the beach. A fearful sight met the eyes – the entire lake stained with blood and crammed with corpses; for there was not a single survivor. During the days that followed a horrible stench hung over the region. The beaches were thick with wrecks and swollen bodies which, hot and steaming in the sun, made the air so foul that the calamity not only horrified the Jews but revolted even those who had brought it about. Such was the outcome of this naval engagement. The dead, including those who earlier perished in the town, totalled 6,700.

After the battle Vespasian held a court-martial in Tarichaeae. Making a distinction between the residents and the newcomers whom he considered responsible for the war, he put the question to his staff whether these too should be spared. The verdict was that it would be against the public interest to set them free: if released they would not keep the peace, being stateless refugees, in a position to induce those who sheltered them to take up arms. Vespasian decided that they did not deserve to be spared, and that if they were released they would injure those who had set them free, but he was not sure of the right way to get rid of them. If he killed them then and there, he suspected that he would antagonize the residents, who would be outraged by the execution of so many suppliants in their midst, and he could not think of letting them go under safe-conduct and then setting upon them. However, his advisers got their way by arguing that Jews had no rights whatever, and that expediency must be preferred to conventional morality whenever the two were in conflict. So he gave the doomed men a guarantee of safety in ambiguous terms, permitting them to leave only by the road that led to Tiberias. Instantly falling into the trap and suspecting nothing, they loaded themselves with their possessions quite openly and set out along the permitted route. Meanwhile the Romans lined the road all the way to Tiberias so that no one could leave it, and shut them up in the city. Vespasian followed and herded them all into the stadium. The aged and useless, 1,200 of them, were disposed of by his orders. From the young men he picked out the 6,000 strongest and sent them to Nero at the Isthmus.[14] The rest of the people to the number of 30,400 he auctioned, except those whom he presented to Agrippa; the men who came from his kingdom Vespasian allowed him to deal with as he pleased, and the king put them too under the hammer. The rest of the mob came from Trachonitis, Gaulanitis, Hippus, and the Gadarene district, and was largely composed of rebels and fugitives whose unsavoury reputation in peacetime made war seem attractive to them. They were captured on the 8th of Gorpiaios.

After the fall of Jotapata some of the Galilaeans had remained in revolt against Rome; but when Tarichaeae was overwhelmed they surrendered, and the Romans took over all the fortresses and towns except Gischala and the garrison of Mount Tabor. These were supported by Gamala, a town opposite Tarichaeae on the far side of the lake. This town was in the territory assigned to Agrippa, as were Sogane and Seleucia. Gamala and Sogane both belonged to Gaulanitis, Sogane being part of Upper Gaulan, as it is called, and Gamala of Lower. Seleucia was near Lake Semechonitis. This lake is three and a half miles wide and seven long. Its marshes stretch as far as Daphne, a pleasant spot in many ways, with springs that feed the Little Jordan under the temple of the golden cow[15] and send it pouring into the Jordan proper. Sogane and Seleucia had been persuaded at the beginning of the revolt to submit to Agrippa[16]; but Gamala had refused to surrender, relying on its inaccessibility even more than Jotapata had done. Sloping down from a towering peak is a spur like a long shaggy neck, behind which rises a symmetrical hump, so that the outline resembles that of a camel; hence the name, the exact form of the word being obscured by the local pronunciation.[17] On the face and both sides it is cut off by impassable ravines. Near the tail it is rather more accessible, where it is detached from the hill; but here too, by digging a trench across, the inhabitants made access very difficult. Built against the almost vertical flank the houses were piled on top of one another, and the town seemed to be hung in mid-air and on the point of tumbling on top of itself from its very steepness. It faced south and its southern crest, which rose to an immense height, served as citadel, resting on an unwalled precipice that went straight down into the deepest ravine. There was a spring inside the wall at the far side of the town.

Nature having thus made the town well nigh impregnable, Josephus had walled it round and given it the additional protection of trenches and underground passages. Thanks to the natural strength of the position its occupants were more confident than the Jotapatans had been, but they had far fewer fighting-men, being so sure of their defences that they would not admit more. For the town was crowded with refugees because of the protection it offered, which was proved by the fact that the forces previously sent by Agrippa to besiege it had made no headway after seven months.[18]

Vespasian set out from Ammathus (i.e. 'warm baths': the town contains a spring of warm water with medicinal qualities) where he had been encamped before Tiberias,[19] and marched to Gamala. Unable to put an unbroken ring of men round the town because of its situation, he posted sentries wherever he could and occupied the hill that overlooked it. When the legions had fortified their camps in the usual way on its slopes, he began to construct platforms at the tail end. In the eastern part of the ridge where rose the highest of the towers the construction was done by the Fifteenth Legion, the Fifth worked opposite the middle of the town, and the filling in of the trenches and ravines was undertaken by the Tenth.

At this juncture King Agrippa approached the walls, and was trying to discuss terms of surrender with the defenders when one of the slingers hit him on the right elbow with a stone. He was immediately surrounded by his own men, but the determination of the Romans to press the siege was redoubled both by indignation on the king's account and by anxiety for their own safety; for men who displayed such savagery towards one of their own race who was advising them in their own interest would stick at no brutality in treating foreigners and enemies.

With so many skilled hands the platforms were soon finished and the engines brought up. Chares and Joseph, the most effective leaders in the town, lined up their armed forces, though they had already lost heart because they had little hope of withstanding the siege for long, being short of water and other necessities. However, their leaders laughed at their fears and led them out on to the wall. For a time they beat back those who were bringing up the engines, but becoming the target for the catapults and stone-throwers they withdrew into the town. Then the Romans brought up the rams at three points, and battering their way through the wall poured in through the breaches with a great blare of trumpets and din of weapons, and shouting themselves hoarse flung themselves upon the defenders of the town. They for a time stood firm against the first waves of attackers, and offering strenuous resistance prevented the Romans from advancing further. But under heavy pressure from all directions they withdrew to the upper parts of the town, and as the enemy pursued them they swung round and counter-attacked vigorously. Swept down the slope and jammed inextricably in the narrow alleys, the Romans suffered fearful casualties. Unable either to resist those above them or to force their way through the advancing mass of their companions, they climbed on to the roofs of the houses where they rested against the slope. Crowded with men and unequal to the weight these quickly collapsed. As one fell it knocked down many of those underneath, and so on to the bottom. The effect on the Romans was devastating. Completely at a loss, even when they saw the roofs falling in they jumped on to them. Many were buried under the debris, many while trying to escape found one limb or another pinned down, and still more were choked by the dust. Seeing in this the hand of God and indifferent to their own losses, the men of Gamala pressed their attack, driving the enemy on to the roofs as they stumbled in the steep, narrow ways, and with a rain of weapons from above dispatching those who fell. The debris furnished them with any number of great stones, and the bodies of the enemy with cold steel: they wrenched the swords from the fallen and used them to finish off those who were slow to die. Many flung themselves to their death as the houses were actually falling. Not even those who fled found it easy to get away; for unacquainted with the roads and choked with the dust, they could not even recognize their friends, but in utter confusion attacked each other. At last after long search they found the exits and escaped from the town.

Vespasian, keeping as close as he could to his struggling soldiers, and deeply moved by the sight of the town falling in ruins about his army, had forgotten his own safety, and without realizing it had gradually reached the highest level of the town, where he found himself in the utmost peril and almost alone. Not even his son Titus was with him at this time, having just been sent to Mucianus in Syria.[20] Flight seemed both dangerous and disgraceful; so remembering his lifetime of struggle and his reputation for prowess he became like one inspired, made his men link their shields to cover their armed bodies, stemmed the wave of attackers that swept down from above, and heedless of the swarms of men and the hail of missiles stood firm, until overawed by his superhuman courage the enemy slackened their attacks. Relieved of their pressure he withdrew step by step, not turning his back till he was outside the walls. Roman losses in this battle were very heavy. One of the fallen was the decurion Aebutius, a man who not only in the action in which he fell but in many earlier battles had shown heroic courage and inflicted very heavy casualties on the Jews. A centurion named Gallus, cut off with ten soldiers in the mêlée, crept into somebody's house. Like the others he was a Syrian, and he overheard the occupants discussing over supper how they would deal with the Romans and look after themselves. In the night he emerged from hiding, cut all their throats, and with his men got back safely to the Roman lines.

Roman morale had suffered severely. Defeat was unfamiliar, disaster on this scale unprecedented, and the soldiers burned with shame to think they had left their commander to his fate. But Vespasian consoled them, suppressing any allusion to himself to avoid the least semblance of reproof. 'What might happen to anyone you must face,' he said, 'like men. Remember, it is in the nature of war that bloodless victories do not happen, and Fortune is a fickle-footed ally. You have killed thousands and thousands of Jews, and her ladyship has only exacted a token payment. If it is vulgar to crow over victory, it is just as cowardly to whine under defeat. You never know how long either will last. A first-class soldier never lets success go to his head; that is why failure never gets him down. As for recent events, they were not due to any slackness of ours or to Jewish prowess: their gain and our loss both came from the difficulty of the ground. With that in mind you might be blamed for your reckless impetuosity: when the enemy retired to the higher ground, you should have restrained yourselves and not run your heads into the danger that hung over you. As you were masters of the lower town, you should have gradually enticed the enemy down to where you could meet them safely on firm ground. Instead, in your headlong dash for victory you forgot all about safety. Such recklessness in war, such crazy impetuosity is foreign to us Romans, who win all our victories by efficiency and discipline; it is the vice of backward races and the chief cause of Jewish defeats. Well then! It is up to us to rely once more on our own superiority and to see red rather than be down in the mouth about an unlucky reverse. The best encouragement each of you will find is his own right arm; that is how you can avenge the killed and punish the killers. For my own part, I shall try, in this and every battle, to be first to get at the enemy and the last to leave the field.'

With this address Vespasian restored the morale of his army. Meanwhile the people of Gamala were for the moment cheered by their success, so unexpected and so overwhelming; but later, when they realized that they had robbed themselves of any hope of coming to terms and knew in their hearts that they could not escape – already they were short of supplies – they became terribly despondent and their courage failed them. However, they did what they could to make themselves safe: the bolder spirits guarded the gaps in the wall, the rest lined those battlements that were still standing. But when the Romans raised the platforms higher and tried a new assault, most of them began to run out of the town, down almost impassable ravines where no pickets had been posted or through the underground passages. The few who remained from fear of being captured were starving, for every corner had been scraped bare to supply the fighting men.

While in spite of these privations Gamala still held out, Vespasian diverted some of his strength to deal with the garrison of Mount Tabor, midway between Scythopolis and the Great Plain. This mountain is no less than 20,000 feet high, with the northern face almost unclimbable: the top is a plateau three miles long with a wall right round.[21] Josephus had built this huge rampart in forty days,[22] obtaining his material and even his water supply from the plain. (The occupants relied entirely on rain.) On this plateau vast numbers had gathered; so Vespasian dispatched six hundred horsemen under Placidus. He, finding the ascent impossible, called on the rank and file to make peace, offering to intercede for them and obtain terms. They came down, intending to meet guile with guile. Placidus had wooed them with honeyed words in order to capture them in the plain; they came down in apparent compliance, intending to attack him off his guard. However, Placidus won the battle of wits; for when the Jews began the fight, he pretended to flee, drew his pursuers far into the plain, and then turned his horsemen about and routed the enemy, killing vast numbers of them and cutting off the rest so that they could not return. These gave up Tabor for lost and fled to Jerusalem; the natives, their safety being guaranteed and their water having failed, handed themselves and the mountain over to Placidus.

At Gamala the more venturesome were slipping away unnoticed, while the combatants sustained the siege and the non-combatants died of starvation. On the 22nd of Hyperberetaios, during the dawn watch, three soldiers of the Fifteenth Legion crept up to the tower that projected opposite them and noiselessly undermined it. In the darkness the sentries on its battlements failed to observe them either during or after their arrival. Working in silence the soldiers rolled away the five stones forming the base. As they jumped out of the way the tower fell with a resounding crash, bringing the sentries down with it. The other sentry-groups fled in panic; many made a bold effort to break through but were cut down by the Romans, among them Joseph, who was killed by a chance shot as he tried to escape through a gap in the wall. Bewildered by the crash, the whole population lost their heads and ran in all directions as if the entire Roman army had broken in. At that moment Chares, confined to bed and in the doctor's hands, expired, his death caused by terror as much as by his illness. The Romans, however, mindful of their earlier failure, made no attempt to force their way in, till on the 23rd of the month Titus returned and, furious at the blow that had fallen on the Romans in his absence, chose two hundred cavalry and some infantry and noiselessly entered the town. Discovering this when he was already inside, the sentry-groups gave the alarm and rushed to their posts. In a moment news of the Roman entry reached the centre of the town. Some snatched their children and dragging their wives with them fled to the citadel, wailing and shouting; others went to meet Titus and were without exception killed. Many were prevented from running up to the heights, and in their helplessness fell into the hands of the Roman guards. There were heart-rending cries as men were slaughtered on every side, and the whole town was deluged with the blood that poured down the slopes.

To deal with those who had retired to the citadel Vespasian came in person at the head of his entire force. The hill-top was rocky and inaccessible on every side, soaring to an immense height, ringed with precipices and thick with people all round. There the Jews inflicted heavy casualties on their attackers, rolling down rocks and hurling missiles of every kind, while they themselves on their lofty perch were almost out of reach. But to ensure their destruction they were struck full in the face by a miraculous tempest, which carried the Roman shafts up to them but checked their own and turned them aside. So violent was the blast that they could neither keep their feet on the narrow ledges, having no proper foothold, nor see the approaching enemy. Up came the Romans and hemmed them in: whether they resisted or tried to surrender, their fate was the same, for the Romans boiled with rage against them all when they remembered those who had perished in the first onslaught. Despairing of escape and hemmed in every way, they flung their wives and children and themselves too into the immensely deep artificial ravine that yawned under the citadel. In fact the fury of the victors seemed less destructive than the suicidal frenzy of the trapped men; 4,000 fell by Roman swords, but those who plunged to destruction proved to be over 5,000. The sole survivors were two women, nieces of Philip son of Jacimus, a man of note who had commanded King Agrippa's army. They survived because when the town fell they eluded the fury of the Romans, who on this occasion did not even spare babies in arms, but seized all they found and slung them from the citadel. Thus Gamala fell on the 23rd of Hyperberetaios, the revolt having begun on the 24th of Gorpiaios.

CHAPTER 14

Factions in Jerusalem

ONLY Gischala, a little town in Galilee, was left unreduced. The inhabitants were anxious for peace – for the most part they were farmers whose only concern was the prospect of a good harvest; but a powerful gang of bandits had infiltrated into their midst and some of the townsmen had been infected. These were incited and organized for revolt by John son of Levi, an impostor expert in every wile, full of ambitions and with a knack of making them succeed.[1] Anyone could see that he was bent on war as a means of becoming dictator. He was the recognized leader of the insurgent element in Gischala; thanks to them the population, who would gladly have sent envoys offering to surrender, were now preparing a warlike reception for the Romans. To crush this opposition Vespasian dispatched Titus with 1,000 horse, removing the Tenth Legion to Scythopolis. He himself returned to Caesarea with the other two, to rest them after their continuous efforts and in the belief that good living in the city would make them fit and keen in readiness for the coming struggles. It was no light task that he saw awaiting him at Jerusalem, for she was the city of kings and capital of the whole race, and into her was flowing a stream of refugees from the war. Her natural strength and formidable walls caused him no small anxiety; and he realized that the daring spirits within would, even without walls, be hard to subdue. So he trained his soldiers like athletes before a contest.

When Titus rode up to Gischala he saw it would be easy to take the town by assault; but he knew that if it was stormed, there would be a wholesale massacre of the population by the soldiery, and he was already sick of bloodshed and grieved that the whole people, without distinction, must share the fate of the guilty. He was therefore anxious to persuade the town to surrender on terms. The wall was crowded with men, mostly members of the corrupt gang; so he asked them what gave them such confidence that, when every other town had fallen, they alone opposed the Roman arms. They had seen much stronger towns overthrown by a single assault, while all who had accepted Roman terms enjoyed their own possessions in safety. The same terms he now offered them, freely forgiving their truculence. To desire freedom was natural enough: to persist when no possibility remained was inexcusable. If they refused to accept his generous proposals and sincere offers, they would experience the remorselessness of his arms, and learn the terrible lesson that to the Roman engines their wall was just a toy – the wall that gave them such confidence that they were the only Galilaeans to show themselves truculent prisoners.

To these overtures none of the townspeople could make any reply – they could not even go on to the wall; the bandits had already occupied it all, and there were sentries at the gates to see that no one slipped out to accept the offered truce or admitted any of the cavalry into the town. But John replied that he welcomed the proposals himself and would either persuade or constrain any dissidents. However, in accordance with the Jewish Law, Titus must allow them that day, the seventh, on which it was an offence either to take up arms or to make peace. It was known even to the Romans that they did no work of any kind when the seventh day came round; if they were compelled to break that rule, the man who compelled them would be as guilty as themselves. The delay would do Titus no harm; what could be attempted in one night except flight, which would be impossible if he camped round the town? It would be a great gain to them not to infringe any ancestral custom, and a gracious act in one who granted an unlooked-for peace to respect the laws of those whose lives he spared. With such pleas John beguiled Titus, being less anxious about the seventh day than about his own skin. He was afraid of being left to his fate the moment the town fell, and pinned his hopes of life on darkness and flight. But clearly God was preserving John to bring destruction on Jerusalem, and it was His doing that Titus not only accepted this pretext for delay, but even pitched his camp further from the town, at Cydassa.[2] This is a strong inland village of the Tyrians, always engaged in bitter strife with the Galilaeans. The size of the population and the strength of the defences enabled it to maintain the struggle against the surrounding nation.

In the night John, seeing no Roman guards round the town, seized his chance, and taking with him not only his armed bodyguard but a large number of non-combatants with their families, fled towards Jerusalem. For two miles or more, though driven along at top speed by fear of prison and death, he managed to carry along a mob of women and children; but as he pressed on further they dropped behind, and agonizing were the lamentations of those thus abandoned. The further each found himself from his own kith and kin, the nearer he imagined himself to the enemy. Believing that their captors were hard on their heels, they lost their heads and turned when they heard the footsteps of their fleeing companions, as if their pursuers were upon them. Many lost their way, and even on the highroad many were crushed in the fight to get to the front. Miserable was the plight of women and children; some even ventured to call their husbands or kinsmen back, shrieking and imploring them to wait. But John's commands were obeyed: 'Every man for himself,' he shouted; 'make for the place where you can avenge those left behind, if they fall into Roman hands.' So as every man made what speed his strength allowed, the column of fugitives lengthened out.

When dawn came Titus advanced to the wall to conclude the treaty. The people opened the gates to him, and coming forward with their families hailed him as a benefactor who had delivered the town from oppression. They told him of John's flight and begged him to spare them and to come and punish the remaining rebels. Titus, deciding that the people's requests must take second place, sent a detachment of horse to pursue John, but they failed to overtake him and he reached Jerusalem in safety. Of those who had set out with him, however, some 6,000 were killed, and nearly 3,000 women and children were rounded up and brought back. Titus was vexed at his failure to inflict immediate punishment on John for his deception; but for his baffled rage he had compensation enough in the mass of prisoners and heaps of dead. So he entered the town amid acclamations, and ordering his men to tear down a short section of the wall in token of capture, used threats rather than punishment to subdue the disturbers of the peace. For many from personal animosity and private enmity would denounce the innocent, if he tried to pick out those who deserved punishment; it was better to leave the guilty in suspense and fear than to destroy any guiltless person with them; for the guilty man would perhaps change his ways from fear of punishment, appreciating the pardon he had received for the past; but for those needlessly put to death there could be no redress. However, he made the town safe with a garrison, by which he could restrain the disaffected and leave the peaceably inclined more secure.

Thus the whole of Galilee was subdued, after giving the Romans plenty of strenuous exercise in preparation for the assault on Jerusalem.[3]

On John's arrival there the whole population turned out, and round each of his companions in flight a vast crowd collected, crying for news of events outside. Still hot and breathless the fugitives could not hide the stress they were under, but they swaggered in their sorry plight, declaring they had not run from the Romans but had come to give them battle on favourable ground. Obviously it would have been senseless and futile to risk their lives in a hopeless struggle for Gischala and other weak little towns, when they ought to save their arms and energies for the united defence of the Capital. Then they mentioned in passing the capture of Gischala, but what they euphemistically described as their withdrawal was generally seen to have been a rout. When, however, the fate of the prisoners became known, utter dismay seized the people, who saw in it an unmistakable omen of their own. John himself, quite unconcerned for those he had left behind, went round urging them one and all to war by false hopes, making out that Roman power was feeble, exaggerating Jewish strength, and ridiculing the ignorance of the inexperienced. Not even if they grew wings could the Romans ever get over the wall of Jerusalem, after being so severely mauled in their attacks on Galilaean villages and wearing out their engines against their walls.

With this nonsense he drew most of the young men into his net and whetted their appetite for war, but of the sensible, older men there was not one but saw what was coming and mourned for the City as if it had perished already. Such was the confused state of the people, but the country population had been torn by dissension before faction reared its head in Jerusalem. (For[4] Titus had left Gischala for Caesarea, and Vespasian had marched from Caesarea to Jamnia and Azotus. These towns[5] he reduced and garrisoned, returning with a mass of people who had surrendered on terms.) Every town was seething with turmoil and civil war, and as soon as the Romans gave them a breathing-space they turned their hands against each other. Between advocates of war and lovers of peace there was a fierce quarrel. First of all in the home family unity was disrupted by partisan bitterness; then the nearest kinsmen severed all ties of blood, and attaching themselves to men who thought as they did lined up on opposite sides. Faction reigned everywhere, the revolutionaries and jingoes with the boldness of youth silencing the old and sensible.

They began by one and all plundering their neighbours, then forming themselves into companies they extended their brigandage all over the country, so that in lawless brutality the Romans were no worse than the victims' own countrymen – in fact those who were robbed thought it far preferable to be captured by the Romans.

The garrisons of the towns, partly to avoid trouble and partly to spite the Jews, did little or nothing to protect those attacked. When at last the leaders of the various gangs of bandits had had enough of plundering the countryside, they came together and formed a single pack of rogues. Then they infiltrated into Jerusalem, a city without military command, where by age-old custom anyone of Jewish race was admitted without scrutiny, and where at this juncture everyone thought that those who were pouring in all came out of kindness as allies. It was this very thing that, quite apart from the faction-fighting, ultimately wrecked the City; for a useless and idle mob consumed supplies adequate for the fighting-men, and in addition to war they brought on themselves faction and starvation. Other bandits from the country slipped into the City, and joining forces with the desperadoes within gave themselves to every imaginable crime. They did not limit their insolence to theft and brigandage, but went so far as to commit murder, not by night or secretly or against the common people, but openly by day, beginning with the most eminent. First they seized and imprisoned Antipas, a member of the royal family[6] and one of the most influential men in the City, entrusted with all the public funds. Next came Levias, an eminent man, and Sophas, son of Raguel, both of royal blood, then all who were prominent in the country. Terror filled the people, and as if the City had been taken by storm no one thought of anything but his own safety.

The terrorists were not satisfied with imprisoning their captives; they thought it unsafe to keep men of influence in such custody for long, as their households were quite large enough to attempt their rescue, and the whole people might be sufficiently incensed by their outrageous conduct to rise in revolt. So they decided to murder the prisoners, choosing for their tool the most bloodthirsty assassin among them, one John, whose father was called in the vernacular Dorcas. He and ten others went into the prison sword in hand and ran the prisoners through. This outrageous crime they justified with a monstrous lie; they alleged that the men had approached the Romans about surrendering Jerusalem, and had perished as traitors to their country.

In fact, they boasted of their crimes as if they were benefactors and saviours of the City. The result was that the people became so cowed and abject, and the terrorists so rabid, that they actually got control of the appointment of high priests.[7] Setting aside the families which provided them in succession,[8] they appointed obscure persons of no family, to gain partners in crime; those who without deserving it found themselves in the highest office were inevitably the creatures of those who had put them there. Again, they sowed dissension between their rulers by various tricks and scandalous stories, turning the squabbles of those who might have restrained them to their own advantage, till, sated with their crimes against men, they transferred their insolence to the Deity and entered the Sanctuary with their polluted feet.

The populace were now seething with discontent, urged on by the oldest of the high priests, Ananus,[9] a man of the soundest judgement who might have saved the City if he had escaped the hands of the plotters. These made the Temple of God their stronghold and refuge from popular upheavals, and the Sanctuary became the centre for their illegal operations. Through their atrocities ran a vein of ironic pretence more exasperating than the actions themselves. For to test the submissiveness of the people and prove their own strength, they attempted to appoint the high priests by lot, though as we said before the succession was by birth.[10] The excuse given for this arrangement was ancient custom; they said that from time immemorial the high priesthood had been conferred by lot. In reality this was a reversal of the regular practice and a device for consolidating their power by arbitrary appointments. Assembling one of the clans from which high priests were chosen, a clan called Eniachin, they drew lots for a high priest. The luck of the draw furnished the clearest proof of the depths to which they had sunk. The office fell to one Phanias, son of Samuel, of the village of Aphtha, a man not only not descended from high priests but too boorish to have any clear notion of what the high priesthood might be. Anyway they dragged him willy-nilly from his holding and disguised him from head to foot like an actor on the stage, robing him in the sacred vestments and teaching him his cues. To the perpetrators this shocking sacrilege was the occasion for ribald mirth, but the other priests, watching from a distance this mockery of their law, burst into tears, cut to the heart by this travesty of the sacred rites.

Such impudence was more than the people could stand: one and all determined to bring tyranny to an end. Natural leaders like Gorion, son of Joseph, and Symeon, son of Gamaliel,[11] by passionate appeals to public meetings and by a door-to-door canvass urged them to act now, punish the destroyers of freedom, and purge the Sanctuary of these blood-guilty men. The most respected of the high priests, Jeshua, son of Gamaliel,[12] and Ananus, son of Ananus, held meetings at which they took the people severely to task for their indifference and incited them against the Zealots; for 'Zealots' they called themselves, as if they were devoted to good works, not zealous for all that was vile – vile beyond belief.[13] The populace flocked to a mass meeting where everyone denounced the invasion of the Sanctuary, the rapine and bloodshed, but no one was prepared to resist, as it was obvious that the Zealots would be very difficult to tackle. So Ananus stood up in the middle, and turning again and again to the Sanctuary with his eyes full of tears began thus:

'How wonderful it would have been if I had died before seeing the house of God full of countless abominations and its unapproachable, sacred precincts crowded with those whose hands are red with blood! Yet I who wear the vestments of a high priest and answer to the most honoured and august of names, am alive and in love with life, and cannot face a death that would be the glory of my old age! And so I'll go alone, and as if no one else existed, I'll give my one life for God. What is the use of living among people blind to calamity and no longer capable of tackling the troubles on their hands? You are plundered without a protest, beaten without a murmur, witnesses of murder without one audible groan. What unbearable tyranny! But why blame the tyrants? Don't they owe their existence to you and your lack of spirit? Wasn't it you who shut your eyes when the gang was first formed – a mere handful then – encouraged its growth by your silence, and by standing idly by while they were arming turned those arms against yourselves? The right thing would have been to nip their attacks in the bud when they were pouring abuse on your own flesh and blood; but by your utter indifference you encouraged these ruffians to plunder. When houses were ransacked, nobody cared; so they seized their owners too, and dragged them through the middle of the City without anyone raising a finger to defend them. Next they flung into jail the men you had let down – I will not say how many or of what character. Uncharged, uncondemned, they were imprisoned without a soul coming to the rescue. The natural consequence was that these same men were seen murdered. We saw this too – they were like a herd of dumb animals from which the best victims were dragged away one by one; yet not a murmur was uttered, not a hand raised!

'Take it calmly then, take it calmly, when you watch your Sanctuary trampled underfoot. You yourselves built every one of the steps by which these sacrilegious wretches have climbed so insolently; do not grumble if they have reached the top. Why, by now they would undoubtedly have reached still dizzier heights, if there had been anything greater than the Sanctuary to destroy!

'They have seized the strongest place in the City – from now on the Temple must be spoken of as a citadel or fort; tyranny is strongly entrenched and the enemy can be seen over your heads; but what do you mean to do? how can you quieten your fears? will you really wait for the Romans to recover our holy places? have things gone so far in the City, are we so sunk in misery, that we are an object of pity even to our foes? Why don't you rise, you spiritless creatures, and turn to meet the blows, and, as you see beasts do, kick out at your tormentors? Why don't you remember your own personal miseries, set before your eyes what you have suffered, whet your appetite for their blood? Have you really lost the most honourable and deep-rooted of our instincts, the longing for freedom? Are we in love with slavery and devoted to our masters, as if our fathers had taught us to be doormats? Why, again and again they fought to the bitter end for independence, defying the might of both Egypt and Persia rather than take orders from anyone! But why talk about our fathers? our present struggle with Rome – never mind whether it is profitable and advantageous or the opposite – what is its object? Isn't it freedom? Then shall we refuse to yield to the masters of the world and put up with tyrants of our own race? Yet submission to a foreign power might be put down to one crushing blow of fortune; but subservience to the scum of our own nation would prove us wilful degenerates.

'Having once mentioned the Romans, I will make no secret of what occurred to me as I spoke and turned my thoughts in their direction. Even if we fall into their hands – I do not suggest we shall – we cannot suffer any worse treatment than these men have subjected us to. Could anything be more galling than first to see offerings left in the Temple by our enemies,[14] then spoils seized by men of our own race who have robbed and massacred the nobility of our capital city, murdering men whom even the Romans would have spared in the hour of triumph? The Romans never went beyond the bounds set for unbelievers,[15] never trampled on one of our sacred customs, but reverently gazed from a distance at the walls of the Sanctuary; and men born in this country, brought up in our customs and called Jews, stroll where they like in the Inner Sanctuary, their hands still reeking with the slaughter of their countrymen! In face of that can anyone dread a foreign war, and enemies by comparison far kinder to us than our own people? Why, if we are to call things by their right names, we might well find that the Romans are the champions of our Law, and its enemies are inside the City!

'But that these plotters against our liberty are the scum of the earth, that for what they have done no one could devise the punishment they deserve, I am sure you were all satisfied when you left home, and before I uttered a word you were furious with them because of the things they have made you suffer. Possibly most of you are terrified by their numbers and their temerity, and also by the advantage of their position. But these are the results of your inaction, and now will grow worse still if you procrastinate. Indeed their numbers are increasing daily, since birds of a feather flock together; their temerity is inflamed by the complete lack of opposition; and they will naturally make use of their commanding position and fortify it too, if we give them the chance. But rest assured that if we go over to the offensive, they will be defeated by their own guilty conscience, and the advantage of height will be cancelled out by anxiety. Perhaps the Deity they have offended will turn their missiles against themselves, and the ungodly wretches will die by their own weapons. We have only to show ourselves and they are finished! Even if there is some danger involved, it will be a splendid thing to die before the sacred gateways and to sacrifice our lives, if not for our wives and children, yet for God and His Temple. I will champion your cause with head and hand; I will do everything I can think of to secure your safety, and every ounce of my bodily strength is at your disposal.'

With this eloquent appeal Ananus roused the populace against the Zealots, though well aware that they would be most difficult to suppress now, numerous, young, and intrepid as they were, and with such terrible crimes on their consciences; for they would hold out to the last, having no hope of pardon for what they had done. Nevertheless he was ready to endure anything rather than look on when affairs were in such a parlous state. The people for their part clamoured for him to lead them against the enemies he had denounced, every man most anxious to be in the forefront of the fight. But while Ananus was enlisting suitable men and organizing them for battle, the Zealots got wind of what was afoot, as they were kept informed of all that the people were doing. They were furious, and charged out of the Temple en masse and in large gangs, sparing no one they encountered. The citizens' forces were quickly mustered by Ananus, superior in numbers, but in equipment and training far inferior to the Zealots. However, enthusiasm made up for the deficiencies on both sides. Those from the City fortified themselves with rage more powerful than weapons, those from the Temple with animal courage for which no numbers were a match; the former were convinced that it was impossible to stay in the City unless they rid her of the terrorists, the Zealots that unless they triumphed they would be spared no punishment. So they joined battle, with their passions in command. They started by pelting each other with stones in the streets and in front of the Temple and by hurling spears at long range. When either side retired the victors used their swords. The slaughter on both sides was frightful and the wounded could not be counted. Casualties on the people's side were carried into the houses by their relatives; if a Zealot was hit he went up into the Temple, leaving bloodstains on the sacred floor. It might indeed be said that their blood alone polluted the sacred floor.

In these encounters the sudden sorties of the bandits were always successful; but the citizens' forces, blazing with fury and constantly growing in numbers, heaped abuse on all who wanted to surrender, while those who turned tail were unable to retire because of the men pushing forward from the rear. Thus they turned their whole strength against their opponents. The latter, unable to withstand this onslaught any longer, slowly retired into the Temple, Ananus and his men charging in with them. Alarmed by the loss of the first court, they took refuge in the inner and at once locked the gates. Ananus could not bring himself to attack the sacred gateways, especially as the enemy were hurling missiles from above, and he deemed it unlawful, even if the attack succeeded, to bring in the City crowd unpurified; so he detailed 6,000 armed men to guard the colonnades.

These were relieved by others, and every man had to take his turn as sentry; but many members of the upper classes were allowed by their superiors to hire men of humbler means to take their place on guard.[16]

The whole of this citizen army was later destroyed – thanks to John, who, as the reader knows, had ratted from Gischala.[17]

CHAPTER 15

Atrocities in the City. Vespasian's Intervention

JOHN was as crafty as a fox. He was eaten up with the love of despotic power and had long been engaged in treasonable activities. In the present crisis he pretended to be on the citizens' side and went every-where with Ananus, whether to discuss the situation with the leading men by day or to visit the guardposts by night, afterwards betraying his secrets to the Zealots.[1] Thus every question discussed by the citizens, even before a decision had been reached, was communicated by him to their mortal enemies. In his determination to avoid sus-picion he showed the utmost obsequiousness to Ananus and the leaders of the citizens. But his efforts to impress produced the opposite result; for his lick-spittle attitude brought him under greater suspicion, and his habit of pushing his nose in everywhere without an invitation made it look as if he was betraying secrets. For evidently their enemies knew all their intentions, and no one had invited the suspicion of having disclosed them more than John. To get rid of him was another matter; he had strengthened his position by his atrocious conduct, and in any case was not one who could be disregarded; and he had built up a large following among members of the Sanhedrin; so it was decided to make him take an oath of loyalty. John swore readily enough to be loyal to the citizens, to betray neither action nor in-tention to their enemies, and to put his powers of body and mind at their service for the destruction of their assailants. Ananus and his friends, satisfied with these oaths, now forgot their suspicions and invited him to their discussions[2]: they even commissioned him to arrange a truce with the Zealots; for they were anxious that no act of theirs should desecrate the Temple and that no Jew should fall in its precincts.

John, however, as if he had sworn loyalty *to* the Zealots and not against them, went in, and placing himself in their midst declared that he had often run into danger for their sakes, to keep them in-formed of all the secret measures concerted against them by Ananus and his friends; now he was face to face with the greatest possible danger, and so were they all, unless providence came to their aid.

Ananus was on the move; he had persuaded the people to send a delegation to Vespasian,[3] requesting him to come with all speed and take over the City; and to injure the Zealots he had announced a purification ceremony for the morrow, so that his men could gain admittance either as worshippers or by force and attack them at close quarters. He did not see how they could hold out for long or stand up to such vast numbers. He added that it was by divine providence that he was the one commissioned to arrange a truce; Ananus was making these overtures in the hope of catching them off their guard. They must therefore either humbly beg their besiegers to spare their lives or obtain some help from outside. Anybody who cherished hopes of being pardoned if they suffered defeat must have forgotten their own black record, or imagine that when the offenders expressed regret their victims were obliged to forgive them at once. In actual fact wrongdoers often caused only disgust by eating humble pie, and the wronged were all the more furious when they found they had the whip hand. Lying in wait for the Zealots were the relatives and friends of the murdered, and a mass of people enraged by the suppression of laws and lawcourts. Even if a tiny section of these was sorry for them, the furious majority would obliterate it.

Such was the fanciful story John told to frighten them all. Precisely what 'help from outside' he had in mind he did not venture to explain, but he was hinting at the Idumaeans.[4] To rouse the Zealot leaders to special fury he insinuated that Ananus was a savage brute whose threats were particularly meant for them. The leaders were Eleazar, son of Simon, judged the most capable of devising suitable measures and carrying them out, and one Zachariah, son of Amphicalleus, both members of priestly families. When these two heard the general threats and then those directed against them personally, and were told that Ananus and his friends in their determination to make themselves dictators were calling in the Romans – another of John's slanders – they were quite at a loss what to do, being so desperately short of time; for the citizens were prepared to attack them quite soon, and the speed of this design had cut off all hope of reinforcement from outside, as they would be finished entirely before any of their allies was any the wiser. All the same they decided to call in the Idumaeans, and wrote a brief letter saying that Ananus had deceived the people and was betraying the Capital to the Romans; that they themselves had revolted in defence of their freedom and as a result were imprisoned in the Temple; that a few short moments would decide whether they should survive; and that unless the Idumaeans came to their aid with all speed, they would soon be in the hands of Ananus and their mortal enemies, and the City in the hands of the Romans. Further details the messengers were to communicate to the Idumaean chiefs orally. To convey the message they chose two men of great energy, fluent and convincing speakers on public affairs, and – still more important – exceptionally good runners. They knew the Idumaeans would promptly agree, as they were an excitable and un-disciplined race, always on the look-out for trouble and with an appetite for revolution, ready at the least flattery from those who sought their aid to take up arms and dash into battle as if to a banquet. The message had to be delivered with all speed – this the messengers (both called Ananias) were only too eager to do, and they very soon reached the Idumaean headquarters.

The rulers, amazed by the letter and the explanations of the bearers, raced about the country like madmen, proclaiming mobiliza-tion. The muster was complete before the time appointed, and every man seized his arms to defend the freedom of the Capital. Forming an army 20,000 strong they marched to Jerusalem commanded by four generals, John and James the sons of Sosas, Simon son of Cathla, and Phineas son of Clusoth.

Neither Ananus nor the sentries had noticed the departure of the messengers, but they could not miss the arrival of the Idumaeans. Aware of it in good time Ananus barred the gates against them and posted sentries on the walls. Anxious however not to antagonize them completely he decided to try persuasion before resorting to arms. So taking his stand on the tower facing them Jeshua, the senior high priest after Ananus, made this appeal.

'Many different disorders have gripped this city: no trick of fortune has astonished me so much as the way scoundrels have received sup-port from unexpected quarters. You, for instance, have come here to help these dregs of humanity against us with more alacrity than could be expected even if the Capital had called on you to resist a foreign attack. If I saw any resemblance between you and those who have fetched you here, your enthusiasm would seem natural enough; no bond is as close as similarity of character. But actually, if they were examined one by one, none of them would be found fit to live a moment longer. The dregs, the scum of the whole country, they have squandered their own property and practised their lunacy upon the towns and villages around, and finally have poured in a stealthy stream into the Holy City, bandits so utterly ungodly that they have dese-crated even hallowed ground. They may be seen now shamelessly getting drunk in the Sanctuary and spending what they have stolen from their victims to satisfy their bottomless appetite. But your great army in its shining array is a sight that would be welcomed if the Capital had by common consent invited you to support us against a foreign enemy. What could anybody call this but one of fortune's meanest tricks, when he sees an entire nation take up arms for the sake of the most despicable scoundrels?

'For a long time I have been asking myself what on earth made you move so suddenly. Without good cause you would never have armed yourselves from head to foot to support bandits against your kith and kin. When we heard Rome and treachery mentioned – that is what some of you were shouting a little while ago, and how you had come here to guard the freedom of the Capital – nothing these impudent wretches ever did surprised us as much as this lying inven-tion. Men who are born lovers of liberty, and for liberty above all are ready to fight a foreign enemy, could in no other way be incited against us than by framing a charge that we were betraying their beloved liberty. Think who are the slanderers and who are their victims, and gather the truth not from fairy tales but from known facts. Whatever could induce us to sell ourselves to the Romans now? We need not have revolted at the start; and when we had done so, we could quickly have made our submission, before our countryside was ravaged. Now, even if we wanted to, we could not easily obtain an armistice, when the Romans despise us for the loss of Galilee, and it would be a disgrace worse than death to cringe to them when they are on our doorsteps. For myself, I would prefer peace to death, but once war has begun and battle been joined I would rather die bravely than live as a prisoner.

'Which do they say – that we, the citizens' leaders, sent secretly to the Romans, or that the citizens voted us authority to proceed? If they blame us, let them name the friends we sent, the stooges who put the dirty business through! Was anyone spotted on his way there or caught on the way back? Are they in possession of any letters? How did we keep it dark from all these thousands of citizens with whom we rub shoulders all day long, while a handful of men, blockaded and unable even to leave the Temple for the City, were informed of secret goings-on in the country? Has the information reached them only now, when they must pay the penalty for their crimes? and while they had no fear for themselves, was none of us suspected of treachery? If on the other hand they lay the blame on the citizens, everything was discussed in public, wasn't it? There was a full attendance at the meeting, so that before your informants arrived rumour would have brought you the news quite openly. Then again, wouldn't they have sent ambassadors if they had voted for an armistice? Who was elected? Let them name him. Gentlemen, this is simply the pretence of men afraid to die and fighting to escape the punishment that is coming to them. Why, if the City *had* been destined to be betrayed, no one but our slanderers would have been vile enough to do it; the list of their villainies is complete already but for this one – treason.

'But now that you are here in arms, your prime duty is to defend the Capital and help us exterminate the usurpers who have suppressed our courts of justice, trampled on our laws, and settled all disputes with their swords. Men of mark, charged with no offence, they have dragged from the middle of the market-place fettered and humiliated, and deaf to protests and entreaties have murdered them. You are free to enter – though not by right of war – and see for yourselves the proofs of what I say: houses emptied by their rapacious hands, wives and children of the murdered men in black, tears and laments in every corner of the City. There is no one who hasn't felt the hand of these grasping scoundrels. Into such a frenzy of madness they have plunged that they have transferred their impudent banditry not only from the country and outlying towns to the very heart of the Jewish world, but even from the City to the Temple! This they have made their headquarters and fortress, the base for their operations against us; and the spot venerated by the whole world and honoured by foreigners from the ends of the earth is trampled on by beasts bred in our midst. Now in their despair they are deliberately setting district against district, town against town, and enlisting the nation to tear out its own vitals. Therefore the right and proper course for you, as I said before, is to help us to exterminate the ruffians, and to punish them for cheating you by daring to call you in as allies when they ought to have feared you as avengers.

'But if you can't disregard the appeals of such men, it is still

possible to lay aside your arms, come into the City by right of kinship, and serve as arbitrators holding the balance between both sides.
Think what they will gain by your judgement on charges unanswer-
able and very serious. *They* would not hear a word in defence of men
charged with no offence at all: still, let them reap the benefit of your
coming. But if you will neither share our indignation nor act as
judges, there is a third course – to dissociate yourselves from both
sides and neither rub salt into our wounds nor give any support to
those who wish to destroy the mother-city. However much you
suspect that some of us have been in contact with the Romans, you
have only to watch the approaches; if any of these slanderous suggestions is found to be true, then you can come and defend the Capital
and punish those whose guilt is proved. The enemy couldn't catch
you off your guard while you are so near the City. If none of these
proposals seems to you acceptable or reasonable, don't be surprised
that the gates remain shut as long as you carry arms.'

Jeshua's speech fell on deaf ears. The Idumaean rank and file were
furious at not being instantly admitted, while their generals were
enraged by the invitation to lay down their arms; they might as well
be prisoners as throw them away under compulsion. Simon, son of
Cathla, one of the generals, managed at last to quieten the uproar of
his men, took his stand where the high priests could hear him, and
made his reply.

'It is no longer surprising that the champions of liberty are confined
in the Temple, when our people are shut out of the city that belongs
to us all – shut out by men who are ready to admit the Romans,
perhaps with garlands on the gates, but who converse with Idumaeans
from the towers, and order them to throw away the arms they have
taken up in defence of liberty – men who will not trust their kinsmen
with the defence of the Capital yet expect those very people to
arbitrate in their disagreements, and accuse others of putting men to
death without a trial when they themselves are condemning the whole
nation to ignominy. The gates of this city have always been wide
open to every foreigner for worship,[5] and now you have walled them
up against your own countrymen! We were racing here to cut your
throats, of course, and to attack our own people – we, who were only
hastening to keep you free! No doubt those you are blockading have
wronged you in the same way, and you have collected an equally
convincing assortment of suspicions against them! Then while

confining everyone in Jerusalem who cares about the welfare of the state, after shutting your gates without distinction against the peoples who are nearest to you in blood and ordering them about in this insulting way, you complain that you are under the thumb of usurpers and hurl a charge of despotism against the victims of your own usurpation! Who could stomach your hypocrisy when he sees your words contradicted by the facts? – unless perhaps it is you who are being shut out of the Capital by the Idumaeans, the men *you* are excluding from their ancestral rites! One might reasonably blame the men besieged in the Temple because, when they were brave enough to punish the traitors whom you, being equally guilty, call "men of mark, charged with no offence", they didn't start with you and hack off first of all the most vital limbs of this treasonable plot. But if they showed foolish leniency, we Idumaeans will defend the House of God and fight for our common country, firmly resisting both the enemy from without and the traitors within. Here before the walls we shall remain in arms, till the Romans tire of paying attention to you, or you come over to the side of freedom.'

This speech was vociferously applauded by the Idumaean rank and file. Jeshua withdrew in despair, seeing them incapable of moderation and the City assailed from two sides. Not that the Idumaeans were in a happy frame of mind. They were furious and insulted at their exclusion from the City, and the failure of the Zealots, who seemed to be in a strong position, to give them any assistance so bewildered them that many were sorry they had come. But the disgrace of going home with nothing whatever accomplished outweighed their regrets, and they stayed where they were before the wall, encamped in the greatest discomfort. During the night a devastating storm broke; a hurricane raged, rain fell in torrents, lightning flashed continuously, the thunderclaps were terrifying, and the earth quaked with deafening roars. Disaster to the human race was plainly foreshadowed by this collapse of the whole framework of things, and no one could doubt that the omens portended a catastrophe without parallel.

The Idumaeans and the people in the City drew the same conclusion. The former felt that God was angry about the expedition and that they would not escape punishment for bearing arms against the Capital; Ananus and his friends were sure that they had gained a victory without a battle and that God was championing their cause. But this guess was wide of the mark – they were predicting for their enemies the fate that awaited their friends. For the Idumaeans pressing close together kept each other warm, and by making a roof overhead with their long shields were little the worse for the downpour; and the Zealots, more anxious about them than about the danger to themselves, met to discuss the possibility of helping them. The hotheads favoured using their weapons to force a way through the lines of guards, and then charging into the middle of the City and defiantly opening the gates to their allies. The guards would fall back confused by their unexpected move, especially as most of them were unarmed and had seen no fighting, while the citizen army could not easily be mustered, as they were confined to their own houses by the storm. If this meant danger, it was their duty to put up with anything rather than stand by while such a huge army perished miserably because of them. The more sensible people on the other hand opposed the use of force, seeing not only that the guards encircling them were at full strength, but that because of the Idumaeans the City wall was carefully guarded. They assumed also that Ananus was everywhere, visiting the guards at all hours. On other nights such was indeed the case, but on this night it was omitted, not through neglect on Ananus' part, but because Fate was determined that he should perish and all his guards with him. It was she who as the night advanced and the storm reached its height put to sleep the sentries guarding the colonnade, and gave the Zealots the idea of borrowing some of the Temple saws and cutting through the bars of the gates. The noise was not heard, thanks to the roar of the wind and the continuous crash of thunder.

They stole out of the Temple and made for the wall; then plying the same saws they opened the gate in front of the Idumaeans. The latter panicked at first, thinking that Ananus and his men were making an attack, and every man grasped his sword to defend himself; but they soon realized who had come, and passed through the gateway. If they had flung themselves on the City, nothing could have prevented the citizens from perishing to a man, such was their fury; but they were anxious to free the Zealots from their confinement first, as the men who had admitted them implored them not to forget that those they had come to assist were in dire peril, or involve them in greater danger. When they had overwhelmed the guards, they could easily attack the City; but if they once roused the City, they would never overcome the guards; for as soon as they realized the situation, the citizens would form up and block every way to the Temple.

Convinced by this reasoning, the Idumaeans passed through the City and up the slope to the Temple. When they appeared inside, the Zealots, who had been on tenterhooks till they arrived, emerged full of confidence from the inner courts, and mingling with the Idumaeans attacked the pickets, knifing some of the advanced sentries in their sleep. The shouts of those who were awake roused the whole force. Completely taken aback they snatched their weapons and rallied to the defence. As long as they thought that only the Zealots were attacking them they fought confidently, hoping to win by weight of numbers, but when they saw others streaming in from outside, they grasped the fact of the Idumaean irruption. Most of them lost hope, flung away their arms, and gave themselves up to lamentation; but some of the younger men, putting up a wall of shields, fought the Idumaeans tooth and nail and for a long time sheltered the feebler folk. Their cries informed the people in the City of the disastrous situation; but none of these ventured to help them when they learnt that the Idumaeans had broken in; they merely replied with futile shouts and groans, and loud shrieks went up from the women who all had relations in danger among the guards. The Zealots echoed the war-cry of the Idumaeans, and the din from every side was made more terrifying by the tempest. No one was spared by the Idumaeans, by nature most barbarous and bloodthirsty, and so knocked about by the storm that they vented their rage on the men who had shut them out, making no distinction between those who cried for mercy and those who fought. Many who reminded them of the ties of blood and begged them to reverence the Temple they shared were run through with swords. There was no room for flight, no hope of safety; they were crushed together and cut down until most of them, driven back, with no way of retreat left, relentlessly assailed by their murderous foes and, in a hopeless position, flung themselves headlong into the City, choosing for themselves a fate more pitiable, it seems to me, than the one they were fleeing from. The entire outer court of the Temple was deluged with blood, and 8,500 corpses greeted the rising sun.

This holocaust did not satisfy the Idumaean appetite for blood. Turning to the City they plundered every house and killed anyone they met. Then thinking the common people not worth bothering about they went after the high priests. It was against them that the main rush was made, and they were soon caught and killed. The murderers, standing on their dead bodies, ridiculed Ananus for his devotion to the people and Jeshua for his speech from the wall. So devoid of decency were they that they threw out the dead bodies without burial, though the Jews pay so much regard to obsequies that even those found guilty and crucified are taken down and buried before sunset. I should not be far wrong if I said that the fall of the City began with Ananus' death, and that the overthrow of the wall and the destruction of the Jewish state dated from the day when they saw the high priest, the champion of their cause, assassinated in the middle of the City. For he was a man looked up to on every account and entirely honest, and although so distinguished by birth, position, and reputation, he loved to treat even the humblest as equals. Utterly devoted to liberty and with a passion for democracy, he always made his own interests take second place to the public advantage and made peace the aim of his life; for he knew that Rome was invincible. But when he had no option he made careful preparations for war, in order that, if the Jews would not end hostilities, they might carry on the fight efficiently. In short, had Ananus lived, hostilities would indeed have ended; for he was an eloquent speaker who could mould public opinion and had already silenced his opponents: if war it was to be, the Jews would have held up the Roman advance a very long time under such a general.[6]

His yoke-fellow was Jeshua, not on his level perhaps, but far above the rest. But I think God had sentenced this polluted city to destruction and willed that the Sanctuary should be purged by fire, and so cut off those who clung to them and loved them so dearly. Thus men who a little while before had been clad in the sacred vestments, had conducted the worship renowned through the world and had been revered by visitors from every land on earth, were thrown out naked, to be devoured by dogs and wild beasts before all eyes. Virtue herself wept for these splendid men, I believe, lamenting her total defeat at the hands of Vice. Yet such was the end of Ananus and Jeshua.

With these two out of the way, the Zealots and a solid mass of Idumaeans fell upon the population and butchered them like a herd of unclean animals. Ordinary people were killed where they were caught; the young nobles were arrested, fettered, and locked up in prison: in the hope that some would join the rebels, their execution was delayed. But not a man did so – rather than align themselves with scoundrels against their own country they all chose death. For this refusal they paid a terrible price; they were flogged and racked, and only when their bodies could endure no more torture were they allowed to die by the sword. Those arrested in the morning were finished off at night, and the bodies brought up and thrown out to make room for the next batch. The people were so petrified with fear that no one dared either to be seen weeping for a dead kinsman or to bury him, but they kept their tears secret behind locked doors, and made sure that none of their enemies could hear them before they uttered a groan; for the mourner promptly received the same treatment as the mourned. By night they took up a little dust in their hands and sprinkled it on the bodies – or by day, if a man was exceptionally bold. 12,000 of the young nobles died in this way.

Disgusted now with haphazard slaughter, the Zealots set up sham courts and faked trials. They had decided to liquidate one of the most distinguished citizens, Zachariah, son of Baruch, as they were annoyed by his burning hatred of wrong and love of freedom, and his wealth made them hope not only to plunder his property but also to get rid of a man capable of destroying them. They therefore issued a categorical order, summoning seventy men in public positions to the Temple, where they turned them into a stage jury with no authority. Then they charged Zachariah with trying to betray their country to Rome and sending an offer of treason to Vespasian. There was no proof of the charges, no evidence at all, but they said that they themselves were quite convinced of his guilt and claimed that that should satisfy anyone. Zachariah realized that his fate was sealed: he had been treacherously summoned to a prison, not a court. But certain death was not going to deprive him of free speech – he stood up, scoffed at the incredibility of the charges, and in a few words disposed of the whole indictment. Then, turning the tables on his accusers, he methodically detailed all their illegalities and mercilessly exposed their mismanagement of affairs. The Zealots howled with rage and could hardly keep their hands off their swords, determined as they were to play out this farce, this sham trial to the end, and eager also to find out whether the jurors would risk their own lives in the cause of justice. But the seventy brought in a unanimous verdict of Not Guilty, choosing to die with the defendant rather than bear the responsibility for his destruction. The Zealots greeted his acquittal with shouts of indignation, and were all enraged with the jury for not realizing that the authority bestowed on them was a mere sham. Two of the most unscrupulous fell upon Zachariah, murdered him in the middle of the Temple, and jested over his dead body: 'Now you have got our verdict too, and your trials are over.' With that they threw him out of the Temple and into the valley beneath. Then they showed their contempt for the jurors by belabouring them with the backs of their swords and driving them from the precincts. For one purpose only they refrained from murdering them – that they might go into every part of the City and let all the citizens know that they were slaves.

The Idumaeans now felt sorry they had come and were disgusted with the goings-on. One of the Zealots came to them privately and held a meeting at which he denounced the excesses they had committed jointly with those who had called them in, and listed the damage done to the Capital. They had taken up arms on the ground that the high priests were betraying the Capital to the Romans, yet they had found no evidence of treason whatever. But her defenders so-called were all out for war and personal domination. The right time to stop all this had been at the outset; but having once formed a partnership to shed their country's blood, they ought at least to set a limit to their misdeeds and not go on assisting the destroyers of all they held dear. If some of them were vexed at the closing of the gates and the refusal to let them enter at once with their weapons, those responsible had certainly paid for their opposition. Ananus was dead, and in a single night the population had been almost wiped out. This had produced an unmistakable revulsion of feeling in many of their own people, but those who had called them in displayed unparalleled savagery and not a trace of respect for their deliverers. Before the very eyes of their allies they perpetrated the vilest atrocities, and their excesses would be laid at the Idumaeans' door until someone either ended or repudiated what was going on. And so, as the allegation of treason had been exploded and there was no Roman invasion on the horizon, while the City was at the mercy of a caucus that could not be dislodged, their right course was to go back home and have nothing more to do with these contemptible people, and so blot out the memory of all the crimes in which they had been tricked into playing a part.

Accepting his advice the Idumaeans first released from prison about

2,000 citizens who at once left the City and fled to Simon,[7] of whom we shall speak by and by; then turning their backs on Jerusalem they went home.[8] Their departure had a paradoxical effect on both sides: the citizens, unaware of the revulsion of feeling, recovered their spirits for a time as if rid of an enemy, while the Zealots became more arrogant still, not as if they were deserted by allies, but as if relieved of men who frowned upon and interfered with their excesses. No longer was there any hesitation or circumspection about their outrages: they reached all their decisions with the utmost speed and executed them more quickly still. Chief objects of their lust for blood were the brave and the nobly born, the former being victims of their fear, the latter of their envy: they felt that their whole safety depended on their leaving no one who counted alive. Along with many others they murdered Gurion,[9] a man with a reputation and of good family, but democratic and passionately devoted to liberty, if ever a Jew was. He owed his ruin mainly to his plain speaking, as well as the advantages he enjoyed. Niger the Peraean did not escape their clutches. He had shown amazing courage in the campaigns against the Romans[10]; but now, protesting loudly and displaying his scars, he was dragged through the middle of the City. When pulled outside the gates he despaired of life and pleaded for burial; but they made it brutally clear that the grave he so desired would never be his, and then did the foul deed. As he died, Niger called down on their heads the vengeance of Rome, famine and pestilence, battle and slaughter, and as a final disaster, a death-grapple with their fellow-citizens. All these things heaven visited on the godless wretches; and the retribution was most just, for through their party-strife they were to taste before long the mad fury of their fellow-citizens.

Niger's death lessened their fear of being overthrown, but there was no section of the people for whose destruction they did not invent an excuse. Those with whom any of them had quarrelled had long ago been put away; those who had not collided with them in peacetime were subjected to carefully chosen accusations: if a man never came near them at all, he was suspected of arrogance; if he approached them boldly, of contempt; if he was obsequious, of conspiracy. The most serious accusations and the most trifling were alike punished with death, and no one could escape unless he was quite insignificant owing to humble birth or poverty.[11]

In the Roman camp all the generals treated the enemy's internal divisions as a godsend, and in their eagerness to march on the City begged Vespasian, as commander-in-chief, to lose no time. Divine providence, they said, had upheld their cause by setting their enemies at each other's throats; but the pendulum would soon swing back, and at any moment the Jews might be reunited through weariness of mutual injury or some revulsion of feeling. Vespasian replied that they were wide of the mark and were hankering after a theatrical display of armed warriors – a dangerous pose – oblivious to safety and commonsense. If he did march on the City at once, he would only reunite the enemy and turn their full strength against himself; if he waited, he would find their numbers reduced by their internal divisions. He might safely leave the generalship to God, who was handing over the Jews to the Romans without their lifting a finger, and making them a present of victory with no danger to the army. Very well then; while their opponents, torn by calamitous internal divisions, perished by their own hands, the right thing for them to do was to watch the dangerous conflict from a safe distance, not to get mixed up with suicidal maniacs locked in a death struggle. 'If anyone thinks', he went on, 'that victory without a fight won't taste so sweet, he had better realize that to win success by biding your time is a sounder policy than courting disaster by plunging into battle. And again, those who shine in physical combat are no more entitled to fame than those who accomplish just as much by self-discipline and brains.' Furthermore, while the enemy were growing weaker, his own army would recover from its continuous toil and be stronger than at present. Finally, this was not the time to set their hearts on a dazzling victory. The Jews were not busy making weapons, building walls or recruiting auxiliaries, in which case postponement would injure those who granted it, but were being bled to death by dissension and civil war, and suffering daily greater miseries than they would themselves inflict on them if they attacked and overwhelmed them. If then safety was to be the criterion, those who were destroying each other should be left to continue the good work; if they asked what kind of success would win the most fame, they would be fools to attack a sick community; for there would be no denying that the victory was due, not to them, but to Jewish divisions.

Vespasian's arguments were accepted by the officers, and any doubt as to the soundness of his judgements was soon dispelled; a steady stream of deserters eluded the Zealots. But flight was difficult as every exit was guarded and anyone caught going out, whatever the reason, was assumed to be on his way to the Romans and dispatched forthwith. However, if he paid enough they let him go, and only if he failed to pay was he a traitor, so that the rich purchased their escape and only the poor were slaughtered. Dead bodies along all the main roads[12] were heaped up high, and many who were anxious to desert decided instead to perish in Jerusalem, for hope of burial made death in their own city seem the lesser evil. But their enemies reached such a pitch of barbarity that they would allow no one, whether killed in the City or on the roads, so much as a hole in the ground. As if they were pledged to destroy the laws of their country and of Nature too, and along with their crimes against mankind to pollute the Deity Himself, they left the dead bodies rotting under the open sky. For those who buried a kinsman, as for deserters, the penalty was death, and anyone who gave burial to another soon needed it himself. In short, no other lofty emotion disappeared so completely amid the horrors of the time as pity; things that deserved compassion were the things that provoked these wretches, who switched their venom from the living to those they had murdered, and from the dead back to the living. Paralysed with fear the survivors envied those already dead – they were at peace – and the tortured occupants of the jails declared that compared with them even the unburied were fortunate. Their persecutors trampled on every ordinance of man, scoffed at the laws of God, and ridiculed the oracles of the prophets as the inventions of tricksters. Yet those prophets clearly discerned the laws of right and wrong, by breaking which the Zealots caused the prophecies against their country to be fulfilled. For there was an age-old saying of inspired men that the City would be taken and the most Holy Temple[13] burnt to the ground by right of war, if ever the citizens strove with each other and Jewish hands were the first to pollute the house of God. The truth of this the Zealots did not question; but they made themselves the means of its fulfilment.

By now John had set his heart on one-man rule and, not content to be on an equality with his fellows, gradually built up a following of the worst types and cut adrift from the rebel organization. He paid no heed whatever to the decisions of the rest and issued his own orders like a lord, obviously aiming at sole sovereignty. Some gave way to him through fear, some were genuine adherents; for he was very clever at winning support by the orator's tricks. Many thought their own skins would be safer if the crimes already committed were laid at one door, not many; and his activity with both hand and brain won him henchmen in plenty. However, a large number of dissidents left him,[14] to some extent prompted by envy and unwillingness to submit to a former equal, but in the main put off by dread of a sovereign ruler; for they could not hope to pull him down easily once he was master, and he would have a handle against them as they had opposed him at the start.[15] Every man chose to face war with all its miseries rather than throw away his liberty and die like a slave. This, then, was the explanation of the rift in the insurgent ranks, and John faced his opponents like a rival monarch. However, they did little more than watch each other's movements, and there was little or no actual fighting: their only rivalry was at the expense of the people – who would bring home the most loot was the point at issue. Now that the storm-tossed city was at the mercy of the three greatest calamities, war, tyranny, and party-strife, by comparison the citizens felt that war was almost endurable. Anyway they fled from their own people and sought sanctuary with foreigners, finding in the Roman camp the safety they had no hope of finding in their own city.[16]

And now a fourth calamity was coming on the doomed nation. Not far from Jerusalem was a well-nigh impregnable fortress built by the kings of long ago for the safe keeping of their treasures and their personal security in the hazards of war. It was called Masada, and was in the hands of the so-called Sicarii.[17] Hitherto they had merely raided the districts near by to procure supplies: fear prevented any further ravages; but when they heard that the Roman army was making no move, while the Jews in Jerusalem were torn by party-strife and domestic tyranny, they launched out on more ambitious schemes. During the Feast of Unleavened Bread (kept by the Jews in memory of their escape, ever since they were freed from slavery in Egypt and returned to their ancestral home) they eluded those who lay in their path and made a night raid on a little town called Engedi. Those who might have put up a resistance were scattered before they could seize their weapons and form up, and thrown out of the town; those who could not fly, women and children more than 700 in number, were butchered. Then they stripped the houses bare, seized the ripest of the crops,[18] and brought the loot to Masada. They proceeded to plunder all the villages round the fortress and ravage the whole area, their numbers being daily swelled by a flow of ruffians like themselves from every side.

In all districts of Judaea there was a similar upsurge of terrorism, dormant hitherto; and as in the body if the chief member is inflamed all the others are infected, so when strife and disorder broke out in the capital the scoundrels in the country could plunder with impunity, and each group after plundering their own village vanished into the wilderness. There they joined forces and organized themselves in companies, smaller than an army but bigger than a gang of bandits, which swooped on sanctuaries[19] and cities. Those they attacked suffered as severely as if they had lost a war, and were unable to retaliate as the raiders, like all bandits, made off as soon as they had got what they wanted. In fact, every corner of Judaea was going the way of the capital.

All this was reported to Vespasian by deserters; for though the insurgents guarded all the outlets and killed those who went near them, whatever the reason, there were some, nevertheless, who eluded them and fled to the Roman camp, where they begged the commander-in-chief to protect the City and save the remnant of the people – it was because of their loyalty to Rome that so many had lost their lives and danger threatened the survivors. Vespasian, already moved by their misfortunes, set out as if to besiege Jerusalem, but really to end the existing siege. But he was obliged first to reduce the places that were left, so as to leave nothing outside the City to interfere with the siege. He therefore proceeded to Gadara, the strongly fortified capital of Peraea, entering the city on the 4th of Dystros.[20] The authorities, unseen by the insurgents, had sent a deputation to him with an offer of surrender, partly from a longing for peace and partly to safeguard their possessions, many Gadarenes being very rich. Of this deputation their opponents knew nothing; Vespasian was nearly there before they discovered it. They despaired of holding the town themselves, as their enemies within outnumbered them and the Romans could be seen not far away. So they decided to flee, but could not bear to do so without spilling blood and wreaking vengeance on those who had brought things to this pass. They seized Dolesus, by birth and reputation the first citizen, but believed to be responsible for the deputation, killed him, and in their uncontrollable rage mutilated his dead body before fleeing from the town. The Roman force now arrived, and the people of Gadara welcomed

Vespasian with acclamation and received from him guarantees of protection, and also a garrison of horse and foot to deal with sudden attacks by the fugitives. They had pulled down their walls without orders from the Romans, so as to prove their devotion to peace by their inability to make war even if they wanted to.

To deal with those who had fled from Gadara Vespasian sent Placidus with 500 horse and 3,000 foot, while he himself with the rest of the army went back to Caesarea. When the fugitives suddenly caught sight of the pursuing horsemen, they crowded into a village named Bethennabris[21] before contact was made. Here they found a large number of young men and armed them willy-nilly. Then with utter recklessness they rushed out to attack Placidus. At the first onset his men gave a little ground, scheming to draw the enemy away from the walls; then, when they had got them where they wanted them, they encircled them and shot them down. Those who fled the cavalry cut off, those who were pinned down the infantry destroyed without mercy. In their death-struggle the Jews could do no more than display their fearlessness; for as they hurled themselves on the massed Romans behind their impenetrable barrier of steel, they could find no chink for their missiles to enter or means of breaking the enemy ranks, while they themselves were easy targets for Roman missiles and like the wildest of wild beasts charged the opposing steel and perished, some struck with the sword as they faced the enemy, some scattered by the cavalry.

Placidus was determined to block their dashes for the village, so he kept his cavalry moving past them on that side, and then wheeled round and instantly discharged a well-aimed volley, killing those who were near and scaring away the rest, till the bravest of them forced their way through and sought the protection of the walls. The sentries found themselves in a quandary: they could not bear to shut out the men from Gadara and with them their own friends; and if they let them in they would perish with them. This was exactly what happened; for when the Jews forced their way inside the ramparts, the Roman cavalry almost managed to burst in with them, and though the gates were shut in the nick of time, Placidus launched an attack, and after battling fiercely till evening captured the wall and the entire village. The non-combatants were exterminated, the able-bodied fled, the houses were ransacked by the soldiery, and the village set on fire. Those who escaped raised all the countryfolk, and by exaggerating their own calamities and saying that the entire Roman army was coming against them drove them all out on every side in terror, and with the whole mass fled towards Jericho; this was the only city left strong enough, at least in the size of its population, to nourish the hope of survival. Placidus, relying on his cavalry and encouraged by his earlier successes, pursued them to the Jordan, killing all he could catch; and when he had penned the whole mass on the bank of the river, where they were stopped by the current, which was swollen by rain and unfordable, he deployed his forces opposite them. Necessity compelled them to fight, having no way of escape; so they extended their line along the bank as far as they could and faced the missiles and the charges of the horsemen, who wounded many of them and threw them into the swirling waters below. Those who perished by Roman hands numbered 15,000; those who were forced to leap into the Jordan of their own accord could not be counted at all. Some 2,200 were taken prisoner, and there was a rich haul of asses, sheep, camels, and oxen.

The Jews had never suffered a heavier blow than this, and it seemed even heavier than it was; for not only was the whole path of their flight one long trail of slaughter and the Jordan rendered impassable by dead bodies, but the Dead Sea too was filled with corpses which the river carried down into it by the thousand. Placidus, seizing his advantage, launched attacks against the little towns and villages round about, captured Abila, Julias, Besimoth, and all the rest as far as the Dead Sea, and drafted into each the most suitable of the deserters. Then putting the soldiers on board ship he rounded up those who had sought safety on the lake. Thus all Peraea submitted or was crushed as far as Machaerus.[22]

CHAPTER 16

Vespasian Emperor

A T this time news was received of the rising in Gaul, and how Vindex
and the native chiefs had revolted from Nero,[1] as described in
detail by other writers. Vespasian's reaction was to step up his campaign; he already foresaw the coming civil wars and the danger to
the whole Empire, and felt that if he quickly pacified the eastern areas
he would lighten the anxiety of Italy. While therefore the winter
lasted he secured the conquered towns and villages with garrisons,
posting centurions in the towns and decurions in the villages, and rebuilt many that had been destroyed. In the early days of spring he set
out from Caesarea with most of his army and marched to Antipatris.
There he stayed two days to settle the affairs of the town, and the next
day marched on, destroying and burning all the villages around. After
reducing the toparchy of Thamna and the neighbouring districts he
went on to Lydda and Jamnia. As these two were subdued already,[2]
he settled there a sufficient number of those who had submitted, and
advanced to Emmaus. After seizing the approaches to the capital of
this area he fortified a camp, and leaving the Fifth Legion there
marched with the rest of his forces to the toparchy of Bethleptepha.
He ravaged with fire this and the neighbouring district together with
the outlying regions of Idumaea, building guardposts in strategic
positions. Then he captured two villages in the very middle of
Idumaea, Betaris and Caphartoba, killed over 10,000 inhabitants,
took over 1,000 prisoners, expelled the rest of the population, and
placed there a large part of his own forces. These overran and laid
waste all the hill country. Then at the head of his remaining forces he
returned to Emmaus, and from there went through Samaritis, past
Neapolis, known locally as Mabartha,[3] and down to Coreae, encamp-
ing there on the 2nd of Daisios. The next day he arrived at Jericho,
where Trajan, one of his generals, joined him with the force from
Peraea,[4] the whole area beyond Jordan being subdued already. The
bulk of the population, without waiting for their arrival, had fled
from Jericho to the hill country opposite Jerusalem, but a large section

which had stayed behind was put to death. The Romans found the city deserted.

Jericho is situated in a plain above which rises a bare, treeless mountain range of very great length, stretching northwards to the Scythopolis district, and southwards to the region of Sodom and the far end of the Dead Sea. This ridge is uneven all the way along and uninhabited because of its infertility. Beyond Jordan rises a parallel range beginning at Julias in the north and running southwards to Somorrhon, which borders on Petra in Arabia. In this range is the so-called Iron Mountain jutting out into Moab. The country between the two ranges is called the Great Plain,[5] stretching from the village of Ginabrin to the Dead Sea, and measuring a hundred and forty miles by fourteen. It is bisected by the Jordan and has two lakes in it, the Dead Sea and Lake Tiberias, opposite in character: the former is salt and sterile, the latter sweet and prolific. In summer time the plain is burnt up and the absolute drought makes the air unwholesome; for it is entirely waterless except for the Jordan, this being the reason why the palm-groves on the river-banks are more flourishing and bear heavier crops than those at a distance.

However, near Jericho there is an abundant spring, admirably suited for irrigation. It gushes out near the old city, the first in the land of Canaan to be stormed by the Hebrew commander Joshua the son of Nun.[6] This spring, it is said, at first not only blighted fruit-crops but produced miscarriages in women, in fact proved unwholesome and destructive of everything, but was sweetened and changed into a most wholesome and life-giving stream by the prophet Elisha, friend and successor of Elijah. When he had been made welcome by the people of Jericho and most hospitably entertained by them, he repaid them and their country with an undying favour. He went out to the spring and threw into the running water an earthenware jar full of salt, then raised his godly right hand towards heaven and poured atoning libations on the ground, beseeching earth to purify the water and open sweeter veins, and heaven to blend the waters with more life-giving airs and to give the people round about fruits in plenty and children to succeed them, not letting them ever lack water to give these birth, so long as they remained righteous. With these prayers, accompanied by many ritual acts based on deep study, he transformed the spring, so that the water that had hitherto brought childlessness and famine upon them, from then on furnished them with children and all good things.[7] Indeed, for irrigation it is so effective that if it merely comes in contact with the land, it benefits the crops more than waters that soak right in. So while the other streams, even if freely used, do little good, this tiny stream does a great deal. In fact it waters more land than all the rest, covering a plain eight and a half miles by two and a half, and satisfying the needs of very numerous and very lovely parks. Of the palms which it waters there are many varieties differing in taste and name: the richer ones when trodden underfoot actually yield a large quantity of 'honey', nearly as good as the real thing. Bees too abound in the district, which also produces balsam, the most valuable local crop, the cypress and the ben-nut[8]; so that it would be no exaggeration to call the place divine – a place where the rarest and loveliest things are found in such abundance. For as regards its other crops, it would be hard to find another region in the wide world to compare with it, so large is the yield from the seed sown. This is due, I think, to the warmth of the air and the fertilizing power of the water; the warmth draws out the growing plants and makes them spread, the moisture encourages root-growth in them all and supplies strength for the summer, when the district is so burnt up that no one goes out if he can help it. If the water is drawn before sunrise and then exposed to the air, it becomes extremely cold and quite unlike the atmosphere round it; on the other hand, in winter it warms up and bathers find it most comfortable. The air too is so mild that the inhabitants dress in linen when the rest of Judaea is under snow. Jericho is eighteen miles from Jerusalem and seven from the Jordan.[9] The country between the two cities is a rocky desert; between Jericho and the Jordan and Dead Sea it is more low-lying, but just as barren a desert.

Of Jericho and its great natural advantages enough has been said; but we must also describe the characteristics of the Dead Sea. This, as I said, is bitter and sterile, but brings even the heaviest things thrown into it to the surface because of their relative lightness; in fact it is not easy to go down into the depths even by deliberate effort. Thus when Vespasian came to examine it, he ordered some non-swimmers to be thrown into deep water with their hands tied behind them, and found that they all came to the surface as if blown upwards by a strong wind. In addition to this the changing colour is remarkable: thrice daily it alters its appearance and reflects the sun's rays with varying tints. Moreover in many places it throws up black lumps of asphalt,[10] which float and resemble headless bulls in shape and size. The lakeside workers row to the spot, seize the lumps one by one and haul them into their boats. When these are full it is not easy to get the asphalt away, as the boat sticks to the glutinous mass until they loosen it with a woman's menstruous blood and urine, the only things to which it yields. It is useful not only for caulking ships but also for curing bodily sickness: it is included in many medical prescriptions.

The length of this lake is sixty-seven miles, measured from Zoar in Arabia, the width seventeen.[11] Next to it lies the land of Sodom, once rich in crops and in the wealth of its cities, but now dust and ashes. They say that owing to the impiety of its inhabitants it was burnt up by lightning [12]; indeed, there are still marks of the fire from heaven and the outlines of five cities to be seen, and ashes still form part of the growing fruits, which have all the appearance of eatable fruit, but when plucked with the hand dissolve into smoke and ashes.[13] To this extent the stories about the land of Sodom are confirmed by the evidence of our eyes.

In order to make the encirclement of Jerusalem complete, Vespasian constructed camps in Jericho and Adida,[14] garrisoning each with a mixed force of Romans and allies. He also sent Lucius Annius to Gerasa,[15] giving him a squadron of cavalry and an ample number of infantry. Annius took the town by assault, put to death 1,000 of the younger men – all who had failed to escape, enslaved the women and children, and allowed the soldiers to plunder everything of value, finally setting fire to the houses before he marched against the surrounding villages. The strong fled, the weak perished, and all that was left went up in flames. Now that the war had engulfed the whole region of mountain and plain, it was impossible to leave Jerusalem; those who wanted to desert were watched by the Zealots, and those who did not yet favour the Romans were shut in by the army which surrounded the City on every side.

Vespasian had returned to Caesarea, and was getting ready to march his entire force against Jerusalem itself when he received the news that Nero had met a violent end after reigning thirteen years and eight days.[16] I might relate how Nero abused his position by entrusting the management of affairs to those utter scoundrels, Nymphidius and Tigellinus, two worthless freedmen; how when they plotted against him, he was deserted by all his guards, ran away with four faithful freedmen, and died in the suburbs by his own hand; and how those who had brought him down soon paid the penalty. I might give an account of the war in Gaul and explain how it ended, how Galba on being invited to mount the throne returned to Rome from Spain, and how he was accused of meanness by the soldiers, assassinated in the middle of the Roman Forum and succeeded by Otho. I might describe Otho's campaign against Vitellius' generals and his overthrow; the disturbances that followed under Vitellius and the fighting round the Capitol, and the way in which Antonius Primus and Mucianus destroyed Vitellius and the German Legions and so brought the civil war to an end.[17] But I must excuse myself from describing any of these events in detail, because they are matters of common knowledge and have been dealt with by many Greek and Roman writers [18]; to secure continuity and coherence in the narrative I have summarized the various incidents.

Vespasian's immediate response was to put off his expedition against Jerusalem, waiting anxiously to see who would step into Nero's shoes. Then, when he heard that Galba was on the throne, he refrained from all military activity pending the receipt of a new directive, but sent his son Titus to pay homage and seek the Emperor's instructions for settling the Jewish problem.[19] With the same object Agrippa embarked for Rome along with Titus. But while they were sailing along the Greek coast in warships because it was winter, Galba was assassinated, after a reign of seven months and as many days,[20] and his office went to Otho, who laid his own claim to the headship of the state. Agrippa decided to complete his journey as if nothing had happened; Titus by a divine impulse sailed back from Greece to Syria and proceeded with all speed to Caesarea to rejoin his father. In their suspense – for the Roman Empire was rocking and everything was in the melting-pot – the two commanders held up operations against the Jews, feeling that while they were so anxious about things at home an invasion of a foreign country would be inopportune.

But there was to be no peace for Jerusalem. There was a young hothead called Simon, son of Gioras, a Gerasene by birth. He was less crafty than John who was master of the City, but superior in physique and daring – the quality which had caused Ananus the high priest to turn him out of his toparchy of Acrabata, so driving him into the arms of the bandits who had seized Masada.[21] At first they eyed him warily, and only allowed him into the lower part of the fortress with the women he brought with him, occupying the upper part themselves. Later, as a kindred spirit and to all appearance trustworthy, they took him on their plundering expeditions and raids round about Masada. His eloquence, however, failed to persuade them to attempt anything more ambitious; they were used to the fortress and dared not venture far from their lair. But Simon had made up his mind to usurp supreme power, and when he heard that Ananus was dead he withdrew to the hill country. There he proclaimed liberty for slaves and rewards for the free, so collecting the scum of the whole district. As soon as his force was strong enough he overran the villages in the hill country, until the constant flow of recruits encouraged him to descend to lower levels. Soon he was an object of dread to the towns, and many men of good position were led astray by his strength and continual success, so that his army no longer consisted only of slaves and bandits, but included many respectable citizens who obeyed him like a king. He next overran the toparchy of Acrabata and the whole area as far as Great Idumaea[22]: near a village called Nain he had built a wall which he used to secure himself from attack; and in the valley of Pharan he found a number of convenient caves and enlarged many others, using them all to safeguard his treasure and to house the loot. There too he stored the corn he had seized and accommodated most of his armed gangs. It was obvious that he was training his army in readiness to attack Jerusalem.

Alarmed at his designs and determined to nip the growing threat in the bud, the Zealots marched out in force under arms. Simon met them and gave battle, inflicting heavy casualties and driving the survivors into the City. He was not yet so sure of himself as to assault the walls: he embarked first on the conquest of Idumaea,[23] setting out for the frontier at the head of 20,000 well-armed men. The Idumaean authorities promptly collected the best fighting-men in the country, about 25,000 of them, and leaving all the rest to guard their homes against raids by the Sicarii from Masada, awaited Simon at the frontier. Battle was joined and raged all day long, ending without victory to either side. Simon returned to Nain and the Idumaeans dispersed to their homes. Not long after Simon with a larger force again invaded their territory, and encamped near a village called Tekoa. From there he sent Eleazar, one of his staff, to the garrison of Herodium near by to induce them to surrender the fort.[24] Eleazar was readily admitted by the guards, who did not realize what he had come for; but when he mentioned surrender, they drew their swords and chased him until, unable to fly any further, he flung himself from the wall into the ravine below and was instantly killed. But the Idumaeans were now thoroughly alarmed by Simon's strength, and decided not t o give battle till they had reconnoitred the enemy forces.

For this duty Jacob, one of their officers, eagerly offered his services with the intention of turning traitor. Setting out from Olurus, the village where the Idumaean army was concentrated at the time, he went straight to Simon and made a compact with him. In return for a solemn undertaking that he should always occupy a position of influence, he would first hand over his own home town, and then help Simon subdue the whole of Idumaea. On this understanding he was lavishly entertained by Simon, and buoyed up with dazzling promises returned to his own lines. When he had undermined the morale of the officers, and gradually of the whole army, by pretending that Simon's army was many times its real size, he urged them to receive Simon and hand over all authority to him without a struggle. During the negotiations he sent messengers to invite Simon, promising to disperse the Idumaeans, as indeed he did. As the army drew near he was the first to leap on to his horse and flee with his companions in crime. Panic seized the whole defending force, and before battle could be joined they left their posts and every man fled to his own home. Having in this unexpected way swept into Idumaea without bloodshed, Simon by a surprise attack captured the little town of Hebron, where he seized a vast quantity of booty and got possession of ample corn supplies. If the inhabitants are to be believed, Hebron is more ancient than any town in the country – older even than Memphis in Egypt; its age is reckoned as 2300 years. They affirm that it was the home of Abraham, the ancestor of the Jews, after his migration from Mesopotamia, and that his descendants went down into Egypt from there. Their tombs are pointed out to this day in the little town, of the finest marble and beautifully fashioned.[25] Three quarters of a mile from the town[26] can be seen an immense terebinth, said to be as old as creation.[27] From there he advanced through the whole country, not only sacking villages and towns but ravaging the countryside: in addition to the heavy infantry he had 40,000 men with him, so that he could not supply his immense host even with the necessities of life. Quite apart from his needs, his brutal nature and vindictiveness against the Idumaean people were major reasons for the devastation of their land. Just as in the wake of locusts we may see a whole forest stripped bare, so in the rear of Simon's army there was nothing left but a desert. Some places they set on fire, others they demolished; everything that grew anywhere in the country they destroyed, either trampling it down or devouring it, and their heavy feet made cultivated land harder than barren soil. In short, not a sign remained to show that what they destroyed had ever existed.[28]

All this roused the Zealots to fresh activity. They dared not face Simon in the open, but they laid ambushes in the passes and captured his wife and many of her servants. Then, as delighted as if they had taken Simon himself prisoner, they went back to the City in the belief that he would at once lay down his arms and plead for the return of his wife. Her capture, however, moved him not to pity but to fury; he came up to the walls of Jerusalem, and like a wounded animal that cannot catch the hunter, he vented his rage upon everyone he met. All who went outside the gates to gather herbs or firewood, old people without arms, he seized and tortured to death. In his boundless indignation he was ready to feed on their dead bodies. Many he sent back after cutting off their hands, in an attempt to terrify his opponents and stir the people to revolt against those responsible. They were ordered to say that Simon swore by God, the Lord of all, that if they did not instantly give him back his wife, he would break down their wall and inflict the same punishment on every person in the City, sparing neither young nor old and treating guilty and innocent alike. These threats terrified not only the citizens but the Zealots too, and they sent his wife back to him. Pacified for the time being he took a brief respite from continual bloodshed.

It was not only in Judaea that sedition and civil war were rife, but in Italy too. Galba had been assassinated in the middle of the Roman Forum and his successor Otho was at war with Vitellius, who claimed the throne as the nominee of the legions in Germany. At Bedriacum in Northern Italy battle was joined with Valens and Caecina, Vitellius' generals. On the first day Otho had the better of it, on the second the army of Vitellius. The carnage was frightful, and when Otho at Brixellum learnt of his defeat he committed suicide, after a reign of only three months and two days.[29] His troops went over to Vitellius' generals, and Vitellius himself marched into Rome with his army.

Meanwhile Vespasian left Caesarea, and on the 5th of Daisios launched a campaign against those parts of Judaea that had not yet submitted. Climbing into the hill country he occupied two top-archies, those of Gophna and Acrabata, and then two small towns, Bethel and Ephraim.[30] After garrisoning these he rode as far as Jerusalem, slaughtering many of those he met and taking prisoners by the score. Cerealis, one of his officers,[31] took a small body of horse and foot and ravaged Upper Idumaea, taking Caphethra (which calls itself a town) in his stride and setting it on fire, and after a preliminary assault laying siege to Capharabin too. The wall was very strong indeed, and he was resigning himself to a long wait when without warning the inhabitants opened the gates, came forward with olive-branches in their hands, and gave themselves up. After accepting their surrender Cerealis made for Hebron, another, very ancient, city, situated, as we have seen, in the hill country not far from Jerusalem. Forcing an entry he slaughtered all he found there, old and young alike, and burnt the city to the ground. Every place had now been reduced but Herodium, Masada, and Machaerus, which were in the hands of the bandits: the target of the Romans was now Jerusalem itself.

When Simon had got back his wife from the Zealots, he returned to what remained of Idumaea, and harrying the nation from every direction forced the majority to flee to Jerusalem. He followed them to the City himself, and again encircling the wall killed any working men he caught going out into the country. The people found Simon outside more terrifying than the Romans, and the Zealots inside more savage than either: of these the Galilaean contingent was pre-eminent in the originality and audacity of their crimes. It was they who had put power in the hands of John, and he from the pinnacle on which they had set him rewarded them by leaving every man free to do as he liked. Their passion for looting was insatiable: they ransacked rich men's houses, murdered men and violated women for sport, and *drank* their spoils washed down with blood: through sheer boredom they shamelessly gave themselves up to effeminate practices, adorning their hair and putting on women's clothes, steeping themselves in scent and painting under their eyes to make themselves attractive. They copied not merely the dress but also the passions of women, and in their utter filthiness invented unlawful pleasures; they wallowed in slime, turning the whole city into a brothel and polluting it with the foulest practices. Yet though they had the faces of women, they had the hands of murderers; they approached with mincing steps, then in a flash became fighting-men, and drawing their swords from under their dyed cloaks ran every passer-by through. Those who ran away from John had a more murderous reception from Simon, and anyone who eluded the tyrant within the walls was killed by the tyrant outside the gates. Thus for those who wished to desert to the Romans every way of escape was cut off.

But John's forces were in a mutinous state, and the entire Idumaean contingent[32] detached itself and attacked the usurper from jealousy of his power as well as hatred of his brutality. They joined battle and wiped out many of the Zealots, chasing the rest into the royal palace built by Grapte, a kinswoman of the king of Adiabene, Izates.[33] The Idumaeans poured in with them, then driving them from there into the Temple set about looting John's effects: it was in this palace that he himself was living and storing the spoils of his tyranny. Meanwhile the mass of Zealots scattered all over the City joined forces with the fugitives in the Temple, and John got ready to lead them down against the citizens and the Idumaeans. The latter, being better fighters, feared their onset less than their madness: in the night they might slip out of the Temple, murder their opponents and burn the City to the ground. So they held a joint meeting with the chief priests to discuss the best means of guarding against their onslaught. But God, it seems, turned their thoughts to foolish courses, and to save their lives they chose a remedy worse than death: in order to overthrow John they voted to admit Simon, and olive-branch in hand to bring in a second tyrant to be their master. The resolution was carried out, and they sent the high priest, Matthias,[34] to implore Simon to enter – the man they so greatly feared! The invitation was supported by those citizens who were trying to escape the Zealots and were anxious about their homes and property. He in his lordly way expressed his willingness to be their master, and entered with the air of one who intended to sweep the Zealots out of the City, acclaimed by the citizens as deliverer and protector. But when he and his forces were inside his one purpose was to establish his own supremacy, and he looked upon those who had invited him as enemies no less than those he had been invited to suppress.

Thus in Xanthicos of the third year of the war Simon became master of Jerusalem. John and the Zealots, unable to leave the Temple and with all their possessions in the City lost – for their property had been instantly plundered by Simon's men – saw no hope of safety. Aided by the citizens Simon began an assault on the Temple; the enemy took their stand on the colonnades and battlements and beat off their attacks. Many of Simon's men were killed and many were carried away wounded; for from their commanding position it was easy for the Zealots to aim their shafts with telling effect. Having already the advantage of position, they further constructed four immense towers to enable them to hurl their missiles from a still greater height – one at the north-east corner, one above the Gymnasium and the third at another corner opposite the Lower City, while the last was set up over the roof of the priests' chambers,[35] where it was the custom for one of the priests to stand and proclaim by trumpet-blast the approach of the seventh day in the late afternoon and its close the next evening, calling on the people in the first case to cease work and in the second to resume it. On these towers they mounted spear-throwers and stone-throwers along with archers and slingers. Simon's attacks now grew more hesitant, most of the men being dispirited; all the same he hung on, having the advantage in numbers, though the artillery with its longer range accounted for many of the men engaged.

While all this was happening[36] Rome herself suffered severe shocks. Vitellius had arrived from Germany dragging along with his army a vast mob of hangers-on[37]; and as the accommodation provided for the soldiers was inadequate, he turned the whole City into a camp and filled every house with armed men. These were unused to the sight of Roman wealth and the silver and gold that glittered all around them; they could hardly restrain their covetous desires, but turned to plunder and the murder of any who got in their way. Such was the state of affairs in Italy.

Vespasian, having crushed all opposition in the neighbourhood of Jerusalem, went back to Caesarea. There he heard of the upheavals in Rome and the accession of Vitellius.[38] He knew how to obey as well as how to command, yet the news angered him; he could not accept as master one who had madly seized on the Empire as if it were derelict; and in his distress at what had happened he suffered unbearable agony and could not give his attention to wars elsewhere while his home-land was being ravaged. But while anger drove him to her defence, the thought of the distance restrained him; the possibility that fortune might play many a scurvy trick before he could cross to Italy, especially if he sailed in the winter season,[39] curbed his indignation which was fast getting out of control.

But his officers and men in informal groups were already talking openly of revolution and exploding with rage. 'The soldiers in Rome, living in luxury and afraid of the very word "war", vote anyone they fancy on to the throne, and appoint emperors with one eye to the main chance. We, who have toiled and sweated and grown old in the service, let others enjoy this privilege, even when we have in our own camp a candidate with much stronger claims. What better way shall we find of repaying his kindness to us, if we throw this chance away? Vespasian's claim to the throne is far stronger than Vitellius's – just as we are far better soldiers than those who appointed him. The wars we have carried through were hardly trifles compared with those in Germany, and as soldiers we can stand comparison with those who brought *that* tyrant with them! But no contest will be necessary – neither Senate nor people will put up with a filthy lout like Vitellius instead of a clean-living man like Vespasian, or turn down a kindly leader in favour of a despotic brute, or choose a childless man as their chief rather than a father; for the best guarantee of peace is the outstanding excellence of princes. If then it takes the experience of years to make good government, we have Vespasian; if the vigour of youth, Titus: the advantages of both ages will be combined. And not only shall we supply strength to those we appoint – we have three legions and contingents from the kings; but they will be backed by all the east and as much of Europe as is safely out of Vitellius's reach, and by the allies in Italy, as well as Vespasian's brother and another son. One of these will be joined by many young men of distinction[40]; the other has already been entrusted with control of the City[41] – an immense asset for any candidate for imperial honours. In short, if we lose our chance, the Senate will most likely appoint the very man whose own soldiers, after helping him guard the Empire, have passed him over.'

Such were the remarks passed by the knots of soldiers, who then joined forces and, urging each other on, declared Vespasian emperor and called on him to save the tottering Empire. He indeed had long been anxious about the general weal, but had never sought office for himself; for though aware that in view of his services he had a good claim, he preferred the safety of private life to the dangers of exalted position. But when he turned down their invitation, the officers were all the more insistent, and the rank and file surrounded him sword in hand, and threatened to kill him if he refused the life that was his due. After earnestly impressing on them his many reasons for declining office, in the end, as he could not convince them, he accepted their nomination.

Mucianus[42] and the other officers now pressed him to assume the sovereignty, while the lower ranks loudly demanded that he should lead them against any that opposed him. But his chief anxiety was to get control of Alexandria, knowing that Egypt was the most important part of the Empire because it supplied corn.[43] Once master of Egypt he felt sure that if hostilities dragged on he could make Vitellius' position impossible, as the people of Rome would not be content to go hungry; secondly he wished to obtain the support of the two legions at Alexandria[44]; and lastly he planned to make the country his shield against the incalculable tricks of fortune. For Egypt is difficult to enter by land, and the coast is almost harbourless; on the west it is protected by the waterless regions of Libya, on the south by Syene (separating Egypt from Ethiopia) and the unnavigable cataracts of the Nile, and on the east by the Red Sea, which extends as far as Coptus. Its northern bulwarks are the district adjoining Palestine and the Egyptian Sea, where there is no anchorage at all. Thus Egypt is walled in on every side. Its length from Pelusium to Syene is about two hundred and thirty miles; the distance by sea from Plinthine to Pelusium is a little over four hundred.[45] The Nile can be navigated as far as the city of Elephantine,[46] beyond which further progress is barred by the cataracts mentioned above. It is difficult even in peacetime for ships to approach the harbour of Alexandria; the entrance is narrow, and submerged rocks make a straight course impossible. The left side is shut in by artificial moles; on the right the island of Pharos lies off shore, and from this rises an enormous lighthouse whose fires are visible thirty-five miles away, warning visiting ships to anchor at night well away from the shore because of the difficulty of making the port.[47] The island is surrounded by immense artificial defences; hurling itself against these and breaking round the barriers opposite, the sea makes the channel rough and the narrow entrance treacherous. Inside, however, the harbour is perfectly safe, and is three and a half miles long.[48] To this port is brought everything the country lacks for life and comfort; in return what the land produces in excess of requirements is exported to every part of the world.

Naturally Vespasian was anxious to gain control there and so ensure the stability of the whole Empire. He wrote at once to the governor of Egypt and Alexandria, Tiberius Alexander, informing him of the army's enthusiasm and asking for his help and co-operation, since he himself was being forced to shoulder the burden of empire. After reading this letter aloud, Alexander enthusiastically called on soldiers and civilians alike to swear allegiance to Vespasian[49]; both were delighted to obey, knowing what an excellent man he was from his campaigns near by. Invited thus to prepare the way for Vespasian's accession, he got everything ready for his arrival; and in a flash rumour spread the news of the emperor in the east, and every city celebrated the good news and offered sacrifices on his behalf. The Moesian and Pannonian legions, still furious at the impudence of Vitellius, were even more delighted to swear allegiance to Vespasian. He, setting out from Caesarea, came to Berytus, where many deputations from Syria and many from the other provinces met him, bringing from all the cities crowns and addresses of congratulation. Mucianus, governor of the province, arrived too with news of the universal enthusiasm and the swearing of allegiance in every city.

Everywhere things were going well for Vespasian and with few exceptions were combining to further his ends. He now felt that divine providence was helping him to seize the reins of office and that some just destiny was choosing him as monarch of the world. In one place after another a succession of omens had foretold his reign: he specially remembered the words of Josephus, who while Nero was still alive had dared to address him as Emperor.[50] He was grieved to think that the man was still a prisoner in his hands; so he sent for Mucianus and his other officers and friends, and after first enlarging on Josephus' outstanding energy and the difficulties he had created for the Romans at Jotapata, he went on to describe the predictions which he himself had suspected at the time of being fictions springing from fear, but which had been proved by time and the course of events to be truly inspired. 'It is shocking,' he said, 'that the man who prophesied my rise to power and was the mouthpiece of God should still be treated as a prisoner and endure the lot of a captive'; then summoning Josephus he ordered him to be set free. Seeing a foreigner receive such recompense, the officers felt they could confidently expect wonderful things for themselves; but Titus, who was present with his father, exclaimed: 'Father, it is only right that Josephus's disgrace should be removed as well as his fetters. It will be equivalent to a free pardon if instead of unfastening his chains we cut them through.' This is the usual procedure in the case of a man unjustly fettered. Vespasian agreed, and a man came forward and severed the chain with one blow of an axe. Josephus, having thus recovered his civil rights as a reward for his past prophecies, was now believed capable of foretelling what was still to come.

After replying to the deputations Vespasian made a careful choice of governors for the various provinces and then proceeded to Antioch. There he considered what course to take, and decided that his journey to Alexandria was less urgent than a settlement in Rome, since Alexandria was his already but Rome was in a ferment because of Vitellius. So he sent Mucianus to Italy with a formidable body of horse and foot. Mucianus, afraid to sail in the depth of winter, marched his army overland through Cappadocia and Phrygia.[51]

Meanwhile Antonius Primus, at the head of the Third Legion from Moesia, where he was in command,[52] was rapidly advancing to do battle with Vitellius. Vitellius sent Caecina Alienus with a large force to oppose him, having complete confidence in this officer in view of his defeat of Otho. Setting out with all speed from Rome he came face to face with Antonius near Cremona, a Gallic town just over the Italian frontier.[53] But when he saw the size and discipline of the enemy force he had no stomach for a fight, and as retreat seemed dangerous he decided to change sides. Assembling his centurions and tribunes he urged them to go over to Antonius, minimizing the resources of Vitellius and magnifying the strength of Vespasian. The one, he said, was sovereign only in name, the other in fact; it was better for them to recognize the inevitable and adapt themselves to it, and as they were bound to be defeated if they gave battle, they must escape the danger by their wits. Vespasian was quite capable, without their assistance, of winning all that was not yet in his grasp: Vitellius, even with it, could not hold what he had.

Speaking to this effect at considerable length Caecina persuaded his whole force to desert to Antonius. But that very night the soldiers changed their minds, realizing with horror that the man who had sent them might prove the winner. So drawing their swords they dashed off to kill Caecina, and would have carried out their intention if the tribunes had not fallen on their knees and begged them not to. They refrained from killing him, but bound the traitor with the intention of sending him to Vitellius. Informed of this, Primus at once summoned his men and led them fully armed against the mutineers. These formed a line and resisted for a while, but soon turned tail and made for Cremona. Primus at the head of his cavalry prevented their entrance, encircled and destroyed the bulk of them before the city, and sweeping in with the survivors gave his troops permission to loot the town. The consequence was that many foreign business men and many of the inhabitants lost their lives, as well as Vitellius' entire army of 30,200 men: of the soldiers from Moesia 4,500 perished.[54] Antonius set Caecina free and sent him to Vespasian to report his triumph. On his arrival Caecina was received with such unexpected honours that his shocking treachery was soon forgotten.

At Rome too Sabinus was more confident now that he knew Antonius was approaching; so collecting the cohorts of armed watchmen he seized the Capitol in the night. At daybreak he was joined by many of the nobles, among them Domitian, his brother's son, the chief pillar of his hopes of victory. Vitellius cared little about Primus, but was furious with those who were supporting Sabinus in his revolt, his congenital brutality making him thirst for noble blood. The part of his army which had returned with him to Rome he flung against the Capitol. The utmost heroism was displayed both by these men and by those who defended the temple; but in the end numbers told and the troops from Germany captured the hill. Domitian and many leading citizens had a remarkable escape, but the rest of the garrison was annihilated. Sabinus was brought before Vitellius and put to death, while the soldiers stripped the temple of its treasures and set it on fire. Next day Antonius marched in with his army; the soldiers of Vitellius met him, joined battle in three areas of the City, and perished to a man. Out of the palace came Vitellius, drunk, and as a last fling gorged to the eyes like the glutton he was. Dragged through the crowd, insulted and tormented in every possible way, he was knifed to death in the heart of his capital, after a reign of eight months and five days: if he had happened to live longer I doubt whether the Empire could have satisfied his lust. Other known casualties totalled more than 50,000 dead. All this took place on the 3rd of Apellaios.[55]

The next day Mucianus entered with his army and stopped further slaughter by Antonius' men, who were still searching the houses and killing many of Vitellius' soldiers and many supposed partisans among the civilians, letting their rage forestall any careful discrimination. He then put forward Domitian, recommending him to the assembled citizens as head of the state till his father arrived. The people, free at last from fear, acclaimed Vespasian as Emperor, and held a combined celebration for his establishment on the throne and Vitellius' overthrow.

After arriving at Alexandria Vespasian received the good news from Rome, and envoys came from all over the world to congratulate their new sovereign, so that the City – bigger than any but Rome – proved too small for the swollen population. Now that the whole Empire was secure and the supremacy of Rome so surprisingly re-established, Vespasian turned his attention to the final stages of the Judaean campaign. He was eager, however, to embark for Rome in person as soon as winter ended, and was putting all his energy into getting things straight in Alexandria; but he sent Titus[56] with the pick of his army to destroy Jerusalem. Titus marched overland to Nicopolis two and a half miles from Alexandria. There he put his army on board naval vessels and sailed up the Nile past the district of Mendes to the city of Thmuis. Disembarking there he marched to the little town of Tanis, where he camped for the night. His second stopping-place was Heracleopolis, his third Pelusium. Here he rested his army for two days, and the next morning crossed the Pelusian river-mouths, and after marching all day across the desert pitched camp by the temple of Casian Zeus, going on the next day to Ostrakine. At this stopping-place there was no water – the inhabitants have to fetch it from elsewhere. After this he broke his journey at Rhinocorura, marching on from there to Raphia, his fourth stopping-place, a town on the Palestinian frontier. His fifth camp he pitched at Gaza, and then he went on to Ascalon, Jamnia, and Joppa, ending up at Caesarea, where he had decided to assemble his other units.

CHAPTER 17
The Siege of Jerusalem – First Stages

TITUS, having crossed the desert from Egypt to Palestine in the way we have described, arrived at Caesarea, where he had decided to concentrate his forces. While he was still at Alexandria helping his father to establish the sovereignty newly entrusted to them by God, the faction-fight in Jerusalem had broken out again; a three-cornered fight now, as one party had split in two – in such a miserable situation the best and most providential thing that could happen. The Zealots' attack on the citizens, for the City the beginning of the end, has been described already, with a detailed account of its origin and disastrous progress. We should not be far wrong if we described this as a faction within a faction, like a maddened beast driven by lack of other food to devour its own flesh.

Eleazar, son of Simon, who had at the start separated the Zealots from the citizens and removed them into the Temple precincts, professed indignation at the outrages daily committed by John, whose appetite for blood was still unsatisfied. The truth was that he could not bear to be under the thumb of a usurper who had come on the scene after him: he had set his heart on absolute power and one-man rule. He therefore broke away, taking with him Judas, son of Chelcias, and Simon, son of Ezron, both influential men, together with Hezekiah, son of Chobari, quite a well-known person. As each of these was followed by an appreciable number[1] of Zealots, they were able to seize the inner court of the Temple and take up positions over the Holy Gates on the sacred pediment. Provisions were ample, and they had no fears on that score: there was an unlimited supply of sacred commodities for those who had no scruples. But they were alarmed by the smallness of their numbers, and for the most part sat still and made no move. John on the other hand had the advantage in numbers, but this was cancelled out by the awkwardness of his position[2]: with his enemies overhead he could not attack them with any confidence, and if he remained inactive his rage choked him. He suffered more damage than he could do to Eleazar and his men, yet he would not suspend operations: there were constant sorties and showers of missiles, and murder desecrated every corner of the Temple.

Simon, son of Gioras, whom the people in their distress had called in, hoping for aid but saddling themselves with one tyrant the more, was master of the Upper City and much of the Lower. He now launched more violent attacks on John's men, since they were being assailed also from above: he himself had to approach them from beneath, as they did those above them. Attacked from both sides, John gave as good as he received, and what he lost by being lower than Eleazar he gained by being higher than Simon. So while easily fighting off with light weapons the attack from below, he used his engines to counter the spears showered on him from the Temple above; for he had plenty of spear-throwers, catapults, and stone-throwers, with which he not only repulsed the attackers but killed many of those who offered sacrifice. For though mad enough to commit any sacrilege, they admitted those who wished to make offerings – natives with suspicion and after cautious search, foreigners with less hesitation. But these, though they gained admission by making the Zealots ashamed of their cruelty, often became victims of the sedition; for the heavy missiles came over with such velocity that they reached the Altar and the Sanctuary, falling on priests and sacrifices; and many who had hastened from the ends of the earth to visit this famous place, which all men held sacred, were themselves struck down before their offerings, and sprinkled with their own blood the Altar revered by Greeks and barbarians everywhere. The bodies of natives and aliens, priests and laymen, were piled on each other, and the blood of men and beasts formed lakes in the sacred courts. Unhappy City! what have you suffered from the Romans to compare with this? They entered your gates to purge with fire the filthiness within you: you were no longer the place of God; you could not continue, now that you were the burial-place of your own sons and had turned the Sanctuary into a common grave for those who had slain each other. Even now you might be restored to life, if only you would make atonement to God who destroyed you! But even the deepest emotions must be stifled in obedience to the laws of history: this is not the time for private lamentation but for a record of the facts. So I will explain the subsequent course of the insurrection.

The plotters against the City were now divided into three. Eleazar and his party, who had the sacred first-fruits[3] in their hands, made

John the target of their drunken rage: John and his men plundered the citizens and directed his attacks against Simon: Simon in his struggle against the rival factions was dependent for supplies on the City. Whenever John was assailed from both sides, he made his men face both ways, raining missiles from the colonnades on those who came up from the City, and using his artillery to repel those who showered spears on him from the Temple. Whenever the pressure from above was relaxed – it was often interrupted by drunkenness and exhaustion – he made bolder, large-scale sallies against Simon's lines. To which-ever part of the City he turned, he never failed to set fire to the houses that were stocked with grain and supplies of every kind; when he withdrew, Simon advanced and followed his example. It was as if to oblige the Romans they were destroying all that the City had laid up against a siege and hamstringing their own powers. The result at any rate was that all the buildings round the Temple were burnt to the ground, the City became a desolate no man's land where they flung themselves at each other's throats, and almost all the grain – enough to support them through many years of siege – went up in flames. It was hunger that defeated them, a thing that could never have happened if they had not brought it upon themselves.[4]

The entire City was the battleground for these plotters and their disreputable followers, and between them the people were being torn to bits like a great carcase. Old men and women, overwhelmed by the miseries within, prayed for the Romans to come, and looked for-ward to the war without, which would free them from the miseries within. Fear and utter despondency filled the hearts of loyal citizens: they had no chance to effect a change of policy, no hope of com-promise or flight if they desired it. Guards were everywhere and the bandit chiefs, quarrelling about everything else, executed as common enemies all who were for peace with the Romans or were suspected of intending to desert, and agreed on only one thing – to murder those who deserved to live. The shouting of the combatants went on cease-lessly day and night; more frightful still was the terrified moaning of the bereaved. Their disasters furnished one cause of grief after another, but their cries were bottled up by overwhelming dread: afraid to voice their anguish they were racked with stifled groans. The living no longer counted for anything with their kinsfolk: the dead no one troubled to bury. The reason in either case was that everyone des-paired of his own life; those who belonged to no party had no interest in anything – they would soon be dead anyway. Trampling on the bodies heaped upon each other the partisans were locked in strife, and drawing in draughts of frenzy from the corpses under their feet they became more savage still. They were constantly devising some new means of self-destruction, and, relentlessly putting all their resolves into effect, they left no method of outrage or barbarity untried. John actually purloined the sacred timber for the construction of engines of war. The high priests and people had once decided to underprop the Sanctuary and increase its height by thirty feet, and the necessary timber had been brought from Lebanon by King Agrippa at very great labour and expense, baulks astonishingly straight and of immense size.[5] But the war had put a stop to the work and John cut them up and built towers with them, as he found them long enough to reach his enemies on the Temple above. These towers he pushed forward and stationed behind the court over against the western recess, the only possible place, as the other sides were completely cut off by staircases.[6]

With the engines so impiously constructed he hoped to defeat his enemies, but God made his efforts useless by bringing the Romans upon him before he had posted a single man on the towers. For Titus had collected part of his forces, ordering the rest to meet him at Jerusalem, and was marching from Caesarea at the head of the three legions which at his father's bidding had laid waste Judaea, and the Twelfth, which under Cestius had once suffered defeat, but which at all times was renowned for its courage and now, remembering what had happened to it, was advancing the more eagerly to seek revenge.[7] Of these he ordered the Fifth to meet him via Emmaus and the Tenth to go up via Jericho.[8] He himself moved off with the rest, accompanied by much larger contingents from his royal allies and many auxiliaries from Syria. The four legions which Vespasian had depleted by selecting men to go with Mucianus to Italy[9] were brought up to strength with those who had arrived with Titus: he had with him 2,000 picked men from the armies at Alexandria and 3,000 from the garrisons on the Euphrates. With them too came a friend of the most tried loyalty and wisdom, Tiberius Alexander. He had recently been administering Egypt for the Romans, and now was entrusted with the command of the armies[10] as a reward for having been the first to welcome the newly emerged imperial house and with splendid faith to throw in his lot with theirs when the future was uncertain. Years and experience, too, had made him a most competent adviser amid the uncertainties of war.

Titus advanced into enemy country behind a vanguard formed of the royal troops and all the allied contingents. Next came roadmakers and camp-constructors, then the officers' baggage with its armed escort. Behind these came the commander-in-chief with his spearmen and other picked soldiers, followed by the legionary cavalry. These marched in front of the engines, with picked men behind them commanded by tribunes and prefects of cohorts; then came the eagle, surrounded by the standards, with their trumpeters in front, and after them the main column, marching six abreast. The servants belonging to each legion came next, preceded by the baggage; and last of all the mercenaries[11] under the watchful eye of a rearguard. Leading his forces on in good order, as is the Roman way, Titus advanced rapidly through Samaritis into Gophna, occupied by his father earlier on and now garrisoned. Having spent one night there he set off at daybreak, and after marching all day pitched camp in the valley which the Jews call the Valley of Thorns near Gabath Saul (Saul's Hill), a village about three and a half miles from Jerusalem. From there with about 600 of his best cavalry he went forward to ascertain the strength of the City and the temper of the Jews – would they at the sight of him be frightened into surrender before a blow was struck? For he had been informed, truthfully enough, that the citizens, though under the thumb of insurgents and terrorists, were anxious for peace, and submitted only because they were too weak to rebel.

As long as he rode straight along the highway leading to the walls, no one showed his face outside the gates; but when he left the road and led his body of horse slantwise towards the tower Psephinus,[12] a horde of Jews suddenly poured out by the Women's Towers[13] through the gate facing Helena's Monuments,[14] burst through his cavalry, and lining up in front of those still galloping along the road prevented him from joining those who had turned aside, so cutting off Titus with a mere handful of men. He could not advance, as all the ground outside the wall was trenched for gardening purposes and divided up by cross-walls and a number of fences; and to withdraw to his own men he realized was impossible with such a mass of enemies in between. Moreover the men on the highway had turned tail, and as most of them had no idea that the prince[15] was in danger but thought that he had turned about as they had, there was no holding them. Titus, seeing that nothing but his own prowess could save him, wheeled his horse, and shouting to his little group to follow, charged into the middle of the foe, determined to hack his way through to his own men. Then, if ever, it became evident that the fortunes of war and the fate of princes are in the hands of God; for when missiles were raining down on Titus, who had neither helmet nor breastplate, having gone forward as I said not to fight but to observe, not one touched his person, but as if badly aimed on purpose every spear whizzed past harmlessly. He with his sword again and again scattered those to right and left of him, and striking down many who opposed him from the front trampled the fallen under his horse's hooves. Caesar's dazzling courage called forth an answering shout and cries of 'Go for him!' But whichever way he rode, his opponents instantly scattered in all directions. Those who shared his peril closed in on him, assailed as they were from flank and rear; for their one chance of survival lay in opening a way through with Titus before they were encircled. Two indeed were further off than the rest; one of these was surrounded and struck down with his horse, the other dismounted but was killed and his horse led away; with the remainder Titus got through safely to his camp. Success in their first attack roused the Jews to unreasoning optimism, and Fortune's fleeting smile filled them with boundless confidence in the future.

During the night Caesar was joined by the legion from Emmaus; at daybreak he set out for Mount Scopus, the first point from which could be seen the City and the shining mass of the Temple – hence the propriety of the name 'Look Out'[16] for this slight eminence adjoining the northern region of the City. Three quarters of a mile from the City he ordered a single camp to be constructed for the two legions,[17] with the Fifth six hundred yards to the rear, as he thought that men tired out by a night march were entitled to protection, so that they could build their rampart in safety. As soon as they had begun their task the Tenth Legion arrived from Jericho, where a body of infantry was stationed to guard the pass previously occupied by Vespasian. This legion had been ordered to encamp about three quarters of a mile from Jerusalem on the Mount of Olives, which faces the City on the east and is separated from it by a deep ravine known as Kidron.

Within the City the warring factions now for the first time put an end to their incessant, suicidal strife in view of war suddenly descending on them from without in all its fury. The partisans, seeing with

consternation the Romans building three separate camps, made an
unholy alliance and asked each other what they were waiting for, and
what ailed them that they allowed the erection of three fortifications
that would suffocate them. The enemy were building a rival city with
impunity while they, as if they were watching something wonderful
being done in their interest, sat behind their battlements, hands on
laps and weapons laid by. 'Are we only capable of injuring ourselves?'
they shouted: 'are the Romans, as the result of our party quarrels, to
capture the City without losing a man?' Urging each other on in this
way and combining their forces, they seized their weapons, made a
sudden sortie against the Tenth Legion, tore across the ravine with
blood-curdling yells, and fell upon the enemy at work on their
fortifications. They had dispersed to speed their labours, and had
grounded most of their arms, never imagining that the Jews would
dare to sally out – if they were disposed to do so, their efforts would be
stultified by their dissensions. As a result they were surprised and
thrown into disorder. Leaving their tasks some promptly retreated;
many ran to their weapons but were struck to the ground before they
could turn and face the enemy. The number of Jews was steadily
increasing as their early successes encouraged others to join them, and
seemed both to them and to the Romans far greater than it really was,
as things were going so well for them. Men highly organized and
trained to fight according to the book and in obedience to orders are
most quickly demoralized by unorthodox and enterprising tactics. So
on this occasion the Romans, having left the initiative to the Jews,
gave way before the onslaught. Whenever some of them were overtaken and faced about, they held up the onrush of the Jews, and
catching them off their guard in the excitement of pursuit inflicted
casualties on them, but as more and more Jews poured out of the City
their confusion grew, till at last they were chased from their camp.
It is likely that the situation of the whole legion would have been
precarious had not Titus, informed of the position, at once gone to the
rescue. Denouncing their cowardice in no uncertain terms he rallied
the runaways; then falling on the Jews from the flank at the head of
the picked men who were with him he killed many, wounded more,
routed them all, and drove them into the ravine. On the downward
slope they suffered severely, but when they had crossed they turned
about and with the stream between them put up a determined
resistance. So it went on till midday; then a few minutes after noon

Titus lined up the reinforcements he had brought and the men from the cohorts and sent the rest of the legion to resume their fortification on the ridge.

The Jews took this for a rout, and when the watchman posted on the wall waved his cloak, a mass of men, quite fresh, sprang into the open with such ferocity that it was like the charge of a herd of buffaloes.[18] Indeed, not one of their opponents awaited the impact, but as if struck by an artillery barrage they broke ranks, turned, and fled up the hillside leaving Titus with a handful of men halfway up the slope. He was strongly urged by the friends who in loyalty to their commander disregarded their danger and stood firm, to retire before these suicidal Jews and not to risk his life for men whose duty was to stay and defend him; he should bear in mind his unique position and not play the part of a private soldier when he was commander-in-chief of the army and master of the world, or run into such extreme danger when everything depended on him. To such appeals Titus shut his ears. He stood his ground against those who were charging up the slope to get at him, and boldly attacking them as they pressed on cut them up; then falling on the masses behind he drove them in a body down the slope. His amazing courage and strength terrified them, but even so they did not retreat into the City, but opening out in both directions to get out of his way went hard on the heels of those fleeing up the slope. So he attacked them from the flank and checked their onrush.

Meanwhile those who were constructing the camp above, seeing the men lower down in flight, were again filled with panic and terror and the whole legion scattered, thinking that the Jewish onrush was irresistible and that Titus himself had been put to flight: the others surely would never have fled while he remained. As if in the grip of panic fear they ran off in all directions, till some caught sight of the general in the thick of the fight, and in great fear for his safety shouted to the whole legion to tell them of his danger. Shame turned them back, and reproaching each other less for their flight than for their abandonment of Caesar they rounded fiercely on the Jews, and after once turning them back pushed them off the hillside into the valley. The retreating Jews disputed every inch, but enjoying the advantage of position the Romans drove them all into the ravine. Titus kept up the pressure on those in front of him, sending the legion back to their camp-building, while he with the same men as before firmly opposed the enemy advance. Thus if truth must be told without adding anything in flattery or subtracting anything through envy, it was Caesar himself who twice saved the whole legion from destruction and enabled them to fortify their camp in safety.[19]

As soon as there was a momentary respite from external war, internal faction again raised its head. When the day of Unleavened Bread arrived (the 14th of Xanthicos,[20] on which the Jews believe they first escaped from Egypt), Eleazar's men half opened the gates to admit citizens who wished to worship within. But John used the Feast to screen his treacherous intentions, and equipping the most insignificant members of his gang – most of them unpurified – with hidden weapons, managed to get them into the Temple unnoticed with orders to seize it before they were detected. As soon as they were inside they whipped off their disguise, and suddenly showed themselves armed to the teeth. Utter disorder and confusion at once reigned all round the Sanctuary: the people who had had nothing to do with party quarrels supposed that the attack was directed against all without distinction, the Zealots that it was against them alone. They, however, abandoned their watch at the gates, jumped down from the battlements, and before a blow was struck concealed themselves in the Temple vaults, while the people from the City, cowering by the Altar and crowding round the Sanctuary, were trampled on and savagely beaten with swords and cudgels. Through private animosity and hatred many harmless persons were taken for rival partisans and murdered by their enemies: any man who had got across one of the conspirators in the past was now recognized as a Zealot and led away to his doom. When the utmost cruelty had been inflicted on the guiltless, a truce was granted to the guilty, who came out of the vaults and were allowed to go. Now that they had seized the inner courts of the Temple and all that was stored in it, the invaders could snap their fingers at Simon. Thus what was recently a three-cornered fight was once more a struggle between two parties.

Titus now decided to leave Mount Scopus and encamp nearer to the City. To deal with any sorties he posted what he considered an adequate body of horse and foot, instructing the rest of his forces to level the ground as far as the walls. Every fence and hedge which the occupiers had put round their gardens and orchards were thrown down, every fruit-tree in the area felled, the dips and hollows filled in, the rocky projections demolished with iron implements, and the whole space flattened from Mount Scopus to Herod's Monuments[21] alongside the Serpents' Pool.[22]

At this stage the Jews devised an ingenious ruse to catch the Romans. The more daring of the insurgents streamed out of the Women's Towers, and as if they had been expelled by the peace party and dreaded an attack by the Romans, huddled together in a cowering mass. Others lined the walls and pretended to be ordinary citizens; they clamoured for peace, begged for protection, and invited the Romans in, promising to open the gates. While they shouted thus they pelted their own men with stones, as if attempting to drive them from the gates. They in turn pretended to be trying to force an entry and appealing to the men inside, and repeatedly made a dash for the Roman lines, then turned tail with every sign of panic. The Roman soldiers fell for the trick: they thought they had one group in their power and ready for execution, and hoping that the others would open the gates started out to settle the business. But Titus smelt a rat. Only the previous day he had, through Josephus,[23] invited them to come to terms without receiving a civil answer, so now he ordered the soldiers to stay where they were. However, some of the men posted in front of the works had already seized their weapons and charged at the gates. Those who had apparently been expelled gave ground before them at first, but when the Romans were between the towers of the gate, the Jews sallied out, surrounded them and attacked them from the rear, while from the battlements came a hail of stones and missiles of every kind, killing many and wounding far more. For it was not easy for the Romans to escape from the wall under pressure from the rear, and besides, shame at their blunder and fear of their officers forced them to persist in their mistake. So for a long time they kept up the fight with spears, suffering severely at the hands of the Jews, but certainly giving as good as they received, till at last they broke out of the circle. But as they retired the Jews pursued them as far as Helena's Monuments, pelting them all the way. Then cock-a-hoop over their success they mocked the Romans for being taken in by a trick, and brandishing their shields danced and yelled with delight.

Meanwhile the soldiers were received with threats from their officers and an angry outburst from Caesar. The Jews, he said, whose only leader was desperation, did everything with forethought and commonsense, planning stratagems and ambushes with every care, and their devices were crowned with success because of their obedience and unswerving loyalty to each other; whereas the Romans, who because of their discipline and quickness to obey their leaders could always command success, were now humiliated through behaving in the opposite way out of a lack of self-control and, as a crowning disgrace, through fighting without a leader in the presence of Caesar. What a blow to the laws of the Service! What a blow to his father when he learnt of this defeat! For in a lifetime of warfare he had never suffered such humiliation; and the laws always punished with death those guilty of the smallest breach of discipline, whereas now they had seen a whole army leaving its post. However, those reckless fools should soon learn that with the Romans even victory, if won without orders, counted for nothing. With such vehemence did Titus address his officers that it seemed evident he would deal with all the offenders according to the law. They abandoned all hope, expecting to die immediately as they deserved[24]; but the legions swarmed round Titus and pleaded for their comrades, begging him to overlook the rashness of a few men in view of the good discipline of them all: they would atone for their present blunder by exemplary conduct in the future.

Caesar saw that it was in his own interest to yield to their entreaties; for he thought that while an individual punishment should be actually carried out, collective punishments should not go beyond words. He therefore pardoned the soldiers after warning them most emphatically to be more careful another time. Then he considered privately how to make the Jews pay for their stratagem. Four days were spent in levelling the ground right up to the walls. Then wishing to get his baggage-train and supernumeraries by in safety, Titus deployed his effective forces opposite the wall on the north and west, in a formation seven deep, infantry drawn up in front, cavalry behind, each in three ranks, with a seventh line in between formed of archers. This huge concentration put a stop to Jewish sorties, and the transport of the three legions and the supernumeraries marched by without fear. The general himself pitched his camp about four hundred yards from the wall near the corner opposite the tower called Psephinus, where the encircling wall bent back from the north to the west. The other section of the army threw up a fortification facing the tower known as Hippicus,[25] at the same distance of four hundred yards from the City. The Tenth Legion remained where it was on the Mount of Olives.

Jerusalem[26] was defended by three walls except where it was shut in by impassable ravines; there a single rampart was enough. It was built on two hills facing each other and separated by a central ravine, at which the terraces of houses ended. Of these hills the one occupied by the Upper City was much the higher and straighter along its length; being so strong it was called the Stronghold by King David, father of Solomon who first built the Temple, though known to us as the Upper Market. The second, called the Citadel and covered with the Lower City, was dome-shaped.[27] Opposite this was a third hill, by nature lower than the Citadel and originally cut off from it by another wide ravine; later, however, when the Hasmonaeans were reigning they filled the ravine in, wishing to join the City to the Temple; they also removed the top of the Citadel to reduce its height[28] so that the Temple could be seen beyond it. The Valley of the Cheese-makers, which as we said separated the hills of the Upper and Lower Cities, goes down to Siloam – such was the name we gave to that sweet and never failing spring. On the outside the City's two hills were surrounded by deep ravines, and the steep cliffs on either side made access everywhere impossible.

Of the three walls the Old, thanks to the ravines and the hill above them on which it was built, was almost impregnable; and apart from the advantage of the situation it was also strongly constructed, David and Solomon, and later kings too, having tackled the work with enthusiasm. Starting in the north at the Hippicus Tower it stretched to the Gymnasium, then joining the Council-chamber ended at the west colonnade of the Temple. Running in the other, westward,[29] direction from the same starting-point, it went down through the area called Bethso to the Essene Gate, then turned south above the fountain of Siloam,[30] from which it bent again eastwards towards Solomon's Pool and going on as far as a place called Ophel joined the east colonnade of the Temple.

The Second Wall started at the Gennath,[31] a gate in the first wall. It enclosed the northern quarter only and went up as far as Antonia. The Third started at the Hippicus Tower from which it ran as far north as the Psephinus Tower, then going down opposite the Monuments of Helena (daughter of King Izates who became queen of Adiabene), and continuing a long way past the Caves of the Kings bent at a corner tower near the Fuller's Tomb, and joining the old precinct wall[32] came to an end at the Kidron Valley. This wall was built by

Agrippa to protect the newest parts of the City, hitherto defenceless; for as the population overflowed, the City gradually crept beyond its limits, and uniting the area north of the Temple to the hill,[33] the people pushed out so far that houses covered a fourth hill, Bezetha. Situated opposite Antonia, this hill was cut off from it by a deep trench,[34] dug purposely so that the foundations of Antonia should not be in contact with the hill and be approachable and too low: the relative height of the towers was greatly increased by the depth of the ditch. The new housing estate was known locally as Bezetha, which might be translated 'New City'. When he saw the occupants of the estate in need of protection, the father of the present king, like him called Agrippa, began the wall mentioned above, but fearing that when Claudius Caesar saw how massive the ramparts were he would suspect him of planning revolt and insurrection, he stopped when he had only laid the foundations.[35] If the wall had been finished as it was begun, the City could never have been taken, for it was built of bonded stones 30 feet long and 15 broad, so that it would have been very difficult to undermine with iron tools or shake with engines. The wall itself was 15 feet thick, and its height would no doubt have been greater if the enthusiasm of its designer had not been damped. Later, though its erection by the Jews was hasty, it rose to 30 feet and was surrounded by battlements 3 feet and ramparts $4\frac{1}{2}$ feet high; so the total height reached $37\frac{1}{2}$ feet.[36]

From the wall rose towers 30 feet wide and 30 high, square and solid like the wall itself, the stones as beautiful and perfectly fitted as in a temple. Above the compact mass that towered up 30 feet there were magnificent halls, and over these upper rooms and tanks to hold rainwater. Each tower had a wide spiral staircase. The Third Wall had 90 such towers 100 yards apart; the Middle Wall was divided up by 14 towers, the Old by 60. The whole circuit of the City was $3\frac{3}{4}$ miles.[37] The whole of the Third Wall was wonderful, but not so wonderful as the Psephinus Tower, which rose at the north-west corner near the spot where Titus later pitched his camp. It was 105 feet high, and when the sun was up it afforded a prospect of Arabia and the farthest extent of Hebrew possessions as far as the sea. It was octagonal.

Opposite this tower was Hippicus and near to it two others, built by King Herod in the Old Wall, and superior in size, beauty, and strength to any in the whole world. For apart from his love of grandeur and his ambitions for the City, the king made the splendour of these works a means of expressing his own emotions, naming the towers after the three persons he cared for most, his brother, friend, and wife, to whose memory he dedicated them. His wife, as related already, he had himself killed through passionate love[38]; the other two had fallen in battle, covered with glory. Hippicus, named after the friend,[39] was of square section, 37½ feet each way, and 45 feet high, with no empty space anywhere in it. On top of this solid structure of fitted stones was a reservoir to hold rain-water 30 feet deep, and over this a two-storey building 37½ feet high divided into various chambers. Above this again rose a ring of turrets 3 feet high with ramparts 4½ feet high, making the total height 120 feet.

The second tower, named Phasael after Herod's brother, was of equal length and width, 60 feet each way, the height of the solid part being also 60 feet. Round the top ran a colonnade 15 feet high, protected by breastworks and bulwarks. Rising from the middle of the colonnade was another tower, divided into splendid apartments which even included a bathroom, that the tower might lack nothing to make it seem a palace. The top was equipped with ramparts and turrets. The total height was about 135 feet, the general appearance like that of the tower at Pharos that shows the light of its fires to sailors approaching Alexandria[40]; but the measurement round was much greater. During the siege it served as headquarters for the autocrat Simon.

The third tower, Mariamme – for this was the queen's name – was solid for the first thirty feet, and was also 30 feet long and of equal width. The building on top was more splendid and elaborate than the others, as the king felt it incumbent on him to make the one named after a woman more ornate than those named after men, while theirs were sturdier than hers. The total height in this case was 82½ feet.

The great size of these three towers seemed much greater still because of their site. For the Old Wall in which they were placed was built on a high hill, and above the hill a sort of crest rose 45 feet higher. Erected on this the towers gained enormously in height. Another remarkable feature was the size of the stones: they did not consist of ordinary small stones or lumps that men might carry, but of white marble, cut into blocks, each 30 feet long, 15 wide, and 7½ deep, so perfectly united that each tower looked like a single rock, sent up by mother earth and later cut and polished by artists' hands into shape and angles; so invisible from any viewpoint was the fitting of the joints.

A little way south of these towers and sheltered by them was the king's Palace, which no tongue could describe. Its magnificence and equipment were unsurpassable, surrounded as it was on every side by a wall 45 feet high, with ornamental towers evenly spaced along it, and containing huge banqueting halls and guestrooms with 100 beds. Words cannot express the varied beauty of the stones, for kinds rare everywhere else were here brought together in quantity. There were ceilings remarkable for the length of the beams and the splendour of the ornamentation, and rooms without number, no two designed alike, and all luxuriously furnished, most of their contents being of gold or silver. On every side were numbers of intersecting colonnades, each differing in the design of its pillars. The open spaces between them were all green lawns, with coppices of different trees traversed by long walks, which were edged with deep canals and cisterns everywhere plentifully adorned with bronze statues through which the water poured out. Flanking the streams were numerous cotes for tame pigeons. But indeed no words are adequate to portray the Palace, and the memory of it is agonizing, since it brings to mind the destruction wrought by the bandits' fires. For the Palace was not fired by the Romans but, as we said earlier, by the plotters within the City, who when the revolt began lit a fire at Antonia which spread to the Palace and reached the upper storeys of the three towers.[41]

The Temple, as stated earlier, was built on a strong hill. At first the level ground at the top was hardly spacious enough for Sanctuary and Altar, as it was surrounded by steep cliffs. King Solomon, who originally founded the Sanctuary, walled up the eastern side and erected a single colonnade on the platform thus created: on the remaining sides the Sanctuary was bare. In successive generations the people kept extending the platform, and the flat hilltop grew wider. Then they cut through the north wall and took in all the ground later included within the circuit of the whole Temple.[42] Having walled in the hill from its base on three sides and completed a task to stagger the imagination – a task on which they spent long ages and all their sacred treasures, replenished as they were by tribute sent from every corner of the world as a gift to God – they built round the Sanctuary both the upper enclosures and the lower Temple courts. These where the ground was lowest had to be built up 450 feet, in some places even more.[43] The whole depth of the foundations did not meet the eye, as the ravines were largely filled in from a wish to level the streets of the town. Stones 60 feet long were used in the building[44]; for the unlimited funds and popular enthusiasm resulted in undertakings beyond belief, and a task with no end in sight was through patience and the passage of time completed.

Of such foundations the works above were entirely worthy. The colonnades were all double, the supporting pillars were $37\frac{1}{2}$ feet high, cut from single blocks of the whitest marble, and the ceiling was panelled with cedar. The natural magnificence of it all, the perfect polish and the accurate jointing afforded a remarkable spectacle, without any superficial ornament either painted or carved. The colonnades were 45 feet wide and the complete circuit of them measures three quarters of a mile, Antonia being enclosed within them. The whole area open to the sky was paved with stones of every kind and colour. Anyone passing through this towards the second court found it enclosed within a stone balustrade $4\frac{1}{2}$ feet high, a perfect specimen of craftsmanship. In this at equal intervals stood slabs announcing the law of purification, some in Greek and some in Roman characters.[45] No foreigner was to enter the holy area[46] – this was the name given to the second court. Fourteen steps led up to it from the first: the elevated area was rectangular and had a protecting wall of its own. The height of this on the outside was 60 feet, but it was concealed by the steps: on the inside it was only $37\frac{1}{2}$ feet. For the interior was perched up at the top of the steps and so could not all be seen, concealed as it was by being higher up the hill. Beyond the fourteen steps there was a space of fifteen feet to the wall, quite flat. From there other flights of five steps led up to the gates. On the north and south the gates numbered eight, four in each case; on the east there were bound to be two, for on this side a special place was walled off for the women to worship in, necessitating a second gate, which opened facing the first. On the other sides there was one north and one south gate through which the Court of the Women could be entered; for women were neither admitted through the others nor allowed to go past the dividing wall via their own gate. This court was open for worship alike to native women and to Jewesses from abroad. The western part had no gate at all, there being no openings in the wall on that side. The colonnades between the gates faced inwards from the wall in front of the treasury,[47] and rested on pillars of exceptional height and beauty; they were single, but apart from size were in every way equal to those round the lower court.

Of the gates nine were completely covered with gold and silver, as were the posts and lintels, but the one outside the Sanctuary was of Corinthian bronze, and far more valuable than those overlaid with silver or even with gold. Every gateway had double doors, each half being 45 feet high and 22½ wide. On the inner side however the gateways widened out, and on either hand there was a gate-room 45 feet square, shaped like a tower and over 60 feet high. Each room was supported by two pillars 18 feet round. The other gates were all of the same size, but the one beyond the Corinthian Gate, opening out from the Court of the Women on the east and facing the gate of the Sanctuary, was much bigger; for its height was 75 feet, that of the doors 50, and the decoration was more magnificent, the gold and silver plates being extremely thick. This plating was the gift of Alexander, father of Tiberius.[48] Fifteen steps went up from the women's enclosure to the Greater Gate, shallower steps than the five at the other gates.

The Sanctuary itself, the Holy Temple, situated in the middle, was reached by a flight of twelve steps. Seen from the front it was of the same height and width, 150 feet each way, but behind it was 60 feet narrower, for the entrance was flanked by shoulders, as it were, projecting 30 feet on either side. The first gate was 105 feet high and 37½ wide; it had no doors, thus revealing instead of excluding the vast expanse of heaven. The face was covered with gold all over, and through the arch the first chamber could all be seen from without, huge as it was, and the inner gate and its surrounding wall, all glistening with gold, struck the beholder's eye. The Sanctuary was divided into two chambers, but only the first[49] was visible all the way up, as it rose 135 feet from the ground, its length being 75 and its width 30. The gate of this was, as I said, covered with gold all over, as was the entire wall surrounding it. Above it were the golden grape-vines, from which hung bunches as big as a man. (The Sanctuary was two storeys high and so appeared lower inside than outside[50].) There were golden doors 82½ feet high and 24 wide. In front of these was a curtain of the same length, Babylonian tapestry embroidered with blue, white linen thread,[51] scarlet and purple, a marvellous example of the craftsman's art. The mixture of materials had a clear mystic meaning, typifying all creation: it seemed that scarlet symbolized fire, linen the earth, blue the air, and purple the sea. In two cases the resemblance was one of colour; in the linen and purple it was a question of origin, as the first comes from the earth, the second from the sea.[52] Worked in the tapestry was the whole vista of the heavens except for the signs of the Zodiac.

Passing through the gate one entered the ground-floor chamber of the Sanctuary, 90 feet high, 90 long, and 30 wide. But the length was again divided. In the first part, partitioned off at 60 feet, were three most wonderful, world-famous works of art, a lampstand, a table, and an altar of incense. The seven lamps branching off from the lampstand symbolized the planets, the twelve loaves on the table the Zodiac circle and the year.[53] The altar of incense, by the thirteen spices from sea and land, inhabited and uninhabited, with which it was kept supplied, signified that all things are from God and for God.[54]

The innermost chamber measured 30 feet and was similarly separated by a curtain from the outer part. Nothing at all was kept in it; it was unapproachable, inviolable, and invisible to all, and was called the Holy of Holies.

Along the sides of the lower part of the Sanctuary were a number of intercommunicating chambers on three floors, approached by passages on both sides of the entrance. The upper part had no such chambers, as it was narrower; it rose 60 feet higher and was less ornate than the lower part. Thus with the 90 feet of the bottom storey we get 150 as the total height.

Viewed from without the Sanctuary had everything that could amaze either mind or eyes. Overlaid all round with stout plates of gold, in the first rays of the sun it reflected so fierce a blaze of fire that those who endeavoured to look at it were forced to turn away as if they had looked straight at the sun. To strangers as they approached it seemed in the distance like a mountain covered with snow; for any part not covered with gold was dazzling white. From the very top rose sharp gold spikes to prevent birds from perching on the roof and soiling it. Of the stones in the building some were $67\frac{1}{2}$ feet long, 9 wide, and $7\frac{1}{2}$ deep.[55] In front of the Sanctuary stood the Altar, $22\frac{1}{2}$ feet high and as much as 75 feet long and 75 wide, with the four corners jutting out like horns, and with a gentle slope leading up to it from the south. It was built without the use of iron, and no iron ever

came in contact with it. Round the Sanctuary and the Altar ran a
graceful parapet of beautiful stone about 18 inches high, separating the
laity from the priests inside.

Sufferers from venereal disease or leprosy were debarred from
entering the City at all; from the Temple women were excluded
during their monthly periods, and even when ceremonially clean they
could not go beyond the barrier already described. As for men, those
not thoroughly sanctified were not admitted to the inner court, nor
were priests during their time of ceremonial cleansing.

Of those who were priests by descent any disqualified by physical
defect from officiating were allowed inside the parapet like those
fully qualified and received the portions to which their birth entitled
them, but wore ordinary clothes: vestments were worn by the officiating priests alone. Priests without blemish went up to the Altar and
Sanctuary robed in fine linen, rigorously abstaining from strong wine
through respect for their ministry, lest they should transgress in any
way while officiating. The high priest went up with them, not always
but on sabbaths and new moons, and whenever a traditional feast or
annual assembly of the nation occurred. He officiated in breeches that
covered his thighs to the crutch, with a linen shirt and over that an
ankle-length blue robe, circular and tasselled; to the tassels were
attached alternately golden bells and pomegranates, thunder being
signified by the bells and lightning by the pomegranates. The sash that
bound the robe to the breast was adorned by five bands in different
colours – gold, purple, scarlet, linen, and blue, with which, as we said,
the Sanctuary curtains also were embroidered. The same combination
appeared in the high priest's ephod, gold being most prominent. It
was shaped like a fitted breastplate, and secured by two round gold
brooches, which were set with very large and very lovely sardonyxes
engraved with the names of the tribes that make up the nation. To the
other side were attached twelve more stones in four groups of three –
sardius, topaz, and emerald; carbuncle, jasper, and sapphire; agate,
amethyst, and jacinth; onyx, beryl, and chrysolite. On each of these
again was engraved the name of one tribe. On his head the high priest
wore a linen mitre wreathed with blue and encircled by a crown of
gold, which bore in relief the sacred letters – four vowels.[56] He did not
normally wear these vestments: he put on less ornate garments except
when he entered the inmost shrine, which he did once a year – alone –
on the day observed by all as a fast to God.[57] The City, and the

Sanctuary with its customs and laws, we shall describe in greater detail in a later work,[58] for we have only touched the fringe of the subject.

Antonia, situated at the junction of two colonnades of the first Temple court, the western and northern, was built on a rock 75 feet high and precipitous on every side. It was the work of King Herod and revealed in the highest degree the grandeur of his conceptions. In the first place, from the very bottom the rock was faced with polished stone slabs, both for ornament and to ensure that anyone who tried to climb up or down would slip off; next, before the actual tower was a 4½ foot wall, and inside this the whole elevation of Antonia rose 60 feet into the air. The interior was like a palace in spaciousness and completeness; for it was divided into rooms of every kind to serve every need, colonnades, bathrooms, and wide courtyards[59] where troops could encamp, so that in having all conveniences it was virtually a town, in its splendour a palace. In general design it was a tower with four other towers attached, one at each corner; of these three were 75 feet high, and the one at the south-east corner 105 feet, so that from it the whole Temple could be viewed. Where it joined the Temple colonnades stairs led down to both,[60] and by these the guards descended; for a Roman infantry unit was always stationed there, and at the festivals they extended along the colonnades fully armed and watched for any sign of popular discontent.[61] The City was dominated by the Temple and the Temple by Antonia, so that Antonia housed the guards of all three. The Upper City had a stronghold of its own – Herod's Palace. Bezetha Hill was cut off, as I mentioned, from Antonia. This hill, on which part of the New City was built, was the highest of them all, and on the north it alone obscured the view of the Temple. I intend in a later work to describe the City and its walls in much greater detail, so for the present this must suffice.[62]

CHAPTER 18

Two Walls Captured

INSIDE the City the partisan fighters[1] under Simon's command, not counting the Idumaeans, numbered 10,000 under fifty officers, with Simon as commander-in-chief. His Idumaean allies were 5,000 strong, with ten officers, of whom Jacob, son of Sosas, and Simon, son of Cathla, were the accepted leaders. John, after his seizure of the Temple, had 6,000 fully armed men under twenty officers. Later he was joined by the Zealots, who had laid aside their quarrel. These numbered 2,400, led by their old commander Eleazar and Simon, son of Arinus. While these factions, as we said, were fighting each other, the citizens were assailed from two directions at once, and those who would not be accessories to crime were plundered by both parties. Simon held the Upper City and the Great Wall[2] as far as the Kidron, with as much of the Old Wall as bent eastward from Siloam and went down to the palace of Monobazus, king of Adiabene east of Euphrates. He also held the Fountain and part of the Citadel, or Lower City, as far as the castle of Helena, Monobazus' mother. John held the Temple and much of the surrounding area, with Ophel and the Kidron Valley. Everything that lay between them they burnt down to leave room for their fratricidal conflict. For even when the Romans were encamped close to the walls the internal strife continued to rage. At the time of the first sortie[3] they had momentarily recovered their wits; but their frenzy had quickly returned, co-operation was at an end, and the internal struggle was resumed as if their one desire was to play into the hands of the besiegers. They suffered nothing worse at Roman hands than they had endured at each other's, and when they had finished there was nothing new left for the City to undergo – she went through greater agony before she fell, and her destroyers accomplished something greater. I mean that her internal divisions destroyed the City, and the Romans destroyed the internal divisions, which were far more firmly established than her walls; and the misery of it all could reasonably be put down to her own people, the justice of it to the Romans. But everyone must interpret the facts in his own way.

Such being the state of affairs within the City, Titus with some picked horsemen rode round outside, looking for the best point for an assault on the walls. Seeing no hope anywhere else, as where the valleys ran there was no access and elsewhere the first wall[4] seemed too solid for his engines, he decided to deliver his assault near the tomb of John the high priest[5]; for there the first rampart was lower and the second was not joined to it,[6] little trouble having been taken with the fortifications where the New City was thinly populated, while it was easy to approach the third through which he planned to invade the Upper City, force his way through Antonia, and capture the Temple. While he was riding round an arrow struck one of his staff, Nicanor, in the left shoulder, as a result of his approaching too near with Josephus in an endeavour to put peace proposals before the sentries on the walls, who knew him well. This brought home to Caesar their determination, for they would not leave unmolested even those who came near to save them: it spurred him on to begin the siege, and he at once gave his infantry leave to devastate the suburbs, and ordered timber to be collected and platforms constructed. Dividing his army into three sections for this work, he stationed the spearmen and bowmen between the platforms and in front of these the spear-throwers, catapults, and stone-throwers, to prevent any enemy sorties directed against the works and any attempted interference from the wall. The felling of the trees at once stripped the suburbs bare, but the collection of the timber for the platforms and the concentration of the whole army on the work were accompanied by feverish activity on the Jewish side. Consequently the citizens who had been at the mercy of robbers and cut-throats now recovered their spirits, confident that they would have a breathing-space while the enemy without kept their persecutors busy, and that they would be revenged on them if the Romans were victorious.

John, however, though his men were eager to attack the Romans, was immobilized by fear of Simon. Simon on the other hand was active enough, being nearer to the besiegers. He mounted his artillery along the wall, the weapons taken from Cestius earlier on and those captured when they overwhelmed the defenders of Antonia.[7] These, however, most of the men were unable to use owing to inexperience, but following instruction from deserters a few managed to use their engines after a fashion, besides showering stones and arrows on the builders from the wall and dashing out in company strength to engage them hand to hand. The workmen were shielded from the missiles by wicker screens laid across palisades, while the artillery halted the sorties. The engines of all the legions were masterpieces of construction, but none were equal to those of the Tenth; their spear-throwers were more powerful and their stone-throwers bigger, so that they could repulse not only the sorties but also the fighters on the wall. The stone missiles weighed half a hundredweight and travelled four hundred yards or more; no one who got in their way, whether in the front line or far behind, remained standing. At first the Jews kept watch for the stone – it was white, so that not only was it heard whizzing through the air but its shining surface could easily be seen. Look-outs posted on the towers gave them warning every time a stone was shot from the engine and came hurtling towards them, by shout-ing 'Baby on the way!'[8] Those in its path at once scattered and fell prone, a precaution which resulted in the stone's passing harmlessly through till it came to a stop. The Roman counter was to blacken the stone. As it could not then be seen so easily, they hit their target, destroying many with a single shot. But in spite of their casualties the Jews did not allow the Romans to raise their platforms in safety; every device of inventiveness and daring was called into play as they fought night and day to keep them out.

When the works were finished the engineers measured the distance to the wall by throwing lead and line from the platforms: no other way was possible under the barrage from above. When they found that the battering-rams could reach it, they brought them up. Titus next posted his artillery nearer to prevent the Jews from keeping the rams away, and ordered the battering to begin. From three sides a frightful din suddenly resounded round the City, a shout went up from those within and the partisans were as terrified as the rest. Both parties seeing the common danger realized at last that they must make a common defence. The rivals shouted across to each other that they were giving the enemy every possible assistance, when the right thing, even if God did not give them permanent concord, was for the moment at any rate to set aside their mutual animosities and unite against the Romans. Simon then announced that everyone was free to proceed from the Temple to the wall, and John gave his permission though suspicious of Simon. Hatred and private differences utterly forgotten, they became one body, and manning the wall they flung firebrands by the hundred against the engines, and showered weapons continuously on the men shoving the battering-rams. The bolder spirits sprang forward in tight groups, tore to pieces the screens over the engines, and falling on the crews overpowered them, not so much by skill as by reckless courage. Titus himself never failed to come to the help of those in difficulty; he placed the cavalry and bowmen on either side of the engines, beat off the fire-throwers, repulsed those who were hurling missiles from the towers, and got the battering-rams into action. Yet the wall did not give way under the blows, except that the Fifteenth Legion's ram knocked away the corner of a tower. The wall itself was undamaged: it was not in the same immediate danger as the tower, which projected a long way and could not easily involve the collapse of any part of the actual rampart.

Suspending their sorties for a while the Jews kept watch on the Romans, who had scattered to their tasks and about the camps under the impression that the defenders had withdrawn through exhaustion and terror. Suddenly they poured out en masse by a hidden gate near the tower Hippicus, armed with brands to set fire to the works and bent on reaching the Roman fortifications. At their shouts the front-line troops manned their posts and the supports came running up. But the reckless courage of the Jews was too quick for the solid defence of the Romans: they routed their foremost opponents and swept on to attack the reserves. A furious battle was joined round the engines, one side straining every nerve to set them on fire, the other to prevent it: a babel of sounds arose from both and many of those in the forefront were killed. The Jews were gaining the advantage through sheer desperation, the works were catching fire and would probably have been completely destroyed, engines and all, had not the picked troops from Alexandria with few exceptions stood fast, surpassing their own reputation for gallantry; for in this battle they put more famous legions in the shade. At last Caesar brought up the flower of his cavalry and charged the enemy. Twelve of the leading Jews he killed with his right hand. Their fate broke the resistance of the rest: Titus followed, drove them in a body into the City, and saved the works from the flames. It happened that in this battle one of the Jews was taken alive. Titus ordered him to be crucified before the walls, hoping that the sight would terrify the rest into surrender. After the withdrawal John, the Idumaean leader, was talking to a soldier of his acquaintance before the wall when he was struck in the breast by an

Arab arrow and died instantly – a terrible shock to the Idumaeans and a grief to the insurgents; for his prowess and ability were both outstanding.

The next night the Romans were thrown into confusion by a surprising occurrence. Titus had ordered the construction of three towers 75 feet high, to be set up on three platforms so that from them he might bombard the defenders on the wall. But in the middle of the night one of these fell down spontaneously with a tremendous crash, causing panic in the army. Convinced that an attack was imminent all rushed for their weapons, and wild confusion seized the legions. As no one could say what had occurred, they scattered in all directions with cries of anguish, and when no enemy appeared they grew scared of each other, and everyone anxiously asked his neighbour for the password as if the Jews had broken into their camps. They were like men in the grip of panic fear, till, learning what had occurred, Titus ordered it to be explained to them all, and at long last they recovered from their confusion.

The Jews stood up obstinately to every other form of attack but were in great difficulty from the towers. From them they were pelted by the lighter engines and by the spearmen, bowmen and stone-throwers. On their lofty perch these men were beyond the reach of Jewish weapons, and there was no way to capture the towers, which were difficult to overturn because of their weight and could not be set alight because of the iron that encased them. So they withdrew out of range, abandoning the attempt to hold off the assaults of the Romans, which by their incessant blows were little by little effecting their purpose. Already the wall was giving way before Victor (so the Jews nicknamed the biggest Roman battering-ram, as being victorious over everything) and they had long been worn out by fighting and sentry-go and night-duty far from the City. Besides, through laziness and their habit of deciding wrongly, they thought it a waste of effort to defend this wall as there remained two more behind it. Most of them slacked off and retired; and when the Romans climbed through the breach made by Victor, they all left their posts and ran helter-skelter to the second wall. Those who had broken through then opened the gates and let in the whole army. Having thus mastered the first wall on the fifteenth day of the siege, the 7th of Artemisios, the Romans demolished a large part of it,[9] together with the northern suburbs of the City, so recently destroyed by Cestius.

Titus now accommodated his troops within the first wall in the traditional Camp of the Assyrians,[10] occupying all the intervening ground as far as the Kidron, but out of bowshot from the second wall, and at once began probing attacks. Dividing their forces the Jews kept up an obstinate defence from the wall, John's men fighting from Antonia and the northern colonnade of the Temple and before the tomb of King Alexander,[11] Simon's brigade[12] occupying the approach near the tomb of John the high priest and defending the ground as far as the gate by which water was brought in to the Hippicus Tower. Over and over again they sprang out from the gates and fought at close quarters; and though chased back to the wall and worsted in these hand-to-hand struggles, being far less skilled than the Romans, they scored in the wall-fighting. The Romans were upheld by the combination of strength with experience, the Jews by reckless courage nourished by fear, and by their characteristic obstinacy amid disasters; and they still had hopes of survival, as the Romans had of a quick victory. Neither side showed any sign of flagging: assaults, wall-fighting, sorties at company strength went on continuously all day long: no method of attack was left untried. Dusk hardly availed to break off the battles begun at dawn, and there was no sleep for either side – indeed the night was less endurable than the day, the Jews expecting every moment the capture of the wall, the Romans an assault on their camps. Both passed the night in arms; yet the first glimmer of dawn found them ready for battle.

Among the Jews the great ambition was to show outstanding courage and earn the gratitude of their officers. Simon was held in special respect and awe, and so devoted to him was every man under his command that none would have hesitated a moment to kill himself at Simon's bidding. With the Romans, the great inducements to valour were the habit of victory and unfamiliarity with defeat, their constant campaigning and uninterrupted training, and the greatness of the Empire – above all the fact that always, in every place, by every man stood Titus. To show weakness when Caesar was there fighting at their side was unthinkable, while the man who fought valiantly did so before the eyes of the one who would reward him; indeed, he was paid already if Caesar had recognized his courage. As a result many showed courage beyond their strength through sheer enthusiasm. Here is an instance. On one of those days the Jews were drawn up before the wall in force, and the opposing lines were still exchanging

spears at long range. Suddenly Longinus, a cavalryman, leapt out of
the Roman ranks and charged the very middle of the Jewish phalanx.
Scattering them by his onslaught he killed two of the most stalwart,
striking one in the face as he came to meet him, withdrawing the spear
and transfixing the other through the side as he turned away. Then
back from the middle of the enemy he ran to his own lines unscathed.
When he had given this demonstration of prowess, there were many
who imitated his valour. The Jews on their side, heedless of the damage
they suffered, were concerned only with what they could inflict, and
death had no terrors for them if only it fell on one of the enemy too.
But Titus was as anxious for the safety of his men as for victory itself.
He declared that incautious enthusiasm was utter madness, and heroism was heroic only when it went with prudent regard for the hero's
own safety. His men were forbidden to risk their own lives in order to
display their fearlessness.

He now brought up the battering-ram against the middle tower of
the north wall. There a cunning Jew named Castor lay in ambush with
ten others like himself, the rest having withdrawn to escape the
arrows. These for a time kept quiet, crouching behind the parapet, but
when the tower began to disintegrate they stood up and Castor,
holding out his hands as if in supplication, called on Caesar and in
heart-rending tones besought him to pity them. Guileless himself,
Titus believed him, and hoping that the Jews had at last come to their
senses, stopped the blows of the ram, allowed no arrows to be aimed
at the supplicants, and invited Castor to state his wishes. When he
replied that he would like to come down under a guarantee of
impunity, Titus expressed delight at his good sense; he would be still
more delighted if everyone felt the same, and gladly gave the City
his word. Of the ten men five pretended to join in Castor's supplication, but the rest loudly protested that they would never be slaves of
the Romans while they could die as free men. During the long
wrangle that followed the assault was held up, and Castor sent to
Simon bidding him take his time in deciding the necessary steps, as he
could delude the Roman command indefinitely. At the same time as
he sent this message he made it appear that he was urging the objectors
to accept the guarantee. They made a show of indignation, brandishing their naked swords above the parapet, then struck their own
breastplates and fell down as if run through. Titus and his staff were
dumbfounded at the extraordinary courage of the men, and being

unable to see from below just what had happened admired their fortitude and pitied their misfortune.

At this point someone shot an arrow and hit Castor at the side of his nose. He at once drew it out and showed it to Titus, complaining of unfair treatment. Reprimanding the archer Caesar deputed Josephus, who was standing by, to convey the guarantee to Castor and shake hands on it. But Josephus refused to go himself, since the petitioners meant no good, and restrained those of his friends who were anxious to take his place. However Aeneas, one of the deserters, said he would go, and when Castor called for someone to receive the money that he had with him, Aeneas spread out his garments to catch it and ran towards him more eagerly. Castor promptly picked up a huge stone and flung it at him. Aeneas dodged out of the way, but it injured another soldier who had come forward. When Caesar saw how he had been tricked, he realized that it was fatal to show pity in war: sterner measures gave the trickster less opportunity. Furious that he had been fooled, he stepped up the assaults of the battering-ram. As the tower was on the point of collapse, Castor and his men set fire to it, and then leapt through the blaze into the vault beneath, thus again giving the Romans an impression of bravery by apparently flinging themselves into the fire.

Caesar captured the wall at this point four days after capturing the first, and as the Jews had retired from it he entered with 1,000 heavy infantry and his special bodyguard, in that part of the New City where the wool-shops, forges, and cloth-market were, and the streets ran slantwise to the wall. If he had without hesitation demolished a longer stretch of the wall, or after entering had by right of conquest sacked what he had taken, his victory would not, I think, have been cancelled out by a reverse. As it was, hoping to shame the Jews by waiving his right to do them hurt, he refrained from widening the breach to ensure an easy retreat: he never imagined they would repay his kindness with treachery. So after his entry he forbade his men to kill any prisoners or set the houses on fire; the partisans he informed that, if they wished to fight without harming the citizens, they were free to march out; to the citizens he promised the return of their property. For his chief concern was to preserve the City for himself and the Temple for the City.

The people had been ready from the first to accept his demands, but the war-party took humanity for weakness and imagined that it was through inability to take the rest of the City that Titus made these offers. Threatening the townsfolk with death if there was any suggestion of surrender, and murdering all who mentioned the word 'peace', they attacked the Romans inside the wall, some pouncing on them in the narrow streets or from the houses, while others made a dash outside the wall from the upper gates. In hopeless confusion the guards on the wall jumped down from the towers and withdrew to their camps. A clamour arose from those within, completely encircled by the enemy, and from those without, in fear for those left behind. The Jews, every minute more numerous, and at a great advantage through familiarity with the streets, wounded many and by relentless pressure forced them towards the exit. They, having no other choice, continued to resist; for it was impossible to escape in a body through the narrow gap in the wall. It is probable that all who had entered the City would have been cut to pieces had not Titus come to the rescue. Placing his bowmen at the ends of the streets and taking his own stand where the enemy were thickest, he stopped their advance with his arrows, aided by Domitius Sabinus,[13] who in this battle again showed his worth. Firm as a rock, Caesar kept up a constant stream of arrows and pinned down the Jews till all his men had got clear.

Thus the Romans after capturing the second wall were driven out again. The war-party in Jerusalem were elated, carried away by their success, and convinced that if the Romans ever did venture to set foot in the City again they were doomed to defeat. For God was blinding their eyes because of their transgressions, and they saw neither the strength of the remaining Roman forces – so much more numerous than those they had ejected – nor the famine that was creeping towards them. It was still possible to feed on the public miseries and drink the City's life-blood, though want had long been assailing honest men and for lack of necessities many were at death's door. But the partisans welcomed the destruction of the people: it left more for them. The only people who, in their opinion, deserved to survive were those who had no use for peace and only lived to defeat the Romans: the masses who opposed them were a mere drag, and they were glad to see them go. Such was their attitude to those within the walls; and when the Romans again tried to break in, they held them up by filling the breach and walling it up with their bodies. For three days they stood their ground, resisting with the utmost determination; but on the fourth Titus delivered a violent onslaught which overcame their defence and forced them to retire as before. Once more in possession of the wall, he at once threw down the northern stretch from end to end, and placing garrisons in the towers on the portion towards the south began to plan the assault on the third wall.

He now resolved to suspend the siege for a time and so afford the partisans an interval for deliberation, in the hope that they would be inclined to surrender in view of the demolition of the second wall or through fear of starvation; for plunder would not keep them going for long. This interval he turned to his own advantage as follows. When the soldiers' pay-day arrived, he ordered the officers to parade their troops in full view of the enemy and there count out the money to each man. In accordance with custom the soldiers removed their armour from its protective coverings and advanced in full panoply, the horsemen leading their chargers decked in all their trappings. Every yard of ground before the City shone with silver and gold, a spectacle that filled the Romans with delight, their enemies with terror. Spectators crowded the whole length of the Old Wall and the north side of the Temple, and behind the wall eyes could be seen peering from every window – nowhere in the City was there an inch of ground not hidden by the crowds. Utter consternation seized even the boldest when they saw the entire army assembled, the splendour of their armour and the perfect discipline of the men. I have little doubt that at this sight the partisans would have abandoned their stand, had not the limitless mischief they had done to the citizens destroyed all hope of pardon by the Romans. Death by torture awaited them if they turned back now: death in battle was greatly to be preferred. Fate, too, ordained that with the guilty should perish the innocent, and with the warring factions the entire City.

In four days the Romans completed the payment of all the legions. On the fifth, as no request for peace came from the Jews, Titus divided his legions into two groups and began building platforms in front of Antonia and the Tomb of John, planning to invade the Upper City at the Tomb and the Temple via Antonia: if the Temple was not taken, not even possession of the town would be secure. At each of these points work on two platforms was begun, every legion being responsible for one. The men working alongside the Tomb were hindered by the Idumaeans and Simon's infantry, who made surprise sorties; those before Antonia by John's men and the Zealot groups. These attackers had the advantage not only because they were hurling their missiles from a greater height, but also because they had now learnt to use their engines; for daily practice had steadily increased their skill. They had three hundred spear-throwers and forty stone-throwers, enabling them to make work on the Roman platforms difficult. Titus knew that the survival or destruction of the City mattered very much to himself; so while he prosecuted the siege he did not fail to urge the Jews to reverse their policy, combining military activity with good advice. Knowing too that very often the sword is less effective than the tongue, he called on them repeatedly to save themselves by handing over the City, virtually his already, and sent Josephus to talk to them in their own language, thinking they would perhaps yield to the persuasions of a fellow-countryman.

Josephus circled the wall, striving to keep out of range but within hearing,[14] and appealing to them again and again to spare themselves and their people, their country and their Temple, and not to show themselves more indifferent than were foreigners. The Romans, who had no share in them, respected their enemies' holy places and till now had kept their hands off them, while those who had been brought up in them, and if they survived would alone possess them, were doing their best to destroy them. Did they not see their strongest walls lying flat, and only the weakest one still standing? Did they not know that the might of Rome was invincible, and submission to her an everyday experience? If it indeed was right to fight for freedom, they should have done so at the start; once they had been crushed, and had submitted for many years, to try then to shake off the yoke was to show, not a love of freedom, but a morbid desire for death. It might well be reasonable to disdain meaner masters, but not the lords of the whole world. What corner of the earth had escaped the Romans, unless heat or cold made it of no value to them? From every side fortune had passed to them, and God, who handed dominion over from nation to nation round the world, abode now in Italy. It was an immutable and unchallenged law among beasts and men alike, that all must submit to the stronger, and that power belonged to those supreme in arms. That was why their ancestors, in soul and body and in resources far superior to themselves, had submitted to Rome – which they could not have borne to do if they had not known that God was on the Roman side.

As for themselves, what gave them confidence to hold out, when most of the City was already captured and those inside, even if the walls were still standing, were worse off than if the City had fallen? The Romans were well aware of the famine within,[15] which was now destroying the civilian population and would soon destroy the fighting-men as well. Even if the Romans suspended operations and made no armed assault on the City, yet a war there was no resisting was raging in their midst and growing every hour – unless they could take arms and fight against famine itself, and alone among men master even hunger! They had better change their ways, he went on, before it was too late, and veer to a safer course while they could: the Romans would bear them no grudge for their past folly unless they brazened it out to the end: they were by nature merciful in victory, and they never allowed bitter feelings to stand in the way of their interests, which would not be served by having the City uninhabited or the country desolate. And so Caesar was ready even now to offer them guarantees; but he would not spare a single man if he took the City by storm, least of all if even at their last gasp they turned down his offers. That the third wall would be quickly captured was evident from the capture of the other two: even if that barrier defied attack, hunger would fight for the Romans and against them.

These appeals of Josephus were received by the defenders generally with howls of derision or execration, sometimes with showers of stones. As frank advice was lost on them, he turned to the story of the nation's past.[16]

'You wretched people!' he cried, 'you forget your real allies. Are you fighting the Romans with weapons and your own right hand? Whom else have we defeated in that way? and when did God our Creator fail to avenge our wrongs? Turn round and look at the place you are setting out from to the fight, and think how powerful an Ally you have grossly insulted! Have you forgotten the miraculous achievements of your fathers, and the terrible wars this place has won for you in days gone by? For my part, I shudder to recall the works of God in your unworthy hearing – listen all the same, and realize that you are fighting not only the Romans but God as well.

'Pharaoh Necho, king of Egypt at the time, descended on this land with an immense army and seized Sarah the Princess, mother of our nation. And what did her husband, our forefather Abraham, do? Did he avenge the insult by force of arms? Yet he had three hundred and eighteen officers under him, with unlimited manpower at their disposal! Did he not regard them as valueless without the help of God,

and stretch out clean hands towards the place you now have dese-
crated, enlisting the Almighty as his Helper? Wasn't the queen sent
back to her husband the very next evening, unsullied, while the
Egyptian, reverencing the place stained by you with your countrymen's blood and shaken by terrible dreams in the night, fled, showering silver and gold on God's beloved Hebrews?[17]

'Need I speak of our fathers' sojourn in Egypt? They were crushed
and subject to foreign rulers for four hundred years; but though they
might have resisted with weapons and their own right hand, they
committed their cause to God. Who has not heard of Egypt, overrun
with every wild beast and wasted by every disease, the barren land,
the shrunken Nile, the ten plagues in swift succession, and the consequent departure of our fathers, sent on their way with no bloodshed
and no danger, led forth by God to establish His temple-worship?[18]
Again, when the Syrians carried off our sacred Ark, did not Philistia
and Dagon the idol, did not the whole nation of plunderers rue the
day? Their hidden parts suppurating, their bowels prolapsed, they
brought it back with the hands that stole it, propitiating the Sanctuary
with the sound of cymbals and timbrels and with peace-offerings of
every kind. It was God whose generalship won this victory for our
fathers, because they placed no trust in their right arm or their weapons
but committed to Him the decision of the issue.[19]

'When the king of Assyria, Sennacherib, brought all Asia with him
and encamped round this City, did he fall by human hands? Wasn't
it when those hands were unarmed and raised in supplication that an
angel of God in one night destroyed that innumerable army, so that
when he arose in the early morning the Assyrian found 185,000
corpses, and fled with the survivors from unarmed Hebrews who
attempted no pursuit?[20] You know too of the bondage in Babylon,
where the people lived in exile for seventy years, and never tried to
shake off the yoke till Cyrus granted them liberty as an offering to
God. They were sent on their way by him to re-establish the temple-
worship of their Ally.[21]

'In short, on no occasion did our fathers succeed by force of arms,
or fail without them after committing their cause to God. If they
took no action, they were victorious as it seemed good to their Judge:
if they gave battle, they were beaten every time. For instance, when
the king of Babylon was besieging this city, and our king Zedekiah
disregarding Jeremiah's prophecies gave battle, he was taken prisoner

himself and saw the town and the Temple razed to the ground.[22] Yet how moderate that king was compared with your leaders, and his subjects compared with you! Jeremiah shouted from the housetops that they were hated by God for their iniquities against Him, and would be taken into captivity unless they surrendered the City; yet neither king nor people put him to death. But you! I will say nothing of happenings in the City – I have no words to describe the atrocities you have perpetrated; but when I appeal to you to save yourselves you greet me with howls of execration and showers of stones, enraged at being reminded of your sins and unable to endure any mention of the outrages you openly commit day after day!

'Again, when Antiochus Epiphanes was blockading the City and had committed gross sacrilege, and our ancestors advanced in arms against him, what happened? They were cut to pieces in the battle, the town was plundered by the enemy, and the Sanctuary was desolated for three years and a half. Need I go on with the story? But who enlisted the Romans against our country? Wasn't the impiety of the inhabitants responsible? And what began our servitude? Wasn't it civil strife among our ancestors, when the insane rivalry of Aristobulus and Hyrcanus brought Pompey against the City and God put beneath the Roman heel those who did not deserve to be free? After three months' siege they surrendered, though they had not sinned against the Sanctuary and the Law as you have done – and were far better equipped for war. And we know the end of Antigonus, the son of Aristobulus, don't we? In his reign God by a further capture of the City smote the people for their iniquities: Herod, Antipater's heir, brought Sosius, and Sosius a Roman army, which blockaded and besieged them for six months,[23] till as the punishment of their sins they saw the City captured and plundered by their enemies.

'Thus it was never intended that our nation should bear arms, and war has invariably ended in defeat. It is the duty, I believe, of those who dwell on holy ground to commit all things to the judgement of God, and to scorn the aid of human hands whenever they can reach the ear of the heavenly Judge. But which of the things blessed by the lawgiver have *you* done? Which of the things cursed by him have you left undone? How far those who were defeated in earlier days fell short of your impiety! You have not eschewed the secret sins – theft, treachery, adultery; in plundering and murder you vie with each other; you open up new avenues of vice. The Temple has become a sink for the nation's dregs, and native hands have polluted the hallowed spot that even Romans venerated from a distance, setting aside many of their own customs from regard for your Law.

'After all this do you expect Him you have dishonoured to be your ally? You are indeed righteous suppliants and it is with clean hands that you beseech your Helper! With such hands no doubt our king made supplications for aid against the Assyrian, when in one night that mighty army was struck down by God! Are the Romans behaving so like the Assyrian that you can expect a like vengeance on them? Isn't the truth that whereas he received money from our king on the understanding that he would not sack the City, and then descended on us, in defiance of his oaths, to burn the Sanctuary, the Romans are only demanding the customary tribute which our fathers paid to theirs?[24] When they obtain this, they will neither sack the City nor lay a finger on your holy places: they will give you everything else, the freedom of your children, the security of your property, and the preservation of your holy Law. It is madness to expect God to treat the just as He treated the unjust!

'Again, He knows how to take immediate vengeance when there is need; thus on the very night the Assyrians pitched their camp by the City He crushed them. So if He had judged our generation worthy of liberty or the Romans of chastisement, He would immediately have fallen upon them as He fell upon the Assyrians. When? – when Pompey meddled with our affairs, when later Sosius came against us, when Vespasian was laying Galilee waste, and last of all now when Titus was drawing near the City. And yet Magnus[25] and Sosius not only suffered no setback but took the City by assault, and Vespasian made his war against us the stepping-stone to the throne, while for Titus the very springs flow more abundantly, springs that had dried up for you! Before his advent you know that Siloam was falling, as were all the springs outside the town, so that water had to be bought by the pailful; but now they are in such full flood for your enemies that there is more than enough not only for them and their beasts but even for gardens. The same portent you saw happen once before at the capture of the City,[26] when the Babylonian already referred to marched against it, took the City and Sanctuary and burnt them both, though that generation was surely guilty of no such impiety as yours. So I am sure the Almighty has quitted your holy places and stands now on the side of your enemies. Why, when a good man will quit a licentious house and abominate its occupants, do you think God can endure the wickedness of His household – God, who sees each hidden thing and hears what is wrapped in silence? But what do you wrap in silence or keep hidden? What have you not paraded before your enemies? You boast of your unspeakable crimes and daily vie with one another to see who can be the worst, as proud of your vices as if they were virtues!

'In spite of all, a way of salvation still remains if you will follow it, and the Almighty is ready to pardon those who confess and repent. You obdurate fools! throw away your weapons, take pity on your birthplace at this moment plunging to ruin, turn round and gaze at the beauty of what you are betraying – what a City! what a Temple! what gifts from all the Gentile world! Against these will any man direct the flames? Does any man wish these things to pass away? What better deserves to be kept safe than these, you inhuman, stony-hearted monsters! If the sight of these things leaves you unmoved, at least pity your families, and let each man set before his eyes his wife and children and parents, so soon to perish by famine or the sword. I know that danger threatens my own mother and wife, a family of great promise and a house famous from of old; and perhaps you think it is for their sake I advise you. Kill them! take my flesh and blood as the price of your own salvation! I too am ready to die, if that will teach you wisdom.'

CHAPTER 19

The Horrors of the Siege

TEARS ran down Josephus' face as he concluded his vehement appeal. The partisans would not give way as they thought a change of front would be disastrous, but among the common people there was a movement in favour of desertion. Some sold all their property at a dead loss, others parted with the more valuable of their treasures. Then to frustrate the bandits they swallowed their gold pieces, and deserting to the Romans had only to empty their bowels to have ample provision for their needs.[1] For most of them were allowed by Titus to go through into the countryside in any direction they chose. This made them still more ready to desert, as they would thus escape from the horrors within the City without being enslaved by the Romans. The supporters of John and Simon made greater efforts to keep these men in than to keep the Romans out, and anyone who afforded even a shadow of suspicion was promptly put to death.

For the wealthy it was just as dangerous to stay in the City as to leave it; for on the pretext that he was a deserter many a man was killed for the sake of his money. As the famine grew worse, the frenzy of the partisans increased with it, and every day these two terrors strengthened their grip. For as corn was nowhere to be seen, men broke into the houses and ransacked them. If they found any, they maltreated the occupants for saying there was none; if they did not, they suspected them of having hidden it more carefully and tortured them. Proof of whether or not they had food was provided by the appearance of the unhappy wretches. If they still had flesh on their bones, they were deemed to have plenty of stores; if they were already reduced to skeletons, they were passed over, for it seemed pointless to dispatch those who were certain to die of starvation before long. Many secretly exchanged their possessions for one measure of corn – wheat if they happened to be rich, barley if they were poor. Then they shut themselves up in the darkest corners of their houses, where some through extreme hunger ate their grain as it was, others made bread, necessity and fear being the only guides. Nowhere was a table laid –

they snatched the food from the fire while still uncooked and ate like wolves.

The sight of such misery would have brought tears to the eyes, for while the strong had more than enough, the weak were in desperate straits. All human feelings, alas, yield to hunger, of which decency is always the first victim; for when hunger reigns, restraint is abandoned. Thus it was that wives robbed their husbands, children their fathers, and – most horrible of all – mothers their babies, snatching the food out of their very mouths; and when their dearest ones were dying in their arms, they did not hesitate to deprive them of the morsels that might have kept them alive. This way of satisfying their hunger did not go unnoticed: everywhere the partisans were ready to swoop even on such pickings. Wherever they saw a locked door they concluded that those within were having a meal, and instantly bursting the door open they rushed in, and hardly stopped short at squeezing their throats to force out the morsels of food! They beat old men who held on to their crusts, and tore the hair of women who hid what was in their hands. They showed no pity for grey hairs or helpless infancy, but picked up the children as they clung to their precious scraps and dashed them on the floor. If anyone anticipated their entry by gulping down what they hoped to seize, they felt themselves defrauded and retaliated with worse savagery still.

Terrible were the methods of torture they devised in their quest for food. They stuffed bitter vetch up the genital passages of their victims, and drove sharp stakes into their seats. Torments horrible even to hear about they inflicted on people to make them admit possession of one loaf or reveal the hiding-place of a single handful of barley. It was not that the tormentors were hungry – their actions would have been less barbarous had they sprung from necessity – but rather they were keeping their passions exercised and laying in stores for use in the coming days. Again, when men had crawled out in the night as far as the Roman guardposts to collect wild plants and herbs, these marauders met them just when they thought they had got safely away from the enemy lines and snatched their treasures from them. Piteous entreaties and appeals to the awful Name of God could not secure the return of even a fraction of what they had collected at such risk: they were lucky to be only robbed and not killed as well.

While the humbler folk suffered thus at the hands of mere

henchmen, men of position or wealth were dragged before the party chiefs. Some of them were falsely accused of plotting and destroyed, others were charged with betraying the City to the Romans; but the favourite device was to pay an informer to allege that they were planning to desert. When a man had been stripped by Simon he was sent to John: when someone had been plundered by John, Simon took him over. They drank each other's health in the blood of their countrymen and divided the carcases of the wretches between them. In their desire for domination the two were at daggers drawn, but in their crimes they were blood-brothers; for the one who did not give his partner a share in the fruits of other people's misery was deemed an utter scoundrel, while the one who received no share, as if robbed of a prize, was furious at being excluded from the savagery. To give a detailed account of their outrageous conduct is impossible, but we may sum it up by saying that no other city has ever endured such horrors, and no generation in history has fathered such wickedness. In the end they brought the whole Hebrew race into contempt in order to make their own impiety seem less outrageous in foreign eyes, and confessed the painful truth that they were slaves, the dregs of humanity, bastards, and outcasts of their nation. The overthrow of the City was their work, though they forced the unwilling Romans to be credited with a melancholy victory, and almost hurried the flames to the Sanctuary as if they were too slow! It is certain that as they watched it burning from the Upper City, they did not turn a hair or shed a tear, though the Romans were deeply moved. But of this I shall speak later at the proper time, giving a full account of the circumstances.[2]

On the Roman side the platforms were nearing completion, though the defenders' missiles caused many casualties among the soldiers. Titus himself detailed a section of the cavalry to ambush those who sallied out along the valleys in search of food. Some of these were fighting-men no longer satisfied with what they could steal, but the majority were penniless workers, afraid to desert lest their families should be penalized; for they knew the partisans would catch them if they tried to get their wives and children through the lines, and they could not bear to leave them behind for the bandits to murder in their stead. But hunger gave them courage for these sallies, the only thing left being to slip out and fall into enemy hands. When caught they were forced to offer resistance, and when the fighting ended it seemed too late to sue for mercy. Scourged and subjected before death to every torture, they were finally crucified in view of the wall. Titus indeed realized the horror of what was happening, for every day five hundred – sometimes even more – fell into his hands. However it was not safe to let men captured by force go free, and to guard such a host of prisoners would tie up a great proportion of his troops. But his chief reason for not stopping the slaughter was the hope that the sight of it would perhaps induce the Jews to surrender in order to avoid the same fate. The soldiers themselves through rage and bitterness nailed up their victims in various attitudes as a grim joke, till owing to the vast numbers there was no room for the crosses, and no crosses for the bodies.

So far were the partisans from changing their policy in view of this calamity that they went to the opposite extreme in tricking the rest of the people. They dragged the families of the deserters on to the wall with those members of the public who were ready to accept Roman assurances, and showed them what happened to men who deserted to the enemy, declaring that the victims were suppliants, not prisoners. This caused many who were eager to desert to remain in the City, until the truth came out; but some crossed over without further delay, knowing the fate that awaited them but regarding death at enemy hands as a deliverance, compared with starvation. Many of these prisoners Titus ordered to have their hands cut off, that they might not be thought to have deserted and might be believed because of their horrible treatment. Then he sent them to Simon and John, urging these two to put an immediate end to their resistance and not compel him to destroy the City, but to reap the benefit of a change of heart, belated as it was, and save their own lives, their wonderful birthplace, and the Sanctuary that was theirs alone. At the same time he went from platform to platform urging on the workers, to show that he would shortly follow up words with deed. In answer the men on the wall hurled insults at Caesar himself and at his father, and shouted that they cared nothing for death, but preferred it to slavery, as men should. They would do all possible damage to the Romans while they had breath in them. What did their birthplace matter to those who, as he himself said, were doomed to die? As for the Sanctuary, God had a better one in the world itself; but this one too would be saved by Him who dwelt in it, and having Him on their side they would laugh at every threat not backed by deeds; for the issue lay with God. Such were the retorts which they yelled, along with mere abuse.

At this time Antiochus Epiphanes[3] arrived with a large force of heavy infantry and a bodyguard of so-called Macedonians, all just out of their teens, tall, and trained and equipped in the Macedonian manner – hence the title, though few of them bore much resemblance to that martial race! As it happened, the most prosperous of Rome's vassals was the king of Commagene – until his luck changed. In his old age he declared that no man should be called happy before his death.[4] But Antiochus, who had arrived while his father still flourished, expressed amazement that the Romans should hesitate to approach the wall. He himself was a born fighter, naturally venturesome, and so phenomenally strong that his audacity rarely failed to achieve its end. Titus smiled and said that they were partners in the struggle; so without more ado Antiochus led his Macedonians in a sudden onslaught on the wall. He himself, thanks to his strength and skill, was untouched by the Jewish missiles as he shot his arrows at them. But his youngsters were severely battered, except a very few; for to fulfil their promise they fought tooth and nail, and when they at last retired many had become casualties. No doubt they said to themselves that even real Macedonians could only conquer if they had Alexander's luck!

The Romans had begun work on the 12th of Artemisios, but they only completed the platforms on the 29th, after seventeen days of continuous toil; for all four were of vast size. One, facing Antonia, was raised by the Fifth Legion opposite the middle of the Quince Pool[5]; another, built by the Twelfth, was thirty feet away. A long way from these, to the north of the City, was the work of the Tenth, near the Almond Pool[6]; forty-five feet from this the Fifteenth built theirs by the High Priest's Monument. But from within the City John tunnelled through the ground near Antonia, supporting the galleries with wooden props, and by the time the engines were brought up he had reached the platforms and left the works without solid support. Next he carried in faggots daubed with pitch and bitumen and set them alight, so that as soon as the props were burnt away the entire tunnel collapsed, and with a thunderous crash the platforms fell into the cavity. At once there arose a dense cloud of smoke and dust as the flames were choked by the debris; then when the mass of timber was burnt away a brilliant flame broke through. This sudden blow filled the Romans with consternation, and the ingenuity of the Jews plunged them into despondency; as they had felt sure that victory was imminent, the shock froze their hope of success even in the future. To fight the flames seemed useless, for even if they did put them out their platforms were already swallowed up.

Two days later Simon's forces assaulted the other two platforms; for the Romans had brought up their battering-rams on this side and were already rocking the wall. A certain Tephthaeus, who came from Garis in Galilee, and Magassarus, one of the royal troops and an attendant of Mariamme,[7] accompanied by a man from Adiabene, the son of one Nabataeus, nicknamed Ceagiras, 'the Cripple', because of a disability, picked up firebrands and rushed at the engines. In the whole course of the war the City produced no one more heroic than these three, or more terrifying. They dashed out as if towards friends, not massed enemies; they neither hesitated nor shrank back, but charged through the centre of the foe and set the artillery on fire. Pelted with missiles and thrust at with swords on every side, they refused to withdraw from their perilous situation till the engines were ablaze. When the flames were already shooting up, the Romans came running from the camps to the rescue. But the Jews advanced from the wall to stop them, grappling with those who attempted to quench the flames and utterly disregarding their personal danger. The Romans tugged at the battering-rams while the wicker covers blazed; the Jews, surrounded with the flames, pulled the other way, and seizing the red-hot iron would not leave go of the rams. From these the fire spread to the platforms, outstripping the defenders. Meantime, the Romans were enveloped in flames, and despairing of saving their handiwork began to withdraw to their camps. The Jews pressed them hard, their numbers constantly swelled by reinforcements from the City, and emboldened by their success attacked with the utmost violence till they actually reached the Roman fortifications and engaged the defenders.

There is an armed picket, periodically relieved, which occupies a position in front of every Roman camp and is subject to the very drastic regulation that a man who retires, no matter what the circumstances, must be executed. These men, preferring death with honour to death as a penalty, stood their ground, and their desperate plight shamed many of the runaways into making a stand. Spear-throwers were set up on the wall to drive off the mass of men that poured out of the City without the slightest thought for their own safety. These grappled with all who stood in their path, falling recklessly upon the Roman spears and flinging their very bodies against the foe. It was less by actions than by supreme confidence that they gained the advantage, and it was Jewish audacity rather than their own casualties that made the Romans give ground.

At this crisis Titus arrived from Antonia, to which he had withdrawn to choose a site for more platforms. He expressed the utmost contempt for the soldiers, who after capturing the enemy's walls were in danger of losing their own, and were enduring a siege themselves through letting the Jews out of prison to attack them! Then he put himself at the head of a body of picked men and tried to turn the flank of the enemy, who, although assailed from the front, wheeled round to meet this new threat and resisted stubbornly. In the confusion that followed, blinded by the dust and deafened by the uproar, neither side could distinguish friend from foe. The Jews stood firm, not so much through prowess now as through despair of victory; the Romans were braced by respect for the honour of their arms, especially as Caesar was in the forefront of danger. The struggle would probably have ended, such was the fury of the Romans, with the capture of the whole mass of Jews, had they not forestalled the crisis of the battle by retreating to the City. With their platforms destroyed the Romans were downhearted, having lost the fruits of their prolonged labours in a single hour; many indeed felt that with conventional weapons they would never take the City.

Titus held a council of war. The more sanguine spirits were for bringing the whole army into action in a full-scale assault. Hitherto only a fraction of their forces had been engaged with the enemy; if they advanced en masse the Jews would yield to the first onslaught, overwhelmed by the rain of missiles. The more cautious urged either that they should reconstruct the platforms, or that, abandoning them, they should merely blockade the City and prevent the inhabitants from making sallies or bringing in food, leaving them to starve and refraining from combat. For there was no battling with despair, when men desired only to die by the sword and so escape a more horrible fate. Titus himself thought it unwise to let so large a force remain idle, while there was no point in fighting those who were certain to destroy each other. To throw up platforms was a hopeless task with timber so scarce, to prevent sallies still more hopeless. For to form a ring of men round so big a City and over such difficult terrain was impracticable, and highly dangerous in view of sudden attacks. The known paths might be blocked, but the Jews would contrive secret ways out, driven by necessity and knowing the ground. Again, if provisions were smuggled in, the siege would be prolonged still further, and he was afraid that the lustre of his triumph would be dimmed by its slowness in coming. Given time, anything could be accomplished, but reputations were won by speed. If he was to combine speed with safety he must build a wall round the entire City. That was the only way to block every exit and force the Jews to abandon their last hope of survival and surrender the City. If they did not, hunger would make them easy victims. For he would not wait for things to happen, but would resume construction of the platforms when resistance had been weakened. If anyone thought the task too great to carry out, he must remember that little tasks were beneath the dignity of Rome, and that without hard work nothing great could be achieved, unless by a miracle.

Having thus convinced the generals, Titus ordered them to divide up the work between their units. An inspired enthusiasm seized the soldiers, and when the circuit had been marked out there was competition not only between legions but even between cohorts. The private was eager to please his decurion, the decurion his centurion, the centurion his tribune; the tribunes were ambitious for the praise of the generals; and of the rivalry between the generals Caesar himself was judge. He personally went round several times every day to inspect the work. Starting at the Assyrians' Camp, where his own quarters were, he took the wall to the New City below, and from there across the Kidron to the Mount of Olives. Then he bent the line towards the south enclosing the Mount (as far as the rock called the Dovecot) and the next eminence, which overhangs the valley near Siloam. From there he went in a westerly direction down into Fountain Valley,[8] then up by the tomb of Ananus the high priest,[9] embracing the hill where Pompey's camp had been.[10] Then turning north he passed the village called The House of Peas, and rounding Herod's Tomb[11] went east till he finished up at his own camp, the starting-place. The wall measured 4½ miles, and outside were built on thirteen forts with a combined circumference of over a mile. Yet the whole task was completed in three days, though it might well have taken months – the speed passed belief.[12] Having surrounded the City with this wall and garrisoned the forts, Titus himself took the first night watch and went the rounds; the second he entrusted to Alexander[13]; the third was assigned to the legion commanders. The guards drew lots for periods of sleep, and all night long they patrolled the intervals between the forts.

The Jews, unable to leave the City, were deprived of all hope of survival. The famine became more intense and devoured whole houses and families. The roofs were covered with women and babies too weak to stand, the streets full of old men already dead. Young men and boys, swollen with hunger, haunted the squares like ghosts and fell wherever faintness overcame them. To bury their kinsfolk was beyond the strength of the sick, and those who were fit shirked the task because of the number of the dead and uncertainty about their own fate; for many while burying others fell dead themselves, and many set out for their graves before their hour struck. In their misery no weeping or lamentation was heard; hunger stifled emotion; with dry eyes and grinning mouths those who were slow to die watched those whose end came sooner. Deep silence enfolded the City, and a darkness burdened with death. Worse still were the bandits, who broke into the houses of the dead like tomb-robbers, stripped the bodies, snatching off their wrappings, and then came out laughing. They tried the points of their swords on the corpses, and even trans-fixed some of those who lay helpless but still alive, to test the steel. But if any begged for a swordthrust to end their sufferings, they contemptuously left them to die of hunger. Everyone as he breathed his last fixed his eyes on the Sanctuary, turning his back on the partisans he was leaving alive. The latter at first ordered the dead to be buried at public expense as they could not bear the stench; later, when this proved impossible, they threw them from the walls into the valleys. When in the course of his rounds Titus saw these choked with dead, and a putrid stream trickling from under the decomposing bodies, he groaned, and uplifting his hands called God to witness that this was not his doing.

While such were the conditions in the City, the Romans were exuberant, for none of the partisans sallied out now that they too were despondent and hungry. There was an abundance of corn and other necessities from Syria and the neighbouring provinces, and the soldiers delighted to stand near the wall and display their ample supplies of food, by their own abundance inflaming the hunger of the enemy. But when suffering made the partisans no more ready to submit, Titus took pity on the remnant of the people, and in his anxiety to rescue the survivors again began constructing platforms, though it was difficult to get timber. Round the City it had all been cut down for the previous works, and the soldiers had to collect new supplies from more than ten miles away. Concentrating on Antonia, they raised platforms in four sections, much bigger than the earlier ones. Caesar made the round of the legions, speeding the work and showing the bandits they were in his hands. But they alone seemed to have lost all sense of remorse, and making a division between soul and body acted as if neither belonged to them. For their souls were as insensitive to suffering as their bodies were to pain – they tore the carcase of the nation with their fangs, and filled the prisons with the defenceless.

Simon actually put Matthias, who had made him master of the City, to death by torture. He was a member of a high-priestly family, the son of Boethus,[14] and he enjoyed the absolute trust and respect of the people. When the masses were being roughly handled by the Zealots whom John had already joined, he persuaded the people to accept Simon's aid, having made no pact with him but expecting no mischief from him. When however Simon arrived and got the City into his power, he treated Matthias as an enemy like the rest, and the furtherer of his cause as a mere simpleton. Matthias was brought before him and accused of favouring the Romans, and without being allowed to defend himself, was condemned to die with three of his sons. The fourth had already made his escape to Titus. When Matthias begged to be killed before his children, pleading for this as a favour because he had opened the gates to Simon, the monster ordered him to be killed last. So his sons were murdered before his eyes and then his dead body was thrown on to theirs, in full view of the Romans. Such were the instructions that Simon had given to Ananus, son of Bagadates, the most brutal of his henchmen; and he mockingly enquired whether Matthias hoped for assistance from his new friends. Burial of the bodies was forbidden. After their deaths an eminent priest named Ananias, son of Masbalus, and the clerk of the Sanhedrin, Aristaeus, whose home was Emmaus, together with fifteen distinguished citizens, were put to death. Josephus' father was kept under lock and key, and an edict forbade anyone in the City to associate with him through fear of betrayal. Any who condoled with him were executed without trial.

Seeing all this Judas, son of Judas, a subordinate whom Simon had entrusted with command of a tower, partly through disgust at these brutal murders but chiefly with an eye to his own safety, collected the ten most reliable of his men. 'How long,' he asked, 'shall we endure these horrors? What hope of survival have we if we remain loyal to a scoundrel? We are starving already and the Romans have almost got in. Simon is betraying his best friends and is likely soon to jump on us; but the word of the Romans can be trusted. So come on! Let us surrender the wall and save ourselves and the City! Simon had lost hope already! It won't hurt him if he gets his deserts a bit sooner.' This argument convinced the ten, and at dawn he sent off the rest in different directions to avoid discovery. Three hours later he shouted from his tower to the Romans, but some of them were scornful, others mistrustful, the majority uninterested: in any case the City would soon fall into their lap. Titus advanced with his heavy infantry towards the wall. But Simon stole a march on him, occupied the tower first, arrested the men, executed them before the eyes of the Romans, and threw their mutilated bodies over the wall.

At this time, as he went round making yet another appeal, Josephus was struck on the head by a stone and fell to the ground unconscious. Seeing him fall the Jews ran out, and would have dragged him into the City had not Caesar promptly sent men to protect him. While they fought Josephus was picked up, knowing little of what was going on. The partisans thought they had disposed of the man they hated most, and whooped for joy. When the report spread through the City, the survivors of the populace were overcome with despair, believing that they had really lost the man with whose help they hoped to desert. When Josephus' mother was told in prison that her son was dead, she said to the guards that she had foreseen this ever since Jotapata; while he was alive she might as well have had no son. Privately she lamented to her maids that this was the only result of bringing children into the world – she would not even bury the son whom she had expected to bury her. But the false report neither grieved her nor cheered the bandits for long. Josephus soon recovered from the blow, and went forward to shout that it would not be long before they paid the penalty for wounding him, and to implore the people to trust him. His reappearance brought new hope to the common folk, to the partisans' consternation.

Some of the deserters, seeing no other way, promptly jumped from the wall. Others advanced as if to battle armed with stones, then fled to the Romans. Their fate was worse than if they had stayed in the City, and the hunger they had left behind was, as they discovered, less lethal than the plenty the Romans provided. They arrived blown up by starvation as if by dropsy, then stuffed their empty bellies non-stop till they burst – except for those who were wise enough to restrain their appetites and take the unaccustomed food a little at a time. Those who escaped this danger fell victims to another disaster. In the Syrian camp[15] one deserter was caught picking gold coins out of his excreta. As I mentioned, they swallowed coins before leaving, because they were all searched by the partisans,[16] and there was a great deal of gold in the City. In fact it fetched less than half the old price. But when the trick was discovered through one man, the rumour ran round the camps that the deserters were arriving stuffed with gold. The Arab unit and the Syrians cut open the refugees and ransacked their bellies. To me this seems the most terrible calamity that happened to the Jews: in a single night nearly two thousand were ripped up.

When Titus learnt of this atrocity he was on the point of surrounding the perpetrators with his cavalry and shooting them down. But far too many were involved; in fact those to be punished far outnumbered their victims. Instead he summoned both the auxiliary and the legionary commanders, some of whose men were accused of participating, and spoke angrily to both groups. Was it possible that some of his own soldiers did such things on the off chance of gain, and had no respect for their own weapons that were made of silver and gold? The Arabs and Syrians, serving in a war that was not the concern of their own nation, began by indulging their passions in an undisciplined fashion, and ended by letting Romans take the blame for their bloodthirsty butchery and their hatred for the Jews; for some of his own soldiers shared their evil reputation. The foreigners therefore he threatened to punish with death if any man was caught after this committing such a crime. The legionary commanders he instructed to ferret out suspected offenders and bring them before him.

But avarice, it seems, scorns every penalty and an extraordinary love of gain is innate in man, nor is any emotion as strong as covetousness. At other times these passions are kept within bounds and overawed by fear. But it was God who condemned the whole nation and turned every means of escape to their destruction. So what Caesar forebade with threats was still done to the deserters in secret, and the refugees, before the rest noticed them, were met and murdered by the foreign soldiers, who looked round in case any Roman saw them, then ripped them up and pulled the filthy money out of their bowels. In few however was any found, the majority being victims of an empty hope. Fear of this fate caused many of the deserters to return.

When there was nothing left that John could extort from the people, he turned to sacrilege and melted down many of the offerings in the Sanctuary and many of the vessels required for services, basins, dishes, and tables, not even keeping his hands off the flagons presented by Augustus and his consort. For the Roman emperors honoured and adorned the Temple at all times.[17] But now this Jew stole even the gifts of foreigners, telling his companions that they need not hesitate to use God's property for God's benefit, and that those who fought for the Sanctuary were entitled to live on it. Accordingly he emptied out the sacred corn and oil which the priests kept in the inner court of the Temple to pour on burnt offerings, and shared them out to the crowd, who without a qualm swallowed a pailful or smeared it on themselves. I cannot refrain from saying what my feelings dictate. I think that if the Romans had delayed their attack on these sacrilegious ruffians, either the ground would have opened and swallowed up the City, or a flood would have overwhelmed it, or lightning would have destroyed it like Sodom. For it produced a generation far more godless than those who perished thus, a generation whose mad folly involved the nation in ruin.

But why should I describe these calamities one by one? While they were happening Mannaeus, son of Lazarus, fled to Titus and told him that through a single gate which had been entrusted to him 115,880 corpses had been carried out between the 14th of Xanthicos, when the Romans pitched their camp near the city, and the 1st of Panemos. All these were the bodies of paupers. Though he was not himself in charge, he had to pay the expenses out of public funds, and so was obliged to keep count. The rest were buried by their own kin, who merely brought them out and threw them clear of the City. After Mannaeus many distinguished citizens deserted, and these reported that in all 600,000 pauper bodies had been thrown out at the gates: of the others the number was unknown. When it was no longer possible to carry out the penniless, they said, the corpses had been heaped up in the biggest houses and the doors locked. The price of corn was fantastically high, and now that the City was walled round and they could not even gather herbs, some were in such dire straits that they raked the sewers and old dunghills and swallowed the refuse they found there, so that what once they could not bear to look at now became their food.

When the Romans heard of all this misery they felt pity: the partisans, who saw it with their own eyes, showed no regrets but allowed these things to come upon them too; for they were blinded by the doom that was closing in on the City and on themselves.

CHAPTER 20

Antonia Captured and Destroyed

As the days wore on the plight of Jerusalem grew steadily worse, the partisans being goaded to greater fury by successive calamities, while the famine that devoured the people now preyed on themselves. The innumerable corpses piled up all over the City not merely were a revolting sight and emitted a pestilential stench: they obstructed the fighting-men as they made their sorties; for like men marching across a battlefield littered with thousands of dead they were forced to trample on the bodies. But as they trod them underfoot they gave no shudder, felt no pity, and saw no ill omen to themselves in this insult to the departed. Their hands drenched with their country's blood, they rushed out to battle with foreigners, reproaching the Almighty, it seems to me, for His slowness in punishing them; for it was not hope of victory but despair of deliverance now that emboldened them for the fight. The Romans, though it was a terrible struggle to collect the timber, raised their platforms in twenty-one days, having, as described before, stripped the whole area in a circle round the town to a distance of ten miles. The countryside like the City was a pitiful sight; for where once there had been a lovely vista of woods and parks there was now nothing but desert and the stumps of trees. No one – not even a foreigner – who had seen the old Judaea and the glorious suburbs of the City, and now set eyes on her present desolation, could have helped sighing and groaning at so terrible a change; for every trace of beauty had been blotted out by the war, and nobody who had known it in the past and came upon it suddenly would have recognized the place: he would have gone on looking for the City when he was already in it.

To Romans and Jews alike the completion of the platforms brought a new terror. The Jews felt sure that unless they burnt these too the City would fall, the Romans that it would never be taken if they went the way of the others. For no more timber was available, and the soldiers' physical strength had been sapped by toil and their morale by constant reverses. Indeed, the disastrous conditions in the City proved more discouraging to the Romans than to the inhabitants: they found the fighting-men not in the least subdued by their severe reverses, while their own hopes were continually frustrated, their platforms rendered useless by stratagems, their engines by the strength of the wall, and their skill in close combat by the daring of their adversaries. Worst blow of all, they discovered that the Jews had an inner courage that rose superior to faction, famine, war, and disasters beyond number. They began to think the onslaughts of these men irresistible, and their equanimity amidst disasters unshakable – what would they not endure if fortune favoured them, seeing that calamity only whetted their appetite for battle? Small wonder, then, that the Romans made the guard-posts of the platforms stronger still.

John's forces in Antonia were building up their strength for eventualities, in case the wall was thrown down. At the same time they forestalled the onslaught of the rams by an assault on the Roman earthworks. The attempt was a failure: they advanced torch in hand, but before nearing the platforms lost hope completely and turned back. In the first place there seemed to be no agreed plan – they dashed out a few at a time, at intervals, with hesitation and fear – in short, unlike Jews; there was little sign of the national characteristics, boldness, dash, the massed charge and the refusal to acknowledge defeat. But while the customary vigour was lacking in their advance, they found the Romans formed up in unusual strength; with their mail-clad bodies they surrounded the platforms with so complete a bulwark as to leave no chink anywhere for the passage of a firebrand, and every man braced himself to die rather than budge from his post. For apart from the destruction of all their hopes if these works too went up in flames, the soldiers could not bear the thought that trickery should triumph every time over prowess, desperation over skill at arms, numbers over experience, and Jews over Romans. Furthermore the artillery co-operated by dropping missiles on the leading Jewish files: the fallen held up those immediately behind, and the risk of going to the fore quenched their ardour. Of those who pushed beyond the beaten zone, some before coming to close quarters took fright at the disciplined and serried ranks of the enemy, others took to flight only when pricked by their lances. At last flinging the word 'coward' at each other, they withdrew with nothing to show. It was on the 1st of Panemos that the attempt was made.

After the Jewish withdrawal the Romans brought up the battering-rams,[1] though they were being pelted with lumps of rock from

Antonia, with firebrands, arrows, and every weapon with which necessity furnished the Jews; for though they felt sure of their wall and despised the engines, they nevertheless tried to prevent them from being brought up. The Romans, assuming that the anxiety of the Jews to avert an assault on Antonia was due to the weakness of the wall, and hoping that the foundations were unsound, made strenuous counter-efforts. The wall stood up to the blows, but the Romans under a deluge of missiles paid no heed to any danger from above and kept the battering-rams constantly at work. As, however, they were awkwardly placed and crushed by the lumps of rock, other men working under a roof of shields[2] strove with hands and crowbars to undermine the foundations, and by strenuous efforts levered out four stones. Darkness ended the activities of both sides, but in the night, at the point where John had undermined the wall by the measures which he had devised against the earlier platforms, the tunnel fell in and the wall, already shaken by the rams, suddenly collapsed.

This occurrence had an astonishing effect on both sides. The Jews, who might have been expected to lose heart because the collapse was unlooked for and they were unprepared for it, took it quite calmly as Antonia remained; but the Romans' unlooked for delight at the downfall was quickly extinguished by the sight of another wall which John's men had built just behind. Certainly this one appeared easier to assail than the other: to climb up over the ruins seemed a simple matter, and it was assumed that the wall was much weaker than that of Antonia, and that as it had been erected in an emergency it would quickly disintegrate. However, no one dared to climb up: for those who led the way it meant certain death.

Believing that zest for battle is roused most effectively by words of encouragement, and that incentives and promises often make men oblivious of danger, sometimes contemptuous of death itself, Titus got together the élite of his army and put them to the test.

'My fellow-soldiers,' he began, 'to urge men on to actions involving no risk is a deliberate insult to them and an unmistakable proof of the speaker's cowardice. Incentives, surely, are needed only for dangerous enterprises: the other sort men will undertake without any inducement. So I tell you here and now that the ascent to this wall is a formidable task: the point I would emphasize is that the first duty of those who pride themselves on their courage is to battle with difficulties, that it is a splendid thing to die with honour, and that the heroism of those who lead the way will be amply rewarded. In the first place, what might well be a deterrent to some should be an incentive to you – the endurance of these Jews and their fortitude in distress. It would be scandalous for men who are Romans and my soldiers, in peacetime trained for war, in war accustomed to triumph, to be outshone by Jews in strength or determination, and that on the brink of victory and with God to assist us! For our setbacks are the result of Jewish desperation; their difficulties are increased both by your prowess and by God's assistance. Faction, hunger, siege, walls that fall when no engine is at work – what else can be the cause but God's anger with them and co-operation with ourselves? So to be outdone by our inferiors and to betray God our Ally as well would be unworthy of us. It would be utterly disgraceful that Jews, whose reputation suffers little from defeat as they have learnt to endure slavery, should despise death in order to escape from it and repeatedly sally out against our full strength, not in the hope of victory but merely to prove their courage, while you, the lords of almost every land and sea, who could not hold up your heads if victory escaped you, never once hazarded a direct encounter with the enemy, but waited for starvation or bad luck to bring them to their knees, while you sat idle with such weapons in your hands, and that when at a trifling hazard you could win a resounding victory! Once we are on top of Antonia, the City is at our mercy; for even if there is some further fighting against the men inside – I do not anticipate any – we shall be sitting on top, squeezing the breath out of them; and that means victory, speedy and complete.

'I have no intention at this moment of singing the praises of death in battle and the immortality given to those who are killed when fighting-mad; as for those who are not made that way, curse them, I hope they will die in a bed of disease, condemned body and soul to the grave. For every good soldier knows that souls set free from the flesh on the battlefield by the sword are given a welcome by the purest element, ether, and set among the stars, and that as friendly spirits and genial heroes they appear to their own descendants; while souls that waste away in sick bodies, even if completely free from spots and stains, vanish into darkness underground and sink deep into oblivion, life, body, and memory too annihilated at one stroke. But if it is fated that all men must die and the sword is a kindlier minister of

death than any sickness, how contemptible it would be not to give
to the service of our country what we must yield up to fate!

'I have spoken so far as if those who make the attempt cannot possibly come through alive; but it *is* possible for those who play the man
to come safely through the very greatest dangers. First, the ruined
wall will be easy to climb; then all the new structure will be easy to
throw down. More and more of you must call up your courage for the
task and give each other encouragement and support; your determination will soon take the heart out of the Jews. It is quite possible that
you will win a bloodless victory once you take the first step. As you
climb they will presumably try to stop you; but if you once force
your way through undetected, there will be no further resistance,
even if only a few of you get there. As for the man who takes the lead,
I should be ashamed if when honours are awarded I did not make
him an object of envy. Finally the survivor shall be promoted over
his present equals, and the fallen shall receive the coveted meed of
valour.'

Listening to this speech the bulk of the army were appalled by the
greatness of the danger; but in one of the cohorts there was a man
called Sabinus, a Syrian by race, who in prowess and courage proved
himself outstanding. And yet anyone who had seen him before would
have concluded from his physical appearance that he was not even an
average soldier. His skin was black, his flesh lean and shrunken; but
in his frail body, far too slender for its own prowess, dwelt a heroic
soul. Springing to his feet he cried: 'I gladly offer you my services,
Caesar. I am the first to scale the wall. I trust my strength and determination will have the benefit of your usual luck; but if I am thwarted
in my efforts, rest assured I am quite prepared for failure and for your
sake have chosen death with my eyes open.'

So saying, with his left hand he held his shield in front of and over
his head, and drawing his sword with his right stepped out towards
the wall, just about midday. He was followed by eleven of the others,
the only ones to emulate his courage; but he went on far ahead of
them all, driven by some supernatural impulse. The guards on the
battlements flung spears at them, discharged volleys of arrows from
all directions and rolled down great lumps of rock, which swept
away some of the eleven; but Sabinus, charging into the missiles
and buried under the arrows, did not falter for a moment till he had

got to the top and routed the enemy. For the Jews, astounded by his
dynamic energy and remorseless determination, and thinking too that
others had climbed up, turned tail. And here one might well complain
of Fortune, so jealous of heroic deeds and ever ready to prevent brilliant successes. For this brave man, just as he achieved his purpose,
tripped up, and stumbling over a big stone fell flat on top of it with
a great crash. The Jews swung round, and seeing him alone and on the
ground pelted him from all directions. He got up on one knee, and
covering himself with his shield for a time fought back, wounding
many who came near him; but soon, riddled with wounds, he lost
the use of his right hand and at length, before he breathed his last, he
was buried under the arrows. So brave a man deserved a better fate,
yet his fall was a fitting end to such an enterprise. Of the others, three
who had already reached the top were battered to death with stones,
the other eight were dragged down wounded and carried back to
camp. This incident took place on the 3rd of Panemos.

Two days later twenty of the men guarding the advanced posts on
the platforms got together, and calling on the standard-bearer of the
Fifth Legion, two soldiers from the cavalry squadrons and one trumpeter, at 2 a.m.[3] moved forward in silence through the ruins of
Antonia. Disposing of the first sentries in their sleep, they got possession of the wall and ordered the trumpeter to sound. The other guards
instantly leapt to their feet and ran away without staying to see how
many had climbed up; for the trumpet-call and the resulting panic
deluded them into thinking that the enemy had climbed up en masse.
When Caesar heard the signal he armed his forces with all speed, and
with his generals and picked troops led the way to the top. The Jews
had taken refuge in the Temple, and the Romans poured in through
the tunnel which John had dug to the Roman platforms. The partisans of both groups, John's and Simon's, drawn up separately,
blocked their way, displaying strength and determination to the very
limit; they realized that a Roman entry into the Sanctuary would be
the beginning of the end, while the Romans saw in it the dawn of
victory. Round the entrances they grappled in a life and death struggle,
the Romans driving on relentlessly to get possession of the Temple,
the Jews pushing them back towards Antonia. Arrows and spears
were of no use to either side; they drew their swords and closed; in
the milling mass it was impossible to distinguish one side from the
other, as the men were locked together inextricably in the confined

space, and amidst the uproar their shouts conveyed no meaning to the ear. The carnage on both sides was terrible, and the mail-clad bodies of the fallen were trampled and crushed by the combatants. Whichever way the tide of battle swung, the cheers of the victors and the groans of the routed were always to be heard. There was room for neither flight nor pursuit: in the confused struggle the turns of the scale, the movements this way and that, were infinitesimal. Those in front must either kill or be killed – there could be no retreat; for on either side those behind pressed their own men forward and left no space between the opposing lines. But the time came when Jewish fury got the better of Roman skill and the line began to give from end to end. After all, they had fought without a break from 2 a.m. till 1 p.m., the Jews in full strength and with the danger of utter defeat as a spur to their valour, the Romans with only a tiny part of their army, since the legions which the men actually fighting counted on had not yet followed them up the slope. So it was sufficient for the present to be in possession of Antonia.

Standing by Titus' side in Antonia was a centurion from Bithynia called Julianus, a man of note and far more remarkable for skill in arms, physical strength, and fearless spirit than anyone I met with from beginning to end of the war. When he saw the Romans already giving way and putting up a poor defence, he sprang forward and drove back the already victorious Jews, unaided, as far as the corner of the inner court of the Temple. The whole mass fled, convinced that such strength and audacity could not be those of a mere man. This way and that he charged through their midst as they scattered, killing all he could reach: never had Caesar beheld so amazing a sight, or the other side one so terrifying. But he too was pursued by Fate, from whom there is no escape for mortal man. He was wearing the ordinary military boots studded with masses of sharp nails, and as he ran across the stone pavement he slipped and fell flat on his back, his armour clanging so loudly that the runaways turned to look. A shout went up from the Romans in Antonia, alarmed for their champion's safety, while the Jews crowded round him and aimed blows from all directions with their lances and broadswords. Many heavy blows he stopped with his shield; time after time he tried to stand up but was knocked down by the mass of assailants. Even then as he lay he stabbed many with his sword; for he could not be finished off easily, as he was protected in every vital part by helmet and breastplate and kept his head down. But at last, when all his limbs were slashed and no one dared come to his aid, he ceased to struggle.

Caesar was greatly distressed at the death of so gallant a soldier, killed before so many eyes. He himself was prevented by his situation from going to the rescue, though anxious to do so. Those who might have gone were too terrified. So Julianus, after a long fight for life in which he allowed few of his assailants to go unscathed, at long last received the *coup de grâce*, leaving behind him, not only with Caesar but even with his foes, a glorious reputation. The Jews snatched the body and again drove the Romans back, shutting them up in Antonia. Those on their side who distinguished themselves in this battle were Alexas and Gyphthaeus among John's followers, among Simon's Malachias, Judas, son of Merto, and Jacob, son of Sosas, commanding the Idumaeans, and of the Zealots two brothers, sons of Jairus, by name Simon and Judas.

Titus ordered the soldiers with him to lay Antonia flat and make the ascent easy for the whole army. Then he put up Josephus to speak; for he was informed that on that day, the 17th of Panemos, through lack of lambs the so-called Continual Sacrifice[4] had been discontinued, and that the people were consequently in the depths of despair. Josephus was to make John the same offer as before: if he was possessed by some morbid craving for a fight, he was free to come out with as many men as he liked and join battle without at the same time bringing destruction on the City and Sanctuary; but he must stop polluting the Holy Place[5] and offending against God. Moreover he was permitted to choose any Jews he liked to offer the discontinued sacrifices.

Josephus took his stand where he could be heard not only by John but by the masses and delivered Caesar's message in Aramaic, appealing to them eloquently to spare their birthplace, to beat out the flames already enveloping the Sanctuary and to restore to God the due oblations. Listening to him the people remained silent and dejected; but the chief gangster poured abuse and curses on the head of Josephus, finally adding that he would never be afraid of capture, as the City was God's. Josephus loudly retorted:

'Of course, you have kept it perfectly pure for God, and the Holy Place[5] remains unpolluted! You have never dishonoured your hoped-for Ally! He still receives the customary sacrifices! If anyone robbed you of your daily food, you godless creature, you would regard him as your enemy; and do you think you can count on God, whom you have denied His everlasting worship, to be your Ally in the war? And do you blame your own sins on the Romans, who have throughout respected our Law and are now pressing you to restore to God the sacrifices which you have interrupted? Who would not groan with anguish at the astounding change that has come over the City, when foreigners and enemies atone for your ungodliness and you, a Jew, cradled in the Law, do more hurt than they? But consider, John! To turn your back on evil ways is no disgrace, even at the last moment. If you wish to save your birthplace, you have a splendid example before you in Jehoiachin, king of the Jews. When the king of Babylon made war on him through his own fault, he left the city of his own accord before its capture, and with his family submitted to voluntary imprisonment rather than surrender these holy places to the enemy and see the House of God go up in flames.[6] For that he is celebrated by all Jews in the sacred record, and memory, flowing through the ages eternally new, passes him on to future generations immortal. A splendid example, John, even if it were dangerous! But I can guarantee your pardon from the Romans. Remember, this is the advice of a fellow-countryman and the promise of a Jew; it is sensible to consider who is counselling you and where he comes from. I trust that never while I live shall I become such an abject slave as to deny my birth or forget my heritage!

'Once more you rage against me with loud-mouthed abuse. I deserve even worse for flying in the face of fate to advise you, and fighting to save men damned by God. Who doesn't know the writings of the old prophets and the oracle pronounced against this unhappy city and now about to be fulfilled? They foretold the day of her fall – the day when some man began the slaughter of his fellow countrymen.[7] And aren't the City and Temple full of your dead bodies? It is God then, God Himself who is bringing with the Romans fire to purge the Temple and is blotting out the City, brimful of corruption, as if it had never been.'

As Josephus spoke thus, with groanings and tears, sobs choked his voice. Even the Romans were moved by his distress and applauded his determination; but John's party were the more incensed with the Romans, and mad to get Josephus into their clutches. However, many citizens of good family were shaken by his speech. Some of them were too frightened of the partisan guards to move, though they had given up themselves and the City for lost; but a few watched their opportunity to escape and sought asylum with the Romans. These included the chief priests Joseph and Jeshua and several sons of chief priests, three sons of Ishmael, who was beheaded in Cyrene,[8] four of Matthias and one of another Matthias; this man had run away after the death of his father, who had been murdered by Simon, son of Gioras, with three sons, as explained above.[9] Many other citizens of good family went over with the chief priests. Caesar received them with all possible kindness, and knowing that foreign customs would make life distasteful for them he sent them to Gophna, where he advised them to remain for the time being: he would restore every man's possessions as soon as he had got the war off his hands. So they retired to the little town allotted to them in perfect safety and supremely content.

When they did not reappear, the partisans again spread the tale that the Romans had butchered the deserters, obviously in the hope that the rest would be too frightened to run away. As before, the trick worked for a time; terror effectively put a stop to desertions. But when the men were brought back from Gophna by Titus and ordered to go round the wall with Josephus under the eyes of the people, there was a wholesale flight to the Romans. All the fugitives joined together, and standing in front of the Roman lines wept and wailed as they besought the partisans, if they could bring themselves to do it, to fling their gates wide open to the Romans; if not, at least to withdraw from the Temple and save their Sanctuary: the Romans would never bring themselves, unless absolutely driven to it, to burn down the sacred buildings. This appeal provoked a violent reaction; a volley of abuse was hurled at the deserters, and above the sacred gates spear-throwers, catapults, and stone-throwers were set in line, so that the Temple courts, littered with bodies, were like a vast graveyard, the Sanctuary itself like a fortress. Into the sacred, untrodden precincts they poured armed to the teeth, their hands still dripping with the blood of their own countrymen. So monstrous was their conduct that the indignation the Jews might well have felt, if the Romans had committed such outrages against them, was felt by the Romans now against the Jews who profaned their own holy ground. In fact, among the soldiers there was not a man who was not filled with reverent awe when his eyes rested on the Sanctuary, or who did not pray that the terrorists would see the light before all was lost. Greatly distressed, Titus again reproached John and his supporters.

'You disgusting people! Didn't you put up that balustrade to guard your Holy House? Didn't you at intervals along it place slabs inscribed in Greek characters and our own, forbidding anyone to go beyond the parapet? And didn't we give you leave to execute anyone who did go beyond it, even if he was a Roman?[10] Why then, you guilty men, are you now trampling dead bodies inside it? Why are you polluting your Sanctuary with the blood of foreigner and native? I call the gods of my fathers and any god that ever watched over this place – I do not believe there is one now – I call my own army, the Jews in my camp, and you yourselves to witness that *I* am not compelling you to desecrate your Temple. If you change the battle-ground, no Roman shall go near your holy places or insult them: I will protect the Sanctuary for you, whether you wish it or not.'

As Josephus made known this promise on Caesar's behalf, the terrorists and their chief, assuming that not good-will but cowardice lay behind his exhortations, received them with scorn. When Titus saw that these men had no mercy on themselves and no concern for the Sanctuary, he resumed hostilities, though much against his will. It was not possible to bring up his whole army against them as there was not room enough; so he picked out from every century the thirty best soldiers and put a tribune in charge of every thousand, the entire force being under the command of Cerealis, with orders to attack the guardposts an hour before sunrise. He was himself in arms and ready to go down with them, but his friends held him back because the danger was so great, and because the officers insisted that he would do more good by sitting quietly in Antonia in general control of the operations of his men than by going down into the forefront of the battle; if Caesar was watching every man would fight to the death. Yielding to their arguments Caesar explained to the men that he was staying behind for one purpose only – to be judge of their exploits, so that no brave man should go unrewarded, no coward unpunished, through not being seen, and to be an eyewitness of every deed, able as he was both to punish and to reward. So he sent them to their task at the time mentioned above, and going himself to an excellent forward observation-post he remained in Antonia, anxiously awaiting the outcome.

However, the task-force did not find the guards asleep, as they hoped; they leapt to their feet with loud yells and a hand-to-hand struggle instantly began. When the shout of the sentries was heard

within, the rest of the guard poured out in a body. Under the onslaught of the leading ranks the Romans stood firm; those who
followed collided with their own troops and many treated friends as
foes. They could not distinguish voices because of the confused hub-
bub, nor faces because it was night. They were blinded also, some by
fury, some by fear; consequently they struck out indiscriminately at
all in their path. The Romans locked their shields together and charged
in their units, so suffering less from this bewilderment; and every
man remembered the password. The Jews were continually scattering, their attacks and retreats were haphazard, and they repeatedly
took each other for enemies; in the darkness any man who moved to
the rear was invariably received by his friends as an advancing Roman.
In fact more were wounded by their comrades than by the enemy,
till day broke and it was possible to see what was happening in the
battle. The two sides now separated into opposing formations and
began to hurl missiles in an orderly engagement. Neither side gave an
inch or showed any sign of weariness. The Romans, as Caesar was
watching, individually and by companies vied with each other, every
man convinced that his promotion would date from that day if he
distinguished himself in the fight: the Jews had as judge of their prowess their fear for themselves and for the Temple, and the tyrant[11]
who stood over them rousing them to action, some with encouragement, some with threats or the lash. In the main the battle was station-
ary, the ebb and flow very slight and very rapid: flight and pursuit
were alike impossible. All the time the shouts from Antonia changed
with the fortunes of their own men: at every advance they were loudly
cheered, at every retreat they were urged to stand fast. It was like a
battle in an amphitheatre: Titus and his staff could see every detail of
the fighting. At last, after battling from before dawn to nearly midday,
they broke off the fight, without either side having really budged the
other from the spot where the first blow was struck, and without any
decision being reached. On the Roman side many had fought magnificently; on the Jewish, of Simon's followers Judas, son of Merto, and
Simon, son of Josiah, of the Idumaeans Jacob and Simon, sons of Sosas
and Cathla respectively, of John's men Gyphthaeus and Alexas, and
of the Zealots Simon, son of Jairus.

Meanwhile the rest of the Roman army had in one week laid
Antonia flat and engineered a wide road to the Temple. Advancing
near to the first rampart the legions now set to work on four

platforms, one opposite the north-west corner of the inner court of the Temple, one near the northern arcade between the two gates, and of the other two one opposite the western colonnade of the outer court, the other farther out opposite the northern. The progress of the work, however, cost them much toil and sweat, as they had to fetch the timber from over eleven miles away.[12] Sometimes they suffered losses through Jewish stratagems, as their crushing superiority made them over-confident just when despair of survival made the Jews more daring than ever. For instance some of the mounted men, every time they went out to collect firewood or fodder, used to let their horses graze free and unbridled while they were foraging; these the Jews would seize and carry off by a sudden sortie in strength. This happened so often that Caesar, correctly diagnosing the cause of these losses as less the valour of the Jews than the negligence of his own soldiers, decided to take a measure of unusual severity to ensure better care of the horses in future. He commanded one of the men who had lost their mounts to be led off for execution, so terrifying the rest that he made sure their horses would be safe. They never again left them behind to graze, but took them on all their forays as if horse and rider were one. So the war against the Temple continued and the platforms neared completion.

The very day after the advance of the legions many of the partisans, as the supply of loot was running out and hunger was pressing, made a united attack on the Roman posts on the Mount of Olives an hour before sunset, hoping that they would catch them off their guard and already busy with their personal needs, and so force their way through without difficulty. But the Romans saw them coming, and instantly closing in from the neighbouring guard-posts prevented them from climbing over the camp wall or cutting through it by force. There followed a fierce struggle, with many instances of heroic courage on both sides, the Romans showing a combination of strength and tactical skill, the Jews unlimited vigour and uncontrollable fury. Shame was in command of one side, necessity of the other: to let the Jews slip out of the net that enveloped them seemed to the Romans an appalling disgrace: their opponents had one solitary hope of survival – to break through the wall by sheer force. A mounted man from one cohort, by name Pedanius, seeing the Jews at last routed and pushed down into the valley, drove his horse alongside at a furious pace and snatched up one of the enemy as he fled, a young man of sturdy build and in full armour too, seizing him by the ankle – so far did he lean over from the saddle, so magnificently did he display strength of hand and body combined with magnificent horsemanship. Then as if he had got hold of a treasure he rode off with his prisoner to Caesar. Titus congratulated the captor on his amazing strength, and ordered the captive to be executed for his part in the attempt on the wall, then turned his personal attention to the battle for the Temple and the speedier construction of the platforms.

The Jews were suffering so severely in every engagement, as the war slowly but surely approached its culmination and crept nearer to the Sanctuary, that, as if dealing with a diseased body, they cut off the affected limbs to prevent the spread of the infection. They set fire to the section of the north-west colonnade that was joined to Antonia, and then demolished some thirty feet of it, thus beginning the burning down of their holy places with their own hands. Two days later, on the 24th of the last-named month (Panemos), the adjoining colonnade was fired by the Romans.[13] When the flames had advanced over seventy-five feet, the Jews as before cut away the roof, and showing no regard whatever for this masterpiece of architecture, severed the link it provided with Antonia. With this in mind, though they had a chance to stop the lighting of the fire, they did not even lift a finger as the flames approached, and regarded the progress of the fire in the light of their own advantage. Around the Temple there was no break in the fighting, battle raging continuously between small raiding parties of both sides.

During this period one of the Jews called Jonathan, a man of small stature and nothing much to look at, whose birth and attainments were negligible, stepped forward opposite the tomb of John the High Priest, heaped contempt and abuse on the heads of the Romans, and challenged the bravest of them to single combat. Of the Romans lined up at that point the majority treated him with contempt; some in all probability were frightened, while a few were struck by the very reasonable thought that a man who was looking for death was not one to be engaged at close quarters: those who despaired of their lives might well have uncontrollable passions and the willing help of the Almighty; and to risk everything in a duel with one whose defeat would be nothing to boast of, and whose victory would be disgraceful as well as dangerous, was an act not of courage but of recklessness. For a long time no one came forward and the Jew hurled a volley of gibes at their cowardice, for he had a great admiration for himself and contempt for the Romans. But at last one Pudens, a member of a cavalry squadron, sickened by his arrogant vapourings and no doubt foolishly over-confident because of his small stature, ran out, joined battle, and was getting the better of it when fortune left him in the lurch: he fell, and Jonathan ran up and dispatched him. Then standing on the body he brandished his dripping sword and with his left hand waved his shield, shouting vociferously at the troops, crowing over the fallen man, and mocking the Romans as they watched. At length, while he still jumped about and played the fool, Priscus, a centurion, shot an arrow which pierced him through; at this shouts went up from Jews and Romans – very different in character. Jonathan, spinning round in his agony, fell down on the body of his foe, clear proof that in war undeserved success instantly brings on itself the vengeance of heaven.

The partisans in the Temple never slackened their overt endeavours to cause daily losses to the soldiers working on the platforms, and on the 27th of the same month they devised the following ruse. In the western colonnade they filled the space between the joists and the ceiling below them with dry wood, bitumen, and pitch, then withdrew as if tired out. Thereupon many thoughtless soldiers, carried away by reckless eagerness, charged after those retreating, and erecting ladders ran up to the colonnade. The more sensible men, suspicious of the unexplained Jewish withdrawal, made no move. However, the colonnade was crowded with the men who had climbed on to it, and at that moment the Jews fired it from end to end. As the flames shot up suddenly all round, the Romans who were out of danger were seized with utter consternation, the trapped men with complete helplessness. Encircled by the blaze some flung themselves down into the City behind them, some into the thick of the foe; many in the hope of escaping with their lives jumped down among their own men and broke their legs; most for all their haste were too slow for the fire; a few cheated the flames with their own daggers. Even those destined for a different end were promptly trapped by the wide extension of the conflagration. Caesar, though angry with the victims for having climbed on to the colonnade without orders, was at the same time moved with human compassion; and though no one could hope to rescue them, it was some comfort to the dying men to see the one for whom they were giving their lives so distressed; for as he called out to

them, and dashed forward and urged those around him to do everything possible to help them, he could be seen by all. Taking with him
those shouts, that sympathy, like a glorious winding-sheet, every man
died happy. Some indeed retired to the wide colonnade wall and got
clear of the fire, but they were trapped by the Jews, and, after long
holding out in spite of their many wounds, finally perished to a man.

Last to fall was a young man named Longus, who added glory to
the whole tragic tale and, though every single one of the men who
died deserved to be mentioned, outshone them all. Full of admiration
for his prowess and in any case unable to get at him, the Jews invited
him to come down to them under a pledge of safety; his brother
Cornelius, on the other hand, adjured him not to tarnish his own
renown and disgrace the Roman army. Convinced that he was right,
Longus held up his sword in the sight of the opposing lines and plunged
it into his heart. Among those trapped by the flames one Artorius
saved his life by a trick. He called to him a fellow-soldier, Lucius,
who shared his tent, and yelled: 'I will leave you everything I have
if you will come close and catch me.' Lucius eagerly ran to his aid;
then Artorius jumped on top of him and survived, but his weight
dashed his rescuer to the stone pavement, killing him instantly.

For a time this terrible blow filled the Romans with despondency;
but it helped them in the long run by making them more wary and
putting them on their guard against Jewish traps, in which they
suffered chiefly through ignorance of the ground and through the
character of their opponents. The colonnade was burnt down as far
as the tower which John in his struggle with Simon had built over the
gates opening on to the Gymnasium[14]; the rest, now that the men who
had climbed on to it had been wiped out, the Jews cut away. The next
day the Romans took a turn, setting light to the entire northern
colonnade as far as its junction with the eastern where the angle
between the two overhung the Kidron Valley, to which there was a
terrifying drop. Here for the present we leave the struggle for the
Temple.

In the City famine raged, its victims dropping dead in countless
numbers, and the horrors were unspeakable. In every home, if the
shadow of something to eat was anywhere detected, war broke out
and the best of friends came to grips with each other, snatching away
the most wretched means of support. Not even the dying were believed to be in want; at their last gasp they were searched by the

bandits in case some of them had food inside their clothes and were feigning death. Open-mouthed with hunger like mad dogs, the desperadoes stumbled and staggered along, hammering at the doors like drunken men, and in their helpless state breaking into the same houses two or three times in a single hour. Necessity made them put their teeth in everything; things which not even the filthiest of dumb animals would look at they picked up and brought themselves to swallow. In the end they actually devoured belts and shoes, and stripped off the leather from their shields and chewed it. Some tried to live on scraps of old hay; for there were people who collected the stalks and sold a tiny bunch for four Attic drachmas![15]

But why should I speak of the inanimate things that hunger made them shameless enough to eat? I am going now to relate a deed for which there is no parallel in the annals of Greece or any other country,[16] a deed horrible to speak of and incredible to hear. For myself, I am so anxious that future ages should not suspect me of grotesque inventions that I would gladly have passed over this calamity in silence,[17] had there not been countless witnesses of my own generation to bear me out; and besides, my country would have little reason to thank me if I drew a veil over the miseries that were so real to her.

There was a woman, Mary, daughter of Eleazar, who lived east of Jordan in the village of Bethezub ('House of Hyssop'). She was of good family and very rich, and had fled with the rest of the population to Jerusalem, where she shared in the horrors of the siege. Most of the property she had packed up and moved from Peraea into the City had been plundered by the party chiefs; the remnants of her treasures and any food she had managed to obtain were being carried off in daily raids by their henchmen. The wretched woman was filled with uncontrollable fury, and let loose a stream of abuse and curses that enraged the looters against her. When neither resentment nor pity caused anyone to kill her and she grew tired of finding food for others – and whichever way she turned it was almost impossible to find – and while hunger was eating her heart out and rage was consuming her still faster, she yielded to the suggestions of fury and necessity, and in defiance of all natural feeling laid hands on her own child, a baby at the breast. 'Poor little mite!' she cried. 'In war, famine, and civil strife why should I keep you alive? With the Romans there is only slavery, even if we are alive when they come; but famine is forestalling slavery, and the partisans are crueller than either. Come, you must be food for me, to the partisans an avenging spirit, and to the world a tale, the only thing left to fill up the measure of Jewish misery.' As she spoke she killed her son, then roasted him and ate one half, concealing and saving up the rest.

At once the partisans appeared, and sniffing the unholy smell threatened that if she did not produce what she had prepared they would kill her on the spot. She replied that she had kept a fine helping for them, and uncovered what was left of her child. Overcome with instant horror and amazement, they could not take their eyes off the sight. But she went on: 'This child is my own, and the deed is mine too. Help yourselves: I have had my share. Don't be softer than a woman or more tender-hearted than a mother. But if you are squeamish and don't approve of my sacrifice – well, I have eaten half, so you may as well leave me the rest.' That was the last straw, and they went away quivering. They had never before shrunk from anything, and did not much like giving up even this food to the mother. From that moment the entire city could think of nothing else but this abomination; everyone saw the tragedy before his own eyes and shuddered as if the crime was his. The one desire of the starving was for death; how they envied those who had gone before seeing or hearing of these appalling horrors!

It was not long before the dreadful news reached the Romans. Some of them refused to believe, some were distressed, but on most the effect was to add enormously to their detestation of the Jewish race. Caesar disclaimed all responsibility in the sight of God for this latest tragedy. He had offered the Jews peace and self-government with an amnesty for all offenders; but they had rejected concord in favour of strife, peace in favour of war, plenty and abundance in favour of hunger, and with their own hands had tried to burn down the Temple which the Romans were safeguarding on their behalf; so this food was just what they deserved. Nevertheless he would bury this abomination of infanticide and cannibalism under the ruins of their country, and would not let a city in which mothers fed themselves thus remain on the face of the earth for the sun to look upon. It was even more revolting for mothers to eat such food than for fathers, who even after such appalling tragedies remained in arms. While he made this clear, he was thinking also of the desperation of these men: they would never see reason after enduring all the agonies which they might so easily have avoided by a change of heart.

CHAPTER 21

The Temple Burnt and the City Taken

By now two of the legions had completed their platforms, and on the 8th of Loös Titus ordered the rams to be brought up opposite the western recess[1] of the outer court of the Temple. For six days before they arrived the most powerful battering-ram of all had been pounding the wall incessantly without result: this like the others made no impression on stones so huge and so perfectly bonded. At the northern gate a second team attempted to undermine the foundations, and by tremendous efforts they did lever out the stones in front; but the inner stones supported the weight and the gate stood firm, till despairing of all attempts with engines and crowbars they set up ladders against the colonnades. The Jews were in no hurry to stop them, but when they climbed up they were violently assailed; some were pushed backwards and sent headlong, others clashed with the defenders and were killed; many as they stepped off the ladders were unable to get behind their shields before they were run through with swords, while a few ladders crowded with heavy infantry were pushed sideways at the top and overturned; the Jews too suffered severe losses. Those who had brought up the standards fought hard for them, knowing that it would be a terrible disgrace if they were captured; but in the end the Jews even captured the standards, destroying every man who climbed up. The rest, demoralized by the fate of the fallen, withdrew. On the Roman side not a man died till he had accomplished something; of the partisans all who had distinguished themselves in earlier battles shone once more in this, as did Eleazar, nephew of the party chief Simon. Titus, seeing that his attempts to spare a foreign temple meant injury and death to his soldiers, ordered the gates to be set on fire.

At this time two men deserted Simon, Ananus from Emmaus, the most bloodthirsty of his henchmen,[2] and Archelaus, son of Magaddatus, expecting a free pardon as they were quitting the Jews when they were getting the better of it. Denouncing this as another of their dirty tricks and aware of their habitual cruelty to their own people, Titus was strongly inclined to kill them both, pointing out that they had been forced to it by necessity and had not come by free choice, and that men did not deserve to live if they first set their own city on fire and then jumped clear. However, anger could not stand against his own pledged word and he let the men go, though he did not grant them the same privileges as the others.

By now the soldiers were setting fire to the gates. The silver melted and ran, quickly exposing the woodwork to the flames, which were carried from there in a solid wall and fastened on to the colonnades. When the Jews saw the ring of fire, they lost all power of body and mind; such was their consternation that not a finger was raised to keep out or quench the flames; they stood looking on in utter helplessness. Yet their dismay at the present destruction made them no wiser for the future, but as if the Sanctuary itself was already in flames they whipped up their rage against the Romans. All that day and the following night the flames were in possession: the colonnades could not be fired all at once but only bit by bit.[3]

The next day Titus ordered a section of his army to put out the fire, and to make a road close to the gates to facilitate the approach of the legions. Then he summoned a council of war, attended by the six senior generals – Tiberius Alexander, the camp prefect; Sextus Cerealis, Larcius Lepidus,[4] and Titus Phrygius, commanding the Fifth, Tenth, and Fifteenth Legions respectively; Aeternius[5] Fronto, tribune in charge of the two legions from Alexandria; and Marcus Antonius Julianus, procurator of Judaea.[6] After these the other procurators[7] and tribunes were brought in, and Titus invited opinions on the question of the Sanctuary. Some insisted that they should enforce the law of war: there would be continual revolts while the Sanctuary remained as a rallying-point for Jews all over the world. Others argued that if the Jews evacuated it and no armed man was allowed on it, it should be spared, but if they climbed on it for military purposes it should be burnt down; it would in that case be a fortress, not a sanctuary, and from then on the impiety would be blameable not on the Romans but on those who forced their hands. Titus replied that even if the Jews did climb on it for military purposes, he would not make war on inanimate objects instead of men, or, whatever happened, burn down such a work of art: it was the Romans who would lose thereby, just as their empire would gain an ornament if it was preserved. Fronto, Alexander, and Cerealis now confidently came over to this opinion. Titus thereupon adjourned

the meeting, and instructing the officers to give the remainder of the
army time for rest, so that he should find them full of new vigour
when fighting was resumed, he ordered the picked men of all the
cohorts to make a road through the ruins and put out the fire.[8]

All that day exhaustion and consternation subdued the enterprise
of the Jews; but on the next, having recovered both strength and
confidence, they made a sortie through the East Gate against the garrison of the outer court of the Temple at about 8 a.m. Their onslaught
met with stubborn resistance from the Romans, who sheltered behind a wall of steel and closed their ranks, though it was obvious
that they could not hold together long, as the raiding party surpassed
them in numbers and determination. Anticipating the collapse of
the line Caesar, who was watching from Antonia, came to the rescue
with his picked horsemen. The Jews broke before their onset, and
when the front-rank men fell the rest withdrew. But whenever the
Romans gave ground they whipped round and pressed them hard:
when the Romans turned about they retreated again, till at about
11 o'clock they were overpowered and shut up in the inner court.

Titus retired to Antonia, intending to launch a full-scale attack at
dawn the next day and surround the Sanctuary completely. It had,
however, been condemned to the flames by God long ago: by the
turning of time's wheel the fated day had now come, the 10th of
Loös, the day which centuries before had seen it burnt by the king of
Babylon.[9] But it was the Jews themselves who caused and started this
conflagration. When Titus had retired, the partisans remained quiet
for a time, then again attacked the Romans, the garrison of the
Sanctuary clashing with those who were putting out the fire in the
inner court, and who routed the Jews and chased them as far as the
Sanctuary. Then one of the soldiers, without waiting for orders
and without a qualm for the terrible consequences of his action but
urged on by some unseen force, snatched up a blazing piece of wood
and climbing on another soldier's back hurled the brand through a
golden aperture giving access on the north side to the chambers
built round the Sanctuary.[10] As the flames shot into the air the Jews
sent up a cry that matched the calamity and dashed to the rescue,
with no thought now of saving their lives or husbanding their
strength; for that which hitherto they had guarded so devotedly
was disappearing before their eyes.

A runner brought the news to Titus as he was resting in his tent after the battle. He leapt up as he was and ran to the Sanctuary to extinguish the blaze. His whole staff panted after him, followed by the excited legions with all the shouting and confusion inseparable from the disorganized rush of an immense army. Caesar shouted and waved to the combatants to put out the fire; but his shouts were unheard as their ears were deafened by a greater din, and his gesticulations went unheeded amidst the distractions of battle and bloodshed. As the legions charged in, neither persuasion nor threat could check their impetuosity: passion alone was in command. Crowded together round the entrances many were trampled by their friends, many fell among the still hot and smoking ruins of the colonnades and died as miserably as the defeated. As they neared the Sanctuary they pretended not even to hear Caesar's commands and urged the men in front to throw in more firebrands. The partisans were no longer in a position to help; everywhere was slaughter and flight. Most of the victims were peaceful citizens, weak and unarmed, butchered wherever they were caught. Round the Altar the heap of corpses grew higher and higher, while down the Sanctuary steps poured a river of blood and the bodies of those killed at the top slithered to the bottom. The soldiers were like men possessed and there was no holding them, nor was there any arguing with the fire. Caesar therefore led his staff inside the building and viewed the Holy Place of the Sanctuary[11] with its furnishings, which went far beyond the accounts circulating in foreign countries, and fully justified their splendid reputation in our own. The flames were not yet effecting an entry from any direction but were feeding on the chambers built round the Sanctuary; so realizing that there was still time to save the glorious edifice, Titus dashed out and by personal efforts strove to persuade his men to put out the fire, instructing Liberalius, a centurion of his bodyguard of spearmen, to lay his staff across the shoulders of any who disobeyed. But their respect for Caesar and their fear of the centurion's staff were powerless against their fury, their detestation of the Jews, and an uncontrollable lust for battle. Most of them were also spurred on by the expectation of loot, being convinced that the interior was bursting with money and seeing that everything outside was of gold. But they were forestalled by one of those who had gone in. When Caesar dashed out to restrain the troops, that man pushed a firebrand into the hinges of the gate. Then from within a flame suddenly shot up, Caesar and his staff withdrew, and those outside were free to start what fires they liked. Thus the Sanctuary was set on fire in defiance of Caesar's wishes.

Grief might well be bitter for the destruction of the most wonderful edifice ever seen or heard of, both for its size and construction and for the lavish perfection of detail and the glory of its holy places[12]; yet we find very real comfort in the thought that Fate is inexorable, not only towards living beings but also towards buildings and sites. We may wonder too at the exactness of the cycle of Fate: she kept, as I said, to the very month and day which centuries before had seen the Sanctuary burnt by the Babylonians. From its first foundation by King Solomon to its present destruction, which occurred in the second year of Vespasian's reign, was a period of 1,130 years, 7 months and 15 days; from its rebuilding in the second year of King Cyrus, for which Haggai was responsible, to its capture under Vespasian was 639 years and 45 days.[13]

While the Sanctuary was burning, looting went on right and left[14] and all who were caught were put to the sword. There was no pity for age, no regard for rank; little children and old men, laymen and priests alike were butchered; every class was held in the iron embrace of war, whether they defended themselves or cried for mercy. Through the roar of the flames as they swept relentlessly on could be heard the groans of the falling: such were the height of the hill and the vastness of the blazing edifice that the entire city seemed to be on fire, while as for the noise, nothing could be imagined more shattering or more horrifying. There was the war-cry of the Roman legions as they converged; the yells of the partisans encircled with fire and sword; the panic flight of the people cut off above into the arms of the enemy, and their shrieks as the end approached. The cries from the hill were answered from the crowded streets; and now many who were wasted with hunger and beyond speech found strength to moan and wail when they saw the Sanctuary in flames. Back from Peraea and the mountains round about came the echo in a thunderous bass.

Yet more terrible than the din were the sights that met the eye. The Temple Hill, enveloped in flames from top to bottom, appeared to be boiling up from its very roots; yet the sea of flame was nothing to the ocean of blood, or the companies of killers to the armies of killed: nowhere could the ground be seen between the corpses, and the soldiers climbed over heaps of bodies as they chased the fugitives. The terrorist horde pushed the Romans back, and by a violent struggle burst through into the outer court of the Temple and from there into the City,[15] the few surviving members of the public taking refuge on the outer colonnade. Some of the priests at first tore up from the Sanctuary the spikes with their lead sockets and threw them at the Romans. Then as they were no better off and the flames were leaping towards them, they retired to the wall, which was twelve feet wide, and stayed there. However, two men of note, in a position either to save their lives by going over to the Romans or to face with the others whatever came their way, threw themselves into the fire and were burnt to ashes with the Sanctuary – Meirus, son of Belgas, and Joseph, son of Dalaeus.

The Romans, judging it useless to spare the outbuildings now that the Sanctuary was in flames, set fire to them all – what remained of the colonnades and all the gates except two, one on the east end, the other on the south, both of which they later demolished. They also burnt the treasuries which housed huge sums of money, huge quantities of clothing, and other precious things; here, in fact, all the wealth of the Jews was piled up, for the rich had dismantled their houses and brought the contents here for safe keeping.[16] Next they came to the last surviving colonnade of the outer court. On this women and children and a mixed crowd of citizens had found a refuge – 6,000 in all. Before Caesar could reach a decision about them or instruct his officers, the soldiers, carried away by their fury, fired the colonnade from below; as a result some flung themselves out of the flames to their death, others perished in the blaze: of that vast number there escaped not one. Their destruction was due to a false prophet who that very day had declared to the people in the City that God commanded them to go up into the Temple to receive the signs of their deliverance. A number of hireling prophets had been put up in recent days by the party chiefs to deceive the people by exhorting them to await help from God, and so to reduce the number of deserters and buoy up with hope those who were above fear and anxiety. Man is readily persuaded in adversity: when the deceiver actually promises deliverance from the miseries that envelop him, then the sufferer becomes the willing slave of hope. So it was that the unhappy people were beguiled at that stage by cheats and false messengers of God, while the unmistakable portents that foreshadowed the coming desolation they treated with indifference and incredulity, disregarding God's warnings as if they were moonstruck, blind and senseless. First a star stood over the City, very like a broadsword, and a comet that remained a whole year. Then before the revolt and the movement to war, while the people were assembling for the Feast of Unleavened Bread,[17] on the 8th of Xanthicos at 3 a.m. so bright a light shone round the Altar and the Sanctuary that it might have been midday. This lasted half an hour. The inexperienced took it for a good omen, but the sacred scribes at once gave an interpretation which the event proved right. During the same feast a cow brought by someone to be sacrificed gave birth to a lamb in the middle of the Temple courts, while at midnight it was observed that the East Gate of the inner court had opened of its own accord – a gate made of bronze and so solid that every evening twenty strong men were required to shut it; it was fastened with iron-bound bars and secured by bolts which were lowered a long way into a threshold fashioned from a single slab of stone. The temple-guards ran with the news to the Captain,[18] who came up and by a great effort managed to shut it. This like the other seemed to the laity to be the best of omens: had not God opened to them the gate of happiness? But the learned perceived that the security of the Sanctuary was dissolving of its own accord, and that the opening of the gate was a gift to the enemy; and they admitted in their hearts that the sign was a portent of desolation.

A few days after the Feast, on the 21st of Artemisios,[19] a supernatural apparition was seen, too amazing to be believed. What I have to relate would, I suppose, have been dismissed as an invention, had it not been vouched for by eyewitnesses and followed by disasters that bore out the signs. Before sunset there were seen in the sky, over the whole country, chariots and regiments in arms speeding through the clouds and encircling the towns. Again, at the Feast of Pentecost, when the priests had gone into the inner court of the Temple at night to perform the usual ceremonies, they declared that they were aware, first of a violent movement and a loud crash, then of a concerted cry: 'Let us go hence.'

An incident more alarming still had occurred four years before the war at a time of exceptional peace and prosperity for the City. One Jeshua, son of Ananias, a very ordinary yokel, came to the feast at which every Jew is expected to set up a tabernacle for God.[20] As he stood in the Temple he suddenly began to shout: 'A voice from the east, a voice from the west, a voice from the four winds, a voice against Jerusalem and the Sanctuary, a voice against bridegrooms and brides, a voice against the whole people.' Day and night he uttered this cry as he went through all the streets. Some of the more prominent citizens, very annoyed at these ominous words, laid hold of the fellow and beat him savagely. Without saying a word in his own defence or for the private information of his persecutors, he persisted in shouting the same warning as before. The Jewish authorities, rightly concluding that some supernatural force was responsible for the man's behaviour, took him before the Roman procurator. There, though scourged till his flesh hung in ribbons, he neither begged for mercy nor shed a tear, but lowering his voice to the most mournful of tones answered every blow with 'Woe to Jerusalem!' When Albinus – for that was the procurator's name – demanded to know who he was, where he came from and why he uttered such cries, he made no reply whatever to the questions but endlessly repeated his lament over the City, till Albinus decided that he was a madman and released him. All the time till the war broke out he never approached another citizen or was seen in conversation, but daily as if he had learnt a prayer by heart he recited his lament: 'Woe to Jerusalem!' Those who daily cursed him he never cursed; those who gave him food he never thanked: his only response to anyone was that dismal foreboding. His voice was heard most of all at the feasts. For seven years and five months he went on ceaselessly, his voice as strong as ever and his vigour unabated, till during the siege after seeing the fulfilment of his foreboding he was silenced. He was going round on the wall uttering his piercing cry: 'Woe again to the City, the people, and the Sanctuary!' and as he added a last word: 'Woe to me also!' a stone shot from an engine struck him, killing him instantly. Thus he uttered those same forebodings to the very end.

Anyone who ponders these things will find that God cares for mankind and in all possible ways foreshows to His people the means of salvation, and that it is through folly and evils of their own choosing that they come to destruction. Thus the Jews after pulling down Antonia made the Temple square, in spite of the warning in their pro-phetic books that when the Temple became a square the City and Sanctuary would fall.[21] But their chief inducement to go to war was an equivocal oracle also found in their sacred writings, announcing that at that time a man from their country would become monarch of the whole world. This they took to mean the triumph of their own

race, and many of their scholars were wildly out in their interpretation. In fact the oracle pointed to the accession of Vespasian; for it
was in Judaea he was proclaimed emperor.[22] But it is not possible
for men to escape from fate even if they see it coming. The Jews
interpreted some of the prophecies to suit themselves and laughed the
others off, till by the fall of their city and their own destruction their
folly stood revealed.

As the partisans had fled into the City, and flames were consuming
the Sanctuary itself and all its surroundings, the Romans brought
their standards into the Temple area, and erecting them opposite the
East Gate sacrificed to them there,[23] and with thunderous acclamations hailed Titus as *Imperator*.[24] So laden with plunder was every
single soldier that all over Syria the value of gold was reduced by
half. With the priests holding out on the Sanctuary wall was a lad
parched with thirst. He begged the Roman guards to give him safe
conduct, openly admitting his thirst. They felt sorry that a mere child
should be suffering so, and granted the safe conduct. He came down,
drank what he needed, filled the vessel he had brought with water,
and dashed off full speed to his friends aloft. He was far too quick for
the guards, who swore at him for breaking his word; but he retorted
that he had done no such thing, for the agreement had not been that
he should stay with them, but only that he should come down and get
some water. That was exactly what he had done, so how had he
broken his word? Such sharp practice in one so young astounded the
victims of his trickery. However, after four days the starving priests
came down and were taken by the guards to Titus, whom they begged
to spare their lives. He replied that the time for pardon was past, that
the one thing that would have justified their being spared had gone,
and that the duty of priests was to perish with their sanctuary. Then
he pronounced sentence of death.

The partisans and their chiefs, beaten in the war on all sides and
shut in by a wall[25] that left them no possibility of escape, invited Titus
to a parley. Such was his natural kindness that he was eager to save
the town, and urged by his friends, who concluded that the terrorists
had at last come to their senses, he took his stand on the west side of
the outer court of the Temple; for here above the Gymnasium there
were gates, and a bridge linked the Temple with the Upper City;
this now separated the party chiefs from Caesar. On either side stood
a dense crowd – Jews round Simon and John on tiptoe with hope of

pardon, Romans eager to see how Titus would receive their appeal. Titus called on his men to control their fury and their weapons, and placing his interpreter by his side exercised the victor's privilege and spoke first.

'Are you satisfied now, gentlemen, with the sufferings of your country? you who, in utter disregard of our strength and your weakness, have through your reckless impetuosity and madness destroyed your people, your city, and your Sanctuary, and richly deserve the destruction that is coming to yourselves; you who from the moment Pompey's forces crushed you have never stopped rebelling, and now have made open war on Rome. Did you rely on numbers? Why, a tiny fraction of the Roman army sufficed to deal with you! Well then; on the trustworthiness of your allies? And which of the nations outside our empire was going to prefer Jews to Romans? Or on your wonderful physique? Yet you know that the Germans are our slaves. On the strength of your walls? What wall could be a better obstacle than the open sea that is the bulwark of Britain? But Britain was brought to her knees by the arms of Rome! On your invincible determination and the wiles of your generals? Yet you know that even Carthage was overwhelmed!

'There is only one answer. You were incited against the Romans by Roman kindness. First we gave you the land to occupy and set over you kings of your own race; then we upheld the laws of your fathers, and allowed you complete control of your internal and external affairs; above all, we permitted you to raise taxes for God and to collect offerings, and we neither discouraged nor interfered with those who brought them[26] – so that you could grow richer to our detriment and prepare at our expense to make war on us! Then, enjoying such advantages, you flung your abundance at the heads of those who furnished it, and like beasts you bit the hand that fed you!

'No doubt you despised Nero for his idleness, and like lesions or sprains you remained quiescent but malignant for a time, and then, when a more serious illness broke out,[27] you came out into the open and let your limitless ambitions grow into insolent presumption. My father came into the country, not to punish you for what you did in Cestius' time, but to caution you. If he had come to put an end to the nation, the right thing would have been to go straight to the root of your strength and sack this city at once. In actual fact he ravaged Galilee and the outlying districts, giving you time to come to your senses. But you took generosity for weakness, and our gentleness only served to increase your audacity. When Nero died you sank to the lowest level of depravity and took advantage of our difficulties at home: when my father and I had gone away to Egypt, you jumped at the chance to prepare for war,[28] and you shamelessly created difficulties once we were emperors, though when we were generals you had found us so considerate. When the whole Empire had come to us for protection, when all its inhabitants were enjoying the blessings of peace and countries outside were sending embassies to congratulate us, once again the Jews rose against us. You sent embassies beyond the Euphrates to stir up a revolt[29]; you rebuilt your city walls; there were faction-fights, rival party chiefs, civil war – just what we should expect from men so depraved!

'I came to the city bearing sombre injunctions which it had pained my father to give. When I heard that the citizens were peacefully inclined, I was delighted. You others I begged to desist before hostilities began; long after you had begun them I spared you, giving safe conduct to deserters and keeping faith with them when they came to me for protection. For many prisoners I showed pity: the warmongers I punished with torture and death.[30] Most unwillingly I brought engines to bear on your walls: my soldiers, ever thirsting for your blood, I held in leash: after every victory, as if it was a defeat, I appealed to you for an armistice. When I got near to the Temple, I again deliberately forwent my rights as victor and appealed to you to spare your own holy places and preserve the Sanctuary for your own use, offering you freedom to come out and a guarantee of safety or, if you wished, a chance to fight on other ground. Every proposal you treated with scorn, and your Sanctuary you set on fire with your own hands![31]

'After all that, you disgusting people, do you now invite me to a conference? What have you to save that can be compared with what has gone? What security do you think you deserve after the loss of your Sanctuary? Why, even now you stand in arms, and not even at your last gasp so much as pretend to be asking for mercy. You poor fools, what are you pinning your faith on? Aren't your people dead, your Sanctuary gone, your city in my power, your very lives in my hands? Do you think you will win renown for your courage by putting off death till the last moment? I shall not compete with you in craziness. If you throw down your arms and surrender your persons,

I will grant you your lives; like an easy-going head of a house, I will punish what cannot be cured and spare the rest for my own use.'

To this they replied that they could accept no terms from him as they had sworn never to do so; but they asked leave to go out through the circumvallation with their wives and children, in which case they would go away into the desert and leave the City to him. Titus, furious that men no better than prisoners should put forward demands as if they had defeated him, ordered it to be announced that it was no longer any use their deserting or hoping for terms, as he would spare no one: they must fight to the last ditch and save themselves in any way they could; from now on he would insist on all his rights as victor. Then he gave his men leave to burn and sack the City. They did nothing that day, but on the next they fired the Muniment Office, the Citadel, the Council Chamber, and the area known as Ophel. The fire spread as far as Helena's Palace in the centre of the Citadel, consuming the narrow streets and the houses full of the bodies of those who had died of starvation.

On the same day King Izates' sons and brothers,[32] joined by many prominent citizens, besought Caesar to grant them protection. Though furious with all the survivors, he lived up to his character and received the applicants. For the time being he kept them all in custody; the king's sons and kinsmen he put in chains and later conveyed to Rome to serve as hostages.

The partisans made a rush towards the Palace, which was so solidly built that many had stored their property there. They drove away the Romans, slaughtered the people who had crowded into the building, 8,400 in number, and looted the riches. They also took two of the Romans alive, a cavalryman and an infantryman. The infantryman they butchered then and there and dragged round the City, as if by proxy they were revenging themselves on all the Romans. As the cavalryman said that he had something to suggest that might save their lives, he was taken into Simon's presence; but when he got there he had nothing to say, so was handed over to Ardalas, one of the officers, to be executed. Ardalas tied his hands behind him and blindfolded him, then marched him forward in full view of the Romans with the intention of cutting off his head; but by a sudden movement the man dashed away to the Roman lines just as the Jew drew his sword. As he had made his escape from the enemy Titus could not very well put him to death, but deciding that he was unfit to be a soldier of Rome as he had let himself be taken alive, he stripped him of his arms and expelled him from the legion, to a man with any self-respect a punishment worse than death.

Next day the Romans drove the terrorists from the Lower City and burnt the whole place as far as Siloam. They were glad enough to see the town destroyed but got precious little loot, as the whole area had been cleaned out by the partisans before they withdrew to the Upper City. These men felt no remorse for the mischief they had done – they boasted as if they were proud of it: when they saw the City burning, they laughed heartily and said they were happily awaiting the end; for, with the people slaughtered, the Sanctuary burnt to the ground, and the town blazing, they were leaving nothing to the enemy. Yet to the very last Josephus never wearied of appealing to them to spare what was left of the City, though however much he might say against their savagery and impiety, however much advice he might give them for their own good, he got nothing but ridicule in return. As they could not very well surrender because of their oath and were unable now to fight the Romans on equal terms, they were like caged animals, so used to killing that they thirsted for blood. They scattered through the outskirts of the City and lay in wait among the ruins for would-be deserters. Many in fact were caught, and as hunger had left them too weak even to run away, all were butchered and their bodies thrown to the dogs. But any kind of death was more bearable than starvation, so that although they had no hope now of mercy from the Romans, they still fled to them, falling into the murderous hands of the partisans with their eyes open. Not one spot in the whole City was empty: every single one had its corpse, the victim of hunger or faction.

The last hope that bolstered up the party chiefs and their terrorist gangs lay in the underground sewers. If they took refuge in them they did not expect to be tracked down, and their intention was to come out and make good their escape after the final capture of the City and the subsequent departure of the Romans. But this was only an idle dream: they were not fated to escape from either God or the Romans. At the time, however, they had such faith in their bolt-holes that they lit more fires than did the Romans. Those who fled from the burning buildings into the sewers they killed without hesitation and plundered; if they found anyone with food they snatched it away and swallowed it, dripping with the wretched man's blood. By now they were actually fighting each other for the loot; and I have little doubt that if capture had not forestalled it, their utter bestiality would have made them get their teeth into the very corpses.

Owing to the steep approach on every side it was not feasible to master the Upper City without platforms, so on the 20th of Loös Caesar divided up the work among the troops. It was difficult to transport the timber since, as mentioned before, all the neighbourhood for over eleven miles had been stripped bare for the earlier platforms.[33] The four legions raised their earthworks on the west side of the City opposite the Palace, while the whole body of allies and the rest of the army worked near the Gymnasium, the bridge and Simon's tower, built during the struggle with John as a stronghold for himself.[34]

At this time the Idumaean chiefs at a secret meeting discussed the question of piecemeal surrender, and sent five men to Titus to implore his protection. Hoping that the party chiefs too would give in if they lost the support of the Idumaeans who had made so large a contribution to the war, Titus hesitated at first, but finally granted them their lives and sent the men back. But as they got ready to go, Simon saw what was afoot, immediately put to death the five who had gone to Titus, seized the chiefs of whom the most prominent was Jacob, son of Sosas, and threw them into prison. On the Idumaean rank and file, at a loss without their leaders, he kept a careful eye, posting more efficient sentry-groups along the wall. However, the sentries were unable to cope with the deserters: though many were killed, far more got away. The Romans received them all, Titus through kindness of heart disregarding his earlier proclamation, and the men holding their hands because they were sick of killing and hopeful of gain. For only the townsmen were kept back – all the rest were sold along with the women and children, the retail price being very low, as supply was far in excess of demand. In spite of his earlier announcement that no one must desert alone, but must bring his family with him, he nevertheless received such people; but he appointed officers to separate from them anyone deserving punishment. The number sold was enormous: the number of townsmen spared was over 40,000; these were free to go wherever they thought fit.

During this same period a priest named Jeshua, son of Thebuthi, obtained from Caesar a sworn guarantee of safety on condition that he should hand over some of the sacred treasures. He came out and

handed over from the Sanctuary wall two lampstands closely resembling those kept in the Sanctuary, as well as tables, basins, and cups, all
of solid gold and very heavy. He also handed over the curtains, the
vestments of the high priests with the precious stones, and many other
articles required for the Temple services. In addition the Temple
treasurer Phineas, when taken prisoner, produced the tunics and
girdles of the priests and a large supply of purple and scarlet kept in
store for repairing the great curtain, together with cinnamon in bulk,
cassia, and quantities of other spices, which were blended and daily
burnt as incense to God. He handed over many of the other treasures
too, with Temple ornaments in abundance, thus earning though a
prisoner the pardon granted to deserters.

   In eighteen days the platforms were ready for use, and on the 7th of
Gorpiaios the Romans brought up their engines. Some of the partisans,
already despairing of the City, withdrew from the wall to the Citadel,
while others plunged into the sewers; but many ranged themselves
along the ramparts and tried to repulse the crews of the battering-
rams. These too the Romans overwhelmed by numbers and by force,
and above all by confidence in face of despondency and half-hearted-
ness. When a section of the wall was broken through and some of the
towers gave way before the assault of the rams, there was an immediate flight from the battlements, and even the party chiefs were filled
with terror unjustified by the situation: before the enemy got through,
they were stunned and ready to fly, and men once arrogant and
bragging about their ungodly deeds could now be seen abject and
trembling, insomuch that even in these vile scoundrels it was pitiful
to note the change. Their one desire was to dash for the wall that
shut them in, repulse the guards and hack their way through to
safety; but when their old faithful supporters were nowhere to be
seen – they had been forced to scatter in all directions – and when
runners announced that the whole west wall was down, or that the
Romans had broken in and were just round the corner seeking them,
while others blinded by terror declared that from the towers they
could actually see the enemy, they fell on their faces bewailing their
own insane folly, and as if hamstrung were incapable of flight.

   What happened would serve as an object-lesson, showing both the
power of God over the wicked and the luck of the Romans. For the
party chiefs divested themselves of their safety, and of their own
accord came down from the towers[35] on which they could never

have been subdued by force but only by starvation; and the Romans, who had toiled so hard to break through the weaker walls, captured by sheer luck those which their engines could not touch; for no mechanical device could have made any impression on the three towers described elsewhere. Abandoning these, or rather driven down from them by God, they took refuge for a moment in the ravine below Siloam; later, when they had recovered somewhat from their terror, they made a dash for the nearest section of the circumvallation. But their strength was broken now by terror and disaster, and their courage could not rise to the occasion; so they were repulsed by the guards, scattered this way and that, and plunged into the sewers.

Masters now of the walls, the Romans set up their standards on the towers and with clapping and singing celebrated their victory, having found the end of the war much easier than the beginning. They had surmounted the last wall without losing a man – it seemed too good to be true – and when they found no one to oppose them, they could make nothing of it. They poured into the streets sword in hand, cut down without mercy all who came within reach, and burnt the houses of any who took refuge indoors, occupants and all. Many they raided, and as they entered in search of plunder, they found whole families dead and the rooms full of the victims of starvation: horrified by the sight, they emerged empty-handed. Pity for those who had died in this way was matched by no such feeling for the living: they ran every man through whom they met and blocked the narrow streets with corpses, deluging the whole City with gore so that many of the fires were quenched by the blood of the slain. At dusk the slaughter ceased, but in the night the fire gained the mastery, and on the 8th of Gorpiaios the sun rose over Jerusalem in flames – a city that during the siege had suffered such disasters that if she had enjoyed as many blessings from her foundation, she would have been the envy of the world, and a city that deserved these terrible misfortunes on no other account than that she produced a generation such as brought about her ruin.

When Titus entered he was astounded by the strength of the city, and especially by the towers which the party chiefs in their mad folly had abandoned. Observing how solid they were all the way up, how huge each block of stone and how accurately fitted, how great their breadth and how immense their height, he exclaimed aloud: 'God has been on our side; it is God who brought the Jews down from these strongholds; for what could human hands or instruments do against such towers?' At that time he made many such remarks to his friends, and he set free all persons imprisoned by the party chiefs and found in the forts. Later, when he destroyed the rest of the City and pulled down the walls, he left the towers[36] as a monument to his own luck, which had proved his ally and enabled him to overcome impregnable defences.

As the soldiers were now growing weary of bloodshed and survivors were still appearing in large numbers, Caesar gave orders that only men who offered armed resistance were to be killed, and everyone else taken alive. But as well as those covered by the orders the aged and infirm were slaughtered: men in their prime who might be useful were herded into the Temple and shut up in the Court of the Women. To guard them Caesar appointed one of his freedmen, and his friend Fronto[37] to decide each man's fate according to his deserts. Those who had taken part in sedition and terrorism informed against each other, and Fronto executed the lot. Of the youngsters he picked out the tallest and handsomest to be kept for the triumphal procession[38]; of the rest, those over seventeen were put in irons and sent to hard labour in Egypt, while great numbers were presented by Titus to the provinces to perish in the theatres by the sword or by wild beasts[39]; those under seventeen were sold. During the days in which Fronto was sorting them out starvation killed 11,000 of the prisoners, some because the guards hated them too bitterly to allow them any food, others because they would not accept it when offered; in any case there was not even enough corn to fill so many mouths.

All the prisoners taken from beginning to end of the war totalled 97,000; those who perished in the long siege 1,100,000.[40] Of these the majority were Jews by race but not Jerusalem citizens: they had come together from the whole country for the Feast of Unleavened Bread and had suddenly been caught up in the war, so that first the overcrowding meant death by pestilence, and later hunger took a heavier toll. That so many could crowd into the City was shown by the census held in Cestius' time. Wishing to bring home the strength of the city to Nero, who despised the nation, Cestius instructed the chief priests to hold a census of the population, if it was possible to do so. They chose the time of the Passover Feast, at which sacrifice is offered from 3 to 5 p.m., and as it is not permissible to feast alone, a sort of fraternal group is formed round each victim, consisting of at least ten adult males, while many groups have twenty members. The count showed that there were 255,600 victims; the men, reckoning ten diners to each victim, totalled 2,700,000,[41] all ceremonially clean; for persons suffering from leprosy, venereal disease, monthly periods, or any form of defilement were debarred from participation, as were the foreigners who came from abroad in large numbers to be present at the ceremonies.

But now fate had decreed that one prison should confine the whole nation and that a city solid with men should be held fast in war's embrace. No destruction ever wrought by God or man approached the wholesale carnage of this war. Every man who showed himself was either killed or captured by the Romans, and then those in the sewers were ferreted out, the ground was torn up, and all who were trapped were killed. There too were found the bodies of more than 2,000, some killed by their own hand, some by one another's, but most by starvation. So foul a stench of human flesh greeted those who charged in that many turned back at once. Others were so avaricious that they pushed on, climbing over the piles of corpses; for many valuables were found in the passages and all scruples were silenced by the prospect of gain. Many prisoners of the party chiefs were brought up; for not even at their last gasp had they abandoned their brutality. But God rewarded them both as they deserved: John, starving to death with his brothers in the sewers, after many scornful refusals at last appealed to the Romans for mercy, while Simon after battling long against the inevitable, as will be described later,[42] gave himself up. John was sentenced to life-imprisonment, but Simon was kept for the triumphal procession and ultimate execution. The Romans now fired the outlying districts of the town and demolished the walls.

So fell Jerusalem in the second year of Vespasian's reign, on the 8th of Gorpiaios, captured five times before and now for the second time utterly laid waste. Shishak king of Egypt,[43] followed by Antiochus, then Pompey, and after that Sosius and Herod together, captured the City but spared it. Earlier on the king of Babylon had stormed it and laid it waste 1,468 years and 6 months from its foundation.[44] It was originally founded by a Canaanite chieftain called in the vernacular 'King of Righteousness', for such he was. On that account he was the first priest of God and the first to build the Temple and in its honour to give the name of Jerusalem to the City, previously called

Salem.[45] The Canaanite inhabitants were driven out by the Jewish king David, who settled his own people there; then 477 years and 6 months after his time it was utterly destroyed by the Babylonians. From King David, the first Jew to reign in it, to the destruction by Titus was 1,179 years.[46] But neither its long history, nor its vast wealth, nor its people dispersed through the whole world, nor the unparalleled renown of its worship sufficed to avert its ruin. So ended the siege of Jerusalem.

CHAPTER 22

Jerusalem Destroyed: Roman Celebrations

THERE was no one left for the soldiers to kill or plunder, not a soul on which to vent their fury; for mercy would never have made them keep their hands off anyone as long as action was possible. So Caesar now ordered them to raze the whole City and Sanctuary to the ground, leaving the towers that overtopped the others, Phasael, Hippicus, and Mariamme, and the stretch of wall enclosing the City on the west – the wall to serve as protection for the garrison that was to be left, the towers to show later generations what a proud and mighty city had been humbled by the gallant sons of Rome.[1] All the rest of the fortifications encircling the City were so completely levelled with the ground that no one visiting the spot would believe it had once been inhabited.[2] This then was the end to which the mad folly of revolutionaries brought Jerusalem, a magnificent city renowned to the ends of the earth.

To guard the site Caesar decided to leave the Tenth Legion with a few troops of horse and companies of foot[3]; and having now settled all problems arising from the war, he desired to congratulate the whole army on its achievements and to bestow suitable rewards on those whose services were outstanding. A wide dais was erected for him in the middle of his old camp-site, and on it he took his stand flanked by his staff, where the whole army could hear him. He thanked them heartily for their unfailing loyalty to him, and praised their obedience throughout the war, shown along with personal heroism in many dangerous situations. By their own efforts they had increased the power of their country and had made it plain to all men that neither the number of their enemies, the strength of their defences, the size of their cities, nor the reckless daring and brutal savagery of their warriors could ever hold out against Roman valour, even if some of them found in fortune a constant ally. It had been a magnificent feat to bring to an end a war that had raged so long: they could not have wished for anything better when they embarked on it. But it was a much more splendid and brilliant achievement to have elected and sent home as rulers and governors of the Roman Empire men whom all were delighted to welcome, and whose decisions they loyally obeyed, full of gratitude to those who had chosen them.[4] He was full of admiration and affection, he went on, for them all, knowing that every man's ability had been fully equalled by his enthusiasm; some however, blest with superior strength, had fought with greater distinction, not only shedding glory on their own lives by their gallant deeds, but making his campaign a more brilliant success by their exploits: on these he would at once bestow their honours and distinctions, and no one who had been prepared to put more into it than the next man should get less than his due. He would, indeed, give this matter his closest attention, as he was more interested in rewarding the courage and initiative of his fellow-soldiers than in punishing slackers.

Accordingly he at once ordered officers detailed for the task to read out the name of every man who in the course of the war had performed any outstanding exploit. Calling them by name he praised them as they came forward, as delighted as a man could be over his own exploits. He put golden crowns on their heads, gave them gold torques, miniature gold spears and standards made of silver,[5] and promoted every man to higher rank. In addition he assigned to them out of the spoils silver, gold, and garments, with any amount of other booty. When he had rewarded them all according to his own opinion of their deserts, he offered prayers on behalf of the whole army, stepped down amidst thunderous applause, and then turned his attention to sacrifices in honour of his victory. A great number of bullocks were herded round the altars: all these he sacrificed and divided among the troops for a victory feast. He himself spent three days celebrating with his senior officers, and then dispatched the bulk of his army to the destinations selected for the various units: the Tenth Legion he detailed to guard Jerusalem instead of sending it to the Euphrates where it had been before. Remembering that while Cestius was in command the Twelfth Legion had given way before the Jews, he banished it from Syria altogether – it had earlier been stationed at Raphanaeae – and sent it away to Melitene, beside the Euphrates between Armenia and Cappadocia. Two legions he decided should stay with him till his arrival in Egypt, the Fifth and the Fifteenth. Then he went down with his army to Caesarea on the coast, where he deposited the bulk of the spoil and arranged for the custody of the prisoners, the voyage to Italy being impossible now that the summer was over.

At the time when Titus Caesar was busy directing the siege of Jerusalem, Vespasian had embarked on a merchantman and crossed from Alexandria to Rhodes. From there he sailed in a fleet of triremes, calling at every city on the way and welcomed everywhere with enthusiasm. From Ionia he went on to Greece, and from there via Corcyra to the Promontory of Iapyx,[6] whence he continued his journey overland.

From Caesarea on the coast Titus marched to Caesarea Philippi, where he stayed a long time exhibiting shows of every kind. Many of the prisoners perished here, some thrown to wild beasts, others forced to meet each other in full-scale battles. Here also Titus was informed of the capture of Simon, son of Gioras, which had happened as follows. During the siege of Jerusalem Simon had been in the Upper City; but when the Roman army was inside the walls sacking the entire city he took his most trustworthy friends, and with them some tunnellers equipped with the tools of their trade and supplies of food sufficient for several weeks, and thus accompanied went down into one of the concealed sewers. They advanced through the old tunnel as far as it went, and when they reached solid earth they tried to hack through it, hoping to push ahead till they could emerge at a safe spot and get clear away. But the hope was baffled when the task was attempted; for progress was slow though the miners toiled hard, and in spite of careful rationing the food was on the point of giving out. So Simon, thinking to frighten the Romans by a trick, dressed himself up in several short white tunics with a crimson cape fastened over them, and at the very spot where the Temple had once stood he appeared out of the ground. At first those who saw him were too taken aback to move, but after a while they came nearer and asked who he was. This Simon refused to tell them: they must summon the general. They ran to fetch him, and Terentius Rufus, left in command of the garrison,[7] came at once. Learning the whole truth from Simon he kept him fettered and sent an account of his capture to Caesar.

Thus as the just punishment of his brutality to his fellow-citizens, whom he had subjected to such savage tyranny, Simon was put by God beneath the heel of his most bitter enemies. He had not been brought into their power by force but had voluntarily thrown himself in the way of vengeance – the very thing for which he had put so many to a horrible death on the false charge of going over to the Romans. For wickedness cannot evade the divine wrath, and Justice is not weak: in time she overtakes those who offend against her, and brings heavier vengeance on the wicked when they think they are out of her reach because punishment has not been immediate. This was brought home to Simon himself when he fell into the hands of the furious Romans. His emergence from the ground meant that in the next few days a great many more partisans were discovered in the sewers. When Caesar returned to Caesarea by the sea, Simon was brought before him in fetters, and was ordered to be reserved for the triumphal procession through Rome which he was planning.

While he remained there he celebrated his brother's birthday[8] in the grand style, reserving much of his vengeance on the Jews for this notable occasion. The number of those who perished in combats with wild beasts or in fighting each other or by being burnt alive exceeded 2,500. Yet all this seemed to the Romans, though their victims were dying a thousand different deaths, to be too light a penalty. Caesar next went on to Berytus, a city in Phoenicia and a Roman colony.[9] Here he made a longer stay, celebrating his father's birthday[10] with a still more lavish display, both in the magnificence of the shows and in the originality of the other costly entertainments. Vast numbers of prisoners perished in the same way as before.

It happened about this time that the surviving Jews in Antioch were the targets of accusations that might well have meant their destruction; for the local population had been roused against them both by slanders of which they were at present the victims and by events that had occurred shortly before. Of these I must first give a short account, in order to make my exposition of what occurred later easier to follow.

Men of Jewish blood are dispersed in great numbers among the native populations all over the world, especially in Syria, where the two nations are neighbours. The biggest Jewish colony was at Antioch, partly because of the size of the city but more because the kings who followed Antiochus[11] had made it safe for them to settle there. Antiochus Epiphanes indeed had sacked Jerusalem and looted the Sanctuary; but his successors restored all the offerings of bronze to the Jews of Antioch as a gift for their synagogue, and further gave them the same civic privileges as the Greeks.[12] As the later kings treated them in the same way, they grew in numbers, and with their elaborate and costly offerings beautified the Temple. All the time they were attracting to their worship a great number of Greeks, making them virtually members of their own community. But at the time of the declaration of war, when Vespasian had just landed in Syria and when the universal hatred of the Jews was at its peak,[13] a certain Antiochus, a Jew himself and greatly respected because of his father, the magistrate responsible for the Antioch Jews, took advantage of a public gathering to go into the theatre and denounce his own father and the others, accusing them of a conspiracy to burn down the whole city in a single night. He also handed over some Jews from abroad as accomplices in the plot. When the people heard this, they could not control their anger, and demanded that those handed over should be at once consigned to the flames, and then and there they were all burnt to death in the theatre. The crowd then hurled themselves at the main body of Jews, thinking that on their swift punishment the safety of their own home-town depended. Antiochus whetted their anger still more: he thought he could provide proof of his conversion and his hatred of Jewish customs by sacrificing according to Greek rites,[14] and suggested that the others should be forced to do the same, as refusal to do so would show who were in the plot. When the Antiochenes applied the test, a few gave way and those who refused were put to death. Antiochus now borrowed soldiers from the Roman general and began to tyrannize over his fellow-citizens, not allowing them to rest on the seventh day, but forcing them to do everything just as on the other days. Such strong compulsion did he bring to bear that not only at Antioch was the seventh-day rest abolished, but starting from there the new rule was enforced in the other cities too for a short time.

Such miseries having befallen the Antioch Jews at that time, they were now struck by a second disaster,[15] to the story of which the last paragraph will serve as prologue. It happened that a fire destroyed the Square Market, the City Hall, the Record Office, and the Law Courts, and it proved difficult to check the flames as they violently swept on through the whole city. With responsibility for this Antiochus saddled the Jews. Even if they had not already viewed them with bitter hostility, in the uproar that followed the incident the Antiochenes would have been deceived by this slander: after what had happened earlier they were much more ready to swallow everything this man said, and to convince themselves they had as good as seen with their own eyes the fires being lit by the Jews. So as if they had gone mad they all rushed in an absolute frenzy upon the victims of the slander. It was with the greatest difficulty that their impetuosity was checked by Gnaeus Collega, the governor's deputy, who insisted that they should allow Caesar to be informed of what had occurred; for though Caesennius Paetus had already been sent out by Vespasian as governor of Syria, it happened that he was not yet on the spot. By painstaking enquiry Collega found out the truth. Of the Jews on whom Antiochus had laid the blame not one had had any share in the business, which was entirely the work of some unscrupulous wretches who, unable to settle their debts, decided that, if they burnt the Market and the public records, they could not be called on for repayment. So with these accusations hanging over them the Jews were still anxious about the future, tossed as they were on a sea of painful fears.[16]

When Titus Caesar received news of the delight with which his father's arrival had been greeted in all the cities of Italy, and of the matchless enthusiasm and splendour of his welcome in Rome, his pleasure and satisfaction knew no bounds; all anxiety on his father's behalf had been most happily dispelled. For long before Vespasian appeared, the whole population of Italy was paying him homage in their hearts as if he was already there; eager anticipation made them mistake the prospect of his coming for his actual arrival, and their devotion to him was entirely spontaneous. The Senate had not forgotten the disastrous consequences of the rapid succession of emperors: it was a godsend to have once again an emperor possessing the dignity of mature years and a magnificent record in war, whose supremacy, they were well aware, would only be for the safety of his subjects. The people, worn out by the miseries of civil war, were still more eager for his coming: now at last they would be freed for ever from their wretchedness, and would again enjoy security and prosperity too, without a doubt. Above all the soldiery pinned their faith on him: they knew better than anyone the magnitude of the wars he had won, and having seen for themselves the incompetence and cowardice of the other emperors, they were eager to close that long and painful chapter, and prayed that the one man who could give them safety and honour should be at their head. Amidst all this devotion on every side citizens of distinguished status could no longer bear to wait, and hastened a very long way from Rome to be the first to welcome him. Nor indeed could any of the humbler folk endure the delay in meeting him: they all felt it was simpler and easier to go than to stay behind; so they all streamed out in such masses that the City itself enjoyed the unwonted pleasure of finding itself sparsely inhabited; for those who went outnumbered those who stayed behind. But when his imminent arrival was announced, and those who had gone ahead exclaimed over the friendly welcome he had given to every group, all the rest of the population with their wives and children now lined the roadside to cheer; each group as he passed was so delighted to see him, and so impressed by the gentleness of his bearing, that they uttered cries of every kind, greeting him as 'benefactor', 'saviour', and 'the only worthy emperor of Rome'. The whole City was as full of garlands and incense as a temple. Making his way with difficulty through the crowd that thronged him to the palace, he offered personal sacrifices to the household gods in thanksgiving for his arrival. The crowd then turned to celebration, and feasting by tribes, families, and neighbourhoods they offered prayers and libations to God, asking that Vespasian himself might remain for very many years at the helm of the Roman state, and that the throne might be preserved unchallenged for his sons and all the generations of their descendants.

After this enthusiastic reception of Vespasian the city of Rome made a rapid advance to great prosperity; but earlier on, while he was at Alexandria and Titus was busy with the siege of Jerusalem, a large section of the Germans had been roused to revolt, and their Gallic neighbours had made common cause with them, sharing their high hopes that they might even throw off the Roman yoke. The motives that induced the Germans to engage in this revolt and take the field were these: first, their national character, incapable of logical thought and ready to rush into danger with little grounds for hope; secondly, hatred of their masters, for they know that only the Romans have ever forced their race into subjection. But nothing did so much to give them confidence as the opportunity then presented. They saw the Roman Empire paralysed at the centre by the continual changes of emperor, and were informed that every corner of Rome's wide-flung dominions was in a state of excitement and agitation; so they felt that this was a splendid opportunity presented to them by the calamitous dissensions of the enemy. Their plan was abetted and their fantastic hopes encouraged by Classicus and Civilis, two of their chiefs, who had evidently set their hearts on this rebellion a long time back, and were encouraged by this opportunity to declare their intention: they were to find the masses only too ready to take the plunge.

A large section of the Germans had already agreed on revolt and the rest had raised no objection when Vespasian, as if by divine providence, sent dispatches to Petilius Cerealis, hitherto commander in Germany, conferring on him the rank of consul and ordering him to proceed to Britain as the new governor. He accordingly set out for his new command; but on receiving news of the German revolt he fell on them when they had assembled their forces and in a pitched battle inflicted immense casualties, compelling them to abandon their mad scheme and learn sense. Even if Cerealis had not come on the scene so expeditiously, they were fated to meet their deserts before long. For the moment that news of their revolt burst on Rome and reached the ears of Caesar Domitian, he, though only in his teens, did not hesitate as anyone else would have done at his age, but shouldered this immense burden of responsibility. He had inherited his father's fighting spirit and had progressed beyond his years in the school of war: now he instantly hurled himself at the barbarian hordes. At the rumour of his approach their courage failed: they submitted to him without a blow, reaping from their terror the great reward of being brought once more under the same yoke without suffering disaster. As soon as he had put all the affairs of Gaul on such a sound basis that no further disturbance was ever likely to occur there, Domitian returned to Rome covered with glory and admired by all for exploits amazing in one so young, and worthy of his father.[17]

The German revolt which I have described coincided with a bold Scythian attack on the Romans. A very large Scythian tribe called the Sarmatians crossed unnoticed to the right bank of the Danube, and launched a very violent attack so completely unexpected that resistance was swept aside. Many of the Roman guards were killed, and when the consular legate Fonteius Agrippa advanced to meet them and put up a strenuous fight he too fell. The whole of the province was overrun and stripped bare. When news of these events and of the devastation of Moesia reached Vespasian, he sent out Rubrius Gallus to punish the Sarmatians. Rubrius slaughtered vast numbers of them in a series of battles, the panic-stricken survivors scurrying back to

their own country. Having brought the war to this conclusion the
general provided for security in the future by stationing garrisons in
greater number and strength about the area, so that the natives were
denied the least chance of getting across again. Thus the Moesian war
was very quickly settled.[18]

Titus Caesar spent some time in Berytus, as we mentioned before.
From there he passed through a number of Syrian towns, exhibiting
in them all lavish spectacles in which Jewish prisoners were forced
to make a show of their own destruction. As he travelled he saw a
river whose character merits description. Flowing between Arca in
Agrippa's kingdom[19] and Raphanaeae, it has a remarkable peculi-
arity. When it flows it fills its channel and the current is strong;
then it fails completely at its source and for six days the bed is bone-
dry; after that, just as if nothing had happened, the water gushes
out on the seventh day exactly as before. From this timetable it has
never been known to deviate; so it is called the Sabbatical River
after the seventh day which the Jews keep holy.[20]

When the citizens of Antioch learnt that Titus was near, they were
too delighted to stay within their walls and ran out to meet him, proceeding nearly four miles, not only men but crowds of women with
their children pouring out of the city. When they saw him coming,
they lined both sides of the road, extending their right arms in salute,
then calling down every kind of blessing on his head escorted him to
Antioch; but all their acclamations were mingled with a constant
appeal for the expulsion of the Jews. Titus took no notice of this appeal
but listened impassively to what was said, so that having no clue to his
thoughts and intentions the Jews were kept in prolonged and painful
suspense. For Titus did not stay in Antioch but marched on immediately to Zeugma on the Euphrates. There he was met by envoys
from the Parthian king, Vologeses, who bestowed on him a golden
crown in honour of his victory over the Jews. Accepting this he
feasted the king's emissaries, then returned to Antioch. After repeated
invitations from the city council and the people to visit the theatre,
where the whole population had crowded in to greet him, he
graciously gave his consent. But when they again pressed him with
extreme earnestness and continuous appeals to drive the Jews out of
the city, his reply was brief and to the point: 'Their own country, to
which, as they are Jews, we should have to banish them, has been
destroyed, and they would not be admitted anywhere else now.' As

that appeal had failed the Antiochenes tried another: they asked him to remove the bronze tablets engraved with the Jews' privileges.[21] Titus would not grant that either; but leaving the position of the Antioch Jews exactly as it was he set out for Egypt.

On the way he called at Jerusalem. There he contrasted the grievous desolation that met his eyes with the splendour of the city that was, and calling to mind the mighty structures in ruins now but once so beautiful, he was pained by the city's destruction. Unlike anyone else, he did not boast that, though it was so great and so strong, he had taken it by storm, but cursed and cursed again those who had instigated the revolt and caused this retribution to fall on the city: so clear did he make it that he would never have wished the terrible punishment that had been inflicted to serve as proof of his prowess.[22] Of the city's great wealth quantities were still being found among the ruins. Much of this was dug up by the Romans, but still more came into their hands as a result of information from the prisoners – gold and silver and the most valuable articles of other kinds, which in view of the incalculable chances of war the owners had stowed underground.

Resuming his interrupted journey to Egypt, Titus crossed the desert by the shortest route and arrived at Alexandria.[23] His intention being to sail for Italy, he sent the two legions that had accompanied him back to their old stations, the Fifth to Moesia, and the Fifteenth to Pannonia. Of the prisoners he ordered the leaders, Simon and John, with seven hundred of the rank and file picked out for their exceptional stature and physique, to be conveyed to Italy without a moment's delay, intending to display them in his triumphal procession. The voyage went according to plan, and Rome gave him as warm a welcome as it had given his father; but it was a more glorious occasion for Titus because his father himself came out to welcome him. The throng of citizens could not contain their joy when they saw all three together.[24] A few days later they decided to celebrate a single triumph in common in honour of their exploits, though the Senate had decreed a separate triumph for each. Notice was given in advance of the day appointed for the victory procession, and not one person stayed at home out of the immense population of the City: everyone came out and, although there was only standing-room, found a place somewhere, so that there was barely enough room left for the procession itself to pass.

While it was still night all the soldiers had marched out under their commanders by centuries and cohorts, and had formed up not round the gates of the Upper Palace[25] but near the Temple of Isis[26]; for there the victorious generals had slept that night. As soon as day began to break Vespasian and Titus came out wreathed with bay and wearing the traditional crimson robes, and proceeded to the Portico of Octavia[27]; for there the Senate and senior magistrates and knights were awaiting their arrival. A dais had been set up in front of the colonnades, and on it placed ready for them were ivory chairs. On these they proceeded to sit; whereupon the soldiery shouted acclamations, one and all bearing full testimony to their prowess. The central figures were unarmed, in silken robes and wreathed with bay. Having received their acclamations Vespasian, though they had more to say, gave the signal for silence. A complete hush fell on all and the emperor, rising from his seat and wrapping most of his head in his cloak, offered the customary prayers, Titus then doing the same. After the prayers Vespasian made a short speech to the whole gathering, dismissed the soldiers to the breakfast which it was customary for victorious generals to provide, and himself retired to the gate which took its name from the triumphal processions that always pass through it.[28] There they first tasted food, then put on the triumphal robes and sacrificed to the gods that stand on either side of the gate, and finally resumed their triumphal advance, driving through the theatres[29] to give the crowds a better view.

It is impossible to give a satisfactory account of the innumerable spectacles, so magnificent in every way one could think of, whether as works of art or varieties of wealth or rarities of nature; almost all the treasures that have ever come one at a time into the hands of fortune's favourites – the priceless marvels of many different peoples – were brought together on that day, showing forth the greatness of the Roman Empire. Masses of silver and gold and ivory in every shape known to the craftsman's art could be seen, not as if carried in procession but like a flowing river. There were hangings borne along, some in the rarest shades of purple, others embroidered with life-like portraits by Babylonian artists; transparent stones, some set in golden crowns, some in other mounts, were carried past in such numbers that we could see how foolish we had been to suppose any of them rare. In the procession too were images of the Roman gods wonderful in size and of true artistic merit, every one of them made from costly

materials; and animals of many kinds were led past, all decked with
the proper trappings. Every item in the procession was escorted by a
large group of men arrayed in garments of genuine purple dye[30]
interwoven with gold; those chosen to take part in the procession
itself had about them the choicest and most astonishing wealth of
ornament. Furthermore, not even the host of captives went un-
adorned: under their elaborate and beautiful garments any dis-
figurement due to physical sufferings was hidden from view.

But what caused the greatest wonder was the structure of the
travelling stages; indeed their immense size caused alarm through
mistrust of their stability, as many of them were three or even four
storeys high, while their lavish equipment was viewed with delighted
surprise. Many were hung with curtains interwoven with gold, and
all were framed in wrought ivory and gold. Numbers of tableaux
showed the successive stages of the war most vividly portrayed. Here
was to be seen a smiling countryside laid waste, there whole formations of the enemy put to the sword; men in flight and men led off to
captivity; walls of enormous size thrown down by engines, great
strongholds stormed, cities whose battlements were lined with
defenders utterly overwhelmed, an army streaming inside the ramparts, the whole place reeking of slaughter, those unable to resist
raising their hands in supplication, temples set on fire and houses torn
down over the heads of their occupants, and after utter desolation
and misery rivers flowing, not over tilled fields, supplying drink to
men and animals, but through a countryside still blazing on every
hand. Such were the agonies to which the Jews condemned themselves when they embarked on this war; and the art and marvellous
craftsmanship of these constructions now revealed the incidents to
those who had not seen them happen as clearly as if they had been
there. Placed on each stage was the commander of a captured town
just as he had been when captured. A number of ships followed.

Most of the spoils that were carried were heaped up indiscriminately, but more prominent than all the rest were those captured in the
Temple at Jerusalem – a golden table weighing several hundredweight,
and a lampstand similarly made of gold but differently constructed
from those we normally use.[31] The central shaft was fixed to a base,
and from it extended slender branches placed like the prongs of a
trident, and with the end of each one forged into a lamp: these
numbered seven, signifying the honour paid to that number by the

Jews. After these was carried the Jewish Law,[32] the last of the spoils. Next came a large group carrying images of Victory, all fashioned of ivory and gold. Behind them drove Vespasian first with Titus behind him[33]: Domitian rode alongside, magnificently adorned himself, and with his horse a splendid sight.

The procession finished at the Temple of Jupiter on the Capitol, where they came to a halt: it was an ancient custom to wait there till news came that the commander-in-chief of the enemy was dead. This was Simon, son of Gioras, who had been marching in the procession among the prisoners, and now with a noose thrown round him was being dragged to the usual spot in the Forum while his escort knocked him about. That is the spot laid down by the law of Rome for the execution of those condemned to death for their misdeeds.[34] When the news of his end arrived it was received with universal acclamation, and the sacrifices were begun. When the customary prayers had been offered and the omens proved favourable, the emperor and his sons went back to the Palace. They entertained some people at the imperial table; for all the rest, sumptuous banquets had been prepared at home. All day long the City of Rome celebrated the triumphant issue of the campaign against her enemies, the end of civil strife, and the beginning of hope for a joyful future.

When the triumphal ceremonies were over, as the Roman Empire was now most firmly established, Vespasian made up his mind to build a temple of Peace. This was completed with remarkable speed and surpassed all human imagination. Not only did he have unlimited wealth at his disposal; he also adorned it with paintings and statues by the greatest of the old masters. In fact, in that temple were collected and deposited all those works that men had hitherto travelled over the whole world to see, longing to set eyes on them even when scattered in different lands.[35] There too he laid up the golden vessels from the Temple of the Jews,[36] for he prided himself on them; but their Law and the crimson curtains of the Inner Sanctuary he ordered to be deposited in the Palace for safe keeping.

CHAPTER 23

Cleaning-up Operations

A NEW legate had been sent to Judaea, Lucilius Bassus, who took over the command from Cerealis Vetilianus.[1] He first secured the submission of the fortress at Herodium together with its defenders[2]; then concentrating all available troops, hitherto very widely dispersed and including the Tenth Legion, he determined to march against Machaerus. It was absolutely necessary to destroy this fortress, for fear that its strength might tempt large numbers to revolt, since the character of the terrain might well fill its defenders with confident hopes of survival and its assailants with despondency and fear. The defended area is itself a rocky hill rising to an immense height, and for that very reason it is almost impregnable; and nature has found means to make it unapproachable too. For it is trenched on every side with ravines too deep for their bottoms to be seen, difficult to cross and quite impossible to fill in. The one which shuts it in on the west stretches for seven miles, ending at the Dead Sea; somewhere in this region the soaring peak of Machaerus itself towers aloft. The ravines to the north and south are considerably smaller, but just as serious an obstacle to an attacker; that to the east is found to be at least a hundred and fifty feet deep, and it extends as far as a mountain situated opposite Machaerus.

Realizing that the site had many natural advantages, the Jewish king Alexander had been the first to build a fortress there – a fortress demolished by Gabinius in his war against Aristobulus.[3] When Herod came to the throne he decided that no place would better repay attention and the strongest fortification, especially in view of the proximity of Arabia; for its situation was most opportune, commanding as it did a view of Arab territory. So he surrounded a large area with walls and towers and founded a city there, from which an ascent led up to the ridge itself. Not content with that he built a wall round the very summit and erected towers at the corners, each ninety feet high. In the middle of this enclosure he built a palace, breath-taking in the size and beauty of the various rooms; and at carefully chosen spots he constructed a number of tanks to receive rain-water and maintain a constant supply. He might well have been competing with nature in the hope that the impregnability the place had received from her might be outdone by his own artificial defences. He further provided an ample store of weapons and engines, and managed to think of everything that could enable the occupants to snap their fingers at the longest siege.[4]

There grew in the palace a plant of rue of an astonishing size – it was every bit as tall and stout as a fig-tree. It was popularly believed to have been there since Herod's time, and it might well have lived much longer if it had escaped the axes of the Jewish settlers. In the ravine that protects the town on the north is a place called Baaras, where grows a root of the same name. This is flame-coloured, and at dusk it sends out brilliant flashes so that those who come near in the hope of plucking it cannot take hold of it, as it slips away and will not stay still until it is drenched with a woman's urine or menstrual blood. Even then to touch it means certain death, unless one happens to have brought an exactly similar root dangling from the wrist. It can also be secured another way without risk, thus – they dig right round it, so as to leave the smallest possible piece of root in the ground; then they tie a dog to it, and when he springs forward to follow the man who tied him it is easily pulled up, but the dog dies instantly, a substitute for the person who was going to remove the plant; for no danger remains for those who subsequently handle it. Despite the greatness of the danger it has one virtue that makes it sought after; for the so-called devils – in reality the spirits of evil-doers that enter the living and kill them if they are not rescued – are quickly cast out by this plant if it so much as touches the possessed. Here too flow springs of hot water, differing widely in flavour, some being bitter and others very sweet indeed. There are also many fountains of cold water, and these do not all issue from wells on low ground in a row: the truth is more surprising, for there is a cave to be seen near by, not hollowed out to any great depth, but sheltered by a rock that juts out. Above this protrude, as it were, two breasts a little way apart, sending out water, in one case icy, in the other boiling hot. When mixed these furnish a most pleasant bath, beneficial in many sicknesses and giving special relief to tired muscles. The region also contains sulphur and alum mines.

After viewing the position from various angles Bassus decided to approach by filling in the ravine to the east. He promptly set to work, endeavouring to raise the platform with the utmost speed and thereby making the siege easy. The Jews trapped inside separated themselves from the gentiles[5]: these they considered a useless mob and forced to stay in the town below to face the first onslaught, while they themselves seized and held the fortress above, both because of the strength of its defences and to ensure their own safety: they felt certain they could win pardon by surrendering the place to the Romans. First, however, they wanted to test their prospects of escaping a siege; so they made vigorous sorties every day and grappled with all whom they encountered,[6] at heavy cost to both sides. On every occasion it was the circumstances of the moment that decided the issue in favour of one side or the other – of the Jews if they caught the Romans off their guard, of the men on the platforms if they had seen the attack coming and were lined up to meet it. However, it was not this skirmishing that was to terminate the siege: a fortuitous and astonishing occurrence forced the Jews to surrender the fortress.

Among the besieged was a young man, bold in enterprise and energetic in action, named Eleazar. He had been prominent in the sorties, inciting the majority of the defenders to issue forth and interrupt the building of the platforms, and in the encounters doing a great deal of damage to the Romans; for those who dared to sally out with him he smoothed the way to the attack, and made retreat safe by being the last to withdraw. One day, when the battle had been broken off and both sides had retired, he, confidently supposing that none of the enemy would start further fighting now, stayed outside the gates talking to the defenders on the wall and with no thought for anyone else. A soldier from the Roman camp, an Egyptian named Rufus, saw his chance and performed a breath-taking feat: he made a sudden rush, picked the man up armour and all, and before the spectators on the wall could recover from their astonishment, carried him off to the Roman camp. The commander ordered him to be stripped, taken where he would be most clearly seen by the watchers in the town, and flogged with whips. The Jews were terribly distressed by the young man's agony, and the whole town burst into tears, showing most unusual concern for one unfortunate individual. Seeing this, Bassus proceeded to play a trick on the enemy, wishing to aggravate their grief, and so to induce them to surrender the fortress in return for the man's life; and in this he succeeded. He ordered a cross to be set up as if he would crucify Eleazar forthwith. When the defenders saw this they were filled with still greater distress, and their shrieks were deafening as they cried out that they could not endure the horror of it. Then Eleazar implored them not to stand by while he suffered the most pitiable of deaths, but to save their own lives by submitting to the might and fortune of Rome, by which all others had now been crushed. Such an appeal was irresistible, and many inside the town pleaded on his behalf, for he came of an eminent and very numerous family; so, contrary to their nature, they yielded to pity and hastily dispatched a delegation to discuss the surrender of the fortress, on the understanding that they should be free to go away, taking Eleazar with them. To this the Romans and their commander agreed.

When the people in the town below learnt of the separate agreement reached by the Jews, they decided that their own best plan was to steal away in the night. But as soon as they opened the gates, those who had come to terms with Bassus informed him of what was happening, perhaps grudging the others their lives, perhaps through fear that they themselves might be held responsible for their escape. The boldest of those who left the town succeeded in breaking through and getting clear, but of those left behind the men were massacred, 1,700 of them, the women and children enslaved. Feeling that he must honour the agreement made with those who had surrendered the fortress, Bassus let them go and sent Eleazar back.

Having settled these problems, he made a rapid march to the Forest of Jardes, for news had reached him that many who had earlier escaped from the sieges of Jerusalem and Machaerus had collected there. Arriving at the spot and finding the information correct, he first encircled the whole area with his cavalry, so that any Jews who tried to break through would find their flight cut off; then he ordered the infantry to cut down the trees amongst which they were hiding. These measures compelled the Jews to attempt some heroic feat, in the hope that by a supreme effort they might get clear. So rushing out en masse with loud hurrahs they fell on the encircling enemy. They met with stubborn resistance, and as one side fought with the fury of despair, the other with the utmost pertinacity, the battle was greatly prolonged; but it ended very differently for the combatants, Roman casualties being no more than twelve killed and a handful wounded, whereas of the Jews not one survived the encounter; three thousand in all, they perished to a man. Among them was their general, Judas, son of Jairus, who, as stated already, commanded a unit at the siege of Jerusalem, and by making his way through some of the sewers slipped unnoticed through the Roman lines.[7]

About the same time Caesar sent a message to Bassus and Laberius Maximus the procurator,[8] instructing them to lease out all Jewish territory.[9] He founded no city there but treated the country as his own property, merely allowing 800 men discharged from the forces to settle in Emmaus three and a half miles from Jerusalem.[10] He imposed a tax on the Jews wherever they lived, ordering them to pay each year into the Capitol two drachmas a head, the sum they had previously paid into the Temple at Jerusalem.[11] Here for the moment we will leave the affairs of the Jews.

In the fourth year of Vespasian's reign the king of Commagene, Antiochus,[12] found himself and all his family in a most disastrous situation. It happened thus. Caesennius Paetus, governor of Syria at the time – either in good faith or to spite Antiochus, it is not certain which – sent a dispatch to Caesar alleging that Antiochus and his son Epiphanes intended to revolt from Rome and had reached an understanding with the king of Parthia[13]: preventive action was therefore called for, to forestall a sudden move that would throw the whole Empire into a state of war. Caesar could hardly overlook an urgent report of such a character; the proximity of the two monarchs made the matter particularly pressing. Samosata, the biggest city of Commagene, lies on the Euphrates, making it very easy for the Parthians, if they had a mind to it, to get across, and guaranteeing them a friendly reception. So Paetus, being trusted and empowered to use his own judgement, wasted no time: suddenly, before Antiochus and his staff had any suspicion, he invaded Commagene at the head of the Sixth Legion, supported by some cohorts and a few troops of horse, and further assisted by the kings of Chalcidice and Emesa, Aristobulus[14] and Soaemus. Their invasion was unopposed, as none of the inhabitants was prepared to lift a hand against them. Antiochus, suddenly faced with the news, did not for a moment contemplate war with Rome, but decided to leave his kingdom just as it was and slip away with his wife and children, thinking thereby to convince the Romans of his innocence. So he travelled fourteen miles from the city and encamped in the plain.

Paetus sent a force to occupy Samosata, thus securing the city while he with the rest of his troops set off in pursuit of Antiochus. Not even his desperate situation could tempt the king to take any warlike measures against the Romans: bewailing his lot he awaited what was coming to him. His sons on the other hand, young, experienced in war and phenomenally strong, could not bring themselves to submit to such a calamity without a struggle, and so Epiphanes and Callinicus resorted to arms. The battle was violent and lasted the whole day, the two leaders displaying noteworthy courage: their forces were intact when dusk broke off the struggle. But not even when the battle ended thus did Antiochus see fit to stay: he took his wife and daughters and fled with them into Cilicia, doing irreparable damage to the morale of his own men; for as he had evidently written off his own kingdom, they mutinied and went over to the Romans, and there was no mistaking the universal despair. So before they were completely bereft of allies, Epiphanes and his brother were obliged to run from the enemy, no more than ten horsemen crossing the Euphrates with them: from there they rode without interference to the Parthian court, where Vologeses, so far from despising them as runaways, received them, as if they still enjoyed their old prosperity, with all honour. When Antiochus arrived at Tarsus in Cilicia, Paetus sent a centurion to dispatch him in fetters to Rome. But Vespasian refused to let the king be brought to him in this condition, thinking it better to honour their old friendship than to make the war a pretext for relentless animosity. He gave instructions that while he was still on the way he should be freed from his fetters, and instead of continuing his journey to Rome should remain for the present in Sparta. He further assigned him a large revenue, enabling him to live not only in luxury but in royal state. When news of this reached Epiphanes and his brother, who had hitherto been extremely anxious about Antiochus, it was a very great load off their minds. They had hoped that Caesar would be reconciled to them, as Vologeses had intervened on their behalf; for though they were living in comfort, they were most unwilling to live outside the Roman Empire. Caesar graciously promised them safe conduct, and they travelled to Rome where their father at once joined them from Sparta. They were treated with all honour and settled in the City.

In an earlier chapter we referred[15] to the Alani, a Scythian tribe living near the Don and the Sea of Azov. At this stage in the story, as they planned a raid into Media and beyond in search of loot, they negotiated with the king of Hyrcania, as master of the pass which King Alexander had closed with gates of iron.[16] He granted them admission, and they poured through en masse; then falling on the unsuspecting Medes, they plundered a populous countryside full of livestock of every kind, meeting with no opposition at all. Pacorus, king of the district,[17] had fled in terror to his hide-outs leaving everything behind except his wife and concubines, who had been taken prisoner and whom he recovered only by the payment of 100 talents. So they continued their raids with the utmost ease and without opposition, advancing as far as Armenia and leaving a trail of destruction behind them. Armenia was ruled by Tiridates,[18] who met them and gave battle, but came within an inch of being taken alive during the fighting; he was lassoed from a distance and would have been dragged off if he had not whipped out his sword and slashed the rope just in time. This battle made the invaders still more savage: they turned the countryside into a desert, and carrying off a large part of the population and quantities of booty from both kingdoms returned to their own country.

In Judaea Bassus had died and the new governor was Flavius Silva, who, seeing the rest of the country reduced to impotence and only one fortress still holding out, marched against it with all available forces. The fortress was Masada, occupied by the Sicarii[19] under the command of an influential man called Eleazar, a descendant of the Judas who had persuaded many Jews, as recorded earlier, not to register when Quirinius was sent to Judaea to take a census.[20] At that time the Sicarii[21] combined against those prepared to submit to Rome, and in every way treated them as enemies, looting their property, rounding up their cattle, and setting their dwellings on fire: they were no better than foreigners, they declared, throwing away in this cowardly fashion the freedom won by the Jews at such cost, and avowedly choosing slavery under the Romans. In reality this was a mere excuse, intended to cloak their barbarity and avarice. The proof lay in their own actions; for people who joined the Sicarii in their revolt and fought by their side against Rome then suffered worse atrocities at their hands, when the Sicarii, convicted of hollow pretence, maltreated those who tried to clear themselves by condemning the wickedness of the Sicarii.

Somehow those days had become so productive of every kind of wickedness among the Jews as to leave no deed of shame uncommitted; and even if someone had used all his powers of invention, he could not have thought of any vice that remained untried: so corrupt was the public and private life of the whole nation, so determined were they to outdo each other in impiety towards God and injustice to their neighbours, those in power ill-using the masses, and the masses striving to overthrow those in power. One group was bent on domination, the other on violence and on robbing the rich. First to begin this lawlessness and this barbarity to kinsmen were the Sicarii, who left no word unspoken, no deed untried, to insult and destroy the objects of their foul plots. Yet even they appeared gentle by the side of John.[22] He not only put to death all advocates of just and profitable courses, treating such as his most bitter foes among the citizens, but by his public actions he subjected his country to countless woes, as a man was sure to do if he had already dared to be impious even towards God. On his table he had unlawful dishes served, and the purifications observed by our fathers he set aside; so it was no longer surprising if gentleness and kindness towards men were not shown by one too mad to show piety towards God.

Think too of Simon, son of Gioras. What crime did he not commit? What outrage was not done to free citizens by the men who gave him unlimited power? What friendship or kinship was there that did not increase the wantonness of their daily murders? The ill-treatment of aliens they looked on as the work of a common criminal, but thought it a proof of brilliance to savage their own kith and kin. But even their madness was nothing to the frenzy of the Idumaeans. These disgusting people butchered the high priests[23] so that no trace of divine worship should be left, and then destroyed everything that remained of civil organization, permeating the whole system with utter lawlessness. In this no one could equal the so-called Zealots, a party which justified its title by its deeds; they followed every bad example, and there was no crime in the records that they did not zealously reproduce. And yet they gave themselves this title in view of their zeal for what was good, either mocking their victims, brutes that they were, or regarding the greatest evils as good! Thus it was that each of them found a fitting end, God sentencing them all to the penalty they deserved. Every torment mankind can endure fell upon them to the very end of their lives, when they came face to face with death in all its most agonizing forms. Yet it would be true to say that they suffered less misery than they had caused: to suffer what they deserved was impossible. But this is not the time to lament for the victims of their savagery, richly as they deserve it; so I will take up the story where I broke it off.

Against Eleazar and the Sicarii who held Masada with him came the Roman general at the head of his forces. He at once subdued the whole area, and stationing garrisons at strategic points threw a wall right round the fortress[24] so that none of the besieged should find it easy to escape, and posted sentries. He established his own headquarters at a place that seemed most opportune for directing the siege, where the rocks on which the fortress stood were linked to the mountain near by, though it was an awkward position for bringing up necessary supplies.[25] For not only was food brought from a distance at the cost of painful toil for the Jews detailed for the task; even drinking-water had to be fetched to the camp as the neighbourhood possesses no spring. These preliminary dispositions completed, Silva began the siege-operations, which called for great skill and immense exertions in view of the strength of the fortress, which I will now describe.

A rock with a very large perimeter and lofty all the way along is broken off on every side by deep ravines.[26] Their bottom is out of sight,[27] and from it rise sheer cliffs on which no animal can get a foothold except in two places where the rock can be climbed, though with difficulty. One of these paths comes from the Dead Sea to the east, the other from the west – an easier route. They call the first one the Snake because of its narrowness and constant windings: it is broken as it rounds the projecting cliffs and often turns back on itself, then lengthening out again a little at a time, manages to make some trifling advance. Walking along it is like balancing on a tight-rope. The least slip means death; for on either side yawns an abyss so terrifying that it could make the boldest tremble. After an agonizing march of three and a half miles[28] the summit is reached, which does not narrow to a sharp point but is a sort of elevated plateau. On this the high priest Jonathan first built a fortress[29] and named it Masada: later King Herod devoted great care to the improvement of the place. The entire summit, measuring three quarters of a mile round, he enclosed within a limestone wall 18 feet high and 12 wide, in which he erected thirty-seven towers 75 feet high: from these one could pass through a ring of chambers right round the inside of the wall.[30] For the plateau was of rich soil more workable than any plain, and the king reserved it for cultivation, so that, if ever there was a shortage of food from without, this should not injure those who had entrusted their safety to these ramparts. He built a palace, too, on the western slope, below the fortifications on the crest and sloping down northwards.[31] The palace wall was of great height and strongly built, with 90 foot towers at the four corners. The design of the interior apartments, the colonnades, and the bathrooms was varied and magnificent, with supporting pillars cut from a single block in every case, and the walls and floors of the room tiled with stones of many hues.[32] At every spot where people lived, whether on the plateau, round the palace, or before the wall, he had cut out in the rock numbers of great tanks to hold water, ensuring a supply as great as where spring water can be used. A sunken road led from the palace to the hill-top, invisible from outside. Even the visible roads were not easy for an enemy to use: the eastern one, as already explained, was by nature unusable; the western was guarded by a large fort at its narrowest point, at least five hundred yards from the crest. To pass this was impossible, to capture it by no means easy, while it had been made difficult even for innocent travellers to get away. So strong had the fortress's defences against enemy attack been made both by nature and by human effort.

The provisions stored inside were even more astonishing in their abundance and diversity, and in their perfect preservation. The stores included a great quantity of corn – more than enough to last for many years – and quantities of wine and oil, with pulse of all varieties and dates in great heaps.[33] All these Eleazar found when he and his Sicarii made themselves masters of the fortress by a trick; they were perfectly fresh and just as good as on the day they were laid in. Yet from that day to the capture by the Romans was about a hundred years![34] In fact, the Romans found what was left of the various foods in excellent condition. We should not be far wrong if we put down their preservation to the atmosphere, which at the height of the plateau is free from any earthy, filthy taint. There was found too a quantity of weapons of every kind, stored there by the king, and enough for 10,000 men, as well as unwrought iron and bronze and a store of lead. For these preparations, indeed, there were very strong reasons: it is believed that Herod equipped this fortress as a refuge for himself, suspecting a double danger – the danger from the Jewish masses, who might push him off his throne and restore to power the royal house that had preceded him, and the greater and more terrible danger from the Egyptian queen, Cleopatra. For she did not conceal her intentions but constantly appealed to Antony, begging him to destroy Herod and requesting the transfer to herself of the kingdom of Judaea.[35] The surprising thing is not that there should have been any question of his gratifying her, but that he did not yield to her demands, hopelessly enslaved as he was by his passion for her. Such were the fears that made Herod fortify Masada, little dreaming that he was to leave it to the Romans as their very last task in the war against the Jews.

As he had now finished the projected exterior wall encircling the whole position, to make absolutely sure that no one slipped out, the Roman commander actively prosecuted the siege, though he had found only one place where it was possible to construct platforms. Behind the tower that guarded the road leading from the west to the palace and the ridge was a rocky projection, quite wide and running out a long way, but 450 feet below the level of Masada: it was called the White Cliff. So climbing up and taking possession of this Silva ordered the troops to heap earth on it. They worked with a will and with ample man-power, and soon a solid platform had been raised to a height of 300 feet.[36] As this did not, however, seem either strong or big enough to carry the engines, they built on top of it a pier composed of great stones fitted together, 75 feet wide and the same height. The engines were similar in construction to those devised by Vespasian first and later by Titus for their siege-operations. Further, a tower was erected 90 feet high and covered all over with iron plates[37]: on this the Romans mounted a number of spear-throwers and stone-throwers which pelted the defenders, driving them from the battlements and forcing them to keep under cover. Meanwhile Silva had had a great ram constructed: now by his orders it was swung continuously against the wall till at long last a breach was made and a small section collapsed.

Inside however the Sicarii had lost no time in building a second wall, which even the engines were likely to find a tougher proposition: it was pliant and capable of absorbing the impetus of the blows owing to its peculiar construction. Huge baulks were laid lengthwise and fastened together at the ends: these were in two parallel rows separated by the width of a wall and with the space between filled with earth. So that the soil should not fall out as the height increased, they laid beams across the long baulks to secure them. To the enemy the rampart looked like a normal construction, but the blows of the engines falling on yielding earth were absorbed: the concussion shook it together and made it more solid. Seeing this Silva decided that fire was the best weapon against such a wall and instructed his men to direct a volley of burning torches at it. Being made mostly of wood it soon caught fire: owing to its loose construction the whole thickness was soon ablaze and a mass of flame shot up. Just as the fire broke out a gust of wind from the north alarmed the Romans: it blew back the flame from above and drove it in their faces, and as their engines seemed on the point of being consumed in the blaze they were plunged into despair. Then all of a sudden as if by divine providence the wind veered to the south, and blowing strongly in the reverse direction carried and flung the flames against the wall, turning it into one solid blazing mass. God was indeed on the side of the Romans, who returned to camp full of delight, intending to assail the enemy early next day, and all night long kept watch with unusual vigilance to ensure that none of them slipped out unobserved. But Eleazar had no intention of slipping out himself, or of allowing anyone else to do so. He saw his wall going up in flames; he could think of no other means of escape or heroic endeavour; he had a clear picture of what the Romans would do to men, women, and children if they won the day; and death seemed to him the right choice for them all. Making up his mind that in the circumstances this was the wisest course, he collected the toughest of his comrades and urged it upon them in a speech of which this was the substance:

'My loyal followers, long ago we resolved to serve neither the Romans nor anyone else but only God, who alone is the true and righteous Lord of men: now the time has come that bids us prove our determination by our deeds. At such a time we must not disgrace ourselves: hitherto we have never submitted to slavery, even when it brought no danger with it: we must not choose slavery now, and with it penalties that will mean the end of everything if we fall alive into the hands of the Romans. For we were the first of all to revolt, and shall be the last to break off the struggle. And I think it is God who has given us this privilege, that we can die nobly and as free men, unlike others who were unexpectedly defeated. In our case it is evident that daybreak will end our resistance, but we are free to choose an honourable death with our loved ones. This our enemies cannot prevent, however earnestly they may pray to take us alive; nor can we defeat them in battle.

'From the very first, when we were bent on claiming our freedom but suffered such constant misery at each other's hands and worse at the enemy's, we ought perhaps to have read the mind of God and realized that His once beloved Jewish race had been sentenced to extinction. For if He had remained gracious or only slightly indignant with us, He would not have shut His eyes to the destruction of so many thousands or allowed His most holy City to be burnt to the ground by our enemies. We hoped, or so it would seem, that of all the Jewish race we alone would come through safely, still in possession of our freedom, as if we had committed no sin against God and taken part in no crime – we who had taught the others! Now see how He shows the folly of our hopes, plunging us into miseries more terrible than any we had dreamt of. Not even the impregnability of our fortress has sufficed to save us, but though we have food in abundance, ample supplies of arms, and more than enough of every other requisite, God Himself without a doubt has taken away all hope of survival. The fire that was being carried into the enemy lines did not turn back of its own accord towards the wall we had built: these things are God's vengeance for the many wrongs that in our madness we dared to do to our own countrymen.

'For those wrongs let us pay the penalty not to our bitterest enemies, the Romans, but to God – by our own hands. It will be easier to bear. Let our wives die unabused, our children without knowledge of slavery: after that, let us do each other an ungrudging kindness, preserving our freedom as a glorious winding-sheet. But first let our possessions and the whole fortress go up in flames: it will be a bitter blow to the Romans, that I know, to find our persons beyond their reach and nothing left for them to loot. One thing only let us spare – our store of food: it will bear witness when we are dead to the fact that we perished, not through want but because, as we resolved at the beginning, we chose death rather than slavery.'

Such was Eleazar's appeal. It did not meet with the same response from all his hearers: some were eager to do as he said, and filled with something like rapture at the thought that death was so noble; others less heroic were moved by pity for their wives and families, and certainly too by the prospect of their own end; and as they exchanged glances the tears in their eyes betrayed the repugnance they felt. When he saw them playing the coward and their spirits quailing before the bold sweep of his plan, Eleazar was afraid that even those who had not flinched when they heard his proposal might be unmanned by other men's tears and laments. So instead of abandoning his appeal he roused himself, and bursting with ardour began a more dazzling display of oratory on the immortality of the soul. Looking hard at his wet-eyed listeners and complaining bitterly he began:

'I made a sad mistake in thinking I had the support of loyal followers in the struggle for freedom, men resolved to live honourably or die. You are not a bit different from the common herd in courage and boldness, you who fear death even when it means the end of utter misery, although you ought not to hesitate or wait for someone to urge you on. Ever since primitive man began to think, the words of our ancestors and of the gods, supported by the actions and spirit of our forefathers, have constantly impressed on us that *life* is the calamity for man, not death. Death gives freedom to our souls and lets them depart to their own pure home where they will know nothing of any calamity; but while they are confined within a mortal body and share its miseries, in strict truth they are dead.[38] For association of the divine with the mortal is most improper. Certainly the soul can do a great deal even when imprisoned in the body: it makes the body its own organ of sense, moving it invisibly and impelling it in its actions further than mortal nature can reach. But when, freed from the weight that drags it down to earth and is hung about it, the soul returns to its own place, then in truth it partakes of a blessed power and an utterly unfettered strength, remaining as invisible to human eyes as God Himself. Not even while it is in the body can it be viewed; it enters undetected and departs unseen, having itself one imperishable nature, but causing a change in the body; for whatever the soul touches lives and blossoms, whatever it deserts withers and dies: such a superabundance it has of immortality.

'Sleep will provide you with the clearest proof of what I say. In sleep souls left to themselves and free from bodily distractions enjoy the most blissful repose, and consorting with God whose kin they are, they go wherever they will and foretell many of the things to come. Why, pray, should we fear death if we love to repose in sleep? And isn't it absurd to run after the freedom of this life and grudge ourselves the freedom of eternity?

'It might be expected that we, so carefully taught at home, would be an example to others of readiness to die. But if we do need the testimony of foreigners, let us look to those Indians who profess to practise philosophy.[39] They are men of true courage who, regarding this life as a kind of service that we must render to nature, undergo it with reluctance and hasten to release their souls from their bodies; and though no misfortune presses or drives them away, desire for immortal life impels them to inform their friends that they are going to depart. No one tries to stop them, but everyone congratulates them and gives them messages for his dear ones: so confidently and so truly do they believe that the souls share a common life. Then after receiving these commissions they consign their bodies to the flames, that the soul may be as pure as possible when it is separated from the body, and hymns are sung to them as they die. In fact they are sent off more happily by their dearest ones to death than other men are sent by their fellow-citizens on a long journey: the bereaved may weep for themselves, but the departed they deem happy, ranked now among the immortals. Well then! Are we not ashamed to show a poorer spirit than Indians, and by our want of courage to bring the Law of our fathers, the envy of all the world, into utter contempt?

'Even if from the very first we had been taught the contrary belief, that life is indeed the greatest good of mankind and death a disaster, the situation is such that we should still be called upon to bear it with a stout heart, for God's will and sheer necessity doom us to death. Long ago, it seems, God issued this warning to the whole Jewish race together, that life would be taken from us if we misused it. Do not fasten the blame on yourselves or give the Romans the credit for the fact that we are all ruined by the war against them: it is not through their power that these things have happened – a mightier hand has intervened to give them the outward shape of victory. What Roman weapons slew the Jews who lived in Caesarea? Why, they had no thought of rebelling against Rome, but were in the middle of their seventh-day ceremonies when the Caesarean mob rushed at them, and though they offered no resistance, butchered them with their wives and children, paying no heed to the Romans who were treating none as enemies except ourselves, who had in fact rebelled.[40] No doubt I shall be told that the Caesareans had a permanent quarrel with the Jews in their midst and simply seized their chance to vent their old hatred.[41] Then what are we to say of the Jews in Scythopolis? They had the effrontery to make war on us to please the Greeks, and would not join with us, their own kith and kin, to drive out the Romans. Much good they got from their faithful support of the Greeks! They were brutally massacred by them, they and their entire households – such was the reward their alliance brought them! What they saved

the Greeks from suffering at our hands they themselves endured as if
it was they who had wished to inflict it![42] It would take too long to
speak now about every individual case: you know that of all the
towns in Syria there isn't one that hasn't exterminated its Jewish
inhabitants, though they were more hostile to us than the Romans.[43]
As a single instance, the Damascenes, though they couldn't even fake a
plausible excuse, made their own city reek with the most loathsome
slaughter, butchering 18,000 Jews and their wives and families as well.[44]
As for those tortured to death in Egypt, it was stated that the number
was something over 60,000.[45]

'They, perhaps, died in this way because in a foreign land they
could find no answer to their enemies; but all those who took up
arms against Rome in their own had everything, hadn't they, that
could give them hope of certain victory? Weapons, walls, impregnable
fortresses, and a spirit that in the cause of liberty no danger could
shake, encouraged all to rebel. But these things were effective for a
very short time: they raised our hopes only to prove the beginning of
worse misfortunes. All were captured; all came into the enemy's
hands as if provided specially to make their victory more splendid,
not to save the lives of those who fashioned them! Those who died in
battle we may well congratulate: they died defending their freedom,
not betraying it. But the masses who are now under the thumb of
Rome who would not pity? Who would not hasten to die rather than
share their fate? Some of them have been broken on the rack or tortured to death at the stake or by the lash; some have been half-eaten
by savage beasts and then kept alive to be their food a second time,
after providing amusement and sport for their enemies.[46] Of them all
we have most cause to pity those who are still alive; for they pray and
pray for the death that never comes.

'Where is the mighty city, the mother-city of the whole Jewish
race, secure within so many encircling walls, sheltering behind so
many forts and lofty towers, chock-full of equipment for war, and
defended by thousands and thousands of determined men? Where
now is the city that was believed to have God for her Founder? She
has been torn up by the roots, and the only memorial of her that is
left is the camp of her destroyers that still occupies her ruins! Old
men with streaming eyes sit by the ashes of the Shrine, with a few
women kept by the enemy as victims of their lust.

'Which of us, realizing these facts, could bear to see the light of day, even if he could live free from danger? Who is such an enemy to his country, who so unmanly and so wedded to life as not to be sorry that he is alive today? If only we had all died before seeing the Sacred City utterly destroyed by enemy hands, the Holy Sanctuary so impiously uprooted! But since an honourable ambition deluded us into thinking that perhaps we should succeed in avenging her of her enemies, and now all hope has fled, abandoning us to our fate, let us at once choose death with honour and do the kindest thing we can for ourselves, our wives and children, while it is still possible to show ourselves any kindness. After all, we were born to die, we and those we brought into the world: this even the luckiest must face. But outrage, slavery, and the sight of our wives led away to shame with our children – these are not evils to which man is subject by the laws of nature: men undergo them through their own cowardice, if they have a chance to forestall them by death and will not take it. We were very proud of our courage, so we revolted from Rome: now in the final stages they have offered to spare our lives and we have turned the offer down. Is anyone too blind to see how furious they will be if they take us alive? Pity the young whose bodies are strong enough to survive prolonged torture; pity the not-so-young whose old frames would break under such ill-usage. A man will see his wife violently carried off; he will hear the voice of his child crying "Father!" when his own hands are fettered. Come! while our hands are free and can hold a sword, let them do a noble service! Let us die unenslaved by our enemies, and leave this world as free men in company with our wives and children. That is what the Law ordains, that is what our wives and children demand of us, the necessity God has laid on us, the opposite of what the Romans wish – they are anxious that none of us should die before the town is captured. So let us deny the enemy their hoped-for pleasure at our expense, and without more ado leave them to be dumbfounded by our death and awed by our courage.'

Eleazar had many more arguments to urge, but all his listeners cut him short and full of uncontrollable enthusiasm made haste to do the deed. As if possessed they rushed off, everyone anxious to be quicker than the next man, and regarding it as proof positive of manliness and wisdom not to be found among the last: so irresistible a desire had seized them to slaughter their wives, their children, and themselves. It might have been thought that as they approached their task their determination would have weakened; but they clung resolutely to the purpose they had formed while listening to the appeal, and while they all retained feelings of personal affection, reason, which had urged what was best for their dear ones, won the day. For at the very moment when with streaming eyes they embraced and caressed their wives, and taking their children in their arms pressed upon them the last, lingering kisses, hands other than their own seemed to assist them and they carried out their purpose, the thought of the agonies which they would suffer at the hands of the enemy consoling them for the necessity of killing them. In the end not a man failed to carry out his terrible resolve, but one and all disposed of their entire families, victims of cruel necessity who with their own hands murdered their wives and children and felt it to be the lightest of evils!

Unable to endure any longer the horror of what they had done, and thinking they would be wronging the dead if they outlived them a moment longer, they quickly made one heap of all they possessed and set it on fire; and when ten of them had been chosen by lot to be the executioners of the rest, every man flung himself down beside his wife and children where they lay, put his arms round them, and exposed his throat to those who must perform the painful office. These un-flinchingly slaughtered them all, then agreed on the same rule for each other, so that the one who drew the lot should kill the nine and last of all himself[47]: such perfect confidence they all had in each other that neither in doing nor in suffering would one differ from another. So finally the nine presented their throats, and the one man left till last first surveyed the serried ranks of the dead, in case amidst all the slaughter anyone was still left in need of his hand; then finding that all had been dispatched, he set the palace blazing fiercely, and summon-ing all his strength drove his sword right through his body and fell dead by the side of his family. Thus these men died supposing that they had left no living soul to fall into the hands of the Romans; but an old woman escaped, along with another who was related to Eleazar, in intelligence and education superior to most women, and five little children. They had hidden in the conduits that brought drinking-water underground while the rest were intent upon the suicide-pact. These numbered nine hundred and sixty, women and children included. The tragedy was enacted on 15th of Xanthicos.[48]

Expecting further resistance, the Romans armed themselves at dawn, bridged the gap between platform and ramparts with gang-ways and then made their assault. Seeing no enemy, but dreadful solitude on every side, fire within, and silence, they were at a loss to guess what had happened. At last, as if giving the signal for a volley, they shouted, in the hope that some of those inside would show themselves. The noise came to the ears of the women, who emerged from the conduits and gave the Romans a detailed account of what had happened, the second of them providing a lucid report of Eleazar's speech and the action that had followed.[49] They found it difficult to believe her and were sceptical of such astounding resolution; but they attempted to extinguish the blaze and quickly cut a way through to the inside of the palace. When they came upon the rows of dead bodies, they did not exult over them as enemies but admired the nobility of their resolve, and the way in which so many had shown an utter contempt of death in carrying it out without a tremor.

Masada having fallen thus, the general left a garrison in the fortress and returned with the rest of his army to Caesarea. For nowhere was there an enemy left: the whole country had been subdued in the long war which had made itself felt by many even of the remotest inhabitants and had endangered their peace.

The next incident occurred in Egypt, and cost the lives of many Jews. Some members of the party of the Sicarii had managed to escape to Alexandria,[50] where not satisfied with being still alive they started a subversive movement, urging many of their hosts to claim their freedom and to regard the Romans as no whit their superiors, honouring God as their only master. When certain Jews in prominent positions objected, they were murdered: the rest were constantly urged to revolt. Seeing the mad folly of the agitators, the leaders of the council of elders[51] decided that it was no longer safe to overlook what was going on, and summoning all the Jews to a mass meeting exposed the mad folly of the Sicarii, showing them to be the cause of all the trouble. Now, they went on, not even after their escape had they any certain hope of safety, since once recognized by the Romans they would instantly be killed; so they were trying to bring the disaster due to themselves on those who had had no part in their crimes. They therefore urged the gathering to take care that these men did not bring them to ruin: they could justify themselves to the Romans by handing them over. Recognizing that the danger was very real the audience accepted their advice, and making a furious rush at the Sicarii rounded them up. Six hundred were caught then and there: a number escaped into Egypt and Egyptian Thebes, but were soon apprehended and brought back. There was universal astonishment at the fortitude and desperation – or was it strength of mind? – that they displayed. Subjected to every form of torture and bodily suffering that could be thought of, for the one purpose of making them acknowledge Caesar as lord, not a man gave in or came near to saying it, but rising above the strongest compulsion they all maintained their resolve, and it seemed as if their bodies felt no pain and their souls were almost exultant as they met the tortures and the flames. But nothing amazed the spectators as much as the behaviour of young children; for not one of them could be constrained to call Caesar lord. So far did the strength of a brave spirit prevail over the weakness of their bodies.

Lupus, who was in charge of Alexandria at the time,[52] promptly reported this disturbance to Caesar. He, viewing with suspicion the continual turbulence of the Jews, and fearing that they might again assemble their forces and win new adherents, instructed Lupus to pull down the Jewish sanctuary in the so-called 'District of Onias'.

This is in Egypt, a settlement that was founded and received its name in the following circumstances. Onias, son of Simon, one of the chief priests in Jerusalem, fled from Antiochus the Syrian king during his war with the Jews and came to Alexandria, where he was given a friendly reception by Ptolemy, who detested Antiochus.[53] Onias declared that he would win him the support of the whole Jewish race if he would agree to his suggestions. When the king undertook to do all he could, Onias asked leave to build a Sanctuary somewhere in Egypt where he could worship God as his fathers had done. This would make the Jews still more hostile to Antiochus, who had plundered their temple at Jerusalem, and more friendly disposed to himself, and freedom of worship would bring many of them to his side.

Pleased with this suggestion, Ptolemy gave him a piece of ground twenty-one miles from Memphis: the district is called the Nome of Heliopolis.[54] There Onias constructed a fortress and built his Sanctuary – not like that in Jerusalem but resembling a tower – built of large blocks of stone and rising to a height of ninety feet. But in designing the altar[55] he copied the one at home, and he enriched the Temple with the same kind of offerings, except for the shape of the lampstand. He did not make a stand at all, but simply had a lamp hammered out of gold: it gave a bright light and was hung by a gold chain. The whole temple precincts were encircled with a wall of baked brick, in which the gateways were of stone. The king further allotted him a large district to bring him in revenue, so that the priests should enjoy abundance and God should have ample provision for His worship. Unfortunately the motive of Onias in doing all this was not to his credit: he was anxious to outdo the Jews in Jerusalem, as he bore them a grudge for his exile, and thought that by raising this temple he could induce the masses to leave them for it.[56] There had been, too, an ancient prophecy made about six hundred years before: Isaiah was the name of the man who foretold that this Sanctuary would be raised in Egypt by a Jew.[57] So it was that the Temple came to be built.

On receipt of this dispatch Lupus proceeded to the temple, brought out some of the offerings and shut up the building. Soon afterwards Lupus died and Paulinus, the new governor,[58] stripped the temple bare, threatening the priests with dire consequences if they did not produce every single offering. He then forbade would-be worshippers to come near the precincts, and locking the gates put the place entirely out of bounds, leaving not a vestige of divine worship there. The time from the building of the sanctuary to its closure was 343 years.[59]

The towns in the neighbourhood of Cyrene were also infected by the mad folly of the Sicarii. Into Cyrene there slipped an unprincipled scoundrel called Jonathan, by trade a weaver,[60] who persuaded a number of men of the poorer classes to listen to him, and led them out into the desert promising to show them signs and portents.[61] Few of the citizens were aware of his fraudulent activities, but the leading Jews in Cyrene reported his exodus with all his paraphernalia to the governor of Libyan Pentapolis, Catullus,[62] who promptly dispatched contingents of horse and foot. They easily crushed the unarmed mob, destroying the majority in the engagement: the few who were taken alive were brought before Catullus. The ringleader, Jonathan, escaped for the moment, but a long and very careful search of the whole country led to his ultimate capture. Brought before the governor, he contrived to save his own skin but gave Catullus a pretext for shocking injustice. Against the wealthiest of the Jews he brought the monstrous charge that they had given him his instructions, and Catullus, welcoming these charges with delight, grossly exaggerated the significance of what had happened, dramatizing it with a vengeance in order that he too might be credited with a victory over the Jews. But what was crueller still – besides being absurdly credulous he even gave the Sicarii lessons in the art of lying. Thus he ordered Jonathan to name one of the Jews, Alexander, whom he had fallen foul of some time before – the quarrel was public knowledge – and then implicated Alexander's wife Berenice in the charges also. Having got rid of these, he next murdered all the wealthier Jews to the number of 3,000: in doing this he felt quite safe, as he confiscated their possessions for the benefit of Caesar's revenues.

For fear that some of the Jews elsewhere might show up his iniquitous conduct, he increased the scope of his calumnies, inviting Jonathan and some of his fellow-prisoners to prefer a charge of subversive activities against the most respectable Jews in both Alexandria and Rome. One of the objects of this trumped-up charge was Josephus, the writer of this history.[63] However, Catullus did not profit as he had expected from his fabrication. He arrived in Rome bringing Jonathan and his associates in fetters, satisfied that the lies told in his presence and at his prompting would be accepted without question. But Vespasian smelt a rat and enquired into the facts, and finding no justification for the accusation brought against the men, acquitted them of the charges at the instance of Titus and gave Jonathan the punishment he deserved: he was first tortured, then burnt alive. Catullus for the time being profited by the leniency of the two emperors and received no more than a reprimand; but soon afterwards he succumbed to a complicated sickness beyond remedy and died miserably, not only chastened in body but suffering from a much more terrible disease of the mind. He was tormented by terrors, constantly calling out that he saw the ghosts of those he had murdered standing before him; and losing control of himself he would spring from his bed as if he himself was being tortured and burnt. His malady grew rapidly worse and worse, and his bowels were eaten through and fell out. Such was his end – proof, if ever there was one, of the providence of God, who executes judgement on the wicked.

*

And here we bring our story to an end – the story which we promised to set down with the utmost accuracy for the benefit of those who wished to learn how the Romans fought this war against the Jews. Its literary merits must be left to the judgement of the readers: as to its truth, I should not hesitate to declare without fear of contradiction that from the first word to the last I have aimed at nothing else.

Notes

1. The original Aramaic version is not extant; see the Introduction.

2. For much fuller personal information, see *V* 1–12.

3. A hope apparently largely unfulfilled.

4. Josephus distorts chronology in this paragraph. The Jewish revolt in 66 had no connection with the risings of Vindex in Gaul in 68 and of the Batavians in 69 or with the deposition of Nero in 68 and the ensuing civil war.

5. The oldest communities of the Diaspora (the Dispersion), descendants of Jews who had been taken into exile by Nebuchadnezzar in 587 B.C. but had chosen not to return when freed by the Persian conquest of Babylon in 538. On Adiabene, see note 39 to p. 161.

6. Here and often elsewhere Josephus uses the word 'tyrant' – the Greek term for an unconstitutional and absolute but not necessarily harsh ruler – for the leaders of the Jewish nationalist groups. In this translation it is usually rendered 'party chief' (e.g. later in this paragraph), but occasionally the literal 'tyrant' is more appropriate.

7. The title 'Caesar' was conferred on both Vespasian's sons when he became emperor. From p. 292 Josephus frequently refers to Titus simply as 'Caesar'.

8. In this translation, *stasiastēs*, 'rebel', is usually rendered 'insurgent' up to p. 296; after that 'partisan' is used.

9. In this translation, *lēstēs* (on which see Appendix A) is usually rendered 'bandit', but from p. 226 'terrorist' is also sometimes used.

10. Josephus later changed his mind, and in the early books of the *AJ* covered Jewish history from Adam.

11. Apart from 1 and 2 Maccabees, the works of none of these are extant.

12. The correct form of the name, always spelt Sossius by Josephus.

13. Upper and Lower Galilee (p. 192).

14. A reference to Josephus' *Vita*.

15. The three north walls; see pp. 487–9.

16. In this translation, the Greek word *naos*, denoting the central shrine (for which *to hagion*, 'the holy place', is sometimes used as a

synonym), is rendered 'Sanctuary', and *hieron*, denoting the enclosure and everything within it, 'Temple'.

17. A recurrent theme from p. 314. Josephus is anxious to exonerate Titus of responsibility for the destruction of the Temple.

CHAPTER I : HEROD'S PREDECESSORS

1. Hellenistic rulers regularly received or claimed divine honours. Antiochus IV (175–163), one of the most powerful of the Seleucid dynasty of Syria, took the title Epiphanes, 'god made manifest', *c.* 171.

2. Literally 'the control of the whole of Syria', which is historical nonsense. Palestine, which is clearly meant, was one of three areas at various times called *Koile* (Coele), 'hollow', Syria. It appears that through similarity of sound *koile* was erroneously rendered into Aramaic as *kol*, 'whole', which was then translated back into Greek as 'the whole of Syria'.

3. In addition to personal rivalry, there was dissension between an orthodox party led by Onias and a Hellenizing party led by the Tobiad family, which had recently emerged and was prepared to use foreign aid to achieve its ends.

4. 167–164.

5. The story is given in full on pp. 406–7. On the Jewish settlement, cf. note 82 to p. 52.

6. Of a new fortress, Acra, 'the citadel', built by Antiochus to control Jerusalem.

7. Hence the name Hasmonaean for the dynasty which he established.

8. Nicknamed Maccabaeus, 'the hammer'. For much fuller accounts of the Maccabaean struggle for independence, see *AJ* xii–xiii and 1 Macc.

9. Rome was by this time the dominant power in the Mediterranean, to whom victims of aggression looked for help. The treaty (of which texts are given in *AJ* xii.417–18 and 1 Macc. 8.23–30, though neither can be taken as authentic) is usually dated 161, after Antiochus IV's death (below). It brought the Jews no practical help, however, against Syria.

10. One of many unidentified places mentioned in the *BJ*. They are not commented on in later notes.

11. In 161.

12. i.e. he renewed the treaty with Rome, *c.* 143 – necessary because a treaty lapsed with the death of the ruler who had made it.

13. An error: the current Syrian king was not Antiochus V, Epi-

phanes' son (p. 34), but Antiochus VI, infant son of the usurper Alexander Balas and nominal king, 145–138. In 150/49 Balas had appointed Jonathan both high priest and governor of Judaea – an important step towards Jewish independence.

14. Simon inherited his brother's dual position in 142. Joppa and Jamnia gave the Jews valuable access to the sea, and the expulsion of the Syrian garrison in 141 made them in effect politically independent.

15. Antiochus VII, king 138–129 after defeating Trypho's attempt to usurp the throne.

16. i.e. he was confirmed in the high priesthood which he already held. By a decree of the Jewish assembly dated 140 he also received the secular position of ethnarch (1 Macc. 14.27–47).

17. From the foundation of the Seleucid dynasty, which was of Macedonian origin, in 312.

18. In 135 or 134.

19. But Antiochus' attack on Jerusalem brought the Jews, in effect, temporarily back under Syrian control.

20. Antiochus' death on this campaign enabled the Jews to reassert their independence and resume territorial expansion.

21. The schismatic Samaritan temple on Mount Gerizim.

22. The capture of Adora and Marisa brought Idumaea (Edom) under Jewish control; its inhabitants were forcibly Judaized by the imposition of circumcision.

23. p. 81.

24. Antiochus VIII.

25. A necessary correction of the 'thirty-three' of the MSS.

26. In 104.

27. The first of Josephus' arithmetical errors. The exiles returned in 538.

28. The Feast of Tabernacles in October.

29. On the topography, buildings and defences of Jerusalem, see pp. 487–9.

30. The only reference in the *BJ* to the annexation of Galilee, which was forcibly Judaized like Idumaea.

31. See pp. 133–7.

32. pp. 82–3.

33. In 103.

34. Alexander Jannaeus. He married Aristobulus' widow, Alexandra Salome (p. 42), as Jewish law required a man to do if his brother died childless.

35. The capture of these two cities brought Peraea under Jewish rule.

36. Also Strato's Tower, which was in Jewish hands by Jannaeus'

death (*AJ* xiii.395), and probably Dora. The Jews now controlled the whole coastal strip from Mount Carmel to the Egyptian frontier.

37. The numerous non-Jews now under Jewish rule.

38. Demetrius III of Syria. The text here has no variants, but elsewhere his nickname is 'the Ready'!

39. Little reliance can be placed on any of Josephus' figures for armies and less on those for casualties and prisoners. The parallel account in *AJ* has even higher ones.

40. Not a normal Jewish method of execution – hence Josephus' protest at Jannaeus' 'impiety'.

41. Antiochus XII, *c.* 86–85, not actually the last Seleucid; Antiochus XIII succeeded and reigned until Rome annexed Syria in 64.

42. Ruler of Chalcis.

43. King of Nabataea.

44. Here denoting the Greco-Syrian area east of the upper Jordan; cf. note 2 to p. 33.

45. He also took Dium, Gadara, Hippus and Abila. Gerasa soon regained her independence.

46. This brought Gaulanitis under Jewish control. Jannaeus' kingdom was now of virtually the same extent as the Davidic kingdom.

47. In 76.

48. The appointment of a queen meant that political and religious power, united in the hands of the Hasmonaean high priests both before and after they had the title king, were now separated.

49. The party of the Pharisees (p. 137) had its roots in the opposition to the Hellenizing movement of the second century (note 3 to p. 33) which had led to the Maccabaean rising. But the increasing secularization of the later Hasmonaeans had caused a rift between the monarchy and the Pharisees which was now healed by Alexandra Salome.

50. In 69. Lucullus was the Roman commander in the war against Mithridates of Pontus and his ally Tigranes, who had invaded Syria. Cleopatra IV, expelled from Egypt, married four Syrian kings in turn.

51. Machaerus and others, some of which his mother had misguidedly put into his custody (*AJ* xiii.417).

52. pp. 81, 83.

53. In 67.

54. And high priest. Hyrcanus had reigned for only three months.

55. The father of Herod the Great; cf. p. 51. His later rise to power as Hyrcanus' chief minister and at times the effective ruler of the country resulted ultimately in the Hasmonaeans being supplanted by the dynasty of the Herods.

56. In 65. Pompey had taken over the command from Lucullus in 66. Scaurus, Metellus and Lollius were his subordinates.

57. In 64.

58. The predecessor of Herod's viaduct across the Valley of the Cheese-makers.

59. The defensive fosse in front of the north wall of the Temple enclosure.

60. The northern end of the Valley of the Cheese-makers – not a 'ravine' comparable with Gehenna or the Kidron; but Josephus uses this word for any valley.

61. *Chōma*, 'heaped-up earth', an artificial mound on which artillery was mounted, in this translation always rendered 'platform'.

62. In 63, probably about midsummer. In *AJ* xiv.66 the date is given as 'the day of the fast', i.e. the Day of Atonement in October. But all other chronological indications are against this (cf. note 14 to p. 74), and Josephus has probably misinterpreted a gentile source which put the capture on 'a fast day', meaning on a Sabbath, which gentiles falsely believed to be a fast day.

63. Only the Holy of Holies (here 'the Holy Place') was barred to everyone but the high priest, and it was empty. The lampstand etc. were in the main body of the Sanctuary (p. 304).

64. Hyrcanus was not allowed to become king, but he was apparently given the less prestigious title of ethnarch. He now owed his position to Rome and would retain it only at her pleasure: i.e. Palestine became a client kingdom.

65. This emphasized the country's dependence on Rome.

66. i.e. Pompey deprived the Jews of most of the non-Jewish terri-tory annexed by the Hasmonaeans, their most serious loss being that of the coastal cities. The Jewish realm was thus reduced to Judaea, Galilee, Samaritis (the name which distinguishes the district from the city of Samaria), and the part of Idumaea centred on Adora (that centred on Marisa being 'freed'). The Transjordanian cities were now linked with others in Syria as the Decapolis, the 'league of ten cities'.

67. Annexed by Pompey in 64.

68. After storming the Temple defences, Pompey evidently razed at least part of the city wall; p. 53.

69. In 57.

70. The re-fortification of the cities 'freed' by Pompey surrounded the Jews with a ring of powerful as well as hostile cities. Two prob-ably incorrect names are replaced by 'Dora' and 'Gaza'.

71. The generally accepted correction of 'Gadara' of the MSS.

72. Gabinius' division of the country into five apparently independ-ent administrative units, each ruled by a council ('an aristocracy'),

effectively deprived Hyrcanus of his powers as ethnarch. It is, however, not heard of again, and was possibly meant to be – as in fact it turned out to be – only temporary.

73. Ptolemy XI Auletes ('the Flute-player').

74. Many Jews resident in Egypt served in the Ptolemaic army, and the fact that they were entrusted with the vital frontier post at Pelusium testifies to their reliability; cf. note 82 below.

75. This probably means that the country was reunified and that Hyrcanus regained at least some of his secular powers, on which Antipater's own ambition to rule through him depended.

76. In 55. This blatant theft shows how illusory Jewish independence was. *AJ* xiv.105 puts the gold decorating the Temple at 8,000 talents.

77. A subordinate of Crassus, who took over the province on his death. Later, as one of the 'liberators' (the murderers of Julius Caesar), he was back in the East independently (pp. 56–9).

78. If Josephus ever kept this promise, the work has not survived.

79. In 49, at the start of the civil war.

80. Hyrcanus and Antipater, and Herod later, became adept at changing sides in the Roman civil war!

81. These minor princes were taking help to Caesar on his Alexandrian campaign in 48.

82. The Jewish settlement near the tip of the Delta (p. 33) had developed into a military colony responsible for the defence of the important road from Pelusium to Memphis.

83. Caesar travelled through Palestine in 47, en route for his campaign in Asia Minor ('I came, I saw, I conquered').

84. Since this was hereditary, the Jews later had a Roman citizen as king.

85. Documents issued by Caesar in the East show that Hyrcanus also recovered his position as ethnarch (*AJ* xiv.190–98). In addition Caesar restored Joppa, which gave the Jews the access to the sea that was essential for a return to economic prosperity and political importance, and regulated taxation.

CHAPTER 2: HEROD'S RISE TO POWER

1. The word here translated 'commissioner' is the normal Greek equivalent of 'procurator', on which see Appendix B. Possibly Antipater was responsible for the collection of the tribute payable to Rome.

2. Inaccurately used of Hyrcanus here and elsewhere.

3. About twenty-five. Note that he and Phasael were appointed by their father, not by Hyrcanus.

4. See Appendix A.

5. This episode was an attempt to reassert the rights of the Sanhedrin, in which alone capital jurisdiction was officially vested, against the growing Antipatrid power.

6. Sextus may have been acting *ultra vires*, but as a Roman citizen Herod was to some degree under Roman protection.

7. As military governor of the Decapolis and the city of Samaria, parts of the province of Syria (p. 48), Herod was now temporarily in the direct service of Rome.

8. In 46. Herod evidently returned home on his patron's death, to be 'sent' back almost at once.

9. In 44. He had effectively become supreme in Rome after Pharsalus, 48.

10. In Josephus always the town north-west of Jerusalem, except on p. 391, the sole reference to the village of Luke 24.13.

11. i.e., as the Caesarian cause now seemed lost in the East, Antipater and Hyrcanus hastily transferred their allegiance to the 'liberators'. With Cassius' requisition cf. Crassus' action (p. 51).

12. In 43. Josephus regularly calls Octavian, Julius Caesar's great-nephew and adopted son and later the emperor Augustus, 'Caesar'; he rarely uses 'Augustus' or its Greek equivalent, 'Sebastos'.

13. i.e. Cassius trusted Herod and his father enough to reappoint him to the post which he had held under Sextus Caesar ('Coele Syria' being substituted here, from *AJ* xiv.280, for the certainly incorrect 'all Syria' of the text; see note 2 to p. 33).

14. A dubious statement: Rome had no reason to contemplate putting Herod over his father's head.

15. In the summer of 43. The East was now wholly in the control of the 'liberators'.

16. To Greece, to face Caesar's avengers at the battle of Philippi in 42.

17. p. 51.

18. The son of the marriage between Hyrcanus' only child, Alexandra, and one of the sons of his brother Aristobulus, uniting the two sides of the family, could be expected to be acceptable as a successor to both Hasmonaean factions. But if Hyrcanus died before that boy came of age, a regent would be needed, and the obvious candidate would be the husband of the boy's elder sister; that was to be Herod. The actual marriage was postponed till 37 (p. 73).

19. p. 49.

20. In 40. A satrap was governor of a section of the Parthian empire.

21. To Parthia, Rome's great enemy, who had used Rome's distraction over the civil war as an opportunity to overrun the province of

Syria, an anti-Roman king in Palestine would be an asset. But by accepting Parthian aid Antigonus shortsightedly forfeited all hope of ever securing Roman recognition for himself (cf. p. 64).

22. Presumably the cup-bearer. Pacorus the prince would have negotiated with Phasael and not asked him to go and meet Barzapharnes (below).

23. An error for Alexandra, mother of Herod's fiancée Mariamme.

24. Herod's ancestral home and the only part of Palestine not in the hands of Antigonus' partisans.

25. The MSS. give 'brothers', which cannot stand with 'the youngest of his brothers' below. Only one sister is known, Salome.

26. p. 83.

27. The successor of Aretas. Antipater's relations with Malchus have not been mentioned before.

28. His plan was now to go to Rome. The normal route was by ship from Alexandria.

29. A fabrication for Herod's glory? At this time, the winter of 40–39, no campaign was imminent.

30. Voyages were made outside the sailing season, 10 March–11 November, only in cases of extreme urgency.

31. Antony and Octavian had come to blows during 40. News of the pact made between them by the treaty of Brundisium in October had evidently not yet reached the East.

32. King, not merely ethnarch, to compensate for the fact that as an Idumaean Herod could never be high priest and to put him on a level with the usurping 'king' Antigonus in his struggle for the throne.

33. Julius Caesar, his adoptive father.

34. An incongruous inauguration for the reign of a king of the Jews! But at heart Herod, an Idumaean, was more a pagan than a Jew, as his conduct throughout his reign was to show. The Idumaeans were still regarded by the Jews as semi-foreigners, and Herod would inevitably be an unpopular ruler – an advantage from the Roman point of view, since he could be relied on for loyalty to the power on which his throne depended.

35. The resolution of the Senate officially making the appointment, which Antony could only recommend.

CHAPTER 3: HEROD MASTER OF PALESTINE

1. He was holding Idumaea for Herod (p. 62).

2. In 39. In two years of campaigns he drove the Parthians out of Syria.

3. See note 85 to p. 52. In Joppa his enemies also controlled the country's only access to the sea.

4. 39–38.

5. A tribute to Herod's governorship of Samaria and Coele Syria in 46 (p. 55).

6. p. 54.

7. In 38. Antigonus' cause was now effectively lost.

8. The capital of the kingdom of Commagene west of the upper Euphrates, an ally of Parthia.

9. An error. Antony spent the winter of 38–37 in Athens, his head-quarters at the time, with his legal wife.

10. A village about 20 miles north of Jerusalem, substituted here from *AJ* xiv.458 for the geographically impossible 'Cana' (Galilee) of the MSS.

11. In the spring of 37. The same Greek word means 'winter' and 'storm', and this phrase could equally well be rendered 'when the winter ended'.

12. p. 59.

13. Testimony to the strength of the rebuilt fortifications (p. 53). It was by now the summer (*AJ* xiv.473).

14. In the fuller account in *AJ* xiv.470–80 Herod's forces take six weeks after completing the earthworks to storm the Lower City and the outer court of the Temple and a further two to storm the Upper City to get possession of the inner courts. The fall of the city is put on the anniversary of the capture by Pompey (ibid. 487, with the 'third month' perhaps an error for the 'third year' of the Olympiad mentioned there).

15. The feminine form of the name.

16. Gentile gifts to the Temple were welcomed; cf. pp. 164, 247–8, 322, 355.

17. He is usually known as Herod the Great, but the epithet so trans-lated occurs only once, in a genealogical passage (*AJ* xviii.130–42), where it probably means merely 'the elder', distinguishing the king from other members of the family with the same name. It does not appear on his coins as a title.

18. This deprived the Jews once more of their only port, Joppa.

19. In 34.

20. In 32.

21. Malchus also had leased back territory which Antony had given to Cleopatra, with Herod standing surety for his rent – an obvious source of friction if, as soon happened, Malchus fell into arrears (*AJ* xv.92–4, 106–8).

22. A minor textual correction of a place-name that makes no sense.

23. In 31. The count is here not from Herod's appointment in 40 but from 37, when he effectively became king. Both counts were apparently used, and some of the chronological confusions in Josephus' narrative can be explained by a dual system of dating.

24. On the speeches in Josephus' works, see the Introduction, pp. 23–4. In the parallel account in *AJ* xv.127–46 Herod is provided with a quite different and much longer speech.

25. By the conventions of ancient warfare envoys were sacrosanct, and to molest them was sacrilege.

26. This position is obscure – Malchus remained king – and is never mentioned again.

27. A flatteringly exaggerated assessment of Herod's prestige!

28. Josephus' accounts here and in *AJ* xv.187–93 of a private interview are presumably based on Herod's *Memoirs*, to which he had access (*AJ* xv.174).

29. Can we really believe that Herod gave Antony this advice?

30. Herod could well claim Octavian's trust. Like his father, he had shown that he would loyally support whatever Roman warlord was currently in the ascendant.

31. They had been training in Asia Minor for service under Antony. Didius, governor of Syria, intercepted them on their way to Egypt after Actium.

32. In 30. Note that Herod's grand gesture was made outside his kingdom.

33. i.e. Herod regained much of the territory lost in 63, as well as Joppa, regained in 47 but lost to Cleopatra.

34. It was probably now that Nicolas of Damascus, tutor to Cleopatra's children, entered Herod's court to become his lifelong friend and counsellor and historian of his reign. Josephus depends heavily on his work.

35. In 23. The four-yearly games in honour of the victory at Actium provided a system of dating (very rarely used), apparently from September, 27.

36. Lysanias of Chalcis (p. 60) had been executed by Antony on a charge of collusion with Parthia brought by Cleopatra (*AJ* xv.92), and Octavian had allowed his son Zenodorus to rule his father's Trans-jordanian territories.

37. In 20. This patently absurd statement may conceal an appointment over the Decapolis, with 'all Syria' an error for Coele Syria (cf. note 2 to p. 33); or it may mean that Herod became financial adviser to the governor of Syria, though there is no record of his ever acting in that capacity.

38. Also in 20 Paneas, Ulatha and Gaulanitis.

39. Another flattering exaggeration. M. Vipsanius Agrippa was Augustus' closest friend and adviser, and also his son-in-law, till his death in 12 B.C.

40. 23, Herod's fifteenth year counted from 37 and his eighteenth (*AJ* xv.380) counted from 40; see note 23 to p. 76.

41. Herod's new Temple, the Antonia (dated by its name to before Antony's defeat at Actium), and his Palace, built in the north-west angle of the city wall to supersede the Hasmonaean Palace, are described fully on pp. 301–6.

42. The worship of a ruler as divine or semi-divine had long been the regular expression of loyalty, affection etc. in the East. Such worship was offered to Augustus spontaneously, and he then introduced the practice into the West. Herod's inclusion of a temple of the imperial cult in the new city-fortress on the site of the former Samaria showed that it was to be Greco-Syrian in character.

43. The feminine form of the adjective *sebastos*, the Greek equivalent of *augustus*, 'more than human'. This title was bestowed on Octavian in 27 as a name, in recognition of his achievement in restoring peace. Coins of Sebaste use an era running from 27 or 26.

44. Capital of the largely non-Jewish district of Paneas, and later renamed Caesarea Philippi (p. 138).

45. p. 231.

46. p. 83.

47. An exaggeration. Despite his desire to Hellenize his kingdom, Herod seems to have refrained from any attempt to impose emperor-worship on the predominantly Jewish areas.

48. Syria? See p. 84.

49. A temple of the imperial cult.

50. Nero Claudius Drusus, younger son of Livia, Augustus' second wife, and brother of the future emperor Tiberius. Traces of the great mole still survive.

51. One of the Seven Wonders of the World.

52. The imperial cult officially honoured the city of Rome personified as a goddess by the side of the emperor.

53. The provision of Greco-Roman cultural amenities (including a stadium; p. 138) shows that Caesarea was designed as a gentile city. But many Jews also settled there, with resultant friction (pp. 148, 150–51). The inaugural festival, here loosely dated to 12–8 B.C., seems from other confused evidence to have been held in 12.

54. No such gate is mentioned in the description of the Temple (pp. 302–3).

55. p. 300.

56. Herodium has been excavated. The palace sunk into the top of

the hill can be seen, and four reservoirs, the aqueduct, and traces of the town on the lower slopes have been found. Herod also strengthened the Hasmonaean fortresses of Masada (pp. 395–6), Machaerus (pp. 387–8), Alexandreum and Hyrcania, providing them also with palaces as comfortable refuges if he were ever driven from Jerusalem by unpopularity.

57. The official in charge originally of the Gymnasium (the cultural centre) of a Hellenistic city, but by this time of public works in general.

58. These lavish gifts, an outlet for the ostentation which Herod could not show among his Jewish subjects and a way of securing prestige among his gentile neighbours, are evidence of the economic prosperity of Palestine.

59. Probably in 12, on his second visit as king (p. 88; his first, in 16, is not mentioned in the *BJ*).

CHAPTER 4: HEROD'S MURDER OF MARIAMME AND HER CHILDREN

1. The quarrels in Herod's family occupy a disproportionate amount of space in Josephus' narratives, here and in the *AJ*.

2. pp. 59, 73.

3. In 40.

4. Herod had invited Hyrcanus back to Palestine soon after 37 'for auld lang syne' (*AJ* xv.11–21) – and as a safeguard against Parthia setting him up as a pretender. He executed him on a false charge of treason (ibid. 161–78) before going to meet Octavian after Actium; for he could not be sure that Octavian would not reinstate him in revenge for Herod's support of Antony.

5. cf. note 10 to p. 88.

6. In 36. Jonathan, also called Aristobulus, was by 37 the obvious candidate for the vacant high priesthood, as the only surviving male Hasmonaean (Hyrcanus being disqualified; p. 63). For fear lest his appointment should invite a coup to make him king, Herod had chosen an outsider, but almost immediately had been forced by pressure from the boy's mother, Alexandra, backed by Cleopatra, to give Jonathan the post. The demonstration had shown that pro-Hasmonaean feeling was as strong as he had feared.

7. See note 36 to p. 80.

8. In 29. But the story given here is more or less that told in *AJ* xv.67–73, 80–87 concerning Herod's absence on a visit to Antony in Syria in 35, which ends with the execution of Joseph. According to *AJ* xv.202–36, when Herod went to meet Octavian after Actium, the same instructions were given to a friend, who similarly betrayed

them and lost his life; and Salome then used Mariamme's increasing estrangement from Herod to trump up a charge that she was planning to poison him.

9. The immediate effect of the remorse which was to warp his personality for the rest of his life was a serious nervous and physical breakdown (*AJ* xv.240–46).

10. Alexander and Aristobulus were in Rome *c.* 23–*c.* 16. Their education at the imperial court not only instilled in them the gentile outlook which would further Herod's aim of Hellenizing his kingdom, but also gave the king a useful means of maintaining personal contact with Augustus.

11. In 14.

12. In 23 Augustus had given Herod the right, not normally granted to client kings, of nominating his successor (*AJ* xv.343).

13. In 13, accompanying Agrippa (note 39 to p. 81) on his return from a command in the East.

14. In 12. Herod may not have dared, as a client king, to try sons who were still possible successors on a capital charge himself.

15. From Rome Antipater had run a campaign of slander against his half-brothers which had convinced Herod that they were plotting against him (*AJ* xvi.87–9).

16. i.e. his right to nominate his successor was confirmed.

17. No territorial division between the three sons is given in this will, but *AJ* xvi.133 vaguely suggests that Mariamme's sons were to be subordinate to Antipater in some way.

18. Grades in the hierarchy of a Hellenistic court. Some Hellenistic features had been gradually introduced into the Hasmonaean monarchy, and Herod had accelerated the process.

19. Had he?

20. The plural is a slip; only Pheroras was still alive.

21. Temenus was an obscure son of Hercules. Darius was the Persian king who had led the attack on Greece in 490.

22. Ten in all, and after Mariamme I's death not in succession (p. 104). Polygamy, though no longer the norm, was still permitted, and the requirement to marry the widow of a deceased, childless brother implied it: a man would hardly remain celibate just in case he had to inherit a brother's relict!

23. A third visit (cf. note 59 to p. 84)? The question is controversial, and this may be an error by Josephus or a reference to an unfulfilled intention.

24. Pheroras had married Mariamme's younger sister in the 20s. In 20 he had received the subordinate but responsible post of tetrarch of Peraea, to lighten Herod's administrative load.

25. A son of Phasael. Probably there is confusion or textual corruption here and the reference should be to Phasael's own murder by the Parthians (p. 63).

26. Mariamme I.

27. See note 8 to p. 87 for Joseph. Costobar was an Idumaean noble whom Herod had appointed governor of Idumaea; Salome divorced him when he was found to be plotting a political breakaway, perhaps in the mid 20s (*AJ* xv.253–66).

28. Some time before 12 Syllaeus, the effective ruler of Nabataea since Malchus had been succeeded by the incompetent Obodas *c*. 30, had visited Herod and fallen in love with Salome; but because he could not agree to Herod's price for her hand – circumcision and the acceptance of Judaism – he had become his bitter enemy (*AJ* xvi.220–25).

29. Presumably several years have now passed since the trial in Rome in 12. The precise chronology of the family quarrels of Herod's last years is not always clear, but it is less important than the vivid picture of steadily deteriorating relationships.

30. Apparently Alexander did not in fact go to Rome.

31. Actually their great-grandfather.

32. pp. 88–9.

33. Again, great-grandfather.

34. In the next paragraph 'Volumnius the procurator' appears. Probably there is no error of title here and two men of the same name are involved. Herod could hardly have sent an imperial procurator on an errand, but he had Romans – or at any rate men with Roman names – among his officers (see pp. 99, 126).

35. C. Sentius Saturninus, legate (governor; see Appendix B) of Syria 10/9–7/6 B.C. His 'legates' (only two in all, below) were members of his staff.

36. Executed in Syria (p. 51).

37. In 7 or thereabouts.

CHAPTER 5: HEROD'S MURDER OF HIS HEIR, AND DEATH

1. King of Chalcis from 41 (p. 143).

2. See pp. 139, 142–3.

3. Mother of the Salome who asked for 'the head of John the Baptist on a charger'.

4. In *c*. 23 Herod had married a second Mariamme, whose father he had then appointed high priest (*AJ* xv.319–22). Her only child, though nominated for the succession at one point (pp. 106, 108, 109), attained no historical importance.

5. p. 93.

6. After the execution of Mariamme I.

7. Mariamme I.

8. According to *AJ* xvii.10 Livia persuaded Salome that it would be politic to give Syllaeus up!

9. Mariamme I.

10. The Pharisees, sticklers for the Law (p. 137), were consistently opposed to Herod's secular rule. The first confrontation had occurred *c.* 20, when Herod had instituted an oath of loyalty to himself, a feature of Hellenistic monarchy, but had exempted the Pharisees because of their conscientious objections (*AJ* xv.368–70). More recently he had demanded an oath of loyalty to himself and Augustus, and, when the Pharisees again refused, had imposed a fine, which Pheroras' wife had paid (*AJ* xvii.41–2).

11. Between 12 and 9 Herod had had to take measures against Nabataean raids on his territory, and in so doing had incurred Augustus' displeasure, even though he had not overstepped his powers by using military force; Nicolas of Damascus (note 34 to p. 80) had eventually gone to Rome and cleared up what may have been basically a mere misunderstanding (*AJ* xvi.271–99, 335–55).

12. Aretas IV, who succeeded Obodas *c.* 9. This obscure paragraph is of little importance.

13. One of Hercules' Twelve Labours was the destruction of the hydra of Lerna, a many-headed water snake. When one head was crushed, two grew in its place.

14. Mariamme II was, not surprisingly, divorced. Her father could not survive her disgrace and lost his post (*AJ* xvii.78).

15. Half-brothers, with different mothers. Now possible heirs, they were being educated at the imperial court, as Mariamme I's sons had been (p. 86).

16. Voyages between Italy and Syria were made either via Alexandria or, as here, via the Aegean and the south coast of Asia Minor.

17. The full name of Herod's new city (pp. 82–3) was 'Caesarea beside the Augustan Harbour'.

18. P. Quintilius Varus (later of Teutoberg Forest notoriety), legate 7/6–4 as successor to Saturninus, and about to play the same role in Antipater's trial as his predecessor had in that of Alexander and Aristobulus.

19. According to *AJ* xvii.92, this is his first wife, daughter of the Hasmonaean Antigonus, whom he had married in the 30s, not his new wife (p. 105).

20. See note 34 to p. 80.

21. This suggests that there had recently been further trouble from

the Nabataeans (cf. note 11 to p. 106), but nothing is known of it or of Antipater's part in dealing with it.

22. 'Lover of his father' – a type of title fashionable among Hellenistic dynasties.

23. Presumably Herod needed Augustus' authorization to execute his heir; cf. note 14 to p. 88.

24. p. 99.

25. Details on p. 117.

26. Perhaps in the technical sense of the emperor's *consilium* (note 8 to p. 122), also known as his *amici*, 'friends'.

27. Literally 'sophists', Josephus' regular term for rabbi.

28. All representations of the human form were forbidden by Jewish law, even in secular contexts, but the Second Commandment was interpreted as forbidding only 'graven images' designed for worship, and purely decorative animal figures and the like had been allowed even in Solomon's Temple. Herod's eagle evidently had some connotation, possibly religious, offensive in Jewish eyes, but what it was is conjectural.

29. Not a normal Jewish form of execution. Herod also deposed the high priest 'as being partly to blame for the incident' (*AJ* xvii.164).

30. Of the various diagnoses suggested for Herod's complaint, arteriosclerosis seems the most convincing.

31. Literally 'Lake Asphaltitis' (pp. 272–3).

32. Jericho had an amphitheatre also (p. 118). Herod had attempted to introduce his Jewish subjects to Greco-Roman cultural amenities, and even built a theatre, an amphitheatre and a hippodrome in Jerusalem (*AJ* xv.268; and below, p. 124).

33. If this is true, it harmonizes with the ferocious punishment of the removers of the eagle as evidence that Herod's physical condition was causing acute mental instability. But, like the 'Massacre of the Innocents' (Matthew 2.16), it may be no more than a legend of the type invented posthumously to blacken the names of tyrants.

34. Philip also was nominated a tetrarch (below). i.e. he and Antipas were to be subordinate rulers under Archelaus, who would control the whole country as king.

35. Herod died shortly before the Passover (p. 121) in 4 B.C.

36. Josephus actually says thirty-four and thirty-seven years. In the East the period, however short, from a king's accession to the New Year counted as his first year; subsequent regnal years, except the last, were calendar years. This system often gives a count one year higher than our reckoning.

37. Of Galilee and Peraea.

38. Foreign mercenaries in service under Herod; for the Gauls see p. 80.

39. The grave has not been found.

CHAPTER 6: THE RISE AND FALL OF ARCHELAUS

1. Literally merely 'duties', but explained in *AJ* xvii.205 as 'duties levied on public purchases and sales and exacted ruthlessly'.

2. The successor of the high priest deposed after the eagle episode (note 29 to p. 117) was understandably regarded as the tool of the tyrant. But there was probably also a hope that under a new king the increasingly secularized post might recover its predominantly spiritual character.

3. On Herod's army see Appendix B.

4. This apparently means that from Herod's Palace the cavalry skirted round the outside of the north wall of the city to reach the Temple.

5. Perhaps the successor of Volumnius (p. 100). As a financial official he evidently assumed that this was his responsibility.

6. p. 115.

7. Presumably this meant a return to theocracy – rule by a high priest instead of a secular king – under Roman oversight.

8. A meeting of the emperor's *consilium* or privy council. Gaius, then aged twenty, and his younger brother had been adopted as sons by their grandfather and designated his heirs.

9. i.e. since Augustus had allowed Herod to nominate his successor, opposition to his nominee was tantamount to opposition to the emperor, which it was Archelaus' duty to put down.

10. See note 32 to p. 117.

11. Herod's non-mercenary troops were, significantly, not Jews; cf. Appendix B.

12. p. 54.

13. Josephus means the district, Samaritis.

14. Sebaste.

15. In Jewish tradition the 'war of Varus' later came to rank with the wars of A.D. 66–70 and 132–5.

16. See note 7 to p. 122.

17. The Jewish community in Rome, probably dating back at least to the mid-second century B.C., had been vastly increased by the thousands of prisoners captured by Pompey in 63, taken to Rome to walk in his triumph, and sold into slavery there.

18. See note 8 to p. 122.

19. A piece of anti-Herodian nonsense.

20. An error. The Exile had ended with Cyrus' defeat of Babylon in 538, fifty years before Xerxes' reign.

21. These anti-monarchists however presumably wanted some degree of internal autonomy under a high priest; cf. the earlier request (note 7 to p. 122).

22. Antipas and Philip were to be independent of Archelaus, however, not subordinate as in Herod's will (note 34 to p. 118). 'Paneas' is restored for an unintelligible place-name in the MSS. Zenodorus' former territory (note 36 to p. 80) is called Ituraea in Luke 3.1, a term actually covering territory extending further north than that ruled by Herod or his son.

23. These three cities (with the old name of Caesarea used anachronistically) are mentioned because, although in Archelaus' territory, they had Greek-style municipal autonomy.

24. The only coastal city that never came under Jewish rule.

25. The Greek name for Puteoli on the north of the bay of Naples, the main port for Rome (the Tiber not being navigable by large boats). This is the earliest evidence for a settlement of Jews there, almost certainly traders.

26. This episode is evidence for the survival of strong pro-Hasmonaean feeling.

27. Actually the tenth, A.D. 6 (AJ xvii.342, with, of course, ten cornears instead of nine, below). Josephus' information about Herod's three successors is very scanty, probably because Nicolas of Damascus, his main source for Herod's reign, apparently retired to Rome at Herod's death.

28. pp. 133–7.

29. Probably the daughter of his half-brother Aristobulus (p. 103), previously married to his half-brother Antipater (p. 105).

30. In Jewish law, marriage to a dead husband's brother (in this case only a half-brother) was incestuous if there was issue of the first marriage (though obligatory if there was not). This tale may be a posthumous invention emanating from outraged orthodox feeling.

CHAPTER 7: JUDAEA UNDER ROMAN RULE

1. Josephus generally, as here, uses the Greek word which normally translates the Latin 'procurator' for the governors of the province of Judaea from A.D. 6; see Appendix B.

2. Capital jurisdiction in political cases belonged to all provincial

governors. The question of Jewish powers of capital punishment in religious cases (raised by the accounts of Christ's trial) is another matter, and a controversial one.

3. On his rising and his sect, see Appendix A.

4. Almost certainly Qumran was one (Appendix E).

5. Or 'offer prayers to it (the sun) as if beseeching it to rise', rather surprisingly implying sun-worship. But cf. their extraordinary respect for 'the rays of the god' (p. 136).

6. Probably for use as charms or amulets.

7. Its use is given on p. 136.

8. Moses.

9. The lowest three are presumably the novices passing through the three years of probation (above).

10. Josephus' account of the war of 66–70 contains no reference to Roman attacks on the Essenes, or indeed to the Essenes themselves except for the rather surprising appointment of one of them as a military commander (p. 180).

11. Hesiod, *Works and Days* 169 ff.; Pindar, *Olymp.* 2, 77 ff.

12. Notorious sinners who suffered picturesque punishments to fit their crimes.

13. The Greek here makes little sense. This suggestion of a possible meaning is based on the Latin translation of Josephus ascribed to the fourth-century writer Rufinus.

14. They stood for strict adherence to the law of Moses in every particular. The Pharisaic scholars and teachers, the rabbis, by discussion and interpretation of the basic law produced a vast quantity of traditional, oral law to supplement it and regulate every aspect of daily life.

15. cf. p. 219, where again acceptance of the doctrine of the transmigration of souls (i.e. the reincarnation of the dead for further lives on earth) held by the Greek philosophers Pythagoras and Plato is attributed to the Pharisees.

16. The Sadducees were the wealthy aristocracy from whom the high priests were drawn.

17. This happened under Coponius' successor, who was in office *c.* 9–12. The toparchy of which Jamnia was the administrative centre is meant. Livia became 'Julia' when adopted into the Julian family under Augustus' will.

18. Reckoned from Julius Caesar's death in 44. A more logical count would be from the battle of Actium.

19. Three of these foundations date from Augustus' lifetime. Coins struck (in all probability) in Caesarea Philippi are dated from 2 B.C.; the renaming of Bethsaida as Julias after Augustus' daughter Julia

(*AJ* xviii.28) must have occurred before her exile in 2 B.C.; and Antipas' Julias, formerly Betharamatha (ibid. 27), was originally 'Livias'.

20. Pontius Pilatus, in 26, as the fifth governor.

21. Caesarea was the Roman administrative and military head-quarters, but the Antonia in Jerusalem was also garrisoned. A standard was a pole bearing circular plaques, usually about four. The explanation of the episode probably is that previously, out of respect for Jewish feelings, units with aniconic standards had been stationed there, but that Pilate had substituted one with standards bearing portraits of the emperor – 'graven images' of religious significance. (In fact *all* Roman military standards were objects of cult – p. 363 – and not merely those bearing imperial portraits.)

22. i.e. the unit was replaced; standards and unit were inseparable.

23. The fund raised by the Temple-tax – half a shekel or two drachmas, its equivalent in Greek currency (p. 391), paid annually by all adult male Jews throughout the world; cf. Matthew 27.6; Mark 7.11. When the upkeep of the Temple had been met from it, the surplus could be used on the fabric of the city. Pilate may have taken more than the surplus, or he may have appropriated it without permission.

24. Only half this length in *AJ* xviii.60, and even that may be an exaggeration. An aqueduct traced for about 12 miles from south-west of Bethlehem may be Pilate's.

25. Luke 13.1 may refer to this episode. Josephus here abandons Pilate without reference to the episode which ended his governorship late in 36 (note 61 to p. 146).

26. In the very full account of Agrippa's career in *AJ* xviii.143-256, the purpose of his return in 36 (ibid. 126) to Rome, where he had lived from childhood until 23, is merely to restore his fallen fortunes. His successful attack on Herod Antipas came later (see below).

27. Great-grandson of Augustus and Tiberius' only surviving great-nephew. Aged twenty-five, he was clearly a more promising candidate for the throne than the only other possibility, Tiberius' teenage grandson.

28. In March, 37.

29. In 34.

30. In 40. The charges were complicity in a plot against Tiberius in 31 and recent treasonable dealings with Parthia (*AJ* xviii.250-52).

31. Gaius' self-deification was a very different matter from the voluntary offering of divine honours to Augustus. His attack on the Temple is here implied to be an act of retaliation for the Jews' refusal to accept it. In the much fuller, and in detail very different, account given by Philo of Alexandria (*Leg.* 186-348) it is his revenge for the Jews' destruction of an altar of the imperial cult built by the gentile minority

in Jamnia, probably in the winter of 39–40. The erection of a statue of Gaius (singular in Philo and in *AJ* xviii.261–309) in the guise of Zeus (*Leg.* 346) would have turned the Temple into a temple of the imperial cult.

32. P. Petronius, legate of Syria, 39–42. The legate of Syria with his four legions had oversight over the province of Judaea with its junior governor and very small garrison for the whole period 6–66, and could intervene there spontaneously (p. 150), on request (p. 145), or, as here, on instructions from Rome.

33. But politically in the province of Syria.

34. The capital of Antipas' tetrarchy. (He himself was in Rome; see above.) The proposed outrage affected Galilaean Jews no less than Judaean, but Petronius may have hoped that he could calm the situation down more easily at a distance than in Jerusalem on the site of the proposed outrage.

35. Jewish law allowed sacrifice for temporal overlords, and since A.D. 6 (or perhaps from the time of Herod) two lambs and a bull had been offered daily for the emperor.

36. Late autumn, when the rains began. But Philo synchronizes the demonstrations with the grain-harvest in the early summer (*Leg.* 249), and this, not Josephus' date, seems to be correct, since the news of the episode reached a Jewish delegation from Alexandria in Italy in about August.

37. This fairy-tale ending, chronologically incompatible with demonstrations in the early summer (since Gaius did not die till January 41), is irreconcilable with Philo's version, in which Agrippa persuades Gaius, by argument and the citing of imperial precedents for respecting the Jewish religion, to rescind his order.

38. The cohorts of the praetorian guard, units created by Augustus to serve, *inter alia*, as the imperial bodyguard. After the murder of Gaius some guards roaming through the palace are said to have found Claudius, his uncle, and declared him emperor.

39. i.e. to revert to republican government – an unrealistic proposal.

40. p. 139. He was remaining over the winter, till the sailing season opened in March.

41. The praetorian camp just outside Rome, to which the guards had taken their nominee for safety. Agrippa had been a friend of Claudius since the days when he had lived in Rome, and Claudius' mother had given him valuable help on several occasions.

42. A stylistic variation for 'senators'. The ancient division between patricians and plebeians meant virtually nothing now, and many senators were plebeians.

43. The account of Agrippa's part in Claudius' elevation to the throne

in *AJ* xix.236–71 differs considerably from this one, making Agrippa take the initiative; and the story as a whole, clearly a Jewish tradition glorifying Agrippa, does not harmonize with the Roman tradition. For discussion see M. V. Scrammuzza, *The Emperor Claudius*, 1940, 51–9.

44. i.e. the province of Judaea was disbanded and added to Agrippa's existing kingdom. Josephus here forgets that he had ruled Philip's former territory since 37 (p. 139).

45. See pp. 299, 488–9. It was completed in 66–7 (pp. 179, 188).

46. In 44; *AJ* xix.343–50 and Acts 12. 20–23 give the story.

47. The new province comprised Antipas' former territory of Galilee and Peraea as well as the old province, though not the northern territories of Trachonitis etc., which were probably administered with Syria till 53 (p. 146).

48. 44–6 and 46–8 respectively. Tiberius Julius Alexander was an apostate Alexandrian Jew; cf. the Introduction, p. 18. The few incidents recorded in *AJ* xx.2–14, 97–103, under these two governors give a rather less rosy picture than this.

49. Tigranes IV and V, under Augustus and Nero respectively.

50. Herod died in 48, but the dating of the start of the revolt in May 66 to Agrippa II's seventeenth year (p. 150) gives an interregnum of a year or so before his appointment to Chalcis.

51. 48–52.

52. The figure is 20,000 in *AJ* xx.112 – also an exaggeration, but evidence that it was a serious episode.

53. See Appendix A. This is their first appearance in the province in the *BJ*. But trouble from them is recorded under Fadus and Alexander (*AJ* xx.5, 102), and before that there was Barabbas.

54. Having been bribed by the Samaritans not to interfere, according to *AJ* xx.119.

55. And also four of his five infantry units (*AJ* xx.122). The title 'Sebasteni' could be a translation of 'Augustans' (see note 43 to p. 81) or could refer to the city from which the unit was originally recruited (Appendix B).

56. See note 32 to p. 140.

57. Jonathan had been high priest for a few months back in 37, but ex-high priests retained the title.

58. Probably the current high priest.

59. Captain of the Temple (*AJ* xx.131), second-in-command to the high priest.

60. A new character in the story, though 'the' implies a previous mention and his punishment (below) implies a heinous crime.

61. In 52, the date given (AJ xx.137) in connection with the appointment of Felix (below). The end of Pilate's career had been identical (AJ xviii. 85–9) – dismissal by the legate of Syria in response to a complaint by his subjects.

62. One of the group of freedmen very powerful at Claudius' court. His influence is clear in this almost unprecedented appointment of a freedman to a provincial post.

63. In 53. Varus and his domains are obscure.

64. Claudius died in October 54. Agrippina, his niece and fourth wife, was the mother of Nero by a previous marriage.

65. His step-brother, Britannicus.

66. Notably Tacitus, *Annals* xiii–xvi, and Suetonius.

67. Herod of Chalcis.

68. i.e. he confirmed Felix in his post, which had officially been terminated by the death of Claudius who had appointed him.

69. See Appendix A.

70. p. 145. The nomination of the high priests, in the procurators' hands 6–41, had been given to Herod of Chalcis in 44 (AJ xx.15–16) and had passed to Agrippa II in 48. Both naturally found it politic to choose men likely to be acceptable to Rome – and therefore unpopular with the nationalists.

71. False messiahs pursued the same nationalist ends as the terrorists but by different methods (Appendix A). The earliest, Theudas, had appeared under Fadus and been put down in the same way (AJ xx.97–8). If he is the Theudas of Acts 5.36, the reference is an anachronistic insertion into a speech delivered years earlier.

72. A rather surprising description of auxiliaries, who were less heavily armed than legionaries.

73. St Paul was later mistaken for this man (Acts 21.38, where his followers more credibly number 4,000).

74. pp. 82–3. It appears that the Jewish settlers were now claiming equality of citizen-rights with the Greco-Syrian citizen-body, who wanted to keep them in the inferior position of aliens with only the right of residence.

75. This may mean recruitment from Syria into the units still called 'Sebastenians' (note 55 to p. 145).

CHAPTER 8: WAR CLOUDS

1. 58/9–62.

2. 62–4. He is named in connection with an episode dated October 62 (pp. 361–2).

3. The Greek has two words similarly unconnected etymologically but alike in sound.

4. The picture given of Albinus in *AJ* xx.204-10, 213-15, is rather less black than this, suggesting an inability to cope with a deteriorating situation rather than corruption.

5. 64-6. At this point Josephus closes the *AJ* with a general paragraph on Florus' oppressive administration.

6. Legate of Syria 65/6-67. On his visit cf. note 32 to p. 140.

7. Cestius made a rough calculation of the adult male population (pp. 371-2); the figures given both there and here are impossibly high even when the city was crammed with pilgrims.

8. In 66. Josephus uses the Macedonian calendar for his narrative of the war. Appendix D gives the approximate modern equivalents.

9. The sting of this parody of a Jewish sacrifice lay in the fact that Leviticus 14.1-7 prescribed the offering of a bird in an earthenware vessel for a cleansed leper – a reference to the anti-Semitic version of the Exodus story which made the Jews lepers, ejected from Egypt.

10. It is hard to see why Florus treated the rescuing of sacred objects from possible desecration as an offence.

11. A single cohort, it appears (p. 155) – presumably an infantry unit with some cavalry attached.

12. Though the word is the same as that translated previously as 'high priest', and though ex-high priests kept their title (p. 145), the men so designated during the war often seem to be a group much larger than could comprise only ex-high priests. A different translation implying senior members of the priestly class therefore seems appropriate in many places.

13. In the Upper City.

14. It is interesting to find Jews of Jerusalem, at this fairly early date, with Roman citizenship (which legally exempted them from degrading punishments) and even equestrian status.

15. The former procurator of Judaea (p. 143), technically 'prefect' of Egypt.

16. The Hasmonaean Palace, used by Agrippa II on his visits to Jerusalem (p. 156).

17. The Nazarite vow; cf. Acts 21.23-6.

18. The only definite evidence for a garrison in Herod's Palace, the procurator's residence, as well as in the Antonia; but such a stronghold is not likely to have been undefended even before the crisis of 66.

19. i.e. one of the two just arrived, not the one which Florus had brought with him (p. 151).

20. Literally 'from the permitted area', the area outside the balustrade

marking off the inner courts (p. 302), sometimes called (without ancient authority) the Court of the Gentiles. Other cases of Romans paying their respects to the Temple are recorded; cf. the general statements on pp. 164–5, 247–8, 322.

21. The 'Xystos', the 'polished place', is taken to mean the gymnasium with polished flagstones built during the Hellenizing period under Antiochus Epiphanes, and is rendered 'Gymnasium' throughout this translation.

22. Though Josephus is likely to have been in Agrippa's audience and to be reproducing his general argument fairly accurately, one may suspect that the historical illustrations and the detailed survey of the Roman empire, much of which would have meant little or nothing to the average Jew, are an elaboration of his own, designed to display his erudition to his readers; cf. the Introduction, p. 24.

23. But provincial governors were appointed by Rome, and the imperial postal service was designed to keep them in touch with the authorities at home!

24. Wishful thinking!

25. In 480 B.C. the Persian invasion force crossed the Dardanelles on a bridge of boats and cut a canal across the neck of the Mount Athos peninsula. Athens was evacuated and then burnt.

26. The Spartans made a valiant but vain attempt to hold Thermopylae in 480 which was counted more glorious than victory, and were mainly responsible for the final defeat of the Persians at Plataea in 479. The Spartan king Agesilaus campaigned against Persia with some success in 396–394.

27. Fortune.

28. The bundle of rods symbolizing the power of summary jurisdiction vested in senior magistrates in the early Roman republic, and still carried before them by lictors after they had lost those powers.

29. The province of Asia (north-west Asia Minor).

30. Peoples round the Black Sea, who had come under Roman rule a few years previously.

31. Provinces in the north, east and south of Asia Minor.

32. Thrace had been annexed in A.D. 46.

33. Josephus actually means, not Illyricum, by now united with Dalmatia as a single province, but the province of Moesia south of the lower Danube.

34. From the first Roman campaigns in southern Gaul in 125 B.C. to the end of Julius Caesar's campaigns of conquest, 58–50.

35. The Straits of Gibraltar.

36. During the summer of 66 the Parthian prince Tiridates received the crown of Armenia from Nero's hand in Rome. Unless this occurred

early enough for news to have reached Judaea by May, Josephus has inserted the allusion himself, oblivious of the anachronism.

37. Peoples along the north coast of Africa.

38. Alexandria was founded by Alexander as a Greco-Macedonian city, and retained its non-Egyptian, exclusive character throughout its history.

39. cf. note 3 to p. 27. The Mesopotamian Diaspora (note 5 to p. 27) had expanded greatly since the sixth century B.C., and there were considerable numbers of Jews in Adiabene, east of the upper Tigris.

40. Ten years of war between Rome and Parthia had ended in 63, though the final concordat was not reached until 66 (above).

41. p. 46.

42. There is ample literary and other evidence to substantiate this statement for Mediterranean countries as far west as Italy from the first century B.C. For Gaul and Spain the evidence is later, but silence does not prove that Jews did not settle there also early.

43. This prophecy was fulfilled in Syria (pp. 169–70) and Alexandria (pp. 171–3).

44. Not mentioned before; but possibly Florus had pillaged the Temple treasury (p. 151) because taxes were in arrears and he was genuinely short of money.

CHAPTER 9: THE OUTBREAK OF WAR

1. Sicarii under Menahem (pp. 166, 266, 393 ff.). There is no evidence to show whether the Romans had garrisoned Masada since 6, since 44, or only recently when the situation became threatening.

2. See note 59 to p. 143.

3. See note 35 to p. 141.

4. The Corinthian Gate (p. 303).

5. Possibly including some Jews; Herod the Great had settled a military colony of Babylonian Jews in Batanaea (*AJ* xvii.23–6).

6. A plural; but the word is normally used in the plural to denote a single building. Berenice is not known to have had a separate establishment in Jerusalem, and she was popularly, though perhaps erroneously, believed to live in incest with her brother.

7. To distinguish Herod's Palace from the Hasmonaean one.

8. In 6 (p. 133 and Appendix A). Menahem, a leader sixty years later, was more probably Judas' grandson than his son.

9. p. 164.

10. pp. 299–300

11. In the grounds of Herod's Palace (p. 301).

12. The first sign of the disunity which was to hamper the Jewish war effort throughout.

13. The first occurrence of this famous term, but probably misplaced – unless it is used here in the general sense of 'fanatics' and not as a title. Menahem was leader of the Sicarii, by now based on Masada, and the Zealots were a separate party. See Appendix A.

14. pp. 393 ff. Probably a cousin of Menahem, if both were grandsons of Judas (note 8 to p. 166 and note 20 to p. 393).

15. The *Megillath Ta'anith*, a Jewish calendar of days when fasting was forbidden, includes the commemoration of 'the Romans' departure from Jerusalem' on a date in the early autumn which would fit this event.

16. Surely an exaggeration. The attackers were rioting mobs, not armed troops, and on p. 190 Ascalon is still 'strongly fortified'.

17. The term probably covers both proselytes and gentiles following Judaism informally but not committed fully by circumcision, people often described as 'God-fearers'.

18. Though west of the Jordan, Scythopolis had never come back under Jewish rule after being 'freed' in 63 B.C. (p. 48).

19. Of Emesa in Syria.

20. The first reference to a Roman garrison in Machaerus. Like Herodium (p. 83), Machaerus had a civilian settlement round the fortress (p. 387).

21. Josephus appears to imply here that the Jews had citizenship in Alexandria on a level with the Greeks. But the weight of other evidence is against this, indicating rather that the Jews formed a separate, autonomous political unit within the city, distinct from the Greek citizen-body, with its own officials, council (p. 405) and assembly. The friction which by this time was endemic seems to have arisen from agitation by at least some Jews for admission to the Greek citizen-body.

22. Alexandria was divided into five sections, denoted by the first five letters of the Greek alphabet. The Jews had Delta.

23. In the Hellenistic period some Jews had served in Macedonian mercenary units in Egypt, and their descendants retained the title 'Macedonian', which had neither ethnic nor civic significance, until at least the first century A.D.

24. Julius Caesar, who was in Alexandria in 48–47 B.C. (p. 52).

25. As non-citizens, the Jews were, indeed, gate-crashers.

26. The prefect of Egypt (p. 152), with his residence in Alexandria.

27. An improbable figure, as usual, but evidence for the gravity of the incident.

28. One of the permanent Syrian garrison of four legions.

29. Auxiliary units.

30. Antiochus IV of Commagene.

31. This prosperous commercial city, with little to gain by revolt, remained steadfastly pro-Roman except for a short lapse in the winter of 66-7 when she went over to Josephus (pp. 180, 186-7).

32. Because it was within the week of the festival.

33. Monobazus, his mother Helena, and his elder brother Izates, whom he had recently succeeded, had become proselytes to Judaism in the 40s (*AJ* xx.17-53, 92-6), had built residences in Jerusalem (p. 307), and were eventually buried there (p. 291).

34. A prominent leader throughout the war.

35. To the north-east, commanding an extensive view (p. 292).

36. Agrippa I's new north wall enclosing Bezetha had been left half-built (p. 143).

37. Florus' last appearance. Josephus evidently found Cestius' failure to press his advantage incomprehensible (cf. below), and so produced this unconvincing explanation. But winter was at hand, and the offer from the peace-party (below) could have been a trap.

38. Probably the high priest murdered in the 50s (p. 147).

39. Latin *testudo*.

40. One of the Syrian legions which had sent a detachment (p. 173).

41. *Oxybelēs*, literally 'an engine for projecting sharp objects' – i.e. some sort of catapult, but evidently not identical with a *katapeltēs*, as both appear together on occasion (e.g. p. 195). Both engines projected weapons (p. 202), as distinct from the *ballista*, which hurled stones.

42. pp. 308, 317.

43. An error for 'thirteenth'; it was by now after the anniversary of Nero's accession in October.

CHAPTER 10: JOSEPHUS GOVERNOR OF GALILEE

1. p. 244.

2. Nero was spending a year in Greece, displaying his artistic talents at all the religious festivals.

3. High priest for three months in 62 (*AJ* xx.197-203).

4. i.e. to complete Agrippa I's north wall (p. 132; cf. note 36 to p. 176).

5. An extremist leader prominent almost to the end of the war.

6. Under their leader Eleazar (cf. note 13 to p. 167) they were to become one of the most important nationalist factions (Appendix A).

It is strange that Josephus mentions them casually here and on p. 188 but does not explain their name till p. 246.

7. One would not expect the Essene way of life (pp. 133–7) to produce military commanders.

8. The historian himself. His full account in the *BJ* of his operations is supplemented, and in places contradicted, by his even fuller account in the *Vita*: see the Introduction, p. 17. He says virtually nothing about operations in the other five commands (note 24 p. 188).

9. At Arbela (*V* 188), a favourite haunt for guerrillas (p. 68).

10. John of Gischala, a prominent leader to the end of the war, qualifies by his bitter hostility to Josephus for a detailed, and perhaps unnecessarily derogatory, character sketch (pp. 181–2).

11. cf. the long account of the Roman army on pp. 195–7.

12. Foreign-produced oil would not be *kosher*, pure, as it might have been contaminated by unclean vessels.

13. A Roman amphora (large earthenware storage jar for liquids) held about 6 gallons, a Greek one apparently about 9.

14. Josephus himself, who had not dared to refuse John permission to buy up the oil (*V* 74–6).

15. Technically part of the kingdom of the pro-Roman Agrippa II (p. 146).

16. Also technically part of Agrippa's kingdom (p. 146).

17. Josephus is here gullible enough to admit the man who has just instigated an attack on his life. The order of the narrative in *V* 85 ff. is more convincing: John's ruse to get into Tiberias precedes the attack on Josephus at Tarichaeae.

18. i.e. to John of Gischala. Gabara in north Galilee is substituted here for the geographically improbable 'Gadara' or 'Gamala' of the MSS.

19. This is not true. Tiberias was recovered by force of arms (*V* 326–35) and Gischala remained in John's hands (below and p. 240).

20. From the Jewish viewpoint: the city resumed its loyalty to the pro-Roman Agrippa.

21. An obvious correction of the 'unarmed' of the MSS.

22. p. 260.

23. Simon, from Gerasa (p. 274) but presumably Jewish, seems to have been working against rather than under the district commander, possibly with the aim of social revolution for the benefit of the poor; cf. p. 275.

24. This paragraph and an account of an attack on Ascalon (pp. 190–91) are all that Josephus gives about the other five military districts.

CHAPTER 11: THE COMING OF VESPASIAN AND TITUS

1. He was fifty-seven. Soldiers were discharged at forty-six.

2. He had commanded one of the four legions comprising Claudius' invasion force in 43, and during the following years had subjugated southern England from Sussex to Dorset or Devon.

3. p. 146.

4. Only the elder, Titus. Domitian was a mere boy of fifteen.

5. Normally stationed in Pannonia on the Danube (p. 383), but temporarily in Egypt after serving in recent campaigns against Parthia.

6. The first reference to a Roman garrison in Ascalon, outside the province of Judaea. It was possibly established after the earlier Jewish attack (p. 169).

7. This Jewish venture, though ill-prepared and disastrous, made strategic sense: they might have been attacked in the rear from Ascalon while facing the Roman offensive from the north.

8. In the spring of 67.

9. p. 174.

10. *AJ* xv.294. They formed a useful military colony guarding the narrow entrance to Esdraelon.

11. Hardly! Galilee had 204 towns and villages, according to *V* 235.

12. Late August, when Sirius the Dog-star rises.

13. Josephus expresses himself badly. Machaerus was in Peraea, Pella and Philadelphia its neighbours over the frontier.

14. Or the rather difficult Greek here may mean 'since it slopes down towards the coastal plain (from a ridge extending) all the way ...'.

15. Apparently an alternative name for Bethleptepha (p. 270); that name, not Pella, occurs in the list of toparchies given by Pliny, *Nat. Hist.* v. 70.

16. Idumaea and Engedi seem to be the two toparchies of the district of Idumaea, otherwise ignored in this survey. Probably 'Idumaea' comprised the area centred on Marisa until its destruction in 40 B.C. (p. 63), and Engedi had replaced Adora as capital of the eastern toparchy.

17. Formerly Bethsaida (note 19 to p. 138).

18. The Tenth was one of the permanent garrison of Syria. The Fifth had not yet returned to its station in Moesia (p. 383) after serving in the recent Parthian war. The Twelfth, disgraced at Beth-horon, took no part in the war till 69 (p. 290).

19. The regular garrison of Judaea.

20. Taking a legion as roughly 5,000 men, one does not get this total. But it is not a wild exaggeration.

21. Sculptured monuments show the longer weapon on the soldier's right – the spectator's left!

22. This, together with Josephus' description of the marching-order of Vespasian's army (pp. 198–9), provides the best extant account of the Roman army in the first century A.D., comparable with Polybius' account of the army in the second century B.C., which was perhaps its prototype.

23. Rome did not use mercenaries. Josephus may be careless in his choice of word here and mean the rest of the auxiliaries, those other than the light-armed and the bowmen mentioned at the beginning of his description.

24. If Josephus really believed all this, why did he then join his run-away troops in Jotapata, especially when Vespasian was already obviously preparing to besiege it?

25. Repeated on p. 216 but surely an exaggeration, even though Josephus had shown more military ability than anyone else so far.

26. This extramural Jewish camp must soon have been abandoned.

27. Josephus seems to have been short-sighted. He says the same thing about the height of the south-east corner of the Temple enclosure above the Kidron (*AJ* xv.412) and about Machaerus and Masada (pp. 387, 395) – though the last two statements presumably depend on hearsay.

28. Little of the defences of Jotapata can be seen today.

CHAPTER 12: JOSEPHUS THE PRISONER OF VESPASIAN

1. Presumably men armed with small catapults.

2. Evidently an outsize version of the battering-ram, the term used of it below.

3. The singular and the definite article suggest some sort of stone-thrower *par excellence*.

4. A *testudo* (p. 176).

5. The earliest recorded use of this weapon, so popular in the Middle Ages.

6. *Faenum Graecum* ('Greek hay'), which flowers about midsummer.

7. Near Nazareth; 'the largest village in Galilee' (*V* 230).

8. The father of the future emperor.

9. With their age-old hostility towards the Jews, the Samaritans had so far stood aside from the revolt. The fact that this movement was centred on the holy mountain of Gerizim suggests a messianic character (cf. a similar gathering there in 36; *AJ* xviii.85–7), and any form of messianism was suspect to Rome; cf. p. 147.

10. Josephus consistently gives the name incorrectly as 'Cerealius'. The correct form and the full name Sextus (p. 356) Vettulenus (corrupted by Josephus into 'Vetilianus'; p. 387) are known from inscriptions.

11. This figure is repeated on p. 221. But from Josephus' arrival on the 21st of Artemisios (p. 200), a few days before the siege began in earnest, to the capture of the town on the 1st of Panemos (p. 216) is actually only about five weeks.

12. See note 25 to p. 200.

13. Josephus' friendship with one of Titus' officers is puzzling. But Nicanor, not an Italian to judge from his Greek name, may have been serving under Agrippa II and have met Josephus on a visit to Jerusalem, where he was known to the Jews (p. 308).

14. One of the tenets of the Stoic philosophy, with which the Pharisees had a certain amount in common (*V* 12).

15. As a Pharisee (*V* 12) Josephus accepted belief in a future life and the transmigration of souls (note 15 to p. 137).

16. The Hebrew equivalent was Sheol.

17. Exodus 20.5; John 9.2; etc.

18. No such law is given in the Pentateuch. It may have been part of the oral law of the time, but it is not found in the oral law as codified in the Mishnah (p. 492).

19. Or to trickery by Josephus? – as the Slavonic version explicitly states (see Appendix F). One cannot but wonder how much of the last four pages is historical fact and how much literary embellishment.

20. Titus was actually four years younger than Josephus, who was now thirty.

21. A messianic prophecy that a world ruler was shortly to arise in Judaea was current at this time (pp. 362-3), and several prophecies of Vespasian's elevation to the throne are recorded by Roman historians. Josephus' foreknowledge of the three short-lived emperors between Nero and Vespasian (pp. 274, 277, 280-86) must be a later insertion.

CHAPTER 13: VESPASIAN'S CONQUERING ADVANCE

1. Several campaigning months of 67 remained but Vespasian realized already that they would not suffice to crush the revolt and therefore began preparations for wintering in good time.

2. pp. 173-4.

3. This endangered both Vespasian's lines of communication and also the food supply of Rome, since at this season north-west winds prevented direct voyages from Alexandria to Italy, and the Egyptian corn-fleet had to sail via the coasts of Palestine and Asia Minor and the Aegean.

4. Andromeda was chained to a rock to be devoured by a sea-monster, which had been sent to ravage the land as punishment for the

impiety of her mother – the only expiation which would end the nuisance. She was rescued in the nick of time by Perseus.

5. Tiberias, after much wavering, had ended up under Josephus' control (p. 187), but pro-Roman feeling there was still strong (below). Tarichaeae, having once joined the rebels, had remained on that side.

6. See note 66 to p. 48.

7. p. 183. The father's name is restored from that passage and V 66, 134.

8. See note 9 to p. 28.

9. p. 212.

10. p. 180. But in V 155–6 Tarichaeae is fortified first.

11. A typical pre-battle pep-talk from the pen of the historian; see the Introduction, pp. 23–4.

12. Built on the site of Paneum (p.). 138

13. Lake Huleh, now drained to form fertile arable land.

14. To work on his great project, soon to be abandoned, of a Corinthian canal.

15. After the division of Solomon's kingdom, Jeroboam in the north established rival sanctuaries to Jerusalem at Dan (here) and Bethel, with golden calves among their furnishings (1 Kings 12.25–30).

16. After temporarily declaring for the rebels (p. 180).

17. Josephus supposes that the K of kamēlos (in Greek) had degenerated into G. But the name is Hebrew or Aramaic, which have gama and gamla respectively for 'camel'.

18. From the spring to the autumn of 67.

19. p. 227. The hot springs (Hebrew hamath) are about a mile and a half south of Tiberias.

20. Legate of Syria in succession to Cestius Gallus, and one of Vespasian's staunchest friends. The purpose of Titus' visit is unknown, but he was soon back (p. 238).

21. The mountain actually rises some 1,300 feet from the plain, and its flat summit is roughly 1,000 by 400 yards.

22. It is, however, omitted from the list on p. 180.

CHAPTER 14: FACTIONS IN JERUSALEM

1. pp. 181–6.

2. Probably Kudditha, two miles south-east of Gischala, in the coastal strip under the political control of Tyre.

3. It was now late in 67, and apart from minor operations such as the securing of Jamnia and Azotus (below), the winter was to be spent resting in the bases at Caesarea and Scythopolis.

4. A 'footnote' on contemporary Roman operations late in 67, inserted awkwardly.

5. And apparently also Lydda, in Roman hands on p. 270.

6. A relation of Agrippa II (pp. 165, 179).

7. Despite the rhetorical plural, they only made the one irregular appointment about to be described.

8. From the time of Herod the Great the succession had not been hereditary, as it had been with the Hasmonaeans, but most of the high priests had been members of half a dozen families. One high priest, Ananus, had had five sons who had all held the post, the youngest being the Ananus mentioned below. The nationalists were hostile to the established high-priestly aristocracy because it was inevitably pro-Roman (note 70 to p. 147).

9. See note 3 to p. 179.

10. The high priest now deposed was Matthias, son of Ananus' brother Theophilus, who had been appointed shortly before the war (*AJ* xx.223). The Matthias of pp. 279 and 332 may be a different person; see the notes to those pages.

11. A rabbi, leader of the Pharisees.

12. High priest from 63/4 (*AJ* xx.213) and predecessor of the deposed Matthias.

13. cf. p. 394 and Appendix A.

14. cf. note 16 to p. 75.

15. The balustrade round the inner courts of the Temple (p. 302); cf. note 20 to p. 156.

16. After this incident the city was geographically divided between the various factions.

17. pp. 240–41.

CHAPTER 15: ATROCITIES IN THE CITY. VESPASIAN'S
INTERVENTION

1. This unholy alliance between John of Gischala and the Zealots under Eleazar, son of Simon, broke up after a few months (pp. 266, 287).

2. Josephus makes Ananus remarkably gullible!

3. This allegation against Ananus, hotly denied (p. 254 ff.), was later found to be groundless (p. 262).

4. A part of the country over which the Romans had not yet recovered control.

5. Gentiles were allowed not merely to present gifts to the Temple (note 16 to p. 75) but also to worship by paying for a sacrifice (p. 164).

6. This encomium on Ananus contrasts strongly with Josephus' picture of his brief high priesthood in 62, when, as 'an impetuous and exceptionally daring man', he deliberately acted *ultra vires* to irritate the procurator (*AJ* xx.199–203). But that was a very different matter from taking on the Roman legions, and to call him a turncoat would be to do him less than justice. Rather, his emergence early in the war as a man of moderation and the leader of the peace party shows that he had developed into a political realist, aware of the ultimate hopelessness of the Jewish cause.

7. Simon, son of Gioras (p. 188), now in Masada (p. 274).

8. Some of them in fact stayed in Jerusalem to the end (pp. 279, 368).

9. Gorion, son of Joseph (p. 246)?

10. pp. 175, 180, 190–91.

11. The Zealots' aim, largely realized, was the elimination of the moderates, who might have sued for peace.

12. The reference is to extra-mural burial.

13. Or the Holy of Holies. This prophecy is otherwise unknown.

14. i.e. his alliance with the Zealots began to break up.

15. The Greek is obscure. Possibly a negative has dropped out and the meaning should be 'he would have a hold on them if they did not oppose him from the start'.

16. The story of how rabbi Johanan ben Zakkai, who was to lead the religious re-establishment after the war, escaped to the Romans in a coffin, feigning death, probably belongs to this period. It implies, it is true, that Jerusalem was under siege at the time, and may therefore belong to 70, when some people still managed to escape (p. 323). But the rabbinic tradition that Johanan prophesied to Vespasian that he would become emperor is against the later date.

17. pp. 164, 166, 168. Simon, son of Gioras, and his supporters were there also (p. 188).

18. The Passover was taken to mark the start of the grain harvest and Pentecost its completion.

19. Presumably synagogues are meant.

20. This operation opens the campaigning season of 68.

21. Probably the modern Beth Nimrin, twelve miles south-west of the site of Gadara/Gadora, and on the road to Jericho (below).

22. In the Jews' hands (p. 171).

CHAPTER 16: VESPASIAN EMPEROR

1. The beginning of the movement that led to Nero's dethronement in June 68.

2. From this it appears that Lydda had been secured with Jamnia and Azotus the previous autumn (p. 243).

3. An anachronistic use of the name Flavia Neapolis (now Nablus) given to the city founded shortly after the war on the site of the village of Mabartha near Shechem.

4. Presumably the Tenth Legion, which Trajan commanded (p. 212), had supplied the detachment which had just subjugated Peraea.

5. This term normally denotes the plain of Esdraelon, not, as here, the Jordan valley.

6. Joshua 6.

7. An elaboration of 2 Kings 2.19–22.

8. This identification of the *myrobalanos* is not certain.

9. Actually sixteen and five miles.

10. i.e. bitumen. Hence the Greek name for the Dead Sea, Lake Asphaltitis.

11. Actually it is some forty-seven miles long, and about ten wide at its widest.

12. Genesis 18.16–19, 29.

13. The 'apple of Sodom' produces a fruit with a soft, attractive yellow skin but only a few dry seeds inside.

14. Near Lydda. Camps had already been established at Emmaus and in Idumaea (p. 270).

15. Clearly this cannot be the city of the Decapolis but must be a site near Jerusalem (with the well-known name possibly having displaced an obscure one in the text).

16. He committed suicide on 9 June, after a reign of thirteen years and almost eight months (not 'days').

17. This paragraph summarizes events to the end of 69, 'the year of the four emperors'. The capture of Rome by Vespasian's supporters Primus and Mucianus established him on the throne.

18. Notably Tacitus' *Histories*.

19. With the death of Nero, who had appointed him, Vespasian's command automatically lapsed. He therefore dared not undertake major operations without orders from the new emperor, though common-sense required him to maintain his position by minor ones, if necessary, until a fresh mandate, or a successor, arrived. But during the period of political instability following Nero's death no further instructions were sent to Vespasian, who consequently spent a year in virtual inaction until resuming operations on his own initiative in the summer of 69 (p. 278).

20. On 15 January, 69. Vespasian evidently did not send Titus as soon as he heard the news of Galba's accession, but waited until late in the year in the vain hope of receiving confirmation of his command.

In winter (cf. note 30 to p. 64) a direct voyage from Alexandria to Italy would not be attempted.

21. p. 188.

22. Eastern Judaea was the only area which Vespasian had not yet attempted to recover.

23. Recently overrun by Vespasian (p. 270) but evidently not securely held.

24. The occupation of the Judaean Herodium by the rebels has not previously been mentioned.

25. And they still are to *this* day, within a rectangular enclosure of splendidly preserved masonry so similar to that of the Temple enclosure that it can be attributed to Herod the Great even though not listed by Josephus among his buildings.

26. At Mambre (Ramat el-Khalil), where there is an enclosure of Hadrianic date over unfinished Herodian work.

27. Genesis 13.18; 14.13; 18.1.

28. Despite Simon's conduct, some Idumaeans joined him (p. 307).

29. On 17 April, 69.

30. On resuming operations now in the summer of 69, Vespasian's first task was to get control over the area which had fallen into Simon's hands. This paragraph gives events later than those in and around Jerusalem which it interrupts; see p. 279, Xanthicos.

31. p. 214.

32. See note 8 to p. 263.

33. As proselytes (note 33 to p. 175) the Adiabenian royal family had two residences in Jerusalem (p. 307). Grapte is otherwise unknown.

34. The high priest deposed in the previous year (p. 245)? But see note 14 to p. 332.

35. Along the sides of the actual Temple (p. 304).

36. The story is now interrupted by an account of Vespasian's elevation to the throne, and is resumed on p. 287.

37. In late May or early June.

38. News of events in Italy will have taken a month or more to reach Caesarea.

39. i.e. after the sailing season closed in mid-November. Vespasian at this stage apparently visualized spending the summer besieging Jerusalem and thus finishing the war before going to the rescue of Rome.

40. Domitian, by now nearly eighteen.

41. Sabinus (p. 285).

42. See note 20 to p. 236.

43. Four months' supply for Rome annually (p. 160).

44. The regular garrison of Egypt.

45. Pelusium to Syene (Assuan) is actually about 650 miles. Plinthine, clearly on the western frontier, has not been identified, but the figure 400 is certainly too high, since the distance from Pelusium to the western mouth of the Delta is only something over 200 miles.

46. An island near Assuan.

47. From the location of this lighthouse, one of the Seven Wonders of the World, *pharos* became the Greek term for a lighthouse.

48. The Great Harbour was less than half this length, but possibly by this time the causeway linking Pharos to the mainland and separating the Great Harbour from the one to the west of it had been broken down.

49. On 1 July, 69. Since oaths of allegiance were taken only to the emperor, this amounted to proclaiming Vespasian emperor.

50. p. 221.

51. It was by now the autumn of 69.

52. Actually commander of one of the three legions in Pannonia. But the Third Legion, from Moesia, took the lead in supporting Vespasian.

53. On the Po, in the area which had formerly been the province of Cisalpine Gaul but had by now been incorporated in Italy for over a century.

54. This short and unbalanced account of the campaign which culminated in the sack of Cremona in October, 69, largely conceals the fact that a major battle was fought. For a full account see Tacitus, *Hist.* iii.1–35.

55. 20 or 21 December.

56. Titus went as far as Alexandria with his father (a fact not previously mentioned) to collect reinforcements (p. 290).

CHAPTER 17: THE SIEGE OF JERUSALEM – FIRST STAGES

1. Figures for the various factions are given on p. 307, after the losses of p. 295.

2. Holding part of the Lower City and the outer court of the Temple, he was sandwiched between the Zealots whom he was besieging and Simon, son of Gioras (below).

3. A common term for the Temple-tax (note 23 to p. 139).

4. According to Jewish tradition, the year which ran from the autumn of 68 had been a sabbatical year. If that is correct, no replenishments were available during the current year, 69–70. By the time the next harvest was gathered, in April–May, 70, Jerusalem was invested. Among the many references to the acute food shortage during the siege, see especially pp. 323–4, 352–4.

5. Agrippa II had the oversight of the Temple and was responsible for its fabric. The foundations had subsided, apparently a considerable time before, and part of the Temple had in consequence collapsed and then been left lower than the height originally intended (*AJ* xv.391).

6. Apparently between the west wall of the enclosure and the rear of the Temple, where there were no entrances through the wall forming the inner courts (p. 302).

7. In the spring of 70; see the Passover (p. 295).

8. The garrisons established in the summer of 68 (pp. 270, 273).

9. p. 284.

10. As camp prefect (p. 356), an unusual post for a man of his rank; cf. Glossary.

11. See note 23 to p. 199.

12. p. 299.

13. Unknown.

14. The so-called 'Tombs of the Kings' near the present Anglican cathedral.

15. Literally 'king', a most unconstitutional term!

16. The meaning of *skopos*.

17. The Twelfth and the Fifteenth.

18. Literally 'the most savage beasts', unspecified.

19. As in the reconnaissance (p. 292) and in some later episodes, it is a matter of opinion whether Titus showed laudable courage or foolhardiness inexcusable in a commander-in-chief.

20. Every Jewish month began with the new moon, and the Passover occurred at the full moon of Nisan, to which Xanthicos roughly corresponded.

21. Unknown, but possibly a building connected with Herod of Chalcis. No members of Herod the Great's family are known to have been buried near Jerusalem.

22. Possibly the reservoir Birket Mamilla west of the city.

23. The historian, used several times later also as an intermediary.

24. The archaic punishment for mutiny or cowardice, decimation (the execution of one man in every ten, chosen by lot), was still occasionally used.

25. p. 300.

26. On Josephus' description of Jerusalem, cf. pp. 487–9.

27. Hence Ophel, 'the hump'.

28. A reference to the demolition of Antiochus Epiphanes' fortress (note 6 to p. 33)?

29. Actually southwards, from the north-west corner.

30. It must actually have been running roughly east here!

31. The precise location is not known.

32. The Temple enclosure at its north-east corner.

33. On which the Upper City stood.

34. The fosse north of the Temple.

35. p. 143 and *AJ* xix.326–7.

36. pp. 179, 188.

37. This is approximately correct for the more northerly of the two possible lines. But Josephus' figures are too unreliable (and mutually inconsistent: a wall with 90 towers 100 yards apart would be over 5 miles long!) for this to be used as an argument in its support.

38. Mariamme I, p. 87.

39. Strangely, he is never mentioned in the narrative of Herod's reign in either *BJ* or *AJ*.

40. p. 282.

41. pp. 166–7.

42. Here Josephus starts describing Herod's work.

43. This probably refers to the south-east corner of the enclosure, where the ground slopes steeply towards the Kidron and the surviving Herodian wall stands to a height of 130 feet above bedrock.

44. The longest still *in situ* in the enclosure wall is actually well under 40 feet long.

45. One complete Greek copy survives, in the Archaeological Museum in Istanbul, and half of another, in the Rockefeller Museum in Jerusalem. The penalty for transgression was death (p. 347).

46. *To hagion* (see note 16 to p. 30) here clearly denotes the inner courts round it as well as the actual Temple building.

47. The treasury chambers were apparently built against the inner side of the wall forming the Court of the Israelites.

48. Tiberius Julius Alexander; his father, brother of Philo, had been one of the wealthiest Jews in Alexandria.

49. i.e. the eastern part open to the priests, with the Holy of Holies beyond.

50. An apparently misplaced sentence, interrupting the description of the façade with a reference to the interior, and using the word translated above as 'divided into two chambers' (on the same level) in a clearly different sense (cf. the 'ground-floor chamber' and the 'lower part' and 'upper part' of the Sanctuary, below).

51. 'White' is inserted, since 'linen' appears as a 'colour' in the high priest's sash (p. 305).

52. Purple dye was made from a shellfish, the *murex*.

53. The shewbread – Exodus 25.23–30; Levit. 24.5–9. No reason is given for the number twelve in these passages. The obvious later interpretation was that the loaves represented the twelve tribes.

54. To the four spices prescribed in Exodus 30.34 the rabbis later added nine more.

55. In *AJ* xv.392 the dimensions of 'each of the stones' are 37½ by 12 by 18 feet, which produces a volume almost double that produced by the unbelievable figures here!

56. The tetragrammaton YHWH, the consonants of the name of God, Yahweh, which might never be uttered. In incorrectly saying 'vowels', Josephus may have been thinking of the Greek transliteration IAUE.

57. The Day of Atonement in October.

58. A work on Jewish theology, law and customs is promised in *AJ* i.25 and xx.268, but, if ever written, it has not survived.

59. It is widely believed that the open-air courtyard paved with large flagstones that survives under the Convent of the Sisters of Zion is the courtyard of the Antonia. But recent work suggests that it belongs to the city built by Hadrian after the revolt of 132–5.

60. cf. Acts 21.40.

61. p. 144.

62. The unwritten (?) work (see note 58 above) seems hardly the place for this, and the *AJ* gives less detail than we have here.

CHAPTER 18: TWO WALLS CAPTURED

1. See note 8 to p. 28.

2. Agrippa I's wall.

3. pp. 293–4.

4. The north walls are now numbered from the Roman point of view, the outermost becoming the 'first' and the 'old' wall the 'third'.

5. The Hasmonaean John Hyrcanus I.

6. The Jews' fatal failure to link Agrippa's wall to the existing fortifications near Herod's three towers is very puzzling.

7. pp. 178, 166 (though without reference to artillery).

8. Probably *ha-eben*, 'the stone', was pronounced *habben*, 'the son'.

9. This was essential lest they should be trapped between the outer and second wall. Contrast the disastrous consequences of Titus' failure to demolish the second wall immediately after its capture (pp. 314–15).

10. See pp. 319, 321.

11. The Hasmonaean Alexander Jannaeus. The site is not known.

12. Parallel commands are suggested here, but Simon's earlier proclamation (p. 309) about the Temple, which was in John's hands, implies his seniority, as does also the next paragraph.

13. p. 215.

14. Without a powerful megaphone, this seems barely possible!

15. p. 289.

16. Perhaps likely to cut more ice than the history etc. in the discourse attributed to Agrippa II (pp. 156 ff.), but still probably an embellishment by Josephus as historian of his words as intermediary; see the Introduction, p. 24.

17. A strange variant of the story in Genesis 12.10-20 (and 14.14 for the 318 men) possibly derived from Jewish legend.

18. Exodus 7 ff.

19. I Samuel 5-6, with embellishments.

20. 2 Kings 18.17-19.36

21. 2 Chron. 36.20-23; Ezra 1.

22. Zedekiah did not witness the final destruction of Jerusalem by Nebuchadnezzar, since he had been deposed, blinded, and removed to Babylon ten years previously (2 Kings 24.18-25.12; Jerem. 27; 34; 37-9; 52).

23. pp. 73-4. Rhetoric has here lengthened the siege by over a month.

24. Paid by the Jews as a client kingdom (p. 47) and as a province (pp. 133, 162).

25. Pompeius Magnus, Pompey the Great.

26. Not in the Biblical accounts of Nebuchadnezzar.

CHAPTER 19: THE HORRORS OF THE SIEGE

1. cf. p. 334.

2. Josephus does not actually describe their unconcern on pp. 357 ff.

3. Son of Antiochus IV of Commagene (pp. 173, 194).

4. A saying attributed to the sixth-century B.C. Athenian lawgiver and sage, Solon.

5. Struthion, probably the reservoir under the Convent of the Sisters of Zion, apparently still open at this date. The surviving vaulted roof is almost certainly contemporary with the paved area above (note 59 to p. 306), i.e. very probably Hadrianic rather than Herodian.

6. Amygdalon.

7. One of Agrippa II's sisters. The man had evidently deserted to the Jews.

8. Siloam, presumably.

9. High priest for some ten years from A.D. 6 (*AJ* xviii.26); note 8 to p. 245.

10. Evidently a place commanding the junction of Gehenna and the Kidron. If this reference to Pompey is not an error, he must have en-

camped there temporarily before moving to the north of the city (p. 75).

11. See note 21 to p. 296.

12. Indeed it does!

13. Tiberius Julius Alexander (p. 290).

14. p. 279. If this Matthias was the high priest deposed in the winter of 68–9 (p. 245), Josephus has put him in the wrong family here. (The family of Boethus, like that of Ananus, had provided a number of high priests.) But there were two men named Matthias from high-priestly families in Jerusalem at this time (p. 346).

15. That of the auxiliary units serving in Syria (pp. 194, 290), and probably largely recruited locally.

16. p. 323.

17. Augustus' and Livia's gifts to Herod's Temple are mentioned also by Philo, *Leg.* 157, 319. But no gifts by later emperors are recorded.

CHAPTER 20: ANTONIA CAPTURED AND DESTROYED

1. Though Josephus does not mention other artillery, the Roman cannon-balls, 4 to 18 inches in diameter, still lying below the Convent of the Sisters of Zion, and others in the adjacent Convent of the Flagellation, both near if not on the site of the Antonia, bear dramatic witness to Titus' use of the *ballista*.

2. A *testudo* (p. 176).

3. Here and in the following pages 'the ninth hour of the night' etc. are rendered by modern equivalents.

4. The daily sacrifice, morning and evening. The text is emended from *andrōn*, 'men', to *arnōn*, 'lambs'.

5. *To hagion* (note 16 to p. 30) here clearly needs a different translation from *naos* to produce the effect which Josephus intends.

6. An embroidery on 2 Kings 24.11–16.

7. p. 265.

8. His escape (?) to Cyrene is not recorded. He was probably a victim of the post-war troubles there, though not mentioned in the narrative of them (pp. 407–8).

9. p. 332.

10. p. 302. This is an interesting scrap of evidence for the Sanhedrin's powers of capital jurisdiction.

11. John of Gischala.

12. cf. p. 337.

13. It was now to the interest of both sides to destroy a potential route for attack from or against the Temple.

14. p. 280.

15. Probably the equivalent of four days' wages for a labourer (see Appendix C).

16. Surprisingly, he does not know the parallel in 2 Kings 6.24–30.

17. Would he? He goes into quite unnecessary details, probably invented by himself.

CHAPTER 21: THE TEMPLE BURNT AND THE CITY TAKEN

1. See note 6 to p. 290.

2. The executioner of Matthias (p. 332).

3. It appears from p. 357 that at this point the Jews abandoned the outer court of the Temple and took refuge in the inner courts, though that withdrawal is not given explicitly.

4. He had apparently replaced Trajan.

5. The name is uncertain. The MSS. give 'Heterius' (Haterius?) and 'Heternius'. It may be 'Liternius'.

6. This man, not mentioned before, may have been Gessius Florus' successor, sent out before it was realized that the situation was beyond the capabilities of any procurator.

7. Almost certainly an error for 'prefects' (commanders of auxiliary units), which would balance the (military) tribunes. No other procurators could well be involved.

8. An inadvertent repetition of the first sentence of the paragraph.

9. Loös was the equivalent of the Jewish month Ab. Nebuchadnezzar's destruction of Solomon's Temple is variously dated to the 7th and the 10th of Ab (2 Kings 25.8–9; Jeremiah 52.12–13). But it is the 9th of Ab, the day on which Titus' men first broke into the outer court, which is still kept as the anniversary of the destruction of both Temples and of the collapse of the second Jewish revolt against Rome, A.D. 132–5.

10. In his determination to absolve Titus of responsibility for the destruction of the Temple Josephus here and in the following paragraph gives an unconvincing picture of insubordination in the Roman ranks. But the fourth-century Christian chronicler Sulpicius Severus says that at the council Titus favoured the destruction of the Temple – which carries the more plausible implication that it was fired on his orders. Sulpicius' statement may well be derived ultimately from the lost work 'On the Jews' by an Antonius Julianus who is credibly identified with the procurator (above), an identification which would give the statement some weight. Titus' distress at the destruction of the Temple is not incompatible with the realization that it was inevitable from the military point of view.

11. The Holy of Holies? But see note 63 to p. 47.

12. Patriotic prejudice here probably takes an over-charitable view of a building which must in fact have been distinctly odd and clumsy in appearance, with its huge flat slab of a portico masking and dwarfing the sanctuary behind it.

13. Actually the first period was about 1040 years and the second 589.

14. Josephus does not mention explicitly the rescue of the gold lamp-stand, table and trumpets (p. 385) from the burning Temple. Presumably Romans, not Jews, salvaged them, since they are excluded by implication from the treasures later used for bargaining (p. 369).

15. i.e. the Upper City, where Simon and his followers were enjoying a respite from attack.

16. But see p. 369 for what the priests managed to salvage.

17. The Passover of 66 (p. 150)?

18. i.e. of the Temple; cf. note 59 to p. 145.

19. Five or six weeks later, if the date is correct.

20. The Feast of Tabernacles in October, 62 (see the $7\frac{1}{2}$ years to his death; below), a period not described as one of peace and prosperity by any means on p. 149.

21. This prophecy is unknown. Literally, *tetragonon* is simply a quadri-lateral, but it usually means a square. The Temple enclosure was in fact oblong, and that may be the meaning of the word here, since the removal of the excrescence of the Antonia did not in fact reduce it to a square.

22. See note 21 to p. 221.

23. Military standards, both the legionary eagles and the standards of auxiliary units (note 21 to p. 138) and sections of legions, were objects of reverence and even of cult. This is a unique literary reference to actual sacrifice to them.

24. 'General'. Under the empire this acclamation, given to any victorious commander under the republic, was normally accorded only to emperors – for victories won for them by their generals.

25. The Roman circumvallation.

26. The Temple-tax (note 23 to p. 139). From the time of Julius Caesar, legislation had safeguarded the right of the Diaspora to collect it and transmit it to Jerusalem.

27. Presumably an anachronistic reference, as on p. 27, to the disturbances which led to Nero's dethronement.

28. Surely military common-sense from the Jewish point of view!

29. Against whom? The Mesopotamian Jews were not under Roman rule, and gave no recorded help to the rebels in Palestine. The assistance from Adiabene seems to have been minimal (pp. 175, 328).

30. The Greek is difficult. The reading of the MSS. is followed here. But with a slight emendation the words would seem to mean 'I prevented their oppressors from torturing them'.

31. p. 350, but a somewhat twisted interpretation of the eventual destruction.

32. Possibly including the two members of the Adiabenian royal family mentioned on p. 175.

33. p. 337.

34. On the implications of this sentence see p. 489. Simon's tower, not mentioned before, presumably stood on the west side of the Valley of the Cheese-makers, facing the one built by John to dominate the Gymnasium from the east (p. 280).

35. Hippicus, Phasael and Mariamme.

36. p. 374.

37. p. 356.

38. pp. 383–6.

39. pp. 376–7.

40. An inflated figure, dependent on the inflated estimates of the whole population in 66 (below and p. 150). Tacitus puts the population of the city when under siege at 600,000 (*Hist.* v.13), a figure possibly derived from Roman military records.

41. This elementary arithmetical error must mean a textual corruption of one of the figures.

42. p. 376.

43. *c.* 969 B.C. (1 Kings 14.25–6).

44. Nebuchadnezzar, in 587 B.C.

45. Melchizedek, king of Salem (Genesis 14.18) – though the name may well have meant in reality 'my king is Zedek' (a Phoenician deity).

46. The method of count used to produce the figures in this paragraph is obscure.

CHAPTER 22: JERUSALEM DESTROYED: ROMAN CELEBRATIONS

1. Phasael still stands to the impressive height of 60 feet, forming the base of a tower misleadingly called the 'Tower of David' in the sixteenth-century Citadel. But there is no trace now of the other towers or of the stretch of city wall left standing south of them.

2. An exaggeration. A great deal of the southern part of the Temple enclosure was spared. The whole of the south wall of its successor, the present wall round the Haram es-Sherif, the southern section of the west wall (the 'Wailing Wall', where the fall of Jerusalem is still lamented) and a short stretch of the east wall running up from the southeast corner are Herodian to a considerable height.

3. Auxiliary units supporting the legionary garrison, according to normal Roman military practice.

4. The fact that Vespasian had sons had been a strong point in his favour to the troops backing him as emperor (p. 281).

5. Normal military decorations. Inscriptions record the award of decorations to Larcius Lepidus (p. 356), though Josephus gives none of his exploits, and to Cerealis.

6. On the east side of the 'toe' of Italy.

7. Replacing Larcius Lepidus, but apparently only temporarily (note 1 to p. 387).

8. 24 October.

9. i.e. the city had been raised to the privileged status of a colony, a term which had originally denoted a settlement of Roman veterans, usually in conquered territory. (Such settlements were still occasionally planted; see note 10 to p. 391.)

10. 17 November.

11. Antiochus I (281–261)?

12. This probably means that, as in Alexandria (note 21 to p. 171), the Jews had an independent civic organization parallel to that of the Greeks (see their 'magistrate' – below), but did not share Greek citizenship.

13. Early in 67. Antioch had escaped the wave of anti-Semitic risings during the previous autumn (p. 171).

14. As an apostate he had evidently been able to become a member of the Greek citizen-body, and had risen high in the municipal hierarchy: he could address the assembly, make arrests, and command troops (below).

15. In the winter of 70–71.

16. These charges of intended and actual arson recall the allegation made by Nero (according to Tacitus, *Ann.* xv.44) that Christians had started the fire which devastated Rome in 64. Antioch had had a strong Church for twenty years, and it is possible that the Jews accused there were Christians against whom the apostate felt peculiar animosity.

17. A flattering inexactitude. According to Tacitus, the rebels had already been defeated by the time Domitian arrived (*Hist.* iv.68, 85–6).

18. Though irrelevant to Josephus' main story, this paragraph is valuable in recording an episode not known from any other source.

19. The district of Arca, far to the north of his main territory, had apparently been given to Agrippa II after the war as a reward for his loyalty; see the extent of his kingdom in 66 (p. 193).

20. A river with this behaviour could more accurately be described as a Sabbath-breaker. Pliny more convincingly says that it dried up every Sabbath (*Nat. Hist.* xxxi.18, 24).

21. This seemingly milder request would have had the same effect: it would have deprived the Jews of their political status as authorized residents and degraded them to the position of aliens without the right of domicile, who could then have been summarily ejected.

22. But the basic purpose of this visit was surely to make sure that the city was peaceful and submissive before going home.

23. Where he rejected an appeal by the Greeks, similar to that made in Antioch, that he would deprive the Jews of their civic rights in the city (*AJ* xii.121).

24. i.e. Domitian as well.

25. On the Palatine.

26. In the Campus Martius, the 'field of Mars', the old parade-ground on the flat plain in the north-east of the city, beside the Tiber.

27. A portico named by Augustus after his sister, surrounding a group of buildings between the Tiber and the Capitol.

28. The location and character of the Porta Triumphalis are uncertain. It was not a city gate, since Rome was then unwalled. It may have been an arch in the Campus Martius.

29. Besides the still partially surviving Theatre of Marcellus built by Augustus near the Capitol, there were two older ones, in the Campus Martius.

30. Literally 'made in the sea', i.e. genuine purple dye from the *murex*, not an imitation.

31. This part of the procession is portrayed on one of the two reliefs decorating the passage of the posthumous Arch of Titus in the Forum in Rome. In addition to the lampstand and the table of the Shewbread, the ritual trumpets are shown.

32. Scrolls of the Pentateuch.

33. The other relief on the Arch of Titus shows the emperor's chariot.

34. The Mamertine Prison, in the north-west corner of the Forum, at the foot of the Capitol.

35. In 75. Other ancient writers testify to its magnificence.

36. They were seized by the Vandals and taken to North Africa in 455, recovered and removed to Constantinople, the capital of the eastern empire (the western half of the divided empire based on Rome having by then collapsed under barbarian pressure), in 534, and then, reputedly, sent to a church in Jerusalem, where they remained till the seventh century. They disappeared at an unknown later date.

CHAPTER 23: CLEANING-UP OPERATIONS

1. It appears from this sentence that the former commander of the Fifth Legion (p. 214) had been put in command of the Tenth (cf. p. 375) and left in charge of the province as *locum tenens* until Vespasian decided on its future. As it was now to have a legionary garrison instead of half a dozen auxiliary units, it could no longer be governed by a mere equestrian procurator, but required a legate of senatorial rank; and since the garrison comprised only one legion, the governor was also its commander.

2. The scale of the defences now visible at Herodium suggests that the reduction of the fortress, given very casually by Josephus, was no negligible operation. The date is not indicated, but as Masada fell in May, 73 (p. 404) it is reasonable to put the siege of Machaerus (below) in 72 and the capture of Herodium early in that year or late in 71.

3. pp. 48–9.

4. Machaerus has not yet been excavated.

5. Probably Nabataeans from the vicinity.

6. Translating the reading of the MSS. A slight emendation gives 'with the men building the platform'.

7. p. 344. His escape has not in fact been previously mentioned.

8. See Appendix B.

9. The translation 'sell', once generally accepted, is now agreed to be incorrect. Even if taken literally to exclude Greek and Samaritan property, 'all Jewish property' seems to be too sweeping, implying as it does that Vespasian appropriated the land even of loyal communities like Sepphoris and of deserters, whose property Titus had promised to restore (p. 346). Presumably only land belonging to rebels who had fought to the end was in fact in question.

10. This veteran colony, a stabilizing force and a support for the legion in Jerusalem, was presumably settled on land confiscated from rebels.

11. i.e. the tax previously paid by Jewish men throughout the world for the upkeep of the Temple in Jerusalem, now obsolete, was converted into a tax payable to Rome – for the upkeep of the temple of Jupiter on the Capitol, according to Dio Cassius lxvi.7.2. Receipts from Egypt show, however, that its incidence was now widened to make women and children from the age of three also liable. Through the universal imposition of this tax, though in no other way, Rome made the Jews of the Diaspora suffer for the sins of the Jews of Palestine.

12. The episode of 72–3 now to be related, of little relevance to Jewish affairs, led, though Josephus does not make it very clear, to the annexation of Commagene as part of Vespasian's policy of strengthening the eastern frontier. For Antiochus IV and his son, see pp. 173, 194, 327.

13. Commagene as a client kingdom was not allowed to pursue an independent foreign policy.

14. If Aristobulus is the son of Herod of Chalcis (pp. 143, 146), he may just have received this principality in northern Syria in compensation for Lesser Armenia in eastern Asia Minor, now annexed after he had ruled it for twenty years.

15. Not in the *BJ* as we have it. Josephus may have lifted the whole sentence from his source. This episode has no more relevance to the Jews than the one just narrated.

16. The 'Caspian Gates' was a pass in the Taurus mountains through which Alexander pursued the Persian king Darius, but no literal gate is mentioned elsewhere.

17. Brother of Vologeses of Parthia (above).

18. Another brother of Vologeses.

19. *Pace* Yadin and the title of his superb book on Masada (see the bibliography), its defenders were Sicarii, not Zealots; Josephus is explicit and consistent on this point.

20. p. 133 and Appendix A. Eleazar, son of Jairus (pp. 167–8), was probably Judas' grandson.

21. An anachronistic application of the term, not current till the 50s (p. 166), to Judas' 'sect'.

22. John of Gischala. Josephus has now drifted back from A.D. 6 to the war.

23. p. 260.

24. The circumvallation, over two miles long, and the eight camps associated with it are clearly visible from the summit.

25. The largest of the camps lies a short distance outside the circumvallation, north-west of the fortress.

26. The isolated rock of Masada rises some 1,200 feet from the plain between the Dead Sea and the Judaean mountains and forms a lozenge-shaped plateau, 600 yards north–south and 250 yards east–west.

27. By no means, to normal eyesight.

28. The 'Snake path', now widened and furnished with hand-rails at the worst corners, is actually two miles long. A cable-car provides an alternative and painless ascent.

29. Coin-finds, however, suggest that it was built later, under Alexander Jannaeus (Yadin, *Masada*, 205).

30. Many of these casemates were used by the defenders as dwellings; hearths, cooking pots and many domestic utensils were found in them by the excavators.

31. So literally. A more accurate description would be 'descending in steps'.

32. Despite the words 'on the western slope', this building 'below the

fortifications' and 'sloping down northwards', with a concealed stair-case cut in the rock to the summit (below), is certainly not Herod's large official palace just inside the western wall but his smaller, private, three-tiered palace built on the natural terraces jutting out from the precipitous northern point. Josephus, who is unlikely to have had any first-hand knowledge of the site, seems unaware that there were two palaces, and misplaces the one which he attempts to describe (without any clear conception of its three tiers) on the site of the one more access-ible to visitors.

33. Near the northern end of the fortress over a dozen long narrow storehouses can be seen.

34. Would the stores not have been used and replaced by, success-ively, Herod's garrison, the Roman garrison, and the Sicarii?

35. pp. 75–6.

36. The projecting ends of timbers laid horizontally to bond the earth of the assault ramp which widened and heightened *Leuke*, the 'white cliff', can be seen from the present path up the ramp.

37. cf. Vespasian's similar but smaller towers at Jotapata (p. 212).

38. Reminiscent of *sōma sēma*, 'the body a tomb', a doctrine held by the Greek philosopher Pythagoras which influenced Plato.

39. In *Ap*.i.176–82 Josephus quotes a passage from a pupil of Aris-totle in which the Jews are alleged to be descended from Indian philo-sophers.

40. pp. 168–9.

41. pp. 148, 150–51.

42. pp. 169–70.

43. pp. 169–71.

44. p. 179 (with 10,500 casualties).

45. Strictly speaking, Alexandria, pp. 171–3 (with 50,000 casualties).

46. pp. 376–7.

47. During excavation a group of eleven ostraca (potsherds, used as the ancient equivalent of scrap paper) was found, each bearing a different name. One is 'the son of Jairus', and it is tempting to interpret them as the lots used for the final massacre, Josephus' 'ten' being an error for 'ten plus one'.

48. In 72. This date is not based on the earlier reference to Vespasian's fourth year, which is attached to the Commagenian episode (p. 391), but on the fact that events in Egypt dated to the summer of 73 are explicitly put after the fall of Masada (p. 405; note 58 to p. 407). Dating Masada a year earlier would mean squeezing the Herodium and Machaerus campaigns both into the last months of 71.

49. They will have heard the speeches (though what Josephus gives surely owes much more to his pen than to verbatim reporting), and

they may have witnessed the start of the family massacres. But one wonders how they observed the final executions by the ten from their underground hideout!

50. These may have been Sicarii who had escaped from Herodium and Machaerus, though Josephus speaks of Sicarii only in connection with Masada. The whole episode, over by August, 73 at the latest (note 58 to p. 407), must actually have begun well before the fall of Masada, since it involved an exchange of letters between Alexandria and Rome (p. 406), which is likely to have taken two months or so.

51. As an independent political unit in Alexandria, the Jews had their own council and officials; note 21 to p. 171.

52. The prefect of Egypt.

53. p. 33. In *AJ* xii.387-8 and xiii. 62-73, perhaps a correction of the version here, the refugee is not Onias III, son of Simon, but his son, Onias IV, and he flees shortly after the persecution.

54. At Leontopolis (*AJ*, loc. cit.), evidently quite a small place, not the town Leontopolis sixty miles from Memphis. The site has been identified as Tell el-Yehudieh, 'the Mound of the Jew', north-east of Memphis at the tip of the Delta. A nome was an administrative district centred on a town.

55. It was the only place outside Jerusalem where sacrifice was offered.

56. The obvious site for a temple built with this in mind would have been Alexandria with its large Jewish community, not a village up-country. In fact the sanctuary probably merely served the needs of the local community (note 82 to p. 52). The fact that Philo (Introduction, p. 18, n.) never mentions it is evidence of its insignificance in the religious life of the Jews in Egypt.

57. Isaiah 19.19-23, but regarded as a late insertion.

58. Lupus is last attested in office by dated Egyptian documents in March, 73; Paulinus is first attested before the end of August, 73.

59. Obviously incorrect. Even emendation to 243 would date the foundation to 170 B.C., a little too early even for Onias III.

60. Not mentioned in the narrative of the war.

61. This recalls the pseudo-messianic movements in Judaea under the procurators (p. 147).

62. The governor of the province of Cyrenaica, the most fertile part of which comprised five cities of Greek origin, the Pentapolis.

63. In *V* 424-5 this is amplified: Jonathan was jealous of the privileged position which Josephus now enjoyed as a protégé of Vespasian in Rome and so alleged that he had supplied arms and money for the movement.

Bandits, Terrorists, Sicarii and Zealots

THE word *lēstēs*, usually translated 'bandit' or 'brigand', denotes in Josephus not a highwayman seeking personal gain but a terrorist, a guerrilla, or (from the man's own viewpoint) a freedom-fighter, a man working towards a political goal. Brigandage of this kind was a frequent, if not an endemic, problem in Palestine. Herod's first post was a military commission to put down bandits in Galilee in 46 B.C. (p. 54) – probably the survivors of the party of the deposed Aristobulus. Herod's death in 4 B.C. was followed by a revolt against Roman overlordship in which bands of brigands supporting pretenders to the throne played a part (p. 126). The annexation of Judaea as a province in A.D. 6 intensified Jewish nationalist feeling, which hardened into a militant resistance movement using terrorist and guerrilla tactics.

The brief reference in the *BJ* to a rising immediately after the annexation led by a certain Judas from Galilee, founder of a sect distinct from the Pharisees, Sadducees and Essenes (p. 133), is filled out on p. 393 and in *AJ* xviii.1-10, 23-5. The rising was a protest against a census held by Quirinius, legate of Syria (brought in because the task was evidently considered to be beyond Coponius' capabilities), for the purpose of tax-assessment. Though the rising came to little and Judas was killed (Acts 5.37), the movement resulted in the formation of a 'fourth school of thought', a sect of extreme nationalist views opposed to all temporal rule and regarding 'God alone as leader and master' (a principle which incidentally tells against identifying Judas with the Galilaean homonym who had made a bid for the throne ten years earlier). Josephus attributes to this sect the responsibility for the subsequent internal strife in the province that led to the war. But, having said that, he never mentions it again. In the numerous clashes which he recounts between the Jews and the Roman authorities from the 40s to the 60s it is always the 'bandits' who are involved. Whether these guerrillas were technically members of the sect or not, however, they were no doubt Judas' spiritual heirs, inspired by the same principles, aiming at the same goal of political independence, and hostile not only to Rome but to pro-Roman Jews (p. 393). The story of the Good Samaritan, though fictitious, and other references to 'robbers' in the Gospels reflect the insecurity which they brought to the country. And the Gospels also record in passing the earliest known outbreak of political violence: *c.* 30 the 'robber' (*lēstēs*) Barabbas and other 'rebels' committed murder in an insurrection in Jerusalem and two of them were crucified.

The Sicarii were a splinter group of terrorists formed in the 50s, distinct from the other nationalists not in their aims but in their methods. Their name 'daggermen' (from Latin *sica*, a dagger) – perhaps originally a derogatory nickname given by their opponents – described their insidious *modus operandi* (pp. 147, 166). They developed into one of the most important nationalist groups and during the war operated independently first under Menahem and then under Eleazar, son of Jairus, from their base at Masada, which they seized in 66 and defended to the end in 73.

The famous term Zealot, which modern writers sometimes use anachronistically of the nationalist movement from its inception, does not occur in Josephus before the war. The Zealots appear late in 66 (p. 188) as the main war-party in Jerusalem under Eleazar, son of Simon. With their self-chosen complimentary name denoting their attitude to their cause and their ideals (p. 246), they may in theory have had primarily religious motives; but their methods were no less brutal than those of other nationalist factions. Josephus' solitary, and most probably erroneous, use of 'Zealots' (p. 167) for Menahem's followers, who elsewhere are the Sicarii, has led to confusion between two factions which seem to have been quite distinct.

The false prophets or messiahs who appeared from time to time after 44 were also nationalists, pursuing the same goal of political independence as the 'bandits' but by different methods. Using the pseudo-spiritual appeal of the promise of miracles leading to deliverance from Roman oppression, they collected hordes of gullible followers and staged miniature risings, all of which resulted in heavy casualties when they were suppressed by force. Josephus regards their misuse of religion for political ends as even more sinister than terrorist activity, and equally damaging (p. 147).

APPENDIX B

Roman Provincial Administration and Defence

A PROVINCE was a tract of territory outside Italy under Roman rule. Provinces were acquired first in the western Mediterranean, then in the eastern, and finally further afield from the middle of the third century B.C. as a result of wars or in various other ways, until by the time of the Jewish war the Roman territorial empire stretched from Spain to the Euphrates and from northern England to the edge of the Sahara.

Under the republic each province was administered by a member of the Roman senate who after holding the consulship or the praetorship (a judicial post) for a year in Italy was sent out as governor for a period of from one to three years, with a small staff. The senate exercised general supervision over the provinces in that it decided on the length of a governor's tenure, controlled his funds, and directed his military operations, if any. But its rein was slack, and many provincial governors (all of whom served without salary) used their term of office to make money by numerous dubious or blatantly dishonest means at the expense of their subjects. The unfortunate provincials were also regularly fleeced by the syndicates of *publicani* to whom contracts for the collection of taxes were auctioned by the government. (It was from this abuse that the term *publicani* acquired its unpleasant connotation; its original meaning was neutral – 'men who undertook contracts for public works', such as building roads.) The syndicates were composed of members of the equestrian order, the wealthy class of business and landed men who were outside the narrow oligarchy of aristocratic senatorial families and rarely succeeded in penetrating it and achieving high public office. Their name went back to the very early years of the republic when only men rich enough to own a horse and equip it for battle served as *equites*, cavalry; it survived as a convenient designation for the wealthy non-senatorial class for centuries after losing its literal meaning.

The battle of Actium in 31 B.C. ended twenty years of intermittent civil war and put the final victor, Octavian, in a position of supreme power, which he used four years later to establish himself as permanent emperor under the new name of Augustus. Under the empire (in the constitutional sense of the form of government which he instituted) the republican administrative machinery continued to function, though under the emperor's general oversight, but at the same time some fundamental changes were initiated. One of the most important concerned provincial government.

Augustus divided the control of the provinces between himself and the senate, taking about half of them into his own care. These were the provinces most recently acquired, i.e. those where there was the greatest risk of disorder and which had frontiers with the non-Roman world. Syria, annexed by Pompey in 63 B.C., thus became an 'imperial' province, as did Egypt, annexed shortly after Actium, while Asia (western Asia Minor), old-established and peaceful, remained senatorial. This division enabled Augustus to keep almost the whole of the standing army which he created and stationed along the frontiers of the empire – notably on the Rhine, the Danube and the Euphrates, and in Egypt – in his own hands. This army of some 300,000 men consisted half of legions numbering about 5,000 men each and recruited from Roman citizens, and half of auxiliaries, infantry and cavalry units of 500 (occasionally 1,000) men each, recruited mainly from provincials who did not have Roman citizenship. The provision of permanent garrisons remedied one of the serious defects of the provincial system under the republic, inadequate frontier defence, and in consequence *pax Romana*, the 'Roman peace', was for some two hundred years the rule rather than the exception in most parts of the Roman world and one of the chief blessings conferred by Rome on her subjects.

In the senatorial provinces methods of administration remained much the same as under the republic. In the imperial provinces, however, there were major changes. Technically Augustus himself was governor of them all (just as he was titular commander of every legion). He delegated this responsibility to men whom he chose as his personal representatives, appointing a legate (literally a 'deputy') to take charge of each province for him, usually for a period of about three years. The legate was a senior member of the senate, in most cases a man who had held the consulship, but he was answerable to the emperor alone, without reference to the senate. (Similarly, a senior senator, but never an ex-consul, was appointed as legate to command each legion in the emperor's name.) A procurator, always a member of the equestrian order, junior in rank and almost certainly also in years to the legate, was also appointed to each province, to take charge of the collection of taxes and of other financial aspects of the administration, and the *publicani* never had a chance to get their claws into the imperial provinces. To reduce the temptation to make money out of a provincial command, salaries were paid to legates and procurators. The provincial legate had overriding control over the legions stationed in his territory, since the legionary legates were slightly junior to him.

A few small provinces, including Judaea from its annexation in A.D.

6 until after the war of 66–70, had instead of a legate a procurator who acted as governor as well as financial officer – or, to be quite exact, an equestrian governor for whom the title procurator became established by about the middle of the first century; in the early decades of the century the evidence indicates that, though terminology was still fluid, equestrian governors were normally called 'prefect', the title held by Pontius Pilate on a fragment of a Latin inscription found in Caesarea c. 1960.

A province under an equestrian governor had no resident legion – if only because a legionary legate of senatorial rank could not serve under a governor of lower rank – but a small garrison of auxiliary units under officers drawn from the equestrian order. In the case of Judaea, it was five infantry units and one cavalry unit, each 500 men strong, which at least until the 40s were recruited locally, largely from the non-Jewish cities of Sebaste and Caesarea. (It is probable that they were basically Herod the Great's troops, taken over from Archelaus in A.D. 6; for the core of his army had been 3,000 men from Sebaste, apparently organized on Roman lines in cohorts under officers who, if not actual Romans, had Roman names – pp. 99, 125.) The inadequacy of a garrison of this size, not substantially increased when the province was almost doubled in size in 44, was one reason for the increasing disorder there which eventually erupted into rebellion and war.

APPENDIX C

Money

JOSEPHUS always gives sums of money in Greek denominations, not Hebrew or Roman, although once Judaea had become a province, Roman silver circulated there and only bronze coins of low value were struck locally. He uses talents for large sums and drachmas for small, except for one passage in which a very large sum is expressed in drachmas (p. 130). Attic (i.e. Athenian) drachmas are once specified (p. 353). A drachma, a silver coin, was roughly equal in value to a Roman silver denarius, the 'penny' of the Gospels (Matthew 20.1–15 and Luke 20.24 A.V.) and the '*d.*' that was used to denote a penny in our old coinage. A talent (for which there was no Roman equivalent) was worth 60,000 drachmas.

It is pointless to attempt, in these days of unstable money, to give modern equivalents for ancient currencies, whether in terms of metallic content or in terms of cash. The only valid standard of comparison is purchasing power, but even in that matter the evidence is not comprehensive and the relative values of articles in the ancient world were by no means the same as they are now. For example, compared with a pair of shoes, a book, hand-produced, must have been relatively a great deal more costly in the ancient world than a book is today. But one can get some idea of the value of a drachma or a denarius from such evidence as the parable of the labourers in the vineyard (Matthew, loc. cit.), where a normal day's wage, which would keep a family at subsistence level, was one denarius.

APPENDIX D

Josephus' Calendar

IN giving precise dates during his narrative of the war Josephus follows neither the Roman nor the Jewish calendar but the Macedonian, which was regularly used throughout Asia Minor and Syria. Only rough equivalents for the Macedonian months can be given, since the system was less exact than the Julian calendar, but each month seems to have begun at about the middle of a Julian month. The correlation is:

Dystros	March–April
Xanthicos	April–May
Artemisios	May–June
Daisios	June–July
Panemos	July–August
Loös	August–September
Gorpiaios	September–October
Hyperberetaios	October–November
Dios	November–December
Apellaios	December–January
Audnaios	January–February
Peritios	February–March

Qumran

THE dramatic discovery in 1947 of numerous scrolls and fragments of scrolls which had formed part of a large ancient library concealed in the caves round Qumran to the north-west of the Dead Sea aroused unprecedented interest and controversy among scholars and the general public alike. But the direct relevance of these writings to Josephus' *BJ* is apparently slight. Josephus does not mention the community based on Khirbet Qumran (the excavated residential building) in that work or any other. He does, however, give a long description of the Essene sect, to which it is now generally agreed that that community belonged (pp. 133-7; cf. the shorter parallel in *AJ* xviii.18–22), possibly drawing on the detailed account given by Philo (*Quod Omnis Probus . . . 75–91*).

Archaeological evidence indicates that Khirbet Qumran was captured by Vespasian (presumably in an operation too insignificant for mention by Josephus) after his occupation of Jericho in 68, when he visited the Dead Sea (pp. 272–3). The buildings show destruction by assault and fire, the life of the community came to an abrupt end, and a Roman military post was established on part of the site; and the fact that large numbers of Jewish coins struck in the second year of the revolt were found there but few of the third year and none of the fourth or fifth provides the date. (The coin era may have run from the outbreak of the war but more probably was taken back to Nisan, 66, the Jewish religious New Year in the spring.)

Much of the Qumran library consisted of Biblical texts; portions of all Old Testament books except Esther have been identified. But it also contained Biblical commentaries, hymns and liturgical works peculiar to the sect, and documents setting out the rules for the life and administration of the community. The *Commentary on Habakkuk* may date from the time of Pompey's siege of Jerusalem and reflect the terror felt at the coming of the Kittim ('foreigners', here taken to mean the Romans). But it supplies few, if any, historical facts to supplement Josephus. (Attempts to interpret the conflict in Jerusalem recounted in the work as an allegorization of the murder of Menaham late in A.D. 66 – pp. 167–8 – fail on palaeographical and other grounds.) There may also be references to Pompey in the Psalms of Solomon 2 and 8. The copper scroll listing quantities of gold and silver, amounting to 4,630 talents in all, hidden in and around Jerusalem and Jericho is more likely, in view of the huge sum involved, to be a fantasy based on the tradition of the vast wealth of the Temple (cf. note 76 to p. 51 above) than a genuine inventory of treasures concealed when Titus' siege of Jerusalem was imminent.

The modern literature on the Qumran library is now enormous, and grows constantly. To give even the smallest representative bibliography here would be to devote disproportionate space to a subject which only touches the fringes of Josephus' work. But the main sectarian documents have been made conveniently accessible by G. Vermes, *The Dead Sea Scrolls in English*, 1962, revised 1965 and 1968 (Pelican), who precedes his translation with a clear and concise account of the beliefs, life and practices of the community as revealed in its literature. The definitive publication of the copper scroll is in *Discoveries in the Judaean Desert*, III (1962). For a selective bibliography of the major works on the library up to 1973 the reader should turn to Schürer (rev.), I, pp. 118–22. After that he can move on, if he has the stamina, to *Revue de Qumran*!

The Slavonic Version of The Jewish War

THE Slavonic version of the *BJ* presents considerable problems which cannot be dealt with even in a summary fashion here; only a few bald facts and a brief indication of some of the questions that arise can be given. It is a translation into old Russian, perhaps made *c.* 1250 (though earlier dates have also been suggested), and preserved in a number of MSS. of the fifteenth century and later. It certainly was not made from the text of the *BJ* as we have it; it appears to have been made, not from the original Aramaic version, but from a different Greek version from ours, a version which, according to the ingeniously worked out theory of R. Eisler (*Iesous Basileus ou Basileusas*, Heidelberg, 1929 – 'Jesus the King who was never King'), was Josephus' first draft of his translation from the Aramaic. In some places the Slavonic version abbreviates our text or omits passages, and in others it differs from it in content. An amusing instance of such a discrepancy occurs in the story of Josephus' escape from Jotapata. Where our *BJ* suggests that it was by divine providence or luck that he was one of the last two survivors of the suicide-pact (p. 220), the Slavonic version blandly gives what the cynical reader probably suspects was the truth anyhow: 'he counted the numbers cunningly and so managed to deceive all the others' – a piece of sharp practice later suppressed as too ignoble for the gallant commander and the pensioner of the Flavians.

The Slavonic version also includes a number of passages which have no parallel in the extant Greek version, and of these the ones which have aroused the greatest interest and consequently the loudest controversy are those dealing with Christianity – passages giving highly garbled accounts of John the Baptist and of the ministry, death and resurrection of Jesus Christ (neither of them referred to by name), and a picture of the early Church as a faith-healing movement. There are basically three possible interpretations of them: that Josephus, who is likely to have been aware of the main facts of Christ's life and of the existence of the Church as a schismatic sect, wrote them; that they are wholesale interpretations (but by whom? hardly by a Christian, since such travesties of the New Testament tradition would have done little to promote belief or to enhance the prestige of the Church); or that they are elaborations of shorter, less sensational passages written by Josephus.

Twenty-two of the additional passages are given in English at the end of Vol. II of the Loeb edition of the *BJ* (see the bibliography). A complete Slavonic text is given by V. Istrin, *La prise de Jérusalem de Josèphe le Juif*, 2 vols., Paris, 1934–8, with a French translation by P. Pascal.

Chronological Table

Rome	Palestine	The East
B.C.	B.C.	B.C.
	Hellenizing movement	175–163 Antiochus IV Epiphanes of Syria
	167 Desecration of the Temple by Antiochus	
	165 Maccabaean revolt	
	164 Reconsecration of the Temple	
	164–161 Judas Maccabaeus high priest	163–162 Antiochus V of Syria
	161 Treaty with Rome	c. 160? Temple of Onias built
	161–142 Jonathan high priest	
	c. 143 Treaty renewed	150–145 Alexander Balas
	142–135/4 Simon high priest	145–138 Antiochus VI of Syria
	?141 Syrian garrison expelled; Jews independent	
	?140 Simon appointed ethnarch Annexation of Joppa and Jamnia	138–129 Antiochus VII of Syria

Rome	Palestine	The East
B.C.	B.C.	B.C.
	135/4–104 John Hyrcanus I high priest and ethnarch	133 Annexation of Asia (western Asia Minor) as province
	Annexation of other coastal cities, Samaritis and Idumaea	
	104–103 Aristobulus I high priest and king	
	Annexation of Galilee	
	103–76 Alexander Jannaeus high priest and king	
	Annexation of remaining coastal cities, Greek cities east of Jordan, and Peraea	
	76–67 Alexandra queen	
	Hyrcanus II high priest	
	67 Hyrcanus II high priest and king (three months); Antipater his minister	
	67–63 Aristobulus II high priest and king	
	63 Pompey's siege of Jerusalem	66–63 Pompey's campaigns in East. Annexation of Syria as province
	Hyrcanus II reinstated as high priest and ethnarch:	

Rome		Palestine		The East	
B.C.		B.C.		B.C.	
			Antipater increasingly powerful		
			Aristobulus and sons taken to Rome		
			Cities on coast and east of Jordan detached from Jewish state		
62	Return of Pompey to Rome with Jewish prisoners				
		57–55	Unsuccessful attempts to reinstate Aristobulus and sons	57–55	Gabinius governor of Syria
		55	Temple treasure seized by Crassus	55	Jewish help to Gabinius in Egypt
				55–53	Crassus governor of Syria
				53–51	Cassius governor of Syria
49–45	Civil war between Caesar and Pompeians	49	Death of Aristobulus and elder son		
48	Death of Pompey at Pharsalus	47	Caesar in Judaea	48/7	Jewish help to Caesar in Egypt
			Hyrcanus II's position confirmed		
			Power and honours given to Antipater		

Rome

B.C.	
44	Murder of Caesar
43–42	Civil war between Caesarians and 'liberators'
42	Death of Brutus and Cassius at Philippi
37	Rome and the West under Octavian's control

Palestine

B.C.	
46	Joppa restored; Rebuilding of walls of Jerusalem authorized; Herod in Galilee; Herod in Syria
43	Cassius' demand for money
40	Parthian invasion of Syria and Palestine; Antigonus installed as king; Death of Phasael; In Rome, Herod appointed king
40–37	Herod's campaigns to get possession of Palestine
37	Capture of Jerusalem by Herod and Sosius; Herod's marriage to Mariamme I; Execution of Antigonus

The East

B.C.	
47–46	Sextus Caesar in Syria
43	Cassius (the 'liberator') in Syria
39–8	Roman campaigns against Parthia; East under Mark Antony's control; Antony dominated by Cleopatra

Rome		Palestine		The East	
B.C.		B.C.		B.C.	
		36	Murder of high priest, Mariamme's brother		
		c. 35	Coastal cities, including Joppa, given to Cleopatra by Antony		
31	Defeat of Antony and Cleopatra by Octavian at Actium	32	War between Herod and Malchus of Nabataea		
		31	Death of Hyrcanus II		
		30	Herod's position confirmed by Octavian; Coastal cities and Greek cities east of Jordan restored	30	Annexation of Egypt as province
				c. 30	Malchus of Nabataea succeeded by Obodas
		29	Murder of Mariamme I		
27	Name 'Augustus' given to Octavian; new form of government under emperor established	27/6	Foundation of Sebaste		
		23	Auranitis, Trachonitis and Batanaea added to Herod's kingdom		
		c. 23	Herod's marriage to Mariamme II		
		23	Rebuilding of Temple begun		
		20	Paneas, Ulatha and Gaulanitis added to Herod's kingdom		

Rome		Palestine		The East	
B.C.		B.C.		B.C.	
		16	Herod's first visit to Rome		
		12	Herod's second visit to Rome; trial of Alexander and Aristobulus. Border trouble with Nabataea		
				c. 9	Obodas succeeded by Aretas IV
		c. 7	Execution of Alexander and Aristobulus	10/9–7/6	Saturninus legate of Syria
		c. 6	Birth of Christ		
		5	Eagle episode	7/6–4	Varus legate of Syria
2	Banishment of Julia	4	Execution of Antipater. Death of Herod (March). Civil war. Division of kingdom between Philip, Antipas and Archelaus		
A.D.		A.D.		A.D.	
		6	Deposition of Archelaus. Annexation of Judaea as province	6–?	Quirinius legate of Syria
14	Accession of Tiberius	6–c. 9	Coponius governor		
		c. 10	Death of Salome		
		c. 9–26	Three (or four?) governors, not mentioned in BJ		

Rome		Palestine		The East	
A.D.		A.D.		A.D.	
		26–36	Pontius Pilate governor		
		30 or 33	Crucifixion of Christ		
		c. 34	Death of Philip	35–9	Vitellius legate of Syria
36–7	Agrippa I in Rome	37–41	Governor not mentioned in BJ		
37	Accession of Gaius	37	Birth of Josephus		
			Appointment of Agrippa I as king of Trachonitis etc.	38	Anti-Semitic riots in Alexandria
				39–42	Petronius legate of Syria
40–41	Agrippa I in Rome	40	Gaius' attack on the Temple		
41	Accession of Claudius	41	Deposition of Antipas; Galilee and Peraea added to Agrippa I's kingdom	41	Herod appointed king of Chalcis
			Province of Judaea disbanded; added to Agrippa I's kingdom		
		44	Death of Agrippa I; Province of Judaea reconstituted, with Galilee and Peraea included		

Rome	A.D.	Palestine	A.D.	The East
A.D.	44–?46	Fadus procurator	A.D.	
	?46–48	Tiberius Julius Alexander procurator	48	Death of Herod of Chalcis
	48–52	Cumanus procurator	49	Agrippa II appointed king of Chalcis
	52–58/9	Felix procurator	51–?60	Ummidius Quadratus legate of Syria
54 Accession of Nero		Arrest and imprisonment of St Paul	53	Agrippa II transferred to Trachonitis etc.
		Quarrel in Caesarea referred to Nero		
	58/9–62	Festus procurator		
		Trial of St Paul and appeal to Nero		
	62–4	Albinus procurator		
64 Fire of Rome	64–6	Florus procurator	65/6–67	Cestius Gallus legate of Syria
	66	Cestius Gallus in Jerusalem at Passover	66–9	Tiberius Julius Alexander prefect of Egypt
		Riots in Caesarea	66	Riots in Alexandria
		Outbreak of war (May)		Anti-Semitic risings in cities of Syria
		Florus' attack on Jerusalem		
		Masada captured by Sicarii		

A.D.	The East
67–9	Mucianus in Syria
67	Anti-Semitic riots in Antioch

A.D.	Palestine
67	Roman troops driven out of Jerusalem (Sept.)
	Defeat of Cestius at Beth-horon (Nov.)
	Appointment of Josephus and five other regional commanders
	Arrival of Vespasian and Titus
	Capture of Jotapata (July)
	Subjugation of most of Galilee
	Capture of Gamala (Oct.)
	in Jerusalem, arrival of John of Gischala; his alliance with Zealots; deposition of high priest; faction fighting
68	Subjugation of most of Judaea, Idumaea and Peraea
	Romans inactive from c. July

A.D.	Rome
68	Dethronement of Nero (June)

Rome		Palestine		The East	
A.D.		A.D.		A.D.	
	Accession of Galba		Simon, son of Gioras, in control of parts of Judaea and Idumaea		
			In Jerusalem, reinforcements summoned from Idumaea; alliance between John and Zealots ended		
69	Murder of Galba (Jan.) Accession of Otho Vitellius proclaimed emperor Death of Otho (April) Death of Vitellius and Flavian victory (Dec.)	69	Simon admitted into Jerusalem; fighting between him, John of Gischala and Zealots Roman recovery of territory lost to Simon (spring) Titus left in command by Vespasian (autumn)	69	Vespasian proclaimed emperor (July); in Egypt (winter 69–70)
70	Return of Vespasian	70	Siege of Jerusalem begun (spring) Outer two north walls captured (May) Circumvallation built (May)		

Rome		Palestine		The East	
A.D.		A.D.		A.D.	
			Antonia captured (July) Temple stormed and burnt (Aug.) Upper City captured and burnt (Sept.)	70–71	Fire in Antioch (winter)
71	Triumph of Vespasian and Titus (summer)	71	Titus' visit to Jerusalem (spring) Capture of Herodium (autumn)?	71–3	Caesennius Paetus legate of Syria
				71	Titus' visits to Antioch and Alexandria (spring)
		72	Capture of Machaerus Battle of Jardes forest	71–2	Trouble in Cyrenaica
		73	Capture of Masada (May)	72–3	Trouble in Alexandria and Egypt; temple of Onias closed
75	Dedication of temple of Peace				

Maps and Plans

THE EASTERN MEDITERRANEAN

PALESTINE

Names of cities are given in capitals
Square brackets denote cities of
the Decapolis
Round brackets denote changes of
name made during the Roman period

0 10 20 30 40 50 km
0   10   20   30 miles

Jerusalem in A.D. 70

JERUSALEM is isolated and protected on three sides by the deep valleys of Gehenna and the Kidron. In antiquity it was divided from north to south by the much shallower valley Tyropoeon, 'the Valley of the Cheese-makers', now largely filled up and barely discernible. The original settlement, the Davidic city of the tenth century B.C., was on Ophel, the narrow ridge east of the Tyropoeon valley later known as the Lower City or the Citadel, the north end of which became the site of the Temple. As early as the seventh century the city was expanding on to the northern part of the western hill, the Upper City, and during the Hasmonaean period, when much of the western hill was settled, walls were built to enclose the whole area within the curve of Gehenna and the Kidron. The northern section of this wall ran from a point on the west wall of the Temple enclosure to the site of the Jaffa Gate in the present sixteenth-century walls above the north end of Gehenna, following the southern lip of a shallow valley which provided slight extra protection. From pre-Exilic days the vulnerable north side of the city was further defended by a fort to the north-west of the Temple. The Baris (p. 38; Aramaic for 'fort') was the Hasmonaean fort replacing an earlier one destroyed by Antiochus Epiphanes, and it was itself replaced by Herod's much stronger Antonia (pp. 81, 306). (Antiochus' Acra – note 6 to p. 33 – was on a different but unknown site, possibly on Ophel.) A fosse was also dug parallel to the north wall of the Temple enclosure.

The Hasmonaean north wall of Jerusalem, the 'old' wall of Josephus' description of the city (p. 298), was not demolished when a second was built at an unknown date – possibly when the fortifications destroyed by Pompey were rebuilt (p. 53) or possibly during the reign of Herod the Great, though it is not attributed to him by Josephus. The second north wall ran from a point on the old wall just east of Herod's three towers to the Antonia (or, if pre-Herodian, presumably to the Baris), enclosing part of the suburb Bezetha which was developing outside. Its line is conjectural, but it must have passed south-east of the site of the Church of the Holy Sepulchre, to leave Golgotha 'outside a city wall'. On the plan two possible lines are suggested; for the problem is complicated by the existence of a well-preserved gateway of typically Herodian masonry beside the Damascus Gate in the present north wall.

JERUSALEM in A.D. 70

HPM   *Herod's towers Hippicus, Phasael and Mariamme*
....   *Possible line of the second north wall, if the third followed roughly the line of the present north wall*
- - - -   *Possible line of the second north wall, if the third wall followed the more northerly line*
::::::::::   *Wall inferred from p.368*

The third north wall enclosing the whole of Bezetha was planned and begun by Agrippa I, though not completed until the winter of 66–7 (pp. 179, 188, 298–9). Until fairly recent years it was generally believed to have followed the line of the present north wall, a belief which some scholars still hold. If that is correct, the gateway dates from Agrippa I, with the Herodian style of masonry persisting for some decades after his death, and the second wall enclosed only a fairly small, roughly triangular area. But since 1925 substantial sections of a massive wall have been coming to light, running more or less parallel to the present north wall some 500 yards to the north and provided with north-facing defensive towers. The thesis that this is Agrippa's wall is gaining ground and becoming increasingly convincing as excavation proceeds. Indeed, if this wall is not Agrippa's, it is hard to see what it is. This would date the gateway to the time of Herod and mean that the second wall, whether built or repaired by him, extended that far north.

The wall marked tentatively as running south from the 'old' wall along the western lip of the Tyropoeon valley is not mentioned by Josephus. But the fact that, after mastering the whole of the eastern ridge, Titus did not march straight into the city from that side but had to build siege-platforms 'near the Gymnasium' (p. 368) suggests the existence of substantial defences there.

Of the three towers with which Herod strengthened the north-west angle of the 'old' wall, Hippicus may have been free-standing just outside; see the reference to the gate through which it was supplied with water (p. 312). The Greek at the beginning of Josephus' description of the towers (p. 299) is not entirely clear and could mean that only the 'two others', Phasael and Mariamme, were actually built into the curve of the wall (as Phasael is shown archaeologically to have been). But later he says unambiguously that their position 'in' the wall gave all three an illusion of increased height.

The approximate positions of the Hasmonaean palace and the Gymnasium are known from passages such as that on p. 156. No trace of Herod's Palace, used by the procurators as their residence when in Jerusalem, has yet been found, but recent excavation has shown that it stood on a platform measuring at least 60 yards and possibly up to 140 yards east to west and extending over 300 yards southwards from the towers almost to the south-west angle of the present city wall. As in the case of the Temple enclosure, the sloping ground was levelled up on substructures.

Herod's Temple Enclosure

THE enclosure wall shown is that of the present Haram es-Sherif, which is known to follow the line of Herod's enclosure wall at the south and is assumed to at the north also. Herod extended the enclosure 30 yards southwards, which entailed levelling up the sloping ground on vast vaulted substructures now misleadingly known as 'Solomon's Stables'.

There is no archaeological evidence for the exact position of the Temple within the enclosure, but it is believed that the bare rock in the centre of the late seventh-century Mosque of Omar, the Dome of the Rock, was the site either of the altar or of the Holy of Holies. The position of Titus' earthwork 'opposite the north-west corner of the inner court of the Temple' (p. 349) puts the Temple north of the junction between the enclosure and the 'old' city wall.

The position of the most northerly of the four gates in the western enclosure wall (*AJ* xv.410) is conjectural. There is archaeological evidence for the others, including the enormous first arch of the viaduct. Recent excavation has shown that at the south end of the western wall there was not, as had long been supposed, a second viaduct, but a monumental stairway leading down to a road along the Valley of the Cheesemakers and to the structures along the south wall.

In *AJ* xv.411 Josephus mentions 'gates in the middle' of the south wall. The Double Gate and the Triple Gate have long been known, but recent excavation has discovered a stepped road rising from the Valley of the Cheese-makers to run along the foot of the south wall, and in front of it a handsome paved 'piazza' with steps up to the gates.

The colonnades (mentioned only briefly in the *BJ* account of the Temple – p. 302), of which the Royal Colonnade was the widest, grandest and most ornate, are described in *AJ* xv.411–16. Josephus gives too little information about the colonnades which 'linked Antonia with the Temple' (pp. 154, 162) or 'enclosed' it (p. 302) for them to be drawn, but it is clear that the fortress was virtually an integral part of the Temple, with an extension of the northern and/or the western colonnade (p. 306) leading directly into it.

HEROD'S TEMPLE ENCLOSURE

Herod's Temple

SINCE Josephus, a priest, was familiar with Herod's Temple, his description of it is probably more reliable than that in the tractate *Middoth*, 'Measurements', in the Mishnah (the oral law codified c. A.D. 150), which records the dimensions in the hope of an eventual rebuilding. In some details *Middoth* supplements Josephus, but there are many discrepancies. It is difficult to reconstruct the details of the Temple and its courts accurately, though the general layout is clear, and the plan given here is only a suggestion.

Josephus gives no indication of the sizes of the Court of the Women and the inner courts in relation to each other or to the Temple, and no indication of the number or position of the entrance(s) from the Court of Israelites to the Court of the Priests.

The gate which Josephus clearly regards as the Corinthian Gate (possibly the Beautiful Gate of Acts 3.2 and 10) was also known as Nicanor's Gate. Some scholars think that the gate on the east of the Women's Court was the Corinthian Gate.

HEROD'S TEMPLE

1 Holy of Holies
2 Sanctuary
3 Priests' chambers
4 Vestibule
5 Corinthian Gate

The Herodian Family

This simplified tree shows only members of the family and marriages that were historically important

Glossary of Technical Terms

AUXILIARY UNITS. Units usually of 500 but occasionally of 1,000 men, recruited largely from provincials who did not have Roman citizenship and serving under Roman officers of equestrian rank known as prefects. See Appendix B.

CAMP PREFECT. Normally a very senior n.c.o., a man who had spent his whole life in the army. He ranked third after the commander and the most senior of the tribunes (*q.v.*).

CENTURION. An n.c.o. in charge of a century, a group of a hundred men, the smallest sub-division of a legion or an auxiliary unit.

CLIENT KING. The ruler (not necessarily with the actual title 'king') of a country dependent politically on Rome as a 'client' was dependent on his wealthy and influential 'patron' in Roman society. His appointment was made, or at least ratified, by Rome and could be terminated at any point. He had internal autonomy but was not allowed to pursue an independent foreign policy.

COHORT. (a) The largest sub-division of a legion, which comprised ten cohorts. (b) A unit of auxiliary infantry. (A cavalry unit was a 'wing', *ala*.)

DECURION. An n.c.o. in charge of a troop of ten men in a unit of auxiliary cavalry.

EQUESTRIAN ORDER. The wealthy business class in Roman society, distinct from the senatorial families which monopolized public office until the late first century B.C. The name dates from very early days when only the wealthy could afford to serve as cavalry. From the time of Augustus the equestrian order held a number of posts in the imperial administration. See Appendix B.

ETHNARCH. A Greek term meaning 'ruler of a nation', a less prestigious title than 'king', but still implying a degree of independence under an overlord.

HELLENISM. Greek culture, thought, practices etc.; from 'Hellas', the Greek name for Greece. Hellenization therefore means the implanting of Greek culture in an alien environment.

HELLENISTIC. Belonging to the Greek world after the death of Alexander the Great in 323 B.C.

LEGATE. Literally a 'deputy'. In the imperial administration, a man of senatorial rank serving as either (a) the governor of a large province or (b) the commander of a legion. See Appendix B.

LEGION. A regiment of some 5,000 men, all Roman citizens. During most of the first century A.D. there were twenty-five legions, distinguished by titles as well as numbers, since some numbers were duplicated.

PREFECT. (a) The governor of Egypt, one of the highest posts open to a member of the equestrian order. Egypt was the only province with a legionary garrison not governed by a senator. (b) The commander of an auxiliary unit.

PROCURATOR. An official in the emperor's service, almost invariably of equestrian rank, either (a) the financial officer in a large province governed by a legate, or (b) the governor of a small province. See Appendix B.

SANHEDRIN. The Jewish council of state, with political and judicial functions, meeting under the presidency of the high priest. Though the question is still controversial, many scholars hold that there were two sanhedrins, the primarily Sadducaean political council (to which Josephus often refers) and the primarily Pharisaean Great Sanhedrin of seventy members, with religious and legislative functions, under rabbinic control.

TETRARCH. A Greek term originally meaning the ruler of a quarter of a piece of territory, but by the first century B.C. meaning a dependent prince of fairly lowly status.

TOPARCHY. A small territorial unit comprising a town from which it took its name and a number of villages. Palestine was divided into toparchies for local administration.

TRIBUNE. Strictly 'military tribune' (as distinct from the civil magistrate in the Roman constitution), an army officer. There were six tribunes under the commander of each legion, mostly young men of equestrian rank.

Bibliography

GENERAL WORKS

F. M. Abel, *Histoire de la Palestine*, Vol. I, J. Gabalda, Paris, 1952
S. W. Baron, *A Social and Religious History of the Jews*, Vols. I and II,
 Columbia, New York, 1937; second edition, 1952.
M. Grant, *The Jews in the Roman World*, Weidenfeld & Nicolson,
 London, 1973
J. Jeremias, *Jerusalem in the Time of Jesus*, S.C.M. Press, London, 1969
E. Schürer, *A History of the Jewish People in the Age of Jesus Christ* (195
 B.C.–A.D. 135), a new English version revised and edited by G. Vermes
 and F. Millar, Vol. I, T. T. Clark, Edinburgh, 1973; Vol. II, Vermes,
 Millar and M. Black, 1979. Vol. III, forthcoming, will deal with
 Jewish literature
E. M. Smallwood, *The Jews under Roman Rule*, E. J. Brill, Leiden, 1976

THE HERODS

M. Grant, *Herod the Great*, Weidenfeld & Nicolson, London, 1971
S. Perowne, *The Life and Times of Herod the Great*, Hodder & Stoughton,
 London, 1956; reprinted, 1957
A. Schalit, *König Herodes, der Mann und sein Werk*, W. de Gruyter,
 Berlin, 1969 (the definitive work on Herod)
A.H.M. Jones, *The Herods of Judaea*, Oxford, 1938; reprinted, 1967
S. Perowne, *The Later Herods*, Hodder & Stoughton, London, 1958
H. W. Hoehner, *Herod Antipas*, C.U.P., 1972
M. P. Charlesworth, *Five Men*, Harvard, 1936, Chapter I on Agrippa I

MISCELLANEOUS TOPICS

W. R. Farmer, *Maccabees, Zealots and Josephus*, Columbia, 1956
M. Hengel, *Die Zeloten*, E. J. Brill, Leiden, 1961
R. Furneaux, *The Roman Siege of Jerusalem*, Hart-Davis, London, 1973

ARCHAEOLOGY

K. M. Kenyon, *Jerusalem: excavating 3,000 years of history*, Thames & Hudson, London, 1967

Y. Yadin, *Jerusalem Revealed: archaeology in the Holy City 1968–1974*, Yale, 1976

Y. Yadin, *Masada, Herod's fortress and the Zealots' last stand*, Weidenfeld & Nicolson, London, 1966

I. A. Richmond, 'The Roman siege-works at Masada, Israel' in *Journ. Roman Stud.* lii (1962)

M. Avi-Yonah and E. Stern (edd.), *Encyclopedia of Archaeological Excavations in the Holy Land*, Vols. I–IV, O.U.P., 1975–8

JOSEPHUS

Bellum Judaicum (BJ), 'The Jewish War'
Antiquitates Judaicae (AJ), 'The Jewish Antiquities'
Vita (V), the 'Life'
In Apionem (Ap.), 'Against Apion'

The text of all Josephus' works is given, with an English translation, in the Loeb Classical Library in nine volumes, ed. H. St J. Thackeray and others, Heinemann, London and New York, 1926–65

M. Grant, *The Ancient Historians*, Weidenfeld & Nicolson, London, 1970, Chapter 15

F. J. Foakes Jackson, *Josephus and the Jews*, New York, 1930

R. A. Laqueur, *Der judische Historiker Flavius Josephus*, Giessen, 1920 (old but still valuable)

H. Lindner, *Die Geschichtsauffassung des Flavius Josephus im BJ*, E. J. Brill, Leiden, 1972

R. J. H. Shutt, *Studies in Josephus*, S.P.C.K., London, 1961

H. St J. Thackeray, *Josephus, the Man and the Historian*, New York, 1929; republished KTAV, New York, 1967

P. Vidal-Naquet, *Flavius Josèphe ou 'Du bon usage de la trahison'* (Préface à *La Guerre des Juifs*), Éditions de Minuit, Paris, 1977

G. A. Williamson, *The World of Josephus*, Secker & Warburg, London, 1964

PHILO OF ALEXANDRIA

The text of all his works is given, with an English translation, in the Loeb Classical Library in nine volumes, ed. F. H. Colson and others, Heinemann, London and New York, 1929–62

Legatio ad Gaium (*Leg.*), 'The Embassy to Gaius', ed. E. M. Smallwood with translation and commentary, E. J. Brill, Leiden, 1961; second edition, 1970 (the only treatise of Philo with any direct bearing on Josephus' *BJ*)

E. R. Goodenough, *An Introduction to Philo Judaeus*, Blackwell, Oxford, 1962

For much fuller bibliographies see Schürer (rev.), I, pp. 3–16 (general), 61–3 (Josephus; citing two recent comprehensive surveys)

Index

INSIGNIFICANT people and places, and casual references, are not indexed. Notes are indexed, as 83n.56, if they refer to material not in the text.

499